41: *Afro-American Poets Since 1955,* edited by Trudier Harris and Thadious M. Davis (1985)

42: *American Writers for Children Before 1900,* edited by Glenn E. Estes (1985)

43: *American Newspaper Journalists, 1690-1872,* edited by Perry J. Ashley (1986)

44: *American Screenwriters,* Second Series, edited by Randall Clark, Robert E. Morsberger, and Stephen O. Lesser (1986)

45: *American Poets, 1880-1945,* First Series, edited by Peter Quartermain (1986)

46: *American Literary Publishing Houses, 1900-1980: Trade and Paperback,* edited by Peter Dzwonkoski (1986)

47: *American Historians, 1866-1912,* edited by Clyde N. Wilson (1986)

48: *American Poets, 1880-1945,* Second Series, edited by Peter Quartermain (1986)

49: *American Literary Publishing Houses, 1638-1899,* 2 parts, edited by Peter Dzwonkoski (1986)

50: *Afro-American Writers Before the Harlem Renaissance,* edited by Trudier Harris (1986)

51: *Afro-American Writers from the Harlem Renaissance to 1940,* edited by Trudier Harris (1987)

52: *American Writers for Children Since 1960: Fiction,* edited by Glenn E. Estes (1986)

53: *Canadian Writers Since 1960,* First Series, edited by W. H. New (1986)

54: *American Poets, 1880-1945,* Third Series, 2 parts, edited by Peter Quartermain (1987)

55: *Victorian Prose Writers Before 1867,* edited by William B. Thesing (1987)

56: *German Fiction Writers, 1914-1945,* edited by James Hardin (1987)

57: *Victorian Prose Writers After 1867,* edited by William B. Thesing (1987)

58: *Jacobean and Caroline Dramatists,* edited by Fredson Bowers (1987)

59: *American Literary Critics and Scholars, 1800-1850,* edited by John W. Rathbun and Monica M. Grecu (1987)

60: *Canadian Writers Since 1960,* Second Series, edited by W. H. New (1987)

61: *American Writers for Children Since 1960: Poets, Illustrators, and Nonfiction Authors,* edited by Glenn E. Estes (1987)

62: *Elizabethan Dramatists,* edited by Fredson Bowers (1987)

63: *Modern American Critics, 1920-1955,* edited by Gregory S. Jay (1988)

64: *American Literary Critics and Scholars, 1850-1880,* edited by John W. Rathbun and Monica M. Grecu (1988)

65: *French Novelists, 1900-1930,* edited by Catharine Savage Brosman (1988)

66: *German Fiction Writers, 1885-1913,* 2 parts, edited by James Hardin (1988)

67: *Modern American Critics Since 1955,* edited by Gregory S. Jay (1988)

68: *Canadian Writers, 1920-1959,* First Series, edited by W. H. New (1988)

69: *Contemporary German Fiction Writers,* First Series, edited by Wolfgang D. Elfe and James Hardin (1988)

70: *British Mystery Writers, 1860-1919,* edited by Bernard Benstock and Thomas F. Staley (1988)

71: *American Literary Critics and Scholars, 1880-1900,* edited by John W. Rathbun and Monica M. Grecu (1988)

72: *French Novelists, 1930-1960,* edited by Catharine Savage Brosman (1988)

73: *American Magazine Journalists, 1741-1850,* edited by Sam G. Riley (1988)

74: *American Short-Story Writers Before 1880,* edited by Bobby Ellen Kimbel, with the assistance of William E. Grant (1988)

75: *Contemporary German Fiction Writers,* Second Series, edited by Wolfgang D. Elfe and James Hardin (1988)

76: *Afro-American Writers, 1940-1955,* edited by Trudier Harris (1988)

77: *British Mystery Writers, 1920-1939,* edited by Bernard Benstock and Thomas F. Staley (1988)

78: *American Short-Story Writers, 1880-1910,* edited by Bobby Ellen Kimbel, with the assistance of William E. Grant (1988)

79: *American Magazine Journalists, 1850-1900,* edited by Sam G. Riley (1988)

(Continued on back endsheets)

Dictionary of Literary Biography® • Volume One Hundred Sixteen

British Romantic Novelists, 1789-1832

Dictionary of Literary Biography® • Volume One Hundred Sixteen

British Romantic Novelists, 1789-1832

Edited by
Bradford K. Mudge
University of Colorado at Denver

A Bruccoli Clark Layman Book
Gale Research Inc.
Detroit, London

Matthew J. Bruccoli and Richard Layman, *Editorial Directors*
C. E. Frazer Clark, Jr., *Managing Editor*
Karen L. Rood, *Senior Editor*

Printed in the United States of America

Published simultaneously in the United Kingdom
by Gale Research International Limited
(An affiliated company of Gale Research Inc.)

The paper used in this publication meets the minimum requirements of American National Standard for Information Sciences—Permanence Paper for Printed Library Materials, ANSI Z39.48-1984. ∞™

Library of Congress Catalog Card Number 92-9153
ISBN 0-8103-7593-1

Contents

Plan of the Series

... Almost the most prodigious asset of a country, and perhaps its most precious possession, is its native literary product—when that product is fine and noble and enduring.

Mark Twain*

The advisory board, the editors, and the publisher of the *Dictionary of Literary Biography* are joined in endorsing Mark Twain's declaration. The literature of a nation provides an inexhaustible resource of permanent worth. We intend to make literature and its creators better understood and more accessible to students and the reading public, while satisfying the standards of teachers and scholars.

To meet these requirements, *literary biography* has been construed in terms of the author's achievement. The most important thing about a writer is his writing. Accordingly, the entries in *DLB* are career biographies, tracing the development of the author's canon and the evolution of his reputation.

The purpose of *DLB* is not only to provide reliable information in a convenient format but also to place the figures in the larger perspective of literary history and to offer appraisals of their accomplishments by qualified scholars.

The publication plan for *DLB* resulted from two years of preparation. The project was proposed to Bruccoli Clark by Frederick C. Ruffner, president of the Gale Research Company, in November 1975. After specimen entries were prepared and typeset, an advisory board was formed to refine the entry format and develop the series rationale. In meetings held during 1976, the publisher, series editors, and advisory board approved the scheme for a comprehensive biographical dictionary of persons who contributed to North American literature. Editorial work on the first volume began in January 1977, and it was published in 1978. In order to make *DLB* more than a reference tool and to compile volumes that individually have claim to status as literary history, it was decided to organize volumes by topic, period, or genre. Each of these freestanding volumes provides a biographical-bibliographical guide and overview for a particular area of literature. We are convinced that this organization—as opposed to a single alphabet method—constitutes a valuable innovation in the presentation of reference material. The volume plan necessarily requires many decisions for the placement and treatment of authors who might properly be included in two or three volumes. In some instances a major figure will be included in separate volumes, but with different entries emphasizing the aspect of his career appropriate to each volume. Ernest Hemingway, for example, is represented in *American Writers in Paris, 1920-1939* by an entry focusing on his expatriate apprenticeship; he is also in *American Novelists, 1910-1945* with an entry surveying his entire career. Each volume includes a cumulative index of the subject authors and articles. Comprehensive indexes to the entire series are planned.

With volume ten in 1982 it was decided to enlarge the scope of *DLB*. By the end of 1986 twenty-one volumes treating British literature had been published, and volumes for Commonwealth and Modern European literature were in progress. The series has been further augmented by the *DLB Yearbooks* (since 1981) which update published entries and add new entries to keep the *DLB* current with contemporary activity. There have also been *DLB Documentary Series* volumes which provide biographical and critical source materials for figures whose work is judged to have particular interest for students. One of these companion volumes is entirely devoted to Tennessee Williams.

We define literature as the *intellectual commerce of a nation:* not merely as belles lettres but as that ample and complex process by which ideas are generated, shaped, and transmitted. *DLB* entries are not limited to "creative writers" but extend to other figures who in their time and in their way influenced the mind of a people. Thus the series encompasses historians, journalists, publishers, and screenwriters. By this means

*From an unpublished section of Mark Twain's autobiography, copyright © by the Mark Twain Company

readers of *DLB* may be aided to perceive literature not as cult scripture in the keeping of intellectual high priests but firmly positioned at the center of a nation's life.

DLB includes the major writers appropriate to each volume and those standing in the ranks immediately behind them. Scholarly and critical counsel has been sought in deciding which minor figures to include and how full their entries should be. Wherever possible, useful references are made to figures who do not warrant separate entries.

Each *DLB* volume has a volume editor responsible for planning the volume, selecting the figures for inclusion, and assigning the entries. Volume editors are also responsible for preparing, where appropriate, appendices surveying the major periodicals and literary and intellectual movements for their volumes, as well as lists of further readings. Work on the series as a whole is coordinated at the Bruccoli Clark Layman editorial center in Columbia, South Carolina, where the editorial staff is responsible for accuracy of the published volumes.

One feature that distinguishes *DLB* is the illustration policy—its concern with the iconography of literature. Just as an author is influenced by his surroundings, so is the reader's understanding of the author enhanced by a knowledge of his environment. Therefore *DLB* volumes include not only drawings, paintings, and photographs of authors, often depicting them at various stages in their careers, but also illustrations of their families and places where they lived. Title pages are regularly reproduced in facsimile along with dust jackets for modern authors. The dust jackets are a special feature of *DLB* because they often document better than anything else the way in which an author's work was perceived in its own time. Specimens of the writers' manuscripts are included when feasible.

Samuel Johnson rightly decreed that "The chief glory of every people arises from its authors." The purpose of the *Dictionary of Literary Biography* is to compile literary history in the surest way available to us—by accurate and comprehensive treatment of the lives and work of those who contributed to it.

The *DLB* Advisory Board

Introduction

The Muse of Fiction has of late considerably extended her walk.—Walter Scott

An anonymous critic, reviewing Maria Edgeworth's *Tales of Fashionable Life* for the August 1809 number of the *Quarterly Review*, began the essay with a startling assessment of the social power of the novel. Redefining "the importance of a literary work" in terms of "the effect which it produces upon character and moral taste" rather than the artistic qualities which it may or may not possess, the review provides several insights into a critical controversy too frequently ignored by historians of the novel:

> If the importance of a literary work is to be estimated by the number of readers which it attracts, and the effect which it produces upon character and moral taste, a novel or a tale cannot be deemed a trifling production. For it is not only that a novel even of the lowest order always finds more readers than a serious work, but that it finds readers of a more ductile cast whose feelings are more easily interested, and with whom every impression is deeper, because more new. Productions of this kind, therefore, are by no means beneath the notice of the reviewer, but fall very particularly with his province. The customers of the circulating library are so numerous, and so easily imposed upon, that it is of the utmost importance to the public, that its weights and measures should be subject to the inspection of a strict literary police, and the standard of its morality and sentiment kept as pure as the nature of things will admit.

For this early-nineteenth-century reviewer, as for many of his contemporaries, the novel was a dangerous thing, a popular, pseudoliterary form whose appeal to impressionable readers constituted a serious threat to cultural standards. Without the inspections of "a strict literary police," naive readers, "easily imposed upon," were in danger of taking the bad for the good, of having their emotions unduly excited by the cheap sensationalism of popular fiction. Instead of experiencing the ethereal and instructive pleasures of fine art, such readers were presumed to delight in the superficial pleasures of tawdry tales, compromising the aesthetic and moral standards of British culture. The popular novel was no "trifling production"; it was a powerful and dangerous presence in the literary marketplace.

By 1809 the controversy over the novel was anything but new. Critics had been declaiming against novels for almost a hundred years, insisting time and again that popular fiction constituted an immoral and dangerous influence on lower-middle-class and middle-class readers—especially women. In fact, because the majority of novels in the eighteenth century were both written and read by women, critics, almost exclusively male, often felt compelled to disparage novels in gender-specific terms. For example, a critic writing for the *Monthly Review* in March 1759 complained:

> The most we can do, with respect to those numerous novels, that issue continuously from the press, is to give rather a character than an account of each. To do even this, however, we find no easy task; since we might say of them, as Pope, with less justice, says of the *ladies*, "Most *novels* have no character at all."

Disclaimers to the contrary, the reviewer established a reciprocal relation between women and novels: the majority of both "have no character at all." Moreover, the "numerous" publications coming "continuously from the press" constitute a threat to judicious review. The reviewer's anxiety is twofold: first, the popularity of this new cultural form—the novel—continues to grow unchecked by the monitors of taste; and, second, the form itself constitutes a feminized departure from the masculinized norms of high culture. As John Taylor confirms in his detailed study *Early Opposition to the English Novel* (1949), "In the opinion of those who dreaded the new, two of the greatest contributions of the eighteenth century, women's freedom and the novel, were assisting each other along the road to corruption."

During the last decades of the eighteenth century, critical outrage against the novel intensified. Literary journals, popular magazines, and an almost unending stream of conduct books all warned of the many dangers of novel reading. Hannah More, who would herself become a novelist in an attempt to correct the vices of popular fiction, voiced the common complaint: novels were a "pernicious source of moral corruption." The reasons for this sudden burst of anxiety were threefold. First, the American and French revolutions proved deeply unsettling for Britons. Worried that at any moment their country might erupt into civil war, they became particularly sensitive to all purported causes of moral turpitude. Edmund Burke squared off against Thomas Paine, and the average citizen associated things French—especially their novels—with corruption and self-indulgence. Second, during the 1790s the Gothic novel enjoyed considerable popularity in France as well as in England, a fact that did nothing to improve the reputation of novels generally. Reveling in excess, the Gothic was nothing if not sensational. Castles and ghosts, virginal heroines and scheming villains, mysterious orphans and lost fortunes all ensured that novels remain decidedly suspect in the literary scheme of things. Third, the literary marketplace, that economic environment within which literature was produced and consumed, had changed in a variety of problematic ways. It was clear by the 1790s, for example, that more and more people were reading for entertainment and that an industry of sorts had arisen to meet and encourage and profit from such activity. Men of letters watched with horror as the novel—an untutored, distant relative of "real literature"—became increasingly popular, increasingly influential, and increasingly lucrative. The chief culprit was the new circulating library, which for a small sum allowed readers unlimited access to books that they could not afford to buy. The new middle class, considered most susceptible to the immoral influences of bad fiction, were thus encouraged to procure it. In short, the 1790s witnessed a marked increase in critical hostility toward popular fiction, and even well into the nineteenth century the novel remained a dangerous thing—economically, aesthetically, and politically.

However pronounced the hostilities against the novel, and however important women writers and readers were to that debate, literary historians have generally ignored the controversy, preferring instead to discuss the novels themselves. After all, by 1800 the novel had already generated several prospective masterpieces: among them, Daniel Defoe's *Robinson Crusoe* (1719) and *Moll Flanders* (1722), Samuel Richardson's *Pamela* (1740) and *Clarissa* (1747-1749), and Henry Fielding's *Joseph Andrews* (1742) and *Tom Jones* (1749). In his landmark study, *The Rise of the Novel* (1957), Ian Watt focuses on Defoe, Richardson, and Fielding and outlines what has become the standard account of the evolution of eighteenth-century fiction. Defining "formal realism" as the constitutive aesthetic of the novel, he traces the history of that genre in terms of a changing sense of self and world directly attributable to the expansion of the middle class. Careful to consider as well the influence of a changing literary marketplace, Watt situates the novel within an evolving social and economic context. As convincing as it is ambitious, Watt's study set a standard with which subsequent accounts have had to contend. But because his argument focuses exclusively on a small, select group of novels—all written by men—that argument avoids confronting several related problems. In particular, Watt fails to explore the critical controversy over the immorality of the novel or to consider in any detail women's involvement in the new "literary" form. While he admits that the "majority of eighteenth-century novels were actually written by women," he is quick to add a qualification: "this had long remained a purely quantitative assertion of dominance."

Watt's dismissal of popular fiction, especially that written by and for women, ensures that his history of the novel takes as representative only one small part of a much larger and more complicated scene. Recent critics, however—most notably Nancy Armstrong in *Desire and Domestic Fiction* (1987), Terry Lovell in *Consuming Fiction* (1987), Michael McKeon in *The Origins of the English Novel, 1600-1740* (1987), and Dale Spender in *Mothers of the Novel* (1986)—have proffered significant challenges to Watt's account. Those challenges make clear that the rise of the novel was hardly a smooth and harmonious process; it was instead a contested and acrimonious transition from one kind of literary economy to another, from a male-dominated patronage system that closely monitored literary standards to an open marketplace that put profit before both aesthetic criteria and gender stereotypes. For example, Spender defines a position that has become extremely influential:

> That it was women and not men who made the greater contribution to the development of the

> novel does not seem to me to be surprising upon reflection. It was a logical extension of women's role. When it is realized that women were not debarred from letter writing—and that most early novels took the form of letters—the relationship between women and the novel is more easily discerned. Denied education, disallowed in the public world, women had always been permitted the "indulgence" of letter writing and were even permitted to excel at it. . . . To me it seems quite obvious that it was a cunning move on the part of women to transform their private occupation into a public and professional activity.
>
> They drew on the strengths they had been allowed and transformed their private literary indulgence into a public paid performance, and in the process they gained for themselves a voice and helped to create a new literary form. Women did not imitate the men; it was quite the reverse. And as the women writers produced this novel form, they forged for themselves an occupation which was intellectually stimulating, often lucrative, generally rewarding, and increasingly influential. They did all this before the men quite realized what was going on and began their policy of "containment."

Spender's challenge to Watt's account does more than simply insert women writers into the history of the novel: her argument also challenges the historical and aesthetic values that mandated their original exclusion. The rise of the novel, in other words, has to be seen as more than a chronologically arranged list of famous books, with each book adding incrementally to the achievements of its predecessors. What, after all, constitutes "famous?" And what can literary historians learn if they pay attention to all of the "not-so-famous" novels in addition to the celebrated few? Recent critics would generally agree that as a new literary form, and one peculiarly adapted to the burgeoning middle class, the novel became a kind of battleground, a discursive terrain over which different social groups competed for different kinds of mastery—aesthetic, moral, economic, and political. This argument finds a prime example in the Romantic novel.

According to Watt's account, the Romantic novel, having descended from such a prestigious eighteenth-century lineage, should have taken its place in literary history with authority and self-assurance. In fact, however, the Romantic period—stretching roughly from 1789, the date of William Blake's *Songs of Innocence* and the fall of the Bastille, to 1832, the year of the great Reform Bill—has become known primarily for its poetry. Although students of the period will quickly mention Jane Austen, Walter Scott, and Mary Shelley as proof of high achievement, they would also have to admit that those authors are taught more often than not at the end of a class in "The Eighteenth-Century Novel" or at the beginning of a class in "The Victorian Novel." A course in "The Romantic Novel" is an unusual event, and the standard offering—a class in "English Romanticism"—would generally focus on the six great poets—William Blake, Samuel Taylor Coleridge, William Wordsworth, John Keats, Percy Bysshe Shelley, and George Gordon, Lord Byron. A quick check in the library confirms the suspicion: the shelves groan under the weight of books about the eighteenth-century novel, the Victorian novel, and the Romantic poem. Much less work seems to have been done on the Romantic novel. When then has the Romantic novel received comparatively little attention? Is it because, in the words that the *Monthly Review* borrowed from Alexander Pope, most of the novels had "no character at all?" Or, is there another explanation?

In fact, explanations abound. Looking no farther than the novels themselves, the experienced reader would have to agree that the Romantic period, rather than suffering from a paucity of good fiction, sets the superior standard against which the novels of the eighteenth and nineteenth centuries must be measured. It has been argued, for instance, that Jane Austen wrote the finest novels in the English language; that Walter Scott was, as Gary Kelly claims, "the most influential novelist in world literature"; and that Mary Shelley, by the time she was nineteen, wrote what Eleanor Ty describes as "one of the most famous novels ever published." The Romantic period claims in addition the domestic novels of Maria Edgeworth, Susan Ferrier, and Amelia Opie, the historical novels of Anna Eliza Bray, Thomas Gaspey, and George P. R. James, the Gothic novels of Mary Meeke, James Hogg, and John William Polidori, the satiric novels of Eaton Barrett, Theodore Hook, and Thomas Love Peacock, and the fashionable novels of Charlotte Bury, Catherine Gore, and Caroline Lamb. The novels themselves range in setting from the bucolic English idylls of Mary Russell Mitford, to the classical Rome of John Gibson Lockhart's *Valerius* (1821), to the exotic landscapes of James Justinian Morier's Oriental romances. Of the authors, some, such as Scott and Mary Shelley, were famous then as now. Others, such as Anna

Eliza Bray and Charlotte Bury, were famous then but are unknown now. Still others, such as Jane Austen, lived and wrote in relative obscurity only to acquire fame posthumously. Of course, fame is only one factor in literary history. Many of the novelists represented in this volume were influential without being famous. Mary Meeke, for example, published more than thirty popular novels without becoming a well-known literary personality. Similarly, John William Polidori, who published only two novels, remained obscure despite writing the successful and influential ghost story *The Vampyre* (1819). Clearly the novel thrived during the first decades of the nineteenth century—why then has poetry retained the center stage?

One obvious answer is that Romantic poetry is itself of exceptional quality; and the Romantic poets, passionately opposed to the novel, were successful in passing along that prejudice. Both Wordsworth and Coleridge, for example, declaimed long and hard against popular fiction; both were worried that the superior qualities of poetry were less and less attractive to a reading public more and more cretinized by the easy pleasures of sensational novels.

In the 1800 Preface to *Lyrical Ballads*, arguably the most important of Romantic manifestos, Wordsworth explains his fears about a whole series of factors rapidly transforming British culture:

> a multitude of causes, unknown to former times, are now acting with combined forces to blunt the discriminating powers of the mind, and, unfitting it for all voluntary exertion, to reduce it to a state of almost savage torpor. The most effective of these causes are the great national events which are daily taking place, and the increasing accumulation of men in cities, where the uniformity of their occupations produces a craving for extraordinary incident, which the rapid communication of intelligence hourly gratifies. To this tendency of life and manners the literature and theatrical exhibitions of the country have conformed themselves. The invaluable works of our elder writers, I had almost said the works of Shakespeare and Milton, are driven into neglect by frantic novels, sickly and stupid German Tragedies, and deluges of idle and extravagant stories in verse.—When I think upon this degrading thirst after outrageous stimulation, I am almost ashamed to have spoken of the feeble endeavour made in these volumes to counteract it. . . .

With one rhetorical flourish after another, Wordsworth argues that a new kind of popular culture—specifically newspapers, novels, plays, and certain kinds of poetry—encourages mental lethargy. His phrase "savage torpor," emphasizes both cultural regression—to a savage, uncivilized state—and slow-wittedness. This torpor results, somewhat paradoxically, from a "degrading thirst after outrageous stimulation" that is itself the result of political upheaval, crowded cities, and industrial employment. The "magnitude of the general evil"—of which novels constituted a significant portion—threatens not only to erase Shakespeare and Milton from public memory but also to destroy the whole of British culture.

The same year that he and Wordsworth first published the *Lyrical Ballads* (1798), Coleridge, in a review of Ann Radcliffe's *The Italian* (1797), explained his distrust of modern novels generally and the Gothic novel in particular:

> It was not difficult to foresee that the *modern romance*, even supported by the skill of the most ingenious of its votaries, would soon experience the fate of every attempt to please by what is unnatural, and by a departure from that observance of real life, which has placed the works of Fielding, Smollett, and some other writers, among the permanent sources of amusement. It might for a time afford an acceptable variety to persons whose reading is confined to works of fiction, and who would, perhaps, be glad to exchange dullness for extravagance; but it was probable that, as its constitution (if we may so speak) was maintained only by the passion of terror, and that excited by trick, and as it was not conversant in the incidents and characters of a natural complexion, it would degenerate into repetition, and would disappoint curiosity. (*Critical Review*, June 1798)

For Coleridge, the majority of modern novels "please[d] by what is unnatural." They "excited by trick" and thus departed "from that observance of real life" that characterizes more "permanent sources of amusement." Moreover, the popularity of the modern novel, Coleridge implies, is largely due to a class of readers "whose reading is confined to works of fiction"—that is, readers of low taste and limited education. Writing in his notebook several years later, Coleridge explained:

> For as to the Devotees of the Circulating Libraries, I may not compliment their pastime, or rather *Kill time*, with the name *Reading*. Call it

> rather a sort of beggarly Day-dreaming in which the mind furnishes for itself only laziness and a little mawkish sensibility, while the whole *Stuff* and Furniture of the Doze is supplied *ab extra* by a sort of spiritual *Camera Obscura*, which (*pro tempore*) fixes, reflects, and transmits the moving phantasms of one man's Delirium so as to people the barrenness of a hundred other brains under the same morbid Trance, or '*suspended Animation*' of Common Sense, and all definite Purpose.

Coleridge's disgust could not be more evident. Reading novels is not reading at all; it is a kind of simpleminded daydreaming practiced by those unable to muster the skills necessary for the finer arts.

Wordsworth and Coleridge articulated a distrust of the novel shared by many of their contemporaries. That distrust continues to be influential well after the Romantic period largely because of the centrality accorded Romantic poetry by literary historians. In the traditional view, Romantic poetry marks a crucial shift away from eighteenth-century rationalism and toward a distinctly modern sensibility. By championing the powers of the imagination over reason, of the natural over the commercial, and of the individual over the collective, Romantic poets forged a highly influential and revolutionary aesthetic. Literary scholars have generally agreed with Percy Shelley: "The literature of England," he declared in *A Defence of Poetry* (1821), "has arisen as it were from a new birth." "We live among such philosophers and poets as surpass beyond comparison any who have appeared since the last national struggle for civil and religious liberty." As Shelley's second sentence indicates, his use of the word *literature* in the first does not include novels. Appropriately, this passage is quoted at the beginning of M. H. Abrams's *Natural Supernaturalism: Tradition and Revolution in Romantic Literature* (1973), a highly respected study of "Romantic literature" and one that makes not a single reference to the Romantic novel.

That Abrams should share Wordsworth, Coleridge, and Shelley's distrust of the Romantic novel seems at once surprising and predictable. It is surprising that a scholar such as Abrams, whose work is otherwise scrupulously historical, should ignore an entire area of "Romantic literature." It is predictable, however, if Romantic literature means first and foremost Romantic poetry. Like Wordsworth, Coleridge, and Shelley, Abrams confidently assumes a literary hierarchy that relegates the novel to an inferior position. Recent scholars of Romanticism have been less inclined to take the poets at their word. In 1983, when the influence of Abrams on romantic studies was still considerable, Jerome McGann published *The Romantic Ideology*, a book whose argument quickly changed the way scholars approached Romantic literature. McGann argued that "the scholarship and criticism of Romanticism and its works are dominated by a Romantic Ideology, by an uncritical absorption in Romanticism's own self-representations." Romantic scholarship, in other words, generally prefers to celebrate the beliefs and values of the Romantic poets. As a remedy for this "uncritical absorption," McGann advocated a sociohistorical method capable of keeping past and present in self-conscious dialectical tension. Crucial to this method is the realization that the Romantic period is diverse and conflicted rather than unified and harmonious:

> Not every artistic production in the Romantic period is a Romantic one . . . indeed, the greatest artists in any period often depart from their age's dominant ideological commitments. . . . The Romantic Age is so called not because all its works are Romantic, but rather because the ideologies of Romanticism exerted an increasingly dominant influence during that time.

Calling for a more sophisticated and self-conscious literary history, McGann's study encouraged students of Romanticism to consider more closely the complexities of the period. Romantic fiction qualifies as suitably complex, for despite the objections of Wordsworth and Coleridge, the novel became an increasingly dominant force in the literary marketplace.

During the late eighteenth century the Jacobin novels inspired by the French Revolution, Gothic novels, sentimental novels, historical novels, romance novels, and satiric novels all came to occupy specific, identifiable subgenres, with each subgenre competing in its own unique way for a larger slice of the available readership and a larger piece of the profits. The revolutionary furor of the 1790s encouraged the Jacobin novels of Robert Bage, Elizabeth Inchbald, Thomas Holcroft, and William Godwin as well as the Gothic novels of Matthew Lewis, Mary Meeke, and Ann Radcliffe. In 1800, the Marquis de Sade, whose pornographic novel *Justine* (1791) inspired Lewis to write *The Monk* (1796), explained that Gothic novels were "the fruit of the revolution of which all Europe felt the shock." Regardless of the popularity of the Gothic, however, other kinds of fiction also enjoyed success. Amelia Opie, friend of woman's rights advocate and novelist Mary Wollstonecraft, began her career with *Dangers of Coquetry* (1790), a sentimental romance that preceded Opie's best-known novel, *The Father and Daughter* (1801). By that date, another "novelist of manners," Maria Edgeworth, had published *Castle Rackrent* (1800), a cautious exploration of volatile Anglo-Irish relations. Experimenting with a kind of social realism made famous by her predecessor Frances Burney, Edgeworth was soon to be the most celebrated of British novelists, a position she would hold until the publication of Walter Scott's *Waverley* in 1814.

Walter Scott's literary career is of crucial importance to historians of the novel. It began in 1800 with the publication of the first of his "Border ballads," *The Eve of Saint John*, and ended with his death thirty-two years and fifty books later. Although a versatile man of letters—he wrote poetry, novels, history, biography, and criticism—Scott was considered for the first half of his career primarily a poet, and for the second half primarily a novelist. The abruptness and finality of Scott's decision to become a novelist derived from and serves to highlight his economic rationale: writing novels was simply more lucrative than writing poetry, even popular poetry. This fact, combined with one other—that the Waverley novels are generally seen as the novels that made novel writing respectable—marks Scott's career as an important transition in the history of popular fiction. Criticized in the eighteenth century as subliterary, as a threat to morality and virtue, the novel had become by Scott's death in 1832 an accepted if not respected literary form. The Waverley novels, critics argue, were a significant factor in that transition.

The Waverley novels are historical romances; they return to well-known events in British and European history and dramatize those events in entertaining ways. They were, right from the beginning, extremely popular with British readers. Scott's intention, as he described it in the introduction to *Waverley* was to portray realistically "the characters and passions of the actor;—those passions common to men in all stages of society, and which have alike agitated the human heart, whether it throbbed under the steel corslet of the fifteenth century, the brocaded coat of the eighteenth, or blue frock and white dimity waistcoast of the present day." His strategy proved successful, and even William Hazlitt—who was horrified by Scott's conservative, Tory politics—was forced to acknowledge Scott's effective use of history. Writing on Scott in *The Spirit of the Age* (1825), Hazlitt explained:

> Sir Walter has found out (oh, rare discovery) that facts are better than fiction; that there is no romance like the romance of real life; and that if we can but arrive at what men feel, do, and say in striking and singular situations, the results will be "more lively, audible, and full of vent," than the fine-spun cobwebs of the brain.

Hazlitt's grudging praise evidences a revealing ambivalence. On one hand, he believes Scott's use of history to be effective; on the other, he is suspicious about the political lessons Scott derives from that history. Eager to challenge ideas about the "Rights of man," for example, Scott repeatedly portrays the forces of history and tradition as "naturally" resistant to political change. Thus, his historical romances, which are ostensibly concerned with past events, also dramatize contemporary political tensions.

That Walter Scott's fictional renderings of the past include a whole series of political overtones serves as an important reminder for all students of the period: early-nineteenth-century fiction provides a dramatic opportunity to glimpse the historical events and political concerns that define British Romanticism. From the unabashedly political novels of William Godwin and Mary Wollstonecraft, to the seemingly apolitical romances of Jane Austen and Susan Ferrier, to the sometimes baffling histories of Walter Scott and George P. R. James, the Romantic novel makes consistent and unavoidable use of contemporary issues. While the temptation may arise for modern readers to view all literature as the repository of eternal and unchanging humanistic truth, such as inclination too often obscures historical specificity and the irreducible difference that specificity enacts. Austen's *Pride and Prejudice* (1813), for example, may well present a timeless love story of universal appeal; but it also dramatizes the hopes and fears of a new middle class eager to assume the best of aristocratic values and anxious to distance itself from the worst of mercantile influences. Inseparable from the tensions of the shifting class structure of early-nineteenth-century Britain, the romance of *Pride and Prejudice* provides a cure for the anxieties of the middle-class family at the same time that it corrects the wayward tendencies of a self-satisfied aristocracy. To ignore the centrality of class tensions in *Pride and Prejudice* would be to miss those details that establish the novel's historical specificity and uniquely "Romantic" character.

The historical events that define the context within which the Romantic novels must be situated are many and complex. It is worth remembering, however, that the literary history with which we are primarily concerned occupies a relatively small portion of a much larger picture. As Marilyn Gaull explains in her useful study *English Romanticism* (1988),

> Most people in England during the opening decades of the nineteenth century showed very little interest in the literature that we now consider important. Those who were literate and able to purchase literary works were primarily concerned with business, politics, war, trade, industry, fashion, sex, status, domestic comfort, horses, servants, marriage, and boxing matches. They discussed their kings: George III's eccentricities, his health, his unruly children, his moralistic attitudes, and his poor taste in political friends; George IV's extravagance, his mistresses, costumes, architectural achievements, and political incompetence. In spite of the loss of the American colonies in the War of Independence, they were cheered by the prospects of a new empire developing through exploration such as Captain Cook's discovery of Australia (1769), through trade and colonization in India, Canada, and South Africa. During the long war against France, they applauded the naval victories of Nelson in Egypt (1798), the continental campaigns of Wellington in Copenhagen (1810), Spain, the Netherlands, and the ultimate victory at Waterloo (1815), which they had financed through the first income tax (1798). In domestic politics their energies were absorbed in debates and shifts of power; the Prime Minister, William Pitt, his cabinet, and an elected Parliament emerged as the true governing body and began an agonizing series of reforms that culminated in the Reform Bill of 1832, enfranchising people of property (£10 householders) while avoiding the trauma of a revolution such as had occurred in France.

Prior to the Reform Bill only 2 percent of the British population could vote. That 2 percent—roughly twenty-seven thousand aristocratic families—owned two-thirds of land. After the Reform Bill the enfranchisement was increased by about two hundred thousand voters, or to one out of every seven adult males. The lower classes—those earning less than one hundred pounds a year—remained without political representation, even though (or precisely because) they comprised two-thirds of the population.

In such a world—a world where an industrious bricklayer earned at best sixty pounds a year (about three hundred dollars then or twelve thousand dollars today) and had no vote, no public education, no health care, and no pension—life for the majority of working men and women was nasty, brutish, and short. Literature was a luxury, and the average novel was extremely expensive. Print technology would not improve dramatically until the 1840s; as a result, a new work of fiction by a known author—Maria Edgeworth, say, or Walter Scott—cost about half a pound, somewhere between seventy-five and one hundred dollars in today's currency. Circulating libraries made those novels available to middle-class patrons, but members of the lower classes, if literate, read mostly newspapers, magazines, and pamphlets. The increasing literacy rate among the underclasses was considered a dangerous development, especially because Britain was experiencing massive population growth and continued political unrest. In Wordsworth's lifetime, for example—that is, from 1770 to 1850—the native population increased from seven to seventeen million; during the same time, civil disturbances continued unabated. The Irish rebellion of 1798, the Luddite riots of 1811-1813, the Blanketeers' March of 1816, the Peterloo Massacre of 1819, and the Cato Street Conspiracy of 1820 marked a period of agitation that would culminate in the late 1830s with the Chartist Movement, which called for universal sufferage. Although by the end of the Romantic period moral outrage against the novel had largely dissipated, middle-class reformers now worried more than ever about the reading materials popular among the newly literate under classes. Literary pleasures, it seems, are always controversial. Even today, of course, who reads what is a matter of great political concern.

Responsible literary history, then, is far more complicated than a recitation of the names and dates of famous books. In addition to the formal complexities of individual works—such as narrative structure, character development, thematic conflicts—and the biographies of individual authors—educational background, religious training, economic status—literary history must concern itself with the social, economic, and political tensions that inform both the literary work and the life of the individual who created it. This volume of the *Dictionary of Literary Biography* is intended to provide information at once historical and critical about the Romantic novelists and their novels. Each entry is a literary biography in miniature, providing a detailed account of the author's life and literary career. In addition, each essay also provides a variety of critical insights into the nature of that author's work and the literary milieu within which it first appeared. Entries also include discussions of current critical debates and bibliographies of recent work. Students of the Romantic novel will thus have access to a "literary history" that functions in a variety of ways, on a variety of levels. Perhaps, however, one should just enjoy Walter Scott's observation that there are two classes of novel readers: "first, those whose attention to history is awakened by the fictitious narrative, and whom curiosity stimulate to study, for the purpose of winnowing the wheat from the chaff, the true from the fabulous. Secondly, those who are too idle to read, save for the purpose of amusement . . . [and who] acquire some acquaintance with history, which, however inaccurate, is better than none."

—Bradford K. Mudge

Acknowledgments

This book was produced by Bruccoli Clark Layman, Inc. Karen L. Rood, senior editor for the *Dictionary of Literary Biography* series, was the inhouse editor.

Production coordinator is James W. Hipp. Projects manager is Charles D. Brower. Photography editors are Edward Scott and Timothy C. Lundy. Layout and graphics supervisor is Penney L. Haughton. Copyediting supervisor is Bill Adams. Typesetting supervisor is Kathleen M. Flanagan. Systems manager is George F. Dodge. The production staff includes Rowena Betts, Steve Borsanyi, Teresa Chaney, Patricia Coate, Rebecca Crawford, Gail Crouch, Henry Cunningham, Margaret McGinty Cureton, Bonita Dingle, Mary Scott Dye, Denise Edwards, Sarah A. Estes, Robert Fowler, Avril E. Gregory, Ellen McCracken, Kathy Lawler Merlette, John Myrick, Pamela D. Norton, Jean W. Ross, Thomasina Singleton, Maxine K. Smalls, and Jennifer C. J. Turley.

Walter W. Ross and Dennis Lynch did library research. They were assisted by the following librarians at the Thomas Cooper Library of the University of South Carolina: Jens Holley and the interlibrary-loan staff; reference librarians Gwen Baxter, Daniel Boice, Faye Chadwell, Jo Cottingham, Cathy Eckman, Rhonda Felder, Gary Geer, Jackie Kinder, Laurie Preston, Jean Rhyne, Carol Tobin, Virginia Weathers, and Connie Widney; circulation-department head Thomas Marcil; and acquisitions-searching supervisor David Haggard.

Dictionary of Literary Biography® • Volume One Hundred Sixteen

British Romantic Novelists, 1789-1832

Dictionary of Literary Biography

Jane Austen

(16 December 1775 - 18 July 1817)

Gary Kelly
University of Alberta

BOOKS: *Sense and Sensibility: A Novel,* 3 volumes (London: Printed for the author by C. Roworth & published by T. Egerton, 1811 [i.e., 1810]);

Pride and Prejudice: A Novel, 3 volumes (London: Printed for T. Egerton, 1813);

Mansfield Park: A Novel, 3 volumes (London: Printed for T. Egerton, 1814);

Emma: A Novel (3 volumes, London: Printed for John Murray, 1816 [i.e., 1815]; 2 volumes, Philadelphia: Published by M. Carey, 1816);

Northanger Abbey and Persuasion, 4 volumes (London: John Murray, 1818 [i.e., 1817]);

Lady Susan, and the Watsons (New York: George Munro, 1882);

Love & Freindship and Other Early Works, Now first printed from the original MS (London: Chatto & Windus, 1922; New York: Frederick A. Stokes, 1922);

The Watsons (London: Leonard Parsons, 1923);

Lady Susan (Oxford: Clarendon Press, 1925);

Fragment of a Novel Written by Jane Austen January - March 1817 [*Sanditon*], edited by R. W. Chapman (Oxford: Clarendon Press, 1925);

Plan of a Novel according to Hints from Various Quarters, edited by Chapman (Oxford: Clarendon Press, 1926);

Two Chapters of Persuasion, Printed from Jane Austen's Autograph (Oxford: Clarendon Press, 1926);

Volume the First [Juvenilia], edited by Chapman (Oxford: Clarendon Press, 1933);

Volume the Third [Juvenilia], edited by Chapman (Oxford: Clarendon Press, 1951);

Volume the Second [Juvenilia], edited by B. C. Southam (Oxford: Clarendon Press, 1963).

Editions: *The Novels of Jane Austen,* 5 volumes, edited by Chapman (Oxford: Clarendon Press, 1923); republished with revisions to notes and appendices by Mary Lascelles (Oxford: Clarendon Press, 1965-1966);

Sense and Sensibility, edited by Claire Lamont, with textual notes by James Kinsley (London, New York & Toronto: Oxford University Press, 1970);

Pride and Prejudice, edited by Frank W. Bradbrook, with textual notes by Kinsley (London, New York & Toronto: Oxford University Press, 1970);

Mansfield Park, edited by John Lucas, with textual notes by Kinsley (London, New York & Toronto: Oxford University Press, 1970);

Emma, edited by David Lodge, with textual notes by Kinsley (London, New York & Toronto: Oxford University Press, 1971);

Northanger Abbey and Persuasion, edited by John Davie, with textual notes by Kinsley (London, New York & Toronto: Oxford University Press, 1971).

Jane Austen is one of the few novelists in world literature who is regarded as a "classic" and yet is widely read. As the contemporary novelist Fay Weldon puts it, for generations of students and the educated reading public in many countries, Austen's novels represent literature with a capital "L." On the other hand, Austen is the only novelist before Charles Dickens who still has

This-pen-and-watercolor sketch, executed circa June 1811, is one of only two authenticated portraits of Jane Austen, both by her sister, Cassandra Austen (National Portrait Gallery, London).

a significant popular readership, and her fictional world—seen as an idyllic bygone time and place unlike, and preferable to, the present—has entered into popular literary culture.

Jane Austen was born into the rural professional middle class. Her father, George Austen (1731-1805), was a country clergyman at Steventon, a small village in the southern English county of Hampshire. He had risen by merit from a Kentish family in trade and the lower professions. Jane Austen's mother, Cassandra Leigh Austen (1739-1827), was from a higher social rank, minor gentry related distantly to titled people, but once she married the Reverend Austen in 1764 she entered wholeheartedly and with humor into the domestic life and responsibilities of managing a household economy by no means luxurious, bearing eight children—six sons and two daughters. In this setting the Austens mingled easily with other gentrified professionals and with local gentry families.

Yet they were also linked, though tenuously in some ways, with the larger world of fashionable society and of patronage, politics, and state. George Austen owed his education at Oxford University to his own merit as a student at Tonbridge School, but he owed his clerical position, or "living," at Steventon to the patronage of a wealthy relative, Thomas Knight of Godmersham Park, Kent, who held the appointment in his gift. Later the Knights, who were childless, adopted one of the Austens' sons, Edward, as their own son and heir to their estates in Kent and Hampshire. One of Jane Austen's cousins, Elizabeth (Eliza) Hancock, married a French aristocrat—Jean Capotte, Comte de Feuillide. The comte was guillotined during the French Revolution, and Eliza later married Jane Austen's brother Henry. Local friends of the Austens included the Reverend George Lefroy and his wife, Anne, sister of an eccentric, novel-writing, obsessively aristocratic Kentish squire, Sir Samuel Egerton Brydges. "Madam Lefroy," as she was known locally, was lively and energetic, wrote verses (some of which got published), enthusiastically embraced the contemporary literature and culture of Sensibility, and engaged in fashionable philanthropy among the local poor. She "took up" the young Jane Austen and encouraged her intellectual development. The closest friends of Jane Austen and her sister, Cassandra, were Elizabeth, Catherine, and Alethea Bigg, whose parents were local gentry and whose brother, Harris Bigg-Wither, later proposed marriage to Jane Austen. Other close friends were Mary and Martha Lloyd, daughters of a neighboring clergyman, whose mother was the daughter of a royal governor of South Carolina.

Austen's brothers, apart from Edward, went in for genteel but demanding professions. Her eldest brother, James (1765-1819), who had literary tastes and intellectual interests, followed his father's path to St. John's College, Oxford, and eventually became his father's successor as rector of Steventon. Her second brother, George (1766-1838), was born handicapped and did not play a part in the family life. The third son was Edward (1767-1852), who was adopted by the Knights and took over the Knight estates in 1797. The fourth child, Henry (1771-1850), was the liveliest, the most adventurous and the most speculative of the Austens. Like James, he went to St. John's College, Oxford, but instead of taking orders

The Reverend George Austen and Cassandra Leigh Austen, the novelist's parents (Jane Austen Memorial Trust)

Steventon Rectory, Jane Austen's birthplace, drawn by her niece Anna Austen in 1814 (Jane Austen Memorial Trust)

Five of Jane Austen's brothers: James and Henry (top), who became clergymen like their father; Edward (center), who was adopted by a wealthy relative, Thomas Knight, in 1783; and Francis and Charles (bottom), who both rose to the rank of admiral in the Royal Navy (top, center, and bottom right: Jane Austen Memorial Trust; bottom left: Collection of Miss Helen Brown)

upon graduation he joined the army, gave that up for the relatively ungenteel line of banking, and married his glamorous widowed cousin, Eliza de Feuillide. When his bank failed in 1816 during the economic crisis following the Napoleonic Wars, he fell back on his father's profession and became a clergyman. The next child, Cassandra (1773-1845), was Jane's closest friend throughout her life and was known in the family for her steady character and sound judgment. Like Jane, she never married. Her fiancé, the Reverend Thomas Fowle, died while serving as a military chaplain in the West Indies in 1797. The two youngest Austen boys, Francis (1774-1865) and Charles (1779-1852), were trained at the Royal Naval Academy at Portsmouth, became officers, served in the French wars, and rose to the rank of admiral.

Though the issues and interests of the wider world may have come from afar somewhat muffled, they did flow through the rectory at Steventon, and later—less muffled—through the other habitations and homes of Jane Austen as well. But the rectory at Steventon with its lively, frank, and intimate yet open family life was her first and formative home. Her parents had a close and happy marriage. Her mother was thoroughly domestic yet commonsensical and humorous; her father was kind, loving, and encouraging to his daughters as well as his sons. Jane, known as "Jenny" in the family, was well liked by her brothers, who were often at home even while students at Oxford or Portsmouth, and who visited their sisters when they were away briefly at school.

The family members were readers, though more in literature of the day than abstruse learning. There was also a great deal of reading aloud in the Austen household. Many families at the time would have one of their members read to the others while they carried out small tasks. Reading aloud was considered a highly valuable professional and social skill, and the Reverend Mr. Austen, not surprisingly, excelled at it. The topic was later made a major point in *Mansfield Park* (1814). Jane Austen was helped by her father to select from his five-hundred-volume library, and there were, of course, books from circulating libraries. These rental libraries, greatly varying in extent of stock and luxury of appointment, specialized in lighter reading. They were the main way that middle-class people, who made up most of the reading public, got access to books and magazines of the day, which were otherwise quite expensive. For example a typical three-volume novel of the kind Austen wrote cost the equivalent of about two weeks' wages for a rural laborer (about half of the laboring class could not read, however). Like other families with literary interests, the Austens also enjoyed putting on plays. There was a vogue for such amateur domestic theatricals in the latter part of the eighteenth century. It was not surprising in such a family for Jane Austen to take to writing before she was even in her teens, and for her to amuse her family throughout her adolescence with burlesques of various kinds of literature.

This early domestic writing shows a firm grasp of the current literary genres as well as literary styles, conventions, and clichés. Prose fiction was the major but not the only object of Austen's parody. "The Visit" and "The Mystery" burlesque popular late-eighteenth-century sentimental comedy. "The History of England from the Reign of Henry the 4th to the Death of Charles the 1st" burlesques the objectivity, factuality, and authoritativeness of historiography, then considered a male discourse, by deliberately inserting attributes that would then have been considered "feminine," such as open prejudice, frank admission of ignorance, and occasional expressive passages, while making fun of the conventions of cause and effect and displaying a prominent interest in the sufferings of historical "women of feeling" such as Mary, Queen of Scots. "A Collection of Letters," with its letter "from a young lady crossed in love to her freind [*sic*]" and letter "from a young lady in distress'd circumstances to her freind," burlesques another kind of desultory sentimental text of the time. Other fragments parody sentimental didacticism and sentimental travel writing.

Austen's main interest, however, was in the varieties of prose fiction. For example "Frederic and Elfrida: A Novel" burlesques the contemporary sentimental novel, with its ideal hero and heroine, interspersed letters and verses, elegant dialogue, noble feelings, pathetic incidents, and plot of delayed courtship. "Jack and Alice: A Novel," "Edgar and Emma: A Tale," "Henry and Eliza: A Novel," and "The Beautiful Cassandra: A Novel in Twelve Chapters" burlesque such novel conventions as the opening in medias res, the use of short racy chapters, names taken from *Burke's Peerage*, scenes of fashionable dissipation, extensive use of correspondence, inset narratives, fatal attractions, and glamorously distressed protagonists. "The Generous Curate: A Moral Tale,"

Jane Austen's only sister, Cassandra Elizabeth Austen (Jane Austen Memorial Trust)

"The Adventures of Mr Harley," "Sir William Mountague," and "Memoirs of Mr Clifford" burlesque the newly popular form of the tale, or brief narrative, often packed with incident and characters lightly sketched, in contrast to the more extended treatment of "sentiment" in novels. The epistolary novel, still much in vogue and the most obviously "sentimental" form of fiction by the 1780s, is burlesqued in "Amelia Webster," "The Three Sisters: A Novel," "Love and Freindship: A Novel in a Series of Letters," and "Lesley Castle: An Unfinished Novel in Letters." The last two, along with "Evelyn" and "Catherine; or, The Bower" are more extended satires on novelistic "heroinism," and several of these burlesques suggest a connection between sentimentalism, which was a common object of criticism in the Austen family, and other kinds of social and even political transgression. A fragment of a burlesque apparently to be called "The Female Philosopher" indicates that Austen was familiar with the increasing tendency in the 1790s to associate Sentimentalism, female appropriation of "philosophy" or social criticism from the period before the French Revolution, and the feminism of writers such as Mary Wollstonecraft and Mary Hays, inspired by the egalitarian doctrines of the Revolution.

Austen's main techniques of satiric undermining are familiar ones. Simply by drastically abbreviating some forms she achieves a burlesque effect, for example packing material that could fill out a three-volume novel into a ludicrously rushed few pages. Other devices are the exaggeration of heroic language into purple patches, mixing vulgar colloquialisms with such language, terminating heroic incidents with bathos, the adoption of a nonchalant and provocatively unprofessional narrative character, and flagrantly disregarding conventions of narrative continuity and plotting. These devices reappear, toned down, in her later, full-length novels. Austen's burlesques are minor but amusing pieces and show excellent familiarity with generic and stylistic conventions of many kinds. Perhaps more important, Austen's will to parody was an acceptably feminine exercise of critical thought, especially applied to the culture of writing. In her time such critical thought was seen as primarily an activity for men, especially in the professions.

Furthermore, critical response to classic and contemporary literature was no mere aesthetic diversion at that time, but a major way of participating in civic culture. "Literature of the day," as it was called, included novels, plays, light verse as well as more serious poetry, magazines, and so on; this literature expressed and reflected the interests and concerns of those who wrote and read it, and these writers and readers were, like the Austens, mainly professional middle-class people. They condemned what they saw as aristocratic snobbery, upper-class decadence, and the patronage system that spread from the royal court and government through the rest of society. They also condemned middle-class emulation of their social "betters" and upper-class cultural domination of society through the fashion system, or "the *ton*." During the 1780s and 1790s, for example, middle-class observers were repeatedly scandalized by the moral misconduct and abuse of social position by the Prince of Wales and his brothers, supposedly the leaders of society. At the same time, the middle classes were becoming increasingly concerned about the condition and the culture of the lower classes. Much middle-class social criticism warned against contamination from the "vulgar." Such warnings became more urgent during the "Revolution Debate" of the 1790s, when the middle and upper classes had to take sides on the nature and significance of the French Revolution for Britain.

At the same time, many social critics complained that "literature of the day" contributed to what it attacked—that it was part of the very "fashion system" it condemned. "Fashionable novels," "indecent plays," and "sentimental" writing of various kinds were condemned for spreading decadent upper-class values and practices to eager middle-class—and especially female—readers. The Austen family kept up with "literature of the day" and were aware of its important and controversial place in civic life. Some of the Austens were even willing to contribute to this literature. James and Henry Austen had literary tastes, and at Oxford University they published a literary magazine called *The Loiterer* in 1789-1790. In genteelly satirical style it promotes the professionalization of culture, attacks decadent court culture and emulation of it by the middle classes, and criticizes the fashionable literature of Sensibility as a form of aristocratic culture in disguise. Yet *The Loiterer* also advances thoroughly Tory, loyalist politics and defends the established Church. These themes, not unusual for the time, illustrate the way interconnections of politics, religion, and culture were taken for granted. Austen herself probably contributed an ironic letter to the editors from "Sophia Sentiment," purporting to complain about the magazine's neglect of feminine literary interests.

The education of Austen and her sister was not nearly as thorough and systematic as that offered their brothers. While the men would have to prepare for a profession and therefore spend their formative years accumulating intellectual and moral capital for the future, the only career open to women of the Austens' class was that of wife and mother. The sisters were prepared accordingly with some training in "accomplishments," that is, "elegant" skills such as music, drawing, dancing, and comportment. Too close emotionally to be separated for schooling, despite their difference in age, the sisters were taken to study with Ann Cooper Cawley, the widow of a head of an Oxford college, in 1783. She then took her charges and their cousin Jane Cooper to Southampton, where the three girls caught typhus and were taken home by their mothers; unfortunately Mrs. Austen's sister caught the fever and died. In 1784 the sisters were sent to the Abbey School in Reading, where intellectual training was little emphasized. In December 1786 the girls returned home, where they received the majority of whatever education they ever had and largely educated themselves. Jane Austen acquired a good knowledge of the literature and culture that were thought valuable at the time, she had a modest talent for music, and she loved dancing. She especially admired the writings of Samuel Johnson and the poetry of William Cowper. With the rest of her family, she shared Johnson's Tory politics, practical piety, Anglican theology, fine sense of language in everyday as well as literary use, and commitment to emergent national cultural institutions. Cowper was the great poet of middle-class sensibility and gave epic scope and even heroic grandeur to middle-class life before the Romantic poets also attempted to do so.

All the Austens were novel readers and, as Jane Austen herself later boasted, were unashamed of the fact, unlike many of their contemporaries. The Austens realized and appreciated the potential of the novel for social criticism and moral discourse at a time when most critics condemned novels as immoral, disseminators of decadent court culture, and subliterature fit only for women (though dangerously seductive for the supposedly weak female intellect and strong female imagination). Austen admired the novels of Samuel Richardson, especially *Sir Charles Grandison* (1754), which she reread many times in her lifetime; with her niece Anna Austen she even tried adapting it into a play for performance by children of the family sometime after 1812. She and her family, with their gentry connections and professional standing, probably appreciated Richardson's portrayal of a landed gentleman thoroughly imbued with middle-class virtues. Richardson's novel not only argues for a fusion of gentry and professional middle-class cultures—a fusion that appealed strongly to the largely middle-class reading public; it also develops new techniques of "realism," or artistic persuasiveness, for representing the individual who is meritorious inwardly—intellectually and morally—rather than merely socially—by birth and rank.

As the Austens would have known well, the "Richardsonian revolution" in the novel was developed from the 1760s to the 1780s by women writers, especially Frances Burney, whose *Evelina* (1778) and *Cecilia* (1782) represent the novelistic version of the middle-class discourse of merit through a heroine rather than a hero. In *Cecilia* Burney also shifts from the Richardsonian episto-

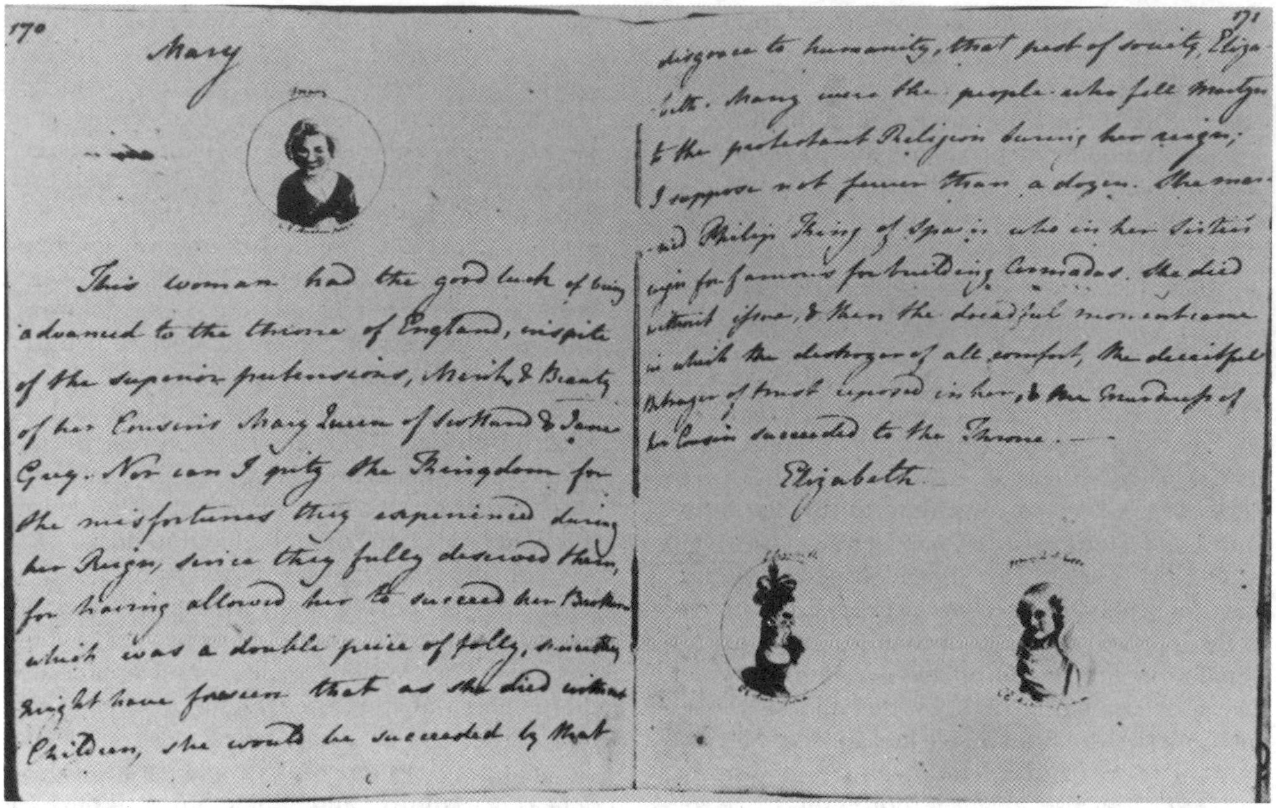
170

Mary

This woman had the good luck of being advanced to the throne of England, inspite of the superior pretensions, Merit, & Beauty of her Cousins Mary Queen of Scotland & Jane Grey. Nor can I pity the Kingdom for the misfortunes they experienced during her Reign, since they fully deserved them, for having allowed her to succeed her Brother which was a double piece of folly, since they might have foreseen that as she died without Children, she would be succeeded by that

171

disgrace to humanity, that pest of society, Elizabeth. Many were the people who fell martyrs to the protestant Religion during her reign; I suppose not fewer than a dozen. She married Philip King of Spain who in her Sister's reign was famous for building Armadas. She died without issue, & then the dreadful moment came in which the destroyer of all comfort, the deceitful Betrayer of trust reposed in her, & the Murderess of her Cousin succeeded to the Throne.—

Elizabeth

Pages from the manuscript for "The History of England," written by Jane Austen and illustrated by her sister, Cassandra (Add. MS 59874, f. 170-171; British Library)

lary form to authoritative third-person narration, using the new technique of "free indirect discourse," the narrator's filtered reporting of the character's inward thoughts and feelings. This device sustains the reader's sympathetic identification with the character while retaining distance, control, and "objectivity" for the narrator. The forms of the novel used by Burney were those taken up by Austen when she began seriously to write novels in the 1790s, and though she abandoned the epistolary form, letters do have important functions in her novels. Not surprisingly, when Burney published her third novel, *Camilla*, by subscription in 1796, Austen's father signed up for a copy for his literary daughter. Once again the Austens' response as a family to the literary culture of the day, including its social and political implications, was decisive in Austen's formation as a writer.

Until 1801 Austen lived in her family home at Steventon, reading the literature of the day, rereading her favorite authors, maintaining her local visiting network, discussing the characters and vicissitudes of new acquaintances and old friends, visiting her brother Edward and his family in Kent, dancing at balls given by the local gentry, accompanying her family to Bath for the recreations and social life of an elegant spa town, and keeping up with issues of the day, such as the long trial (1788-1794) in the House of Commons of Warren Hastings, first governor general of British India, on charges of corruption and abuse of office. (The Austens were pro-Hastings.) Austen closely followed the careers of her brothers, especially the naval officers, who were at war from 1793 until the final defeat of Napoleon in 1815. She shared the happiness, occasional bereavements, and disappointments of brothers and friends as they married, began families of their own, and lost their loved ones.

In December 1795 she fell in love herself, with Thomas Langlois Lefroy, a graduate of Trinity College, Dublin, who was visiting his uncle and aunt. Recognizing that the young man would be disinherited if he married the daughter of a penniless clergyman, Madam Lefroy cut short the courtship by sending her nephew away.

All the while Austen observed the successive feasts and holy days of the established Church, from quiet, but firm, personal conviction and not just from family duty. In the 1790s she also left behind writing the spirited literary satires with which she had amused her family from about the age of eleven to the age of eighteen. At first without her family's knowledge, she began to write novels that were meant to be full-length and seriously literary, if still humorous and even satirical.

Yet there is continuity between Austen's "juvenilia" and her maturer works. Both grew out of a family literary culture. As Lord David Cecil puts it, "Many authors start writing in order to relieve their private feelings; Jane Austen began in order to contribute to family entertainment. Her early works were examples of a family activity and expressions of a family outlook." But it was a family outlook confident in being representative of the reading public at large, a reading public dominated by the values and culture of the middle classes, led by the professionals and in many ways linked to the progressive elements of the landed gentry. Austen's novels continued to reflect and advance this outlook.

The novel was being used extensively in the Revolution debate of the 1790s: the struggle to lead the "political nation" and its immediate supporters and dependents (which could be equated with the reading public) into coalition either with politicized artisans and the lower-middle classes or with the landed gentry. In the late 1790s and early 1800s, however, writers turned to representing the reconciliation of social differences and conflicts that had threatened to take Britain, like France, over the brink of revolution in the early and mid 1790s and that continued to cause concern for the preservation of Britain's unity and empire against challenge from Napoleonic France. Women, conventionally seen as social mediators, were quick to take up the theme of national reconciliation in their writings, while avoiding overt discussion of the "unfeminine" subject of politics. Yet such writers wanted to continue the long-standing, middle-class critique of upper-class decadence, lower-class unreason, and middle-class social emulation of either.

Austen's novels participate in this post-Revolutionary literary movement. Austen began several novels in the latter half of the 1790s, though they were not published for some years, and then they were much altered. An epistolary novella, published after her death by her nephew as *Lady Susan*, in the second edition of his *Memoir of Jane Austen* (1871), depicts a selfish and witty courtly coquette. The text is partly a satirical exaggeration of the fashionable novels that portrayed such characters with apparent disapproval for fascinated and scandalized middle-class readers. In 1795 she wrote, again probably in epistolary form, a story titled "Elinor and Marianne," and began to revise it two years later in third-person narrative form as the novel that would be published in 1811 as *Sense and Sensibility*. In 1796 and 1797 she worked on a novel titled "First Impressions," probably also in letter form; this novel was later revised and published in 1813 as *Pride and Prejudice*. Late in 1797 Austen's father offered "First Impressions" as a novel "comprised in three Vols. about the length of Miss Burney's *Evelina*" to the prominent London publishers Thomas Cadell and William Davies. He hinted at willingness to pay the expense of printing if the novel were accepted, but it was turned down. In 1798 and 1799 Austen wrote most of a novel that was later revised, bought by the publisher Richard Crosby, and advertised in 1803 as "In the Press, SUSAN; a novel, in 2 vols." It remained unpublished, however, and was later revised again and brought out at the end of 1817, after Austen's death, as *Northanger Abbey*.

Austen's mother was in poor health, and in 1800 her father suddenly decided to retire, hire his son James as his curate, and settle in Bath. Austen fainted when told of the decision, but when she moved to Bath with her parents in May 1801 she determined to like the place. It was still an important health spa, holiday center, and place of fashionable resort for the gentry and well-to-do middle classes. While the Austens vacationed on the coast at Sidmouth in Devon in summer 1801, Austen seems to have met and fallen in love with a young clergyman. The Austens apparently expected that he would propose marriage and be accepted, but he died suddenly. More than a year later, while visiting her close friends the Bigg sisters, Austen was proposed to by their brother. Because his fortune would insure her against a fate she feared—spending her old age in poverty—she accepted him even though he was younger and temperamentally unsuited to her, but she broke off the engagement the next morning and returned immediately to Bath. It was at this time that Austen began a novel depicting sisters apparently condemned to the fate Austen feared for herself, though in the novel eventually a marriage of true minds and sufficient means would avert this. The novel was never completed and the surviving fragment was published after her death as *The Watsons* in the second edition of her nephew's *Memoir of Jane Austen*.

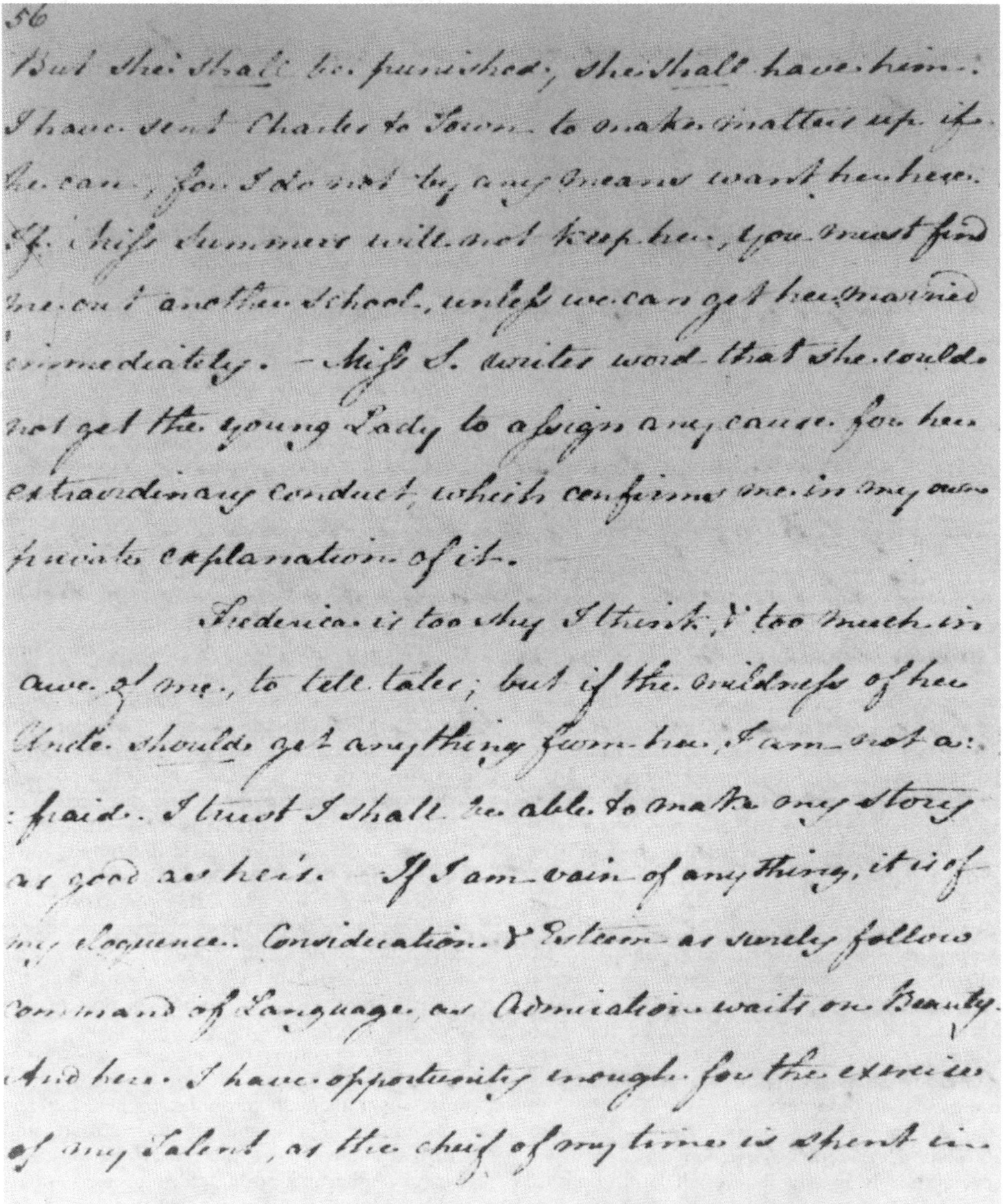
56
But she shall be punished, she shall have him. I have sent Charles to Town to make matters up if he can, for I do not by any means want her here. If Miss Summers will not keep her, you must find me out another School, unless we can get her married immediately. — Miss S. writes word that she could not get the young Lady to assign any cause for her extraordinary conduct, which confirms me in my own private explanation of it.

Frederica is too shy I think, & too much in awe of me, to tell tales; but if the mildness of her Uncle should get anything from her, I am not afraid. I trust I shall be able to make my story as good as her's. If I am vain of anything, it is of my eloquence. Consideration & Esteem as surely follow command of Language, as Admiration waits on Beauty. And here I have opportunity enough for the exercise of my Talent, as the chief of my time is spent in

Pages from the manuscript for Lady Susan *(MA 1226; Pierpont Morgan Library)*

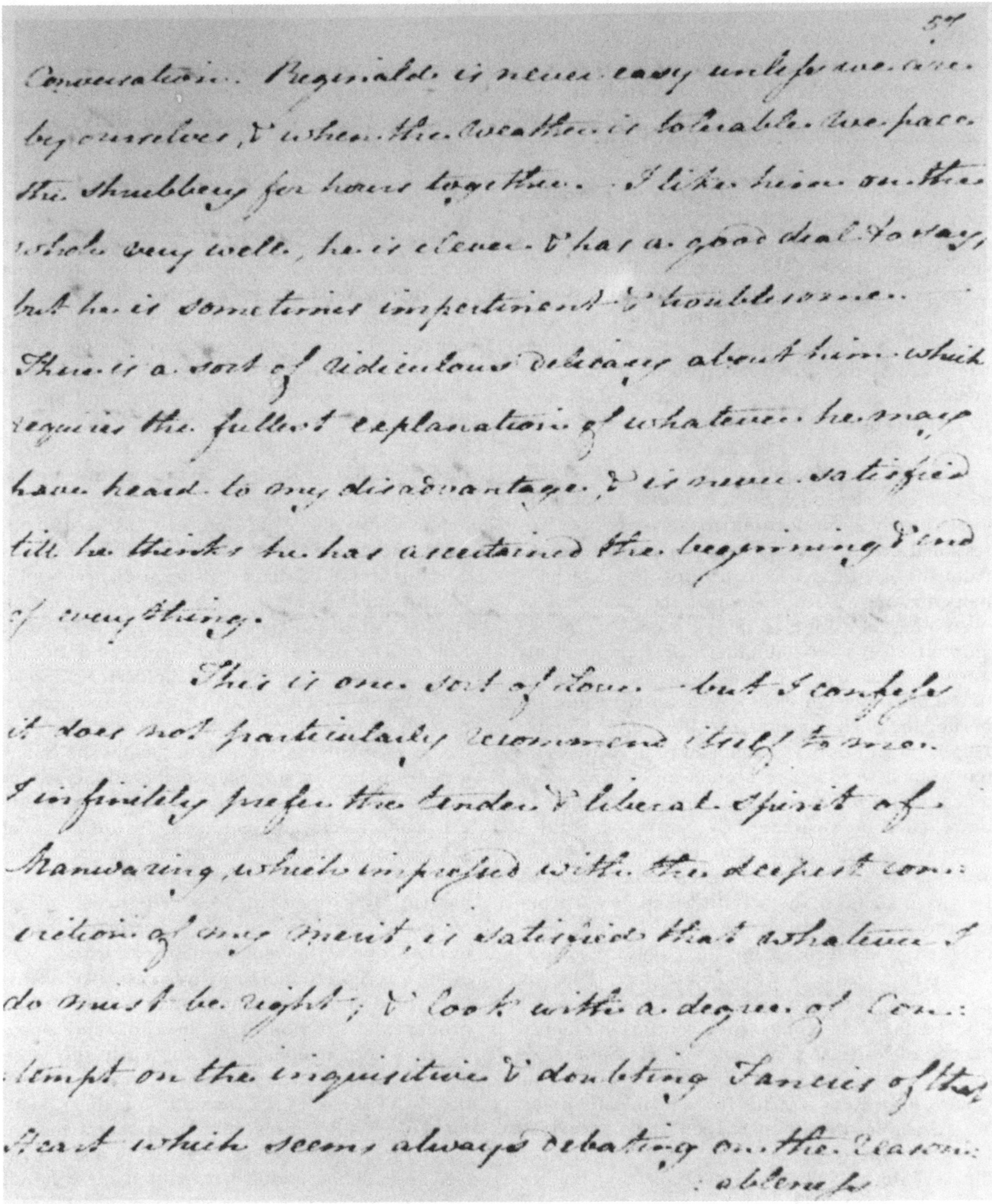
57
Conversation. Reginald is never easy unless we are
by ourselves, & when the weather is tolerable we pace
the shrubbery for hours together. I like him on the
whole very well, he is clever & has a good deal to say,
but he is sometimes impertinent & troublesome.
There is a sort of ridiculous delicacy about him which
requires the fullest explanation of whatever he may
have heard to my disadvantage, & is never satisfied
till he thinks he has ascertained the beginning & end
of everything.
This is one sort of Love - but I confess
it does not particularly recommend itself to me.
I infinitely prefer the tender & liberal spirit of
Manwaring, which impressed with the deepest con:
:viction of my merit, is satisfied that whatever I
do must be right; & look with a degree of Con:
:tempt on the inquisitive & doubting Fancies of that
Heart which seems always debating on the reason:
:ableness

One reason for Austen's failure to push a book through to publication during these years may have been a series of personal losses and the anxiety of living near the edge of socially degrading circumstances. In December 1804 her close friend and early encourager, the lively Madam Lefroy, died from a concussion sustained in a riding accident. In January 1805 Austen's father died. Since his clerical income ended with his death, his widow and daughters were faced with relative penury, but the Austen brothers pooled resources to maintain their mother and sisters, joined by their friend Martha Lloyd, in solid middle-class comfort at Bath. Although Austen had enjoyed the varied social scene at first, she eventually grew to dislike the place and its people. She continued to follow the career, both at sea and ashore, of her brother Frank. In 1805 he just missed participating in the Battle of Trafalgar, an experience he much regretted because he lost not only an opportunity to increase his "professional credit" but also "pecuniary advantage" from the sale of any French ships he might have helped capture. He married in 1806 and invited his mother and sisters to share his house at Southampton. They joined him there after a stay at Clifton near Bristol and a visit to the great country house of Stoneleigh Abbey, Warwickshire, just inherited by their relation the Reverend Thomas Leigh. When Frank was again away at sea the Austen women were left to a quiet and retired existence, visiting little, using the local circulating library, gardening, visiting Edward Austen and his large family (who took the surname Knight in 1812) in Kent and Henry Austen in London, and following news of the war in Spain. Austen became especially close to Edward's daughter Fanny, then in her teens; it was a lifelong friendship.

When Edward's wife died in late 1808, his mother and sisters comforted the family. Edward offered them the choice of a comfortable house on one of his estates, in Kent and Hampshire, so that they would be closer. They chose a house at Chawton, in Kent, not far from their early home at Steventon. In summer 1809 they moved to Chawton, where Austen would live until her final illness. Life at Chawton was simple and neither mean nor grand. The Austen women and Martha Lloyd kept one indoor and one outdoor servant. Austen and her sister managed the household economy with great efficiency and thoroughness. Since they could not afford to keep a carriage, their local social life was limited to places within walking distance and their larger social life was mainly in their brothers' households. Jane Austen was less interested and involved in general socializing than her mother and sister. Mary Mitford, herself an ardent admirer of Austen's novels, recorded the report of a friend that Austen had "stiffened into the most perpendicular, precise, taciturn piece of 'single blessedness' that ever existed," and until *Pride and Prejudice* came out she was "no more regarded in society than a poker or a fire-screen, or any other thin, upright piece of wood or iron that fills the corner in peace and quietness." Cassandra Austen did some philanthropic and educational work among the local poor, but Jane Austen deliberately took second place to her sister, whom she regarded as her superior, and limited herself to affairs in and about Chawton Cottage. She kept up her music, practicing the piano before breakfast so as not to disturb the others. The Austens subscribed to the circulating library in the nearby village of Alton, and Austen also subscribed to a local literary society. This group was a common way of sharing the cost of new books, which would be given to each member of the society for a specified period, after which the book had to be passed to the next member on the list. Austen looked after the household meals and in the evening joined in cards, needlework, games of skill, and conversation. She also read aloud to her companions, an interest and talent she inherited from her father. She interested herself in the doings of the large Austen family, especially her many nieces and nephews. In the morning she read and wrote apart from the others.

This thoroughly feminine, supportive domesticity was not then regarded as degrading, but in fact had gained greatly in prestige in the aftermath of the Revolution debate. Austen's way of life was represented by many writers—and Austen would be prominent among them—as the proper sphere of woman, as repository and reproducer of the "national" culture, not in the sense of high culture but as the moral and ethical practices in local, daily existence that together constituted the nation, especially the political nation. Austen may have been sequestered in a small village and a household of women, but she was well aware of contemporary political and social thinking and would have realized that her life at Chawton in fact resembled the emergent ideal of romantic femininity, rooted in the "domestic affections" and the source of the national character. Not surprisingly, then, she turned once again and with renewed purpose to writing. The novels

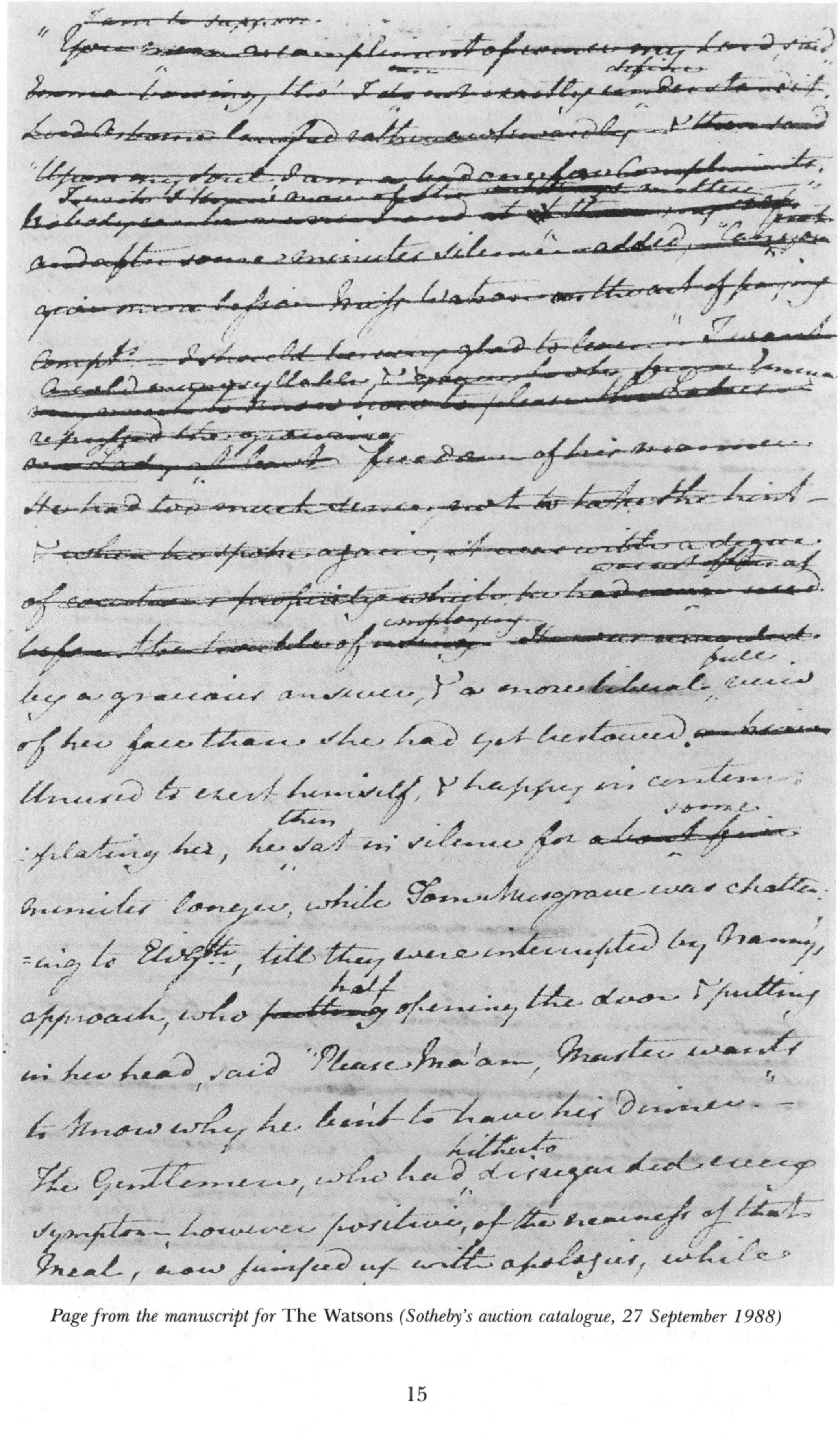
by a gracious answer, & a more full view of her face than she had yet bestowed. Unused to exert himself, & happy in contemplating her, he sat in silence for some minutes longer, while Tom Musgrave was chattering to Elizth, till they were interrupted by Nanny's approach, who half opening the door & putting in her head, said "Please Ma'am, Master wants to know why he be'nt to have his Dinner."— The Gentlemen, who had hitherto disregarded every symptom, however positive, of the nearness of that Meal, now jumped up with apologies, while

Page from the manuscript for The Watsons *(Sotheby's auction catalogue, 27 September 1988)* that she began during this period were developed from the pre-Revolutionary novel of manners, sentiment, and emulation, but they were conceived in the latter part of the Revolutionary decade and rewritten to address the interests and concerns of a post-Revolutionary age, not directly or explicitly but obliquely. Indeed, their obliqueness was essential to their rhetorical effect, for the reading public was disgusted with direct ideological and political warfare in print, perhaps especially in novels.

A further dimension to this obliqueness was Austen's secrecy about her writing as an activity, linked to her profound and genuine aversion to acquiring a public character and life as what would then have been called an "authoress." It does seem likely that, in general, the balance between psychological and social being encourages the development of either a rich domestic life or a dominant social identity. Furthermore, the ideal of domestic woman formulated in the late eighteenth century was accompanied by ambiguity or even hostility toward women appearing in public characters, such as that of a published writer. More particularly, the Revolutionary aftermath saw an aggressive remasculization of literary culture along with an energetic appropriation by male writers of the themes of subjectivity and domesticity that female writers had exploited in order to build professional careers in the decades before 1800. Austen's secrecy about her writing and her rejection of a public character were responses to all these forces rather than what Cecil calls "the nearest thing to an eccentricity in her otherwise well-balanced character."

At Chawton Cottage she wrote away from the others at first, in a chamber that served as both a hallway and a dining room. The room had a squeaky door that Austen prevented from being repaired because it gave warning of anyone approaching. She worked on a writing desk placed on top of a small table and used small slips of paper that could quickly be put out of sight if someone did enter. (Later in her career she would sometimes write in the common sitting room when others were present.) When she wrote to the publisher Crosby in 1809 to ask for the return of the still-unpublished manuscript of "Susan" she used the pseudonym "Mrs Ashton Dennis." The title page of her first published novel, *Sense and Sensibility*, states that it was "By A Lady," and such of her relations as knew of her authorship were enjoined to keep the secret. The title page of her next novel, *Pride and Prejudice*, attributed the work to "The Author of 'Sense and Sensibility,' " and this practice continued with each successive novel.

By the time she returned to novel writing at Chawton, Austen was an experienced novelist, if still an unpublished one, and had strong views on the art of fiction. She expressed these opinions only desultorily, however, in letters to her family. Austen read her niece Anna Austen's manuscript novel "Which Is the Heroine?" and offered detailed comments in letters of May or June, 10 August, 9 and 28 September, and December 1814. Her criticisms were directed to maintaining plausibility in the representation of manners and social conventions and to establishing a clear focus of social relations—"3 or 4 Families in a Country Village is the very thing to work on." Cassandra Austen disliked "desultory novels," Jane Austen advised Anna, or ones with "too frequent a change from one set of people to another" and "circumstances" of "apparent consequence" that actually "lead to nothing." Such structure was in fact fairly common in the Burney type of novel that Jane Austen practiced, and she said that she herself allowed "much more Latitude" in this matter than Cassandra; at least she allowed it to other novelists, for her own novels have an economy of elements and tightness of construction that would have pleased Cassandra very much. Austen was also conscious of the way genres and styles were seen as either "masculine" or "feminine." For example, the novel was widely regarded as a "woman's" form of writing though certain kinds of novels were seen as more appropriate for male writers. To her nephew James Edward Austen, who was trying to write a "man's" novel, Jane Austen protested:

> What should I do with your strong, manly, spirited Sketches, full of Variety and Glow?—How could I possibly join them on to the little bit (two Inches wide) of Ivory on which I work with so fine a Brush, as produces little effect after much labour? (16 December 1816)

Two years earlier, she had complained, tongue in cheek, against Walter Scott's taking up novel writing after a career as best-selling Romantic poet, because he "should not be taking the bread out of other people's mouths." She also made fun of novelists who padded out their works with extraneous matter, such as sermons, travelogues, and literary criticism.

As for the practicalities of composition, Austen fully realized the conflict between sustained

Jane Austen circa 1802 (watercolor by Cassandra Austen; Collection of Mr. A. F. H. Austen)

creativity and domestic responsibility. Admiring the productivity of the novelist Jane West, who managed a farm, Austen wrote to her sister on 8 September 1816, "Composition seems to me Impossible, with a head full of Joints of Mutton & doses of rhubarb." Nevertheless, in 1809 the promise of domestic security at Chawton seems to have renewed her interest in novel writing and her determination to publish. She began by returning to her earlier work. In April 1809 she asked Crosby to publish "Susan," which he had bought for ten pounds in 1803, or to return it to her. The publisher insisted on retaining his rights, and Austen let the matter drop. Eventually she reacquired the manuscript in 1816 but died before it was published, as *Northanger Abbey*, in 1817.

Since she probably did little to revise the manuscript during the short time it was back in her hands, *Northanger Abbey* is generally regarded as her earliest substantially completed novel. Furthermore, since it satirizes the naive reader of popular Gothic "romances" as well as the conventions of that genre, it is usually seen as more closely linked than her later works to her early burlesques and parodies of literary genres and conventions, designed to entertain her family rather than for publication. Nevertheless, as Austen's family would have realized, parody of literary themes, genres, and conventions might be amusing and still have implications of national importance. *Northanger Abbey* certainly deals with the politics of literary discourse in ways that would have been recognized in the mid 1790s or early 1800s, when it was first designed or written, as issues more vital than ever. Unlike such overtly political novels as William Godwin's *Things As They Are* (1794) or Mary Wollstonecraft's *The Wrongs of Woman* (1798), *Northanger Abbey*—like most of its contemporaries—works out issues of immediate political moment at the local level of individual lives; the oblique representation is the more rhetorically effective.

Northanger Abbey is clearly in the line of the Burney novel of a young woman's first entrance into the world—or rather "World," the common self-designation of narrow fashionable society as if it were to be equated with the whole of society. This narrow world is in fact the "political nation"—those of property or incomes sufficient to give them a voice in national affairs, however indirect. This world overlaps with the world of the "reading public"—those who can afford to rent or buy novels. This overlap is what gave novels such as *Northanger Abbey* their importance. Like a Burney novel, though in much shorter compass, with far fewer characters, incidents, and complications of plot, *Northanger Abbey* sets a young protagonist in society peopled by both the fashionable and the vulgar. It follows her trials and errors in "reading" this world and negotiating through it to successful "establishment" there, as a woman married or about to be married to a "proper" man and thus with her otherwise hidden intellectual and moral merit recognized by and instrumental in the "World." Though such novels usually have a female protagonist, she serves as a symbolic device rather than a representation of actual women. There is evidence that as many men as women read novels, and the socially inexperienced novel protagonist may stand for either a man or woman of merit faced with a seductive social reality dominated by considerations other than intellectual and moral merit—especially inherited wealth, rank, and power—and operating by courtly intrigue and patronage. Furthermore, this protagonist's situation must have been common to many novel readers at the time; thus such novels spoke to their real material interests and had powerful significance for them.

The protagonist of *Northanger Abbey*, Catherine Morland, is typical in these respects. Still in her teens and taken from her childhood home to stay with relatives in the fashionable spa of Bath, she and her brother James are taken up by Isabella and John Thorpe, social climbers who affect the fashionable cultures of female sensibility and male gallantry respectively. The Thorpes represent familiar types of upper-middle-class social emulation of their betters, resorting to deception and intrigue to advance their own interests. While Isabella sets her cap at James, John Thorpe hurries Catherine into a semblance of courtship. Catherine's genuine personal merit, despite her lack of worldly experience, is noticed by Henry Tilney, younger son of the socially ambitious General Tilney. John Thorpe's attempt to impress the general by greatly exaggerating Catherine's fortune induces the general to consider her a suitable match for his son and to invite her to his estate, Northanger Abbey. The name is suggestive in several ways. Most obviously it echoes the titles of "Gothic romances." These are novels of description and place, in which residues of medieval culture intrude secretly into the present to exert power over the protagonist. Middle-class readers found these romances intensely interesting. In the imaginary world of Gothic romance such readers could feel, if not consciously perceive, an analogy between the plight of the protagonist and their own situation in a society and culture dominated by what seemed an "alien," semifeudal system of court government, a system operating not through brute force but through the invisible agency of ideology and culture. In the 1790s, "English Jacobin" novelists such as Godwin and Wollstonecraft made the analogy between Gothic romance and the real world more explicit, borrowing elements of such romances to argue that "Gothic" (that is, medieval and feudal) oppression and tyranny were neither in the past nor mere fictional devices, but present political reality.

Austen's novel rejects "English Jacobin" political Gothicism. In the unfamiliar setting of Northanger Abbey, Catherine does make a mistake in interpretation. As often occurs with such protagonists, her inner strength becomes her weakness. Lacking the worldly experience to chasten and direct her subjective power, her "natural" sympathy and imagination, she relies on what she has learned in reading novels and "reads" her present world as if it were that of a Gothic romance. She sees General Tilney as a domestic tyrant and Northanger as a facade for secret horrors. Henry Tilney recognizes her error and reminds her of the present social and political reality:

> Remember the country and the age in which we live. Remember that we are English, that we are Christians. Consult your own understanding, your own sense of the probable, your own observation of what is passing around you—Does our education prepare us for such atrocities [as she has imagined]? Do our laws connive at them? Could they be perpetrated without being known, in a country like this, where social and literary intercourse is on such a footing; where every man is surrounded by a neighbourhood of voluntary spies, and where roads and newspapers lay every thing open?

This speech asserts a particular view of the present constitution of Britain and thus of British society. It is characteristic of Austen's rejection of novelistic excess of all kinds that Henry's perception of Catherine's error does not diminish the value of her character in his eyes, let alone lead him to reject her as a prospective wife—that would be too characteristic of a mere novel.

As Henry soon discovers, Catherine's imaginings about his father have some truth. If not a Gothic tyrant, General Tilney is a modern equivalent, an ambitious squire aiming to advance his position by courtly intrigue and manipulation of the marriage market. When he learns that Catherine is not the great heiress John Thorpe has led him to believe, he sends her packing. Meanwhile, Catherine's brother has been thrown over by Isabella Thorpe in pursuit of the better material prospects offered by Captain Tilney, the general's older son and heir to Northanger Abbey. Austen retains the reformist criticism of courtliness and emulation as real social evils while rejecting the reformist global condemnation of "things as they are." This double move is characteristic of post-Revolutionary literature. The move is formalized in the novel's plot by Catherine's disillusionment with the Thorpes and dismay at the general's inhumanity, Henry Tilney's confrontation with his father and decision to choose Catherine as a wife, and Catherine's prospective re-creation, with subjective merit intact and even enhanced, as wife of a man able both to school her further in the ways of the "World" and to confer on her, as married woman, social validation of her subjective merit.

Austen's social criticism in *Northanger Abbey* is executed not only in the novel's "story," or structured sequence of incidents and related characters, but also in its "discourse," or composition and manner of telling. As with her political argument, Austen links critical reflection on the novel as a genre to the development of the individual's critical thought in general and thus to strengthening of domestic relations and society at large. It is no accident that *Northanger Abbey* includes the best-known comment in English on the novel. Imagining a "miss" apologizing, when caught reading a book, that it is "only a novel," the narrator comments sarcastically that it is "only" Frances Burney's *Cecilla* (1782) or *Camilla* (1796) or Maria Edgeworth's *Belinda* (1801), "or, in short, only some work in which the greatest powers of the mind are displayed, in which the most thorough knowledge of human nature, the happiest delineation of its varieties, the liveliest effusions of wit and humour are conveyed to the world in the best chosen language." This comment could in fact be a reply to Edgeworth's prefatory remarks in *Belinda*, notifying the reader that the work is called a "tale" because "novel" has come to be associated with extravagant and seductive forms of fiction. Readers in her day would probably think of two different forms of fiction—on one hand the fashionable novel glamorously depicting courtly decadence and on the other "English Jacobin," especially Revolutionary feminist, novels depicting emotional extravagance and social and political transgression. Both these kinds of fiction, it was increasingly felt, disseminated false ideology and impractical models, undermining individual morality and thus the "domestic affections," the foundation of the state. The fact that these false fictions were associated with either French courtliness or French Revolutionary culture indicates the importance of the novel as an instrument of political communication.

Austen's move to correct the excesses of the 1790s novel is similar to Edgeworth's. Austen reduces the scope and variety of incidents and characters, avoids narratorial expressivity—in fact adopting narratorial irony—eliminates characters that are mere "humors" or caricatures, as well as any hint of melodrama in incident, and in plotting takes a middle course between mere novelistic coincidence and "English Jacobin necessitarianism," that is, the tight connection of "circumstances," individual character, and the character's ethical action. She aims for a plausible though not inevitable outcome, thereby suggesting that "destiny" is a result of free will operating in a particular social and material horizon of possibility. Not surprisingly, such plotting accords with an Anglican theology of salvation through both true faith (or understanding, in secular terms) and good works (or ethical action in accordance with informed and accurate moral judgment). Throughout her career, Austen followed this same pattern of correcting excessive novel conventions, at times alluding to specific bizarrenesses in particular novels of the day but otherwise cutting against generally well known novel devices. In *Northanger Abbey* this criticism by "rewriting" is especially obvious, as the narrator repeatedly draws the reader's attention to ways in which this novel is not like a common "novel of the day." In her later novels Austen's narrators are less obtrusive in this respect, but the same work is carried on. Rewriting is to effect rereading—not just reading again but reading as a critical and reflective activity. This activity produces true knowledge, a secular version of that "true faith" that is the basis of ethical action necessary to win salvation. As much as her father or her clergymen brothers, Austen addresses a secular life in the light of eternity. Since women in her day could not do this from the pulpit they often chose to do so in the genre assigned to them by social, cultural, and literary convention.

Narrative method plays a central role in this process of reformative reading. The omniscient narrator represents a model consciousness, a figure for the "author," implicitly on the same level as the reader, representing the world of the novel from a superior position, whereas the protagonist is clearly fallible and limited, whether sympathetically or ironically treated by the narrator. As a character in the text, the narrator implicitly arranges all other characters in a hierarchical order over a grid whose coordinates are knowledge and moral judgment. Structurally the narrator represents a level of understanding toward which the protagonist is headed, somewhere beyond the end of the novel. The reader's interest in this progress is underpinned by Austen's use of free indirect discourse, or reported inward thought and feeling. Other novelists who use this device, such as Frances Burney, Ann Radcliffe, and Maria Edgeworth, treat several or many characters this way; Austen focuses almost exclusively on her protagonist, thereby giving a centrality and importance to a character that most other characters regard as unimportant. This device is one of Austen's favorites, used in *Sense and Sensibility*, *Mansfield Park*, and *Persuasion*. But Austen also uses free indirect discourse to encourage the reader to sympathize with the protagonist, to accept her interpretations and judgments of the world around her. In this way the reader is often tricked into going along with the protagonist's errors until brought up short by the narrator's irony or revelation of the "truth." This device creates an irony of reading by which the reader identifies with both narrator and protagonist. In experiencing this irony at certain moments of narratorial revelation the reader vicariously experiences the gap between the protagonist's imperfection and fallibility and the narrator's superior understanding. All human understanding, except the godlike narrator's, is conditional and relative. The narrator's irony reminds us of this mortal fallibility. This reading would be serious matter indeed were it not for the fact that it is presented in what is "only a novel." In political terms, the point does implicitly counter "English Jacobin" ideas of the "perfectibility of man."

Northanger Abbey, substantially completed by 1803, is thus very much a novel of its time, of a particular moment in the evolution in the novel as vehicle of ideological and cultural conflict. At the same time it includes the basic elements of the Austen novel, rapidly developed with greater sophistication and subtlety from Austen's settling at Chawton in 1809 to a few months before her death in 1817.

Through 1809 and 1810 Austen worked on revising "Elinor and Marianne," her epistolary novel of 1795, into *Sense and Sensibility*. When it was complete Henry Austen again served as intermediary between his sister and the publisher, this time Thomas Egerton, who may have been chosen because he had participated in the distribution of James and Henry Austen's Oxford magazine, *The Loiterer*. Jane Austen offered to pay the costs of printing and, not expecting to break even on the book, had saved some money for that purpose. She was to retain copyright, and the publisher was to get a commission for distributing the book. In April 1810 she went to stay with Henry in London to correct proofs and wrote to her sister, "I am never too busy to think of S. & S. I can no more forget it, than a mother can forget her sucking child." It was published in the fall, and the first edition sold out in less than two years, making Austen £140, in those days a sum sufficient to support someone in comfort for a year or more.

Sense and Sensibility: A Novel—the generic designation is important and was in the title of all Austen's novels published in her lifetime—is a more ambitious novel than *Northanger Abbey*. Austen doubles the plot by representing the courtship of two sisters, Elinor and Marianne Dashwood, and by increasing the number of characters and incidents. In scope *Sense and Sensibility* is more like a full-blown Burney novel. Nevertheless, the narrator-protagonist relationship remains focused for the most part on one character, the unglamorous Elinor. In fact, in Elinor and Marianne, Austen foregrounds in one novel the two character types that she preferred to alternate in the later novels—the quiet but right-thinking heroine such as Fanny Price and Anne Elliot and the more outgoing and somewhat quixotic heroine such as Elizabeth Bennet and Emma Woodhouse. *Sense and Sensibility* brings into play another set of issues that were prominent in the Revolution debate and the post-Revolutionary quest for reform with renewed social stability—issues of property, patronage, and gender in the reconstruction of British society.

The widowed Mrs. Dashwood and her three daughters are required to leave their home when the new heir, Mrs. Dashwood's stepson, John, assumes his inheritance with his fashionable and selfish wife, Fanny. Such is the lot of wives and daughters under the system of male primogeniture that was common at the time—and much criticized by feminists such as Mary Wollstonecraft. The Dashwood women are given a home at Barton Cottage on the Devonshire estate of a distant relation, Sir John Middleton, whose family is unfortunately a disorder of snobbery, vulgarity, and mere sociability. One visitor, Colonel Brandon, is interested in the middle daughter, Marianne, but he does not fit her romantic idea of a hero, constructed from her novel reading. She makes no secret of her preference for the dashing Willoughby, who is also visiting in the neighborhood. The eldest daughter, Elinor, is disappointed, however, that Fanny Dashwood's brother Edward Ferrars, a young clergyman with a good estate in prospect, does not visit, for she has fallen in love with him and the feeling has seemed mutual. Other guests at the Middletons' include Charlotte Palmer and her husband, the one silly and the other aloof, and the obsequious Misses Steele, the younger of whom, Lucy, confidentially divulges to Elinor her secret engagement with Edward Ferrars. The Steeles, like the Dashwood women, are dependent on others to prevent a slide from comfort and gentility to poverty and social insignificance. Unlike her mother, Elinor Dashwood is prepared to deal with her situation with conventional feminine virtues of fortitude and forbearance. Her sister Marianne indulges in romantic fantasy. Lucy Steele has evidently taken the worst course, practicing the courtly arts of coquetry to inveigle Edward Ferrars into an imprudent engagement.

When the scene shifts from the country to London the destinies of the Dashwood sisters seem to take a further turn for the worse. Marianne learns that Willoughby is a fortune hunter and is about to marry for money. Fanny Dashwood's mother, old Mrs. Ferrars, suspects her son Edward of being in love with Elinor and snubs the Dashwood women in favor of the Steeles, until Lucy reveals her secret engagement to Edward, who is then disinherited in favor of his younger brother, Robert, a mere man of fashion. Returning to Barton, the Dashwoods stay with the Palmers, where Marianne falls ill. Alarmed, Willoughby arrives and confesses to Elinor that he did love Marianne and must now live out an unhappy marriage. Back at Barton the last movement of the plot unfolds. Marianne recovers, but Elinor is further distressed when told that a Mr. Ferrars, whom she takes to be Edward, has recently married Lucy Steele. But the new husband turns out to be Edward's brother, whom Lucy has turned to as now the better prospect. Edward is freed from his engagement and proposes to Elinor; Colonel Brandon has offered the young clergyman a living in his gift; eventually Marianne comes to see the colonel's quiet domestic and social virtues and marries him.

There is an obvious post-Revolutionary argument in *Sense and Sensibility*, indicated in its title. "Sensibility" as indulgence of personal absolutes, such as romantic love, regardless of social conventions and even laws, was widely seen as a major ideological source of Revolutionary transgression. In the Revolution debate "sense," or "common sense," was often opposed to Revolutionary theory, speculation, and enthusiasm. In Austen's novel the evident triumph of sense over sensibility, and the confinement of sensibility, as domestic and social sympathy, though enacted on the level of common life, would have had political and public implications for readers at the time the novel was published, in part because moral, religious, and educational writers insisted that there was a close connection between small, apparently insignificant transgressions and more serious ones. Furthermore, *Sense and Sensibility* clearly establishes the value of "feminine" passive virtues of the kind possessed from the outset by Elinor and acquired through error and suffering by Marianne. These virtues were proclaimed by numerous writers of the Revolutionary aftermath, beginning at least as early as Hannah More's *Strictures on the Modern System of Female Education* (1799), as central to social order and even to national survival.

At the same time it is clear that *Sense and Sensibility* registers the desperate situation of genteel women deprived of the wherewithal to sustain social dignity or even nobility of mind and feeling. Mary Wollstonecraft argued in *A Vindication of the Rights of Woman* (1792) that this plight drove many women of the middle and upper class to coquetry and courtly intrigue, to the ruin of the domestic affections and thus the corruption of society as a whole. Austen does not explicitly make

The house at Chawton where Jane Austen lived with her mother and sister from April 1809 until shortly before her death in 1817

this kind of protest in *Sense and Sensibility* or elsewhere, but her reticence accords with a post-Revolutionary program of avoiding the explicitnesses that many thought had threatened to tear the country apart in the 1790s. Furthermore, the fact that her novel has a happy ending reflects her Anglican faith in a just and benevolent deity presiding over a universe that is comic in the sense that suffering and injustice have, finally, a beneficial effect. "Wise passiveness" is better in the long run than rebellion. If Austen was a feminist, she was a post-Revolutionary one. Certainly the social criticism of *Sense and Sensibility* takes in a broad sweep of foolish and even vulgar emulation, by gentry and professional middle class alike, of a court culture increasingly seen as threatening ruin to the nation.

With *Sense and Sensibility* published, Austen turned again to "First Impressions," the novel she had completed in 1797 and tried to sell to Cadell. She revised it, gave it the title *Pride and Prejudice: A Novel,* and sold the copyright to Egerton for £110 late in 1812, having asked for £150. It was published early in 1813, anonymously, though Austen's authorship soon became known beyond the family circle. It was very well received; for example, Byron's future wife, Anne Isabella Milbanke, considered it to be "the fashionable novel" of the season. It seems to have been widely read and discussed in fashionable and literary society.

Pride and Prejudice takes another pair of sisters but puts the outgoing one, Elizabeth Bennet, more into the foreground, while keeping the silent suffering one, Jane, much more in the background. Property inheritance again becomes a major factor in the destiny of these two—along with their three younger sisters Mary, Kitty, and Lydia—for their father's small estate is entailed to the nearest male relative, the Reverend William Collins. Entailment was the kind of injustice against women that Wollstonecraft and other Revolutionary feminists had criticized sharply, for it forced women to make their fortune the only way open to them—by speculating on the marriage market. Mr. Bennet has also committed an error attacked by feminists of the time—giving in to the influence of courtly erotic culture and marrying a woman who was merely beautiful and lacking in the intellectual and moral resources necessary to support her own social position with dignity and discretion, to be a true friend and companion to her husband, and to raise children—especially children themselves utterly dependent on such inner resources. Closed up in his gentleman's library for much of the time, Mr. Bennet does not even pass on his own knowledge and discrimination to his children, except to his favorite, Elizabeth. Fortunately, Elizabeth and Jane have also spent time with some cultivated relations, the Gardiners, who were formerly in the ungenteel mercantile middle class. Of the other sisters, Mary is a junior pedant, Kitty is impressionable, and Lydia is a mere ambitious coquette.

When Mr. Bingley, a wealthy young man also from an ungenteel background, rents a nearby manor and arrives with his sister and a friend, Mrs. Bennet's notion that well-managed intrigue will get her daughters husbands seems to have promise. Bingley seems to be falling in love with Jane, despite the condescending discouragement of his sister and the aloof disapproval of his friend, Mr. Darcy. Elizabeth resents their intrusion, especially Darcy's. The Reverend Mr. Collins shows up determined to marry one of the Bennet girls and thereby make some recompense for the harsh terms of the entail. For their part, Lydia and Kitty are delighted with the prospects offered by some officers quartered nearby. A young militia officer, Mr. Wickham, seems especially attracted to Elizabeth, and she is more disposed to return his regard after he tells her Darcy has treated him unjustly. When the recently arrived Mr. Collins learns Jane is already in love he proposes immediately to Elizabeth, who refuses his offer because she cannot love him. Shortly thereafter, however, he is accepted by Elizabeth's friend Charlotte Lucas, whom Elizabeth knows to have too much sense not to see that Collins is a fool. Disillusioned, Elizabeth decides that Charlotte has merely sold herself on the marriage market. When Bingley and his party leave suddenly for London, she concludes that Darcy has talked Bingley out of proposing to Jane. Jane visits the Gardiners in London, where she is treated with mere formal politeness by Miss Bingley, who suggests that her brother is to marry Darcy's sister. Learning that Wickham is courting an heiress merely for her money, Elizabeth is completely disillusioned: all except her sister Jane seem mere courtly and self-interested intriguers, and she can only congratulate herself on not being taken in.

Elizabeth meets Darcy by accident, however, while visiting Charlotte and Mr. Collins, who has a living on the estate of Lady Catherine de Bourgh, a haughty snob and Darcy's aunt. Elizabeth is dumbfounded when Darcy suddenly proposes to her, and angrily rejects him, accusing him of separating Bingley and Jane and of being unjust to Wickham. The next day he gives her a letter explaining and justifying his conduct; at first Elizabeth believes it must be false, but gradually she comes to accept the truth of everything Darcy says. Ashamed, she admits that until this moment she never knew herself, and she now sees all the characters and incidents to this point in the story in a new light. Structurally, this scene is the center of the novel. It is clear to the reader, if not entirely clear to Elizabeth, that she and Darcy would be a match, and the plot now turns to repairing the breach between them.

Against Elizabeth's advice, Mr. Bennet allows Lydia to visit the family of one of the officers, who are at the fashionable resort of Brighton, somewhat notorious at that time as the preferred haunt of the Prince of Wales. Elizabeth herself goes on a tour with the Gardiners through scenic Derbyshire. The Gardiners want to visit Darcy's estate of Pemberley, and when they learn that he is absent, Elizabeth agrees. They are shown over the house, and the housekeeper gives them a glowing report of its master's character and conduct. The Gardiners are surprised, but Elizabeth has more reason than ever to regret her prejudice against the man. When Darcy returns unexpectedly he is all hospitality, and prospects for a new understanding seem to be opening. But these possibilities seem dashed when Elizabeth hears that her sister Lydia has eloped from Brighton with Wickham, who is unlikely to marry someone with little money. By the social conventions of the time the "ruin" of Lydia will affect the marriageability of all her sisters. Distressed at this news, Elizabeth blurts it out to Darcy, and Mr. Gardiner leaves to help Mr. Bennet track down the couple. Later the Bennets learn that Wickham has agreed to marry Lydia and surmise that he has been bribed to do so by Mr. Gardiner. But Elizabeth learns that Darcy arranged everything. When the Bingleys and Darcy return to the neighborhood, Bingley and Jane quickly resume their love for one another and become engaged. To Elizabeth's surprise, however, Lady Catherine de Bourgh arrives and haughtily tries to extract a promise from Elizabeth that she will not marry Darcy. As happens to such domineering intriguers, her aim is undermined by her own actions: Darcy learns of Elizabeth's standing up to his aunt, and to Elizabeth's further surprise—though not the reader's—he comes to propose again. This time he is accepted. In a characteristic final comic touch, Mrs. Bennet is ecstatic at the accomplishment of more than she could have imagined in her plans to marry off her daughters.

In its plot, incidents, and characters *Pride and Prejudice* is an interesting variation on the novel of manners and sentiment. But its originality—more obviously than in *Sense and Sensibility* or *Northanger Abbey*—is in its manipulation of the triangular relationship between narrator, protagonist, and reader. As in the earlier novels, the omniscient narrator retains the power to withhold information from the reader and restrict access to the consciousnesses of characters other than the protagonist. By being let fully into Elizabeth's mind but virtually excluded from all others, the reader is meant to develop a sympathetic identification with Elizabeth's character and judgments. Thus when Elizabeth realizes in the middle of the novel that she, who prided herself on her perspicacity, has been mistaken about all the main points, her confidence in her ability to "read" her world is seriously shaken. Similarly, the reader, who might feel confidently able to decode the story correctly but who has fallen in with Elizabeth's reading, will feel an analogous humiliation. Chastened, though in different ways, Elizabeth and the reader continue their adventures in the text, but it becomes increasingly apparent to the reader that Elizabeth's abandonment of any hope for a return from Darcy is yet another mistake in her "reading" of him and herself. The narrator, too, who has been fairly noncommittal about Elizabeth's "readings" in the early part of the novel, becomes more ironic in the later part. In short, the novel constructs an exercise in reading for both protagonist and reader, and manipulates narrative so as to make the reader conscious of the fallibility and precariousness of reading of any kind. Again, it would not be going too far to see this exercise in terms of Austen's deeply held Anglican faith and its theology of the imperfection yet improvability—though not perfectibility—of humankind.

In June 1813, five months after *Pride and Prejudice* was published, Austen completed a new novel, begun in February 1811. *Mansfield Park: A Novel*, which some scholars feel also had an earlier version, was published by Egerton, though Austen kept the copyright this time and made more than three hundred pounds by the first edition. In *Mansfield Park* Austen returns to a heroine who, like Elinor Dashwood, is right-thinking but socially disregarded from the outset. Fanny Price is one of a large and impecunious family at Portsmouth. Her mother is one of three once-famous beauties, though her sisters married better than she—one, Mrs. Norris, to a country clergyman and the other, Lady Bertram, to a baronet, the owner of the large estate of Mansfield Park. After the death of her husband, Mrs. Norris, who resides near the Bertrams, persuades Sir Thomas Bertram to take in their niece Fanny. Separated from her family and especially her beloved brother William, Fanny remains an outcast at Mansfield, condescended to by her cousins Tom, Maria, and Julia, though her kind cousin Edmund protects her and guides her education. Not surprisingly, she comes to love him for it. Her uncle Sir Thomas leaves to attend to his plantations in Antigua. In the absence of the father the others in the family soon drift into one folly or another, abetted by Mrs. Norris, who dotes on her wealthy nieces and nephews while treating Fanny like a servant.

Maria becomes engaged to Mr. Rushworth, a wealthy neighboring gentleman whose name accurately represents his moral and intellectual value. All the Bertrams become intrigued by Henry and Mary Crawford, a fashionable brother and sister who are visiting their half sister Mrs. Grant, wife of the local vicar, himself an old-style clergyman more interested in the pleasures of the table than in the cure of souls. Together the young people visit Rushworth's estate of Sotherton Court, the name of which suggests the decadent, courtly, more "southern" or Mediterranean than English fashionableness (or ton) pervading the values of all but Fanny and Edmund. The outing is ostensibly to discuss Rushworth's planned "improvements," or ornamental additions to his estate, but new love interests and flirtations develop quickly in the symbolically sultry weather. While the Bertram sisters become rivals in flirting with Henry, Edmund becomes fascinated by Mary, who is, however, dismayed to learn that as the second son he intends to take up a profession in the church. Fanny remains a silently suffering spectator. When Tom brings to Mansfield his vacuous friend Yates, the young people catch the contemporary fad for amateur theatricals and plan to perform *Lovers' Vows*, a translation of August von Kotzebue's *Das Kind der Liebe* (1791, The Love Child). The play is a dubious choice for several reasons. It represents illicit love; it celebrates romantic subjectivity in the face of social convention, in a way that had already given such "German plays" a bad reputation in respectable English society; and it will enable the young people at Mansfield to make love

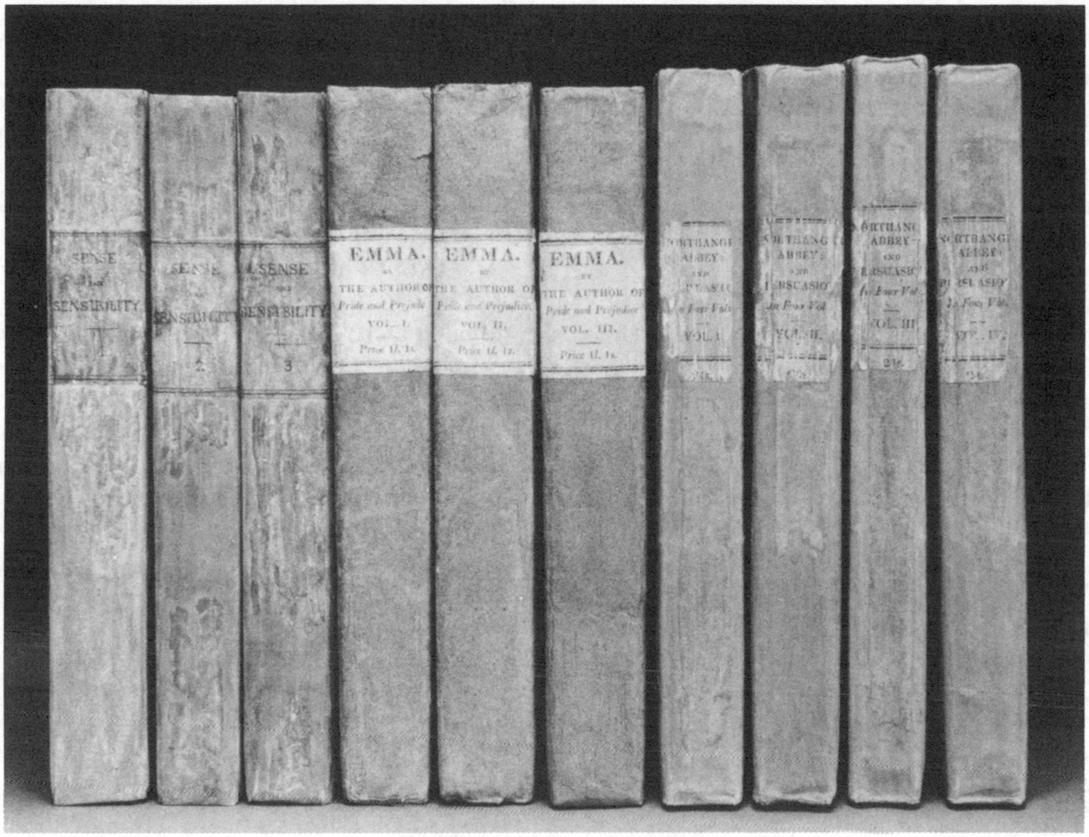

First editions of three Austen novels

speeches to each other that social convention would prohibit them from making in their real characters. Fanny, significantly, wishes to decline any part in it.

Sir Thomas's sudden return from the West Indies puts a stop to these follies, though he allows Maria to marry Rushworth. The next movement of the story focuses on Fanny, who begins to be more noticed by everyone. Mary Crawford tries to make her a confidante regarding Mary's infatuation for Edmund, which she feels is impeded by Edmund's determination to become a "mere" country clergyman. Fanny is treated with consideration by Sir Thomas and with friendly solicitude by Edmund, all to Mrs. Norris's disgust. Even Henry Crawford now finds her interesting enough to wish that he could make her fall in love with him. Fanny's only real delight, however, is in a visit from her beloved sailor brother, whose career is being promoted by Sir Thomas. To Henry's surprise, he finds himself actually falling in love with Fanny, and persuades his uncle, an admiral, to arrange William's promotion to lieutenant. Henry then proposes to Fanny, and the connection between the two actions suggests the kind of leverage used in the patronage system rather than a disinterested courtship. To Sir Thomas's anger and Mary's surprise, Fanny rejects Henry, whom she sees as merely a courtly seducer. To remind Fanny of the degrading life that awaits her if she does not change her mind and accept Henry, Sir Thomas sends her to her vulgar parents' home in Portsmouth. Henry visits her there, and despite his apparent sincerity she finds she still cannot love him, or will not.

The denouement now unfolds, as the Bertram family seems to disintegrate. When Tom Bertram falls seriously ill, Mary writes to Fanny and reveals her true character by expressing the hope that Tom's death will clear the way for Edmund to become heir to Mansfield, and thus the kind of catch Mary wants. The recent bride Maria runs off with Henry, and Julia elopes with Yates. Mary's inability to see Maria and Henry's adultery as morally serious, rather than just socially damaging, shocks Edmund out of his fascination for her. When Fanny returns to Mansfield to lend what comfort she can, even the indolent Lady Bertram is relieved by her presence. Fanny is still the shyly feminine person she has always been, but now, amid so many crises, her steadiness of character and moral authority begin to be recognized by all—she is indeed a woman of "price," in the sense of intrinsic value. Tom's brush with death sobers him into a greater sense of moral and social responsibility, and Fanny marries Edmund. They will continue to sustain Mansfield Park and will spread their wedded virtues through local society from the nearby, and again aptly named, vicarage of Thornton Lacey—uniting the symbol of Christ's sacrifice with an ornament of upper-class dress.

Mansfield Park embodies the timeliest possible message for the novel-reading public of the early Regency and the late stages of the long struggle with Revolutionary and Napoleonic France. Mansfield Park is a figure for England or Britain as rural, leisured, and cultivated but with heavy social, economic, and imperial responsibilities that must be carefully tended and reinvigorated in each generation. It is also a "mansefield," a field for the inspiriting influence of the manse or domestic home of the established church and its theology of true faith, or ideological correctness, and good works, or social responsibility and leadership. This home is of course presided over by a woman, the heart of the nation according to an increasingly powerful ideology of domestic woman as repository and nurturer of the national soul, conscience, culture, and destiny.

Late in January 1814, four months before *Mansfield Park* came out, Austen began work on *Emma*, and she completed it fourteen months later, in March 1815. Here Austen again reverses the character of her heroine, for Emma Woodhouse is quite unlike Fanny Price, subjectively and socially. Emma is the belle of her neighborhood—beautiful, young, and wealthy, the younger and unmarried daughter of a querulous hypochondriac widower. Emma's education was supervised by a kindly governess, Miss Taylor, now married to a neighboring gentleman, Mr. Weston. Miss Taylor was more of a friend than a preceptor, and Emma's mind is neither well stocked nor well trained. She has therefore become an "imaginist," a fictionist or romancer of real life, speculating incorrectly on the characters and intentions of others while presuming on her native talents and her social power to arrange their lives. She prides herself, for example, on having brought about the marriage of Miss Taylor and Mr. Weston. Emma has been freer than ever to indulge in her brand of local patronage since the marriage of her older sister, Isabella, to John Knightley, a London lawyer and younger brother of a local landed gentleman. This gentleman, as his name suggests—Knightley is the knight's ley, or field—epitomizes the best of the rural landed class and its modern chivalric, moral-and-ethical culture. Not surprisingly, he is the only person who dares try to correct Emma's character and point out her errors.

He has his work cut out for him. Soon after the novel opens Emma is already planning another match, between the local clergyman Mr. Elton and Emma's new protégée, Harriet Smith. An impressionable boarding-school girl, Harriet is an illegitimate child of unknown parentage, and Emma imagines she must be the love child of some nobleman. Harriet is attracted to Mr. Martin, a yeoman farmer and tenant of Mr. Knightley's. Knightley thinks Harriet and Martin would make a good couple, but Emma insists on a higher destiny for her client and discourages the match, to Knightley's chagrin. (Yet he and Emma do work well together in smoothing relations between her father and Knightley's brother.) Emma's plans for Harriet and Elton are disastrously—though comically—overset, however, when Elton mistakes Emma's interest as a sign of love for him. Emboldened by too much wine, he proposes. After Emma explains that she has intended him for the lowly Harriet, Elton is offended and goes off to Bath. Chastened, Emma resolves to give up matchmaking.

Yet her imagination is already at work on Frank Churchill, Weston's son by his previous marriage, long ago adopted by a wealthy, childless uncle and aunt. He is soon expected to pay a courtesy call to his father and new stepmother. Frank does not appear on schedule, apparently detained by his imperious aunt. Another visitor arrives, however—the beautiful and talented, but impecunious, Jane Fairfax, orphan granddaughter of a clergyman's widow, Mrs. Bates, who lives in straitened circumstances with her unmarried daughter. While she recognizes her social and material superiority to Jane, Emma feels shamed by Jane's superiority of mind and evident discipline of character. When Frank arrives, Emma is attracted to him and realizes that the Westons hope she can be drawn into marriage with him, but Knightley finds Frank to be an extravagant and self-willed flirt. Emma is further chagrined when Elton returns with a bride who, as a married woman, takes social precedence over Emma. When Elton rudely snubs Harriet at a ball, Knightley comes to the rescue, and when Harriet is later harassed by some gypsies she is rescued by Frank. Emma now projects a match between Frank and Harriet and encourages her young friend not to be deterred from falling in love with a man above her socially, but Knightley suspects some secret between Frank and Jane. Meanwhile, Mrs. Elton, a snobbish busybody, finds a situation as governess for Jane. When the company goes on an outing to Box Hill Frank flirts with Emma and, made careless by his attention, she insults Miss Bates, who dares not stand up to her. Knightley is shocked, and his reproof gives Emma real pain. She realizes she has abused her social position and responsibility, and in a characteristic act of self-abnegation calls on Miss Bates by way of apology.

The death of the dictatorial Mrs. Churchill seems to free her nephew to follow his own wishes in marriage. Emma now expects Frank may propose to Harriet, but a few weeks later she is amazed to learn that he and Jane have been secretly engaged for some time. Emma now fears the ill consequences of having again encouraged Harriet to love a man beyond her reach, but she is stunned to learn that Harriet thought Emma was encouraging her to think of Knightley, not Frank, and she has taken Knightley's kindness to her as a sign of love. With a sickening shock, Emma realizes that she herself loves Knightley and fears that Harriet's surmise may be right. When Knightley calls to console Emma, in case she has allowed herself to be taken in by Frank's flirtation, she at first prevents him from speaking because she thinks he is about to confess his love for Harriet. Then, in another act of self-sacrifice, she invites him to say what he had intended. With a third and even greater shock—Austen was playfully fond of the fairy-tale pattern of threes—Knightley confesses his love for Emma and hopes she can return his feeling. Characteristically, the narrator draws away from Emma's joy with a sudden turn of amused irony. Emma now has the unpleasant duty of telling Harriet, but it soon transpires that Harriet has been seeing Martin, with Knightley's encouragement, and is to marry him. It later turns out that Harriet's father is not a dashing aristocrat but a solid and unromantic tradesman. Emma's "novelizing" of those around her is completely exposed. If this book were a sentimental tale or a Gothic novel the consequences would be tragic; but in Austen's comic novel no real harm has been done. In fact, Emma's errors have helped to educate others, as well as herself, to their human fallibility, as one might expect in a novelistic universe ruled by a benevolent deity much like the one supposed by Austen's Anglican theology to preside over the natural universe.

Like its predecessor, *Emma* shows the centrality of domestic woman to a renewed nation led by a reformed professionalized gentry. Emma resembles heroines in other novels of the time, representing the socially divisive and destabilizing effect of a woman who lacks intellectual resources and moral discipline appropriate to her station and thus misuses her social power. Yet Austen characteristically gives a comic rather than pathetic or tragic cast to this story and greatly diminishes what is too commonly treated melodramatically by other writers. She also denies that extensive social reform is necessary to end the social evil caused by such vitiated female characters. In Austen's benign novelistic universe reform on the individual level is enough to effect social change, provided that a character can practice, in however small and local a way, the virtues of self-correction and self-abnegation, which are in fact, for Austen, Christian and Anglican virtues. Further, the value of marriage, which is a sacrament as well as a property arrangement and legal contract, is shown in the fact that Knightley's more practiced ethical character will support Emma's continued spiritual growth and consequent social usefulness—a much subtler echo of the conclusion to Eaton Stannard Barrett's spoof *The Heroine; or, Adventures of a Fair Romance Reader* (1813), which Austen had read in March 1814.

When she was ready to publish *Emma*, Austen decided to change publishers and offered the work to Byron's publisher, John Murray. He referred it to a leading man of letters, William Gifford, editor of the Tory *Quarterly Review*. Gifford had published two verse satires, the *Baviad* (1791) and *Maeviad* (1795), attacking what he saw as signs of moral and cultural decline, including women authors. He thought very highly of Austen's novel, however, and Murray offered her £450 for the copyright, along with those of *Mansfield Park* and *Sense and Sensibility*. Austen preferred to retain property in her work, however, and Murray published *Emma: A Novel* on commission, in December 1815. Following a suggestion from the Prince Regent's librarian, the Reverend James Stanier Clarke, Austen dedicated the novel, though with no enthusiasm, to the prince.

She had met Clarke in autumn 1815 when he had been sent by the prince to invite Austen,

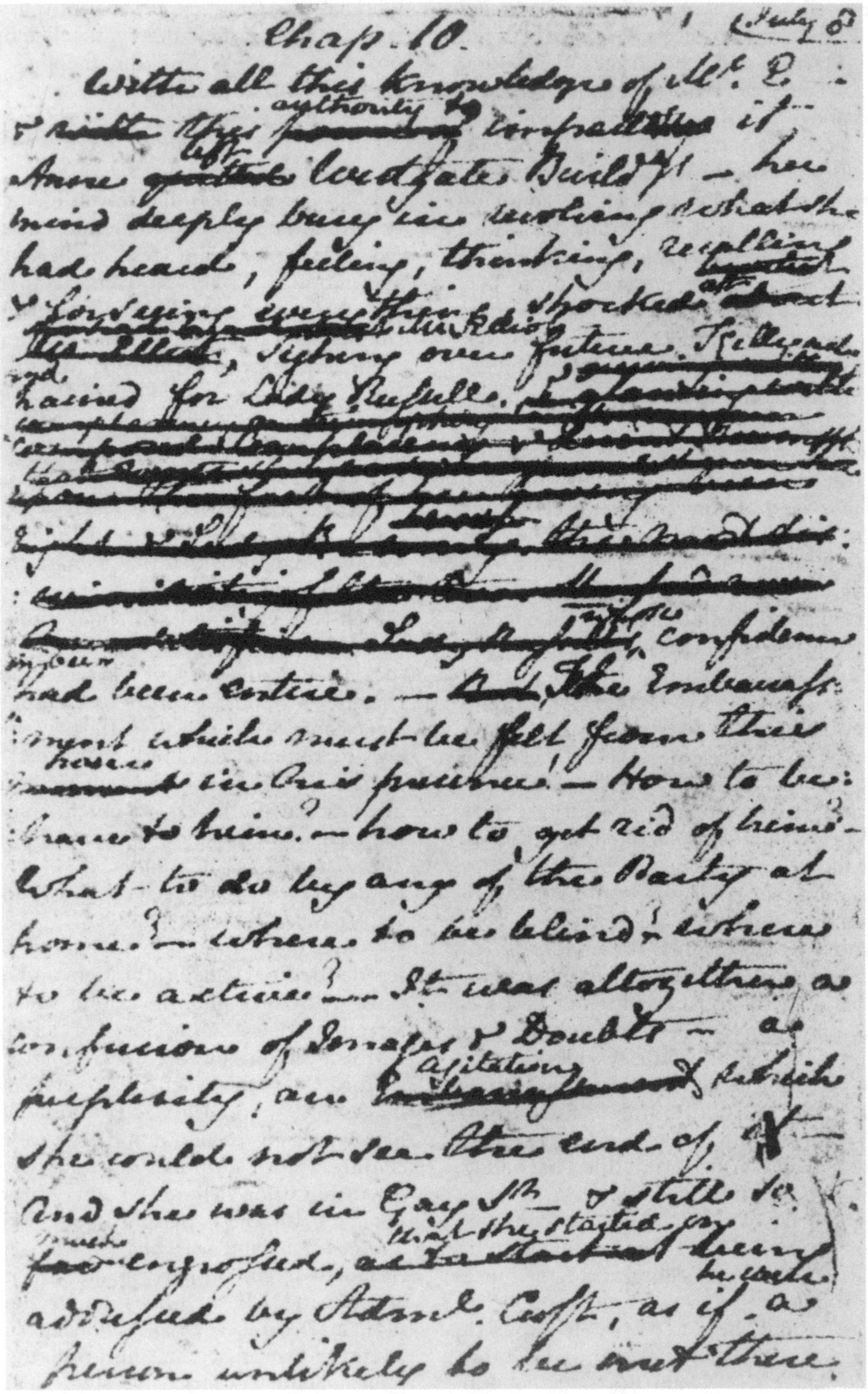
Chap. 10.

With all this knowledge of Mr. E. & this authority to impart it, Anne left Westgate Buildgs — her mind deeply busy in revolving what she had heard, feeling, thinking, recalling & foreseeing everything; shocked at Mr Elliot, sighing over future Kellynch, and pained for Lady Russell, in whose confidence had been entire. — The Embarrassment which must be felt from this hour in his presence! — How to behave to him? — how to get rid of him? — What to do by any of the Party at home? — where to be blind? where to be active? — It was altogether a confusion of Images & Doubts — a perplexity, an agitation which she could not see the end of. And she was in Gay St — & still so much engrossed, that she started on being addressed by Admd. Croft, as if a person unlikely to be met there.

Page from the first of two surviving chapters in the original draft for Persuasion *(British Library)* then in London, to see Carlton House, his London residence. Clarke told her that the prince admired her novels and kept a set in each of his residences. Austen was not overawed. Though she accepted Clarke's suggestion that she dedicate her next novel to the prince, she rejected Clarke's suggestion that she write a novel about a clergyman, evidently somewhat like Clarke himself, and declared:

> The comic part of the character I might be equal to, but not the good, the enthusiastic, the literary. Such a man's conversation must at times be upon subjects of science and philosophy, of which I know nothing; or at least be occasionally abundant in quotations and allusions which a woman who, like me, knows only her own mother tongue, and has read very little in that, would be totally without the power of giving. A classical education, or at any rate a very extensive acquaintance with English literature, ancient and modern, appears to me quite indispensable for the person who would do any justice to your clergyman; and I think I may boast myself to be, with all possible vanity, the most unlearned and uninformed female who ever dared to be an authoress. (11 December 1815)

Obviously if Austen desired, she could use to her own advantage the conventional distinctions between "masculine" and "feminine" genres and styles.

Undeterred, Clarke then hinted that it might be in Austen's interest to write some "historical romance, illustrative of the history of the august House of Cobourg," in view of the impending marriage of the princess Charlotte, heir presumptive to the throne. Austen replied even more emphatically that she realized such a work "might be much more to the purpose of profit or popularity than such pictures of domestic life in country villages as I deal in." Then she added,

> But I could no more write a romance than an epic poem. I could not sit seriously down to write a serious romance under any other motive than to save my life; and if it were indispensable for me to keep it up and never relax into laughing at myself or other people, I am sure I should be hung before I had finished the first chapter. No, I must keep to my own style and go on in my own way; and though I may never succeed again in that, I am convinced that I should totally fail in any other. (1 April 1816)

The reply is less interesting for its apparent modesty than for its clear sense of generic distinctions and the commercialized nature of the literary marketplace.

A few months after she finished *Emma*, Austen did "go on in [her] own way," with *Persuasion*, begun in August 1815 and completed, though not finally polished, a year later. In this novel Austen returns to the silently suffering, stoical heroine disregarded by everyone who applies merely social criteria in judging others. Austen also presents more directly than before the problem, underlying *Mansfield Park*, of reconstructing Britain and its social leadership in the Revolutionary aftermath. Austen and a host of other writers were representing this reconstruction as a progressive dialectic of gentry and professionals, especially the elite professions to which Austen's brothers belonged. In *Mansfield Park* the estate (and state) dangerously divided within is purged of courtly and vulgar elements—or at least such elements are put in their place—and reinvigorated with merit "from below." In *Persuasion* an estate dangerously overextended morally, socially, and financially is not so much reinvigorated as superseded by an estate acquired entirely on merit and able to take into itself the neglected best of the older estate (or state). Not surprisingly, the representatives of merit are, like two of Austen's brothers, navy men.

The novel opens with the vain and vacuous widower, Sir Walter Elliot of Kellynch Hall, contemplating retrenchment of his estate, which his proud extravagance has run into debt. Moreover the estate, like that of Mr. Bennet in *Pride and Prejudice*, is entailed on the nearest male relative. It will not go to any of Sir Walter's three daughters unless one of them marries the heir at law. Sir Walter's youngest daughter, Mary, who has inherited his merely social values, has married a neighboring gentleman, Charles Musgrove, son and heir of a wealthy squire. Sir Walter's other two daughters remain unmarried, but Sir Walter's projects are only for the elder, Elizabeth, who is as vain and superficial as her father. The middle daughter, Anne, is taken for granted by everyone, though the narrator lets the reader see that she is the only one with real inner resources and character, partly thanks to her older friend and adviser, Lady Russell. Reluctantly accepting the advice of his estate agent, Sir Walter agrees to let Kellynch to Admiral Croft and his wife, who are looking for a home now that war with France is over. Sir Walter looks down on such mere men of merit, rushed to prominence and even wealth by the vicissitudes of war. In fact eight years earlier he had, with the help of Lady Russell, persuaded Anne not to marry Mrs. Croft's brother, Frederick Wentworth, a man unsuitable in rank and prospects for a daughter of a baronet. Fortunately the matter was kept secret from other members of both families at the time.

Sir Walter plans to take his family to Bath, where he can maintain his social standing without great expense and where his daughters will have enhanced prospects of finding husbands. He and Elizabeth leave for Bath first, while Anne spends time with her sister Mary's family, the Musgroves, mediating the differences and difficulties of various family members. When Wentworth, now á successful and wealthy man thanks to the fortunes of war, arrives to see the Crofts he evidently harbors resentment against Anne and gaily joins the circle of the sociable flirts Henrietta and Louisa Musgrove as Anne suffers in silence. Wentworth does her several small kindnesses, but he seems determined to value in a woman what he thinks Anne lacked by rejecting him, namely firmness of purpose. The party visits the seacoast town of Lyme Regis, where they meet Wentworth's friends Captains Harville and Benwick. Benwick, who is staying with Harville and his family, is despondent over the death of his fiancée, Harville's sister. Anne continues to act as healer and counselor of other characters' upsets, such as Benwick's romantic grief, and while at Lyme Regis she finds herself being admired by a stranger, who turns out to be the heir to Kellynch, William Walter Elliot. After the impetuous Louisa Musgrove, to whom Wentworth seems drawn, suffers a serious accident because of her own careless folly, it is Anne who takes charge of the situation.

The next movement of the novel opens with Anne's arrival in Bath with Lady Russell to join her father and sister. There she finds William Walter Elliot paying court to her father, who still hopes a marriage between the heir and Elizabeth will keep Kellynch in his line. Anne also finds the insinuating Mrs. Clay, a vulgar older woman who seems determined to marry Sir Walter. Anne visits an old friend, Mrs. Smith, now ill and living at Bath in straitened circumstances. Mrs. Smith seems to know a good deal about William Walter Elliot, whom Anne finds hard to read and suspects of having a double character. Then the Crofts and Wentworth arrive at Bath, and Anne hears with surprise that the apparently heartbroken Benwick has become engaged to Louisa Musgrove. In the great set piece of the novel the various principal characters encounter each other at a concert, where Anne as usual devotes herself to the comfort of others. Later she learns from Mrs. Smith that William Walter Elliot has a vicious character. He has come to Bath to head off Mrs. Clay's designs on Sir Walter because he fears that a marriage between them might result in the male heir needed to keep Kellynch in Sir Walter's line. The Bath party is enlarged when the Musgroves and Harvilles arrive. During one meeting Wentworth appears to be writing a letter for Harville while Harville discusses with Anne the differing perseverance of men and women in loving someone who has been lost to them. Against Harville's claim that women easily turn to new love, Anne protests that men—with their public duties and professional interests—have greater aid in overcoming loss, while women can only silently suffer and endure. When the party leaves, Wentworth comes back and puts a letter in Anne's hand; overhearing her talk with Harville he has realized that he has to ask once more for her love. Anne is afraid she will find no chance to reassure him, but a chance meeting in the street affords the opportunity. This time Sir Walter and Lady Russell approve of the match; William Walter Elliot and Mrs. Clay leave Bath together. The novel closes not on a note of narratorial irony and detachment but with a sense that despite present happiness, with Anne having to fear only some future outbreak of war, some years of conjugal joy and social usefulness have already been needlessly lost because of social prejudice and a feminine weakness in face of merely social persuasion.

As Jane Austen was writing *Persuasion* her brother Henry and his partners found their bank threatened by their overoptimistic speculation and some rather questionable business practices. The postwar economic slump soon brought the bank down, and in March 1816 Henry was bankrupt; worse still, his speculations had involved large sums of his brothers' money. He decided to become a clergyman and became assistant at Chawton. At this time he regained the manuscript for Austen's unpublished novel "Susan" from Crosby, who had held it since 1803. Austen first wanted to publish immediately, but then decided to put it aside. Early in 1816 she began to show symptoms of what was probably Addison's disease, a malfunction of the adrenal cortex resulting in imbalance of the body's mineral metabolism, with symptoms such as physical weakness, skin discoloration, as well as abdominal and back

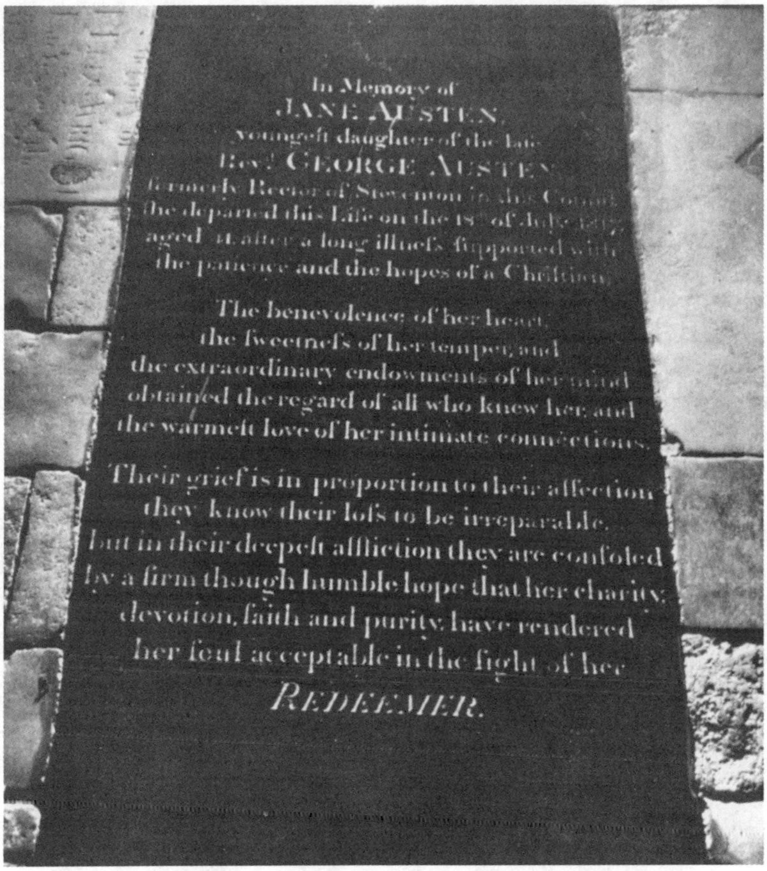

Jane Austen's grave in Winchester Cathedral

pain. Though the disease progressed steadily, Austen enjoyed increased contact with her family, including her young nieces and nephews, especially her brother James's son Edward, who, like his sister Anna, had aspirations to be a novel writer. Austen's brothers Francis and Charles, freed from constant naval duty with the ending of war, came with their families to Chawton.

In January 1817 Austen began drafting a new novel and worked at it until March, when she was too ill to continue; extracts were published in 1871 by her favorite nephew Edward in the second edition of his *Memoir of Jane Austen.* He called it *Sanditon,* though a family tradition held that Austen herself intended it to be called "The Brothers." It opens as Mr. Parker, an entrepreneur developing a seaside health spa named Sanditon, is seeking a physician to serve his new resort. When Parker's coach is overturned on a country road, he is looked after by a local family, the Heywoods. He takes young Charlotte Heywood as his guest to Sanditon, where she meets a variety of individualists seemingly tainted by the new culture of Romanticism, including Parker's brothers and sisters and the literary man of feeling, Sir Edward Denham. Another visitor to Sanditon is the rich West Indian, Miss Lambe. Austen did not get much farther than setting the scene and cast of characters, but her intention was clearly to continue her exploration of class, gender, and culture in post-Revolutionary Britain.

Austen became seriously ill in March 1817, and in May she was taken to consult a surgeon in Winchester, where she stayed in lodgings in College Street. Attended by her faithful sister, Cassandra, she rallied from time to time, and even wrote a comic poem to mark St. Swithin's Day, 15 July, but she died three days later, early in the morning. She was buried in Winchester Cathedral on 24 July. In her will Austen left the remainder of her estate after funeral expenses, £561 and two shillings, to Cassandra.

"Susan" was published as *Northanger Abbey* with *Persuasion* and a "Biographical Notice" of Austen by her brother Henry, at the end of 1817, though it is dated 1818. She was much missed in her family, but her passing caused little stir in the literary world, and her novels were soon virtually forgotten by the reading public. It was not until 1833, when they were republished in the Bentley's Standard Novels series, that her novels began a steady rise in their status to become both commercially successful and recognized as "classics." Of the thousands of novels published in the late eighteenth and early nineteenth centuries, they are among the few to survive their own time. Bentley reprinted the Standard Novels editions into the 1880s; other publishers started putting out their own editions soon after the copyrights began to expire in 1839. By the late nineteenth century, in response to Austen's emergent status as a "popular classic," editions were appearing with introductions by leading men of letters and illustrations by fashionable artists. In 1906 Austen's novels began to be published in the Everyman Library; in 1907 they began to appear in the Oxford World's Classics series; and in 1938 Penguin books began publishing them. In addition to these various popular editions, R. W. Chapman's critical edition was published by the Clarendon Press of Oxford University Press in 1923; in the 1970s Oxford University Press had this edition reedited for the Oxford English Novels series and later republished them in the new Oxford World's Classics series. Other editions are legion, and there are numerous film and television adaptations. Studied in English classes around the world, yet still read by thousands just for pleasure, Austen is now one of the world's most widely read authors.

In Austen's own time her works were praised by the few critics to review them, but not so as to distinguish them in any extraordinary way from other novels of that time. Yet Walter Scott recognized Austen's achievement. He wrote approvingly of her novels in the *Quarterly Review* (October 1815), and ten years later he reread *Pride and Prejudice* "for the third time at least" and confided to his journal:

> That young lady had a talent for describing the involvements and feelings and characters of ordinary life which is to me the most wonderful I ever met with. The Big Bow wow strain I can do myself like any now going but the exquisite touch which renders ordinary common-place things and characters interesting from the truth of the description and the sentiment is denied to me. What a pity such a gifted creature died so early. (14 March 1826)

Mary Mitford at first found Austen's novels lacking in "elegance" and "taste," but by the early 1820s she enlisted them, along with Gilbert White's *Natural History of Selborne* (1789), for her book *Our Village* (1824-1832), her own middle-class appropriation of rural England—one of the most powerful influences on the cultural imagination of the nineteenth and twentieth centuries. Nevertheless, for much of the nineteenth century Austen remained, in Brian C. Southam's words, "a critic's novelist." The modern construction of Austen as a literary *and* popular classic—popular with the educated middle-class reading public—was spurred by the publication in 1870 of James Edward Austen-Leigh's *Memoir of Jane Austen.* Its portrayal of Austen as a feminine and domestic sage simply recording a real world of rural felicity clearly had considerable cultural and political use in an age of ever deeper social, national, and imperial conflicts, of horrific industrial blight and social problems that seemed or were made out to be beyond the power of the state to remedy. Austen, like Mary Mitford, Gilbert White, and many other earlier writers, was brought to serve what Martin Wiener has described as the attack of an upper-middle-class English culture against the industrial spirit, an attack only decisively rebutted, according to Wiener, by Margaret Thatcher.

The late-nineteenth- and early-twentieth-century "Janeites," the uncritical devotees of Austen and the world she was thought to represent, saw Austen's supposed limitations of social scope and psychological depth to be strengths, something peculiarly "English." More important, such devotees often held important positions in governmental, cultural, and educational institutions. They found in Austen a vision of "Englishness" they were looking for and applied to Britain and its empire. Reaction against this complacent late-imperial, anti-industrial culture generated new approaches to and understanding of Austen, especially after the unprecedented horror of World War I and with the rise of professionalized, university-based criticism. In broad terms social historians were exploding the popular myth of an idyllic, preindustrial, Austenian world. R. W. Chapman's critical editions of Austen's novels, early writings, and letters made available materials for better understanding Austen in her own time as well as critical analysis that was more searching than the "appreciations" characteristic of earlier, "Janeite" criticism. J. David Grey and Deirdre La Faye's forthcoming, revised and expanded edition of Austen's letters will make still more information available. Mary Lascelles, Q. D.

Leavis, D. W. Harding, and others showed Austen as a determined, conscious artist and social critic.

After World War II and the further democratization of education, especially at the higher levels, Austen and her work were interpreted in the light of new social issues, including class conflict, feminism, and anti-imperialism. Austen has even become one of the few novelists to have a concordance to her works. Meanwhile, Austen's fiction had served for some time as one model for an emergent form of popular novel known as the "Regency romance." Enterprising writers undertook to "complete" Austen's unfinished works such as *The Watsons* and *Sanditon*. It is true that Austen has not yet been fully accepted as a "Romantic" writer, and as recently as 1975 Alistair M. Duckworth could write, "In spite of a staggering amount of critical attention Jane Austen can hardly be said, in her bicentennial year, to be understood better than she understood herself" ("Prospects and Retrospects," in *Jane Austen Today*). At the same time, as Duckworth goes on to illustrate, Austen's work has been profitably explored in light of recent critical and literary theory, and determined exploration of Austen's relation to her contemporary novelists and contemporary issues is making possible new understandings of her and her work in her time, thus providing new ways of understanding her importance in the present.

Letters:

Jane Austen's Letters to Her Sister Cassandra and Others, edited by Robert W. Chapman, second edition, corrected (Oxford: Oxford University Press, 1959);

Jane Austen's Manuscript Letters in Facsimile: Reproductions of Every Known Extant Letter, Fragment, and Autograph Copy, with an Annotated List of All Known Letters, edited by Jo Modert (Carbondale & Edwardsville: Southern Illinois University Press, 1990).

Bibliography:

David Gilson, *A Bibliography of Jane Austen* (Oxford: Clarendon Press, 1982; corrected, 1985).

Biographies:

Henry Austen, "Biographical Notice of the Author," in *Northanger Abbey and Persuasion: With a Biographical Notice of the Author* (London: John Murray, 1818);

James Edward Austen-Leigh, *A Memoir of Jane Austen* (London: Richard Bentley, 1870); second edition, to which is added *Lady Susan*, and fragments of two other unfinished tales (London: Richard Bentley & Son, 1871);

William and Richard Austen-Leigh, *Jane Austen: Her Life and Letters, A Family Record* (London: Smith, Elder, 1913);

Mary Augusta Austen-Leigh, *Personal Aspects of Jane Austen* (London: John Murray, 1920);

Elizabeth Jenkins, *Jane Austen: A Biography* (London: Gollancz, 1938; revised, 1948);

Mona Wilson, *Jane Austen and Some Contemporaries* (London: Cresset Press, 1938);

R. W. Chapman, *Jane Austen: Facts and Problems*, The Clark Lectures (Oxford: Clarendon Press, 1948);

Jane Aikin Hodge, *The Double Life of Jane Austen* (London: Hodder & Stoughton, 1972);

Lord David Cecil, *A Portrait of Jane Austen* (London: Constable, 1978);

Park Honan, *Jane Austen: Her Life* (New York: St. Martin's Press, 1987);

Jan S. Fergus, *Jane Austen: A Literary Life* (London: Macmillan, 1991).

References:

Harold S. Babb, *Jane Austen's Novels: The Fabric of Dialogue* (Columbus: Ohio State University Press, 1962);

Patricia Beer, *Reader I Married Him: A Study of the Women Characters of Jane Austen, Charlotte Brontë, Elizabeth Gaskell and George Eliot* (London: Macmillan, 1974);

Frank W. Bradbrook, *Jane Austen and Her Predecessors* (Cambridge: Cambridge University Press, 1966);

Julia P. Brown, *Jane Austen's Novels: Social Change and Literary Form* (Cambridge, Mass.: Harvard University Press, 1979);

Lloyd W. Brown, *Bits of Ivory: Narrative Techniques in Jane Austen's Fiction* (Baton Rouge: Louisiana University Press, 1973);

Rachel M. Brownstein, *Becoming a Heroine: Reading about Women in Novels* (New York: Viking, 1982);

Douglas Bush, *Jane Austen* (New York & London: Macmillan, 1975);

Marilyn Butler, *Jane Austen and the War of Ideas* (Oxford: Clarendon Press, 1975);

Wendy A. Craik, *Jane Austen: The Six Novels* (London: Methuen, 1965; New York: Barnes & Noble, 1965);

David D. Devlin, *Jane Austen and Education* (London: Macmillan, 1975);
Alistair M. Duckworth, *The Improvement of the Estate: A Study of Jane Austen's Novels* (Baltimore & London: Johns Hopkins Press, 1971);
Jan S. Fergus, *Jane Austen and the Didactic Novel: Northanger Abbey, Sense and Sensibility, and Pride and Prejudice* (London: Macmillan, 1983);
Sandra M. Gilbert and Susan Gubar, *The Madwoman in the Attic: The Woman Writer and the Nineteenth-Century Literary Imagination* (New Haven & London: Yale University Press, 1979);
Yasmine Gooneratne, *Jane Austen* (Cambridge: Cambridge University Press, 1970);
John Halperin, ed., *Jane Austen Bicentenary Essays* (Cambridge: Cambridge University Press, 1975);
Barbara Hardy, *A Reading of Jane Austen* (London: Peter Owen, 1975);
Jocelyn Harris, *Jane Austen's Art of Memory* (Cambridge: Cambridge University Press, 1989);
Claudia L. Johnson, *Jane Austen: Women, Politics, and the Novel* (Chicago & London: University of Chicago Press, 1988);
Gary Kelly, *English Fiction of the Romantic Period 1789-1830* (London & New York: Longman, 1989);
Joseph Kestner, *Jane Austen: Spatial Structure of Thematic Variations*, Salzburg Studies in English Literature (Salzburg: Institut für englische Sprache und Literatur, Universität Salzburg, 1974);
Robert Kiely, *The Romantic Novel in England* (Cambridge, Mass.: Harvard University Press, 1972);
Margaret Kirkham, *Jane Austen, Feminism and Fiction* (Brighton: Harvester Press / Totowa, N.J.: Barnes & Noble, 1983);
Karl Kroeber, *Styles in Fictional Structure: The Art of Jane Austen, Charlotte Brontë and George Eliot* (Princeton: Princeton University Press, 1971);
Mary Lascelles, *Jane Austen and Her Art* (Oxford: Clarendon Press, 1939);
Queenie D. Leavis, "A Critical Theory of Jane Austen's Writings," *Scrutiny*, 10 (1941-1942): 61-87, 114-142, 272-294; 12 (1944-1945): 104-119;
Laurence Lerner, *The Truthtellers: Jane Austen, George Eliot, D. H. Lawrence* (London: Chatto & Windus, 1967);
Robert Liddell, *The Novels of Jane Austen* (London: Longmans, Green, 1963);
A. Walton Litz, *Jane Austen: A Study of Her Artistic Development* (London: Chatto & Windus, 1965; New York: Oxford University Press, 1965);
Juliet S. McMaster, *Jane Austen on Love*, English Monograph Series 13 (Victoria, B.C.: English Literary Studies, 1978);
McMaster, ed., *Jane Austen's Achievement* (London: Macmillan, 1976);
Hazel Mews, *Frail Vessels: Woman's Role in Women's Novels from Fanny Burney to George Eliot* (London: Athlone Press, 1969);
Kenneth L. Moler, *Jane Austen's Art of Allusion* (Lincoln: University of Nebraska Press, 1968);
David Monaghan, *Jane Austen, Structure and Social Vision* (London: Macmillan, 1980; Totowa, N.J.: Barnes & Noble, 1980);
Monaghan, ed., *Jane Austen in a Social Context* (London: Macmillan, 1981);
Marvin Mudrick, *Jane Austen: Irony as Defense and Discovery* (Princeton: Princeton University Press, 1952; London: Oxford University Press, 1952);
Nineteenth-Century Fiction, special Jane Austen issue, 30 (December 1985);
Norman Page, *The Language of Jane Austen* (Oxford: Blackwell, 1972);
Kenneth C. Phillipps, *Jane Austen's English* (London: Deutsch, 1970);
Mary Poovey, *The Proper Lady and the Woman Writer: Ideology as Style in the Works of Mary Wollstonecraft, Mary Shelley, and Jane Austen* (Chicago & London: University of Chicago Press, 1984);
Joan Rees, *Jane Austen: Woman and Writer* (London: Hale, 1976; New York: St. Martin's Press, 1976);
Warren Roberts, *Jane Austen and the French Revolution* (New York: St. Martin's Press, 1980);
Brian C. Southam, *Jane Austen's Literary Manuscripts: A Study of the Novelist's Development* (London: Oxford University Press, 1964);
Southam, ed., *Jane Austen: The Critical Heritage* (London: Routledge & Kegan Paul, 1968);
Jane Spencer, *The Rise of the Woman Novelist: From Aphra Behn to Jane Austen* (Oxford: Blackwell, 1986);
Studies in the Novel, special Jane Austen issue, 7 (Spring 1975);
Alison G. Sulloway, *Jane Austen and the Province of Womanhood* (Philadelphia: University of Pennsylvania Press, 1989);

Tony Tanner, *Jane Austen* (Cambridge, Mass.: Harvard University Press, 1986);

Stuart M. Tave, *Some Words of Jane Austen* (Chicago & London: Chicago University Press, 1973);

Lionel Trilling, "*Emma*," *Encounter*, 8 (June 1957): 49-59; republished in his *Beyond Culture: Essays on Literature and Learning* (New York: Viking, 1965; London: Secker & Warburg, 1966);

Trilling, "In Mansfield Park," *Encounter*, 3 (September 1954): 9-19; republished in his *The Opposing Self: Nine Essays in Criticism* (New York: Viking, 1955; London: Secker & Warburg, 1955);

Trilling, *Sincerity and Authenticity* (Cambridge, Mass.: Harvard University Press, 1972; London: Oxford University Press, 1972);

Trilling, "Why We Read Jane Austen," *Times Literary Supplement*, 5 March 1976, pp. 250-252;

Joel C. Weinsheimer, ed., *Jane Austen Today* (Athens: University of Georgia Press, 1975);

Joseph Wiesenfarth, *The Errand of Form: An Assay of Jane Austen's Art* (New York: Fordham University Press, 1967);

Judith Wilt, *Ghosts of the Gothic: Austen, Eliot, Lawrence* (Princeton: Princeton University Press, 1980);

The Wordsworth Circle, special Jane Austen issue, 7 (Autumn 1976);

Andrew H. Wright, *Jane Austen's Novels: A Study in Structure* (New York: Oxford University Press, 1953; London: Chatto & Windus, 1953).

Papers:

The majority of Austen's surviving letters and manuscripts are in the Pierpont Morgan Library, New York.

John Banim

(3 April 1798 - 15 August 1842)

Cy Frost
University of Colorado at Denver

BOOKS: *The Celt's Paradise: A Poem in Four Duans* (London: John Warren, 1821);

Damon and Pythias: A Tragedy in Five Acts (London: John Warren, 1821; New York: Murden & Thomson, 1821);

A letter to the Committee appointed to appropriate a Fund for a National Testimonial, Commemorative of His Majesty's First Visit to Ireland (Dublin: Milliken, 1822);

Revelations of the Dead-Alive (London: Printed for W. Simpkin & R. Marshall, 1824); republished as *London and Its Eccentricities in the Year 2023: or Revelations of the Dead Alive, by the Author of Boyne Water* (London: Simkin, Marshall / A. K. Newman, 1845);

Tales by the O'Hara Family, first series, by John and Michael Banim 3 volumes (London: W. Simpkin & R. Marshall, 1825);

The Boyne Water: A Tale by the O'Hara Family, 3 volumes (London: W. Simpkin & R. Marshall, 1826);

Tales by the O'Hara Family, second series, 3 volumes (London: Henry Colburn, 1826);

The Anglo-Irish of the Nineteenth Century: A Novel, 3 volumes (London: Henry Colburn, 1828);

The Croppy: A Tale of 1798, by the Authors of "The O'Hara Tales," by John and Michael Banim (3 volumes, London: Henry Colburn, 1828; 2 volumes, Philadelphia: E. L. Carey & A. Hart, 1839);

The Denounced. By the Authors of "Tales by the O'Hara Family" (3 volumes, London: Colburn & Bentley, 1830; 1 volume, New York: Printed by J. & J. Harper, 1830);

The Smuggler: A Tale, by the Authors of "Tales by the O'Hara Family" (3 volumes, London: Henry Colburn & Richard Bentley, 1831; 1 volume, New York: Printed & published by J. & J. Harper, 1832);

The Chaunt of the Cholera: Songs for Ireland, by the Authors of "The O'Hara Tales" (London: James Cochran, 1831);

The Bit O' Writin' and Other Tales by the O'Hara Family (3 volumes, London: Saunders & Otley, 1838; 2 volumes, Philadelphia: E. L. Carey & A. Hart, 1838);

Father Connell, by the O'Hara Family, by John and Michael Banim (3 volumes, London: T. C. Newby, 1842; 1 volume, New York: Wilson, 1842).

PLAY PRODUCTION: *Damon and Pythias: A Tragedy in Five Acts,* London, Theatre Royal, Covent Garden, 28 May 1821.

> My Dear Michael,
> You have made me shake and shiver, by bringing before my eyes the ticklish ground on which I stand.

Writing to his brother and collaborator Michael in October 1825, John Banim evinced an anxious preoccupation with the politics of his soon-to-be-published novel, *The Boyne Water* (1826). Informed by the political crisis surrounding the Treaty of Limerick and its unfulfilled promise of Catholic Emancipation, the novel tells a story of cultural stress and religious intolerance in late-seventeenth-century Ireland. The treaty, signed on the Treaty Stone at Limerick in 1691 following James II's loss to William of Orange, promised Irish Catholics political and religious freedom, a promise that soon disintegrated when the pact failed ratification in 1695. Despite swings of the political/cultural pendulum across one hundred and thirty years, the Emancipation controversy dogged its English promisors from 1691 well into the nineteenth century; it remained the most volatile political issue of Banim's Ireland in the 1820s. With a radical Catholic Association expanding ominously and the Irish peasantry made restive by the Penal Days of Catholic persecution, 1825 found both houses of Parliament grappling with "the state of Ireland," a long-avoided legislative task that would absorb exorbitant amounts of legislative energy for the rest of the century. Banim, the first novelist of Ireland wholly of Irish-Catholic origin, inflected *The Boyne Water* with

these collusions of politics and religion. Driven by the political yearning and cultural memory of Ireland, superimposing past on present, *The Boyne Water* lobbies hard for fulfillment of the Emancipation promise.

Born on 3 April 1798, John Banim followed his brother Michael in a family headed by Michael Banim, Sr., a farmer and the proprietor of a powder-and-shot shop in the town of Kilkenny, Leinster, and Joannah Carroll Banim, described by John's biographer as possessing "a mind of very superior order and a store of good sense." John aspired to become an artist, while his brother Michael, interested in law, began study at the bar. Although Michael Senior was determined that his sons would receive advanced educations, economic reality partially foreclosed his goal, and Michael, instead of completing the law study he had begun, joined his father in the shop. John enrolled in the Protestant College of Saint John, founded at Kilkenny in the sixteenth century as an adjunct to the Cathedral of Saint Canice. Chartered by James Butler, first Duke of Ormonde, in 1684 and reendowed by James II in 1689, Kilkenny College had a reputation as the country's oldest and most distinguished preparatory school. Sometimes called "the Eton of Ireland," the college's alumni included Jonathan Swift, William Congreve, George Berkeley, and George Farquhar. John's admission seems fortunate, for J. K. L. Doyle, who succeeded Corcoran in 1819 as Catholic bishop of Kildare and Leighlin, opposed mixed education and could have made John's entrance problematic. Banim's literary ambitions emerged after he attended a private performance hosted by the Ormonde family: a reading of *Monologue on National Music* by Thomas Moore, one of many such seasonal events held in the theater at Kilkenny Castle.

Leaving for Dublin in 1813, John briefly studied drawing at the Academy of the Royal Dublin Society. He returned to Kilkenny in 1815, but, determined to make his way in the literary world, he departed again for Dublin in 1820, taking with him a verse fragment he called "Ossian's Paradise." Through the agency of Charles Phillips, the poem found its way to Sir Walter Scott, who found in it "much beauty of language, with a considerable command of numbers and meters." With Scott's endorsement, Banim's completed poem was published in 1821 as *The Celt's Paradise*. The work centers on a religious dialectic, a discussion between Saint Patrick and Ossian on the relative merits of Christianity and paganism. At this same time Banim became friends with Richard Lalor Sheil (1791-1851), an Irish barrister and playwright also from the trading class of Kilkenny. Sheil became Banim's adviser and mentor, encouraging him to write the tragedy *Damon and Pythias*, which debuted successfully at the Covent Garden on 28 May 1821, featuring in its cast William Charles Macready, a well-known tragedian, and Charles Kemble. Buoyed by the successes of *The Celt's Paradise* and *Damon and Pythias*, and after writing a notice commemorating George IV's forthcoming visit to Ireland (1822), Banim married Ellen Ruth of Kilkenny on 27 February 1822 and set out in March for London, aspiring to make a name writing classical verse tragedy. Finding work as an assistant at the English Opera House, Banim spent his available time writing articles for popular magazines, including the *Literary Register*.

Before leaving Kilkenny, John and Michael Banim had discussed John's vague notion of writing a series of tales concerning Irish life. In 1824, after publishing anonymously *Revelations of the Dead-Alive*—a group of satirical essays on such disparate issues as the fashions of the period, phrenology, art critics, and literary reviewers—John began writing in earnest two Irish stories, *The Fetches* and *John Doe*. In Kilkenny Michael worked on a third, *Crohoore of the Billhook*, which he sent to John in sections as completed. *The Fetches* focuses on the subject of an ancient Irish superstition—the "Fetch" or miragelike figure of a living person—and its impact on the psychology of a young couple. Banim situated *John Doe* in Clonmel, County Tipperary, Munster, centering his story on a search by two English officers for John Doe, the anonymous leader of the local terrorist "whiteboys." Banim set down the neophyte officers in the midst of a tangled, confusing Irish milieu, with the reader accompanying them on a convoluted search for John Doe, the emblem of an irreducibly complex and, for these outsiders, unknowable Ireland. Protestant and Catholic currents tug at the story as well, as the English officers' mission is complicated by an affair between one of them and a Catholic woman. Also in *John Doe*, as in Banim's other historical fiction, Ireland's conflicted historical circumstances make inevitable the Irish peasant's hatred of the law. Published on 7 April 1825 as the *Tales by the O'Hara Family*—"the O'Hara Family" was the pseudonym used by John (Abel O'Hara) and Michael (Barnes O'Hara) when collaborating—these three stories received considerable public attention and a favorable critical reception. Gerald Griffin, in a letter to his brother William, called the *Tales* "most vigorous and original things. . . . astonishing in nothing so much as in the power of creating an intense interest without stepping out of real life, and in the very easy and natural drama that is carried through them, as well as in the excellent tact which [Banim] shows, in seizing on all the points of national character. . . ." Yet Banim's narrative transcends the mere stylistic accomplishments particularized by Griffin. By indicting flaws which he acknowledges and atones for, by admitting uncertainties and allowing contradictions to remain unresolved, Banim—forthright about the burden of his fiction—acts to vindicate his countrymen, to redeem publicly Ireland.

As critics have noticed, much of Banim's work, especially *Tales* and *The Boyne Water*, derives from Scott's historical fiction, particularly *Redgauntlet* (1824) and other of the Waverley Novels. Indeed, Banim's use of rural themes, contemporary peasant life, regional dialects, and dualisms owes much to Scott. Patrick Joseph Murray, in his 1857 biography of Banim, asserted that had his health cooperated, Banim "would have been the Scott of Ireland." Following closely in Scott's wake, Banim hoped to do for the Irish what Scott had done for his people; Banim sought to depict an Ireland grasped in the tightened fist of historical contingencies and thus to engender within the reader, particularly the English reader, a new comprehension of and tolerance for the Irish.

Barely three weeks after the publication of *Tales by the O'Hara Family*, John wrote to Michael that he would soon "be ready with a tale in three volumes." John began writing *The Boyne Water* in July of 1825 and by Christmas of that year had completed it. Michael, the less ambitious of the brothers, contributed by surveilling the locale of the Limerick Siege, retracing the route taken by the Sarsfield ambush, and by editing John's prose. A cautious Michael warned John that the overt Catholic sympathies of the book would alienate a substantial number of readers and influential literati. Published early in 1826, *The Boyne Water* indeed suffered a rough critical reception, with commentators reserving their harshest words for the politics of which John had been so self-conscious. Yet Banim's advocacy of Emancipation and religious tolerance had an immense resonance in Ireland, and the public received the book enthusiastically; as a result, the brothers received a substantial advance from the publisher Henry Colburn for a subsequent work by "The O'Haras."

In *The Boyne Water* Eva and Edmund M'Donnell, Catholic sister and brother born into an aristocratic family, double Esther Evelyn and her brother Robert, young Protestant landholders. Banim projects his hopes for tolerance and religious pluralism into the young couples; they become romantically intertwined, their newfound affection and tolerance ironically inverting the ancient hatred and suspicion obtaining between Protestants and Catholics. Upon first meeting, Esther and Eva commiserate over the loss of family members, the Evelyns having been orphaned as children and the M'Donnells having recently lost their mother. After quietly talking to Esther for a few minutes, Eva lifts her eyes "as if silently repeating a prayer," troping the religious toleration and piety of the two families. The upheaval following the Glorious Revolution of 1688 quickly overwhelms intimations of hope and possibility; notwithstanding their tolerance, the M'Donnells and Evelyns soon find themselves on opposing sides of an explosive conflict. While Edmund serves enthusiastically as the commander of a rapparee band of Catholic partisans, Robert—who comes to know three of the conflict's leading figures, Patrick Sarsfield, James II, and William III—serves more reluctantly as an aide to General Friedrich Hermann Schomberg in the army of William III. Banim presents William as a tough-minded but equitable leader who resists advocates of Catholic persecution. Treating James II with strained sympathy, Banim intimates that James's defeat at the Battle of the Boyne resulted less from his cowardice and betrayal of his troops, as generally regarded, than from his inefficient prosecution of the battle. In another of Banim's calculated dualities the violently anti-Papist George Walker, Anglican bishop of Londonderry and a governor during the siege of that city, acts as the embodiment of Protestant extremism, while Walker's counterpart, the moderate priest O'Haggerty, seeks understanding and reconciliation. Rory na Chopple, an indecipherable, foreboding, seemingly primeval figure, tropes—as do Crohoore in Michael Banim's *Crohoore of the Billhook* (1825) and Shawn-a-Gow in John and Michael's novel *The Croppy* (1828)—an ancient, dark, and conflicted Ireland.

Stricken by a degenerative spinal disease that would eventually paralyze his legs, John nevertheless began work in 1826 on a second series of *Tales by the O'Hara Family*, completing its two novels by summer's end. Banim situates *The Nowlans*, the longer of the stories, in Llieuve Ieullem in western Tipperary, one of the so-called disturbed counties near Limerick. Banim designed a didactic fiction, one that would demonstrate how the Evangelicals' ignorance of Ireland made them unwitting dupes of Protestant Orange radicals. Foregrounded by the early-nineteenth-century rise of the New Reformation—an Evangelical movement that attempted to find converts among the Irish peasantry—the story centers on the Nowlan family and their son John, a married priest who, upon learning he is terminally ill, returns to his family to die. A prosperous and conservative farming family whose members differ drastically in their social aspirations, the Nowlans embody the complexities and contradictions inherent in religious and cultural difference. John's marriage to Letty, a Protestant—and Letty's failure to comprehend John's feelings of his apostasy and betrayal of the priesthood—becomes the major theme of *The Nowlans*. Considering the moral authority of the priest in the nineteenth-century Irish Catholic consciousness, the figure of Father John—a conflicted, married recreant—marks Banim's novel as daringly, almost luridly, provocative.

The Denounced. By the Authors of "Tales by the O'Hara Family," which deals with two Gaelic families during the murkily defined and chaotic period following the Irish surrender at Limerick, was published in 1830 with *The Conformists*, which treats the notorious Penal Days, centering on a statute providing that a son or younger brother who joined the Established Church would, under the law, take possession of his family's lands. The novel focuses on the effects of the statute as it demolishes a family. *The Croppy* concerns the Uprising of 1798; its authorship has been the subject of some critical haggling, but critics generally agree that Michael played the greater role in its writing. John's personal history sustains this view, for by 1827 his condition had worsened to such an extent that he could do little work beyond revising *Tales by the O'Hara Family* for a new edition. The title of *The Croppy* derives from the term used by radical Protestant Orangemen to deprecate United Irishmen, who, following French Revolutionary fashion, wore close-cropped haircuts; Orangeman widened the term to apply to Catholics generally. *The Croppy* centers on an uprising in County Wexford, Leinster, in southern Ireland, near the towns of Enniscorthy, Wexford, and New Ross. Under instruction from the government, the Protestant radical Saunders Smily attempts to foment an ill-prepared and thus doomed insurrection among the Irish peasants. Encouraged by the duplicity of Rattling Bill Nale, a mercenary who betrays his fellows for money, and by "the Member from the Committee," a zealot sent from the United Irishmen, radical Catholics undertake the wholesale massacre of Protestants. Each side commits its share of atrocities, and events soon shove the two pivotal figures of the novel, Father Rourke and Shane-a-Gow, away from moderation and toward militancy; each commits murder; each is hanged. As with *The Boyne Water, The Croppy* confronts the cultural/religious complexities of Ireland unflinchingly, if romantically. By devising a melodramatic but determined story, the Banims created a compelling history, one converted from political reality to fictive extravagance.

In 1829, after a protracted dispute with his publisher Henry Colburn, John dissolved their association and moved to Boulogne, where his health deteriorated markedly. While in France, he wrote only sporadically, producing a series of stories later collected as *The Bit O' Writin' and Other Tales by the O'Hara Family* (1838). By the mid 1830s, John's disease left him immobilized; public appeals and subscription enabled him to return in 1835 to Kilkenny, where his countrymen honored him in public ceremony. John and Michael collaborated one last time on another three-volume O'Hara story, *Father Connell* (1842), published in the year of John's death.

Modestly remembered as the first Irish-Catholic novelist and as the author of realistic Irish stories told in dramatic, overwrought prose, John Banim widened the scope and complicated the tone of nineteenth-century Irish literature. Banim's ambitious theory of fiction was moral and redemptive; he attempted nothing less than the uncoiling of ancient prejudices and the rehabilitation of a morally exhausted society. While he sought conciliation to seal the fractures of religious factionalism, Banim refused to turn away from the brutal political exigencies of his time, demanding a fiction as powerful as Irish historical circumstances were destructive. Yet even at his most melodramatic, politics, religion, and culture interlace in works which fail to justify their author's obsolescence. Depicting an Ireland caught up in the disquieting fullness of its historical, cultural, and religious experience, John Banim's thematic accomplishments declare his excesses superfluous.

Biography:

Patrick Joseph Murray, *The Life of John Banim* (London: William Lay, 1857).

References:

Thomas Flanagan, *The Irish Novelists, 1800-1850* (New York & London: Columbia University Press, 1959), pp. 167-202;

T. H. Lister, "Novels Descriptive of Irish Life," *Edinburgh Review*, 52 (January 1831): 410-431;

Michael Sadleir, *XIX Century Fiction*, 2 volumes (London: Constable, 1951; Berkeley & Los Angeles: University of California Press, 1951), I: 23-26;

Robert Lee Wolff, Introduction to *The Life of John Banim*, by Patrick Joseph Murray (New York: Garland, 1978), pp. v-xivi.

Eaton Stannard Barrett

(1786 - 20 March 1820)

Gary Kelly
University of Alberta

BOOKS: *All the Talents: A Satirical Poem, In Three Dialogues, By Polypus* (London: Printed for J. J. Stockdale, 1807); seventeenth edition, enlarged as *All the Talents: A Satirical Poem, In Four Dialogues, to Which Is Added a Pastoral Epilogue. By Polypus* (London: Printed for J. J. Stockdale, 1807; facsimile, New York & London: Garland, 1979);

The Comet: A Mock Newspaper (London: Printed for J. J. Stockdale, 1807);

The Rising Sun: A Serio-Comic Satiric Romance, By Cervantes Hogg (2 volumes, London: Printed for Appleyards, 1807; fourth edition, 3 volumes, revised, corrected, and enlarged, 1807);

The Second Titan War Against Heaven; or, The Talents Buried Under Portland-Isle: A Satirical Poem (London: Printed for H. Colburn, 1807; facsimile, New York & London: Garland, 1979);

The Miss-Led General: A Serio-Comic, Satiric, Mock-Heroic Romance (London: Printed for H. Oddy, 1808);

The Setting Sun; or, Devil among the Placemen; To Which Is Added a New Musical Drama, Being a Parody on The Beggar's Opera. By Cervantes Hogg, 3 volumes (London: Printed by J. D. Dewick for T. Hughes, 1809);

The Tarantula; or, The Dance of Fools: A Satirical Work, 2 volumes (London: Printed for Holmes & Whitteron, 1809);

Woman: A Poem (London: Printed for John Murray; Manners & Miller, Edinburgh; and M. N. Mahon, Dublin, 1810; facsimile, New York & London: Garland, 1979); republished with *Occasional Poems* (London: Printed for Henry Colburn, 1818);

The Metropolis; or, A Cure for Gaming; Interspersed with Anecdotes of Living Characters in High Life. By Cervantes Hogg, 3 volumes (London: Printed at the Minerva Press for A. K. Newman, 1811);

The Heroine; or, Adventures of a Fair Romance Reader (3 volumes, London: Printed for Henry Colburn and sold by George Goldie, Edinburgh, and John Cumming, Dublin, 1813); second edition, "with considerable additions and alterations," published as *The Heroine; or, Adventures of Cherubina* (London: Printed for Henry Colburn, 1814; third edition, with additions, 1815; first American edition, from the second London edition, 2 volumes, Philadelphia: Published for M. Carey, Wm. McCulloch, printer, 1815);

"My Wife! What Wife?": A Comedy, In Three Acts (London: Printed for C. Chapple, 1815);

The Talents Run Mad; or, Eighteen Hundred and Sixteen: A Satirical Poem In Three Dialogues (London: Printed for Henry Colburn, 1816; facsimile, New York & London: Garland, 1979);

Six Weeks at Long's; By a Late Resident, 3 volumes, often attributed to Barrett (London: Printed for the Author, 1817).

Editions: *The Heroine*, introduction by Walter Raleigh (London: Henry Frowde, 1909);

The Heroine, introduction by Michael Sadleir (London: E. Mathews & Marrot, 1927; New York: Frederick A. Stokes, 1928.

PLAY PRODUCTION: *"My Wife! What Wife?,"* London, Theatre Royal, Haymarket, 25 July 1815.

Eaton Stannard Barrett was one of many talented and ambitious Irish men and women of his time who made a name in "literature of the day." These writers included the journalist Pierce Egan, the novelist and writer for children Maria Edgeworth, the poet Thomas Moore, the Gothic novelist Regina Maria Roche, the novelist and playwright Charles Robert Maturin, and the writer of "national Tales" Sydney Owenson, Lady Morgan. A few of Barrett's miscellaneous topical satires in verse and prose had brief but intense popularity. His best-known work, however, was *The Heroine* (1813), a novel parodying the fictional feminisms

Frontispiece for volume one of the revised, fourth edition of Barrett's popular prose satire The Rising Sun, *which went through four editions in 1807. Prominent Whigs are shown kneeling before the Prince of Wales, who was sympathetic to their political views.*

of the 1790s and early 1800s as part of a remasculization of culture and literature.

Barrett's family was from Navan in County Meath, Ireland. He is said to have been born at Cork, Ireland, and educated with his brother Richard at a school in Wandsworth, near London. There he was apparently considered something of a genius for writing and putting on a play. According to D. J. O'Donoghue's *The Poets of Ireland* (1912), he received his B.A. from Trinity College, Dublin, in 1805. While his brother seems to have become a brewer and then editor of a reformist Dublin newspaper called the *Pilot*, Barrett himself decided to train as a lawyer, and in November 1805 he entered the Middle Temple, London, where he met a young man who would become his lifelong friend, John Taylor Coleridge, nephew of the poet Samuel Taylor Coleridge. Barrett does not seem to have been called to the bar, but instead became a literary and political journalist.

While Barrett was still a boy, intellectual and cultural life in Great Britain was divided by an intense debate over the nature and significance of the French Revolution, and especially over the question whether or not the Revolution was a model for reform in Britain. This Revolution debate carried on public issues that had been developing for some time. Before the 1790s literature had increasingly reflected the interests of the largely middle-class reading public. Plays, novels, and narrative poems, as well as newspapers, magazines, and learned and polemical writing expressed criticism of what were seen as a decadent and courtly upper class and an ignorant and violent lower class. Some of this criticism dealt specifically with the bad example being set by the sons of George III, especially George, Prince of Wales. Another major theme in this criticism was the role of women in encouraging or discouraging immorality and corruption and in helping to educate and "improve" the common people. During the 1790s and the war with Revolutionary France these issues became part of the Revolution debate, especially with the work of feminists such as Mary Wollstonecraft and Mary Hays. Conservative social critics saw this feminism as a form of revolutionary subversion and condemned it. Some critics went even further and condemned most writing by women as unfeminine by its very nature, since women were supposed to be private and domestic beings, not public and published ones.

By the end of the 1790s leading voices of the Revolution debate were becoming exhausted or had been suppressed by government censorship and intimidation. New issues of national solidarity were being broached, though there was continued criticism of upper-class corruption and lower-class rebelliousness. This was the situation into which Barrett entered as an ambitious young man of letters, and he began his career with a bang. In 1807, writing as Polypus, he published *All the Talents: A Satirical Poem, In Three Dialogues*, a verse satire on the Whig-dominated government, or ministry "Of All the Talents," avowedly dedicated to political reform, which had come to power in February 1806 and fell in March 1807. The poem went through nineteen editions the same year and Barrett quickly exploited its success with three more political satires. *The Comet: A Mock Newspaper* (1807) and *The Second Titan War Against Heaven; or, The Talents Buried Under Portland-Isle: A Satirical Poem* (1807) did nothing for his fortune, but he achieved modest success writing as Cervantes Hogg, with a prose satire on the Prince of Wales, *The Rising Sun: A Serio-Comic Satiric Romance* (1807), which reached four editions in the same year. "Cervantes Hogg" went on to satirize another of the reprobate sons of George III—Frederick, Duke of York—in *The Miss-Led General: A Serio-Comic, Satiric, Mock-Heroic Romance* (1808). "Cervantes Hogg" then returned to the Prince of Wales and the Whigs in the three-volume prose satire *The Setting Sun; or, Devil among the Placemen* (1809).

These satires all deal predominantly with what many saw as a dangerous alliance of the decadent and courtly Prince of Wales and the opposition Whigs whom he was believed to favor politically. During the 1790s many Whigs were at first sympathetic to the French Revolution, seeing it as an overthrow of the kind of court government and royal interference they had long criticized. Tories and Royalists, however, saw the Whigs as misguided at best and traitors at worst. George III was known to be in uncertain mental health and in case of his having a serious breakdown the Prince of Wales would be named regent, able to dismiss the Tory government and bring his friends, the Whigs, with their program of reforms, to power. In the view of many observers, then, the prince and the Whigs represented a sinister and dangerous alliance of courtly and decadent ambition with reformist disaffection and "democratic" rebelliousness. In fact, when the Whigs came to power without the prince's help, in the government "of all the talents," they were unable to carry out many reforms and they were soon turned out of office. Perhaps more alarming to many was the example of irresponsibility and incompetence set by the Prince of Wales and his brothers at a time of international military crisis in the war with Napoleonic France. Barrett's satires deal with these prominent political issues.

As his pen-name indicates, Barrett wrote his prose satires in the tradition of Miguel de Cervantes's *Don Quixote* (1605, 1615). These satires are less indebted to Cervantes, however, or to François Rabelais and others mentioned by "Cervantes Hogg," than to Samuel Butler's political verse satire *Hudibras* (1663-1678), a favorite model for counterrevolutionary, antireform polemicists of the 1790s and after. *The Rising Sun, The Miss-Led General*, and *The Setting Sun* also belong to the classical tradition of the farrago or Menippean satire, a mixture of forms bringing together a miscellany of social, cultural, and political criticism in a form that suggests the interconnection of all these domains in the body politic. Because such satires are often highly topical, most of them are doomed to a short existence and to subliterary status. Yet, like Barrett's, they often press, or even transgress, conventionally received limits of discourse and decorum, suggesting that the dominant genres and styles serve the corrupt state of "things as they are" and therefore need to be challenged. Such challenges were increasingly common in the aftermath of the Revolution debate of the 1790s, seen in the Romantic writers' experiments with form, including an increasing number of quasi-novels, or novels in which the fictional elements are subordinated to some other discourse incorporated in the text, such as poetry, travelogue, historiography, and of course the kinds of criticism in Barrett's satires.

Barrett's satiric quasi-novels are certainly amusing, lively, pointed, and loaded with material, if also boisterous, desultory, uneven, and obvious. They also brought him some success. But critics and the reading public were ambivalent about satire directed to particular issues and persons, increasingly so at a time of growing concern over social unity and political stability in face of the unprecedented external military threat from Napoleonic France. The debate as to whether satire should be particular or general, should attack vi-

THE

MISS-LED GENERAL;

A

Serio-Comic,

SATIRIC, MOCK-HEROIC

ROMANCE.

BY THE AUTHOR OF THE

Rising Sun.

Brettell and Co. Printers.

LONDON:

PRINTED FOR H. ODDY,
OXFORD-STREET.

1808.

Cover and frontispiece for Barrett's prose satire on Frederick, Duke of York, who had been appointed commander-in-chief of the British army despite his incompetence as a general on the battlefield. The parade of mistresses leading him by the nose is headed by Mary Anne Clarke, who was widely rumored to be selling army commissions on the basis of her supposed power over him. A year after Barrett's book was published, Parliament investigated the scandal, finding the duke not guilty of corruption but dismissing him as commander-in-chief because he had discussed official business with Mrs. Clarke (Bruce Peel Special Collections, University of Alberta Library)

He comes, the Conq-ring Hero comes.

cious individuals or vices in general, was a long-standing one, going back to the seventeenth century at least. Barrett would have been aware of this debate and may also have felt his prominence as a belletristic political commentator on particular events and characters of the day was wearing out; for in 1809 he tried a broader range of social and cultural criticism in the two-volume satire *The Tarantula; or, The Dance of Fools.* While still within the range of the farrago or Menippean satire, it aims to depict a panorama of contemporary vices. According to the *Gentleman's Magazine* (July 1809) the author "seems determined to have a lash at every thing, and spares neither the *ins* nor the *outs*; and treats all the world as fools or knaves."

> Absurd matches, gin-drinkers, and divorces, are all attributed to Lord Chesterfield's mock morals; and army contractors and upstart red-coats have not escaped his scorpion scourge. The second of these delicate volumes has a cut at our senators, drunken elections, and other follies as well as evils of the day. On private card parties, debating societies, Methodists, the Southcotts [a religious sect led by Joanna Southcott], mock auctions, cheap shops, and medical quacks, he is particularly severe.... Against sharping companions, ... the bubbles of many benefit societies, and lotteries, he is very pointed.

Like Barrett's other satires, the text was embellished with engraved prints. Despite such attractions, as well as its breadth and detail, however, *The Tarantula* was barely noticed and sank without a trace.

The following year Barrett tried his hand as a social and cultural critic on a more dignified level with *Woman: A Poem* (1810). His theme was still timely but more general, celebrating the post-Revolutionary ideal of domestic woman as heart and conscience of the nation against other models of woman proposed by the Revolutionary feminists of the 1790s. Barrett was following the example of William Gifford, whose verse satires *The Baviad* (1794) and *The Maeviad* (1795) attacked the intrusion of women into not only politics but literature and culture, and ensured Gifford a career as man of letters. In the widespread remasculization of culture in the aftermath of the Revolutionary decade, Barrett had good reason to expect a similar success. Certainly the poem was as widely reviewed as his first success, *All the Talents*. But *Woman* did not sell as well as the earlier poem had, and Barrett turned to satire on the culture of the decadent upper classes, whose vices were then widely blamed for Britain's domestic and international failures but were also a subject of continuing fascination to the mainly middle-class reading public. Not surprisingly, *The Metropolis; or, A Cure for Gaming; Interspersed with Anecdotes of Living Characters in High Life* (1811), by "Cervantes Hogg," was published by the notorious Minerva Press, purveyor of fashionable novels and scandalous literature. This work was less successful than *Woman*, however.

Barrett fared better with his next work, a literary burlesque published by Henry Colburn (also known as a purveyor of scandalous literature and romans à clef), who had published the second edition of *Woman*. Barrett's three-volume novel *The Heroine; or, Adventures of a Fair Romance Reader* was published in 1813 and revised the next year as *The Heroine; or, Adventures of Cherubina*, and it reached several editions. It is again in the quixote tradition, particularly the line of Charlotte Lennox's *The Female Quixote* (1752). As Marilyn Butler points out in *Jane Austen and the War of Ideas* (1975), during the Revolution debate this line had acquired a distinctive political cast in "Anti-Jacobin" novels. These novels often depict inexperienced and gullible young heroines burdened with false ideals derived from novels of Sensibility such as Jean-Jacques Rousseau's *La nouvelle Héloïse* (1761) and from "philosophy," or pre-Revolutionary and Revolutionary books of social criticism. A recent example of such novelistic satire was Elizabeth Hamilton's *Memoirs of Modern Philosophers* (1800), burlesquing the writings and conduct of the Revolutionary feminists Mary Wollstonecraft and Mary Hays. In the Revolutionary aftermath writers such as Amelia Opie in *Adeline Mowbray* (1804), Maria Edgeworth in *Belinda* (1801) and *The Modern Griselda* (1805), and Jane Austen in *Northanger Abbey* (written in 1803; not published until 1818) tried to depoliticize the theme and return to the quixote tradition in which novel reading leads to dangerous misunderstanding of the world or to foolish abandonment of women's role in domestic and local social life, seen during that period as central to national life and even national survival.

The Heroine is based on the long-standing, widely held assumption that reading constructs the individual subject, for better or for worse. Though it may seem paradoxical, novels were seen by many middle-class critics at that time as disseminators of both decadent court culture, disguised as "sensibility," and plebeian rebelliousness, dressed up as Revolutionary "new philosophy." Both were seen as licensing moral, social, and political transgression and thereby threatening social hierarchy and stability. The transgressor was often depicted as foolish rather than evil, and therefore given the character of a young woman resembling the protagonists of late-eighteenth-century novels of manners—inexperienced in the ways of the world and liable to be deceived by appearances and by the seductive illusions of "romance" and speculative "philosophy." Barrett's novel burlesques not only "English Jacobin" persons, views, and writings of the 1790s, but also post-Revolutionary women writers who were reasserting the centrality of women to a social order, culture, and destiny that were represented as "national" by the middle class. It is not surprising, then, that Barrett dedicated the second edition of his novel to Prime Minister George Canning and a former contributor to the *Anti-Jacobin Magazine*, for *The Heroine* carries the novelistic Revolution debate forward from the 1790s to the 1810s.

Like the protagonists of "English Jacobin" novels such as William Godwin's *Things As They Are; or, The Adventures of Caleb Williams* (1794), Mary Hays's *Memoirs of Emma Courtney* (1796), and Mary Wollstonecraft's *The Wrongs of Woman; or, Maria* (1798), Barrett's "heroine" tells her own story, in a series of letters to her former governess, who seems to have allowed her pupil a free rein in reading. But whereas the English Jacobin autobiographical narrative is meant to be self-authorizing, a personal case of and witness to social "wrongs," Barrett's narrator is meant to be manifestly unreliable from the outset, a poor reader of herself and her world because she has read too much of the wrong things. No doubt this element in *The Heroine* is what appealed to Jane Austen, who read the novel in March 1814, was "very much amused by it," and created a muted version of Barrett's well-meaning but erring heroine in *Emma* (1815), the novel on which she was then beginning work.

Barrett's heroine, Cherry Wilkinson, begins by changing her name to the novelish "Cherubina de Willoughby." She goes on to invent an aristocratic origin for herself, rejecting her own family of well-to-do farming folk and the sensible middle-class man designed to be her husband, Robert Stuart, whose name suggests good Scottish Enlightenment common sense, Barrett's own touchstone. "Cherubina" embarks on a series of adventures in flight from mere bourgeois comfort and happiness in quest of more heroinelike suffering and misery. Ominously, she begins by abetting the imprisonment of her father, who has ordered her novels burned. Cherry persists in seeing everyone and everything she meets in terms familiar to her from sentimental and Gothic novels. At a masquerade an old man named Whylome Eftsoones—two notorious archaisms affected by Romantic medievalist poets—persuades her she is the illegitimate daughter of Lord de Willoughby and Lady Hysterica Belamour. Inspired by Revolutionary feminism, Cherry also assumes an identity and capabilities as a woman, which she does not in fact possess. In pursing her assumed identity as a "heroine" she is inspired by or reenacts scenes from sentimental and Gothic novels such as Rousseau's *La nouvelle Héloïse*, Goethe's *Sorrows of Young Werther* (1774), and Isabelle de Montolieu's *Caroline of Lichtfield* (1786). She is encouraged in her "romantic" excesses by the mad poet Higginson, who is meant to be a literary "son" of the poetaster Higgins, a burlesque version of the English Jacobin philosopher William Godwin in the *Anti-Jacobin Magazine*. Like Austen's Emma, Cherry sees fit to rearrange the world around her, breaking up a match between another couple, William and Mary, because it is too unromantic for her taste. She seeks adventures that result in repeated transgression against the contemporary ideal of domestic femininity, ranging from disregard of "manners" or social convention, appearing in immodest dress, traveling about with men unrelated to her, and performing in public, to leading an uprising of Irish laborers and dabbling in politics.

Like the deluded heroine in Anti-Jacobin novels, she thereby makes herself available to become the ideological dupe and thus the sexual prey of ambitious plebeians. One of these is the reformer Betterton, whose name suggests the optimistic English Jacobin philosophy that under the right government, or no government at all, humanity is "perfectible," or capable of becoming ever "better." The second part of Betterton's name suggests that this philosophy is a mere fad, or part of the *ton*—a French word meaning fashion. Another would-be seducer, and Betterton's coconspirator, is the actor Montmorenci (real name Grundy), whose romantic posturing and claim to illegitimate aristocratic blood suggest the new Romantic style of acting and the pretensions of "star" actors to artistic nobility of soul. Fortunately Cherry's natural goodness gains her the loyalty of Jery Sullivan, an Irish laborer who participated in the Irish rebellion of 1798. Jery represents the gullible lower classes too easily swayed by example, especially bad example, from their "betters," though they are "naturally" good-natured, hardworking, and subordinate.

First Cherry is led to believe that she is heiress to the Welsh property of Lady Gwyn. Lady Gwyn plays Cherry along for the amusement of her sophisticated guests and pretends to have "Cherubina" crowned as a female bard, in the manner of Corinne in Mme de Staël's 1807 novel of that title. At the ceremony Cherry acknowledges her subjective identity with the novels she has read, declaring, "Such as I am, these, these alone have made me." She decides to refurbish as her residence a nearby ruin, Monkton Castle (Monk: title of M. G. Lewis's well-known Gothic novel, 1796; ton: again, the French word for fashion). When she hears that her castle is about to be attacked, she has Jery raise a band of navvies to defend it and promises to reward them with a " 'radical Reform,' " by which she means " 'a revival of the Feudal System.' " When her promises are greeted with shouts of acclaim she observes, "I now found that a popular speech was not difficult; and I judged, from my performance, that the same qualities which have made me so good a Heroine, would, if I were a man, have made just as illustrious a Patriot." Barrett pointedly if crudely makes the connection between what he sees as feminist heroinism and subversive politics. In a later edition of the novel, Barrett took the trouble to point out that Cherry's speech burlesques one by the real-life political reformer, Sir Francis Burdett. More generally, Cherry's plebeian "army" would suggest to readers the recent (1811-1812) Luddite disturbances among the laboring class.

Worse, Betterton and Montmorenci plot to exploit Cherry's heroinism so that Montmorenci can gain possession of her property and Betterton can force her to become his mistress. They exploit her appetite for Gothic incident to stage several episodes at Monkton Castle, including a meeting with her favorite novel heroes and heroines, designed to persuade her to marry Montmorenci. This plot pointedly expresses middle-class fear of a coalition between middle-class intellectuals and lower-class upstarts to seize social power, here represented as contamination and control of middle-class woman. Fortunately, the unheroic but sensible Stuart discovers their plot, breaks it up, and has them arrested. The realization that she has been duped shocks Cherry into a physical illness. Her physical recovery is accompanied by a mental one as well, as her future husband, Stuart, supervises her ideological reeducation, based on close study of Cervantes's *Don Quixote*. Not only does the closure of the novel see Cherry's autobiographical narrative superseded by Stuart's authoritative condemnation of novels as a source of national degeneration, but Stuart also gets the novel's last words, quoted by Cherry. Presumably her moral and intellectual personality is now as effectively covered by her fiancé's as a wife's legal personality was "covered" by that of her husband under the English common law doctrine of "feme covert." Barrett had after all been a student of the law.

The Heroine was a success with the reading public, though not with the critics, and Barrett made "considerable additions and alterations" in new editions. He also seems to have felt that many of the burlesque allusions were being missed, for he added a list of these to a later edition. He next tried to achieve success in the theater, then the most lucrative line for a successful author. *"My Wife! What Wife?": A Comedy, In Three Acts*, was performed at the Theatre Royal, Haymarket, and published in 1815, with the inclusion of lines omitted in performance. It represents marriage in fashionable society as a matter of courtly intrigue and material self-interest. The following year Barrett returned to political verse satire with *The Talents Run Mad; or, Eighteen Hundred and Sixteen*, dedicated to his friend the Tory writer William Gifford. In this renewed attack on the opposition Whigs, Barrett insists on the necessity of continuing to criticize the courtly decadence of the age without going to the extreme of undermining the entire system of government.

In 1817 appeared a three-volume novel titled *Six Weeks at Long's; By a Late Resident*. In his introduction to the 1979 Garland reprints of Barrett's poems Donald H. Reiman points out that in his *Autobiography* (1852) William Jerdan, the editor and man of letters, claimed he and Michael Nugent had written it from material provided by someone else. Nevertheless, the work was attributed to Barrett in J. F. Walker's *Imperial Dictionary of Universal Biography* (1857-1863), and this attribution continues to be accepted. It is easy to see why. Like Barrett's earlier prose "romances," *Six Weeks at Long's* depicts various public characters in the guise of fiction, and reviewers agreed that these "are so strongly represented as to be recognised instantly even by the most superficial observers of the dissipation and depravity, affectation and eccentricity which prevail in the higher classes of society" (*New Monthly Magazine*, April 1817). Though the title page claims the work was "printed for the author" it was published by Henry Colburn, known for gratifying the public taste for scandal in high life by publishing romans à clef such as Lady Caroline Lamb's *Glenarvon* (1816), a fictionalized account of her affair with Lord Byron and discussed in *Six Weeks at Long's*. It is true that *Six Weeks at Long's* does not have the knockabout burlesque of Barrett's earlier topical "romances" such as *The Rising Sun* and *The Miss-Led General*. Like *The Heroine*, however, it depicts an apparently naive (in fact simpleminded) young woman who becomes the prospective sexual and financial prey of a variety of courtly gallants before ending up with the proper man, scion of a mercantile middle-class family.

Another work attributed to Barrett, *Henry Schutze: A Tale; The Savoyard: A French Republican Story; With Other Poems*, was published in 1821, after his death, and is unlikely to be his. In later years Barrett seems to have supported himself in part by reviewing, that great mainstay of Romantic hack writers, and in this respect probably found his relation with William Gifford to be useful. He was a tall man, and, in a letter written to Dublin bookseller John Cumming on 15 August 1818, he admitted to being ugly. An obituary in the *Annual Register* for 1820 reported that he died in March 1820 in Glamorganshire, Wales, from a "rapid decline" after having burst a blood vessel. His work remains witness to the highly commercialized and highly contested character of literature in the Romantic period.

Letters:

"An Old Discovery" [two letters from Barrett to John Cumming and one from Cumming to Barrett], edited by John C. Mendenhall, *University of Pennsylvania General Magazine and Historical Chronicle*, 30 (1927): 10-14.

Bibliography:

Patrick Rafroidi, *Irish Literature in English: The Romantic Period*, volume 2 (Atlantic Highlands, N.J.: Humanities Press, 1972).

References:

Gary Kelly, "Unbecoming a Heroine: Novel Reading, Romanticism, and Barrett's *The Heroine*," *Nineteenth-Century Literature*, 45 (September 1990): 220-241;

Donald H. Reiman, Introduction to *All the Talents; The Second Titan War, or, The Talents Buried under Portland-Isle; The Talents Run Mad* (New York & London: Garland, 1979).

Anna Eliza Bray

(25 December 1790 - 21 January 1883)

Beverly Schneller
Millersville University

BOOKS: *Letters written during a Tour through Normandy, Britanny, and other Parts of France, in 1818* (London: Longman, Hurst, Rees, Orme & Brown, 1820);

Memoirs, including Original Journals, Letters, Papers, and Antiquarian Tracts of the late Charles Alfred Stothard, and some Account of the Journey to the Netherlands (London: Printed for Longman, Hurst, Rees, Orme & Brown, 1823);

De Foix: or, Sketches of the Manners and Customs of the Fourteenth Century, 3 volumes (London: Longman, Rees, Orme, Brown & Green, 1826);

The White Hoods, 3 volumes (London: Printed for Longman, Rees, Orme, Brown & Green, 1828);

The Protestant. A Tale of the Reign of Queen Mary (3 volumes, London: Colburn, 1828; 2 volumes, New York: J. & J. Harper, 1829);

Fitz of Fitz-Ford. A Legend of Devon, 3 volumes (London: Smith, Elder, 1830);

The Talba (3 volumes, London: Longman, Rees, Orme, Brown & Green, 1830; 2 volumes, New York: J. & J. Harper, 1831);

Warleigh; or, The Fatal Oak, 3 volumes (London: Longman, Rees, Orme, Brown, Green & Longman, 1834);

A Description of that Part of Devonshire bordering on the Tamar and the Tavy; Its Natural History, Manners, Customs, Superstitions, Scenery, Antiquities, Biography of Eminent Persons, &c. &c. in a Series of Letters to Robert Southey, 3 volumes (London: J. Murray, 1836);

Trelawny of Trelawne; or, The Prophecy. A Legend of Cornwall, 3 volumes (London: Longman, Orme, Brown, Green & Longmans, 1837);

Trials of the Heart (3 volumes, London: Longman, Orme, Brown, Green & Longmans, 1839; 2 volumes, Philadelphia: Lee & Blanchard, 1839);

The Mountains and Lakes of Switzerland, with Descriptive Sketches of other Parts of the Continent, 3 volumes (London: Longman, Orme, Brown, Green & Longmans, 1841);

Henry de Pomeroy; or, The Eve of St. John, 3 volumes (London: Bentley, 1842);

Courtenay of Walreddon. A Romance of the West, 3 volumes (London: Richard Bentley, 1844);

Trials of Domestic Life, 3 volumes (London: H. Colburn, 1848);

The Life of Thomas Stothard, R. A., with Personal Reminiscences (London: John Murray, 1851);

A Peep at the Pixies; or, Legends of the West (London: Grant & Griffith, 1854);

Handel: His Life, Personal and Professional. With Thoughts on Sacred Music (London: J. Ward, 1857);

The Revolt of the Protestants of the Cévennes; with Some Account of the Huguenots in the Seventeenth Century (London: J. Murray, 1870);

The Good St. Louis and His Times (London: Griffith & Farran, 1870);

Hartland Forest. A Legend of North Devon (London: Longmans, Green, 1871);

Roseteague; or, The Heir of Treville Crewes, 2 volumes (London: Chapman & Hall, 1874);

Joan of Arc and the Times of Charles the Seventh, King of France (London: Griffith & Farran, 1874);

Silver Linings; or, Light and Shade (London: Chapman & Hall, 1880);

Autobiography, edited by John A. Kempe (London: Chapman & Hall, 1884).

Editions: *Novels and Romances of Anna Eliza Bray*, 10 volumes (London: Longman, Brown, Green & Longmans, 1845);

The Novels, Historical, Legendary and Romantic. By Mrs. Bray, 12 volumes (London: Chapman & Hall, 1884).

OTHER: *The Fables and other Pieces in Verse by Maria Colling; with Some Account of the Author in Letters to Robert Southey, Esq. Poet Laureate, By Mrs. Bray* (London: Longman, Rees, Orme, Brown & Green, 1831);

The Monumental Effigies of Great Britain. By Charles Stothard with an Introduction and Descriptions from Stothard's Monumental Effigies of Great

Anna Eliza Bray

Britain. By Alfred John Kempe. With a List of Mrs. Bray's Works, completed by Bray and Alfred John Kempe (London: Printed by J. McCreery for the author & sold by J. Murray, 1832);

Edward Atkyns Bray, *Poetical Remains, Social, Sacred, and Miscellaneous*, 2 volumes, edited by Anna Eliza Bray (London: Longman, Brown, Green, Longmans & Roberts, 1859).

Eliza Bray's novels receive little attention today, but during her lifetime her writings were so popular that two editions of her complete works appeared (1845 and 1884), and her publishers included such leading nineteenth-century firms as Thomas Longman and John Murray. Described as "a modest imitator of Scott" in volume seven of Ernest Baker's *History of the English Novel* (1936), Bray, who published all of her novels and most of her nonfiction under the name Mrs. Bray, was the author of twelve historical novels and a dozen nonfiction books, including biographies of historical figures—all published between 1820 and 1884. Her romances typically involve royalty and their associates in specific historical or local settings, which are described in realistic detail. Bray, who considered herself an amateur historian and artist, strove to create "living history" for the reader through carefully researched and vividly presented descriptions. She emphasized setting and history more than the characters, who were often left undeveloped.

Anna Eliza Kempe, known to her friends as Eliza, was born on 25 December 1790 in the parish of Newington, Surrey. Her father, John Kempe, inherited his position as porteur d'or in the Royal Mint from his father, Nicholas Kempe, one of the founders of the eighteenth-century pleasure garden Ranelagh. Through both her father and her grandfather, young Eliza met many well-known eighteenth-century figures, including the actress Mary Robinson ("Perdita"), who was then an elderly invalid. Eliza's mother, Ann Arrow Kempe, was the daughter of James Arrow of Berkshire and his wife, Elizabeth Jerden Arrow. Near the turn of the nineteenth century, Eliza attended school in the home of her mother's cousin, a Miss Wrather, but she was forced to abandon her studies within two years because of an outbreak of scarlet fever. A few years later she contracted rheumatic fever, and throughout her life she described herself as having a "delicate" constitution. According to her nephew John A. Kempe, who wrote the introduction to her *Autobiography* (1884), both she and her second husband were sensitive to light and often sat in their home with their eyes covered and the curtains drawn.

In 1815 Eliza prepared for a career in the theater. Her father arranged acting lessons for her in London and took her to plays regularly. In May 1816, on her way to Bath to appear as Belvidera in Thomas Otway's *Venice Preserved*, she contracted a cold and was forced to cancel her debut. She never resumed her attempts to become an actress, turning instead to painting. Her father provided her with lessons at the studio of the well-known artist Thomas Stothard, who turned the tutelage of young Eliza Kempe over to his son, Charles. In February 1818, against her parents' wishes, she married Charles Stothard, and the couple left almost immediately for a tour of France. Encouraged by Charles and the bookseller John Nichols, she published the letters she wrote to her mother and brother as *Letters written during a Tour through Normandy, Britanny, and other Parts of France* (1820). These letters reveal her keen ability to describe scenery and her intense love for local history and travel.

During the three years she was married to Charles Stothard, he was actively engaged in sketching historical statuary and funereal art throughout England. Their marriage seemed to be a happy partnership in which each encouraged the other: for example, Eliza provided Charles with a detailed account of her visit to the Arundel tomb, and he provided her with specialized information on fourteenth-century armor for her first novel, *De Foix: or, Sketches of the Manners and Customs of the Fourteenth Century*, which was not published until 1826. They shared interests in history, art, and literature.

Charles Stothard died unexpectedly from a fall in May 1821 at a church in Beer Freers, Devonshire. He had been sketching a painted ceiling when the ladder on which he stood gave way, causing him to fall and strike his head against a pew. Eliza Stothard, who was pregnant at the time, not only lost her thirty-five-year-old husband, but soon after that her only child, Blanche Anna Eliza Stothard, who died in February 1822.

In 1823 Eliza Stothard published her second book, *Memoirs, including Original Journals, Letters, Papers, and Antiquarian Tracts of the late Charles Alfred Stothard*. Although a certain amount of partisanship and passion are to be expected in Eliza Stothard's account of her husband, she is not entirely wrong about his admirable accomplishments. His posthumously published book, *The Monumental Effigies of Great Britain* (1832), is a remarkable collection of historical drawings, with astute commentary provided by Eliza Stothard's brother, Alfred Kempe, himself a respected antiquarian. Most of the *Memoirs* is composed of letters Eliza and Charles Stothard exchanged during 1816 and 1817 along with Kempe's memorial article, first published in the *Gentleman's Magazine* (June 1821). For Eliza, her husband "was an example of how much may be accomplished by unassisted exertions. To those who have mounted the steep ascent of fame and honour, they will show the rare pattern of modesty and humility." The descriptive method, combining facts with a moral observation, is characteristic of Bray's presentation of both real and fictional personalities, for she was always more concerned with the spiritual dimensions of those she knew or created than she was with physical appearance.

In 1822 Eliza Stothard married the Reverend Edward Atkyns Bray of Tavistock, Devonshire. Soon after the marriage, she completed and published *De Foix*, which was followed in 1828 by two more novels, *The White Hoods* and *The Protestant*.

In her *Autobiography*, Bray implied that her habit was to finish one work and immediately take up another. For example, *De Foix* was completed on 17 December 1825; *The White Hoods*, begun on December twenty-sixth and finished in July 1826, was published on 11 February 1828; *The Protestant*, begun on 18 September 1826 and completed on 19 November 1827, was published in November 1828. On 28 August 1828 she began *Fitz of Fitz-Ford* (1830), completing it on 11 October. It seems as though Bray was always correcting proofs, researching, and writing. Initially she was able to vary her prolific output, but as her career progressed, she gave way to redundancy and self-imitation. Bray was caught off guard by the controversy *The Protestant* caused. In this novel, set in the reign of Queen Mary, Owen Wilford, a Protestant, his wife, Alice, and their children, Rose and Edward, are persecuted by Jesuit inquisitors and imprisoned because of their faith. Because the ceremony was not performed by a Roman Catholic priest, the Wilfords have been told their marriage is invalid and that their children are illegitimate. The Catholics are portrayed as despicably cruel and insensitive, while the Protestants are presented as valiant and patient sufferers of many tribulations. In one particularly graphic scene, written with an intensity Bray was never able to replicate, Rose's right hand is burned until it becomes withered and disfigured. At the last moment, the Wilfords, a blind boy and his grandmother, and the Wilfords' servant, Abel, are saved from the heretics' pyre by the accession of Queen Elizabeth. Such contrived and transparent plots are common in Bray's novels.

Urged by her publisher, Henry Colburn, and her brother, Bray sent a review copy of *The Protestant* to the *Quarterly Review*, where her work was brought to the attention of Robert Southey, who had recently written articles for the periodical on the Catholic Emancipation issue. In her *Autobiography*, it was not *The Protestant*, however, but another novel, *The Talba* (1830), which Bray called "the most important of all my writings, as it was the more immediate cause of my becoming known to Robert Southey."

By 1831 Southey was corresponding regularly with Bray, who was by then a well-known historical novelist, travel writer, and biographer. Writing in February 1831, Southey suggested that Bray might turn her "spiritual mind" to writing "a good specimen of local history," directing her "to give not only all the history and biography of the place and to gather up whatever of tradition and manners can be saved from oblivion, but also state everything about a parish that can be made not omitting some of those short and simple annals of domestic life which ought not to be forgotten." The resulting work, which she began in January 1832, was dedicated to Southey and published as *A Description of that Part of Devonshire bordering on the Tamar and the Tavy* (1836). Each volume addresses a specific time, and the number of letters Bray wrote as descriptive sketches for Southey varies from volume to volume. Overall, the three volumes cover the period from February 1832 through October 1835. In composing the ninety-four letters, Bray interspersed quotations from her husband's journals of Devonshire history, anecdotal historical information collected from local people for her by the servant-poet Maria Colling, and material from Thomas Percy's *Reliques of Ancient English Poetry* (1765). After Bray arranged for Colling's poetry to be published in 1831, Colling had become something of a local celebrity in Devonshire.

While collecting information for *The Tamar and the Tavy*, Bray continued to research and write historical romances, beginning *Trelawny of Trelawne* (1837), an epistolary novel, in 1834. She examined actual love letters written in the seventeenth century by first cousins in the Trelawny family, upon whom her story is focused. In *Trelawny of Trelawne* Bray's method of basing her stories "upon the foundation of historical fragments, and family traditions [venturing] to raise a superstructure of fiction" becomes clear as Laetitia Trelawny spurns marriage with Sir Francis Beaumont in order to marry her cousin, Henry Trelawny. In typical Bray fashion he must survive the persecution of the Jesuits in order to marry Laetitia. To authenticate her account Bray included a twenty-three-page introductory essay outlining how she came into possession of the letters through the current Lady Trelawny, how she was invited to write the story, and how the real letters influenced her fictional ones. When the book was published in 1837, Alfred Kempe told her that many people in London thought the letters in her novel were the genuine correspondence of Henry and Laetitia Trelawny.

Eliza Bray's first meeting with Robert Southey came in 1835, just two days after her mother's death in London at the age of ninety. The meeting was brief and unfruitful as Bray was too overcome with grief to enjoy their conversation. Their second meeting, on Christmas Day in 1836 at the Brays' home in Tavistock, was much different. Southey entertained the Brays, Maria Colling, and other guests with recitations of his own verses and those of others. To everyone's satisfaction, Colling also recited her poetry. During Southey's brief visit, the Brays alternately and discreetly took notes of his activities and his subjects of conversation. These are included in the last twenty pages of Bray's *Autobiography*. Southey's 1 January 1837 letter to Katharine Southey provides one of the few glimpses into the Brays' home, as Mrs. Bray wrote nothing of her personal life in the *Autobiography*:

> Mr. Bray's is the only house in which I have eaten upon pewter since I was a child, he has a complete service of it, with his crest engraved upon it; and as bright as silver. The house is a very good one, the garden large and pleasantly laid out; it includes some of the ruins and the door from it opens upon a delightful walk on the Tavy.

Southey's comments suggest that the Brays had a comfortable home life.

Because Bray ended her *Autobiography* with Southey's death in March 1843, specific details about her publications after this date are not readily available. According to John Kempe's preface to her *Autobiography*, Bray planned to continue this book with a discussion of her close friendship with Southey's second wife, poet Caroline Bowles. A draft for this section, which is included in the published book, contains excerpts from the correspondence between Bray and Bowles during Southey's decline. As if she were describing one of her fictional heroines, Bray wrote of Caroline Bowles:

> The fatal affliction which terminated in the complete overthrow of such a mind as his [Southey's] did not come suddenly; nothing could be more afflicting than its slow but certain progress. During this most disastrous period, with a warmth of affection, a sense of duty, a watchfulness, and total disregard for herself, the most praiseworthy did that highly-gifted wife devote herself to the care of a husband, in wedding whom she indeed wedded sorrow in its most trying form. Many of her most interesting letters to me were written in moments of the deepest affliction until death closed the scene.

Caroline Bowles also had a high regard for Bray, and the unhappy widow frequently expressed admiration for Bray's ability to succeed as an author.

The last novel Bray mentions in her *Autobiography* is *Henry de Pomeroy* (1842), which she says was "founded on a wild tradition connected with Berry Pomeroy Castle and St. Michael's Mount," both located in Cornwall. This novel was included in the *Novels and Romances of Anna Eliza Bray*, a ten-volume collection published by Longman in 1845. *Trials of the Heart* (1839), *The White Hoods, Warleigh* (1834), *Trelawny, De Foix, The Talba*, and *Courtenay of Walreddon* (1844) complete the first edition of her collected works.

In 1857 the Reverend Bray died, and Mrs. Bray moved to London, where she continued to reside until her death in 1883. Her next publication was *Handel: His Life, Personal and Professional* (1857). Hardly biographical, this slender ninety-two-page volume is more patriotic than critical or informative. Her narrative of Handel's life is frequently interrupted with her views on motives, jealousy, and filial responsibility. For Bray one of the most important aspects of Handel's personality was his faithfulness to his mother. For example, she writes: "It is pleasing to think of the consolation she must have derived from the visit. To find the son, who left her from motives of filial piety now returning to his home prosperous and happy as a result of his exertions." In addition to having inherited one of the composer's spinet pianos from her father, Bray also seems to have owned some manuscript scores. Bray's enthusiasm for Handel and his works was also encouraged by her attendance at a Handel Festival in 1834. She relied on the memoirs of Georg Philipp Telemann (1681-1767) and those of a rival composer, Johann Mattheson (1681-1764), in addition to Dr. Charles Burney's history of music (1776-1789) for background information. Bray concluded her book with the observation that God must have created Handel with England in mind, "for although born in Germany, he was best placed in England, since a man is ever placed where he can do the most good."

Bray was on hiatus from publishing between 1859 and 1870, when her biography of Saint Louis and an historical work, *The Revolt of the Protestants of the Cévennes*, about a revolt in an early-eighteenth-century religious community in southern France, were published. Her account of the Protestants in the Cévennes was the first written in English. For her research, she relied heavily on Napoléon Peyrat's *Histoire des Pasteurs du Désert* (1842). These two nonfiction works were soon followed by two novels, published in 1871 and 1874, and a biography of Joan of Arc, also published in 1874. From 1874 until her death in 1883, Bray was apparently busy revising all her novels for the Chapman and Hall collected edition of 1884. The brothers George and Edward Dalziel, leading engravers of the nineteenth century, were commissioned to illustrate her works. Bray also wrote her *Autobiography*, and her nephew John A. Kempe added the preface before its posthumous publication. He became acquainted with Bray near the end of her life and found her to be bright, but something of a disappointment, it seems. He remarks that she could have been better known had she written in a more common style and had she corresponded more with the literati whose attention her writings attracted.

Despite Kempe's remarks, Bray was in the mainstream of literature in her time with her fictionalized accounts of real historical people. Her novels were often set in the seventeenth century or earlier, and she was careful to present accurate details of life and speech of the period. Frequently, Bray's novels feature court trials and reflect the themes of filial piety and loyalty to the "cause," whatever it might be. Her characters are generally flat, her scenic descriptions occasionally overbearing, and her plots transparent. Humor rarely figures in Bray's novels, and most of her plots are resolved by contrived sets of circumstances. Yet in her day Bray was a popular success. Amelia Opie wrote to Bray in 1845, "I bought *The White Hoods* when it came out, have read it FOUR times and mean to read it again. And when I was in Ghent in 1835, it was not the pages of the Historians but THINE that impelled me to the localities where thy Heroes and Heroines acted and suffered."

Eliza Bray's books show little stylistic development as her career progressed; they are all competently written, however, and accurately researched. In keeping with the times and popular taste, Bray's historical romances, especially, inform and instruct more often than they entertain.

References:

Ernest A. Baker, *The History of the English Novel*, volume 7: *The Age of Dickens and Thackeray* (London: H. F. & G. Witherby, 1936);

G. C. Boase, "Anna Eliza Bray and her Writings," *Library Chronicle*, 1 (1884): 126;

Charles Cuthbert Southey, ed., *The Life and Correspondence of Robert Southey*, 6 volumes (London: Longman, Brown, Green & Longmans, 1849-1850).

Lady Charlotte Bury

(28 January 1775 - 31 March 1861)

Jacqueline Gray
University of Colorado at Boulder

BOOKS: *Poems on Several Occasions. By a Lady* (Edinburgh, 1797);

Self-Indulgence; A Tale of the Nineteenth Century (2 volumes, Edinburgh: Printed by Thomas Allan for G. R. Clarke and Longman, Hurst, Rees, Orme & Brown, London, 1812; 1 volume, Boston: Printed & published by John Eliot, 1812; Philadelphia: Published by Bradford & Inskeep and Inskeep & Bradford, New York, Jane Aitken, printer, 1812);

Conduct is Fate, 3 volumes (Edinburgh: William Blackwood / London: T. Cadell, 1822);

Suspirium Sanctorium, or Holy Breathings: A Series of Prayers (London, 1826);

"Alla Giornata;" or, To the Day, 3 volumes (London: Printed by S. & R. Bentley for Saunders & Otley, 1826);

Flirtation: A Novel (3 volumes, London: Henry Colburn, 1827; 2 volumes, New York: Printed by J. & J. Harper for Collins & Hannay, 1828);

The Exclusives (3 volumes, London: Henry Colburn & Richard Bentley, 1830; 2 volumes, New York: Sold by Collins & Hannay, 1830);

The Separation: A Novel by the Authoress of "Flirtation" (2 volumes, London: Henry Colburn & Richard Bentley, 1830; 1 volume, New York: Printed by J. & J. Harper for Collins & Hannay, 1830);

Journal of the Heart, Edited by the Authoress of "Flirtation" (London: Colburn & Bentley, 1830; Philadelphia: Printed by James Kay, Jun., for Carey & Lea, 1830);

The Three Great Sanctuaries of Tuscany, Valombrosa, Camaldoli, Laverna: A Poem, with Historical and Legendary Notices (London: John Murray, 1833);

The Disinherited and The Ensnared by the Authoress of "Flirtation," 3 volumes (London: Printed by Samuel Bentley for Richard Bentley, 1834); republished in part as *The Insnared*, 1 volume (Philadelphia: T. B. Peterson, 1847);

The Lady's Own Cookery Book, and New Dinner-Table Directory, second edition (London: Published for H. Colburn by R. Bentley, 1835);

The Devoted. By the Authoress of "The Disinherited," "Flirtation," & c. (3 volumes, London: Richard Bentley, 1836; 2 volumes, Philadelphia: Carey, Lea & Blanchard, 1836);

The Divorced (2 volumes, London: Henry Colburn, 1837; 1 volume, Philadelphia: E. L. Carey & A. Hart, 1837);

Love, by the Authoress of "Flirtation," "The Divorced," & c. (3 volumes, London, 1837; 2 volumes, Philadelphia: Carey, Lea & Blanchard, 1838);

Diary Illustrative of the Times of George the Fourth interspersed with letters from the late Queen Caroline and from other distinguished Persons, volumes 1 and 2 (London: Henry Colburn, 1838; Philadelphia: Carey, Lea & Blanchard, 1839); volumes 3 and 4, edited by John Galt (London: Henry Colburn, 1839); American edition of volumes 3 and 4 published as *Continuation of the Diary Illustrative of the Times of George IV* (Philadelphia: Lea & Blanchard, 1839);

The History of a Flirt. Related by Herself (3 volumes, London: Henry Colburn, 1840);

Family Records; or, The Two Sisters (3 volumes, London: Saunders & Otley, 1841; 2 volumes, Philadelphia: Lea & Blanchard, 1841);

The Manoeuvring Mother. By the Author of The History of a Flirt (3 volumes, London: Printed by F. Shoberl for Henry Colburn, 1842; 1 volume, Philadelphia: T. B. Peterson, 1848);

The Wilfulness of Woman, by the Author of "The History of a Flirt," "The Manoeuvring Mother," and c. (3 volumes, London: Henry Colburn, 1844; 1 volume, New York: William H. Colyer, 1844);

The Roses by the author of "The History of a Flirt," 3 volumes (London: Hurst & Blackett, 1853);

The Lady of Fashion by the author of "The History of a Flirt," 3 volumes (London, 1856);

The Two Baronets: A novel of fashionable life (London & New York: Routledge, 1864).

Lady Charlotte Campbell (later Bury), 1795 (portrait by Anna Tonelli; from Constance Russell, Three Generations of Fascinating Women, *1904)*

Edition: *The Diary of a Lady-in-Waiting*, edited by A. Francis Steuart (London & New York: John Lane, 1908).

A glance at the titles of Charlotte Bury's novels gives one some indication of their content. *Self-Indulgence* (1812), *Conduct is Fate* (1822), *The Disinherited* (1834), *The Ensnared* (1834), *The Devoted* (1836), *The Divorced* (1837), *The History of a Flirt* (1840), all suggest indictment of the women described within their covers. Bury wrote at least seventeen such novels, none of which is in print today, but in the early nineteenth century her books were widely read in the United States as well as in England. Bury's novels include perceptive descriptions of what it meant to be a woman in her time—emotionally, economically, and physically—offering a glimpse at nineteenth-century British nobility through the eyes of one of its members. While appealing to her readership's fascination with the titled upper class, Bury described with conviction and accuracy the experiences and concerns of women. The characters in her novels are far removed from the relentless misery of the poor. Her heroines move from Milan to Vienna, gliding from one assizes ball to another in subtly flounced silk, but when the trappings and settings are pushed aside, several concerns and conditions, common to women of all classes, become evident in Bury's novels. "The outline of a woman's life," wrote Bury in *The Wilfulness of Woman* (1844), "possesses a general character of sameness."

Like Bury herself, the women in her fiction are titled; born into privilege, they are trained to marry well, so as to maintain or increase that status. Unlike other writers of the day, whose employment she described in *Journal of the Heart* as "delineating the vices and follies of high life" while never "seeing or mixing . . . with those they intend to represent," Charlotte Bury knew her turf. Born at Argyll House, London, on 28 January 1775, Lady Charlotte Susan Maria Campbell was the youngest daughter of Elizabeth Gunning,

Duchess of Hamilton and Duchess of Argyll (said to have held more than sixty titles), and John Campbell, fifth Duke of Argyll. Young Charlotte moved through the rooms of Inverary Castle, the family seat in Scotland, witness to an unending parade of the day's noble and celebrated figures. One of these was Matthew ("Monk") Lewis, whom Bury introduced to Walter Scott in 1798.

Lewis was a regular at Inverary and for a time even produced a weekly, handwritten, private newspaper for the castle, *The Bugle*. He also directed theatrical productions given for the amusement of the numerous guests and residents of the castle, productions later described in Susan Ferrier's novel *Destiny* (1831). Lewis was in some measure infatuated with Bury, whom he often addressed in verse. In 1808, for instance, he dedicated his *Romantic Tales* to her. Unlike Scott, who penned lines of encouragement to Bury after reviewing some of her poetry and later used verses from one of her poems to introduce a chapter in *The Heart of Midlothian* (1818), Lewis offered only his cynical view of women writers. After learning of Susan Ferrier's forthcoming novel *Marriage* (1818), for example, Lewis wrote to Charlotte that he had "an aversion, a pity and contempt for all female scribblers." (In an infamous, 18 March 1804 letter to his mother, who had herself taken up the pen, Lewis remarked: "I always consider a female writer as a sort of half-man.") Matthew Lewis was not alone; the world in which Charlotte Bury dared to write her first novel was far more inclined to applaud her beauty and encourage her to marry well than to nurture any indication of literary talent.

Bury was in fact recognized for her beauty. Speaking of her at sixteen, Horace Walpole, who once described Mary Wollstonecraft as "a hyena in petticoats," noted that "everyone admires [her] person and understanding." The Prince of Wales (later George IV) joined the ranks of Bury's admirers, referring to her as the most beautiful woman in England. Anticipating a more promising match, her friends and family were dismayed when on 14 June 1796, she married her cousin Col. John Campbell of Shawfield, the eldest of Eleonora and Walter Campbell's fourteen children. A year later she published, anonymously, *Poems on Several Occasions*, her first work to appear in print. For the next twelve years the Campbells established themselves as a family. Unfortunately, John Campbell died in Edinburgh in 1809 at age thirty-six, leaving his widow with nine children and limited means for their provision. Prompted by financial considerations, she soon accepted a position as lady-in-waiting to Princess Caroline, the estranged wife of the Prince of Wales.

During this time Bury published her first novel, *Self-Indulgence; A Tale of the Nineteenth Century* (1812). As the two-volume work was published anonymously, authorship was credited to several writers, including Bury's niece, Charlotte Clavering, who did in fact help to edit the second edition. The backdrop for *Self-Indulgence* is the rising middle class of England as it collides with nobility of failing means. At the urging of his parents, Lord and Lady Doneraille, Granville Doneraille marries Sophia Dickens, the daughter of a wealthy merchant. Doneraille—whose weak, fickle, and flawed character includes a propensity for "not thinking at all, till necessity compelled him to act"—is already secretly married to Corrisande de Montbazon, lone survivor of a family of French nobility murdered by Robespierre. In all her novels Bury manages to make some serious observations on the circumstances of nineteenth-century women. In *Self-Indulgence*, she laments the failure of English law to protect women like Corrisande by recognizing the validity of their Roman Catholic marriages. An important theme in many of Bury's novels is the sorority of women. When Sophia learns that her husband is a bigamist and that he abandoned Corrisande to marry her, she seeks out the French woman and befriends her, eventually raising Corrisande's son as her own.

Bury thought enough of this plot to make a few superficial changes and sell it in 1830 to Henry Colburn as *The Separation*. In this version, the young bigamist nobleman becomes Fitzharris Milsington; Corrisande becomes Lenora; and the Siege of Saragossa replaces the French Revolution. With bitter wit, Bury describes the marketing of women and the inflated value of men, even those guilty of bigamy and abandonment. As the drama between the two wives of Lord Milsington is played out, Lady Hightower, mother of two single daughters, speculates that the young nobleman will soon be divorced, and is "delighted to think there [will be] another chance in the market for them."

The Separation, like several other early novels, is marked by the influence of the author's time in Italy, where, after nine years as a widow, she married Reverend Edward John Bury on 21 March 1818. This second marriage proved to be as disappointing to her friends and family as her

Bury's childhood home, Inverary Castle, in 1821 (engraving after a drawing by J. P. Neale)

Bury's parents: John Campbell, fifth Duke of Argyll (portrait by Thomas Gainsborough; Collection of the Duke of Argyll) and Elizabeth Gunning, Duchess of Hamilton and Duchess of Argyll (portrait by Gavin Hamilton; Scottish National Galleries)

Lady Charlotte and Col. John Campbell (drawing by Henry Edridge; from Constance Russell, Three Generations of Fascinating Women, *1904)*

first, and was complicated by the fact that "family" now meant her own children. In his journal Walter Scott later called Edward Bury "a thorough paced coxcomb with some accomplishments, however" (9 June 1827) and "an egregious fop but a fine draughtsman" (27 May 1829). Charlotte Bury's granddaughter, Constance Russell, referred to the match in her *Three Generations of Fascinating Women* (1904) as "Lady Charlotte's unfortunate change of name," but Bury herself, after five years of marriage, wrote, "in my husband I am really bless'd. He has his faults, like us all, but as a husband has as few as possible." Her own happiness notwithstanding, the marriage was difficult for Bury's immediate family. The distaste of her offspring for Bury's new husband was compounded by the fact that Bury had traveled to Italy as the tutor to her eldest son, Walter Frederick Campbell. Writing in her journal in 1817 (later published as *A Journey to Florence*, 1951), Bury's third daughter, Harriet Charlotte Beaujolois Campbell, described how her brother begged his mother to at least delay the marriage a few months, allowing "full time for reflection." When she refused, he wrote to Edinburgh requesting that the allowance he paid her be cut off immediately after the wedding. A few weeks after her mother married Edward Bury, Beaujolois, as she was called, wrote in her last journal entry:

> The marriage was celebrated on the 21st of March. I was present . . . I could write much, but I am unable. . . . The last weeks have been a painful trial for me. I am far from happy, everything I see vexes me and in such a condition I could not put myself to write.

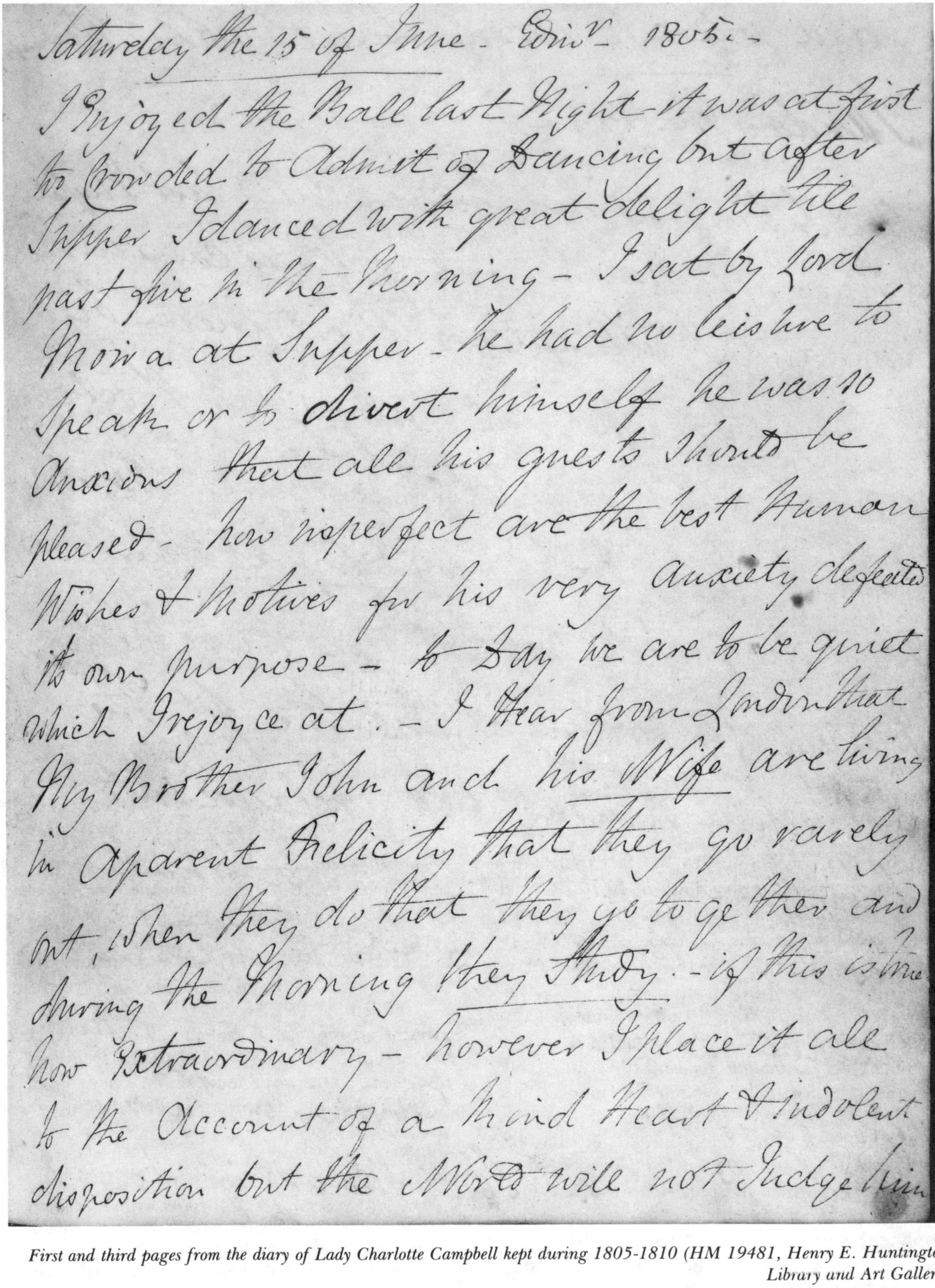
Satturday the 15 of June - Edinr - 1805.-
I Enjoyed the Ball last Night - it was at first
to Crowded to Admit of Dancing but after
Supper I danced with great delight tile
past five in the Morning - I sat by Lord
Moira at Supper - he had no leisure to
Speak or to divert himself he was so
Anxious that all his guests should be
pleased - how imperfect are the best Human
Wishes & Motives for his very anxiety defeated
its own purpose - to Day we are to be quiet
which I rejoyce at. - I Hear from London that
My Brother John and his Wife are living
in Aparent Felicity that they go rarely
out, when they do that they go together and
during the Morning they Study. - if this is true
how Extraordinary - however I place it all
to the Account of a Kind Heart & indolent
disposition but the World will not Judge him

First and third pages from the diary of Lady Charlotte Campbell kept during 1805-1810 (HM 19481, Henry E. Huntington Library and Art Gallery)

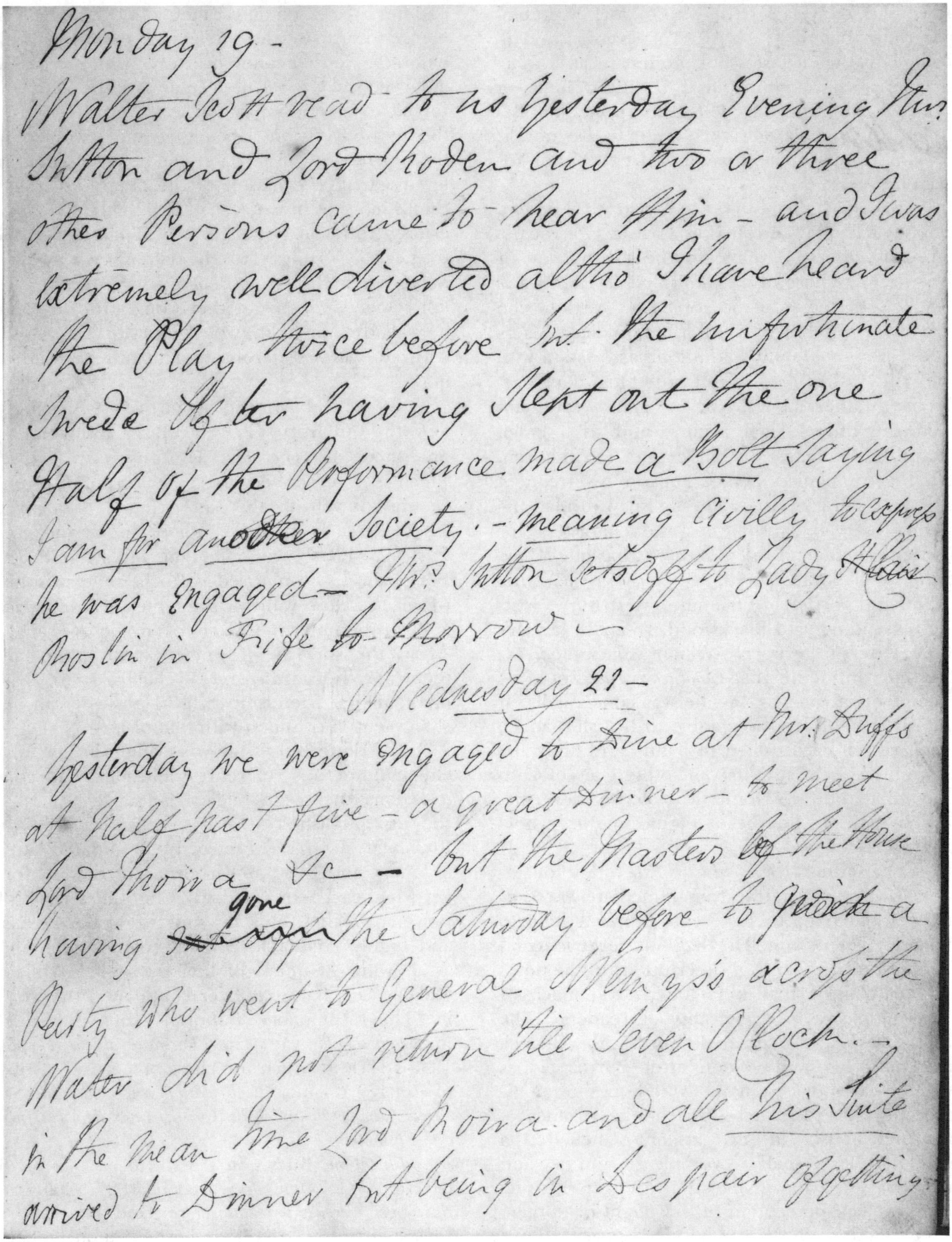

Monday 19 –

Walter Scott read to us Yesterday Evening Mrs Sutton and Lord Roden and two or three other Persons came to hear Him – and I was extremely well diverted altho' I have heard the Play twice before but the unfortunate Swede after having slept out the one Half of the Performance made a Bolt saying I am for another Society. – meaning civilly to express he was Engaged – Mrs Sutton sets off to Lady [illegible] Roslin in Fife to Morrow –

Wednesday 21 –

Yesterday we were engaged to Dine at Mr. Duffs at Half past five – a great Dinner – to meet Lord Moira &c – but the Master of the House having ~~set out~~ gone off the Saturday before to [illegible] a Party who went to General Wemyss's across the Water did not return till Seven O'Clock. – in the mean time Lord Moira and all his Suite arrived to Dinner but being in Despair of getting

Reverend Bury, an artist whose work was compared to that of J. M. W. Turner, was said to have extravagant tastes but modest means, a fact that must have contributed to the volume of work Charlotte produced after marrying him. Between 1822 and 1844 she wrote twelve novels, earning approximately two hundred pounds for each book.

In 1820 the Burys returned to London, where Charlotte was called as a witness for the defense of Queen Caroline in the divorce suit of George IV. There, Bury published *Conduct is Fate* (1822) with the assistance of Susan Ferrier, who submitted it to her own publisher, William Blackwood. Ferrier's family had a long association with the fifth duke of Argyll and his daughter. Ferrier's father, James, had for many years handled the duke's legal affairs, and as a child, Susan, the youngest of the Ferriers' ten children, often accompanied her father on his frequent trips to Inverary Castle. These visits provided the setting as well as some of the characters for Ferrier's fiction. Bury's niece, Charlotte Clavering, collaborated with Ferrier on her first novel, and Ferrier in turn supported Bury's writing by sending it to Blackwood. In an 18 January 1820 letter to Ferrier, William Blackwood expressed confidence that *Conduct is Fate* would be a commercial success, but he was concerned that the novel be made "acceptable to British readers, who are not accustomed to a husband knocking down his wife, nor yet to some other traits of Continental manners." Domestic violence, nevertheless, became an important theme in Bury's novels.

The settings for *Conduct is Fate* follow the author's own travels in the years immediately preceding her marriage to Reverend Bury. Writing to her sister Janet Connell in 1820 Susan Ferrier commented on the beautiful descriptions in the novel but complained that it included "too much of them to please the generality of readers." The main character, orphaned Bertha de Chanci, lives near Lausanne. Soon after Bertha elopes with the Compte D'Egmont—who hopes to gain financially from the match—the compte becomes increasingly abusive in his treatment of her. Bertha wonders: "How shall I ever please him . . . and how know to avoid giving him offence?" Writing out of a keen perception of the plight of women, Bury describes Bertha's wounded spirit: "after a time, she found herself frequently reading over the same page, drawling over the same song, and working, till her hands dropped down listless, and her eyes gazed on vacancy." As D'Egmont's violence toward Bertha accelerates, she receives his embraces and romantic overtures with increasing ambivalence. At last he abandons Bertha, who is forced to accept a position as governess, one of the few professions open to genteel women in the nineteenth century and one generally held in low regard: "the master of the family invariably thinks more of his cook than of his children's governess; the salary which he willingly gives the former he grudges to the latter." As in *Self-Indulgence* and *The Separation*, when Bertha is at last rescued, it is by another woman; in this case, it is Lady Mayfield, who (like Bury) is good-natured, witty, generous, and "doatingly fond of dogs."

In 1826, having given birth to two daughters by John Bury, Charlotte Bury anonymously published *"Alla Giornata;" or, To the Day*, a novel which she described as a "romantic legend." In this novel of the last crusade, Ildegarda Gherardesca is a woman whose "pure and free spirit" governs "every thought and action." For Ildegarda, to be married is "to become prisoner within the close walls of some melancholy palace and to become the slave of domestic cares." Again the sorority of women is an important theme as Ildegarda and Rachaella share "the dawn of first friendship [which] possesses an enchantment in common with that of love."

Charlotte Bury's piety is evident in her novels, in numerous references, allusions, and constructions that echo biblical language. In 1826 she also published *Suspirium Sanctorium, or Holy Breathings: A Series of Prayers*. In an undated letter to Janet Connell, Susan Ferrier commented, "I forget whether I sent you Lady Charlotte's book of prayers, which I think far superior to her novels, and highly creditable both as compositions and as showing so much Biblical research." William Makepeace Thackeray later lampooned the work in "The Fashionable Authoress" (first published in *Heads of the People; or Portraits of the People*, 1840-1841), in which the narrator peruses a copy of *Heavenly Chords; A Collection of Sacred Strains, Selected, Composed, and Edited by the Lady Frances Juliana Flummery*.

Flirtation, Bury's first book to be published by Henry Colburn, appeared in 1827. Colburn, now best known for having rejected Thackeray's *Vanity Fair* (1847-1848), published about ninety percent of the fashionable genre novels between 1825 and 1845. *Flirtation*, which appeared anonymously and quickly sold out three printings, describes two sisters, Lady Emily and Lady Frances, nieces of General Montgomery, who loses most of the ladies' inheritance through an imprudent mining investment. Lady Emily, a character of exaggerated unselfishness, finds happiness "by participation in the promised happiness of others." Her sister, Lady Frances, makes a fashionable but loveless marriage, which eventually drives her to the arms of an unprincipled lover and to an untimely death. In contrast Lady Emily's patient virtue is rewarded by her happy marriage to Lord Mowbray.

The characters in *The Exclusives*, published by Colburn in 1830, when Bury was fifty-five, are thinly disguised ladies and gentlemen of nineteenth-century "ton." Immediately after *The Exclusives* was published, Marsh and Miller produced a pamphlet titled *Key to the Royal Novel The Exclusives*, identifying the characters as well-known socialites. For example, Lady Tilney, who "knew the value of intervals," is Sarah Sophia, Lady Jersey, chief owner of Child's bank in London, and the Duchess of Hermanton is Princess Esterházy, wife of the Hungarian ambassador.

Bury seems compelled to explain her motive in writing such a novel; *The Exclusives* includes frequent interjections insisting that it is not the author's wish to attach "blame to the defects of the individual" but rather "to point out the dangers attendant on their peculiar stations, and to show how far even noble natures are liable to be debased by constant exposure to a baneful influence." If this were not her intention, Bury continues, "contemptible indeed would be the pen, which could waste its powers in tracing the vanities and follies of a race which always has existed in some shape or other, and possibly will always continue to do so." Scathing details concerning each of the many characters who delight "in the vanity of being exclusive" obscure the plot line of this novel.

In 1830 Bury also published *Journal of the Heart*, a collection of poems, musings, and reflections in which she laments:

> How I long for a well-written romance! It would be so refreshing to get off the beaten track of modern novels, away from the lords, and ladies, and fashionables, and would-be representatives of beau-monde, such as the rage for scandal, spite, hatred, malice and uncharitableness renders the idol, the Moloch idol of most publishers, and of many novel readers of the day. . . . But I know not of one publisher who will withdraw the veil of obscurity from before such a work.

Even so, Bury was to publish twelve more novels remarkably like those of her early career. Sometimes she felt her limitations as a writer; in 1810 she told Charlotte Clavering that, after reading Ferrier's work, she felt quite discouraged from writing. Yet Bury was serious about her writing, lamenting the state of fiction and referring, in *Journal of the Heart*, to its "nobler and rightful station—that of delighting the fancy and purifying the heart." But the novel was caught in the new market-driven economy. What Bury and others wanted to say had to be tucked and fitted into what would sell.

In 1832 Bury was widowed for the second time. The next year she produced a lavishly printed poem illustrated by her late husband, *The Three Great Sanctuaries of Tuscany, Valombrosa, Camaldoli, Laverna*. The volume was favorably mentioned in the *Quarterly Review* (June 1834), and Bury sent a copy of the poem to William Wordsworth, who may have borrowed from Bury's work for his poem "The Cuckoo at Laverna."

Bury's financial circumstances remained difficult; in 1833 she wrote a letter regarding a small sum owed her, requesting that the money which was twelve days overdue, be paid immediately. "I cannot complain of any long delay in payment"; wrote Bury, "but my circumstances are so dreadfully narrow, that it puts me to serious difficulties (even sometimes to wanting a dinner) if my remittances do not come to a day"(22 May 1833). The pace at which she produced novels reflects Bury's financial circumstances. Two shorter novels, *The Disinherited and The Ensnared*, appeared together in three volumes in 1834, published anonymously in London by Richard Bentley, Henry Colburn's former partner. In *The Disinherited*, superficial Sir Robert Leslie wants his wife, Lady Leslie, and his daughters, Honoria and Letitia, to "expand" by shopping on the other side of town and giving sherbet to the servants. Sir Robert is determined that they his daughters marry well, and, when Honoria refuses to marry the man her father has chosen for her, he dies of a heart attack. The liquid part of the estate passes to Lady Leslie's son, leaving Lady Leslie and Honoria penniless. Letitia, whose marriage to Lord Macpherson had the blessing of Sir Robert, receives her inheritance but remains insensitive to the plight of her mother and sister.

In publishing *The Ensnared*, Bury intended to "show the ultimate misery and wide-extended

Lady Charlotte Campbell (portrait by John Hoppner; from Constance Russell, Three Generations of Fascinating Women, *1904)*

mischief which are the inevitable consequences of all attachments which are not founded on principle and sanctioned by virtue." Lady Constance begins an adulterous relationship with a man many years her junior, Lord de Courcy, who after a period of time becomes abusive toward her. In the end they suffer a "moral death which makes a greater separation that an actual one."

The Divorced (1837) was the first novel published under Bury's name. Thought by some to be her best work, it is probably based in part on the life of well-known literary hostess Elizabeth Vassall Fox, Lady Holland, whose first husband had divorced her in 1797 on the grounds of her adultery with Henry Richard Vassall Fox, third Baron Holland, whom she married three days after the divorce was finalized. After marrying Lord Vernon, beautiful Laura de Quincy succumbs to the amorous advances of her husband's friend, Lord Howard. She divorces Vernon after giving birth to his son and immediately marries Howard, who grows increasingly frustrated with his wife's ostracism from society and becomes violent and abusive. For years the Howards manage to keep the divorce a secret from their own son and daughter, but they eventually learn the truth, after which the family endures many related tragedies.

Bury's tone reflects her sincere concern for women who succumb to temptation. The social stigma suffered by these women was not the only penalty they paid; there were economic considerations as well. Bury's novel was published twenty years before the reform of the marriage and divorce laws. The Married Women's Property Act came later still. *The Divorced* reflects the failure of English law to protect women. When Lord Howard kills himself, his estate passes to a distant relative, and Lady Howard is left penniless, forced to live off the proceeds from the sale of her jewelry. Like Jane Austen's *Pride and Prejudice* (1813) and other novels of the day that focus on the entailment of property to males, Bury's novel underscores the vulnerability of women, even those in positions of privilege.

Love, also published in 1837, opens with a quotation from Matthew Lewis and examines the marriage of Mabel Elton and Lord Francis Herbert, an extravagant gambler and philanderer. As in Bury's other novels, Lord Herbert's blue blood does not prevent him from abusing his wife physically as well as emotionally. Lady Herbert endures years of ill treatment, justifying it to herself by her belief that "love is the principle whereby everything great and good may be achieved . . . the governing law of the universe." When their only child is born, Herbert curses because the infant is a girl. He has numerous affairs, including one with an Italian singer, La Signora Lanti, on whom he lavishes Lady Herbert's jewelry; he also insists that Lady Herbert invite Lanti to sing in their home. Perhaps more than any of Bury's other novels, *Love* defines Bury's concept of romantic love as indistinguishable from what might be called universal love. Her conviction that "a woman's love is too unselfish to be reasonable" and that "women love on for a length of time, without any probability of being loved in return" may have kept her from questioning why women so often found themselves in oppressive circumstances. Bury stops short of such questioning, merely warning her readership to avoid the pitfalls of scandal, divorce, and illicit love.

In his review of *Love*, which appeared in the 11 January 1838 issue of the London *Times*, Thackeray responds to Bury's scenes of wife abuse with sarcasm:

> If this is exclusive love, it should be a lesson to all men never to marry a woman beyond the rank of a milk-maid and vice-versa. But we may venture humbly to ask, are exclusives, fashionables, lords, or whatever they are called, so continually drunk? . . . Do they kick their ladies out of bed? Do they, after having so ejected them, proceed to flog them as they lie on the floor?

Anticipating such a response, Bury had offered this defense within the context of the novel: "How many marriages are like this one! . . . It is a common practice to say, 'Oh! how unnatural! Oh! how exaggerated!' . . . but . . . a thousand more such could be added to the catalogue of Lady Herbert's life, without any colouring." Certainly the violence against women that Blackwood had earlier feared might offend British readers was not a phenomenon of fiction. In an 1816(?) letter to Charlotte Clavering, Susan Ferrier reported a conversation she had had with Bury and John Wilson, in which they debated "whether a woman of a right way of thinking would not rather be stabbed as kicked by her husband. . . ." Ferrier did not record Bury's opinion, but, she asserted, "I am for a stabber, but I dare say you will be for putting up with a kicker. . . . I maintain there is but one crime a woman could never forgive in her husband, and that is kicking."

Evident throughout her work is the tension Charlotte Bury felt in occupying a position of rank even as she wrote in a genre dominated by writers from the middle class. Surrounded by those with money while her own lack of it was a source of constant difficulty, witness to a persistent parade of women determined that they and their daughters should marry up while she herself twice married down, Charlotte Bury wrote from a place of exile that she had to some extent imposed upon herself. She sealed her isolation in 1838 with the publication of the *Diary Illustrative of the Times of George the Fourth interspersed with letters from the late Queen Caroline and from other distinguished Persons*. The diary was published anonymously, but Bury was quickly identified as the author. A story was circulated that her husband had sold the diary without her consent, but as he had died four years before its publication, this story seems unlikely. The diary was popular in the United States as well as in England. Joining the ranks of those attacking the diary was Thackeray, who lampooned Bury's writing in "Skimmings from the Diary of George IV" (*Fraser's Magazine*, March 1838): "as for believing that Lady Sharlot had any hand in this book, Heaven forbid! She is all gratitude, pure gratitude,—depend on it!" He also wrote a review that was published in the same issue of the *Times* where he lambasted *Love*, saying of the *Diary*: "We never met with a book more pernicious or mean."

By 1840 the English press had forgiven Bury sufficiently to greet the publication of *The*

Lady Charlotte Bury (portrait by Alexander Blaikley; from A. Francis Steuart, The Diary of a Lady-in-Waiting, *1908)*

History of a Flirt with glowing reviews. One advertisement promised that the work was "among the best novels of its kind for many years given to the world by the English press." The *Dispatch* called it "an admirable novel," and the *Morning Post* counseled, "No thoughtless or giddy woman can rise from the perusal of this useful and agreeable work, without feeling that it must be her own fault if the lesson it inculcates is thrown away." Written in 1840 when Bury was sixty-five, *The History of a Flirt* details the experiences of Louisa Vansittart, a literary ancestor of Edith Wharton's Lily Bart. On several occasions, Louisa comes to the brink of social ruin through her flirtations with titled, moneyed, and more often than not older men. After Alfred Jones and Dyneton duel over her and the latter is wounded so severely that he must wear a wooden leg, she chooses to pursue Henry Breton in order to "pique the interest" of yet another suitor, Sir William. When these efforts prove to be in vain, Louisa slinks off to Southampton with a family friend, Susan Partington. Alarmed by the possibility of joining the ghetto of spinsters in which she finds herself, Louisa becomes engaged to an elderly man of property, Mr. Turner Ellis. One day their carriage overturns, and they are rescued by two passing gentlemen, Captain Thelwal and Sir James Langham, who suppose Ellis to be Louisa's father. Disappointed by Louisa's attraction to the younger, more virile Thelwal, Ellis goes off to London where his health declines rapidly.

Susan Partington becomes Lady Langham, and Louisa returns to her family home, where she responds to the amorous advances of Lord Elford, another wealthy suitor of advanced years. Elford's "one dominant passion . . . , the desire to be loved for himself," blinds him to the obvious exchange of youth and beauty for money and position. Promising Louisa that he will be "indulgent in every respect," Elford insists that "my wife is my own property, and she belongs exclusively to myself." He tells his bride to be that he "will never allow a female friend" and then recoils when Louisa compares the lot of women to slavery, asking "What is slavery but dictation carried to excess?" There are other feminist rumblings in this late novel, as Bury more than once warns her readership that "marriage is a lottery."

Published in 1841, *Family Records; or, The Two Sisters* is set in Scotland and recounts the lives of Susan and Margaret Falkland. After Susan Falkland marries Lord de Tracey, whom she does not love, they move to Florence (where Charlotte Bury met her second husband). It quickly becomes obvious that de Tracey is involved in gambling and heavily in debt. (Bury's brother George Campbell, Lord Lorne, an habitual gambler, once ran up a staggering debt of more than thirty thousand pounds, nearly pushing her family into financial ruin.)

Bury's wit is evident as she describes Susan Falkland's response to a tedious dinner guest's lengthy recital of what he named "the malt incident." After the pretentious young man recounts his horror at a young woman's request for a beer at a country dance, Susan turns to the servant behind her and orders a beer for herself. The novel accurately portrays the closeness of sisters and the effect of marriage on that relationship. Bury's later novels often have a philosophical tone as if she is trying to say more than the genre will allow.

In 1842 Henry Colburn published yet another of Bury's novels, *The Manoeuvring Mother*. Almost thirty years after Jane Austen's Mrs. Bennet carried on "the business of her life," which was "to get her daughters married," Lady Gertrude Wetheral takes on the same task, pushing her five daughters with a degree of ambition that Austen's character would have been loath to consider. Sir John and Lady Wetheral had four lovely daughters whose "forms were perfect, and their features . . . faultless," but when a fifth was born, Lady Wetheral rejected her, in part because she "loved . . . an even number; four daughters were not too alarming: five or three [were] an indefinite half-vulgar fraction." At Christobel's birth, Lady Wetheral regrets that "the little animal looks determined to live."

Haunted by "visions of [her] daughters pairing off with curates or lieutenants," Lady Wetheral is ever mindful of the market, insisting that one daughter stay inside so that "the wind will not give her that blue look which I cannot endure." She also requests that the young lady be fed only chicken, telling a servant not to "vulgarise her with nasty brown meats." The girls are "brought up to consider wealth and station a balance to the weight of matrimonial misery." At age seventeen Isabel marries Mr. Boscowen, who is stout, rich, and forty-five. Bury describes the uneasy peace of Isabel's marriage, as she wins "his acquiescence by her tears and gentle self-upbraidings." Against her father's counsel, Julia marries selfish, decrepit Lord Ennismore, "a man perfectly disgusting, had he been unsupported by station and wealth." Ennismore is inseparable from his mother, who maintains "dominion over the imbecile mind of her son." Julia eventually flees from the Ennismores to the home of her friend Penelope. Clara marries "that violent and coarse fellow" Sir Foster Kerrison and after much physical abuse eventually dies. Anna Maria makes a somewhat happier match with Tom Pynsent.

Like Austen's Mr. Bennet, Sir John Wetheral closets himself in the study making light of Lady Wetheral's "manoeuvrings," but Bury's character does fight back. Frustrated by the demands of a culture which requires her to see that her daughters marry well, Lady Wetheral retorts: "you thunder blame from your study, yet never assist yourself in work of so much importance." Lady Wetheral considered one "daughter's singlehood at seventeen years of age a severe blow upon her matronly cares," and her fierce maneuvering is indefensible. Even after Clara's death and Julia's misery under Ennismore's mother, Gertrude Wetheral insists that "All my daughters have married splendidly."

The Wilfulness of Woman, published in 1844, describes the unhappy experiences of two women: Harriet Erskine, who marries John Trelawney, and Lady Sarah Monteith, who marries a "dismal general" many years her senior. One night after the general complains that Lady Sarah has kept him waiting for dinner, commenting that if he fails to dine at his usual hour, he "can never eat with appetite," he learns that his wife has eloped with Captain Fermor. The lovers assume the name of Smith and move to Florence, where Lady Sarah grows tired of hiding from her past and laments that "if he had quitted her to join society, a hundred voices would welcome his return, but her path would be in silent wretchedness for ever." Of particular interest in this novel is Bury's treatment of alcoholism in women and its relationship to "domestic misery." After Harriet's husband deserts her, Dr. Meadows discovers her drinking habit; convinced that idleness is the problem, Meadows recommends that she find employment. Upon leaving her idle life behind, she recovers from her addiction.

In the years between 1827, when Colburn published *Flirtation*, and 1844, when *The Wilfulness of Woman* appeared, Charlotte produced eleven novels. It would be nearly ten years before she published another, *The Roses* (1853), and three more years before *The Lady of Fashion* was published in 1856.

Bury spent her last years in London near her two surviving children, Lady Arthur Lennox and Mrs. William Russell. Her granddaughter, Lady Constance Russell, remembers her in those years, dressed in satin and surrounded by Maltese dogs. On 31 March 1861, at age eighty-six, Charlotte Bury died peacefully in her home at 91 Sloane Street. A final novel, *The Two Baronets*, was published posthumously in 1864.

The titles of Charlotte Bury's novels suggest that women are somehow at fault for conduct aimed at survival in a patriarchal society, where struggling against limitation they are called by those in power—and sometimes by themselves—maneuvering, flirtatious, willful, and ensnaring. It is their misfortune to be disinherited or divorced; their conduct is their fate. Tied by her birth to the Tory political views, Charlotte Bury failed to ask questions which in retrospect seem obvious; yet her descriptions and sympathetic characterizations force the very questions she failed to articulate. Restrained by her strict adherence to nineteenth-century Protestant values, as well as by financial pressure, widowhood, and the considerations of raising eleven children, Bury was a prolific writer of popular fiction. Her ability to accurately portray relationships between women and to address the concerns of domestic violence, alcoholism, and economic powerlessness remains an important contribution.

References:

Charlotte Beaujolois Campbell, *A Journey to Florence in 1817*, edited by G. R. de Beer (London: Geoffrey Bles, 1951);

Bruce E. Graver, "Wordsworth, St. Francis, and Lady Charlotte Bury," *Philological Quarterly*, 65 (Summer 1986): 371-380;

Ian G. Lindsay and Mary Cosh, *Inverary and the Dukes of Argyll* (Edinburgh: Edinburgh University Press, 1973);

Auda Prucher, *Figure Europee del Primo '800 nel Diary di Lady Charlotte Campbell Bury* (Florence: Olschki, 1961);

Matthew G. Rosa, *The Silver-Fork School* (New York: Columbia University Press, 1936);

Constance Russell, *Three Generations of Fascinating Women* (London: Longmans, Green, 1904).

Papers:

The National Library of Scotland has a collection of Bury's papers.

Allan Cunningham

(7 December 1784 - 30 October 1842)

Raymond N. MacKenzie
University of St. Thomas

BOOKS: *Remains of Nithsdale and Galloway Song*, edited by Robert Hartley Cromek (London: T. Cadell & W. Davies, 1810);

Songs: Chiefly in the Rural Language of Scotland (London: Printed for the author by Smith & Davy and sold by J. Hearne, 1813);

Sir Marmaduke Maxwell, A Dramatic Poem; The Mermaid of Galloway; The Legend of Richard Faulder; and Twenty Scottish Songs (London: Taylor & Hessy, 1822);

Traditional Tales of the English and Scottish Peasantry, 2 volumes (London: Printed for Taylor & Hessy, 1822);

Paul Jones; A Romance, 3 volumes (Edinburgh: Oliver & Boyd / London: Longman, Rees, Orme, Brown & Green, 1826; Philadelphia: H. C. Carey & I. Lea, 1827);

Sir Michael Scott, A Romance, 3 volumes (London: Henry Colburn, 1828);

The Lives of the Most Eminent British Painters, Sculptors and Architects, 6 volumes (London: John Murray, 1829-1833); republished in part as *The Lives of the Most Eminent British Painters and Sculptors*, 3 volumes (New York: J. & J. Harper, 1831-1834);

Some Account of the Life and Works of Sir Walter Scott (Boston: Stimpson & Ciapp, 1832);

The Maid of Elvar, A Poem in Twelve Parts (London: E. Moxon, 1832);

The Cabinet Gallery of Pictures, Selected from the Splendid Collections of Art, Public and Private, which adorn Great Britain: With Biographical and Critical Descriptions, 2 volumes (London: J. Major, 1833, 1834);

Biographical and Critical History of the British Literature of the Last Fifty Years (Paris: Baudry, 1834);

Lord Roldan, A Romance (3 volumes, London: John Macrone, 1836; 1 volume, New York: Harper & Brothers, 1836);

The Life and Correspondence of Robert Burns (London: J. Cochrane, 1836);

The Life and Land of Burns (New York: J. & H. G. Langley, 1841);

The Life of Sir David Wilkie, 3 volumes, edited by Peter Cunningham (London: J. Murray, 1843);

Poems and Songs, edited by Peter Cunningham (London: J. Murray, 1847).

OTHER: *The Songs of Scotland, Ancient and Modern*, 4 volumes, edited by Cunningham (London: J. Taylor, 1825);

The Works of Robert Burns, 8 volumes, edited, with a biography, by Cunningham (London: Cochrane & M'Crone, 1834);

"The Land of Burns," in *The Poems, Letters, and Land of Burns*, 2 volumes, edited, with a memoir, by Cunningham (London: G. Virtue, 1838, 1840);

James Thomson, *The Seasons, and The Castle of Indolence*, edited, with a biography, by Cunningham (London: Tilt & Bogue, 1841).

Although Allan Cunningham is best remembered today as a minor poet, anthologist, and biographer, he also produced tales, a drama, and three substantial novels. His fiction enjoyed little success in his own time, but there are elements in it which make it of interest to the modern reader, especially to the reader interested in the history of Scottish literature.

The son of John and Elizabeth Harley Cunningham, Allan Cunningham was born in the parish of Keir, Dumfriesshire, in the southwest of Scotland. In 1784 his father, after an unsuccessful period as a farmer, became gardener and land steward at Blackwood House, the estate of a Mr. Copeland. When Allan was two years old, his father took a similar position working for Patrick Miller at Dalswinton. Miller was also Robert Burns's landlord, and Allan developed an early devotion to Burns that colored his entire life's work. He became a voracious reader, but financial difficulties prevented his schooling beyond his eleventh year. At that time he was apprenticed as a stonemason to his elder brother James, learning a trade that would support him

Engraving by J. Jenkins after a portrait by J. Moore

for the rest of his life. He continued to develop literary interests and began writing poems on Scottish subjects. When Burns died in 1796, Cunningham went to see Burns's body and was a part of the funeral procession; he later wrote a valuable essay on the funerals of Burns and Byron (*London Magazine*, August 1824). He also idolized Walter Scott: when *Marmion* (1808) was published, Cunningham walked all the way to Edinburgh just to lay eyes on the author. After catching sight of Scott returning to his home one evening, Cunningham was satisfied and returned to Dumfriesshire. In 1806, seeking out advice and criticism, he sent some of his poems to a local minister who was respected for his learning, Reverend John Wightman. Wightman's response was only partly encouraging: he did not really approve of poetry though he thought young Cunningham was promising, and he sent him a list of books that he should read to put his education on a more solid footing—chiefly historical and religious works. Cunningham persevered, however, and managed in 1807 to get some poems printed in *Monthly Literary Recreations*, edited by Eugenius Roche in London; this short-lived periodical also published some of Byron's earliest works. In the meantime he was becoming successful in stonemasonry work and was building a strong reputation as a designer and carver.

When a London-based publisher, Robert Hartley Cromek, came to Scotland in 1809 to collect traditional songs and poems from the countryside, he and a partner met with Cunningham, who agreed to do the gathering for him. He did not tell Cromek that he intended to write the poems and songs himself and submit them as "traditional" pieces. It is ironic that Cunningham's literary career was born in a species of forgery, for

Dalswinton Village, in Dumfriesshire, Scotland, where Cunningham lived from the time he was two until he moved to London in 1810

he later acquired the affectionate nickname of "Honest Allan Cunningham," an epithet that stayed with him lifelong. Cunningham himself seems to have seen his imposture as both a means of getting himself into the literary world and a way of enhancing Scotland's literary reputation. On 8 September 1810 he wrote to his brother, "I could cheat a whole General Assembly of Antiquarians with my original manner of writing and forging ballads. Indeed, the poetry of our ancestors is become all the cry. Romance and chivalry will again begin their adventures—distressed damsels relieved—unaccomplishable exploits of knighthood—and a whole Lapland winter of heathen darkness will overspread the land! from which may the Lord deliver us! and let Scotland 'hae ae blink' of true poetic sunshine." Of course, Cunningham's sort of forgery was almost a traditional genre by his time, after the scandalous successes of Ossian (James Macpherson) and Thomas Chatterton a few decades before. The volume was published in 1810 as *Remains of Nithsdale and Galloway Song*. The scholar today who would undertake to sort out which parts of which songs were indeed traditional and which were strictly of Cunningham's invention would have a difficult time. The book was an immediate success, though many (including Walter Scott) were confident that the songs were contemporary productions. During the period of Cunningham's "gathering" the songs, Cromek wrote him frequently from London, urging him to move there at least temporarily, and in April 1810 he did so, returning to Scotland only once, in 1831.

In London he supported himself to some extent by writing for periodicals and newspapers, but he soon found that the only way he could make a reasonable living was to go back into stone work and confine his literary work to evening hours. In 1811 he was joined by his Scottish fiancée, Jean Walker, and they were married in London on July first. In 1813 he put out a second volume, *Songs: Chiefly in the Rural Language of Scotland*, which also enjoyed popular success. In the next year, Cromek introduced him to the sculptor Francis Chantrey, who offered Cunningham work as superintendent of his studio, a post he accepted and held until his death. Chantrey did mostly busts for well-to-do patrons, and his work was already very much in demand. The living Cunningham enjoyed was therefore steady if not exactly affluent.

His first attempts at fiction were a series of tales commissioned by *Blackwood's Edinburgh Maga-*

zine; appearing in 1819-1821, the tales were chiefly satirical, and their primary butts were Cameronian Scots—an extremist dissenting sect, followers of the preacher Richard Cameron (1648-1680). He was also producing tales for the *London Magazine* and published a collection of them in 1822 as *Traditional Tales of the English and Scottish Peasantry*. As with *Remains of Nithsdale and Galloway Song*, this book is a mixture of traditional and invented material. The chief intent of the tales was to document beliefs and customs that were vanishing, rather than to create well-wrought narrative art. With that caveat, *Traditional Tales* still make for enjoyable reading, and they have the feeling (at least) of authenticity about them. "The Selbys of Cumberland" stands out as a vivid tale of fallen aristocrats and class distinctions insisted upon long after they were meaningful. "Judith Macrone, The Prophetess" is a tightly knit story about witchcraft. The best tale in the volume is "Ezra Peden," about a minister who does battle with the devil and is betrayed by his own fleshly desires; in atmosphere and theme, it is comparable to a Hawthorne tale.

In 1820 Cunningham was also working on a tragedy, *Sir Marmaduke Maxwell* (1822). He sent a draft to Sir Walter Scott for criticism, and after some delay Scott wrote from Edinburgh on 14 November 1820 with more criticism than the author had expected. Scott found the play to be diffuse and in need of major revision, whereas Cunningham had regarded it as finished and polished. Scott's letter is a minor masterwork of combining tact with straightforward criticism. After the play was published, Scott wrote on 27 April 1822, suggesting that Cunningham's muse was probably not suited to the tight construction of a drama and offering another observation: "Perhaps something of the dramatic romance, if you could hit on a good subject, and combine the scenes well, might answer." While Cunningham seems to have resented Scott's lack of enthusiasm for his play, he did follow his suggestion to work in the romance genre, and in 1826 he published *Paul Jones; A Romance*.

Paul Jones is certainly Cunningham's best novel, but it also has major weaknesses. The three-volume work is overlong and extremely diffuse. Even making allowances for the exaggerations of romance, there are many scenes that strain credibility beyond the breaking point. But there are also elements in it that are very well handled. The story is loosely based on the life of John Paul Jones, and the major events in Jones's life—his victories at sea in the service of the American Revolution and his subsequent service for the French and Russian navies—are adhered to; indeed, many of the events in Jones's life were so extreme and so apparently unlikely as to make him the perfect subject for a romance writer. Yet Cunningham took major liberties with historical fact as well, primarily in dealing with Jones's youth in Scotland and the forces that motivated him. He adopted a legend of Jones's uncertain parentage and made him the bastard son of Lord Dalveen. Dalveen's legitimate son is the same age as Jones, and the two begin as close friends but gradually become bitter enemies as they reach young adulthood. The young Dalveen is a combination of the Byronic hero and of Samuel Richardson's seducer-villain Lovelace. Seducing the young maidens of his Solway neighborhood and then abandoning them, Dalveen is a powerful character. He alternates between periods of human remorse and true demonic energies, and the story is often at its best when he is prominent in it, as he is in volume one. After Dalveen sets his sights on Jones's sister and—despite Jones's warnings—has her kidnapped and taken off to sea, Jones publicly assaults and challenges Dalveen. He is hauled off to a corrupt local judge, Justice Macmittimus, who commits him to forced sea service. He quickly escapes and, in bitter rage, vows revenge against his native land for allowing class distinction to obscure justice. In the novel's terms this attitude clearly labels Jones an extremist, and his subsequent pirate activities prove that his rage has put him beyond the pale, his revenge turning him into a worse public menace than even Dalveen.

At around this same point in the story Cunningham produced one of his finest scenes, in which Dalveen, walking home through the countryside at night, is accosted by the ghost of the father of one of the women he has ruined. The scene is eerie and powerfully presented, worthy of the Scottish legends Cunningham used in so much of his earlier work. The scene also starts Dalveen on the road to repentance, though the novel does not let him off for his crimes. Much of volumes two and three concerns Jones's adventures abroad. Cunningham vividly depicts the historical battle Jones won in the Irish Sea. His historical research on the battle is evident, but thereafter much of the story loses all plausibility. Returning to America, for example, Jones happens to get George Washington for his guide through the wilderness. A Scottish settlement in America

turns out to be something of a matriarchy headed by his sister Maud, who had escaped from her kidnappers. An Indian guide who befriends Jones turns out to have had a Scottish father. And in a battle in America, Dalveen himself turns up, having joined the British army. He, of course, happens to run into Maud and to beg her forgiveness. He and Jones go their separate ways and keep encountering each other in strained circumstances, such as a battle in Turkey and a hall in Paris during the height of the French Revolution. During the French Revolution, both Dalveen and Jones die in Paris, Jones embittered and alone, Dalveen murdered in an alleyway.

Cunningham invests his story with some interesting thematic elements. Both the main characters are driven to their unhappy lives by the sin of pride. Cunningham sets some scenes near ruins where minor characters explicate the meaning of the ruins for prideful humankind. He also seems to have adapted the Greek notion of a chorus, especially in the Scottish sections, where a group of common people occasionally observes events and comments on them. (This commentary is often in dialect, which the main characters never speak.) The barren and eerie Solway countryside is used effectively in the early parts of the novel, almost as well as Scott used it in *Redgauntlet* (1824). In *Paul Jones*, as in his other novels and most of his tales, Cunningham interweaves ballads and poems with the story itself; while these sometimes impede the progress of the story, they contribute to the tone and atmosphere.

Although *Blackwood's* reviewed *Paul Jones* favorably, the novel had small success. Cunningham nevertheless began work on a new

Portrait from the Fraser's Magazine *"Gallery of Illustrious Literary Characters" (1830-1838)*

novel and published it in 1828 as *Sir Michael Scott*. It suffers from the same diffuseness as *Paul Jones*, but it is a very different sort of production. Its stated purpose is "to present to my countrymen an image of the poetic beliefs of their ancestors; to gather from history, tale, and tradition, the torn and scattered members of popular superstition, and seek to unite them into one consistent narrative. . . ." Opening in 1513 with the battle of Flodden Field, where James IV of Scotland was killed, the story is a wide-ranging allegory of Scotland's past and future, presented through the person of Michael Scott, a traditional wizard from Scottish lore. Scott takes the young James V on a tour of Scotland and England with many digressions into supernatural settings, gradually readying him for kingship. The whole long process culminates in a vision of English and Scottish unity—demonstrating that the real enemy of the Scots was not the English but the pope. Cunningham's anti-Catholicism was not unique in the 1820s, when the question of increased toleration for Catholics was being hotly debated; in the novel Michael Scott shows James that the pope is not so much a religious leader as a potent political threat due to his command over Spain and France. The final scenes concern the defeat of the Spanish Armada in 1588, and the book culminates in a vision of British imperial grandeur. Despite the religious issues, the conception of the book is a grand one, and Cunningham's language throughout is suitably lofty. The description of the defeat of the Armada is couched in long, rolling, biblical sentences; in many passages, this lofty style is quite effective. The book as a whole, however, lacks a clear, unified conception—episode follows episode with no sense of forward movement.

Sir Michael Scott had even less success than *Paul Jones*. Cunningham later corresponded with the popular novelist G. P. R. James, and James, who had liked *Michael Scott*, wrote to Cunningham in 1837, "I am very sorry to hear you say that these well-informed and enlightened times have not done justice to your romances. I'll tell you one great fault they have, which is probably that which prevents the world from liking them as much as it should do: they have too much poetry in them, Allan. . . . " In a sense James was correct: the spirit of poetic mystery pervades the novel, as does the love of language, but Cunningham was unable to combine these gifts with narrative focus.

His final novel was *Lord Roldan*, published in 1836. The weakest of his three novels, it continues the tendency to diffuseness present in the others, and it lacks their good points, especially the strong descriptions of Scottish life and superstitions. The bastard son of wild Lord Roldan (somewhat reminiscent of Lord Dalveen, but lacking his satanic energy), the young Morison grows up under the gentle tutelage of his mother. Eventually kidnapped by Roldan's man, Captain Corsbone, in order to get him out of the way, Morison wanders throughout Europe, rising to military prominence as a general under Napoleon, who says, "I love [Morison]—his courage is great, his presence of mind equal to my own, and the quickness of his conceptions is surpassed by the rapidity of his execution—yet, he is a riddle; there is something mystical and undefined about him; . . . his head is filled with the chimeras of liberty and equality, and he expects to see thrones pulled down, and republics reared, after every victory." When he decides Napoleon does not fully meet his ideal conception of him, Morison makes his way eventually back to Scotland, where he is reconciled with his dying father. Lord Roldan finally sees Morison's true worth, and with his dying words acknowledges him and his mother. The new Lord Roldan, we are told, will restore the family name to the dignity and greatness it once had. In the final pages, Morison learns that the woman he has loved and has always believed to be his sister is not really his sister, and the two are married. The novel, as this brief synopsis will suggest, suffers from the melodramatic, trite, and unbelievable plot conventions of romance, but unlike *Paul Jones*, *Lord Roldan* does not redeem itself by any greater elements of character or incident. The novel met with an indifferent public, and James—always the loyal friend—wrote Cunningham, insisting that "I like what I have read [of the novel] much—very much indeed; and I do not scruple to say that there is more vigorous writing, more fine painting, more truth and perception of character, in that part alone than would make ten of the novels that are daily praised to the skies in all reviews of Great Britain."

James was in a very small minority in praising *Lord Roldan*, and Cunningham made no further attempts to write fiction, devoting himself instead to poetry and nonfiction, most notably his edition of Robert Burns's works, for which he wrote a biography, and his biography of Sir David Wilkie. In 1840 he had a paralytic attack from which he seemed to recover completely. On 29 October 1842, however, he had a second attack and died the next day, at the age of fifty-seven. Cunningham's fiction is seldom read today; the diffuse, overlong nature of his novels is a sin that will probably keep him unknown. At his best, as in the early sections of *Paul Jones*, he was a novelist of some promise, with a unique blend of Scottish sensibility and powerful descriptive abilities. His varied output of fiction, nonfiction, and poetry make him an interesting example of a nearly extinct species, the professional man of letters.

Biography:

David Hogg, *The Life of Allan Cunningham, With Selections from His Works and Correspondence* (London: Hodder & Stoughton / Dumfries: John Anderson & Son / Edinburgh: John Grant, 1875).

Reference:

S. M. Ellis, *The Solitary Horseman, or The Life and Adventures of G. P. R. James* (Kensington: Cayme Press, 1927).

Maria Edgeworth

(1 January 1768 - 22 May 1849)

Gary Kelly
University of Alberta

BOOKS: *Letters for Literary Ladies, to Which Is Added an Essay on the Noble Science of Self-Justification* (London: Printed for J. Johnson, 1795; second edition, corrected and enlarged, 1799; George Town: Published by Joseph Milligan, W. Cooper, printer, 1810);

The Parent's Assistant; or, Stories for Children (3 volumes, London: Printed for J. Johnson, 1796; expanded edition, 6 volumes, London: Printed for J. Johnson by G. Woodfall, 1800; 3 volumes, George Town: Published by Joseph Milligan, Dinsmore & Cooper, printers, 1809);

Practical Education, 2 volumes, by Maria Edgeworth and Richard Lovell Edgeworth (London: Printed for J. Johnson, 1798; New York: Printed for G. F. Hopkins and Brown & Stansbury, 1801); revised, 3 volumes (London: Printed for J. Johnson, 1801); republished as *Essays on Practical Education*, 2 volumes (London: Printed for J. Johnson, 1811);

Castle Rackrent: An Hibernian Tale; Taken from Facts, and from the Manners of the Irish Squires, before the Year 1782 (London: Printed for J. Johnson, 1800; third edition, revised, 1801; Boston: Printed & published by T. B. Wait & Sons, 1814);

Early Lessons, 10 parts in 5 volumes (London: Printed for J. Johnson, 1801-1802): *Harry and Lucy*, parts 1-2; *Rosamond*, parts 3-5; *Frank*, parts 6-9; "The Little Dog Trusty," "The Orange Man," and "The Cherry Orchard," part 10; 4 volumes (Philadelphia: Printed for J. Maxwell, 1821);

Moral Tales for Young People (5 volumes, London: Printed for J. Johnson, 1801; 1 volume, Philadelphia: G. S. Appleton / New York: D. Appleton, 1846);

Belinda, 3 volumes (London: Printed for J. Johnson, 1801); revised edition, in *British Novelists*, edited by Anna Laetitia Barbauld, volumes 49 and 50 (London: Printed for F. C. & J. Rivington, 1810; 2 volumes, Boston: Printed for Wells & Lilly, 1814; fourth edition, corrected and improved, London: Printed for R. Hunter, 1821);

Essay on Irish Bulls, by Maria Edgeworth and Richard Lovell Edgeworth (London: Printed for J. Johnson, 1802; New York: Printed by J. Sevaine, 1803; fourth edition, London: Printed for R. Hunter, 1815);

Popular Tales (3 volumes, London: Printed for J. Johnson by C. Mercer, 1804; 2 volumes, Philadelphia: Printed & sold by J. Humphreys, 1804);

The Modern Griselda: A Tale (London: Printed for J. Johnson, 1805; second edition, corrected, London: Printed for J. Johnson, 1805; George Town: Published by Joseph Milligan, W. Cooper, printer, 1810; third edition, corrected, London: Printed for J. Johnson, 1813; fourth edition, corrected, London: Printed for R. Hunter, 1819);

Leonora, 2 volumes (London: Printed for J. Johnson, 1806; New York: I. Riley & Co., 1806);

Essays on Professional Education, by Maria Edgeworth and Richard Lovell Edgeworth (London: Printed for J. Johnson, 1809);

Tales of Fashionable Life, 6 volumes; volumes 1-3: "Ennui," "Almeria," "Madame de Fleury," "The Dun," and "Manoeuvring" (London: Printed by J. Johnson, 1809; 2 volumes, George Town: Printed for Joseph Milligan, 1809); volumes 4-6: "Vivian," "Emilie de Coulanges," and "The Absentee" (London: Printed for J. Johnson, 1812);

Patronage (4 volumes, London: Printed for J. Johnson, 1814 [i.e., 1813]; 3 volumes, Philadelphia: Published by Moses Thomas, J. Maxwell, printer, 1814); revised edition, in volumes 11 and 12 of *Tales and Miscellaneous Pieces*, 14 volumes (London: Printed for R. Hunter and Baldwin, Cradock & Joy, 1825);

Continuation of Early Lessons, 2 volumes (London: Printed for J. Johnson, 1814; Boston: Printed for Bradford & Read, 1815);

Maria Edgeworth late in life

Comic Dramas in Three Acts [*Love and Law*, *The Two Guardians*, and *The Rose, the Thistle, and the Shamrock*] (London: Printed for R. Hunter, 1817; second edition, 1817; Boston: Printed for Wells & Lilly, 1817);

Harrington: A Tale and *Ormond: A Tale* (3 volumes, London: Printed for R. Hunter and Baldwin, Cradock & Joy, 1817; 2 volumes, New York: Printed for Kirk & Mercein, 1817; Philadelphia: Published by Moses Thomas and Van Winkle & Wiley, New York, 1817; second edition, corrected, London: Printed for R. Hunter and Baldwin, Cradock & Joy, 1817);

Rosamond: A Sequel to Early Lessons, 2 volumes (London: Printed for R. Hunter, 1821; Philadelphia: Printed for J. Maxwell, 1821);

Frank: A Sequel to Frank in Early Lessons (3 volumes, London: Printed for R. Hunter, 1822; 2 volumes, New York: Printed for W. B. Gilley, 1822);

Harry and Lucy Concluded: Being the Last Part of Early Lessons (4 volumes, London: Printed for R. Hunter and Baldwin, Cradock & Joy, 1825; 3 volumes, Boston: Printed for Munroe & Francis, 1825; second edition, corrected, 4 volumes, London: Printed for R. Hunter and Baldwin, Cradock & Joy, 1827; third edition, revised and corrected, London: Printed for R. Hunter and Baldwin, Cradock & Joy, 1837);

Little Plays for Children, volume 7 of *The Parent's Assistant* [*The Grinding Organ*, *Dumb Andy*, and *The Dame School Holiday*] (London: Printed for R. Hunter, 1827); republished as *Little Plays . . . Being an Additional Volume of The Parent's Assistant* (Philadelphia: Thomas T. Ash, 1827);

Garry Owen; or, The Snow-Woman (Salem, Mass.: John M. and W. & S. B. Ives, 1829); republished with *Poor Bob the Chimney-sweeper* (London: Printed for J. Murray, 1832);

Helen: A Tale (3 volumes, London: Printed for R. Bentley, 1834; 2 volumes, Philadelphia: Carey, Lea & Blanchard / Boston: Allen & Ticknor, 1834);

Orlandino, in Chambers' Library for Young People (Edinburgh: Printed for W. & R. Chambers, 1848; Boston: Gould, Kendall & Lincoln, 1848);

The Most Unfortunate Day of My Life: Being a Hitherto Unpublished Story, Together with the Purple Jar and Other Stories (London: Cobden-Sanderson, 1931).

Editions: *Tales and Miscellaneous Pieces*, 14 volumes (London: Printed for R. Hunter and Baldwin, Cradock & Joy, 1825);

Tales and Novels (18 volumes, London: Printed for Baldwin & Cradock, 1832-1833; 9 volumes, New York: J. & J. Harper, 1832-1834);

Tales and Novels (9 volumes, London: Printed for Whitaker & Co.; Simpkin, Marshall & Co., 1848; 10 volumes, New York: Harper & Brothers, 1852);

Tales and Novels, 10 volumes (London: George Routledge & Sons, 1893);

Castle Rackrent and The Absentee (London: Dent / New York: Dutton, 1909);

Castle Rackrent, edited by George Watson (London: Oxford University Press, 1964).

OTHER: "The Mental Thermometer," in *The Juvenile Library*, volume 2 (London: Printed for T. Hurst, 1801);

"Little Dominick," in *Wild Roses: or, Cottage Tales* (London, 1807);

Mary Leadbeater, *Cottage Dialogues Among the Irish Peasantry, with Notes and a Preface by Maria Edgeworth* (London: Printed for J. Johnson, 1811);

Charles Sneyd Edgeworth, *Memoirs of the Abbé Edgeworth; Containing His Narrative of the Last Hours of Louis XVI*, revised by Maria Edgeworth (London: Printed for R. Hunter, 1815);

Richard Lovell Edgeworth, *Readings on Poetry*, preface and last chapter by Maria Edgeworth (London: Printed for R. Hunter, 1816; second edition, corrected, London: Printed for R. Hunter, 1816; Boston: Published by Wells & Lilly and sold by Van Winkle & Wiley, New York, and by M. Carey, Philadelphia, 1816);

Memoirs of Richard Lovell Edgeworth, Esq.: Begun by Himself and Concluded by His Daughter, Maria Edgeworth, 2 volumes, volume 2 by Maria Edgeworth (London: Printed for R. Hunter, 1820; second edition, corrected, London: Printed for R. Hunter, 1821; Boston: Wells & Lilly, 1821);

Garry-Owen; or, The Snow-Woman, in *The Christmas Box*, edited by T. Crofton Croker (London: John Ebers / Edinburgh: W. Blackwood, 1829).

Maria Edgeworth was the best-known novelist in Britain from 1800 until the publication of Walter Scott's *Waverley* in 1814. She was also one of the most important writers of fiction for children in the nineteenth century. She developed the late-eighteenth-century novel of manners and sentiment, as practiced by Frances Burney and other women writers, into a vehicle for representing a national difference-in-unity in the aftermath of a revolutionary crisis that had threatened to break society and the nation apart during the 1790s. She infused the late-eighteenth-century didactic and instructional tale for children, practiced by the sisters Mary Ann and Dorothy Kilner, Sarah Trimmer, and other women writers, with a new complexity, domestic realism, and liveliness, instrumental in founding the main tradition of nineteenth-century children's literature and still influential today. These two spheres of fiction writing were not separate but interdependent. Both were dedicated to constructing the individual as a moral and rational self, independent of merely relative social categories of worth and identity and thus able to construct families and local communities based on relationships of affection rather than social interest and power. These communities in turn would constitute the nation, not so much through laws, institutions, and external modes of power, but internalized within the individual subject by education in the broadest sense, including academic studies, professional training, and socialization or "manners." This vision of self and society, represented in fictions that develop individual psychology with new detail, set in domestic society described with new particularity, was rooted in Enlightenment epistemology and sociology and contributed largely to the emergence and popularization of modern ideas of civil society.

Maria Edgeworth was born at Black Bourton in Oxfordshire, on 1 January, probably in 1768 rather than 1767, the year often cited. She was the second surviving child and first daughter of Anna Maria Elers (1743-1773) and Richard Lov-

Richard Lovell Edgeworth and his first wife, Anna Maria Elers, the mother of Maria Edgeworth

ell Edgeworth (1744-1817). Her father was by far the most important figure in her life. He was an Anglo-Irish landed gentleman, but by family tradition he had been given a broad intellectual and professional education and trained in law in order to be an effective estate manager. As a young man, Edgeworth's father spent much time in England and had seen dissipated upper-class society at firsthand. He was also familiar with leading figures in the provincial and Nonconformist enlightenments centered in the English Midlands. These men—leaders in the commercial and manufacturing revolutions and in campaigns for moral, social, and political reform—included the scientist Erasmus Darwin, the china manufacturer Josiah Wedgwood, the chemist James Keir, the industrialist Matthew Boulton, the educationist and social critic Thomas Day, and the inventor James Watt. Edgeworth's father published a book on the construction of roads and carriages (1813), devised a system of telegraphic communication, and invented various gadgets to increase domestic comfort and lessen domestic labor.

He married four times, and his wives bore him twenty-two children, of which four died very young. Thus his older daughters, especially Maria, were almost mothers to the younger children, the last of whom was born in 1812; his last wife, Frances Anne Beaufort, was slightly younger than Maria. This large and diverse family was dominated by his sheer physical energy, varied scientific, literary, and political interests, commitment to economic and social progress, and dedication to liberal educational ideas of the time. He decided to educate his oldest son according to the principles of Jean-Jacques Rousseau, but neglected Maria Edgeworth, who often expressed herself in tantrums and "naughtiness." Her mother died in March 1773, and her father married Honora Sneyd (1751-1780), whom he had loved for several years, only four months later. She bore him two children. In the late 1770s he turned to the educational ideas of Joseph Priestley, who advocated a system based on Lockean association of ideas and modern subjects, rather than the older tradition of the classics. Edgeworth's father also rejected the traditional reading matter for children—chapbooks of the common people—and used the new children's literature represented by Anna Laetitia Barbauld's *Lessons for Children* (1787-1788). Barbauld's work was based on the same materialist and empirical epistemology of the English provincial Enlightenment that informed all his thought and his daughter's writings. He and his second wife, Honora, even began a series of stories illustrating the modern curriculum, though it was left to Maria Edgeworth to complete this ambitious project years later and over many years, in *The Parent's Assistant* (1796) and *Early Lessons* (1801-1825). Edgeworth herself was sent to boarding schools, where she received the conventional education of an upper-middle-class girl and was fairly happy.

Honora Edgeworth died in April 1780 after exhorting her husband to marry her younger sister Elizabeth in order to provide a mother for the children. Against his will and the resistance of their families, Richard Lovell Edgeworth followed her wishes in December 1780. He was far less engrossed with Elizabeth than he had been with her sister, and thus he had more time and energy for Maria Edgeworth and his other children. Elizabeth Edgeworth bore nine children from 1781 to 1794. Maria Edgeworth was sent to a London boarding school to acquire social graces, but what she felt to be her lack of physical attractions made her feel incapable of a conventional feminine social identity. Instead she turned to intellectual pursuits, which made her the subject of ridicule at school, and to the domestic affections outside of marriage. At the same time, her serious eye disease drew out her father's parental concern for her and her education, beginning their lifelong intellectual and domestic relationship.

These relationships developed rapidly after 1782, when Edgeworth's father, inspired by a new Irish patriotism and desire for reform, returned with his family to the ancestral estate of Edgeworthstown in County Longford, Ireland. The example of the American Revolution inspired many Anglo-Irish landowners and professionals to demand control of Irish politics, economic development, and trade. Edgeworth's father attended an Irish "national convention" and reformed management of his own estate, practicing a form of agrarian capitalism. This work formed the basis for his daughter's representation of national reconstruction after the Revolutionary 1790s. The core of his program was a professionalization of gentry culture, to be achieved through careful education of the young. Maria Edgeworth's father directed the education of his own increasing family to prepare them for the new social order, and she acted as his assistant. He directed her to translate the French education novel *Adèle et Théodore* (1782), by Stéphanie-Félicité Ducrest de Saint-Aubin de Genlis. "Adelaide and Theodore" was apparently printed in 1783, but publication was preempted by another English version. Meanwhile he was elected to the new Irish Academy, designed to improve agriculture and industry, and he continued his enthusiastic pursuit of technological innovations to enhance capitalist estate management and national economic development.

When in 1791 he took a break from these endeavors to renew his intellectual associations in England, Maria Edgeworth was left behind and developed a close and long-lasting friendship with his sister, Margaret Ruxton. Maria Edgeworth later joined her father and stepmother in England, but after her firsthand involvement in her father's progressive projects she found herself highly critical of mere fashionable society. Furthermore, the Revolution in France and the political debate and unrest it inspired in Britain made fashionable society seem irresponsible—another major theme of Edgeworth's later writings. In response to reports of such unrest in Ireland the Edgeworths returned there in 1793. Richard Lovell Edgeworth developed a telegraph system to support defense against a possible French invasion or Irish uprising. He also stood—unsuccessfully—for the Irish parliament and tried to moderate social and political conflict.

Meanwhile Maria Edgeworth articulated her father's views in the acceptably feminine domain of education. The spheres of political action and polemical discourse open to him as a man were closed to her as a woman. He also discouraged her from writing mere fiction, associated in eighteenth-century culture with the subliterary discourse of children, women, the uneducated lower classes, and uncivilized peoples. The novel, with a few exceptions, was condemned for spreading decadent court culture and upper-class values, distracting its readers from "solid and useful" reading necessary to professional training. Many believed—wrongly—that novels were mostly written and read by women and that such books expressed and encouraged their emotional, irrational nature. During the 1790s cultural anxiety about women, authorship, and the novel became

The Edgeworth family in 1787. Maria Edgeworth is seated facing her father, whose third wife, Elizabeth Sneyd, is directly behind him holding William. The other children (standing) are Emmeline, Henry, Charlotte, Sneyd, Lovell, Anna, Bessie, and Honora (watercolor by Adam Buck; from Elisabeth Inglis-Jones, Great Maria, *1959).*

sharper with the work of Revolutionary feminists such as Mary Wollstonecraft and Mary Hays. These writers drew from the same Enlightenment philosophy that influenced Edgeworth's father and thus Edgeworth herself.

In 1795 her *Letters for Literary Ladies* was published by Joseph Johnson, the leading publisher of the English Nonconformist and provincial enlightenments, and for that reason her father's choice. In the 1790s, however, Johnson also published Revolutionary sympathizers and feminists such as Wollstonecraft and Hays. Maria Edgeworth would have preferred another publisher, but Johnson and the successors of his firm remained her publishers until very late in her career. *Letters for Literary Ladies* is in three parts. A pair of letters between two men debates both the capacity of women for literary work and the propriety of their publishing at all. An epistolary novella follows, exhibiting the contrast between the intellectual and chaste Caroline and the enthusiastic and sentimental Julia—an allusion to Julie, the heroine of Rousseau's novel *La nouvelle Héloïse* (1761), who had become an even more controversial figure during the feminist debate of the 1790s. The third part is "An Essay on the Noble Science of Self-Justification," ironically advising weakly feminine women on how to win verbal battles with men. The three parts of the book are separate (even separately paginated) considerations of women's intellectual "nature," at a time when strong claims were being made for woman's rights as the basis of social transformation and stability of the state. Edgeworth's contributions to this debate are framed in the kind of familiar epistolary or essayistic discourse often used by women writers to engage in serious subjects. She uses these forms to engage central topics of Revolutionary feminism obliquely, not in her own voice. Writers such as Wollstonecraft use a personal, expressive, and autobiographical form to validate their feminist arguments from their female experience and observation; Edgeworth's obliqueness thus sets her discussion apart from that of the Revolutionary feminists though it is in many ways parallel to it. This move to revise Enlightenment and Revolutionary feminist ideas away from social and political conflict toward a more conventionally feminine role of mediation would inform all her later work and become especially prominent in the revolutionary aftermath. She continued both to argue for women's intellectual rights and to insist on women staying out of the public political domain to work from the domestic sphere, as she did herself.

Her next work, her most widely read and in many ways her most successful, exemplifies cultural and social criticism that was acceptably feminine and domestic and in which women were leading the way. *The Parent's Assistant* (1796) comprises stories and a play for children written in the early 1790s. An expanded version in a more "elegant" format appeared in 1800 and was republished numerous times in various forms throughout the nineteenth century. The stories continue the work of such pioneering English education writers as Thomas Day, Sarah Trimmer, the Kilner sisters, and Wollstonecraft (several of whom were also published by Johnson), as well as French writers such as Arnaud Berquin and Madame de Genlis, in the three decades before the 1790s. Edgeworth's children's stories are less overtly didactic than her predecessors', blending moralizing into situation, incident, and plot, and exhibiting less religiosity than writers before her (and many of those who came after her). She also constructed a greater sense of probability and authenticity, more detailed domestic "realism" and convincing, characteristic speech, thus creating greater rhetorical effectiveness.

During the mid 1790s Maria Edgeworth also collaborated with her father on *Practical Education*, published in 1798. The treatise is a mixture of theory from John Locke, Francis Hutcheson, Jean-Jacques Rousseau, and Joseph Priestley with practical, anecdotal illustration based on the Edgeworth family's own experience. The plan of education applies the sensationist and associationist epistemology of the Scottish and English provincial enlightenments to what are supposed to be the "natural" stages in the child's growth, aiming to construct a rational and independent individual fit for professional work, social responsibility, and public service. The philosophical background and educational program are in fact close to those of leading "English Jacobins," but the practical emphasis of the book silently moderates theoretical elements that would, by the time the book was published, have been associated by many readers with the dangerous "new philosophy" that was thought to inspire both the French Revolution and its sympathizers in Britain. This moderation was carried further in the cheaper and more "popular" second and revised edition of 1801. Maria Edgeworth continued to popularize the book's educational plan further in fiction—for both adults and children—over the next three decades.

Just when the Edgeworths were completing their plan of domestic education the family life was disrupted by the illness and death of Maria Edgeworth's stepmother Elizabeth. Once again, however, Richard Lovell Edgeworth was remarried quickly: in May 1798 to Frances Beaufort, daughter of a progressive clergyman and landlord and a year younger than Maria Edgeworth. Edgeworth and her new stepmother got on well, and the household was about to settle into its accustomed harmony and activity when public and political developments intruded. In the mid 1790s long-standing social conflicts within Ireland were exacerbated by the French Revolution debate. Both predominantly Protestant middle-class reformers and predominantly Catholic lower-class dissidents expected the French republic to assist an Irish uprising against British rule and gentry domination. In reaction landlords and "loyalists," both Protestant and Catholic, raised local forces of yeomanry or militia to intimidate the politically or socially disaffected. This reign of terror, embittered by sectarian hatred, provoked uprisings in various parts of Ireland in the spring of 1798. These were eventually crushed, and the French invasion in August was soon defeated. During the crisis Edgeworth's father raised a militia of both Protestants and Catholics, leading to charges by his anti-Catholic neighbors that he sympathized with the rebels; at one point he was almost lynched by a loyalist mob.

The crisis convinced many in the British government that Ireland could be made more stable only by merging the Irish parliament with Britain's. The usual government methods of bribery and patronage were used to secure a majority in the Irish parliament for the union. These methods aroused deep resentment among the Irish gentry, including Richard Lovell Edgeworth, who was actually for the union because he believed it would spur economic development and ensure improvement in the lot of Catholics. Accordingly, he spoke in favor of union but voted against it. The bitter debate over union divided Irish society and again showed Maria Edgeworth the evil effect of public affairs on domestic and local social harmony and the importance of moderation and conciliation. In her fiction she combined promotion of these virtues, conventionally ascribed to women, with popularization of her father's political and social views.

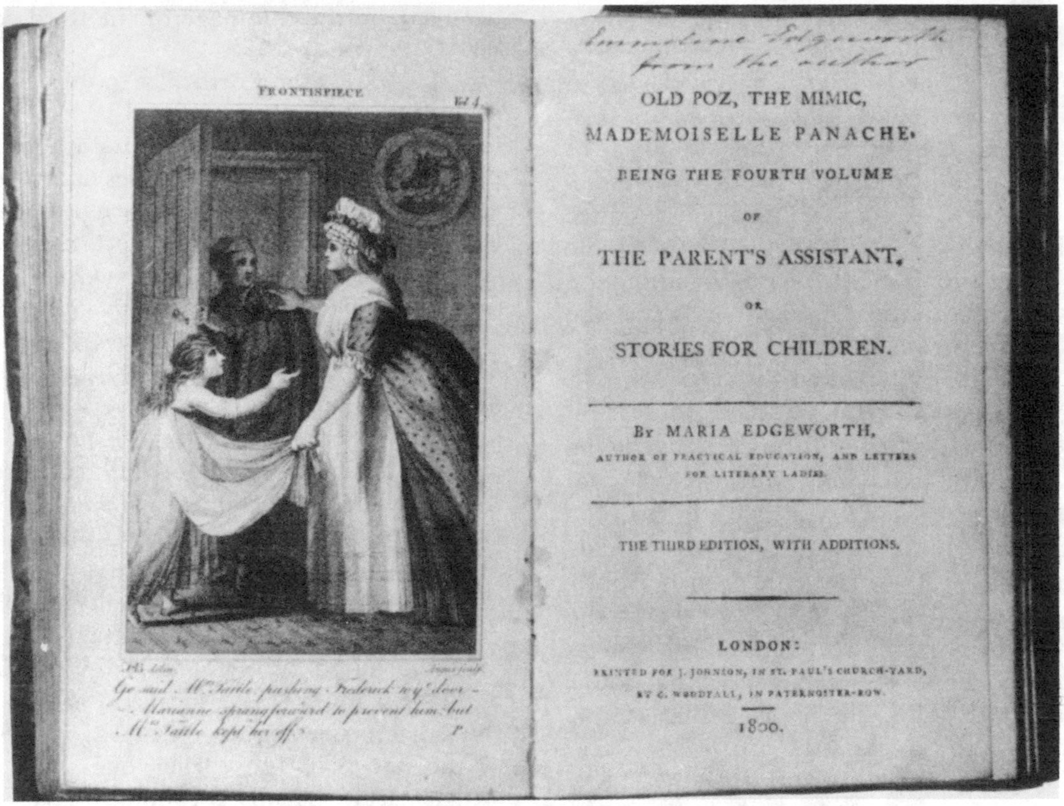

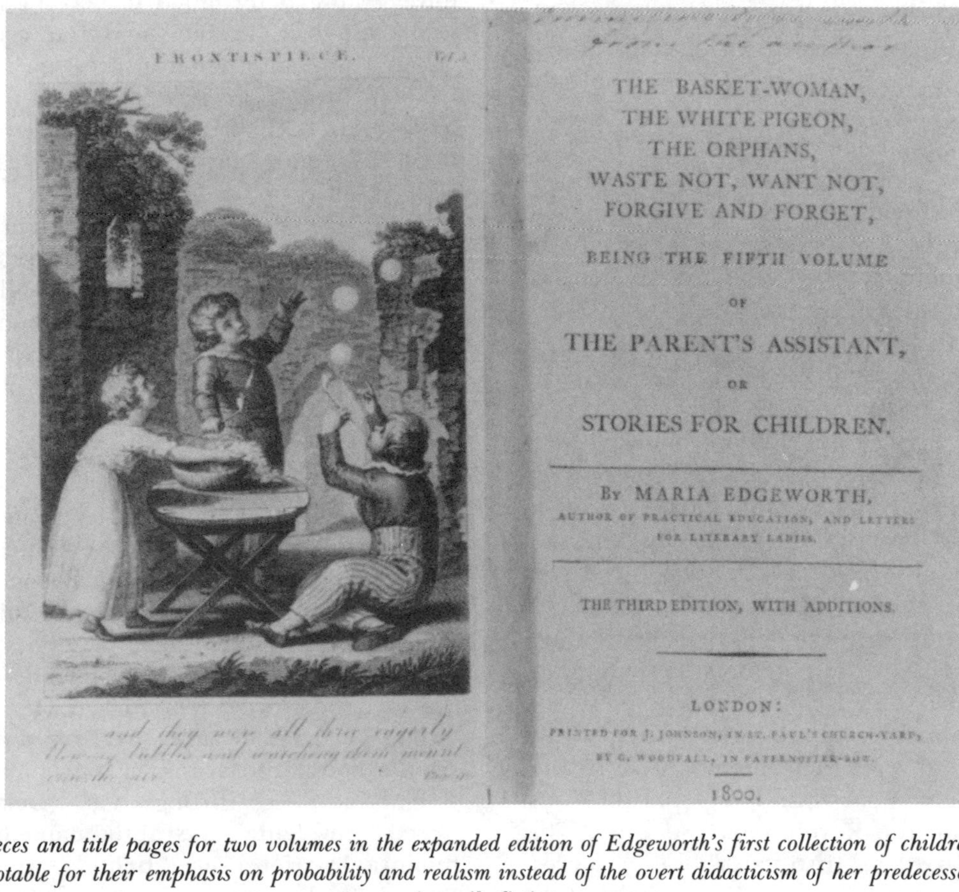

Frontispieces and title pages for two volumes in the expanded edition of Edgeworth's first collection of children's stories, notable for their emphasis on probability and realism instead of the overt didacticism of her predecessors' juvenile fiction

For example, *Castle Rackrent: An Hibernian Tale; Taken from the Facts, and from the Manners of the Irish Squires, before the Year 1782*, published in 1800, incorporated some Edgeworth family history into an extension of her father's mimicry of the phrases, accent, and style of an Irish estate steward. The work criticizes extravagant absentee Anglo-Irish landed gentry and rapacious middle class alike, and shows the former abandoning the peasantry to ignorance, "superstition," and the popular lottery mentality and the latter exploiting both peasants and landlords. The story of four generations of reckless Rackrents is recounted in a much-softened form of Irish brogue by their retainer Thady Quirk. Such monologues in characteristic speech are typical of the short fiction, or conte. Typical too is the fact that Thady is an amusing and sympathetic but obviously unreliable narrator. His irrational loyalty to the Rackrent family represents the mutually debilitating semifeudal bond between gentry and lower class, enabling Thady's son Jason, a sharp attorney, to exploit the weaknesses of the last Rackrent, Sir Condy, and gain control of the estate. Since Thady's views cannot be entirely shared by the reader and the story has no truly admirable characters, the novel seems to lack a hero. But in her anxiety to mediate the Irishness of the themes, settings, characters, and language for the reader in Britain, Edgeworth supplies the story with a preface, glossary, and explanatory notes. In this framing material is found the informed, critical, progressive mentality with which the reader could identity. The "Editor" is the hero in the text, though not in the story.

Edgeworth sets the story in the past and suggests that the abuses depicted in the story no longer prevail, though readers who had just seen the results of upper-class irresponsibility, lower-class violence, and middle-class self-interest—in France as well as Ireland—would have found in the tale obvious implications for the present. Yet the apparently historical setting, humor, complex framing of the story, sympathetic narrator, lively character portraits, and the "Editor's" learned detachment disarm the frightening contemporary relevance of the story for readers who were still facing international and imperial struggle with France and who were determined to overcome Britain's dangerous social and regional divisions, revealed during the Revolutionary decade. This first of Edgeworth's "Irish tales" was a success with the reading public, and Edgeworth added her name to the title page of the third edition in 1801.

In 1801 Edgeworth also published further collections of educational tales. *Early Lessons* was for children older than those for whom *The Parent's Assistant* was designed. It uses narrative and dialogue to teach a variety of sciences and other learning in a systematic yet entertaining way. The lessons are grouped as *Harry and Lucy*, *Rosamond* (who also appears in *The Parent's Assistant*), and *Frank* and were concluded in the early 1820s. *Moral Tales for Young People*, published in five volumes in 1801, was more narrative and less instructional than *Early Lessons*, though no less didactic, and was again designed for older children. Like the other books for children, *Moral Tales* was supposed to use the "natural" pattern of child development and domestic and local "real life" to construct the child as rational, self-disciplined, independent, and thereby socially responsible, a professionalized subject, implicitly able in adulthood to assume a role of local and national leadership. These tales more obviously address issues of the day than the earlier ones. For example "Angelina; or, L'Amie Inconnue" depicts a young novel reader determined to become a "heroine," using "English Jacobin" and feminist jargon of "liberty" to justify her transgression of social convention. In fact she is a "female quixote," a type named after Charlotte Lennox's novel of that title (1752) and a favorite kind of upstart woman with "Anti-Jacobin" novelists of the 1790s. Edgeworth's tale also shows the "female quixote" sowing social disharmony wherever she goes, rather than mediating conflict by cultivating domestic virtues and affections that then spread out into society at large. This theme was central to the argument on women in the Revolutionary aftermath.

It is the central theme of Edgeworth's major literary success of 1801, *Belinda*, a three-volume novel in the manner of Frances Burney. Edgeworth's rational and clear-sighted heroine is left by her aunt with the aptly named, courtly Lady Delacour in order to ensure her success in the marriage market. Belinda soon sees past the glitter of her patroness's merely fashionable social life to discover her moral suffering from an unhappy marriage and her physical suffering from a literal and symbolic cancer of the breast. Belinda also sees through Lady Delacour's professed confidante, the aptly named, masculine feminist Harriot Freke. Belinda attempts to reform Lady Delacour, who comes to believe that

Belinda is as hypocritical as anyone else in fashionable life and plans to marry Lord Delacour once Lady Delacour herself is dead. For a time Belinda stays with the Percivals, a model family based on reason and domesticity, but she returns to Lady Delacour to see her through her successful treatment for the cancer and reconciliation with her now reformable husband. Meanwhile Belinda faces the fairy-tale pattern of three suitors who, like the three main women characters, represent contending forms of male identity. Sir Philip Baddely is the vacuous man of fashion, Mr Vincent the plausible but corrupt gallant, and Clarence Hervey the romantic yet virtuous "philosopher" hero, whose main folly—like the Edgeworths' friend Thomas Day—is attempting to train a model wife, the naive Virginia, whose name recalls the female "child of nature" in Bernardin de Saint-Pierre's popular sentimental tale, *Paul et Virginie* (1787).

As in all her work, Edgeworth attempts to revise fictional themes, elements, and forms that she feels serve false ideologies and cultural models. Like many post-Revolutionary women novelists, she attacks both fashionable society and its literature as well as the literature and culture of Sensibility, which many saw as the source of dangerously transgressive feminism in the Revolutionary decade. Although Edgeworth's preface to *Belinda* polemically denies that it is a mere "novel," the work resembles the novel of manners and sentiment brought to its height before the 1790s by Frances Burney. Like Burney, Edgeworth aims for a high degree of social realism so as to make malevolence, folly, and error seem real threats to the heroine's desires and happiness. Thus Lady Delacour and Belinda's suitor Vincent are made attractive enough to enable the reader to experience vicariously the appeal they might have for the heroine. Edgeworth's main innovation, and part of her critique of "sensibility," was to construct a heroine who is rational and independent yet acceptably feminine and domestic.

Thus the novel models a way beyond conflicts of the 1790s that led Britain and Ireland to the brink of social chaos and France over that brink. Certainly *Belinda* adopts the familiar novel-of-manners story of a young lady's first entrance into "society" from the shelter of home and domesticity. This story had wide literary currency because it depicts the education of the unsocialized but meritorious subject—man or woman—to the dangers of seduction by decadent upper-class court culture or contamination by middle-class or lower-class "vulgarity." Yet this story is less prominent in *Belinda* than themes of social reconciliation and reform—topics of vital interest for readers in the early aftermath of the Revolutionary decade. Edgeworth typically combined familiar literary forms and themes with pressing issues of the day, within a grand project of showing how to reconstruct Britain after the cataclysmic conflicts of the 1790s and in the face of continuing external and internal threats to national unity and even national and imperial survival.

In *Belinda*, as in all her fiction for adults, Edgeworth attempted to strike a middle way between "English Jacobin" social and political critiques of the 1790s, including the Revolutionary feminism of Wollstonecraft and others, and the political, social, and cultural reaction of "Anti-Jacobins" and counterfeminists. Like other writers of the time, Edgeworth constructed her post-Revolutionary middle ground by drawing on pre-Revolutionary intellectual culture. For her this culture was the Scottish and the English provincial and Nonconformist enlightenments, her father's intellectual and literary legacy. These enlightenments also nourished radical reformers of the 1790s, but Edgeworth softens their critical edge by novelizing them in fictional forms of an unassuming kind, such as the tale, or of a somewhat old-fashioned cast, such as the Burney novel of manners and sentiment. At the same time Edgeworth developed a central theme of conservative post-Revolutionary social criticism, such as Hannah More's *Strictures on the Modern System of Female Education* (1799), calling on upper- and middle-class women to reform society and to stabilize the state by operating as moral and rational agents within the domestic sphere. Yet this call was not so different from the insistence of Revolutionary feminists that the progress and stability of civil society depended on women with sufficient knowledge, moral and intellectual training, and public spirit to eradicate court culture (especially amorous culture) from domestic and social life, and thus from politics and the state.

In 1802 Edgeworth and her father published another collaboration, *Essay on Irish Bulls*. It purports to explain "Irish bulls," or unwitting paradoxes and contradictions, to English readers, but in fact it is an experimental text combining fiction, personal observation, political argument, folkloristic observation, linguistic analysis, and irony in a post-Union defense of the common Irish and their culture. The implication of the book is that the Irish are not ignorant as they

Drawing of Edgeworthstown House, 12 September 1836, by Francis Thomas Beaufort, nephew of Frances Beaufort, James Lovell Edgeworth's fourth wife. The window of Maria Edgeworth's room is at the upper left (from Marilyn Butler, Maria Edgeworth: A Literary Biography, *1972).*

seem, that their apparent cultural inferiority to other Britons is often due to culturally based misperceptions, and they are not so different from other Britons as those other Britons may think. In short, the book furthers social, cultural, and economic reconciliation between Ireland and the rest of Britain in the aftermath of the Irish rebellion and the Union.

After the turmoil of the Union debate and her publications of 1800 and 1801, Edgeworth accompanied her father and other family members on a tour through the English Midlands and on to Paris in autumn 1802. Edgeworth's father still hoped that she might meet a suitable husband, though she herself declared she was "not afraid of being an old maid." In Paris the Edgeworths were celebrated as educational writers, and they met French and foreign intellectuals, many of whom were associated with the opposition to Napoleon Bonaparte. In December Edgeworth received a marriage proposal from Abraham Niclas Clewberg-Edelcrantz, a Swedish intellectual and royal official. Despite her father's approval and some pressure from him to accept—and despite her own avowed longing for marriage and children—she declined the offer, mainly because it would have separated her from her family and placed her at a foreign royal court, with all its intrigues and conflicts. The struggle ruined the rest of the trip for her, and, though she did meet the long-admired Mme de Genlis, the Edgeworths soon had to leave France because of a supposed relation to Abbé Edgeworth (Henry Essex, Edgeworth de Firmont), former chaplain of Louis XVI, and because renewal of war seemed imminent. On the way home they visited Edinburgh and Glasgow, where Edgeworth met leading Scottish Enlightenment figures such as Dugald Stewart, James Gregory, John Playfair, and Archibald Alison. Edgeworth also met the novelist Elizabeth Hamilton, whose satires *Letters of a Hindoo Rajah* (1796) and *Memoirs of Modern Philosophers* (1800) have much in common with Edgeworth's novels and tales and whose later *Cottagers of Glenburnie* (1808) draws on Edgeworth's *Popular Tales* (1804).

The *Popular Tales* were written during the late 1790s and early 1800s. They portray social division and reconciliation in various parts of Britain, and one story set in the Orient extends the theme to the empire. Collectively the tales advance a post-Revolutionary vision of Britain and its empire as diverse yet harmonious and do so by using settings in common life, realistic detail of daily domesticity, and characters speaking dialect, sociolect, and idiolect framed by the authoritative "standard" English of an omniscient and moralizing narrator. The tales criticize emulation of court culture by all other classes in society. Several of the tales also criticize the lottery mentality of the lower classes and advance an investment mentality as improvement of an individual's or family's lot in the context of broad social "progress," scientific and technological advance, and economic development. Although partly inspired by the "Cheap Repository" tracts aimed at the lower classes by the Evangelical Hannah More during the Revolutionary crisis of the 1790s, Edgeworth's tales place far less emphasis on the virtue of silent suffering, patience, stoical subordination, religious piety, and reward in the afterlife and more emphasis on individual self-discipline, familial self-help, social and religious toleration, and practical improvement. Thus *Popular Tales* tacitly criticizes "Cheap Repository" and other polemical fiction of the Revolution debate. Furthermore, *Popular Tales* only ostensibly aims at the "popular" or lower classes and, like "Cheap Repository," in effect gives a fantasy version of lower-class reformability for the edification of nervous middle-class readers.

For Ireland and Britain continued in a state of social crisis, despite the Union and the suppression of much middle-class and lower-class political protest. While Richard Lovell Edgeworth fortified his house against further agrarian disturbances, undertook a national telegraph system to warn of a possible French invasion, and visited London on legal affairs, Maria Edgeworth turned again to the central role of domestic woman in preserving the family and thereby the state. Her visit to France had made her more aware of French culture and literature than before. The visit also made her more sharply critical of upper-class courtly decadence, a feeling that became more widespread as Britain failed to turn back military and imperial challenge from Napoleonic France. This failure was increasingly blamed on the incompetence and irresponsibility of Britain's ruling class, whose vices were often portrayed as the result of contamination by French courtliness. The frivolity and decadence of Parisian high society, even under the Revolution and Bonaparte, were bywords in Britain, as was the long-standing belief that such decadence had a bad influence on society in Britain. These attitudes were revived for Edgeworth and others by the example of *Delphine* (1802), by Anne-Louise-Germaine Necker, Mme de Staël. This novel was widely condemned in the circles the Edgeworths knew at Paris. Edgeworth's dislike of the celebration of extravagant subjectivity and the transgression of social convention in the novel would have been reinforced by her acquaintance with Elizabeth Hamilton, who had attacked the same excesses found in novels by English Revolutionary feminists such as Mary Wollstonecraft and Mary Hays.

Accordingly, in 1805 Edgeworth published, without her father's knowledge, *The Modern Griselda*, a satire on the antidomestic, would-be genteel Englishwoman. She extended the theme further in a short epistolary novel, *Leonora* (1806), written to please Edelcrantz and satirizing Frenchified courtliness masquerading as avant-garde ideas and emancipated conduct. *Leonora* also counterbalances *The Modern Griselda* by placing the virtuous, intellectual, and socially responsible domestic woman in the foreground, rather than as a mere foil to the Frenchified villainess of the earlier novella. Such moves reveal Edgeworth's continuing anxiety about the reception of her work, and about its being misunderstood in a complexly conflicted society divided along many lines—especially so in Ireland. At the same time the Edgeworths were concerned that the pressing need for social, economic, political, and cultural reform not be sacrificed to the need to close ranks against external threats to Britain and its empire. These concerns, incorporating Edgeworth's work in representing domestic woman as the center of social virtue and harmony, became the major focus of her fiction for the rest of her career, but especially from the first decade of the 1800s to her father's death in 1817.

The key to the Edgeworths' social criticism was professionalization of society and the state. This interest was expressed in a new book on education, *Essays on Professional Education* (1809), by Maria Edgeworth and her father. Its loose essayistic form again reflects the intention to reach a general readership, it offers a plan for general pre-professional intellectual and moral training, and it prefers professions more likely to ensure independence and less subject to patronage. The themes of the book were fictionalized by Edgeworth in *Tales of Fashionable Life*, written between 1802 and 1812 and published in two sets in 1809 ("Ennui," "Almeria," "Madame de Fleury," "The Dun," and "Manoeuvring") and 1812 ("Vivian," "Emilie de Coulanges," and "The Absentee"). These tales elaborate the tradition of Enlightenment "philosophical tales," such as those of Jean-François Marmontel, that Edgeworth took as models for ideological fiction, against the "mere" novel. To the argumentative form of the "philosophical tale" Edgeworth again added greater particularity of quotidian realism, topics of post-Revolutionary social criticism, and characterization through socially differentiated language. These tales again attack merely fashionable society, plebeian fecklessness and improvidence encouraged by upper-class irresponsibility, and middle-class emulation and self-interest. At the same time they defend reform of society through professionalization, especially of the gentry. In "Ennui," for example, the bored upper-class protagonist is forced into an active life and a profession when it is revealed that he was exchanged at birth with the real heir to his Irish estate. But his hard work and self-discipline in mastering and practicing the law are rewarded with professional success and the patronage of the virtuous great. These in turn are rewarded by the love of an intellectual yet domestic wife and eventual repossession of the estate, earned by merit and not mere accidental privileges of birth.

The weightiest (and one of the most widely read) of the *Tales of Fashionable Life* is "The Absentee," originally written in 1811 as a play for family performance at Edgeworthstown. Like *Castle Rackrent*, it shows the evils of irresponsible landlordism in Ireland, here again a synecdoche for the whole of Britain. Unlike *Castle Rackrent*, however, "The Absentee" presents a model hero in the story. Lord Colambre, like Edgeworth's father in the 1780s, rejects pursuit of fashionable life in London and returns to his family's Irish estate to restore justice, the paternalist social order, and prosperity. "The Absentee" also includes elements of the Burney novel of manners, with a variety of socially representative types from all classes characterized through action and dialogue, especially speech represented as idiolect and sociolect, to which Edgeworth adds dialect. But Edgeworth orders this polyvocal representation of Britain under the aegis of an omniscient narrator using standard English. Thus the linguistic universe of "The Absentee"—as of the great European social-historical novels that took after it from Walter Scott into the twentieth century—represents social diversity harmonized and ordered hierarchically by means of the "standard" language that was the cultural property of the professional class.

Edgeworth had become the most respected and one of the most widely read fiction writers in English, but for several years she had resisted invitations to visit England, declaring that cosmopolitan diversions and being made a literary lion "are as 0 in my scale compared with domestic life." In the spring of 1813, however, she went with her father, stepmother, and sister to England. In Liverpool she met among others William Roscoe, the banker, historian, and onetime friend of Mary Wollstonecraft. In London she finally met the Swiss utilitarian Etienne Dumont, with whom she had corresponded for several years and whom she thought of as a potential husband. She met other leading writers and intellectuals, including Sir James Mackintosh, Thomas Malthus, Thomas Moore, Lord Byron, Mary Berry, and the scientist Jane Marcet, and she maintained correspondence with some of these for years after. Although Edgeworth was well liked by those she met, many found her father too talkative and overbearing, especially in contrast to her. This impression lasted long in literary and fashionable society, causing Edgeworth much pain and reinforcing her alienation from such society.

In December 1813 Edgeworth published *Patronage* (dated 1814), a four-volume Burney novel of manners resembling *Belinda* rather than *Tales of Fashionable Life* and dealing with national reform and harmony at the English center rather than at the Irish periphery. *Patronage* was begun in 1809 and intended for the second series of *Tales of Fashionable Life*, but it originated even earlier in a series of stories Edgeworth's father told his family in the late 1780s, written down by Edgeworth as "The Freeman Family" and reworked by her through the 1790s. *Patronage* follows the destinies of two contrasting families of landed gentry, the independent Percys and the courtly Falconers, as the sons and daughters pursue careers and marriages, partly in relation to the powerful politician Lord Oldborough. The younger Percys are well educated and trained by their parents to depend on their own merit and to seek friends, companions, and spouses like themselves. They refuse patronage, overcome family misfortune and the intrigues of their rivals, making steady progress in their careers and love relationships. The elder Percy is, like Edgeworth's father, a progressive landlord.

Though he loses his estate for a time to a greedy and courtly relation, he and his family are too independent of mere social status to be affected by this reverse, and the fraud is finally exposed by young Alfred Percy, a lawyer. The younger Falconers, by contrast, rely on chance, intrigue, and patronage to get ahead. Though they enjoy success at first, their lack of intellectual ability, professional knowledge, and moral self-discipline eventually leads to their individual and collective downfalls.

Central to the contrast are the women of the two families, and central to the differing destinies of the families' sons and daughters are the marriages they make. While the Falconers marry or try to marry for merely social reasons—money, rank, status, and power—the Percys marry and form friendships on the basis of intellectual equality and moral compatibility. The most prominent of these relationships is the marriage of the model Edgeworth woman, Caroline Percy, with the intellectual yet heroic German Count Altenberg, an idealized version of Edgeworth's Swedish suitor, Edelcrantz. Mediating the contrast of Percys and Falconers is the character and career of the politician and government minister Lord Oldborough. A public personage who conceals his private thoughts and personal affairs from all but Mr. Percy, Oldborough has dedicated himself to his career after an early disappointment in love. Nevertheless, he tries to practice statecraft with honor, probity, and professionalism in the face of political faction, envy, and domestic and international political crisis.

Edgeworth generalized the political context and characters to prevent the novel from being read as a roman à clef, though it is clearly set in the post-Revolutionary period. Because this presumed reference to particular persons was seen as indecorous by some critics, Edgeworth later revised the novel to make dating its events more difficult. Oldborough mediates the public and political sphere with the private lives and professional careers of the Percys and Falconers. At first Oldborough is forced to make use of the Falconers, but he approves the independence and rewards the professional merit of the Percys. In the end he leaves office unreluctantly for the domestic life that the Percys have taught him to value more highly. In a sentimental touch, his retirement is made perfect when, thanks to the Percys, he discovers his long lost son. Edgeworth not only shows the interdependence of the social hierarchy with the political and institutional order but makes that hierarchy and order seem transient and relative in contrast to professionalized subjectivity and domestic and social relations based on such subjectivity.

After *Patronage* Edgeworth published a two-volume *Continuation of Early Lessons* (1814), revised her half brother Charles Sneyd Edgeworth's *Memoirs of the Abbé Edgeworth* (1815), wrote the preface and last chapter of her father's *Readings on Poetry* (1816), published a memoir of the novelist Elizabeth Hamilton in the *Monthly Magazine* (September 1816), and completed *Comic Dramas in Three Acts* (1817). Though Edgeworth was distracted by her father's increasing illnesses she also produced two substantial fictions, *Harrington* and *Ormond*, published together in 1817 and continuing her work of reconciling social differences of all kinds.

In 1815 the American Rachel Mordecai complained to Edgeworth about her stereotypic characterization of Jews, such as the grasping coachmaker Mordicai in "The Absentee." In *Harrington* Edgeworth aimed to redress this wrong in the portrayal of the rich but cultivated, cosmopolitan, honorable, and virtuous Sephardic Jew Montenero and his daughter Berenice (named after the Jewish heroine of Jean Racine's 1670 tragedy of the same name). The novel also includes the characters of a Jewish intellectual, Israel Lyons, and an honest Jewish peddler. The hero of the novel, Harrington, is a young professional man who had developed an irrational fear of Jews as a child. Nevertheless, he falls in love with Berenice, but Montenero will not allow a marriage until Harrington proves he can discipline his overexcitable character, which Montenero fears may be a symptom of incipient madness. The snobbish, envious, extravagant, and anti-Semitic Mowbray seems to compete with Harrington for Berenice's love and plots against Harrington's fulfilling this condition. Eventually Mowbray is exposed, and the marriage takes place. Montenero's coolness in protecting Harrington's parents from an angry mob even overcomes the objections of the hero's family. This reconciliation is qualified, however, when it is revealed that Berenice is after all a Christian. The Jewish theme is only a modification of some of Edgeworth's favorite topics—that the mercantile and industrialist middle class could be cultured, honorable, and public-spirited; that reason should prevail over custom, "prejudice," and superstition; that a professional education was a bet-

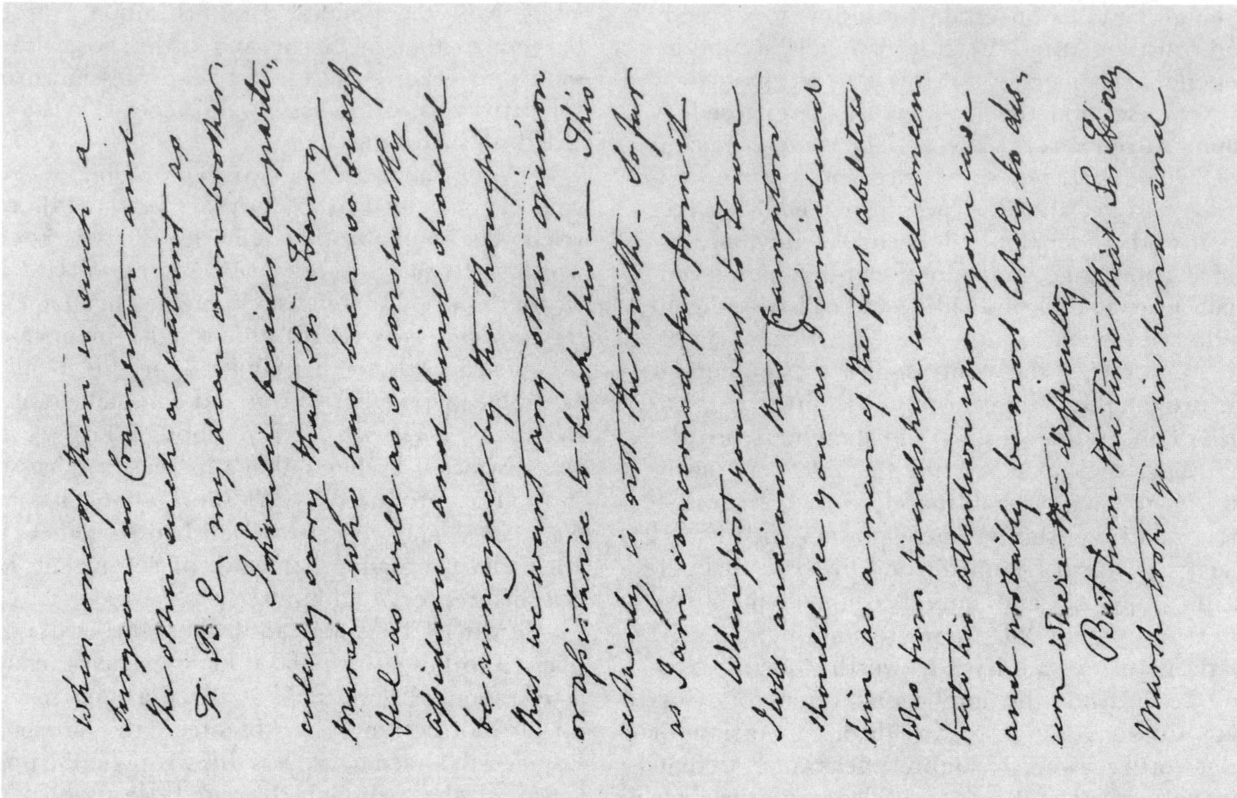

when one of them is such a
surgeon as Crampton and
the other such a patient as
F B E my dear own brother,
I should besides be particularly sorry that Sir Henry
Marsh who has been so much
feel as well as so constantly
assiduous and kind should
be annoyed by the thought
that we want any other opinion
or assistance to back his — This
certainly is not the truth - So far
as I am concerned far from it
When first you went to Town
I was anxious that Crampton
should see you as I considered
him as a man of the first abilities
who from friendship would concentrate his attention upon your case
and probably be most likely to dis-
cern where the difficulty
But from the time that Sir Henry
Marsh took you in hand and

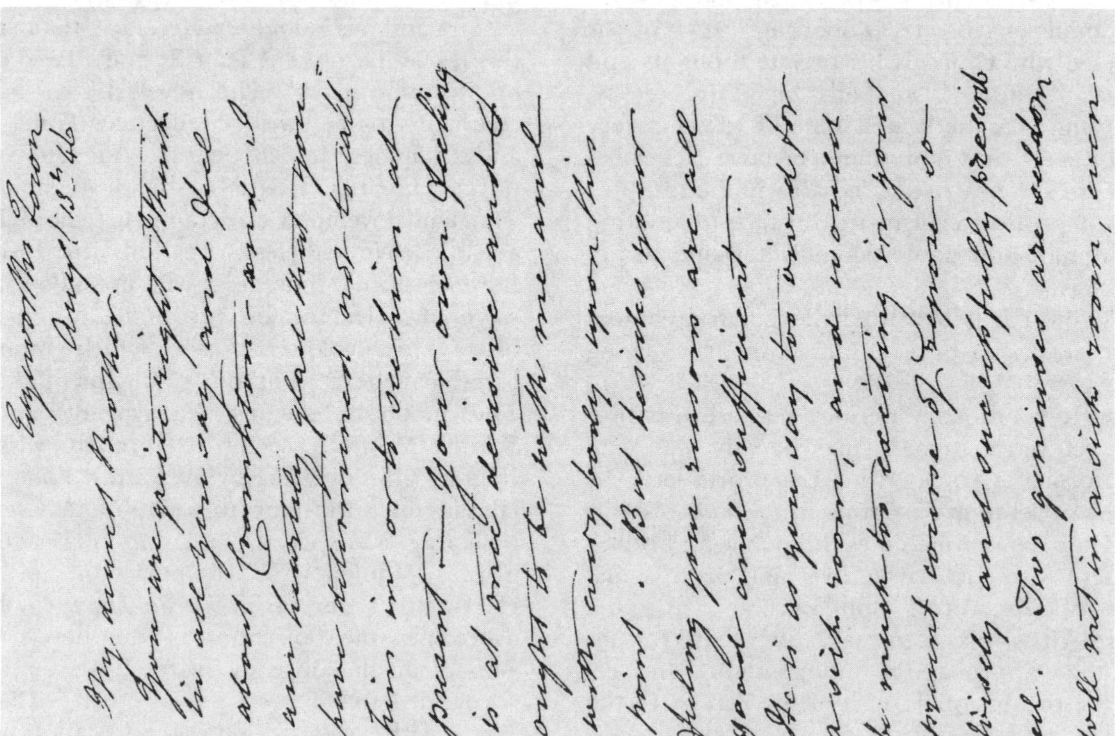

Edgeworthstown
Aug 1st 46
My dearest Brother
You are quite right I think
in all you say and feel
about Crampton - and I
am heartily glad that you
have determined not to ask
him or to see him at
present — Your own feeling
is at once decisive and
ought to be with me and
with every body upon this
point. But besides your
feeling your reasons are all
good and sufficient -
He is as you say too vivid for
a sick room, and would
be much too exciting in your
present course of repose so
wisely and successfully prescribed. Two geniuses are seldom
well met in a sick room, even

Letter from Maria Edgeworth to her brother Francis (from Isabel C. Clarke, Maria Edgeworth: Her Family and Friends, *1949)*

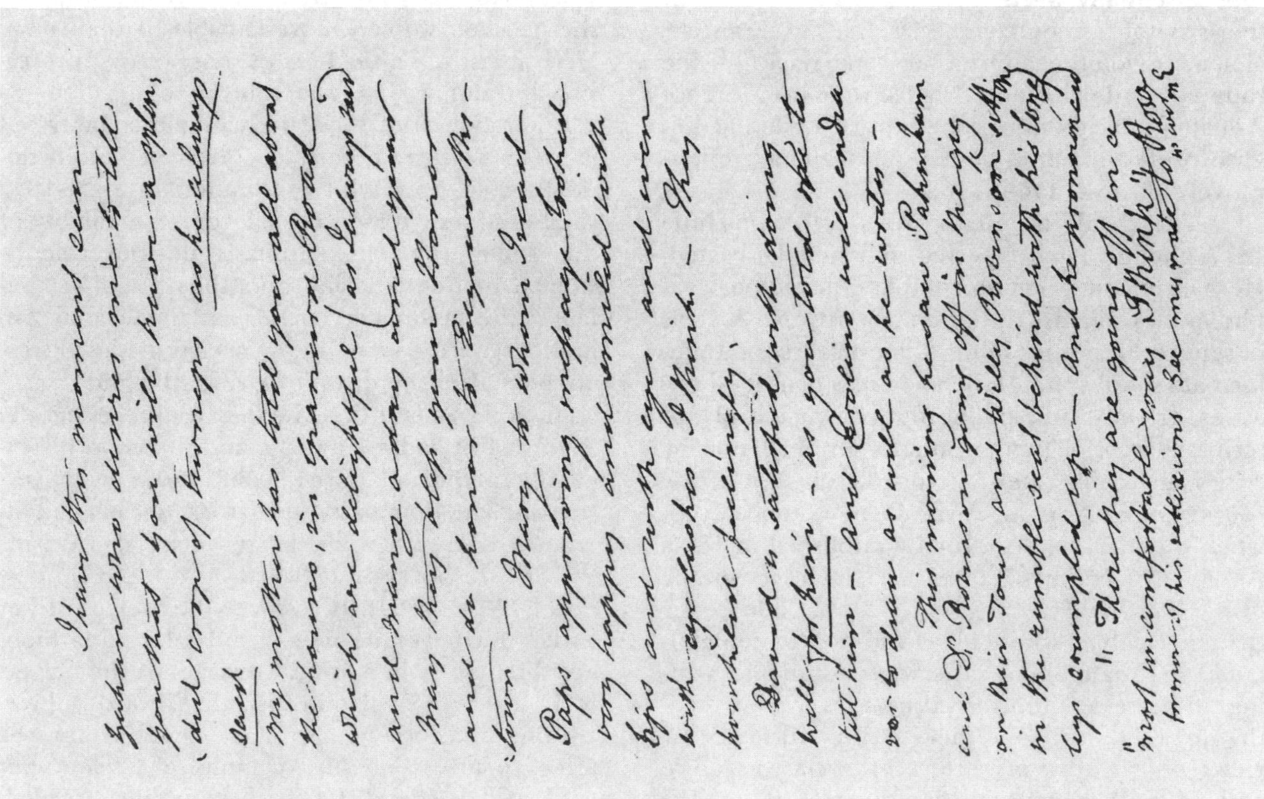

I have this moment seen
Zahan who desires me to tell
you that you will have a splen,
did crop of turneps as he always
said
my mother has told you all about
the houses, in Garrard Road
which are delightful (as I always said
and many a day and year
May they bless your Honor
and do honor to Edgeworthstown — Mary to whom I read
Paps approving message looked
very happy and smiled with
lips and with eyes and even
with eyelashes I think — They
wrinkled feelingly.
David is satisfied with doing
well for him - as you told me to
tell him - and Collins will endea
vor to draw as well as he writes -
This morning he saw Pakenham
and Dr Robinson going off in the gig
on their Tour and Willy Robinson sitting
in the rumble seat behind with his long
legs crumpled up — And he pronounced
" There they are going off in a
"most uncomfortable way I think" Rosa
for more of his reflexions See my note to " " " m E

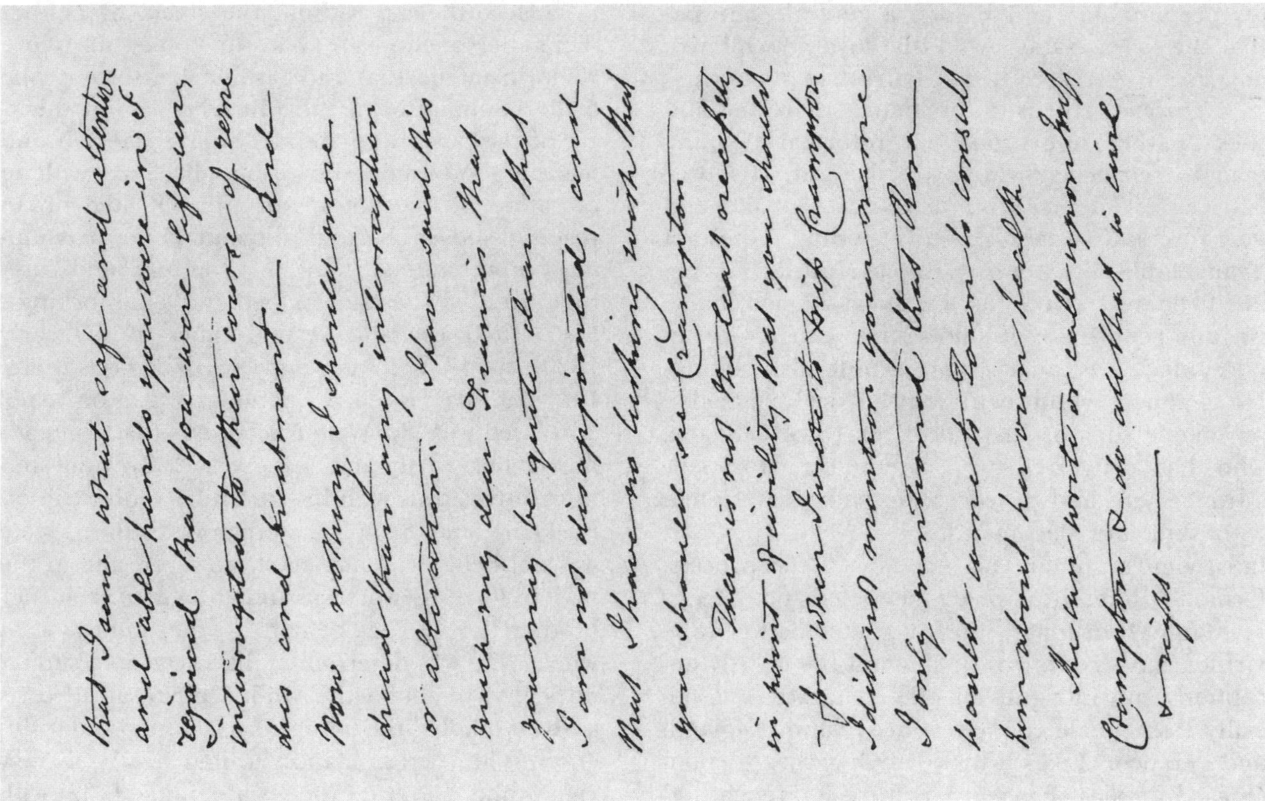

that I saw what safe and attentive
and able hands you were in I
rejoiced that you were left un-
interrupted to their course of reme
dies and treatment.— And
Now nothing I should more
dread than any interruption
or alteration. I have said this
much my dear Francis that
you may be quite clear that
I am not disappointed, and
that I have no hankering wish that
you should see Crampton
There is not the least necessity
in point of civility that you should
- for when I wrote to Miss Crampton
I did not mention your name
I only mentioned that Rosa
would come to Town to consult
him about her own health
She can write or call upon Miss
Crampton & do all that is civil
& right —

ter preparation for life than a genteel one; and that the lower classes would be loyal, disciplined, and useful if treated properly by their "betters."

Ormond returns to the matter of Ireland and uses another impetuous but reformable young man to reconcile different Irish (and thus British) classes and cultures in the face of old and new forces of social division (including Protestant Evangelicalism). One of Ormond's uncles, Cornelius O'Shane, represents the old-fashioned, boorish but generous Catholic squire, clinging to an outmoded, customary, and semifeudal culture. He is almost withdrawn from a world controlled by people such as his cousin Sir Ulick O'Shane, who has converted to Protestantism for self-advancement and practices the patronage system with skill and daring until he overreaches and falls, almost ruining his nephew in the process. Ormond himself, overtly modeled on Henry Fielding's Tom Jones, must negotiate between the virtues and vices of his uncles and the courtly deceptions and intrigues of other characters, especially fashionable coquettes, in Ireland, England, and France. Like Edgeworth's earlier fiction, *Ormond* implies that court culture is French and thus essentially alien, tainting British society at the risk of an outcome like that in France—violent revolution. Ormond's marriage to the rational and virtuous Englishwoman Florence Annaly implicitly unites the best of Irish and English professionalized gentry culture in a prefiguratively "British" family.

The death of Edgeworth's father in June 1817, though long expected, left her devastated. He had enjoined her to complete his autobiography, a task against the grain. Aware that he was not much liked outside his domestic circle and immediate social sphere, she anxiously consulted relatives, friends, and public figures on the manuscript. Fearful of further attacks on her father by critics, she deliberately arranged to be out of the country, traveling in Paris, Geneva, and Lyon, when the *Memoirs* were finally published in 1820. As she feared, her father was attacked in the Tory *Quarterly Review* (May 1820) as little better than a "Jacobin" whose ideas and politics contaminated his daughter's otherwise admirable writings. The review reinforced a widespread antipathy to Edgeworth's father and confirmed her views on the divisive effect of social prejudice and political contention. For the rest of her life she feared publishing fiction for adults lest any defects in her work again be attributed to her father's influence.

Nevertheless, without the shield of her father's personality she had to come out more when in intellectual and fashionable society. She made a point of being introduced to leading thinkers of the day and generally enjoyed herself and made a good impression, especially since, with all her store of anecdotes, turn for wit, and broad reading, she was careful to maintain an unassuming, unpretentious, feminine conduct, and carefully avoided the taint of being a "bluestocking." She visited England several times in the early 1820s, spending longer and longer periods there. In 1823 she visited Scotland and got on especially well with Sir Walter Scott, who had long admired her work and who visited Ireland and Edgeworthstown with his son-in-law, John Gibson Lockhart, in 1825. The Edgeworthstown estate was not being well managed, however, and in the mid 1820s Edgeworth assumed control from her brother Lovell on behalf of the family as a whole. She was determined, like Scott in a similar difficulty, to retain the landed estate at all costs as the symbol of the family's social status and influence. The determination called forth a new vigor, and she ran the estate until 1839 with strict discipline and attention to detail, qualities she believed women more capable of than men. Here at last was a field for exercise of that professional training that was central to her father's and her system of social reform and stability but in which women were usually given an entirely domestic role. In a visit to London in 1831-1832 she found new reason to believe in the validity of this system and its emphasis on the role of women in domestic life and thus the state and fate of the nation. Old friends and intellectual connections were passing away; society had a different tone after the death of George IV and the accession of William IV. The debates preceding the Reform Bill had a language and direction different from the old post-Revolutionary controversies, and late Romantic "silver-fork" society and literature offered new challenges to social criticism.

In response Edgeworth produced a new novel, *Helen* (1834). It resumes the themes of her earlier Burneyesque novels and tales of fashionable life, partly in a critical revision of the "silver-fork" novels of Benjamin Disraeli, Edward Bulwer-Lytton, and others. *Helen* is centered on the affective and domestic relations of Helen; her weak-willed friend Cecilia Clarendon; Cecilia's mother, the aloof but decisive Lady Davenant; and Cecilia's sister-in-law, the philosophical and independent-minded quasi-feminist Esther Clarendon. Helen, who was raised by a clergyman and his wife, is represented as an essentially English and domestic young woman, a version of that favorite type of nineteenth-century fiction, the heroine of private life. Somewhat like a Burney heroine, she tries through much of the novel to manage the necessary transition from her entirely domestic education to a public character and manners. At the same time she learns to steer clear of involvement with various intriguing (in both senses) "silver-fork" characters, such as the witty socialite and epicure Horace Churchill and a variety of fashionable women, who envy Helen her simplicity, naturalness, and consequent attractiveness. The early part of the novel thus emphasizes favorite Edgeworth themes of social criticism, exposing the selfishness, superficiality, and disunity of fashionable courtly society, including fashionable literary society. At the same time the dialogue and scenes of socializing illustrate another favorite Edgeworth theme, the relativity of perception and the way it is affected by situation and personal feeling. True to her upbringing, Helen cleaves to candor and truth and thus avoids seduction by the merely social.

The most severe challenge to her character comes from her own feminine sympathy, and the most dangerous intriguer against her proves to be the person to whom she is closest, her childhood friend Cecilia. In order to protect Cecilia from the consequences of her own merely feminine weaknesses, Helen is drawn into a web of intrigue and deception that costs her the respect and protection of Cecilia's husband, General Clarendon, and separates her from her suitor and General Clarendon's ward, the Ormond-like Granville Beauclerc. Social rivals and an unscrupulous bookseller threaten to publish a partly fictionalized autobiography of the decadent seducer Colonel D'Aubigny. This kind of book was in fact a mainstay of "silver-fork" romans à clef. The book includes extracts from love letters Cecilia once wrote to D'Aubigny. Her husband has an irrational prejudice against a woman's having any romantic attachment with another man prior to marriage, and Cecilia fears a revelation would break up her marriage, in turn causing the death of her mother, who has a weak heart. To keep her secret, Cecilia exploits Helen's sympathy and persuades her to let it be believed the letters are hers, though Beauclerc and Esther continue to believe Helen innocent. Cecilia's guilt at destroying her friend's happiness to save her own affects her health, however, and eventually leads to a confession and reconciliation with her mother, who blames herself for her daughter's weak character: she had neglected Cecilia's education and moral development in order to pursue her own interest in politics. Thus this novel too affirms the primacy of the domestic over the public and political sphere. Helen's essentially passive virtues and domestic character prove superior to all other versions of womanhood in the novel, and once they are united to and moderating the active character of Beauclerc, they will, the novel implies, contribute as female virtues should to the reconstruction of Britain—more so than any Reform Bill.

Edgeworth took five years to write *Helen*, and after it she published only one piece of fiction, *Orlandino* (1848), another story for children, during the rest of her life. She lived quietly at Edgeworthstown, now bereft of most of those who had crowded it during her long life. After a brief illness she died there on 22 May 1849.

Maria Edgeworth was not only the most respected fiction writer from 1800 to the mid 1810s and one of the most successful and influential writers for children of the nineteenth century, she also successfully established a model of the woman writer as intellectual, artistic, and moral, yet feminine and domestic. In creating this literary identity through her writing she sought to reconcile the images of the merely fashionable woman writer on one hand and the transgressive, "bluestocking" feminist on the other. Yet there was a large blot on Edgeworth's literary identity even in her own time—her "failure" (as many saw it) to emphasize the importance of religion. In the revolutionary aftermath many women writers, especially writers of didactic fiction and books for children, took up Evangelicalism as a way of extending acceptably feminine social roles from domesticity and local philanthropy to intervention in national issues. Edgeworth's Enlightenment inheritance, her Irish perspective on the divisive effect of religious zeal, and her recognition of the use of Evangelicalism as a form of class oppression prevented her from taking this turn. Nevertheless, her mediating, post-Revolutionary literary identity proved invaluable for generations of women writers, down to the twentieth century. It is not surprising, then, that this identity was retailed in biographies of her and selections of her letters, until Marilyn Butler's biography of 1972, published at a time when women were at last entering in numbers into the public and even political professional culture of which Edgeworth was, in her own time, a prophet. Yet the very sharpness and specificity of this prophecy has hindered recognition of her work as a literary artist equal in many respects to her less polemical contemporaries such as Jane Austen.

Letters:

A Memoir of Maria Edgeworth, with a Selection from Her Letters, 3 volumes, edited by Frances Edgeworth and others (London: Printed by Joseph Masters & Son, 1867);

The Life and Letters of Maria Edgeworth, 2 volumes, edited by Augustus J. C. Hare (London: Arnold, 1894);

The Black Book of Edgeworthstown 1585-1817, edited by Harold E. Butler and Jessie H. Butler (London: Faber & Gwyer, 1927);

Maria Edgeworth: Letters from England 1813-1844, edited by Christina Colvin (Oxford: Clarendon Press, 1971);

The Education of the Heart: The Correspondence of Rachel Mordecai Lazarus and Maria Edgeworth, edited by Edgar E. MacDonald (Chapel Hill: University of North Carolina Press, 1977);

Maria Edgeworth in France and Switzerland: Selections from the Edgeworth Family Letters, edited by Colvin (Oxford: Clarendon Press, 1979).

Bibliography:

Bertha Coolidge Slade, *Maria Edgeworth 1767-1849: A Bibliographical Tribute* (London: Constable, 1937).

Biography:

Marilyn Butler, *Maria Edgeworth: A Literary Biography* (Oxford: Clarendon Press, 1972).

References:

Marilyn Butler, *Jane Austen and the War of Ideas* (Oxford: Clarendon Press, 1975);

Desmond Clarke, *The Ingenious Mr. Edgeworth* (London: Oldbourne, 1965);

Vineta Colby, *Yesterday's Woman: Domestic Realism in the English Novel* (Princeton: Princeton University Press, 1974);

Donald Davie, *The Heyday of Sir Walter Scott* (London: Routledge & Kegan Paul, 1961);

Thomas Flanagan, *The Irish Novelists 1800-1850* (New York & London: Columbia University Press, 1958), pp. 53-106;

O. Elizabeth M. Harden, *Maria Edgeworth* (Boston: Twayne, 1984);

Harden, *Maria Edgeworth's Art of Prose Fiction* (The Hague: Mouton, 1971);

Mark D. Hawthorne, *Doubt and Dogma in Maria Edgeworth* (Gainesville: University of Florida Press, 1967);

Michael Hurst, *Maria Edgeworth and the Public Scene* (Coral Gables: University of Miami Press, 1969);

Elizabeth Kowaleski-Wallace, *Their Fathers' Daughters: Hannah More, Maria Edgeworth, and Patriarchal Complicity* (New York: Oxford University Press, 1991);

Patrick Murray, *Maria Edgeworth: A Study of the Novelist* (Cork: Mercier Press, 1971);

James Newcomer, *Maria Edgeworth the Novelist* (Fort Wayne: Texas Christian University Press, 1967);

Cóilín Owens, ed., *Family Chronicles: Maria Edgeworth's* Castle Rackrent (Dublin: Wolfhound Press / Totowa, N.J.: Barnes & Noble, 1987).

Papers:

The principal collection of Edgeworth's letters, with those of her family, is in the National Library of Ireland, Dublin; and other letters and manuscripts are in the Bodleian Library, Oxford; Bibliothèque Publique et Universitaire, Geneva; the National Library of Scotland, Edinburgh; the British Library, London; the Royal College of Surgeons, London; the Huntington Library, San Marino; and Birmingham University Library.

Susan Ferrier

(17 September 1782 - 5 November 1854)

David E. Latané, Jr.
Virginia Commonwealth University

BOOKS: *Marriage, a Novel* (3 volumes, Edinburgh: William Blackwood, 1818; 2 volumes, New York: A. T. Goodrich, 1818; revised edition, 1 volume, London: R. Bentley, 1841);

The Inheritance (3 volumes, Edinburgh: W. Blackwood, 1824; 2 volumes, Philadelphia: H. C. Carey & I. Lea, 1824; revised edition, 1 volume, London: R. Bentley, 1841);

Destiny: or, The Chief's Daughter (3 volumes, Edinburgh: Printed for Robert Cadell / London, Whitaker, 1831; 1 volume, Philadelphia: Carey & Lea, 1831; revised edition, London: R. Bentley, 1841).

Editions: *The Works of Susan Ferrier*, Holyrood Edition, 4 volumes (London: E. Nash & Grayson, 1929);

Marriage: A Novel, edited by Herbert Foltinek (London & New York: Oxford University Press, 1971);

The Inheritance (Bampton: Three Rivers, 1984);

Marriage (Bampton: Three Rivers, 1984);

Marriage, edited by Rosemary Ashton (London: Virago, 1986; New York: Penguin, 1986).

As novelists, Jane Austen and Sir Walter Scott have long been contrasted; while she painted exquisite miniatures of the minutiae of life among the English gentry, he used a broad brush and canvas to describe the epic of Scotland's past. Susan Ferrier, a native of Edinburgh and a friend of Scott's, took on the task of describing Scottish manners in her three novels and is thus more akin to Austen and to the Irish novelist Maria Edgeworth than to her countryman. Her works reached a large audience, were translated into French, and were adapted for the stage. Their public success was aided in part by the vogue for matters Scottish instigated by Scott's *Waverley* novels, but readers chiefly admired the interesting situations and quirky characters that Ferrier invented and enlivened with a satiric eye of the first order. Her novels have fared less well with modern readers, as the manners they sketch have disappeared and the novel-reading public has become averse to Ferrier's pious intent.

Susan Ferrier, the youngest of ten children, was raised in a conservative family, dominated—especially after the death of her mother, Helen Coutts Ferrier, in 1797 when Susan was fifteen—by James Ferrier, her eccentric and autocratic father. He was a writer to the Signet and man of business for John, fifth Duke of Argyll, and the family lived in middle-class comfort in Edinburgh's New Town. Susan—nicknamed "Roe" by her father—was a favorite; her delicate health required that she be "transported" at times to the softer climate of England. Early in life she developed a talent for witty mimicry: on one occasion, when their father was absent, the older Ferrier children were engaged in pranks; then from the top of the stairs they were startled by the angry sound of their father's voice—only to discover that it was Susan.

Between the ages of nineteen and twenty-three she lost three brothers who were in the army, including her favorite, James, who died while serving in the Scots Brigade in India in 1804. As siblings died or married, Susan was gradually left alone as head of her father's household, spending most of her time in Edinburgh, or on visits to Inverary Castle, the highland seat of the duke of Argyll, where she became close friends with the duke's youngest granddaughter, Charlotte Clavering. (Much of what is known of Ferrier's life at this time is from the animated correspondence between Susan and Charlotte.) In addition to Walter Scott, a legal colleague of her father's, the family was intimate with the circle of novelist Henry Mackenzie, and Susan Ferrier's autograph album—kept from 1802 to 1814—reveals numerous contributions from other literary men of the day, from James Hogg to William Wordsworth. In a circa 1810 letter to Charlotte Clavering, Ferrier proclaims a natural affinity for the scribbling word: "For know I am descended from a race of Scribes; . . . I was nurtured upon

Engraving by Walker & Boutall after a miniature painted by Robert Thorburn in 1836

ink; my pap-spoon was the stump of an old pen . . . and my cradle a paper poke!"

Ferrier's first novel, *Marriage* (1818), grew out of her correspondence with Charlotte Clavering, in which Ferrier gave free play to her keen satiric sense, skewering everyone from "the old tabbies in town . . . sitting on their sofas with *white sashes* on, ready to faint away at the sight of a man!" (26 September 1809) to the various male "foolies" whose chief use is in "hitching in a hackneyed observation whenever the conversation starts to flag" (26 July 1809). In 1809 Ferrier and Clavering began writing about the possibility of jointly composing a novel, and discussed the difficulties of doing so through the post. "I do not recollect ever," Ferrier wrote, "to have seen the sudden transition of a high-bred English beauty, who thinks she can sacrifice all for love, to an uncomfortable Highland dwelling among tall red-haired sisters and grim-faced aunts. Don't you think this would make a good opening for the piece?" From this promising start, it took eight more years for *Marriage* (with only a short section composed by Clavering) to be published.

When the novel was conceived, Scottish subjects were not yet popular, though the regional examples of Maria Edgeworth and the less-well-known Elizabeth Hamilton (author of *The Cottagers of Glenburnie*, 1808) provided some precedent. By 1817, when Ferrier submitted the book to William Blackwood for publication, the *Waverley* novels were enjoying their huge success. *Marriage* deploys the intersection of Scottish and English society for satiric effect, merged some-

James Ferrier, the novelist's father, in 1794 (miniature by George Place; private collection, from National Library of Scotland, Susan Ferrier, 1782-1854, *Exhibition Catalogue no. 22, 1982)*

what uneasily with moral fables about man and woman, parent and child. Blackwood paid £150 for the book (about $30,000 in 1989) and agreed to keep the secret of the author's identity.

Marriage is set in England and Scotland. In the opening of the first volume, the English Lord Courtland attempts to match his daughter Juliana with a disgusting but wealthy old man; she disobeys and elopes with the Scottish Lord Douglas—a good but impoverished young man. He takes her to Glernfern Castle, a "hideous grim house" in the Highlands that serves as a locale for Ferrier's proto-Dickensian character sketches, chiefly of "three long-chinned spinsters" and "five awkward purple girls," who are her husband's aunts and sisters, respectively. Juliana, temperamental, spoiled, and loving only lapdogs and ease, gives birth to twin daughters, Adelaide and Mary, and then forces Lord Douglas to return to London, leaving Mary behind to be raised by the pious Mrs. Douglas, her aunt. After their money is wasted, Lord Douglas embarks for India, and Juliana moves in with her wealthy brother, devoting herself to the pleasures of her class (one thinks of Mary Wollstonecraft's views of the debilitating effect of the "education" of women in the upper classes). Adelaide is raised à la mode, while her twin, Mary, has the benefit of a simple and pious country education; they thus provide grist for a comparison of the effect of differing educations in girls with the same natural endowment.

The second part of the novel describes what happens when the grown-up Mary leaves her Highland home to meet for the first time her mother and sister, residing at Lord Courtland's estate of Beech Park, near Bath. The difference between the two girls is at all times apparent; when the rakish character of the elegant Lord Lindore is sketched, Adelaide is impressed, thinking "it would be no vulgar conquest to fix and reform one who was notorious for his inconstancy and libertine principles," and she sets her cap for him. "In Mary's well-regulated mind," Ferrier tells us, "other feelings arose . . . and the hope of finding a friend and brother in her cousin, now gave way to the feeling, that in the future she could only consider him as a mere common acquaintance."

Like her mother, Mary falls in love with a man who does not meet with parental approval, but instead of disobedience and flight with Charles Lennox, she exhibits patience and filial obedience, despite the petty persecution of her erratic and flighty mother. Her sister, Adelaide, on the other hand, marries solely for money, and then unable to bear her bargain decamps to the Continent with a lover. The most amusing parts of the novel, however, occur with the arrival of Aunt Grizzy from Scotland. In her tours of English society she encounters Mrs. Fox, who coerces visitors into giving to her favorite charity (herself) and dupes poor Grizzy out of a brooch, and the circle of Mrs. Bluemits—intellectual women who banter about George Gordon, Lord Byron. This string of humorous characters reveals Ferrier's inventiveness and wit, even as the deepening seriousness of her heroine's character shows her concern with the moral impact of the novel.

After the success of *Marriage*, Susan Ferrier was in no hurry to produce another book. Her duty lay first to her father, whose dubiety about female authorship had driven her to read the manuscript of *Marriage* to him from behind a curtain as he lay ill in bed, so that he could not see that she was not reading from a published book. When Susan Ferrier revealed that the book had been written by a woman, he replied, "Nonsense, no woman could ever write a book like that." Susan then confessed her authorship but continued to write secretively. *The Inheritance*, her next book, was offered to the London publisher John Murray by her lawyer brother John in 1823; hearing of his rival's interest, Blackwood offered the large sum of £1,000, and the novel was published by him in 1824.

The Inheritance is a much better crafted novel than *Marriage* and won the hearty admiration of Ferrier's circle. Blackwood, who compared the work to Austen's, reported that Scott was enthusiastic, speaking "*con amore*" and entering completely "into the spirit of the book and of the characters." It begins with a rewording of the famous first sentence of Austen's *Pride and Prejudice* (1813): "It is a truth universally acknowledged, that there is no passion so deeply rooted in human nature as that of pride." Ferrier then proceeds to tell the story of Gertrude St. Clair, a young girl of Scottish origin, raised in France as a result of her father's disinheritance following a rash marriage to a woman of a humble family. After the death of her father, Gertrude and her mother return to the manse of Lord Rossville. A "report" tells her that "Lord Rossville is an obstinate, troublesome, tiresome, well-behaved man; that his sister, Lady Betty . . . is a harmless, dull inquisitive old woman" and that there are "nephews, sister's sons, to one of whom you are probably destined; there is Mr. Delmour, a weak, formal parliamentary drudge . . . Colonel Delmour, a fashionable, unprincipled gamester; and Mr. Lyndsay, a sort of quakerish, methodistical, sombre person—all, of course, brimful of pride and prejudice." The plot which follows is conventional. The willful uncle wishes to marry the heiress off to the dull nephew, while she is courted without scruple by the gaming nephew and watched over with concern by the religious nephew. There is a dark secret about her origin, with a blackmailing American and a scheming mother. In the end she returns to true values, chastised, but with a fortune recouped through the ministrations of an uncouth uncle of her mother's, Adam Ramsey (widely suspected in Ferrier's day of being a portrait of her own crusty father).

The Inheritance, like *Marriage*, delights the reader through its comic situations, the nuance of the narratorial voice, and the sharp ear for dialogue. The characters are better rounded than in *Marriage*. Mrs. St. Clair is twisted into a manipulative and selfish woman, but the author does not let us forget the pressures that deformed her. Uncle Adam is the gruff, self-made, rich eccentric who plays poor, but we also are touched by his strong remembrance of his thwarted love for his "bonnie Lizzie Lundie," amused by his rich Scottish dialect among characters whose aim is to appear English and genteel, and surprised by his guilty secret—an addiction to reading the novels of Walter Scott. As in Ferrier's other books, the women characters come in for the brunt of the satire, and at the same time they are more closely observed. The reader sees Mr. Lyndsay only from the outside, and even then the distinguishing marks are few; he is characteristically bland. Miss Pratt, on the other hand, is more than a gossipy old spinster—she is a quirky counterpart for

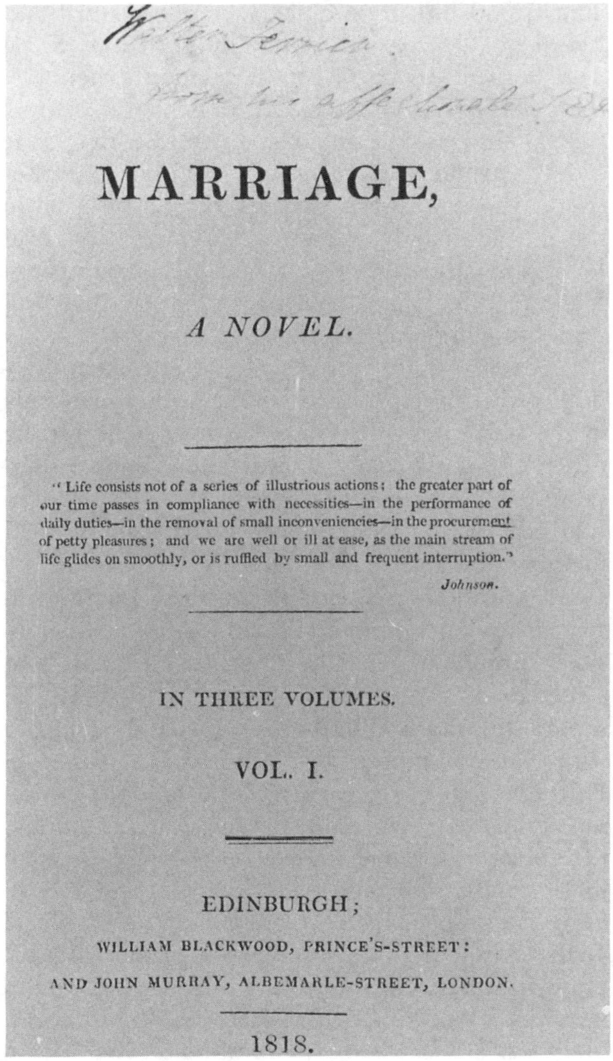

MARRIAGE,

A NOVEL.

"Life consists not of a series of illustrious actions; the greater part of our time passes in compliance with necessities—in the performance of daily duties—in the removal of small inconveniencies—in the procurement of petty pleasures; and we are well or ill at ease, as the main stream of life glides on smoothly, or is ruffled by small and frequent interruption."

Johnson.

IN THREE VOLUMES.

VOL. I.

EDINBURGH;

WILLIAM BLACKWOOD, PRINCE'S-STREET:

AND JOHN MURRAY, ALBEMARLE-STREET, LONDON.

1818.

Charlotte Clavering, the friend who helped Ferrier with her first novel (engraving by Walker & Boutall after a portrait by Kearsley), and the copy of the novel that Ferrier inscribed to one of her brothers (private collection, from National Library of Scotland, Susan Ferrier, 1782-1854, *Exhibition Catalogue no. 22, 1982)*

Lord Rossville, with a hundred inventive ways of getting his goat.

As Mary Cullinan points out, the novel is thematically unified around the interplay of truth and dissimulation. Nearly all the characters lack self-knowledge: "Gertrude stands at the center of this issue: she is not the person she believes she is. Her whole life is based on false premises. . . ." The novel proceeds to test Gertrude's character as she inherits vast wealth, acts against her true character, loses the wealth, and then finds, for the first time, who she really is. Her crucial test comes when her good cousin, Anne Black, who has been prevented from marrying the poor clergyman she loves, appeals for Gertrude to keep a promise and help him to a living. Under the influence of Colonel Delmour Gertrude reneges on her pledge, so that the position can go to a dissolute friend of his. When her real identity becomes known, Gertrude acts honorably—she avoids the temptation to cover up—but falls into despair. Eventually, she is born again as herself, as a Christian, and (no surprise) as the spouse of Mr. Lyndsay. If *Marriage* places great emphasis on education as a determinant, *The Inheritance* adds a sense of an essential goodness; Gertrude's real inheritance is the humble but virtuous blood of her real family.

After the death of her father in January of 1829, Ferrier went to stay with her sister Jane Graham at Stirling, where she continued working on her next novel; in the fall she visited Scott at Abbotsford and admitted her authorship of *Marriage* and *The Inheritance* to "the Great Unknown."

The friendship grew quickly, and her third and last novel, *Destiny* (1831), is dedicated to Scott, who helped secure favorable terms for her with the publisher Robert Cadell. (The novel fetched £1,700 and sold 2,400 copies in the first four months.) While the critics were not quite as enthusiastic, the book was discussed by John Wilson in the influential "Noctes Ambrosianæ" series in *Blackwood's Magazine*, where he proclaimed in September 1831 that "the age of lucre-banished clans" was the unique subject of Ferrier's pen.

Destiny begins with a sketch of an anachronistic Scottish laird, Glenroy, who finds worth only in the trappings of his Highland estate. After the death of his first wife, however, he finds a stepmother for Norman and Edith, their children, in Lady Elizabeth Waldegreave, a light, spendthrift member of the English aristocracy whom he meets on one of his visits to London. Ferrier presents it as a phenomenon of nature that such opposites should mate. The plot, while well constructed, is conventional. After the inevitable separation, Lady Elizabeth returns to England with her daughter by a previous marriage, Florinda, and Glenroy turns his attentions to doting on his heir, Norman. After Norman's premature death, Glenroy fixes on his nephew Reginald as his heir and plans to marry Edith to him. He also schemes to acquire the estate of Inch Orran, a distant cousin, a Scotch original and an honest man. Orran despises Glenroy and wills the estate to Ronald Malcolm, who is seemingly lost at sea. As in *The Inheritance*, Edith loves the wrong man—though this time he is Reginald, the man she is assigned by her father. On a trip to the Continent, however, he falls in love with the glamorous Florinda, and Edith breaks off the engagement. Reginald still inherits Glenroy's estate, but with the return of Ronald (in disguise), she acquires a faithful lover and eventually recoups her fortune.

The minor characters in *Destiny* bear the brunt of entertaining the readers, especially Mr. M'Dow, who is mercilessly sketched as an insincere, greedy minister. As Ronald Malcolm prepares to go to sea, the barbarous M'Dow scents future money and writes a letter proposing marriage to Lucy Malcolm, including "testimonials" which make "the eulogy uttered by Mark Antony over the dead body of Julius Cæsar" sound "tame and cold in comparison of the panegyrics lavished on Mr. M'Dow to his own face." The minister is omnipresent, popping up at the most inconvenient times, almost always to good comic effect. Ferrier manipulates her ensemble of minor characters—M'Dow, Inch Orran, his spouse with her "mean, vacant countenance," Benbowie (Glenroy's sycophant), and others—almost in the manner of Charles Dickens. They surround Edith without giving her any options. It is only in the idyllic family life of the Malcolms that a path can be seen toward living a meaningful existence. As in Ferrier's other books, the moral speaks to the safety of the woman through the suppression of desire and the cultivation of Christian and familial virtues. Critics who find Ferrier's satire undercutting this theme in the first two books note with dismay the extension of the pietistic sections in *Destiny*. It is the only one of the novels not to have a modern edition.

Susan Ferrier chose to place family duty ahead of her art and to publish anonymously and infrequently. In an 1823 letter to her sister Helen, she says, "I never will avow myself . . . ; this is not *facon de parler*, but my real and unalterable feeling. I could not bear the *fuss* of authorism!" After the publication of *Destiny*, she could have made a considerable income from her pen, had the need arisen; on one occasion in 1837 she was approached through a friend, Hope Mackenzie, with an offer of £1,000 "for a *volume anything from you*." On the back of the letter she wrote, "I made two attempts to write *something*, but could not please myself, and would not publish '*anything*.' " New manuscript starts, including one called "Maplehurst Manor," lost their impetus and remained in an extremely sketchy state; her other writing, such as her recollections of visits to Scott's Abbotsford and a brief memoir of her father, were for family consumption. As she grew older her health declined, her eyesight became poor, and she grew more devout. She did have to endure some of "the *fuss* of authorism," especially after Bentley republished her novels in 1841 under her name. Most of her last twenty years were spent quietly, battling ill health and tending to family matters. She died in Edinburgh in 1854, at her brother Walter's house on Albany Street.

While the Victorians rated her works highly, her reputation slipped considerably in the early twentieth century. In her introduction to the Holyrood edition of *Destiny* (1929), Margaret Sackville argued, "Each novel contains a dull section and a brilliant section running side by side as it were; two novels like twin philippina nuts in one shell." The critics of the 1920s, with their excessive horror of Victorian morality, appreciated

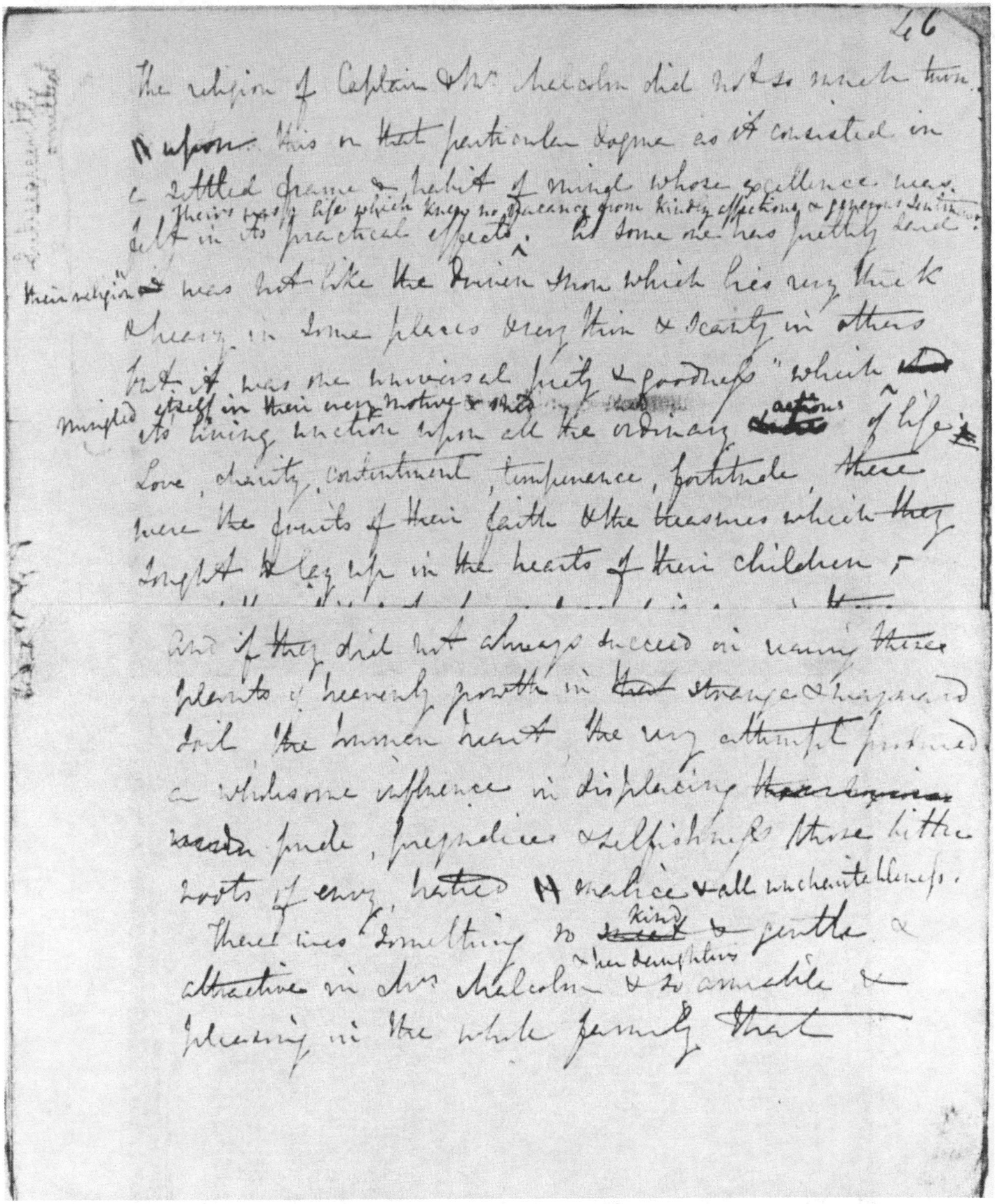

46

The religion of Captain & Mrs Malcolm did not so much turn upon this or that particular dogma as it consisted in a settled frame & habit of mind whose excellence was felt in its practical effects. Theirs was a life which knew no vacance from kindly affections & generous sentiments. As some one has prettily said: their religion was not like the driven snow which lies very thick & heavy in some places & very thin & scanty in others but it was the universal piety & goodness" which mingled itself in their very motives & its living unction upon all the ordinary ~~duties~~ actions of life.
Love, charity, contentment, temperance, fortitude, these were the fruits of their faith & the treasures which they sought to lay up in the hearts of their children,
And if they did not always succeed in rearing these plants of heavenly growth in ~~that~~ strange & ungrateful soil the human heart, the very attempt produced a wholesome influence in displacing ~~[illegible]~~ pride, prejudices & selfishness those little roots of envy, hatred & malice & all uncharitableness.
There was something so ~~sweet~~ kind & gentle & attractive in Mrs Malcolm & her daughters & so amiable & pleasing in the whole family ~~that~~

Page from the original manuscript for Destiny *(private collection, from National Library of Scotland,* Susan Ferrier, 1782-1854, *Exhibition Catalogue no. 22, 1982)*

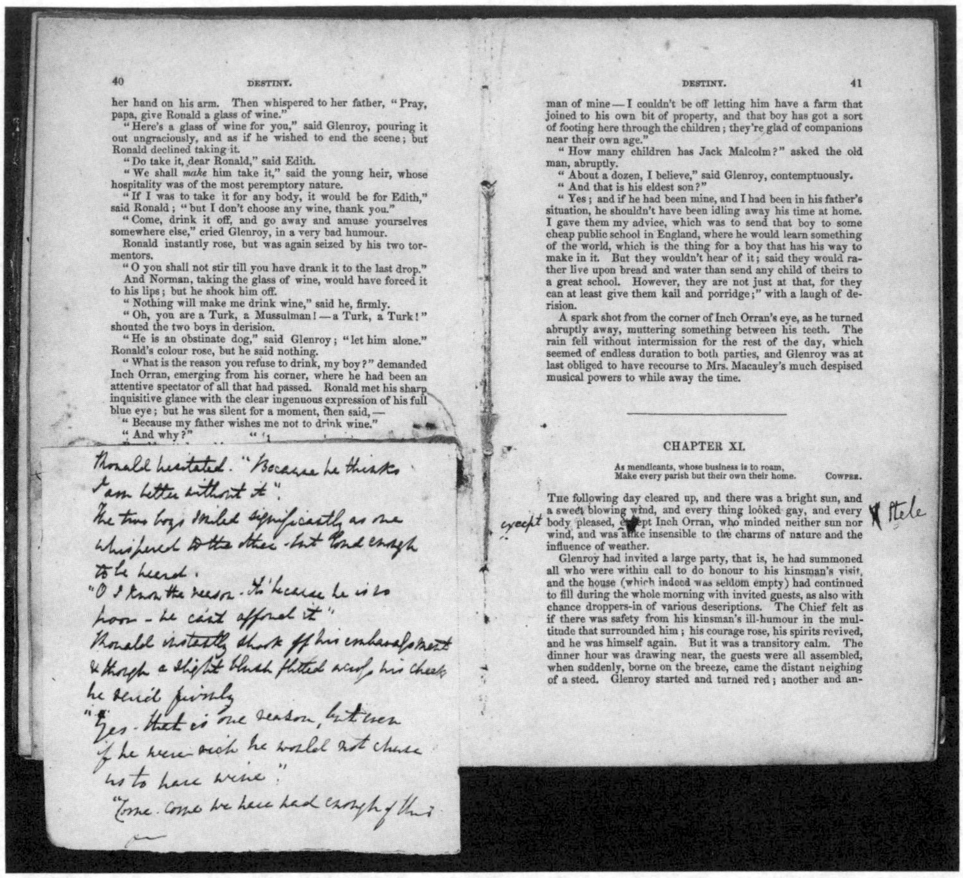

40 DESTINY.

her hand on his arm. Then whispered to her father, "Pray, papa, give Ronald a glass of wine."

"Here's a glass of wine for you," said Glenroy, pouring it out ungraciously, and as if he wished to end the scene; but Ronald declined taking it.

"Do take it, dear Ronald," said Edith.

"We shall *make* him take it," said the young heir, whose hospitality was of the most peremptory nature.

"If I was to take it for any body, it would be for Edith," said Ronald; "but I don't choose any wine, thank you."

"Come, drink it off, and go away and amuse yourselves somewhere else," cried Glenroy, in a very bad humour.

Ronald instantly rose, but was again seized by his two tormentors.

"O you shall not stir till you have drank it to the last drop."

And Norman, taking the glass of wine, would have forced it to his lips; but he shook him off.

"Nothing will make me drink wine," said he, firmly.

"Oh, you are a Turk, a Mussulman! — a Turk, a Turk!" shouted the two boys in derision.

"He is an obstinate dog," said Glenroy; "let him alone." Ronald's colour rose, but he said nothing.

"What is the reason you refuse to drink, my boy?" demanded Inch Orran, emerging from his corner, where he had been an attentive spectator of all that had passed. Ronald met his sharp inquisitive glance with the clear ingenuous expression of his full blue eye; but he was silent for a moment, then said, —

"Because my father wishes me not to drink wine."

"And why?"

Ronald hesitated. "Because he thinks I am better without it".
The two boys smiled significantly as one whispered to the other - but loud enough to be heard.
"O I know the reason - It's because he is so poor - he can't afford it".
Ronald instantly shook off his embarrassment & though a slight blush flitted across his cheek he said firmly
"Yes - that is one reason, but even if he were rich he would not chuse us to have wine".
"Come. Come we have had enough of this —"

DESTINY. 41

man of mine — I couldn't be off letting him have a farm that joined to his own bit of property, and that boy has got a sort of footing here through the children; they're glad of companions near their own age."

"How many children has Jack Malcolm?" asked the old man, abruptly.

"About a dozen, I believe," said Glenroy, contemptuously.

"And that is his eldest son?"

"Yes; and if he had been mine, and I had been in his father's situation, he shouldn't have been idling away his time at home. I gave them my advice, which was to send that boy to some cheap public school in England, where he would learn something of the world, which is the thing for a boy that has his way to make in it. But they wouldn't hear of it; said they would rather live upon bread and water than send any child of theirs to a great school. However, they are not just at that, for they can at least give them kail and porridge;" with a laugh of derision.

A spark shot from the corner of Inch Orran's eye, as he turned abruptly away, muttering something between his teeth. The rain fell without intermission for the rest of the day, which seemed of endless duration to both parties, and Glenroy was at last obliged to have recourse to Mrs. Macauley's much despised musical powers to while away the time.

CHAPTER XI.

As mendicants, whose business is to roam,
Make every parish but their own their home. COWPER.

The following day cleared up, and there was a bright sun, and a sweet blowing wind, and every thing looked gay, and every body pleased, except Inch Orran, who minded neither sun nor wind, and was alike insensible to the charms of nature and the influence of weather.

Glenroy had invited a large party, that is, he had summoned all who were within call to do honour to his kinsman's visit, and the house (which indeed was seldom empty) had continued to fill during the whole morning with invited guests, as also with chance droppers-in of various descriptions. The Chief felt as if there was safety from his kinsman's ill-humour in the multitude that surrounded him; his courage rose, his spirits revived, and he was himself again. But it was a transitory calm. The dinner hour was drawing near, the guests were all assembled, when suddenly, borne on the breeze, came the distant neighing of a steed. Glenroy started and turned red; another and an-

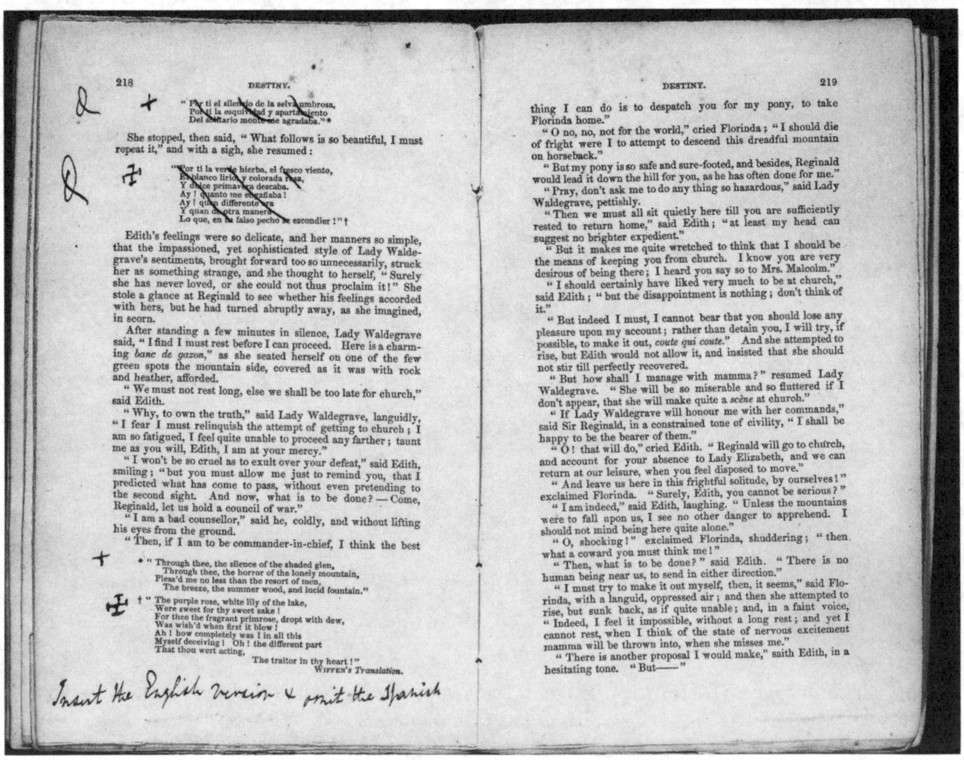

218 DESTINY.

"Por ti el silencio de la selva umbrosa,
Por ti la esquividad y apartamiento
Del solitario monte me agradaba."*

She stopped, then said, "What follows is so beautiful, I must repeat it," and with a sigh, she resumed:

"Por ti la verde hierba, el fresco viento,
El blanco lirio, y colorada rosa,
Y dulce primavera descaba.
Ay! quanto me engañaba!
Ay! quan differente era
Y quan de otra manera
Lo que, en tu falso pecho se escondier!"†

Edith's feelings were so delicate, and her manners so simple, that the impassioned, yet sophisticated style of Lady Waldegrave's sentiments, brought forward too so unnecessarily, struck her as something strange, and she thought to herself, "Surely she has never loved, or she could not thus proclaim it!" She stole a glance at Reginald to see whether his feelings accorded with hers, but he had turned abruptly away, as she imagined, in scorn.

After standing a few minutes in silence, Lady Waldegrave said, "I find I must rest before I can proceed. Here is a charming *banc de gazon*," as she seated herself on one of the few green spots the mountain side, covered as it was with rock and heather, afforded.

"We must not rest long, else we shall be too late for church," said Edith.

"Why, to own the truth," said Lady Waldegrave, languidly, "I fear I must relinquish the attempt of getting to church; I am so fatigued, I feel quite unable to proceed any farther; taunt me as you will, Edith, I am at your mercy."

"I won't be so cruel as to exult over your defeat," said Edith, smiling; "but you must allow me just to remind you, that I predicted what has come to pass, without even pretending to the second sight. And now, what is to be done? — Come, Reginald, let us hold a council of war."

"I am a bad counsellor," said he, coldly, and without lifting his eyes from the ground.

"Then, if I am to be commander-in-chief, I think the best

* "Through thee, the silence of the shaded glen,
Through thee, the horror of the lonely mountain,
Pleas'd me no less than the resort of men,
The breeze, the summer wood, and lucid fountain."

† "The purple rose, white lily of the lake,
Were sweet for thy sweet sake!
For thee the fragrant primrose, dropt with dew,
Was wish'd when first it blew!
Ah! how completely was I in all this
Myself deceiving! Oh! the different part
That thou wert acting,
The traitor in thy heart!"
WIFFEN'S *Translation.*

Insert the English version & omit the Spanish

DESTINY. 219

thing I can do is to despatch you for my pony, to take Florinda home."

"O no, no, not for the world," cried Florinda; "I should die of fright were I to attempt to descend this dreadful mountain on horseback."

"But my pony is so safe and sure-footed, and besides, Reginald would lead it down the hill for you, as he has often done for me."

"Pray, don't ask me to do any thing so hazardous," said Lady Waldegrave, pettishly.

"Then we must all sit quietly here till you are sufficiently rested to return home," said Edith; "at least my head can suggest no brighter expedient."

"But it makes me quite wretched to think that I should be the means of keeping you from church. I know you are very desirous of being there; I heard you say so to Mrs. Malcolm."

"I should certainly have liked very much to be at church," said Edith; "but the disappointment is nothing; don't think of it."

"But indeed I must, I cannot bear that you should lose any pleasure upon my account; rather than detain you, I will try, if possible, to make it out, *coute qui coute*." And she attempted to rise, but Edith would not allow it, and insisted that she should not stir till perfectly recovered.

"But how shall I manage with mamma?" resumed Lady Waldegrave. "She will be so miserable and so fluttered if I don't appear, that she will make quite a *scène* at church."

"If Lady Waldegrave will honour me with her commands," said Sir Reginald, in a constrained tone of civility, "I shall be happy to be the bearer of them."

"O! that will do," cried Edith. "Reginald will go to church, and account for your absence to Lady Elizabeth, and we can return at our leisure, when you feel disposed to move."

"And leave us here in this frightful solitude, by ourselves!" exclaimed Florinda. "Surely, Edith, you cannot be serious?"

"I am indeed," said Edith, laughing. "Unless the mountains were to fall upon us, I see no other danger to apprehend. I should not mind being here quite alone."

"O, shocking!" exclaimed Florinda, shuddering; "then what a coward you must think me!"

"Then, what is to be done?" said Edith. "There is no human being near us, to send in either direction."

"I must try to make it out myself, then, it seems," said Florinda, with a languid, oppressed air; and then she attempted to rise, but sunk back, as if quite unable; and, in a faint voice, "Indeed, I feel it impossible, without a long rest; and yet I cannot rest, when I think of the state of nervous excitement mamma will be thrown into, when she misses me."

"There is another proposal I would make," saith Edith, in a hesitating tone. "But——"

Pages from Ferrier's copy of the revised, 1841 edition of Destiny *with further revisions in her hand (RB 123523, Henry E. Huntington Library and Art Gallery)* only the biting social satire of Ferrier's novels. More recently, critics influenced by feminist thought have begun a reassessment, finding a broader attack on the norms of Victorian patriarchy; the flaw of the argument, however, is in the assimilation of Ferrier's protofeminism to her sincere, conservative views in religion and politics. A contemporary consensus is that her works are fragmented, and that, limited as she was by the choices available to her, she failed to see her appropriate aim as a writer. Barbara Hardy, who highly values the immediacy of Ferrier's letters, concludes that with another path open to her, "she might have concentrated her genius in the essays and sketches of a brilliant journalist."

Letters:

Memoir and Correspondence of Susan Ferrier, 1782-1854, edited by J. A. Doyle (London: John Murray, 1898).

Biography:

Aline Grant, *Susan Ferrier of Edinburgh, A Biography* (Denver: Alan Swallow, 1957).

References:

Nelson Bushnell, "Susan Ferrier's *Marriage* as a Novel of Manners," *Studies in Scottish Literature*, 5 (April 1968): 216-228;

Mary Cullinan, *Susan Ferrier* (Boston: Twayne, 1984);

Barbara Hardy, "The Fruits of Separation," *TLS* (7 June 1985): 641-642;

[George Moir], "Miss Ferrier's Novels," *Edinburgh Review*, 74 (January 1842): 498-505;

W. M. Parker, *Susan Ferrier and John Galt* (London: Published for the British Council and the National Book League by Longmans, Green, 1965);

Nancy L. Paxton, "Subversive Feminism: A Reassessment of Susan Ferrier's *Marriage*," *Women and Literature*, 4, no.1 (1976): 18-29;

George Saintsbury, "Miss Ferrier," in *Collected Essays and Papers*, 4 volumes (London: Dent, 1923-1924), I: 302-329;

Susan Ferrier, 1782-1854, Exhibition Catalogue no. 22 (Edinburgh: National Library of Scotland, 1982).

John Galt

(2 May 1779 - 11 April 1839)

Samuel I. Bellman
California State Polytechnic University, Pomona

See also the Galt entry in *DLB 99: Canadian Writers Before 1890.*

BOOKS: *The Battle of Largs: A Gothic Poem with Several Miscellaneous Pieces* (London: Printed by C. Whittingham for S. Highley, 1804);

Voyages and Travels in the Years 1809, 1810, and 1811; Containing Statistical, Commercial, and Miscellaneous Observations on Gibraltar, Sardinia, Sicily, Malta, Serigo, and Turkey (London: Printed for T. Cadell & W. Davies, 1812);

Cursory Reflections on Political and Commercial Topics as reflected by the Regent's Accession to Royal Authority (London: C. J. Barrington, 1812);

The Tragedies of Maddalen, Agamemnon, Lady Macbeth, Antonia & Clytemnestra (London: Printed by W. Smith for T. Cadell & W. Davies, 1812);

The Life and Administration of Cardinal Wolsey (London: Printed for T. Cadell & W. Davies by Nichols, Son & Bentley, 1812);

Letters from the Levant; Containing Views of the State of Society, Manners, Opinions, and Commerce in Greece and Several of the Principal Islands of the Archipelago (London: Printed for T. Cadell & W. Davies, 1813);

The Life and Studies of Benjamin West, volume 1 (London: Printed by Nichols, Son & Bentley for T. Cadell & W. Davies, 1816; Philadelphia: Moses Thomas, J. Maxwell, printer, 1816);

The Crusade (Edinburgh, 1816);

The Majolo: A Tale, 2 volumes (London: Printed by W. Smith for T. Faulkner, 1816);

The Appeal: A Tragedy in Three Acts: As Performed at the Theatre-Royal, Edinburgh (Edinburgh: Printed for Archibald Constable and Longman, Rees, Orme & Brown, London, 1818);

Glenfell; or, Macdonalds and Campbells (London: Printed for Sir Richard Phillips & sold by W. Sams, 1820);

The Life, Studies, and Works of Benjamin West, volume 2 (London: Printed for T. Cadell & W. Davies, 1820);

All the Voyages Round the World: From the First by Magellan in 1520 to that of Krusenstern in 1807, as Capt. Samuel Prior (London: Printed by W. Lewis for Sir Richard Phillips, 1820; New York: W. H. Colyer, 1840);

The Wandering Jew; or, The Travels and Observations of Hareach the Prolonged, as the Rev. T. Clark (London: Printed for John Souter, 1820);

A Tour of Europe, as the Rev. T. Clark (London: Souter, 1820);

A Tour of Asia, as the Rev. T. Clark (London: Souter, 1820);

The Earthquake: A Tale (3 volumes, Edinburgh: Printed for W. Blackwood and T. Cadell & W. Davies, London, by W. Smith, 1820; 2 volumes, New York: C. S. Van Winkle, 1821; New York: W. B. Gilley, 1821);

Pictures Historical and Biographical drawn from English, Scottish, and Irish History, 2 volumes (London: Printed by W. Lewis for Sir Richard Phillips, 1821);

The National Reader, as the Rev. T. Clark (London: Souter, 1821);

The National Spelling Book, as the Rev. T. Clark (London: Souter, 1821);

The Annals of the Parish; or, The Chronicle of Dalmailing (Edinburgh: Printed for W. Blackwood & T. Cadell, London, by J. Ballantyne, 1821; Philadelphia: M. Carey & Sons, 1821);

The Ayrshire Legatees; or, The Pringle Family (Edinburgh: Printed for W. Blackwood & T. Cadell, London, by James Ballantyne, 1821; New York: W. B. Gilley, 1823);

Sir Andrew Wylie, of That Ilk (3 volumes, Edinburgh: Printed for W. Blackwood & T. Cadell, London, 1822; 2 volumes, New York: Printed for the Booksellers by W. Grattan, 1822);

The Provost (Edinburgh: Printed for W. Blackwood & T. Cadell, London, 1822; New York: Published by E. Duyckinck, and nine others, printed by J. & J. Harper, 1822);

Drawing by Alfred, Count d'Orsay (Scottish National Portrait Gallery)

The Steam-boat (Edinburgh: W. Blackwood / London: T. Cadell, 1822; New York: Printed by J. & J. Harper for S. Campbell & Son, and eight others, 1823);

A New General School Atlas, as the Rev. T. Clark (London: Souter, 1822);

The English Mother's First Catechism for her Children, as the Rev. T. Clark (London: Printed for J. Souter, 1822);

The Entail: or, The Lords of the Grippy (3 volumes, Edinburgh: W. Blackwood and T. Cadell, London, 1823 [i.e., 1822]; 2 volumes, New York: Printed by J. & J. Harper for S. Campbell & Son, and eight others, 1823);

The Gathering of the West (Edinburgh: Printed for William Blackwood and T. Cadell, London, by George Ramsay, 1823);

Ringan Gilhaize; or, The Covenanters (3 volumes, Edinburgh: Printed by & for Oliver & Boyd and for G. & W. B. Whittaker, London, 1823; 2 volumes, New York: E. Duyckinck, 1823);

The Spaewife: a Tale of the Scottish Chronicles (3 volumes, Edinburgh: Printed & published by Oliver & Boyd and G. & W. B. Whittaker, London, 1823; 2 volumes, Philadelphia: H. C. Carey & I. Lea, 1824);

The Bachelor's Wife; A Selection of Curious and Interesting Extracts, with Cursory Observations (Edinburgh: Printed & Published by Oliver & Boyd and G. & W. B. Whittaker, London, 1824);

Rothelan: A Romance of the English Histories (3 volumes, Edinburgh: Printed & published by Oliver & Boyd and Geo. B. Whittaker, London, 1824; 2 volumes, New York: Published by Collins & Hannay, 1825);

The Omen (Edinburgh: Printed for W. Blackwood and T. Cadell, London, by A. & R. Spottiswoode, London, 1825 [i.e., 1826]);

High Street, Irvine, Galt's birthplace, as it appeared during his lifetime (engraving by W. H. Lizars)

The Last of the Lairds; or, The Life and Opinions of Malachi Mailings, Esq. of Auldbiggings (Edinburgh: Printed for W. Blackwood and T. Cadell, London, by James Ballantyne, 1826; New York: Printed by J. & J. Harper, 1827);

Lawrie Todd; or, The Settlers in the Woods (3 volumes, London: Henry Colburn & Richard Bentley, 1830; 2 volumes, New York: Printed by J. & J. Harper, 1830);

Southennan (3 volumes, London: Henry Colburn & Richard Bentley, 1830; 2 volumes, New York: Printed by J. & J. Harper, 1830);

The Life of Lord Byron (London: Henry Colburn & Richard Bentley; Bell & Bradfeite, Edinburgh; Cumming, Dublin, 1830; New York: Printed by J. & J. Harper, 1830);

Bogle Corbet; or, The Emigrants, 3 volumes (London: Henry Colburn & Richard Bentley, 1831);

The Lives of the Players, 2 volumes (London: Henry Colburn & Richard Bentley, 1831; Boston: F. S. Hill, 1831);

Stanley Buxton; or, The Schoolfellows (3 volumes, London: Henry Colburn & Richard Bentley, 1832; 2 volumes, Philadelphia & Baltimore: E. L. Carey & A. Hart, 1833);

The Member: An Autobiography (London: James Fraser, 1832); republished in *Reform* (London: James Fraser, 1833);

The Radical: An Autobiography (London: James Fraser, 1832); republished in *Reform* (1833);

The Stolen Child. A Tale of the Town, Founded on a Certain Interesting Fact (London: Smith, Elder, 1833; Philadelphia: Carey, Lea & Blanchard, 1833);

Eben Erskine; or, The Traveller (3 volumes, London: Richard Bentley, 1833; 2 volumes, Philadelphia: Carey, Lea & Blanchard, 1833);

The Ouranoulogos; or, The Celestial Volume, "The Deluge" by Galt with engravings by John Martin (Edinburgh: W. Blackwood and T. Cadell, London, 1833);

The Autobiography of John Galt, 2 volumes (London: Cochrane & M'Crone, 1833; Philadelphia: Key & Biddle, 1833);

Poems (London: Cochrane & M'Crone, 1833);

Stories of the Study, 3 volumes (London: Cochrane & M'Crone, 1833);

The Literary Life and Miscellanies of John Galt, 3 volumes (Edinburgh: W. Blackwood and T. Cadell, London, 1834);

Efforts By an Invalid (Greenock: Printed for the author by John Mennons, 1835; London: James Fraser, 1835);

A Contribution to the Greenock Calamity Fund (Greenock: Printed for the author by W. Johnston & Son, 1835);

The Demon of Destiny; and Other Poems (Greenock: Printed by W. Johnston & Son, 1839);

The Howdie and Other Tales, edited by William Roughead (Edinburgh & London: T. N. Foulis, 1923);

A Rich Man and Other Stories, edited by Roughead (London & Edinburgh: T. N. Foulis, 1925).

Editions: *Works of John Galt*, 8 volumes, edited by D. Storrar Meldrum (Edinburgh: William Blackwood, 1895; Boston: Roberts, 1895-1896); enlarged and reedited by Meldrum and Roughead, 10 volumes (Edinburgh: J. Grant, 1936).

Considering his vast and diversified literary output, as well as his colorful career as a businessman and promoter of various enterprises, it is ironic that John Galt, a Scots novelist contemporaneous with Sir Walter Scott, should be so little known today. According to George Saintsbury's *History of Nineteenth Century Literature* (1896), Galt's writings are "totally uncritical; his poems, dramas, etc., being admittedly worthless, his miscellaneous writing mostly book-making, while his historical novels are given up by all but devotees." Yet a recent biographer, Ian A. Gordon, calls Galt "a novelist of considerable power, with an assured niche in literary history." Other scholars have agreed, pointing out that novels such as *Annals of the Parish* (1821), *The Ayrshire Legatees* (1821), *The Provost* (1822), and *The Entail* (1822) are valuable reflections of English and Scottish society during the eighteenth and early nineteenth centuries. Galt's novels generally involve the important concerns of his times, and they are important as contributions to the development of the realistic Scottish novel, enhanced by local color derived from minute details of village life day-today and a generous use of vernacular speech. Such realism, however, has contributed to the decline of Galt's popularity. *Annals of the Parish*, entertaining as it is, is practically unreadable today without recourse to an extensive glossary of Scottish words and idioms.

John Galt was born in the west of Scotland, in the seaport town of Irvine, Ayrshire, on 2 May 1779, the oldest of four children of John Galt, a sea captain in command of a merchant ship, and Jean Tilloch Galt. In 1789 the family moved north to another seaport town, Greenock, on the Firth of Clyde, so that the elder Galt could expand his mercantile activities and trade with Jamaica. His bookish son John was schooled in practical subjects pertaining to commerce: penmanship, astronomy, mathematics, English, and French. Between 1795 and 1804 he served as a clerk in Greenock, briefly in the customshouse and then in a mercantile establishment. In 1804 Galt removed to London to enter the world of commerce. During the next five years he attempted several business ventures, all of which ended in failure. He had already begun to write for publication: a "Gothic epic," *The Battle of Largs* (1804) and articles on a variety of subjects for the *Greenock Advertiser* and the *Scots Magazine* were followed by contributions to a newspaper, the *Star*, and the *Philosophical Magazine*.

At about age thirty he made plans to take up residence in Lincoln's Inn and prepare for a career in law. By 1811 Galt had given up that plan, having spent much of the two preceding years traveling in Mediterranean countries and in the Near East, occasionally in the company of George Gordon, Lord Byron, with whom he had developed a friendship of sorts. In the same year Galt embarked on an ambitious plan to frustrate Napoleon's Berlin and Milan decrees, which called for a commercial blockade of British vessels seeking trade with Europe. His scheme involved storing his merchandise on a Greek island and attempting to move the goods into Europe by way of Turkey. Like other Galt enterprises, it was an utter failure. Yet the letters he had sent to his friend James Park became the basis for Galt's first full-length book, *Voyages and Travels in the years 1809, 1810, and 1811*, published in January 1812.

By the time he married Elizabeth Tilloch on 20 April 1813, Galt had published two more books and a pamphlet. In the course of a career that spanned two and a half decades, he wrote novels, biographies, plays, accounts of his travels, poetry, short stories, literary reviews and commentaries, miscellaneous essays, histories and autobiography, as well as school texts and other books for young readers. Many of these works were written to earn the money necessary to support his wife and three sons. He also twice served briefly as editor of new papers: the *Political Review* in 1812, and the *Courier* (London) in 1830. Throughout much of his career he was involved in the literary politics of Edinburgh—particularly through his sometimes-stormy relationship with the powerful editor and publisher William Blackwood—and of London, with its competitive literary journals and book publishers. By 1819 Galt had developed a sizable body of powerful, well-placed friends and acquaintances—through family connections, mercantile ventures, literary contacts, and (not least) his own assiduous efforts at cultivating influential friendships. There were at least sixty members of Parliament on whom Galt felt he could call if conditions required. Accordingly, he was commissioned by the directors of a company established by Parliament for the purpose of constructing a canal between Glasgow and Edinburgh, to lobby his important connections for the passage of a bill to raise revenue for their project. Galt failed to win parliamentary support in 1819, but the next year he succeeded.

Throughout this period Galt's literary production continued at a dizzying rate—with quantity steadily exceeding quality—while he also took on additional lobbying assignments and pursued ancillary business endeavors. At the end of 1820 he was made the agent for a sizable group of settlers in Upper Canada (now Ontario), who were seeking redress from Britain's Colonial Office for losses they had sustained in the War of 1812, when American troops had crossed the border into Canada. After four years of labors on their behalf, Galt was still unable to gain relief for them from the British government.

Seeking another source of financial compensation for his Canadian clients, Galt—through a complicated series of circumstances—in 1826 became superintendent of a huge land-investment organization. The Canada Company had a million acres of government forest land between Lake Huron and Lake Ontario to develop for settlement, sale, and commerce, at a profit. Early on, things looked promising. Galt was instrumental in founding the towns of Guelph and Goderich, and optimistically outlined plans for a new colony, which would be under his administration.

Yet Galt failed, to a large extent because of his mismanagement, lack of judgment, and undiplomatic attitude toward his superiors. He lost his lucrative position with the organization and was obliged to set sail for England, landing at Liverpool in May 1829. More trouble was ahead for him; when he went to Canada in 1826, he had left behind personal debts which were now long overdue. His creditors demanded payment, and he was unable to come up with the money. As a result he was placed under arrest for debt, and on 15 July he was incarcerated in the King's Bench debtors' prison, where he remained until 10 November.

Galt had written little in Canada, but while he was in prison, his facility in writing commercially salable magazine articles and fiction aided him, for he wrote a great deal during his quarter-year's stay in prison, and he wrote vastly more during the decade of life left to him following his release. His first successes as a novelist had come at about the same time he was lobbying for the Canadians. During the years 1820-1822 he wrote six novels for Edinburgh publisher William Blackwood.

The twentieth-century reader of Galt's novels may be put off by their uneven quality, their parochial subject matter, and their Scottish dialect. As critics noted late in the nineteenth century, Galt's writing lacks artistry. He was not often a skilled craftsman with words, nor did he frequently make his characters and situations live on in readers' minds and take on new meaning with the passage of time. It has been noted, however, that Galt did provide a basis for a deeper understanding and continuing appreciation of his novels: a basis rooted not in aesthetics or architectonic skill, but in applied historiography. Galt called this system "theoretical history."

Taking an unconventional approach to the craft of fiction writing, Galt pointedly disputed the importance of plot. He stressed unity of place—though his fictive "theoretical histories" did not always follow this rule—the narrative had to be confined to events within a "circumscribed locality." So that his art might reproduce nature, he employed—according to Ruth I. Aldrich—"the fictional autobiography, the epistolary novel, the interpolated short story, the imitation chronicle, and the episodic and documentary panorama of a place." *Annals of the Parish* (1821), *The Ayrshire Legatees* (1821), *Sir Andrew Wylie of That Ilk* (1822), *The Provost* (1822), *The Steam-Boat* (1822), and *The Entail* (published in December 1822 with 1823 on its title page)—the novels Galt wrote for Blackwood, who insisted (to Galt's annoyance) on certain compositional changes in the interests of

John Galt (portrait by Charles Gray; Scottish National Portrait Gallery)

greater reader appeal—deal for the most part with regional life in western Scotland, Galt's home territory.

The first novel Galt submitted to Blackwood was *The Ayrshire Legatees*, which was serialized in *Blackwood's Edinburgh Magazine* (June 1820 - February 1821) before it was published in one volume in June 1821. A series of letters written by four characters, Galt's novel has been compared to another epistolary narrative, *The Expedition of Humphrey Clinker* (1771), written by a fellow Scot, Tobias Smollett. In Galt's book a legacy is left to a country minister, Dr. Zachariah Pringle, by his late cousin, a Colonel Armour, of Hyderabad, India. To ensure that he will receive the money, he removes—with wife, Janet; son, Andrew (recently called to the bar); and marriageable daughter, Rachel—from his rural parish of Garnock to London, where he is to deal with Armour's agents. Much of the book concerns the experiences and observations of the Pringles in London. They describe London life in their letters to the enthusiastic but unsophisticated folks back home—including Reverend Charles Snodgrass, Dr. Pringle's temporary replacement. National events are discussed (the funeral of George III, the divorce trial of Queen Caroline, wife of George IV), as are women's fashions and political, religious, and philosophical matters. All ends well, as Rachel marries a dashing officer, Captain Sabre. The novel was warmly received by the public, increasing the sales of *Blackwood's* "prodigiously," and did much to encourage sales of future novels by Galt, but *The Ayrshire Legatees* seems now—for all its being a contemporary record of London in 1820—a very modest literary effort.

The February 1821 issue of *Blackwood's*, which included the last installment of *The Ayrshire Legatees*, also included the first part of *The Steamboat*, which ran in the magazine through December of that year. Galt thoroughly revised the novel, adding new material before its book publication in July 1821. Yet this series of tales and anecdotes (some unfinished)—told during steamboat trips between Glasgow and Helensburgh on the Firth of Clyde, and a coach trip from Glasgow to Edinburgh followed by a steamboat journey from there to London—still seems carelessly assembled. The central figure of this conglomeration of story segments and fragments narrated by diverse travelers in their own particular modes of speech is Thomas Duffle, a cloth merchant from Glasgow. The book includes descriptions of London and impressions of the coronation of George IV. Among the characters thrown into *The Steamboat* were the Pringles, from *The Ayrshire Legatees*. Critics have been quite disparaging of *The Steamboat*, although its various speech styles have been singled out for praise.

Before writing the later episodes of *The Steam-boat*, Galt completed the final revisions on what is now generally considered his best work of fiction, *Annals of the Parish*, which Blackwood published in April 1821. Presented as the Reverend Micah Balwhidder's journal records of the rural parish of Dalmailing from 1760 to 1810, the novel is a lively and colorful account of the elderly pastor's career, from his "placing" (over the strong opposition of the parishioners) by his patron, the Laird of Breadloaf, to his retirement, amid the affectionate expressions of appreciation from his flock. The events he records succinctly and convincingly include such local matters as smuggling and church politics, and general matters such as the impact of the American Revolution and the threat of a Napoleonic invasion on village life. The novel covers a broad range of emotional tones, including tragedy (the suicides of a destitute cotton-mill overseer and his wife, despondent over their inability to provide for their children), pathos (the antic behavior of mad Meg Gaffaw, following her mother's death), and comedy (Reverend Balwhidder, now retired, records his decrepit state: "Mrs. Balwhidder is now and then obliged to stop me in my prayers, as I sometimes wander—pronouncing the baptismal blessing upon a bride and bridegroom, talking as if they were already parents").

Among the numerous picturesque characters in the *Annals* are the three wives of the twice-widowed Reverend Balwhidder; Mrs. Malcolm, a poor widow with five children; mad Meg Gaffaw and her mother, Jenny; Mr. Heckletext—a disreputable preacher; and the fiery-tempered newcomer (and future justice of the peace) Mr. Cayenne. *Annals of the Parish* was a popular success. Sir Walter Scott was enthusiastic about it. The reviewer for the *Inverness Courier* (10 May 1821) was only the first critic to liken Galt's novel to Oliver Goldsmith's *Vicar of Wakefield* (1766)—a comparison that must have pleased Galt, who wrote in his *Autobiography* (1833) that as a young boy he had wanted to write a Scottish equivalent of the story.

Sir Andrew Wylie, of That Ilk, published in three volumes in January 1822, is the odyssey of a Scots lad of good parts, Andrew Wylie, from a village in Ayrshire (Stoneyholm, near Galt's native Irvine) to London, where he meets and uses people of quality and influence to advance his career. From time to time he does favors for some of his friends of convenience. He also becomes embroiled in colorful adventures (including one with a band of gypsies). Eventually he gains a seat in Parliament, a baronetcy, enough wealth to purchase a huge estate, and the hand in marriage of his childhood sweetheart, Mary Cunningham, whose father is the laird of Craiglands. Critical opinion of the book, for all its episodic, "novelistic" qualities (which Galt regretted, because they were generally Blackwood's doing), has often been negative. Critics have complained of plot contrivances, poor writing, lack of organization and verisimilitude, vulgarity, and length.

Galt had another novel, *The Provost*, ready for publication in one volume in May 1822. As critics have noted, this novel is at once a "theoretical history" of a Scottish town (the royal borough of Gudetown, closely modeled on Galt's birthplace, Irvine) from about 1760 to late 1816, and a study in local politics. The narrator, an upwardly mobile townsman named James Pawkie (his surname means sly or cunning), in his reminiscences provides interesting social commentary about the different classes and a remarkable psychological self-portrait. Pawkie unwittingly reveals himself to be a consummate egoist and manipulator of others, with a keen understanding of human motives and an armory of defense mechanisms. Beginning as an apprentice to a tailor, Pawkie received a modest legacy from an uncle and set up as a shopkeeper. He married judiciously and used his wife's inheritance to further his business. Entering local politics, he made his way up in the town council from councilor to dean of guild to bailie (magistrate) to provost (chief magistrate), serving three terms in that exalted capacity—all the while accumulating property in Gudetown. Upon his retirement he succeeded in wangling a silver cup with a Latin inscription from the grateful town council.

Drawing of Galt by Daniel Maclise (Victoria and Albert Museum)

Pawkie's wife and some townspeople, such as the greedy rascal M'Lucre, are treated fleetingly in relation to Pawkie himself and his campaign of self-advancement. Among the events in Gudetown that he records are the gruesome hanging of the town harlot, Jean Gaisling, for murdering her newborn babe; the incursion of a press gang into Gudetown; the threat felt by the locals of a Napoleonic invasion of Britain; and a duel (illegal and carrying the death penalty) involving Pawkie's nephew and a young laird. At the outset the book received mixed reviews, and over the decades it has aroused strong pro and con sentiments. Yet in his copy of the novel Samuel Taylor Coleridge wrote, "This work is not for the Many; but in the unconscious, perfectly natural, Irony of self-delusion, in all parts intelligible to the intelligent Reader, without the slightest suspicion on the part of the Autobiographer, I know of no equal in our Literature." This comment seems particularly perceptive, and it may be that much negative criticism of the novel results from a lack of careful reading.

The Entail, a three-volume family chronicle published by Blackwood in December 1822, follows three generations of the Walkinshaw family over most of the eighteenth century. As the title suggests the subject is primarily the *entailment* of family property: the limiting of the inheritance to a designated succession of heirs. The plot focuses on greed and questionable behavior in the building up of a landed estate and the personal suffering that can result from placing land acquisition above all else. Claud Walkinshaw, a poor orphan who is fed by a nurse on dreams of his family's lost property, devotes his crabbed existence to regaining and augmenting that land, at whatever cost. His conniving, through a calculated marriage and other means, to achieve that end and his disinheriting of his eldest son set the tone for an intricate pattern of family quarrels and other unpleasantness that will run through the next two generations, before the family's conflicts can be resolved satisfactorily.

Characterization is effectively handled. Two memorable figures besides Claud are his wife Leddy Grippy (Leddy = Lady; Claud is, technically, laird, or lord, of the Grippy lands), and their retarded son Walter. Leddy Grippy is a forceful, expressive person, while Walter's ridiculous remarks provide somewhat tasteless comic relief. Critical opinion of the book has been divided. Scott and Byron were so taken with the story that each read it three times. Partisans have praised *The Entail* for its narrative power and insightful characterization; opponents have cited its difficult dialectal prose (various levels of Scottish English are used to differentiate social backgrounds), its vulgarity, and the sordidness of its characters. So many writers—including Honoré de Balzac, Charles Dickens, Mark Twain, and John Galsworthy—have employed the consequences of property-obsession as a controlling story idea that Galt's novel seems overly familiar today. Yet, one should not overlook his gallery of colorful characters in an ancient and conservative society that is moving toward political reform and the Industrial Revolution.

After *The Entail* appeared, Galt tired of Blackwood's incessant demands for revisions and offered his next novel, *Ringan Gilhaize; or, The Covenanters*, to the rival Edinburgh firm of Oliver and Boyd, which published the three-volume novel in May 1823. Written partly in response to Scott's *Old Mortality* (1816), which Galt considered disrespectful to the Covenanters, *Ringan Gilhaize* is set during the religious wars in Scotland between 1558 and 1696, when the Kirk—the Presbyterian Church of Scotland, supported by the Covenanters—was in effect embroiled in fierce religious wars: first against Catholicism and later against the Anglican church. The title character is a third-generation member of his family, fighting bitterly with other Covenanters—members of Scottish bands bound by oath to defend their Kirk against foreign ecclesiastical powers and foreign rulers. He loses his entire family in the struggle against the Stuart monarchs and their supporters, and at last has the satisfaction in 1689 of killing his mortal enemy, Viscount Claverhouse, who fought for the return to the throne of the deposed Stuart king, James II.

Despite all the effort that Galt poured into researching and writing this novel it was poorly received by his contemporaries, and modern critics tend to concur with these earlier judgments.

Among the novels Galt wrote for Oliver and Boyd during the years before he left for Canada are two other three-volume historical novels: *The Spaewife* (December 1823), dealing with the reign of James I of Scotland (1406-1437) and the murder plot which ended his life, and *Rothelan* (November 1824), set during the reign of Edward III (1327-1377). Also worthy of mention is *Southennan*, concerned with intrigues in the court of Mary, Queen of Scots, during the years 1561-1565. The three-volume novel, which Galt began soon after his release from debtors' prison in late November 1829 and finished by February 1830, was published by the London firm of Henry Colburn and Richard Bentley in July of that year. These three novels are considerably less ambitious in scope and purpose than *Ringan Gilhaize* and have been held in even lower esteem by critics and reviewers. To the general complaint that Galt simply wrote too much to write well may be added the specific criticism that these historical novels are tedious and unconvincing.

A far more interesting novel of the 1830s is *The Member: An Autobiography*, published in London by James Fraser in January 1832. Fictionalizing his own experiences as a parliamentary lobbyist, Galt provided a valuable picture of British politics in the period just before the passage of the Reform Bill of 1832 extended limited suffrage somewhat and eliminated the "rotten" boroughs with unfair representation in Parliament. The novel is also a fascinating psychological study of calculated, self-serving expediency in the political arena. The narrator, a Scotsman named Archibald Jobbry (always concerned with "keeping [his] eye on the main chance"), returns to his native land after spending a quarter of a century in Bengal, India. He decides to run for Parliament "with the full intention of administering [his] share of the Government patronage with judgment and sensibility, and to keep aloof as much as possible from political matters. . . ."

Working within the existing corrupt system that makes possible the purchase of a seat in Parliament, he succeeds, after much political maneuvering, in obtaining his seat and subsequently in being returned for two more terms. In the course of the novel Jobbry discusses his handling of patronage (always with some advantage to himself), and he tells of his assisting a starving family by using his political connections. A moderate

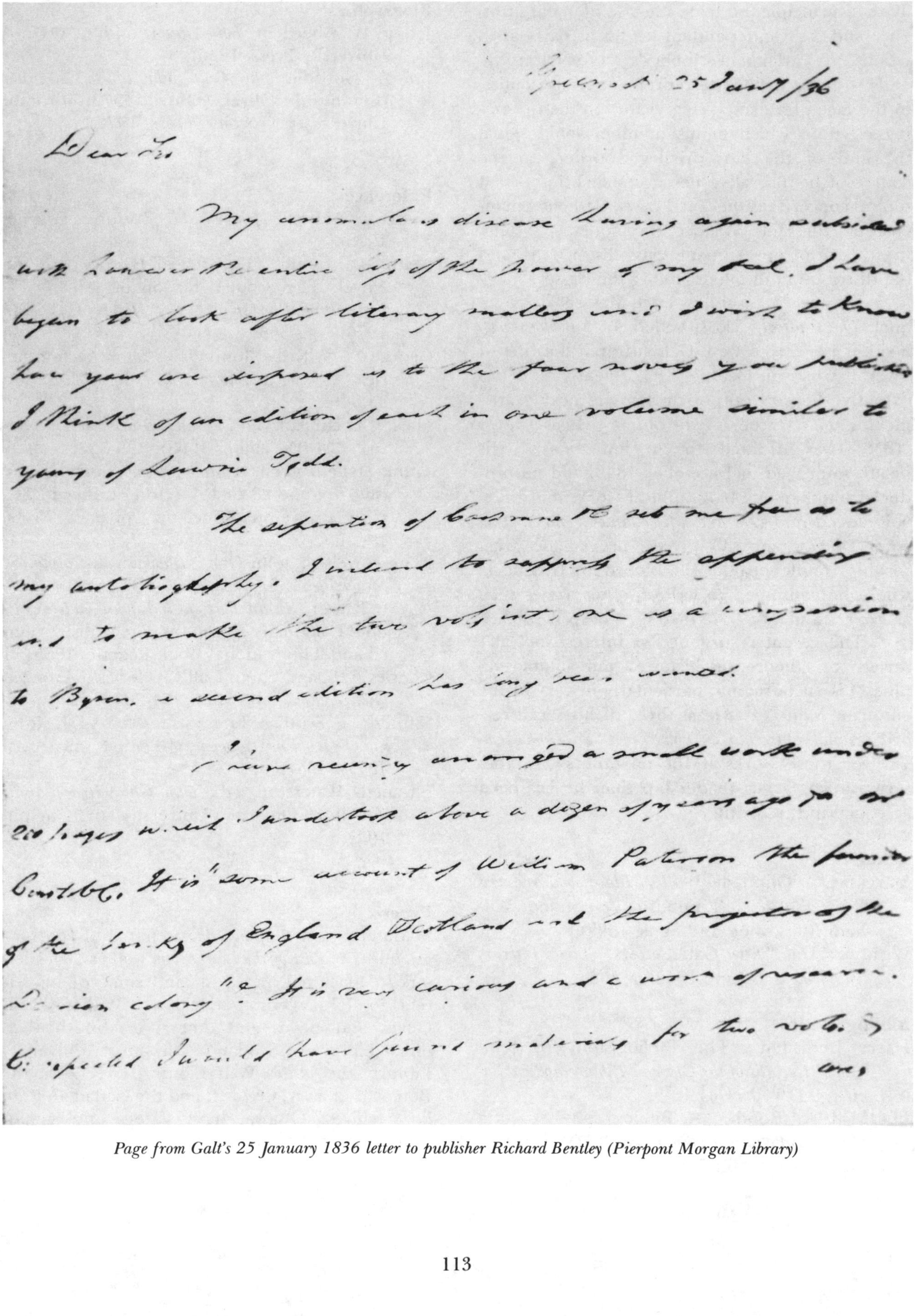

Greenock 25 Jany/36

Dear Sir

My anomalous disease having again subsided with however the entire loss of the power of my body. I have begun to look after literary matters and I wish to know how you are disposed as to the four novels you publisht. I think of an edition of each in one volume similar to years of Lawrie Todd.

The separation of Cochrane sets me free as to my autobiography. I intend to suppress the appendix and to make the two vols into one as a companion to Byron, a second edition has long been wanted.

I have recently arranged a small work under 200 pages which I undertook above a dozen of years ago for Constable. It is "some account of William Paterson the founder of the banks of England & Scotland and the projector of the Darien colony." It is very curious and a work of research. I expected I would have found materials for two vols. one,

Page from Galt's 25 January 1836 letter to publisher Richard Bentley (Pierpont Morgan Library)

Tory in principle, he fears the rise of Whig influence and is an independent (as far as party affiliation) in Parliament. Jobbry's "autobiography" ends with his deliberate retirement from politics, in the face of a likely Whig victory in the upcoming election, which in his opinion would signal the end of the old, privileged order. In the course of his narrative he covers such important topical concerns as the Corn Laws, Catholic Emancipation, the Holy Alliance, the monetary system, the nature of government, class distinctions, and the distribution of talent among the classes.

The Member was followed in May 1832 by a sequel, *The Radical*, also subtitled *An Autobiography*. Neither novel sold well. Galt suffered the first of several strokes in October 1832. Nearly all of his extensive literary output during the next year—including a true, two-volume *Autobiography* (1833)—was dictated to an amanuensis. His health improved in December 1833, and he produced another autobiographical work, the three-volume *Literary Life and Miscellanies* (1834). The strain of work on this project proved too great for his fragile health. He retired to Greenock, where he continued to write for magazines such as *Fraser's* and *Tait's*. He died on 11 April 1839.

The recent resurgence of interest in Galt's novels (or "theoretical histories and autobiographies") is encouraging, particularly in view of the enduring value of at least three of his social records: *Annals of the Parish, The Provost*, and *The Member*. For these works if for no others, Galt deserves a far larger readership than he has been accorded in this century.

Letters:

Margaret O. Oliphant, *William Blackwood and His Sons*, volume 1 (Edinburgh & London: William Blackwood and Sons, 1897);

W. M. Parker, "New Galt Letters," *Times Literary Supplement*, 6 June 1942, p. 288.

Bibliographies:

Harry Lumsden, "The Bibliography of John Galt," *Records of the Glasgow Bibliographical Society*, 9 (1931): 1-41;

Bradford A. Booth, "A Bibliography of John Galt," *Bulletin of Bibliography*, 16 (September-December 1936): 7-9.

Biographies:

Jennie W. Aberdein, *John Galt* (London: Oxford University Press, 1936);

Ian A. Gordon, *John Galt: The life of a writer* (Edinburgh: Oliver & Boyd, 1972; Toronto: University of Toronto Press, 1972).

References:

Ruth I. Aldrich, *John Galt* (Boston: Twayne, 1978);

Keith M. Costain, "Theoretical History and the Novel: The Scottish Fiction of John Galt," *Journal of English Literary History*, 43 (Fall 1976): 342-365;

George V. Griffith, "John Galt's Short Fiction Series," *Studies in Short Fiction*, 17 (Fall 1980): 455-462;

Marion Lochhead, "John Galt," *Blackwood's Magazine*, 304 (December 1968): 496-508;

Frank Hallam Lyell, *A Study of the Novels of John Galt*, volume 28 of Princeton Studies in English (Princeton: Princeton University Press, 1942);

"The Novels of John Galt," *Blackwood's Edinburgh Magazine*, 159 (June 1896): 871-882;

W. M. Parker, *Susan Ferrier and John Galt* (London: Longmans, Green for The British Council and The National Book League, 1965);

Charles E. Shain, "John Galt's America," *American Quarterly*, 8 (Fall 1956): 254-263;

"Studies in Scottish Literature, No. VIII: John Galt," *Dublin University Magazine*, 89 (April 1877): 495-506;

Elizabeth Waterston, ed., *John Galt: Reappraisals* (Guelph, Ontario: University of Guelph, 1985).

Papers:

Manuscripts for *Ringan Gilhaize*, part 1 of *The Howdie*, and *The Last of the Lairds*—as well as Galt's letters to Blackwell and Scott and some of his letters to John Gibson Lockhart, William Tait, Oliver and Boyd, and others—are in the National Library of Scotland. Edinburgh University Library; the James Watt Library, Greenock; the Bodleian Library, Oxford; and the Canadian Public Archives, Ottawa, have letters and manuscripts for poems and sketches.

Thomas Gaspey

(31 March 1788 - 8 December 1871)

Michael Adams
Albright College

BOOKS: *The Mystery; or Forty Years Ago: A Novel* (3 volumes, London: Longman, Hurst, Rees, Orme & Brown, 1820; 2 volumes, New York: E. Duyckink, 1820);

Calthorpe; or, Fallen Fortunes: A Novel (3 volumes, London: Longman, Hurst, Rees, Orme & Brown, 1821; 2 volumes, Philadelphia: T. Desilver, 1821);

Takings; or, The Life of a Collegian: A Poem (London: J. Warren, 1821);

The Lollards; a Tale, Founded on the Persecutions which Marked the Early Part of the Fifteenth Century, 3 volumes (London: Longman, Hurst, Rees, Orme & Brown, 1822);

Other Times; or, the Monks of Leadenhall, 3 volumes (London: Longman, Hurst, Rees, Orme & Brown, 1823);

The Witch-Finder; or, the Wisdom of Our Ancestors: A Romance, 3 volumes (London: Longman, Hurst, Rees, Orme, Brown & Green, 1824);

The History of George Godfrey, Written by Himself, 3 volumes (London: H. Colburn, 1828);

The Self-Condemned: A Romance (3 volumes, London: H. Colburn, 1836; 1 volume, New York: Harper & Brothers, 1836);

"Many-coloured life": or, Tales of Woe and Touches of Mirth (London: H. Cunningham, 1842);

A Pictorial History of France and of the French People: from the Establishment of the Franks in Gaul, to the Period of the French Revolution, by Gaspey and G. M. Bussey (2 volumes, London: W. S. Orr, 1843);

The Life and Times of the Good Lord Cobham, 2 volumes (London: H. Cunningham, 1844);

The Dream of Human Life, 2 volumes (London & New York: London Printing and Publishing Company, 1852);

The History of England; Continued from the Reign of George the Third, 4 volumes (London & New York: London Printing & Publishing, 1852);

The History of Smithfield (London: Willoughby, 1852);

The Political Life of Wellington, volume 3 of *The Life and Times of the Late Duke of Wellington*, 4 volumes, volumes 1, 2, and 4 by W. F. Williams (London and New York: London Printing and Publishing Company, 1853).

Thomas Gaspey, prominent Victorian man of letters, founded his reputation during the late Romantic period as a journalist and novelist, beginning a distinguished career as reporter, reviewer, editor, and newspaper proprietor. He also proved a fine historian: there is perhaps no better compact introduction to Victorian England and its empire than the introduction to Gaspey's multivolume *History of England; Continued from the Reign of George the Third* (1852). Even in fiction Gaspey was an historian at heart, and critics saw him as a follower of Walter Scott. As a reviewer for the *Literary Magnet* (1824) wrote, "It is the brilliant example, joined to his success, of the Author of the Scotch Novels, that has inspired 'minor hands' to attempt something worthy of the age in which they are written. Among these commendable authors, that of the Witch-Finder stands very conspicuously." The presence of history in Gaspey's fiction accounts for its great interest for current readers as well as his contemporaries; yet his misuse of history accounts for the tentative success of his fiction and his now all-but-extinguished reputation.

Little is known of Gaspey's early life. He was born in Hoxton on 31 March 1788, the son of William Gaspey, a navy lieutenant. In his teens Thomas published verse, and by his early twenties he had entered mainstream journalism, first as a contributor to Eugenius Roche's *Literary Recreations*, then as parliamentary reporter on Roche's primary concern, the *Morning Post*. Gaspey was too clever to follow a single line, however, and contributed all manner of occasional pieces, especially political satire, notably the "Elegy on the Marquis of Anglesey's Leg" long attributed to George Canning. Gaspey spent sixteen years at the *Post*—during which he married Ann Camp on 1 September 1811—then left in

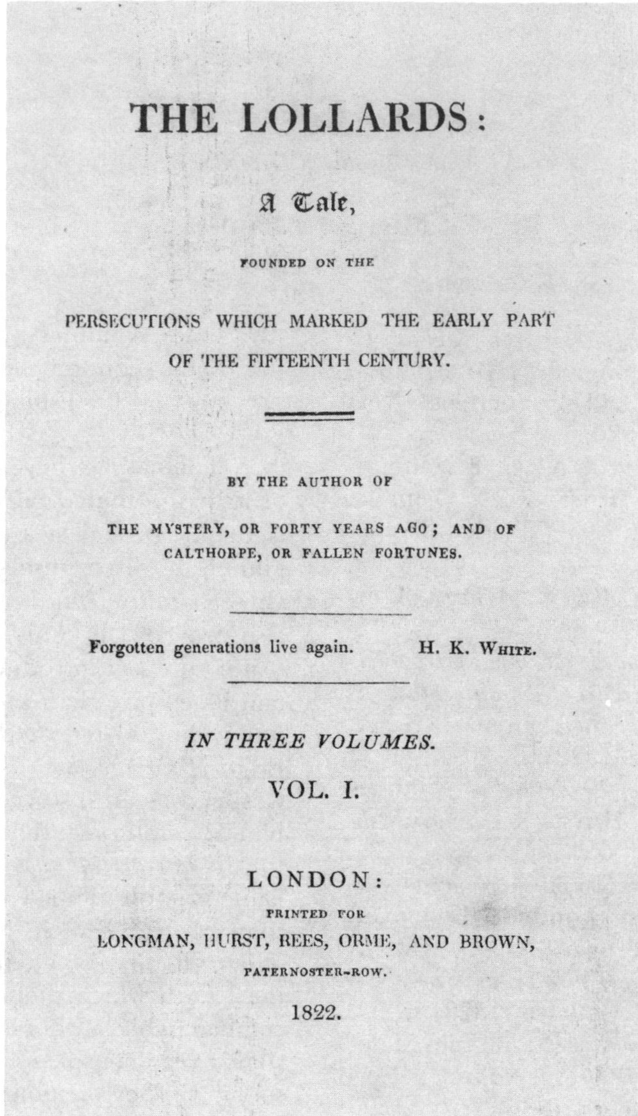
THE LOLLARDS:

A Tale,

FOUNDED ON THE

PERSECUTIONS WHICH MARKED THE EARLY PART
OF THE FIFTEENTH CENTURY.

BY THE AUTHOR OF

THE MYSTERY, OR FORTY YEARS AGO; AND OF
CALTHORPE, OR FALLEN FORTUNES.

Forgotten generations live again. H. K. WHITE.

IN THREE VOLUMES.

VOL. I.

LONDON:
PRINTED FOR
LONGMAN, HURST, REES, ORME, AND BROWN,
PATERNOSTER-ROW.
1822.

Title page for Gaspey's fictional account of the persecution of Sir John Oldcastle, Baron Cobham, and the religious movement he led

1824 to serve as subeditor for a government paper, the *Courier*.

During his last few years on the *Post* Gaspey wrote six novels, the first of which, *The Mystery* (1820), exhibits talents and weaknesses that foretell the rest of his career. As the *Literary Chronicle* (10 February 1821) noted, "the novel . . . was principally founded on facts." It includes an account of the anti-Catholic Gordon Riots of 1780, with a thrilling description of Newgate prison in flames, during which the protagonists are carried along in the mob. *The Mystery* influenced Charles Dickens, who reread it while writing *Barnaby Rudge* (1841), which revolves around these same riots; jests leveled at Ned Dennis, the executioner, in Dickens's novel echo those made about him in *The Mystery*. The terrifying mob scene shows Gaspey at his best, both as historian and storyteller. He found it difficult, however, to frame such vivid and accurate historical passages in a credible narrative.

Charles Harley, the novel's hero, and Amelia Henderson, daughter of his benefactor, Sir George Henderson, ask permission to marry. Although Charles had rescued him from the London mob, Sir George refuses. So disappointed, Charles proceeds to the African interior; Gaspey bases his adventure there on those of Major Daniel Houghton (1740?-1791). After Charles escapes Gambian captors, he is enslaved by Moors, who free him only after he saves their leader's life. Unlike Houghton, Charles returns to England, where he once again presses his suit and is once again denied. Sir George, the reader discovers, believes that Charles is his son by a cousin whom he had seduced; new evidence, however, proves him mistaken, and he finally permits the marriage. The trip to Africa is gratuitous; the "mystery" is solved not because Charles explored Gambia, but because he renewed his proposal.

This unworthy story surrounds much excellent writing in what is, by any account, a mediocre novel. Accustomed to writing for the papers, Gaspey confused editorial with dialogue. While the historical passages exude energy and color, interspersed drawing-room scenes are badly paced. Gaspey devoted the first few chapters to a single conversation about Britain's colonial policy. The speeches that characters make during this conversation add little to the love story, to Gaspey's account of the riots, or to Charles's African adventures. Colonial policy is a subject about which Gaspey had something to say, and what he said will interest students of the period, as it no doubt interested readers in 1820. Yet when he deferred plot in favor of lengthy editorial dressed up as dialogue, when he compromised the novel rather than his journalistic habits of mind, he showed just how much he had to learn before he could write "something worthy of the age."

A quick study, Gaspey improved dramatically in his next novel, *Calthorpe* (1821), which the *Literary Gazette* (6 January 1820 [i.e., 1821]) considered "very superior in interest to its predecessor." The *Anti-Jacobin Review* (March 1821), impressed with his "happy tact for the ludicrous," saw him as descended from Henry Fielding and Tobias Smollett. The novel, filled with what the *Literary Gazette* called "facetious humour," is, in fact, a dark murder mystery. Henry and Harriet Burleigh, children of a prominent London judge, are cast upon Fortune's waves when their father apparently commits suicide. As the *Anti-Jacobin Review* remarked, the plot of the novel is "ingenious," or at least complicated and fraught with coincidence; but "the attention of the reader, notwithstanding some little violations of probability, is kept upon the stretch throughout." By the end of the novel, the Burleighs recover their "fallen fortunes" and more, for they find worthy spouses.

The book will not satisfy modern readers for, as in *The Mystery*, dialogue is often antidialogue, the delivery of moral set pieces. But it shows considerable promise, and the *Anti-Jacobin Review* wondered whether Gaspey would consider writing romances: "We should be glad to witness the effort; for, without that violence of nationality by which our northern neighbours are generally distinguished, we confess that we feel a little jealous of the unremitting and enthusiastic praise which, more from fashion than from correctness of taste, or soundness of judgment, is so lavishly bestowed on *all* the productions of the Scotch novelist." Gaspey soon challenged Scott with *The Lollards* (1822), a full-blown historical romance, which proved his talent even as it risked his reputation, by then well established, not only in England, but in America and France.

First, however, he collaborated with Richard Dagley, a well-known illustrator, on a book called *Takings; or, The Life of a Collegian* (1821), to which Dagley contributed etchings and Gaspey a lengthy narrative poem. *Takings* is merely a jeu d'esprit, amusing rather than edifying, evidence that Gaspey found it difficult to put aside popular satire for mature projects. *The Lollards*, however, is a serious work, which satisfied what the *European Magazine* (July 1822) called "a prevailing rage for historical and antiquarian research." In the preface Gaspey describes himself, not as an author, but as a "compiler." He eschews footnotes as "too formal," yet lists "Maitland, Pennant, Malcolm, Douce, Henry, Beckmann, Baker, Monstrelet, Hollingshed, and Grose" as sources "for most of the historical facts and local representations." Gaspey adjudicated the competing interests of fiction, history, and editorial by giving history priority, a wise decision according to the *European Magazine*, which announced that Gaspey wrote *The Lollards*, "not only with the delightful interest and vivid colouring which attract and charm the general mass of readers, but with an accuracy and general fidelity, that may defy the most cynical of antiquaries."

The Lollards somewhat obliquely recounts the persecution of Sir John Oldcastle, Baron Cobham, a Lollard leader, during the suppression of the religious movement in Henry IV's reign (1399-1413). Lord Cobham escapes captivity early in the novel to refute the claim that he had recanted: "this intrepidity added to the admiration which his conduct had previously inspired," and "the resolution of the man was thought to prove the excellence of his words, and many who found it more easy to adopt than to form an opinion, took it for granted, that because Cobham was resolute he was right." Gaspey, in this respect a writer for his time, portrays Cobham as a Protestant hero.

While Cobham hides from the archbishop of Canterbury, his two children, Edward and Alice, stay with a Lollard called Whittington, brother to the London mayor, and in his company read John Wycliffe's translation of the Bible, the first English Bible, from which Gaspey, painstakingly accurate, quotes in the original language. They meet Jan Huss, whom they accompany to Bohemia, and with whom, in Prague, they meet Hoffmann, a printer half a century ahead of history, who has reproduced the Wycliffite Gospels. Edward takes custody of them, and smuggles Europe's first printed books into England. When Huss is tried and executed for his heresies, Alice is essentially on her own, is lost and found by various protectors, passes safely through France by dressing as a man, and returns to England, just before the archbishop captures and executes her father. Edward is arrested for smuggling the Gospels. The archbishop's spies kill the friend who attempts to find Hoffmann for Edward's defense, and Edward is blamed for the murder. The villain, Roderick Redhand, confesses to murdering Octavius when he meant to kill Edward and also admits to having lost the printed book, the only material evidence against Edward, who is subsequently freed.

Gaspey was no match for Scott; yet *The Lollards* is a respectable attempt to tell English history in the form of romance, and reviewers appreciated both the effort and the effect. The *Literary Chronicle* (20-27 April 1822) praised Gaspey: "In the class of those who have been most successful as historical novelists, we would rank the author of 'The Lollards.'" The *European Magazine* concurred, emphasizing the magnitude of Gaspey's achievement, for *The Lollards* "is not a mere commentary upon the human passions, and a nicely constructed series of incidents and story," but rather it "aspires to the loftier task of identifying remote and important matters of history with the occurances of private life, and the customs and habits of private society."

The Lollards is, in fact, a readable novel, filled with interesting historical information; but it is, perhaps, overly historical: the first chapter sounds more like a textbook than fiction, and textbooklike passages obtrude throughout the story. Many of those who wrote historical fiction in the 1820s, for instance Jane and Anna Maria Porter, often failed to flour their fancy with enough history; in *The Lollards* Gaspey found it difficult to leaven history with sufficient fancy, though his story about the origins of printing is certainly imaginative.

Gaspey's next novel, *Other Times, or, the Monks of Leadenhall* (1823), which takes place during Henry VIII's reign (1509-1547) repeats the antiquarian method of its predecessor. Most modern readers, however, will find its remarkably fanciful plot difficult to bear. Edmund Sherborne, the hero, returns to England from Spain with two friends, Ferdinand and Mariana, who (unknown to Edmund) are children of Edmund's guardian, Lord Thomas Erpingham, from a Spanish marriage. Ferdinand, who does not know about the marriage and is angry at his father's apparent desertion, becomes Erpingham's secretary and attempts to kill him. Erpingham can explain his conduct, and after enjoying tension that nearly leads to parricide, the reader enjoys equally the subsequent reconciliation.

In the meantime Edmund becomes a novice among the monks of Leadenhall, and Mariana joins the neighboring convent. After Edmund discovers that the monastery is the scene of debauchery arranged between the monks and their holy sisters, the abbot attempts to murder Edmund and to seduce Mariana, with support from her prioress. Edmund escapes through a network of underground tunnels and chambers connecting the monastery and the priory. Mariana, liberated in a peasant uprising, finds refuge with none other than William and Margaret Roper, the son-in-law and daughter of Sir Thomas More.

The *New Monthly Magazine* (1 August 1822) reacted harshly, along lines a modern reader can understand: "We cannot help advising the author of 'Other Times' to abstain in future from the representation of such odious excesses as disgraced the iniquitous monks of Leadenhall. The world is so far advanced as to lose its relish for descriptions of this kind, however well executed." But most reviews applauded the novel. The *London Literary Gazette* (5 April 1823) saw its "chief merit" in the way it depicts "the accurate and curious patterns of byegone manners and customs," and noted the "considerable talent and skill displayed in the leading contrivances of the fable itself." It is exactly the "leading contrivances" that detract from the novel, yet the *Gentleman's Magazine* (July 1823) also cast an appreciative vote: "This romance exhibits, in a well-told tale, some excellent sketches of the manners and customs of our ancestors." One can only wonder whether the re-

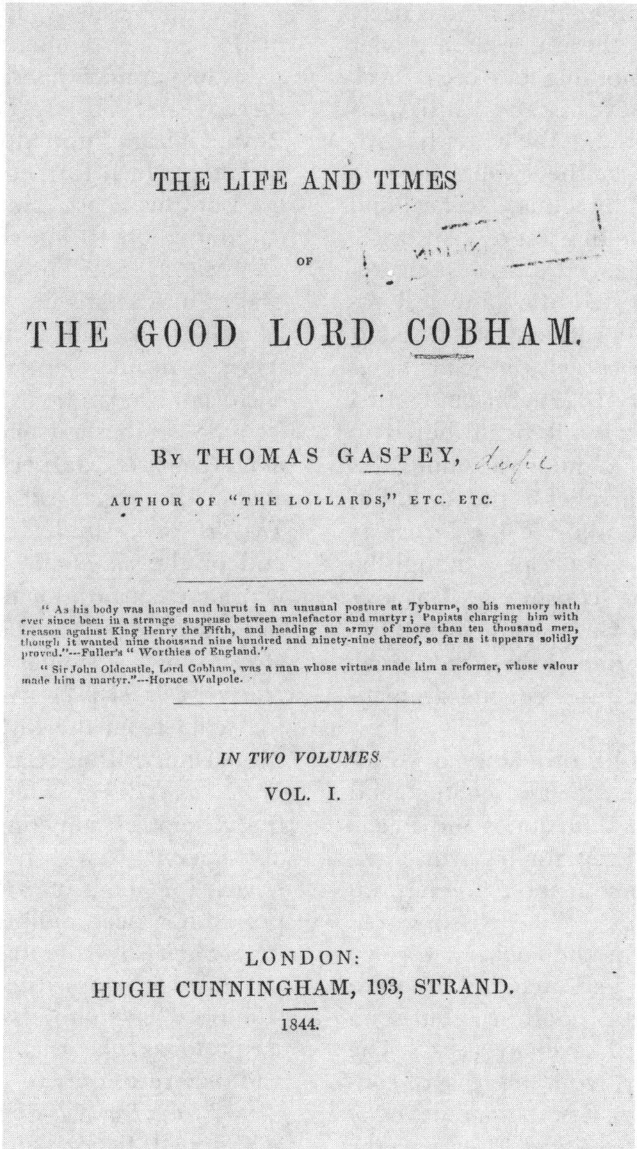

THE LIFE AND TIMES

OF

THE GOOD LORD COBHAM.

BY THOMAS GASPEY,

AUTHOR OF "THE LOLLARDS," ETC. ETC.

" As his body was hanged and burnt in an unusual posture at Tyburne, so his memory hath ever since been in a strange suspense between malefactor and martyr; Papists charging him with treason against King Henry the Fifth, and heading an army of more than ten thousand men, though it wanted nine thousand nine hundred and ninety-nine thereof, so far as it appears solidly proved."---Fuller's " Worthies of England."

" Sir John Oldcastle, Lord Cobham, was a man whose virtues made him a reformer, whose valour made him a martyr."---Horace Walpole.

IN TWO VOLUMES.

VOL. I.

LONDON:
HUGH CUNNINGHAM, 193, STRAND.
1844.

Title page for Gaspey's biography of the Lollard leader whose struggles for religious freedom were the subject of Gaspey's 1822 novel

viewer had read the novel, and of which particular manners and customs he approved.

Encouraged by such praise, Gaspey continued his string of historical romances with *The Witch-Finder* (1824). The preface announces his intention "to exhibit in action the ideas once general on the subject of witchcraft, and to depict the state to which the drama was reduced when monarchy was no more." Gaspey subordinates the "action," the storial aspects of the romance, to "ideas" and their historical context. As usual, he floods the story with context: "The kindness of Antiquarian friends has placed in his hands some of the fruits of their more extended researches, and facts connected with the drama, and with the politics of the day, are given, which, he believes have never appeared in print."

Yet historical emphasis, as the *Ladies' Monthly Museum* (July 1824) saw it, limited the book's appeal: "The story of the 'Witch-Finder' is sufficiently interesting; but it is chiefly valuable for the delineations which it affords of the state of society and manners, and of the usages and superstitions, which prevailed in England in the former part of the seventeenth century." The *Literary Gazette* (5 July 1824) liked the novel but also doubted that Gaspey's antiquarian technique would satisfy typical readers of romance, suggesting that Gaspey "has brought together a variety of singular facts. Some of these the mere reader of romance, who covets nothing but break-neck adventures and hair-breadth escapes, will, perhaps, think might be spared; but the writer has evidently flattered himself that they would give an air of *vraisemblance* to his imaginary scenes, and thus heighten generally the interest of his work."

Gaspey probably realized, after such reviews, that he had exhausted the historical romance and might turn profitably to another genre. He did not write *Richmond, or Scenes in the Life of a Bow Street Runner* (1827), England's first detective novel, though it is often attributed to him. His widow did not mention it among his works when she applied for relief to the Royal Literary Fund, nor did the author of the *Dictionary of National Biography* entry on Gaspey, though he wrote the article after consulting Gaspey's younger son, William. But Gaspey's next venture, *The History of George Godfrey* (1828), did break from his previous fictional practice, and dramatically.

George Godfrey tells his own story, a worldwide picaresque satire on the law, politics, and manners. A cross between Tom Jones and Bertie Wooster, Godfrey is too clever for his own good, involved with too many women, and extremely unlucky until the novel ends. While chasing robbers, George is arrested for the robbery, thrown into Newgate, and nearly executed. As the hero admits, "I have a remarkably good head but soon find that it is not likely to save my neck." The book is uproariously funny, from the table of contents forward. Even though it is the one novel by Gaspey to receive recent critical attention (by Keith Hollingsworth in 1963), it is fair to call it neglected and to wish that it had a late-twentieth-century champion.

In 1828, and for several years following, Gaspey found himself too busy to write fiction. Immediately upon finishing *George Godfrey* he was appointed editor of the *Sunday Times* by its new owner, his latest publisher, Henry Colburn. James Grant reported that under Gaspey's control, the *Sunday Times* "steered a somewhat middle course between the Tories and Liberals," and "rarely expressed an opinion on any great subject of political influence one way or other," but that "under [Gaspey's] management [it] was as readable a paper as one could have wished." In time Gaspey became part proprietor of the paper, but his connection with it ceased by 1835, after which he edited the *Evening Chronicle*.

Gaspey's newspaper work and novels had made him a prominent person of letters. Having paid his annual subscription for the required three years, Gaspey became a member of the Royal Literary Fund in 1827, and thus began an association which formed a major part of his public life until his death. He was elected to the general committee on 10 March 1830, and to the council on 9 March 1836. His prominence in the Royal Literary Fund seems out of keeping with his stature as an author, and he must have worked hard to merit a position among the greatest writers of Victorian England.

So established and once editor of the *Evening Chronicle*, Gaspey found the time to write again. He began with another historical novel, *The Self-Condemned* (1836), about Ireland at the end of the sixteenth century. He followed that with short, inspirational stories and verse in *"Many-coloured Life:" or, Tales of Woe and Touches of Mirth* (1842), and a similar work titled *The Dream of Human Life* (1852). When Ann Gaspey applied for relief from the Royal Literary Fund in 1875, she claimed that Gaspey wrote a play called *Freaks and Follies*, which "played a long time at the Adelphi," sometime around 1846. He may also have written a short novel called *Ivan, or the Immured* ("about 1854"), which his widow reported had been published in one duodecimo volume. She also wrote that she had no copy, and apparently no copy survives today. Someone wrote "doubtful" next to the estimated dates, but the script looks like that of the whole application, and may refer only to the dates.

After *The Self-Condemned* Gaspey essentially abandoned fiction for history. He collaborated with G. M. Bussey on *A Pictorial History of France and of the French People* (1843), and returned to a familiar subject in *The Life and Times of the Good Lord Cobham* (1844). As Gaspey wrote in his preface, he hoped to amplify and correct the historical record of Cobham's life and times; yet the book is partly didactic, as events in Cobham's life "teach a lesson which may be studied with advantage by those who wish for the truth, and who feel that religion is little served by enlisting the passions, prejudices, and interests of men, mixed up with the active business of life, in a theological contest." As it illustrates problems of the day, history becomes news.

The History of Smithfield (1852) expanded glancing references in several of Gaspey's novels, and was followed by the historical works for which Gaspey deserves the greatest respect: he contributed a volume on Wellington's political career to W. F. Williams's *Life and Times of the Late Duke of Wellington* (1853), and produced a massive *History of England; Continued from the Reign of George the Third* (1852), which he intended as a sequel to David Hume's *History of Great Britain* (1754-1762). Preoccupied with such serious work, Gaspey nonetheless continued to contribute pieces to periodicals throughout his life. For instance, during Dickens's editorship, he contributed five essays to *Bentley's Miscellany* (June 1837 - July 1838); in 1844 he contributed to a set of humorous pamphlets called *Young England's Little Library*; and as late as 1867 to 1870, he wrote "Shelah, an Irish Story" in monthly parts for the *Churchman's Family Magazine*.

By the time Gaspey died on 8 December 1871, he had accomplished a great deal as novelist, historian, newspaperman, and philanthropist. We read little of his work today, though *The Lollards, George Godfrey*, the lives of Cobham and Wellington, and *The History of England* certainly reward their readers. Perhaps our lack of interest is understandable; when he died, Gaspey was better known as having written than by his writings. In 1875 John Stewart, just elevated to the Privy Council, wrote to support Ann Gaspey's application to the Royal Literary Fund that Gaspey "was well known to me during the greater part of my long life as an able honourable & respectable man . . . one of his novels called 'the Lollards' had a large sale & I believe was a work of merit." It is difficult to know whether this last compliment was matter of conviction or of hearsay.

References:

E. F. Bleiler, Introduction to *Richmond: Scenes in the Life of a Bow Street Runner Drawn Up from his Private Memoranda*, by T. S. Surr (New York: Dover, 1976), pp. ix-x;

John Butt and Kathleen Tillotson, *Dickens at Work* (London: Methuen, 1957), pp. 77-78;

Nigel Cross, *The Royal Literary Fund 1790-1918* (London: World Microfilms Publications, 1984), reels 77, 125-126;

James Grant, *The Great Metropolis*, second edition (London: Saunders & Otley, 1837), pp. 46-48, 143-145;

Keith Hollingsworth, *The Newgate Novel 1830-1847* (Detroit: Wayne State University Press, 1963), pp. 31-32, 55-60;

Madeline House and Graham Storey, eds., *The Letters of Charles Dickens*, volume 1 (Oxford: Clarendon, 1965), pp. 363 and 639;

The Royal Literary Fund: Address for the Anniversary; Members of the Corporation; Donors not Qualified as Members; Annual Reports (London: John James Metcalfe for the Royal Literary Fund, 1852);

Kathleen Tillotson, ed., *The Letters of Charles Dickens*, volume 4 (Oxford: Clarendon Press, 1977), p. 9.

Catherine Gore

(1800 - 29 January 1861)

Louis J. Parascandola
Long Island University—Brooklyn Center

BOOKS: *Theresa Marchmont, or the Maid of Honour: a Tale* (London: J. Andrews, 1824);

The Bond, a Dramatic Poem (London: Murray, 1824);

The Lettre de Cachet: a Tale; The Reign of Terror: a Tale (London: J. Andrews, 1827);

Hungarian Tales (3 volumes, London: Saunders & Otley, 1829; 2 volumes, New York: Harper, 1829);

Romances of Real Life (3 volumes, London: H. Colburn, 1829; 2 volumes, New York: Harper, 1829);

Women as They Are, or Manners of the Day, 3 volumes (London: H. Colburn & R. Bentley, 1830);

The Historical Traveller: Comprising Narratives Connected with the Most Curious Epochs of European History, and with the Phenomena of European Countries, 2 volumes (London: H. Colburn & R. Bentley, 1831);

Pin Money: a Novel (3 volumes, London: H. Colburn & R. Bentley, 1831; 1 volume, Philadelphia: E. L. Carey & A. Hart / Baltimore: Carey, Hart, 1834);

The Tuileries: a Tale (3 volumes, London: H. Colburn & R. Bentley, 1831; 2 volumes, New York: J. & J. Harper, 1831); republished as *The Soldier of Lyons: a Tale of the Tuileries*, 1 volume (London: R. Bentley, 1841);

Mothers and Daughters: a Tale of the Year 1830 (3 volumes, London: H. Colburn & R. Bentley, 1831; 2 volumes, Philadelphia: E. L. Carey & A. Hart, 1834);

The Opera: a Novel, 3 volumes (London: H. Colburn & R. Bentley, 1832);

The Fair of May Fair, 3 volumes (London: H. Colburn & R. Bentley, 1832); republished as *The Miseries of Marriage; or the Fair of May Fair*, 1 volume (Philadelphia: E. L. Carey & A. Hart / Boston: Allen & Ticknor, 1834);

The Sketch Book of Fashion (3 volumes, London: R. Bentley, 1833; 2 volumes, New York: Harper, 1833);

Polish Tales, 3 volumes (London: Saunders & Otley, 1833);

The Hamiltons, or the New Era, 3 volumes (London: Saunders & Otley, 1834);

King O'Neil; or, The Irish Brigade (London: Chapman & Hall, 1835);

The Diary of a Désennuyée (London: H. Colburn, 1836; Philadelphia: E. L. Carey & A. Hart, 1836; New York: Harper, 1836);

Mrs. Armytage, or Female Domination (3 volumes, London: H. Colburn, 1836; 2 volumes, Philadelphia: Carey, Lea & Blanchard, 1836);

Memoirs of a Peeress, or the Days of Fox (3 volumes, London: H. Colburn, 1837; 2 volumes, Philadelphia: E. L. Carey & A. Hart, 1837; revised edition, London: Knight & Son, 1859);

Stokeshill Place, or the Man of Business, 3 volumes (London: H. Colburn, 1837);

The Maid of Croissey; or Theresa's Vow (London: Chapman & Hall, 1838);

The Heir of Selwood, or Three Epochs of a Life (3 volumes, London: R. Colburn, 1838; 1 volume, Philadelphia: E. L. Carey & A. Hart, 1838);

The Rose Fancier's Manual (London: H. Colburn, 1838);

Mary Raymond and Other Tales (3 volumes, London: H. Colburn, 1838; 1 volume, Philadelphia: Lea & Blanchard, 1838);

The Woman of the World: a Novel (3 volumes, London: H. Colburn, 1838; 1 volume, Philadelphia, 1838);

The Cabinet Minister (3 volumes, London: R. Bentley, 1839; 2 volumes, New York: Harper, 1839; Philadelphia: E. L. Carey & A. Hart, 1839);

The Courtier of the Days of Charles II with Other Tales (3 volumes, London: H. Colburn, 1839; 2 volumes, New York: Harper, 1839);

Dacre of the South, or the Olden Time: a Drama (London: R. Bentley, 1840);

The Dowager, or the New School for Scandal (3 volumes, London: R. Bentley, 1840; 1 volume, Philadelphia: Lea & Blanchard, 1841);

Portrait from the New Monthly Magazine *(March 1837); courtesy of the Special Collections Department, Duke University Library)*

Preferment, or My Uncle the Earl (3 volumes, London: H. Colburn, 1840; 2 volumes, New York: Harper, 1840);

Greville, or a Season in Paris (3 volumes, London: H. Colburn, 1841; 2 volumes, Philadelphia: Lea & Blanchard, 1841);

Cecil: or the Adventures of a Coxcomb: a Novel (3 volumes, London: R. Bentley, 1841; 1 volume, Philadelphia: Lea & Blanchard, 1841);

Cecil: a Peer (3 volumes, London: T. & W. Boone, 1841; 1 volume, Philadelphia: Lea, 1842); republished as *Ormington: or Cecil: a Peer*, 3 volumes (London, 1842);

Paris in 1841 (London: Longman, Brown, Green & Longmans, 1842; Philadelphia: Lea & Blanchard, 1842);

The Man of Fortune and Other Tales (3 volumes, London: H. Colburn, 1842; 1 volume, Philadelphia: Lea & Blanchard, 1842);

The Ambassador's Wife, 3 volumes (London: R. Bentley, 1842);

The Money-Lender, 3 volumes (London: H. Colburn, 1843);

Modern Chivalry, or a New Orlando Furioso, 2 volumes, by Gore, possibly with W. Harrison Ainsworth, 2 volumes (London: John Mortimer, 1843);

The Banker's Wife, or Court and City: a Novel (3 volumes, London: Henry Colburn, 1843; 1 volume, New York: Harper, 1843);

Agathonia: a Romance (London: Edward Moxon, 1844);

The Birthright and Other Tales (3 volumes, London: H. Colburn, 1844);

Quid Pro Quo; or, The Day of the Dupes (London: Published at the National Acting Drama Office, 1844);

The Popular Member: The Wheel of Fortune, etc., 3 volumes (London: R. Bentley, 1844);

Self (3 volumes, London: H. Colburn, 1845; 1 volume, New York: Harper, 1845);

The Story of a Royal Favourite (3 volumes, London:

H. Colburn, 1845; 1 volume, New York: Harper, 1846);

The Snow Storm: a Christmas Story (London & Paris: Fisher, Son & Co., 1845; Boston: Charles H. Peirce, 1848);

Peers and Parvenus (3 volumes, London: H. Colburn, 1846; 1 volume, New York: Harper, 1846);

New Year's Day (London: Fisher, Son & Co., 1846; Boston: Strong & Brodhead, 1846); republished as *The Lost Son: a Winter's Tale* (London: Dean & Son, 1854);

Men of Capital (3 volumes, London: H. Colburn, 1846; 1 volume, New York: W. F. Burgess, 1849);

The Débutante: or the London Season, 3 volumes (London: R. Bentley, 1846);

Sketches of English Character (2 volumes, London: R. Bentley, 1846; revised, 1 volume, 1852);

Castles in the Air: a Novel (3 volumes, London: R. Bentley, 1847; 1 volume, New York: Long, 1848);

Temptation and Atonement, and Other Tales, 3 volumes (London: H. Colburn, 1847);

The Inundation, or Parson and Peace: a Christmas Story (London: Fisher, Son & Co., 1847);

The Diamond and the Pearl: a Novel (3 volumes, London: H. Colburn, 1849; 1 volume, New York: H. Long & Brother, 1849);

Adventures in Borneo: a Tale of Shipwreck (London: H. Colburn, 1849);

The Dean's Daughter, or the Days We Live In (3 volumes, London: Hurst & Blackett, 1853; 1 volume, New York: D. Appleton, 1853);

Progress and Prejudice, 3 volumes (London: Hurst & Blackett, 1854);

Transmutation, or the Lord and the Lout (London: Chapman & Hall, 1854); republished as *The Lord and the Lout* (London: Knight & Son, 1860);

Mammon, or the Hardships of an Heiress, 3 volumes (London: Hurst & Blackett, 1855);

A Life's Lessons, 3 volumes (London: Hurst & Blackett, 1856);

The Two Aristocracies: a Novel, 3 volumes (London: Hurst & Blackett, 1857);

Heckington: a Novel, 3 volumes (London: Hurst & Blackett, 1858).

PLAY PRODUCTIONS: *The School for Coquettes*, London, Theatre Royal, Haymarket, 14 July 1831;

Lords and Commons, London, Theatre Royal, Drury Lane, 20 December 1831;

The Queen's Champion, London, Theatre Royal, Haymarket, 10 September 1834;

Modern Honour; or, the Sharper of High Life, London, Theatre Royal, Covent Garden, 3 December 1834;

The King's Seal, by Gore and James Kenney, London, Theatre Royal, Drury Lane, 10 January 1835;

The Maid of Croissey; or, Theresa's Vow, London, Theatre Royal, Haymarket, 10 July 1835;

King O'Neil; or, the Irish Brigade, London, Theatre Royal, Covent Garden, 9 December 1835;

Don John of Austria, adapted from Casimir Delavigne's *Don Juan d' Austriche*, London, Theatre Royal, Covent Garden, 16 April 1836;

A Tale of a Tub, London, Theatre Royal, Haymarket, 15 July 1837;

A Good Night's Rest; or, Two in the Morning, London, Strand Theatre, 19 August 1839;

Quid Pro Quo; or, the Day of Dupes, London, Theatre Royal, Haymarket, 18 June 1844.

OTHER: Joseph Xavier Bonaparte de Saintine, *Picciola, or, Captivity Captive*, 2 volumes, edited and translated by Gore (London: H. Colburn, 1837);

Charles de Bernard, *The Lover and the Husband*, edited by Gore (3 volumes, London: R. Bentley, 1841; 1 volume, Philadelphia: Lea & Blanchard, 1842);

Fascination and Other Tales, 3 volumes, edited by Gore (London: H. Colburn, 1842);

Andreas Nicolai de Saint-Aubain, *Modern French Life*, 3 volumes, edited by Gore (London, 1842);

T. C. Heiberg, *The Queen of Denmark: an Historical Novel*, edited by Gore (3 volumes, London: H. Colburn, 1846; 1 volume, New York: Harper, 1846).

A character in Catherine Gore's *Women as They Are* (1830) says, "We have perhaps had more than enough of fashionable novels, but as the amber which serves to preserve the ephemeral modes and caprices of the passing day, they have their value." If this statement is true, then Gore's work is a veritable museum, preserving life as it existed in fashionable London during the regency and reign of George IV (1811-1830). In an age of prolific writers, her oeuvre (more than sixty volumes of fiction, drama, and verse as well as

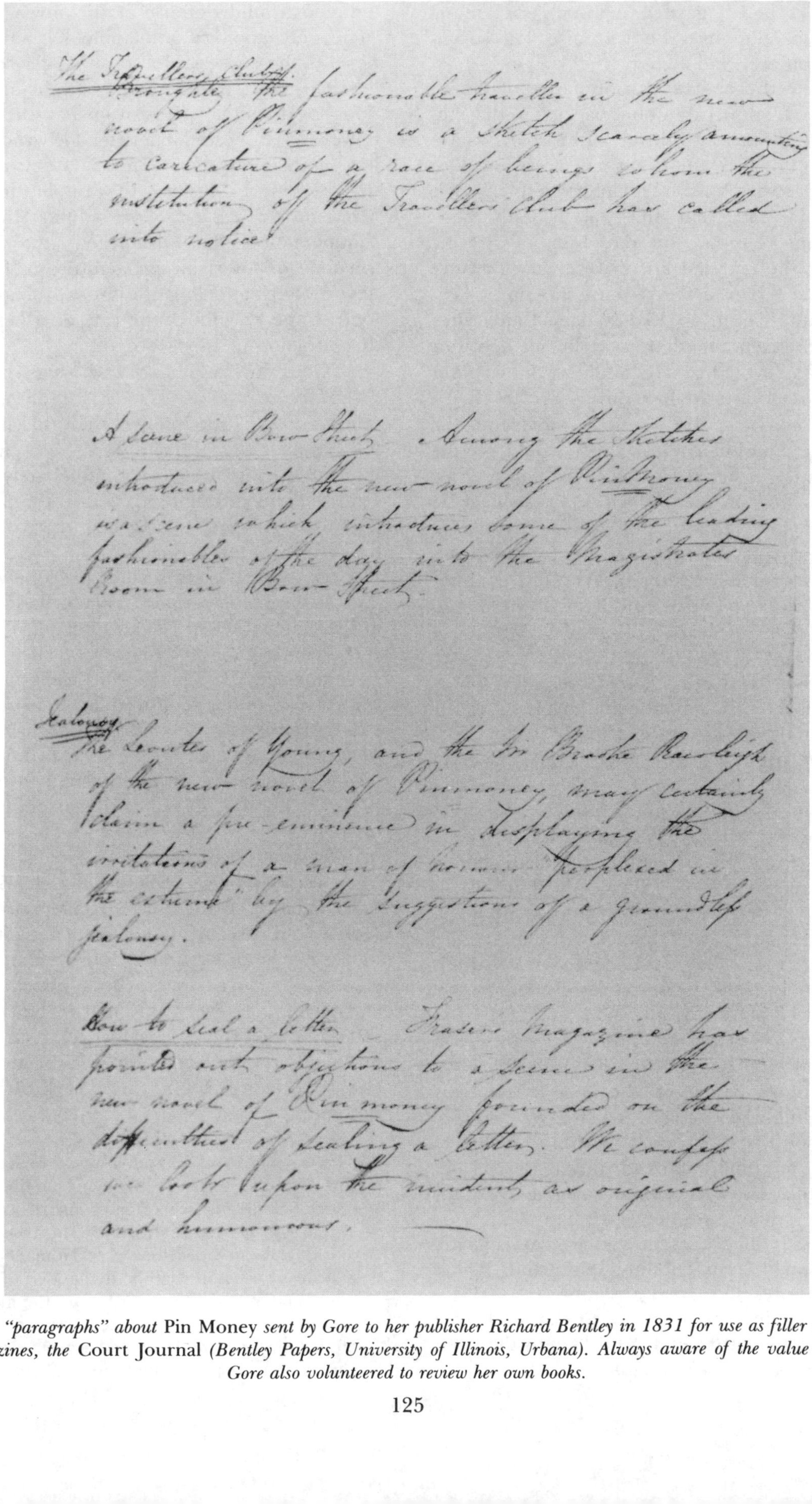

The Travellers Club. Brougnate the fashionable traveller in the new novel of Pinmoney is a sketch scarcely amounting to caricature of a race of beings whom the institution of the Travellers Club has called into notice.

A Scene in Bow Street. Among the sketches introduced into the new novel of Pinmoney was scene which introduces some of the leading fashionables of the day into the Magistrates Room in Bow Street.

Jealousy. The Leontes of Young, and the Mr Brooke Rawleigh of the new novel of Pinmoney, may certainly claim a pre-eminence in displaying the irritations of a man of honour "perplexed in the extreme" by the suggestions of a groundless jealousy.

How to Seal a Letter. Frasers Magazine has pointed out objections to a scene in the new novel of Pin money founded on the difficulties of sealing a letter. We confess we look upon the incident as original and humorous.

Promotional "paragraphs" about Pin Money *sent by Gore to her publisher Richard Bentley in 1831 for use as filler in one of his firm's magazines, the* Court Journal *(Bentley Papers, University of Illinois, Urbana). Always aware of the value of publicity, Gore also volunteered to review her own books.*

travel books and a garden manual) was among the most prodigious. She was also an accomplished composer and etcher.

Despite the enormous popularity of Gore's novels, little is known about her background. Catherine Grace Frances Moody is often said to have been born in 1799 in the small town of East Retford, Nottinghamshire. Papers left by her, however, indicate that she was actually born in 1800 in London, the daughter of a wine merchant. She married an officer, Charles Gore (whether he achieved the rank of captain or lieutenant is uncertain), on 15 February 1823. They had ten children together, and by all accounts Gore was as devoted to her family as the virtuous female protagonists in her novels are to theirs. After her marriage she began to move into the fashionable London circles which would be the subject matter of her most successful novels.

Gore's first novel, *Theresa Marchmont, or the Maid of Honour* (1824), is a historical romance which she wrote in a week. She followed this novel with a dramatic poem, *The Bond* (1824), additional historical romances, and a collection of stories, *Hungarian Tales* (1829). *Women as They Are, or Manners of the Day* (1830), the first of Gore's fashionable novels, was praised by George IV, but it is merely a tedious imitation of novels by Fanny Burney and Jane Austen.

In the preface to *Pin Money* (1831), a more successful work than *Women as They Are*, Gore says that she is attempting "to transfer the familiar narrative of Miss Austen to a higher sphere of society." Frederica Lauceston, the main character, marries Sir Brooke Rawleigh, but she is almost ruined by extravagant expenses and eventually surrenders her financial independence to her husband. The message seems apparent: women should concentrate on family affairs and leave financial matters to the men.

Mothers and Daughters: a Tale of the Year 1830 (1831) shows the dangers of manipulative women. Yearning to belong to the aristocracy, Lady Maria Willingham marries not for love but to raise her social status. Much of the novel has to do with her machinations to advance her social ambitions, while Mary, a woman who marries for love, is the only one who ends up happy.

In 1832 the Gores moved to Paris, where they remained until about 1840 and where Mrs. Gore presided over a salon in the Place Vendôme. Undoubtedly, she was exhausted from her prodigious output in 1831-1832. In the preface to *The Sketch Book of Fashion* (1833) she attempted a mild defense of the silver-fork novel: "The only apology admissible for a fashionable novel is the successful exposure of vices and follies daily and hourly generated by the corruptions of society." Her disgust with the form, however, is indicated in a letter she wrote to the editor of the *Athenaeum*, Charles Wentworth Dilke, urging him to ignore the publication of *The Sketch Book of Fashion*. Gore admits "that general condemnation has rendered me somewhat ashamed of my sickly progeniture of fashionable novels." Such a feeling of disgust probably contributed to the decline in the rate at which she produced fiction in 1834-1835.

One novel published during these years, *The Hamiltons, or the New Era* (1834), is an attempt at a weightier subject than that in the fashionable novels. *The Hamiltons* reflects the popular interest during the years immediately after the First Reform Bill of 1832, and in the politics that led to its passage. Gore's bias toward the Whig (or reform) interest is clear.

Gore also wrote several plays between 1831 and 1835. *The School for Coquettes* had a long run at the Haymarket in 1831. Other plays of this period include *Lords and Commons* (which opened in December 1831), *The Queen's Champion* and *Modern Honour* (both produced in 1834), and three plays premiering in 1835: *The King's Seal, The Maid of Croissey*, and *King O'Neil*. Though they never attained the popularity of her novels, the plays are another indicator of her enormous productivity.

In another of Gore's fashionable novels, *The Diary of a Désennuyée* (1836), Lady Harriet Delaval falls in love with the Byronic Lord Eustace Hartston, a wealthy man who speaks for the poor in the House of Commons. His seeming indifference to her turns out to be a silent admiration and love. They eventually marry, but not before she has a nightmare in which Hartston chastises her (and by extension the wealthy members of Gore's audience) for having a lack of interest in the poor:

> The leavings of your lapdog would be dainties to sustain the strength of this dying family! Do the cries of their anguish offend your delicate ears? *They* are tormented to afford you the means of languishing in an opera-box! . . . Woman! woman! —A heavy account shall be demanded of you for this thing! You shall answer before the most high God for the sufferings of these nursing mothers,— of these young children; and repay in sackcloth and ashes your profligate levity!

First editions of three of Gore's novels: A Life's Lessons *(1856);* Greville, or a Season in Paris *(1841); and* The Dean's Daughter, *1853).*

Upon awakening, Lady Harriet takes steps to aid the poor.

Gore also wrote a nonfashionable novel, *Mrs. Armytage, or Female Domination*, in 1836. A dominating woman, like Lady Maria Willingham, Mrs. Armytage prevents her son from getting his proper inheritance and causes her daughter Sophy's death (of a broken heart) by blocking her marriage. Though some readers may think Mrs. Armytage a great woman because of her forcefulness, Gore presents such a skill as being unnatural in a woman. As one character in the novel says, "What business has a woman with *great* qualities?" This antiwoman tone is also apparent in the preface, where it is stated: "I believe a woman of first-rate faculties would constitute only a third-rate man." "Good women" such as Sophy are, as Bonnie Anderson says, "perfectly happy to accept the woman's world of family, home and marriage to a wise and good man" while "bad women are those who do not recognize the proper limits of women's estate: marriage, home, and family."

Gore's best-known novel, *Cecil: or the Adventures of a Coxcomb* (1841), was published, like much of her work, anonymously. Many thought the novel was written by a man because of its use of classical languages and its details on London clubs (information provided by Gore's friend William Beckford). The book was an immediate sensation in social circles although interest in the fashionable novel was waning. Gore wrote her publisher Richard Bentley, saying that *Cecil* "has enormous success *in society* but I know from experience that this does not make a sale." Part of its appeal may have been its recollection of the bygone era of Regency London. Cecil remarks, "Ten years later, and I should have been born *too* late for my vocation."

Cecil is Gore's only dandy hero. Even his surname "Danby" hints at what he is. Cecil (or "Cis" as he is often called) knows he is a dandy and is proud of it, explaining "that the leading trait of my character had its origin in the first glimpse I caught of myself, at six months old, in the swing-glass of my mother's dressing room. I looked and became a coxcomb for life!" Some dozen variations of the word *coxcomb* are used throughout the novel (including "cockade," "cockadehood," and "coxcombry"). Fittingly, the last word in the novel is "Coxcomb."

Catherine Gore

Cecil, a second son, is scorned by Lord Ormington, who, Cecil only discovers at his mother's deathbed, is not his real father. Young Cecil enters London society, breaks several women's hearts, fights at Waterloo, travels on the Continent with Byron as a companion, finally gains the family fortune, and ends up in the court of George IV. It is appropriate that this male protagonist, as with so many of Gore's female characters, takes comfort at the end in his family. A less successful sequel, *Cecil: a Peer* (1841), soon followed.

Also in 1841, under the pseudonym Albany Poyntz, Gore began publication of a series of articles in *Bentley's Miscellany*. Many of these articles satirize the aristocracy and show sympathy for the poor, particularly in a piece published in the February 1841 issue, "The Children of the Mobility, Versus the Children of the Nobility."

Gore's husband died in 1846, while they were living in Belgium. Four years later she inherited a substantial sum from a relative. Gore showed a shrewd sense of finance in her novels. Norman Russell, in fact, feels that of all nineteenth-century novelists, Gore "seems to be nearest the pulse of society in its real reactions to money and its manifold powers." Despite this knowledge of finance, however, Gore lost most of her money in a bank scandal in 1855. Ironically, *The Banker's Wife, or Court and City* (1843) is about a banker who defrauds his client. Even more ironically, Gore dedicated the book to Sir John Dean Paul, the banker who would later defraud her.

In addition to these financial woes, Gore was troubled by failing eyesight in her final years. She wrote her last novel, *Heckington*, in 1858 and died on 29 January 1861 in Lyndhurst, Hampshire. She was much eulogized in the London newspapers.

Gore's books have many flaws. She wrote more often than she should have, frequently used flabby sentence structures, was devoted to an affected vocabulary and French words (for which she was pilloried by William Makepeace Thackeray in "Lords and Liveries," 1847), showed little profundity of thought, and lacked a sense of characterization. As early as 1831 she admitted, "I was a reader of rubbish long before I became a writer of it." One sentence from *Mothers and Daughters* may serve as an example of Gore's convoluted style (as well as that of many fashionable novelists):

> On returning from Lady Lorimer's party, however, she had somewhat prematurely dismissed her maid—whose care in disposing the satin folds within the wardrobe, and the necklace in the trinket-box, had never before appeared so superfluous—in order that she might moisten her *papillotes* with a few tears while the officious attendant, who had already ascertained from the footman the care with which Sir William Wyndham had handed her young lady to the carriage, and who, with waiting-maid sagacity, had immediately discovered her discomposure, retreated to her own aerial dormitory, under the satisfactory conviction that Miss Willingham had returned home with a proposal still echoing in her ears.

Despite these weaknesses Gore was the most popular of the fashionable novelists. Her novels had an enormous appeal for her audience, especially, as Bonnie Anderson notes, middle-class women: "Female readers no doubt enjoyed the topicality of her references; the novels were also read as accurate guides to social behavior." Though she was no feminist, feeling women should derive their comfort from marriage and family, she wrote, as she stated in the preface to *Pin Money*, novels "of the simplest kind addressed by a woman to readers of her own sex." As Vineta Colby points out, Gore's writing reflected "a female, not a feminine, spirit," which was typical of the times. And although she sometimes wrote tortured sentences, she could also be witty, as in the following skillful use of zeugma from *The Diary of a Désennuyée*: "I entered . . . that long and echoing ballroom, where so many hearts, promises, and fans have been broken." Moreover, with her use of specific details, she gave a realistic portrayal of aristocratic life in the first quarter of the century. Even though her novels generally concern members of the upper classes, she often ridiculed their failures and sympathized with the middle class. A reviewer in the *New Monthly Magazine* (June 1852) commented, "the comedy of artificial life is Mrs. Gore's *forte*; and it is when reproducing, in her brilliant way, the soap-bubbles and sparkling fire-flies of the 'upper ten thousand,' that we feel her power."

Some well-known contemporaries also saw the value of her novels. Leigh Hunt wrote in his poem "Blue-Stocking Revels" (1837), that her satire "wasn't evil, a bit; / But as full of good heart, as of spirits and wit." In a letter to Gore, Charlotte Brontë said of *The Hamiltons*: "I found in its pages not the echo of another mind—the pale reflection of a reflection—but the result of original observation, and faithful delineation from actual life." William Makepeace Thackeray, despite parodying her in "Lords and Liveries" (from the series "Punch's Prize Novelists," *Punch*, 12-26 June 1847), praised her in reviews of *The Snow Storm* (*Morning Chronicle*, 31 December 1845) and *Sketches of English Character* (*Morning Chronicle*, 4 May 1846). The latter book, he felt, gives a faithful depiction of London dandies. Perhaps Edward Bulwer-Lytton sums her up best when he calls her "a remarkably clever woman," one whose "novels have a merit that has never been sufficiently appreciated." Certainly such novels as *Mothers and Daughters*, *Mrs. Armytage*, and *Cecil: or the Adventures of a Coxcomb* still offer their rewards to modern readers.

References:

Bonnie Anderson, "The Writings of Catherine Gore," *Journal of Popular Culture*, 10 (Fall 1976): 404-423;

Vineta Colby, *Yesterday's Woman: Domestic Realism in the English Novel* (Princeton: Princeton University Press, 1974);

Elliot Engel and Margaret F. King, *The Victorian Novel before Victoria: British Fiction during the Reign of William IV, 1830-37* (New York: St. Martin's Press, 1984);

"Female Novelists. No. II.—Mrs. Gore," *New Monthly Magazine*, 95 (June 1852): 157-168;

Matthew W. Rosa, *The Silver-Fork School: Novels of Fashion Preceding Vanity Fair* (New York: Columbia University Press, 1936);

Norman Russell, *The Novelist and Mammon: Literary Responses to the World of Commerce in the Nineteenth Century* (Oxford: Clarendon Press, 1986).

Elizabeth Hamilton

(25 July 1758 - 23 July 1816)

Myra L. Rich
University of Colorado at Denver

BOOKS: *Translation of the Letters of a Hindoo Rajah,* 2 volumes (London: Printed for G. G. & J. Robinson, 1796);

Memoirs of Modern Philosophers, 3 volumes (Bath: Printed by R. Cruttwell for G. G. & J. Robinson, London, 1800);

Letters on the Principles of Education (Bath: Printed by R. Cruttwell for G. G. & J. Robinson, London, 1801); republished as *Letters on the Elementary Principles of Education,* 2 volumes (Bath: Printed by R. Crutwell for G. G. & J. Robinson, London, 1801; Alexandria, Va.: Printed by Cotton & Stewart for S. Bishop, 1803);

Memoirs of the Life of Agrippina, Wife of Germanicus, 2 volumes (Bath: Printed by R. Crutwell for G. G. & J. Robinson, London, 1804);

Letters Addressed to the Daughter of a Nobleman, 2 volumes (London: Printed for Cadell & Davies by W. Flint, 1806);

The Cottagers of Glenburnie (Edinburgh: Printed by J. Ballantyne for Manners & Miller and S. Cheyne, 1808; New York: Printed for E. Sargent, 1808);

Exercises in Religious Knowledge (Edinburgh: Manners & Miller, 1809);

A Series of Popular Essays Illustrative of Principles Essentially Connected with the Improvement of the Understanding, the Imagination and the Heart, 2 volumes (Edinburgh: Printed for Manners & Miller, 1813; Boston: Wells & Lilly, 1817);

Hints Addressed to Patrons and Directors of Schools (London: Printed for Longman, Hurst, Rees, Orme & Brown, 1815);

Memoirs of the late Mrs. Elizabeth Hamilton with a selection from Her Correspondence and other unpublished writings, edited by Elizabeth Benger, 2 volumes (London: Printed for Longman, Hurst, Rees, Orme & Brown, 1818).

Elizabeth Hamilton lived a quiet life as a single woman of letters at the turn of the eighteenth century, one of an increasing number of women who had the courage to breach the walls of propriety prescribed for them by writing for a literary marketplace. Though she was neither so great a novelist as Jane Austen nor so trenchant a polemicist or radical a thinker as Mary Wollstonecraft, she successfully explored a variety of genres, and her work was widely read and appreciated by British readers of her time. In fact, she earned the praise of both Austen and Sir Walter Scott. Through volumes of essays, letters, and novels, she advocated evangelical religion, early childhood education, and the mother's role in the process of nurturance. Her work formed part of the growing body of opinion on education for women. According to Vineta Colby, though Hamilton wrote few novels herself, she "laid down the ideological principles of the evangelical-domestic novel."

Hamilton was born in Belfast, Ireland, 25 July 1758, the third child and second daughter of Charles and Katherine Mackay Hamilton. The family had originated in Scotland but Hamilton's great-grandfather had immigrated to Ireland in the seventeenth century. There the family remained, and Charles Hamilton was engaged in business. He died of typhus in 1759, leaving his wife and three young children. In the years following his death, his widow placed the children one by one in homes where, she believed, they would receive better care and education than she herself could manage. At the age of six, Elizabeth was consigned to the care of her father's sister and her husband, a Mr. and Mrs. Marshall. When her mother died three years later, Elizabeth remained with the Marshalls, moving with them to Scotland in 1772. Until she was thirteen she was educated at a coeducational day school, an institution common at the elementary level in the British Isles at that time. Hamilton reflected on her rural upbringing frequently and with pleasure. "No child," she wrote in her memoirs, "ever spent so happy a life; nor, indeed, have I ever met with anything at all resembling the way in which we lived, except the description

Elizabeth Hamilton (engraving by W. T. Fry after a portrait by Henry Raeburn)

given by Rousseau of Wolmar's farm and vintage." Her guardians encouraged reading and supported her early attempts to write, though Elizabeth remembered once hiding Henry Home, Lord Kames's *Elements of Criticism* (1762) under a chair cushion lest her choice of reading be thought unfeminine.

Through the years of her childhood Elizabeth did not see her older brother, Charles, or her sister, Katherine. Finally, in 1772, her brother reentered her life. Though he departed shortly thereafter for a military post in India, the two were eager to continue their newfound relationship. Charles Hamilton's frequent letters became for Elizabeth Hamilton "a *second* education, in some respects, perhaps more important than any preceding course of instruction." When he returned to England in 1786, she worked with him on his translations of Indian documents. During that year Charles, Elizabeth, and their sister moved to London, where they remained until Charles's death in 1792.

Elizabeth Hamilton's active literary career began after her brother's death. The two sisters retired to the English countryside, where they sought to recover from their loss, first in Hadleigh, Suffolk, and later in Sonning, Berkshire. There, in tribute to her brother, Hamilton wrote *Translation of the Letters of a Hindoo Rajah*, which was published in 1796. In it she describes the education of the Hindu Rajah Zaarmilla in the customs of the English. She embodies herself in the character of Charlotte and her brother in that of Captain Percy. The book thus enabled her to re-create and praise her brother, his work, and his ideas.

By 1800 Hamilton and her sister had moved to Bath in an effort to relieve Hamilton's recurring attacks of gout. Here "they found . . . the superior attraction of an elegant circle of acquaintances, with some of whom they formed attachments never to be broken." In this comfortable environment Hamilton finished a satirical novel, *Memoirs of Modern Philosophers*, which was

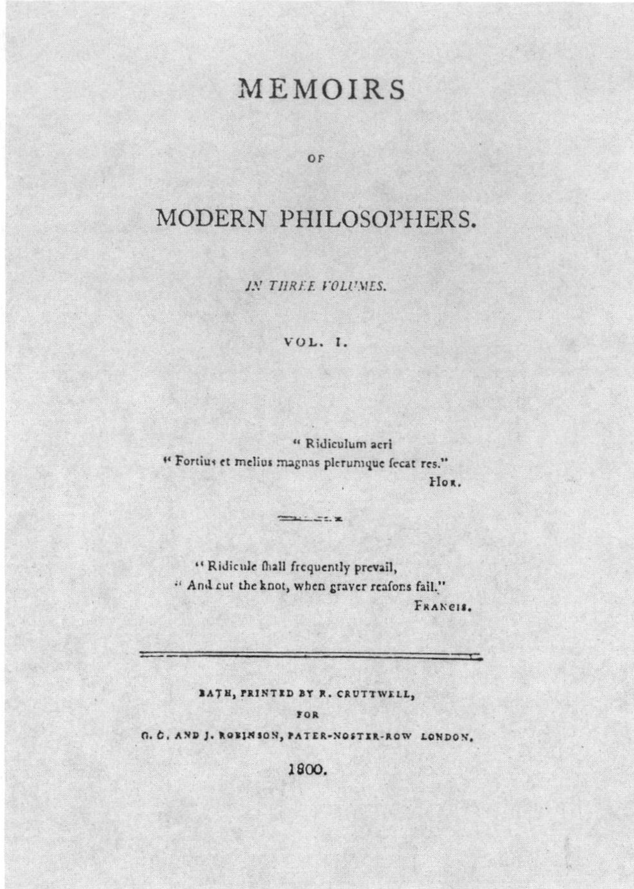
MEMOIRS

OF

MODERN PHILOSOPHERS.

IN THREE VOLUMES.

VOL. I.

"Ridiculum acri
"Fortius et melius magnas plerumque ſecat res."
HOR.

"Ridicule ſhall frequently prevail,
"And cut the knot, when graver reaſons fail."
FRANCIS.

BATH, PRINTED BY R. CRUTTWELL,
FOR
G. G. AND J. ROBINSON, PATER-NOSTER-ROW LONDON.
1800.

Title page for Hamilton's satirical novel on philosophers such as Jean-Jacques Rousseau and William Godwin, whose Political Justice *is "in many parts admirable" but "might, by a bad man, be converted into an engine of mischief, and be made the means of ensnaring innocence and virtue"*

published anonymously in 1800 to great success. A second edition appeared within the year, after which Hamilton acknowledged authorship. In her preface to that edition, which she wrote in the guise of the editor, she says that it was not the author's intention to condemn outright the "ingenious, and in many parts admirable performance" of the modern philosophers, but merely to "expose the dangerous tendency" of the new theories. Hamilton centers the satire on the ridiculous character of Bridgetina Botherim, who, having no principles of her own, is seduced by the new philosophy. Her tragic counterpart is Julia Delmond, a young, beautiful, and naive woman who is corrupted by Mr. Vallaton, a scoundrel disguising his dissolute intentions in the high-minded language of modern philosophy. Through these two women and a host of corresponding characters, Hamilton describes two different modes of "enthusiasm." One, "born of reason and directed by judgment, is noble, discriminating, and effective. The other, the product of an inflammable imagination, is blinded by the glare of its own bewildering light, expends itself upon any object that chance puts in its reach, and is usually unsteady as it is abortive." Obviously the first type of enthusiasm reflects Hamilton's own commitment to reason, religion, tradition, and social stability. The second becomes the object of her satiric wit as she criticizes Jean-Jacques Rousseau, William Godwin, and other modern philosophers who draw unsuspecting people into a vortex of swirling opinions.

Hamilton objects to Rousseau's "system of female education," which she believes is guaranteed to convert women into objects: "A creature instructed in no duty but the art of pleasing, and taught that the sole-end of her creation was to attract the attention of the men, could not be expected to tread very firmly in the paths of virtue." In fact, Hamilton credits Mary Wollstonecraft for exposing "the inconsistency and folly of his system." Referring to Wollstonecraft's *Vindication of the Rights of Woman* (1792), Hamilton has her character Henry Sidney say that it is a "very ingenious" publication. Her only criticism, spoken through Henry, is that "the very sensible authoress has sometimes permitted her zeal to hurry her into expressions which have raised a prejudice against the whole. To superficial readers it appears to be her intention to unsex women entirely."

Thus Hamilton places herself between the ideas of Rousseau, which would make women objects of amusement, and the ideas of Wollstonecraft, which, she believed, would remove women from their proper sphere. Her own middle ground is embodied by Henry Sidney, Harriet Orwell, and Harriet's father, who tells the young people that "each sex, in every situation in life, has its peculiar duties assigned to it by that good Providence which governs all things, and which seems to delight in order." Dr. Orwell says that Jesus Christ "was the first philosopher who placed the female character in a respectable point of view." He treated women, like men, "as beings who were to be taught the performance of duty, not by arbitrary regulations confined to particular parts of conduct, but by the knowledge of principles which enlighten the understanding and improve the heart." Whether or not this interpretation was an accurate reading of Jesus' ideas about women, it provided a way for Christian feminists such as Hamilton to deal with their objections to clerical interpretation while at the same time maintaining fidelity to the scriptures. By arguing for equality in Christ they countered the presumed superiority of the male sphere.

While still in Bath, Hamilton began her *Letters on the Elementary Principles of Education*, published in 1801. As in many of her later works, Hamilton stresses the importance of learning in early childhood, the crucial role of religion and moral content in a system of instruction, and the necessity of better education for women so that they might fulfill their duties to their children, and thence to society. She echoes the argument of Mary Wollstonecraft and other Enlightenment feminists that women's education is inferior and unsuited to the many demands made upon them. Because female education "is conducted upon no regular plan, we acquire no regular associations in our ideas, no accurate arrangement, no habit of mental application." Women have been endowed with adequate intellect, Hamilton believes, but have not been permitted to develop their minds. Nature has "sufficiently qualified us for the sphere in which she evidently intended we should move; and that sphere is neither undignified nor confined, she has rendered evident, from the intellectual facilities with which she has endowed us. Why these should be given to us as a *Sealed* book which ought not to be opened, I confess I cannot comprehend." Plainly, Hamilton accepts the idea of woman's sphere. At the same time she wishes to dignify it and to argue that it is equal in all respects to any of the callings of men. Pursuing the themes of motherhood and education, Hamilton began a new biography. While on an extensive tour through Scotland, she read all she could find on Roman history, and in 1804 *Memoirs of the Life of Agrippina, Wife of Germanicus* was published. Hamilton embarked on this lengthy work in order to "illustrate by biographical examples the speculative principles assumed in the *Letters on Education*." *Memoirs of the Life of Agrippina* is a scrupulously scholarly work, demonstrating complete fidelity to the available sources. Only one scene was reconstructed, and Hamilton painstakingly acknowledged how and why she chose to do so.

Hamilton chose biography over fiction on the grounds that the story of a person who had actually lived could create a deeper interest because of its essential truth. Agrippina became her subject because of the accessibility of evidence and the familiarity of most readers with Roman history. This wife of the Roman general Germanicus Caesar (15 B.C.-A.D. 19) and mother of Emperor Caligula (A.D. 12-41)—as well as a daughter, Agrippina, the mother of Nero (A.D. 37-68)—must also have appealed to Hamilton because of contemporary interest in the Roman and British empires. People in both England and America at the close of the eighteenth century were preoccupied with the fall of the Roman Empire and the lessons that could be learned from it by modern builders of nations. Moreover, historically the life of Agrippina coincided roughly with the life of Christ; thus the parallel between the Roman and early Christian worlds could be clearly drawn—the debauchery, greed, pride, and ambition of the Romans contrasted to the Christian virtues of meekness and humility. Hamilton points out that "this dark and gloomy period, in which vice seemed to reign triumphant over a benighted world, was the season chosen in the councils of Divine Wisdom for the display not of judgment but of grace!" At the same time that, under the Emperor Tiberius, chaos enveloped the Roman Empire, "In the wilderness of

Judea, the voice of John the Baptist was lifted up to proclaim the glad tidings of approaching light." The parallel is complete when we see that Tiberius, who ordered the final suffering and death of Agrippina, was the same person who ordered the crucifixion: "Tiberius, who had so often made innocence suffer, was the ostensible judge of the Savior of the world, for in his name was the iniquitous decree of Pilate pronounced."

The choice of a woman as the subject of such a biography was also significant. It again demonstrated Hamilton's conviction that the education of children by the mother's precept and example is definitive in the formation of character. The instrumental role of the mother in the nurturance of good citizens was a theory widely accepted in the aftermath of the French and American Revolutions. Unfortunately Agrippina, herself the product of complex and often contradictory forces, was doomed to pass similar messages to her children, notwithstanding her good character and virtue. Moreover, the society in which they lived was so fraught with conflict and decadence, that even a mother's virtue in combination with taste, intelligence, and education was inadequate to ward off the multiplicity of malevolent influences.

Agrippina died on 15 November A.D. 33. She was forty-six years old. Hamilton concedes that her reputation, "in the points in which Tiberius maliciously endeavored to attack it, was indeed invulnerable." But she herself judges Agrippina on other grounds. Though she recognizes that in ancient Rome pride and ambition were not antithetical to virtue, still "those who have paid any attention to their consequences, as they have been displayed in the preceding pages, will perceive, that in cherishing pride and ambition, Agrippina cherished the seeds of misery and corruption. She acted up to her ideas of virtue, but her ideas of virtue were imperfect." She was, in other words, the product of a pagan rather than a Christian world. Christianity offered "clearer views of moral excellence, and brighter prospects of future reward, than ever opened on the unfortunate Agrippina!"

Hamilton had completed the biography of Agrippina during a stay in the town of Bowness on Lake Windermere. In the fall of 1804 she and her sister moved once again, this time to Edinburgh, where they remained for many years. During 1805 she spent six months supervising the education of the children of a local nobleman. Her experiences there became *Letters Addressed to the Daughter of a Nobleman*, published in 1806. In these letters, intended for the eldest daughter of the family, Hamilton extends and personalizes the themes of her *Letters on the Elementary Principles of Education*, addressing the responsibilities of a young woman growing up to take her place as wife and mother in privileged society. She warns against that pride of family and class that can supersede the important virtues of hard work, piety, and humility.

In *Letters Addressed to the Daughter of a Nobleman* Hamilton confronts directly the issue of female inferiority. As a Christian she acknowledges that the Bible presents Eve as the first in sin and dooms her "to an additional load of suffering and sorrow. . . ." At the same time she argues that God held out to Eve the possibility of an equal share with Adam in the hope of salvation and mercy. She reminds any woman "who, thinking meanly of her sex, relinquishes all hope all desire of improvement," that when Adam and Eve faced God's judgment, "though the weakness of the woman was not accepted as an apology for her guilt, yet, that to her was granted the promise of salvation, and that she was expressly told by the voice of Omnipotence, that it was the 'seed of the woman which should bruise the serpent's heel.' "

As Hamilton reads Genesis, its lessons "would teach the woman who repines at want of power, and who boldly assumes it as her right, to be humbled by the remembrance of her sex's weakness. It would at the same time prevent any from sinking under a painful sense of inferiority." Hamilton argues that we find the denigration of women not in Scripture itself but in later interpretations. She suggests that God alone could have written a text that combines justice, mercy, and equality. Only the Bible is to be relied upon to understand God's intentions toward women. Successive layers of interpretation eroded the original meaning of the text, which was "soon overwhelmed by the loads of absurd fiction with which it had been decorated by human imagination." If women relied on these later accounts, Hamilton points out, "We should have seen the woman represented as seducing and seduced, the first accounted for by her charms; the latter by her weakness. We should have seen her represented as the cause of ruin; but we should never have heard of her being declared the medium of restoration to the human race."

Through a detailed history of Judaism and Christianity, Hamilton seeks to establish a firm

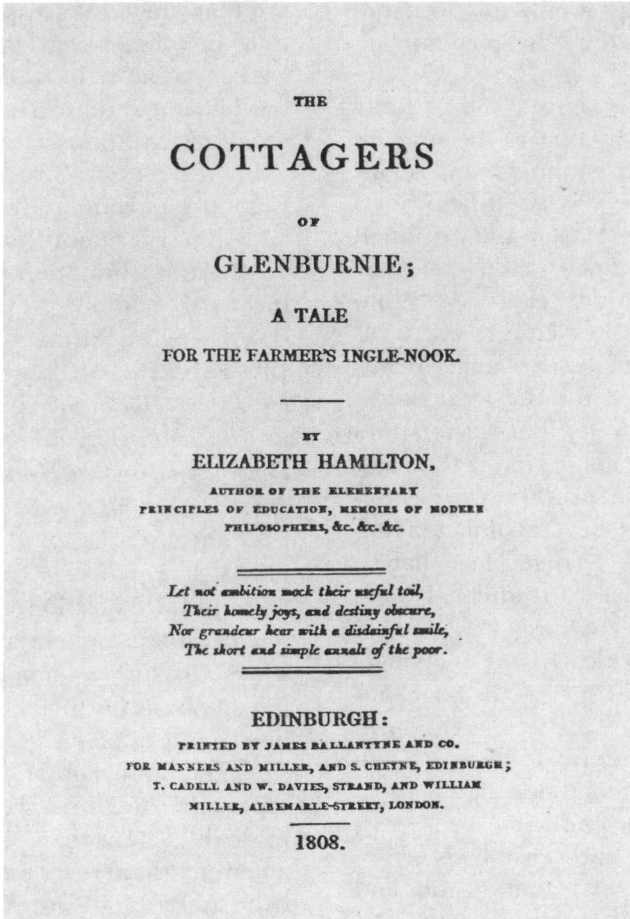

THE

COTTAGERS

OF

GLENBURNIE;

A TALE

FOR THE FARMER'S INGLE-NOOK.

BY

ELIZABETH HAMILTON,

AUTHOR OF THE ELEMENTARY PRINCIPLES OF EDUCATION, MEMOIRS OF MODERN PHILOSOPHERS, &c. &c. &c.

Let not ambition mock their useful toil,
Their homely joys, and destiny obscure,
Nor grandeur hear with a disdainful smile,
The short and simple annals of the poor.

EDINBURGH:

PRINTED BY JAMES BALLANTYNE AND CO.
FOR MANNERS AND MILLER, AND S. CHEYNE, EDINBURGH;
T. CADELL AND W. DAVIES, STRAND, AND WILLIAM MILLER, ALBEMARLE-STREET, LONDON.

1808.

Title page for the novel Hamilton wrote to encourage the poor to develop good work habits

foundation for beliefs that point the way to proper choices in life. An understanding of the Gospels, she believes, would protect people from pride and selfishness, and it would enable them to make independent and appropriate choices rather than succumbing to the latest intellectual and political fads.

Hamilton rejects the idea that woman is inferior. Yet the modest feminism she espouses rests firmly within a Christian context. She embraces religion and the Gospels as the sure guides for women's lives, enabling them to avoid both worldly temptations and fashionable opinions.

The years in Edinburgh were fruitful for Elizabeth Hamilton. Her reputation was assured. Although as a literary figure and a woman she was initially suspect, she overcame any doubts and became something of a fixture in Edinburgh, known for her many friends and cheerful gatherings: "Her house was the resort, not only of the intellectual, but of the gay and even of the fashionable; and her cheerfulness, good sense, and good humor, soon reconciled every one to the literary lady." Hamilton made it her business to support other female writers and, like many single women of her generation, developed a wide network of women friends. She believed that "the bright side of mankind" would "turn out to be—woman!" She had become convinced "that whenever our sex step over the pale of folly . . . they ascend the steeps of wisdom and virtue more readily than the other. They are less encumbered by the load of selfishness; and, if they carry enough ballast to prevent being blown into the gulf of *sentiment* they mount much higher than their stronger associates."

While in Edinburgh, Hamilton actively supported a benevolent organization called the House of Industry, which promoted employment and education for poor women. As a result of this experience, she wrote *The Cottagers of Glenburnie* (1808), a didactic novel directed to the inculcation of good habits among the working poor. The book proved immensely popular throughout Britain, but especially in Scotland, where the publishers printed a "cheap edition" to meet the demand.

The heroine of the novel, Mrs. Betty Mason, leads families one by one to the practice of industry, thrift, order, cleanliness, and sobriety. *The Cottagers of Glenburnie* is a self-help novel for the poor in which Betty Mason, herself raised as a servant, leads so exemplary a life that she bridges the lower and the middle classes. Her conduct and virtue, as well as her kindnesses to his late wife, make her welcome at the home of Mr. Stewart, the estate manager for the local nobleman. Yet she does not forget her station and chooses to live in a nearby village among the peasants, whom she instructs in practical virtues designed to improve their lives. Several of these families resist her attempts to change their habits, partly out of easy adherence to traditional ways, partly out of suspicion of anything new. Others welcome the opportunity to learn and to change. These families, of course, prosper as the novel unfolds. Finally, Mrs. Mason turns her attention to one of Mr. Stewart's daughters, a young woman who has aspired to rise out of her class and in the process has neglected the enduring virtues possessed by her more modest and sensible sister.

Hamilton never suggests that virtue and hard work are keys to social mobility. Rather she asserts that they are the means to gain respectability while remaining within one's class. As Mr. Stewart says to his wayward daughter, Mary, "though, by being factor on the estate at Longlands, I have been brought into the company of higher people, it is by my character, and not by my situation, that I have gained a title to their respect. Depend upon it, Mary, that as long as people in our private station rest their claim to respect upon the ground of upright conduct, and unblemished virtue, they will not fail to meet with the attention they deserve. . . ."

Although she firmly insists on the permanence of social class, Hamilton nevertheless holds out the hope of religion to the poor. At the funeral of a man whose family had rejected her advice, Mrs. Mason reflects that death has removed "those barriers which, in this world, separate man from man. . . . Why, then should those of lowly station envy the trappings of vanity, that are but the boast of a moment, when, by piety and virtue, they may attain a distinction so much more lasting and glorious? To the humble and the lowly are the gates of Paradise thrown open. Nor is there any other path which leads to them, but that which the Gospel points out to all." Salvation, in other words, is available to the poor as well as to the rich. It alone should be the goal of the peasant rather than the false and fleeting rewards of wealth or station.

After several productive and happy years in Edinburgh, Hamilton's health deteriorated. She and her sister moved to England in the fall of 1812. After a brief tour of Ireland in 1813, they returned to Edinburgh, where they remained until shortly before Elizabeth Hamilton's death on 23 July 1816. In 1813 she published *A Series of Popular Essays Illustrative of Principles Essentially Connected with the Improvement of the Understanding, the Imagination, and the Heart*. Her final work, *Hints Addressed to Patrons and Directors of Schools* (1815), follows the theories of the Swiss educator Johann Heinrich Pestalozzi. Critics consider Hamilton's writings on education as among her most enduring because of their analysis of the process by which the human mind acquires knowledge and the emphasis on the importance of proper education to a productive life.

Hamilton observes that, though boys—especially of the lower classes—appear to be more intelligent than girls, the difference is more apparent than real. Because boys engage in active sports and are free to roam with their friends, their powers of observation are enhanced, she says, while those of girls, confined to the house, are not. It is therefore incumbent on the mother to cultivate and apply her own powers of observation in order to set an example and to stimulate her children. It was not enough, she believed, to teach by rote, to cram young minds with facts. Children needed to be encouraged to develop independent powers and habits of attention, observation, and perception, which would enable them to acquire knowledge in adult life.

Hamilton proved to be a dedicated pioneer in the field of women's education. She intended *A Series of Popular Essays* "to enforce the necessity of cultivating the reasoning faculty, and to explain the advantages arising from the capability of taking general and extensive views." Her male friends, apparently, believed that the essays were too difficult for most women to comprehend. Hamilton was happy to report "that their apprehensions were groundless. All the ladies of my acquaintance here have read them with satisfaction; and I have received letters, even from young ladies, upon the subject, which show not only that they understood it, but were capable of weighing, with accuracy, every argument adduced."

Maria Edgeworth, writing in tribute to Hamilton after her death, praised her work on education for opening "to all classes of readers those metaphysical discoveries or observations which had been confined chiefly to the learned. To a sort of knowledge, which had been considered rather a matter of curiosity than of use, she has given real value and actual currency" (*Monthly Magazine*, 1 September 1816). She had made the subject of acquisition of knowledge accessible to a wide audience and showed how it could be applied to the field of education. Hamilton's goal was to show that "a little knowledge of the various powers and faculties of the human mind may be considered essentially instrumental in confirming our religious faith and in improving our moral qualities. . . ." She believed that the psychology of learning could be used in the service of revealed religion.

Elizabeth Hamilton's work is little known today. Twentieth-century critics have been most interested in her writings on education and in her domestic novel, *The Cottagers of Glenburnie*. Yet her work displays an overall consistency of purpose and theme, and her analysis of the problems and possibilities for women and for the laboring classes merits increased consideration by modern readers. Her views were quite conservative, and her commitment to Christianity makes her seem less innovative than the secular and radical writers who were her contemporaries. Yet her ideas claimed a wide and faithful audience in her time. She was an advocate for women and education, but she wrote for a commercial marketplace which accorded her acceptability precisely because she did not offend the sensibilities of readers committed to the traditional religious and social values of the early nineteenth century.

References:

Robert A. Colby, *Fiction with a Purpose: Major and Minor Nineteenth-Century Novels* (Bloomington: Indiana University Press, 1967);

Vineta Colby, *Yesterday's Woman: Domestic Realism in the English Novel* (Princeton: Princeton University Press, 1974);

Kenneth L. Moler, *Jane Austen's Art of Allusion* (Lincoln: University of Nebraska Press, 1968).

James Hogg

(December 1770 - 21 November 1835)

Andrew M. Cooper
University of Texas at Austin

See also the Hogg entry in *DLB 93: British Romantic Poets, 1789-1832: First Series.*

BOOKS: *Scottish Pastorals, Poems, Songs, etc., Mostly Written in the Dialect of the South* (Edinburgh: Printed by John Taylor, 1801);

The Shepherd's Guide: being a Practical Treatise on the Diseases of Sheep (Edinburgh: Printed by J. Ballantyne for Archibald Constable and John Murray, London, 1807);

The Mountain Bard: consisting of Ballads and Songs, founded on Facts and Legendary Tales (Edinburgh: Printed by J. Ballantyne for Archibald Constable and John Murray, London, 1807; enlarged edition, Edinburgh: Oliver & Boyd, and also sold by G. & W. B. Whittaker, London, and William Turnbull, Glasgow, 1821);

The Forest Minstrel; a Selection of Songs, adapted to the most favourite Scottish Airs, by Hogg and others (Edinburgh: Printed for the editor & sold by Archibald Constable, 1810; Philadelphia: M. Carey, 1816);

The Spy (nos. 1-52, Edinburgh, 1 September 1810 - 24 August 1811; 1 volume, Edinburgh: Sold by Constable, 1811);

The Queen's Wake: A Legendary Poem (Edinburgh: Printed by Andrew Balfour for George Goldie and for Longman, Hurst, Rees, Orme & Brown, London, 1813);

The Hunting of Badlewe, A Dramatic Tale, as J. H Craig, of Douglas, Esq. (London: Printed for Henry Colburn & George Goldie, Edinburgh, 1814);

The Pilgrims of the Sun: A Poem (Edinburgh: Printed for William Blackwood and sold by John Murray, London, 1815);

The Ettricke Garland: being Two Excellent New Songs on The Lifting of the Banner of the House of Buccleuch, at the great foot-ball match on Carterhaugh, Dec. 4, 1815, by Hogg and Walter Scott (Edinburgh: Printed by James Ballantyne, 1815);

A Selection of German Hebrew Melodies, lyrics by Hogg (London: Printed & sold by C. Christmas, 1815);

The Poetic Mirror, or The Living Bards of Britain (London: Printed for Longman, Hurst, Rees, Orme & Brown and J. Ballantyne, Edinburgh, 1816; Philadelphia: Published by M. Carey, 1817);

Mador of the Moor; a Poem (Edinburgh: Printed for William Blackwood and John Murray, London, 1816; Philadelphia: Published by Moses Thomas, printed by J. Maxwell, 1816);

Dramatic Tales, 2 volumes (Edinburgh: Printed by James Ballantyne for Longman, Hurst, Rees, Orme & Brown, London, and John Ballantyne, Edinburgh, 1817);

The Long Pack (Newcastle: Printed for John Bell, 1817);

The Brownie of Bodsbeck; and Other Tales (2 volumes, Edinburgh: Printed for William Blackwood and John Murray, London, 1818; 1 volume, New York: Charles Wiley, 1818);

A Border Garland. Containing Nine New Songs, lyrics by Hogg, music by Hogg and others (Edinburgh: Printed for the editor by Walker & Anderson and sold by Nathaniel Gow & Son, 1819); enlarged as *A Border Garland, Containing Twelve New Songs* (Edinburgh: Printed & sold by R. Purdie, n.d.);

Winter Evening Tales, collected among the Cottagers in the South of Scotland, 2 volumes (Edinburgh: Printed for Oliver & Boyd and G. & W. B. Whittaker, London, 1820);

The Poetical Works of James Hogg, 4 volumes (Edinburgh: Printed for Archibald Constable and Hurst, Robinson, London, 1822);

The Royal Jubilee. A Scottish Mask (Edinburgh: William Blackwood and T. Cadell, London, 1822);

The Three Perils of Man; or, War, Women, and Witchcraft. A Border Romance, 3 volumes (London: Longman, Hurst, Rees, Orme & Brown, 1822);

James Hogg (portrait by William Nicholson; Scottish National Portrait Gallery)

The Three Perils of Women; or, Love, Leasing, and Jealousy. A Series of Domestic Scottish Tales, 3 volumes (London: Longman, Hurst, Rees, Orme, Brown & Green, 1823);

The Private Memoirs and Confessions of a Justified Sinner: written by himself: with a detail of curious traditionary facts, and other evidence, by the editor (London: Printed for Longman, Hurst, Rees, Orme, Brown & Green, 1824); republished as *The Suicide's Grave* (London: J. Sheills, 1828);

Queen Hynde. A Poem (London: Printed for Longman, Hurst, Rees, Orme, Brown & Green and William Blackwood, Edinburgh, 1825);

The Shepherd's Calendar, 2 volumes (Edinburgh: William Blackwood and T. Cadell, London, 1829);

Songs, by the Ettrick Shepherd. Now First Collected (Edinburgh: William Blackwood and T. Cadell, London, 1831);

A Queer Book (Edinburgh: William Blackwood and T. Cadell, London, 1832);

Altrive Tales: collected from among the peasantry of Scotland, and from foreign adventurers, with illustrations by George Cruikshank, volume 1 (London: James Cochrane, 1832)—no more published;

A Series of Lay Sermons on Good Principles and Good Breeding (London: James Fraser, 1834);

Familiar Anecdotes of Sir Walter Scott, with a "Sketch of the Life of the [Ettrick] Shepherd" by S. De Witt Bloodgood (New York: Harper & Brothers, 1834); unauthorized, altered edition: *The Domestic Manners and Private Life of Sir Walter Scott* (Glasgow: John Reid & Co. /

Edinburgh: Oliver & Boyd / London: Black, Young & Young, 1834);

Tales of the Wars of Montrose, 3 volumes (London: James Cochrane, 1835);

Tales and Sketches, 6 volumes, edited by D. O. Hill (Glasgow, Edinburgh & London: Blackie & Son, 1837).

Editions: *Noctes Ambrosianae*, by John Wilson, William Maginn, John Gibson Lockhart, Hogg and others, 5 volumes, edited by R. Shelton Mackenzie (New York: Redfield, 1854);

The Works of the Ettrick Shepherd, edited by Rev. Thomas Thomson, 2 volumes (London, Glasgow & Edinburgh: Blackie & Son, 1865);

The Brownie of Bodsbeck, edited, with spelling revised to agree with Ettrick pronunciation, by George Lewis (Selkirk: James Lewis, 1903);

The Private Memoirs and Confessions of a Justified Sinner, edited, with an introduction, by John Carey (London: Oxford University Press, 1969);

James Hogg: Selected Stories and Sketches, edited, with an introduction, by Douglas S. Mack (Edinburgh & London: Scottish Academic Press, 1972; New York: Harper & Row, 1972);

The Three Perils of Man; War, Women, and Witchcraft, edited, with an introduction, by Douglas Gifford (Edinburgh & London: Scottish Academic Press, 1972);

The Brownie of Bodsbeck, edited, with an introduction, by Mack (Edinburgh & London: Scottish Academic Press, 1976).

OTHER: *The Jacobite Relics of Scotland; being the Songs, Airs, and Legends, of the Adherents to the House of Stuart*, collected by Hogg (Edinburgh: Printed for William Blackwood and T. Cadell & W. Davies, London, 1819; second series, 1821).

SELECTED PERIODICAL PUBLICATIONS—UNCOLLECTED: "The Mistakes of a Night," *Scots Magazine*, 61 (October 1794): 624;

"Letters on Poetry, by the Ettrick Shepherd," *Scots Magazine*, 67 (May 1805): 352-354; 68 (January 1806): 17-20;

"Translation from an Ancient Chaldee Ms.," by Hogg, William Blackwood, John Wilson, J. G. Lockhart, and R. P. Gillies, *Blackwood's Edinburgh Magazine*, 2 (October 1817): 89-96.

Known today as the author of *The Private Memoirs and Confessions of a Justified Sinner* (1824), an extraordinary portrayal of the psychology of antinomian Calvinism, James Hogg became famous in his time as the "Ettrick Shepherd" of *Blackwood's Edinburgh Magazine*, a coarsely ingenuous rustic full of opinions sometimes nobly savage in their honesty, sometimes rollickingly satirical, but always more or less offensive to polite Edinburgh society. Although Hogg the young shepherd was largely illiterate, the question of how deliberately Hogg the struggling man of letters exploited his background has long been disputed. What seems clear is that Hogg, always ambitious and often barely solvent whatever the success of his latest book, adopted a variety of literary roles in the course of a writing career that generated scores of ballads and songs, numerous long verse narratives, dozens of short stories (many of them later rewritten and published under different titles), several novels, an autobiography, a controversial life of Sir Walter Scott, and a collaboration with other contributors to *Blackwood's Magazine* that produced the libelous "Chaldee Manuscript" (October 1817) and the sensational *Noctes Ambrosianae* (1822-1835), the latter primarily a forum for the "deevilry" of the *Blackwood's* circle of writers. Most of these works are justly forgotten.

Part of Hogg's great personal charm was an energy and resiliency that enabled him to keep writing in the face of hardship and snobbery that would have silenced others. He is an important cultural figure, and not simply for his close connections with John Wilson, John Gibson Lockhart, and the literati of Edinburgh, or for his amusing, if occasionally unreliable, anecdotes about luminaries such as William Wordsworth and Walter Scott. The problems of identity and audience that confronted many early-nineteenth-century Scottish writers are epitomized by his struggle to choose among writing in vernacular Scots such as Robert Burns preferred; employing English, increasingly the dominant language, and the one used by Scott, Hogg's friend and mentor; or using a combination of the two, as found in the mixed Lowland culture of Hogg's day, a mixture which had been successfully versified by Allan Ramsay and Robert Fergusson but which was beginning to degenerate into sentimental affectation, English sprinkled with picturesque but basically trivial Scotticisms. Hogg's literary distinction lies in his hard-eyed rendering of old Scottish folklore and superstition, which he viewed as

Walter Scott (seated at right) visiting Hogg and his mother while collecting material for his Minstrelsy of the Scottish Border. *He was brought to the Hoggs' cottage by their distant cousin William Laidlaw (seated at left).*

the imaginative core of a way of life already disappearing, but also as the repository of bigotry and hypocrisy quite as narrow-minded as the utilitarian ethic of the emergent urban middle classes.

Although he dated his birth as 25 January 1772, the thirteenth birthday of Robert Burns, the Ettrick parish register gives the baptismal date of James Hogg as 9 December 1770. He was the second son of Robert Hogg, a tenant farmer of Ettrickhouse and Ettrickhall, where James was born. His mother, Margaret Laidlaw, was well-versed in Border ballads and legends, and—as Hogg's older brother, William, told—"to keep us boys quiet would often tell us tales of kings, giants, fairies, kelpies, brownies, etc., etc." Her father was William Laidlaw of Fawhope (or Phawhope), well known as the shepherd Will o' Phaup, whom James described in one of his "Shepherd's Calendar" sketches, "Odd Characters" (first published in *Blackwood's*, April 1827), as "the last man of this wild region, who heard, saw, and conversed with the fairies; and that not once or twice, but at sundry times and seasons." Hogg's own father was, according to William, a devoted Bible reader particularly fond of "the sublime descriptions of Isaiah, the plaintive strains of Jeremiah, or beautiful imagery of Ezekiel"; from him, James acquired an intimate, and ambivalent, interest in puritanism that figures in his later tales and novels. Writing in 1792 for the first *Statistical Account of Scotland*, the parish minister described the remoteness of Ettrick: "This parish possesses no advantage. The nearest market town is 15 miles distant. The roads to all of them are almost impassible.... The snow also, at times, is a great inconvenience; often for many months, we can have no intercourse with mankind." As if such conditions were not hostile enough, when Hogg was six years old his father went bankrupt. The family was evicted from Ettrickhall, and Hogg was compelled to leave school, which he had only begun attending that year. He spent the rest of his childhood working on various local farms. In his first job as cowherd for the neighboring farmer, he earned, for a half-year's work, a ewe lamb and a new pair of shoes. From this time until he was sixteen, Hogg reported, "I neither read nor wrote; nor had I access to any book save the Bible."

At eighteen the semiliterate Hogg embarked on a strenuous program of self-education. According to his "Memoirs of the Author's Life"—first published in *The Mountain Bard* (1807) and revised in 1821 and 1832—the first

Part of Hogg's description of his first visit to the Scotts' home in Edinburgh, from the manuscript for Familiar Anecdotes of Sir Walter Scott *(MA 192, Pierpont Morgan Library)*

books he borrowed to read while tending sheep were theological. The only one he could still remember was Thomas Burnet's work on the "theory of the conflagration of the earth," and "Happy it was for me that I did not understand it! . . . All the day I was pondering the grand millennium, and the reign of the saints; and all the night dreaming of new heavens and a new earth—the stars in horror, and the world in flames!" Such terrifying visions would eventually become the preachings of the fanatical Reverend Wringhim in *The Private Memoirs and Confessions of a Justified Sinner*. Within a few years Hogg had familiarized himself with the masterpieces of English and Scottish literature—his longer verse narratives often imitate the styles of Edmund Spenser, John Milton, and Alexander Pope—as well as the works of contemporaries such as William Wordsworth, Samuel Taylor Coleridge, and Scott, all of whom are aptly parodied in his *Poetic Mirror* (1816). Still a full-time shepherd, he began during the early 1790s to compose verse: "whenever a leisure minute or two offered . . . I sat down and wrote out my thoughts as I found them. This is still my invariable practice in writing prose. I cannot make out one sentence by study, without the pen in my hand to catch the ideas as they arise, and I never write two copies of the same thing." Hogg's method of composing helps to explain at once his prolific output, the unevenness of his writing and the carelessness by which suspenseful plots are sometimes marred with ridiculously abrupt conclusions, and also his tendency when republishing a story in a later edition to rewrite and retitle it rather than simply revising the original version (a tendency that creates much editorial confusion). In the summer of 1797 he learned that Robert Burns was dead. As his "Memoirs" tell it, this event was a turning point in his life; he had then never heard of Burns, but the sad news was accompanied by a recital of Burns's popular "Tam o' Shanter," after which Hogg says he "resolved to be a poet, and to follow in the steps of Burns."

Crucial to his career was his meeting, probably early in 1802, with Scott, then busy gathering old ballads for his collection *The Minstrelsy of the Scottish Border* (1802, 1803). Hogg managed to introduce Scott to his mother, who was steeped in Lowlands folklore and balladry, and he supplied Scott with transcriptions. It was the beginning of a lifelong friendship, not without its tensions, between the two men. Indeed, when the first two volumes of Scott's *Minstrelsy* had appeared in January 1802, Hogg had been dissatisfied with its imitations of ancient ballads and decided he could do better. He soon composed more than a hundred pages of songs and dedicated them to Scott, who as patron undertook to get them published. In the meantime, Hogg spent several summers touring the Highlands and contributing songs to the *Scots Magazine*. These were finally collected in 1807 as *The Mountain Bard*. The volume was a success; Hogg not only earned £214, an amount boosted to almost £300 by publication that year of his award-winning *Shepherd's Guide: being a Practical Treatise on the Diseases of Sheep*, but he began to achieve renown.

Hogg used the proceeds to lease a second farm and continued writing poetry. Within three years both farms were repossessed and Hogg, having presumed to better his station, was no longer employable as a mere shepherd. In February 1810 say his "Memoirs," "in utter desperation I took my plaid about my shoulders, and marched away to Edinburgh, determined, since no better could be, to push my fortune as a literary man." After publishing *The Forest Minstrel* (1810), a collection of poems by various writers ("but the worst of them are all mine"), he began a weekly paper, *The Spy* (1 September 1810 - 24 August 1811), comprised mostly of his own poems, essays, and stories. Unfortunately, such was "the fastidiousness and affectation of the people" that he lost half his subscribers with the publication, in the third and fourth issues, of the indecorous prose tale, "On Instability in One's Calling" (later revised as "The Adventures of Basil Lee" and collected in *Winter Evening Tales*, 1820). The outwardly amoral hero spends a lifetime of picaresque wandering, finally arriving as an old man in Edinburgh, where he prepares to marry a hideous old dowager. He is saved by a miraculous meeting with the widowed Scottish prostitute who loved him in his youth but ended their affair in order to marry a rich American. They forgive one another's failings and marry happily. The tale is one of Hogg's best, and anticipates his lifelong concern with humanity's isolation and suffering, their connection with supernatural mystery, and their potential salvation through community.

The Edinburgh booksellers having decided his genius was not prose but poetry, Hogg achieved his first major success by exploiting the taste for long verse narratives created by Byron and Scott. *The Queen's Wake* (1813) is, like Hogg's previous volumes of poetry, a collection of songs, but it is loosely organized as the story of a competi-

Hogg in 1824 (portrait by William Bewick; Scottish National Portrait Gallery)

tion between twelve minstrels at a festival held by Mary, Queen of Scots, at Holyrood. Deservedly the best-known poem in it is "The Witch of Fife," which contrasts the thrilling nocturnal revels of a group of witches meeting in the bishop of Carlisle's wine cellars with a grotesquely comic account of how the husband of one manages to join them and, after drinking himself silly, is discovered the next morning and burned at the stake. Within six years the volume had gone through as many editions, and had been praised by Francis Jeffrey, the powerful editor of the *Edinburgh Review*. *The Queen's Wake* introduces the technique of multiple perspectives used in much of Hogg's subsequent work; its twelve minstrels offer differing views of the human condition. Its conclusion, in which the Ettrick Shepherd receives only second prize—an older, less ornate harp than that awarded the winner—is not, like Hogg's previous surprise endings, a mere trick upon the reader; for the wily Ettrick Shepherd realizes that his harp affords a deeper, more enduring music. Hogg followed *The Queen's Wake* with several less successful long narrative poems, which kept him in the public eye. During these years it appears Hogg moved back and forth between Edinburgh and the farm of Altrive at Yarrow that he obtained thanks to Harriet, Duchess of Buccleuch, to whom he had dedicated *The Forest Minstrel*. He installed his father, and in 1820 he settled there with his bride, Margaret Phillips, whom he had married in April of that year. Their marriage was a notoriously happy one.

In 1818 Hogg abandoned verse narratives for prose and published a two-volume collection of tales including the short historical novel, *The Brownie of Bodsbeck*. Set in 1685, six years after the defeat of the Cameronian rebellion at the Battle of Bothwell Bridge, the book tells how a Border farmer, Walter Laidlaw, offers refuge to the defeated Covenanters hiding among the hills of his isolated farm of Chapelhope. When the brutal Graham of Claverhouse leads his government troops through the Borders hunting down Covenanters, Laidlaw is taken prisoner and sent to Edinburgh for trial. His danger is aggravated by the townsfolk's growing suspicion that his daughter, Katherine, is in league with the Brownie of Bodsbeck, a monstrous supernatural creature whose favorite haunt is Chapelhope. During Walter's absence his pious wife allows the local curate, Mass John Clerk, to spend the night with Katherine in order to exorcise her; when he attempts rape, she is rescued by the Brownie and his crew. Soon afterward the persecution of the Covenanters ends, Walter is released, and it is finally revealed that the Brownie and his demons are none other than Covenanters who had been in hiding. As the poem "Mess John" and its accompanying note show, Hogg derived much of *The Brownie of Bodsbeck* from traditional Ettrick tales concerning the actual farmhouse of Chapelhope, situated four miles from his birthplace. The novel endorses what Hogg, in his introduction, calls the "traditionary account of the incidents" which supported the Covenanters and condemned the Royalists. But Hogg is less interested in taking political sides than in emphasizing the fundamental humaneness of traditional social values, which ostensibly transcend politics. Says Walter to Katherine at the novel's close: "Deil care what side they war on, Kate! . . . Ye hae taen the side o' human nature; the suffering and the humble side, an' the side o' feeling. . . ."

As Hogg wrote in *Familiar Anecdotes of Sir Walter Scott* (1834), publication of *The Brownie of Bodsbeck* brought him into conflict with his literary mentor. For Scott's *Old Mortality*, published in December 1816, focuses on the same time period and some of the same characters, depicting them from a Tory viewpoint contrary to Hogg's more Whiggish, popular treatment. Since Hogg's book appeared some eighteen months later, it was widely thought to be an imitation or refutation of Scott's. The evidence, however, supports Hogg's claim that he had written *The Brownie of Bodsbeck* before *Old Mortality* appeared; publication of Hogg's book was delayed by his usual difficulties with booksellers and publishers.

The Brownie of Bodsbeck, with its episodic organization as a series of winter evening tales related by Walter Laidlaw, is rendered even more disjointed by Hogg's failure fully to connect its two plots, concerning Katherine and the Brownie on one hand and Walter and the Covenanters on the other. This weakness is surmounted in *The Private Memoirs and Confessions of a Justified Sinner* (1824), where a double plot supplies an ambiguous double perspective that is an essential part of the story. *The Justified Sinner* is divided into three parts: "The Editor's Narrative" giving the story of the protagonist Robert Wringhim's life until he succeeds, through the mysterious death of his older brother, to the Dalcastle estate; Wringhim's own memoirs retelling these events from his increasingly distorted point of view, and carrying the narrative forward to the moment of his death; and the antiquarian editor's concluding account of the discovery of the memoirs and of Wringhim's death as reported in the "traditionary history."

The story begins with the short-lived marriage between tolerant, pleasure-loving old Laird Dalcastle and his lady, a Presbyterian bigot under the sway of "one flaming predestinarian divine alone"—the Reverend Wringhim. They separate, but not before Lady Dalcastle bears two sons, the happy, open-hearted George, and his haughty, misanthropic younger brother, Robert, whom the Laird rejects as a bastard. Wringhim then baptizes the boy in his own name and brings him up according to the strictest puritan tenets, teaching him to pray only for God's elect and to "doom all that are aliens from God to destruction"—particularly Laird Dalcastle and his other son. When George is found murdered, the testimony of the witnesses is curiously ambiguous. The old laird having died, Robert Wringhim, who has been consorting more and more frequently with a mysterious friend able to take on the appearance of whomever he pleases, assumes the lairdship. When the authorities send to question Robert about the murder, neither he nor his mother can be found: both are "lost."

Then follow the confessions proper, Wringhim's written version of these events. According to Wringhim, his life's turning point came when the reverend determined that his adoptive son was a member of God's elect, whose salvation is certain and "justified" despite any future sins he may commit. On the same day, young Wringhim meets an enigmatic friend, Gil-Martin, who shares his beliefs to the point of convincing Wringhim that it is his special privilege to act as a divine scourge. After taking possession of the Dalcastle estate, Wringhim begins to experience

Portrait in the Fraser's Magazine *"Gallery of Illustrious Literary Characters" (1830-1838)*

increasingly prolonged lapses of memory and hallucinations: "When I lay in bed, I deemed there were two of us in it. . . . The most perverse part was, that I rarely conceived *myself* to be any of the two persons." During his lucid intervals, he learns that he is accused of numerous crimes, including rape and matricide. Fleeing Dalcastle estate, the anguished Wringhim seeks anonymity in the country, but his pursuing demons create commotion and suspicion wherever he goes. In despair he apparently commits suicide, assured by Gil-Martin that his elect status protects him from damnation.

To an extent, the two tales complement each other as objective and subjective versions of the same events. Matched against the editor's story, Wringhim's tale reveals his hypocrisy and self-deception. But Gil-Martin possesses a definite reality in both accounts: if he is never quite a figment of Wringhim's religious schizophrenia neither is he so unambiguously supernatural that we can label him the devil. Instead of resolving the question of Wringhim's fate and the nature of his strange tormentor, the editor's closing remarks attempt to rationalize these perplexities with a complacency that hardly seems trustworthy.

Much in *The Justified Sinner* is a culmination of Hogg's best earlier work. The Calvinist Reverend Wringhim develops out of the hypocritical clerk in *The Brownie of Bodsbeck*; Gil-Martin's behavior recalls that of the demon Merodach in "The Brownie of The Black Haggs"; the candid shamelessness with which young Wringhim narrates his misdeeds echoes the tone of "Basil Lee" in *Winter Evening Tales*. If one ignores some important social differences between the characters and the author, George Dalcastle and his brother, Robert

Wringhim, can be seen as two aspects of Hogg himself: the confident, easygoing traditionalist, proud of his family roots and content simply to enjoy life, versus the ambitious writer, struggling uneasily to carve out a career in professional intellectual society while repelled by its Enlightenment rationalism and compromised spirituality. But the rivalry of the two brothers also implies a whole network of social-political conflicts between Whig and Tory, between the emergent middle class and the old gentry, between town and country, between individualism and tradition—conflicts which Hogg saw to be growing increasingly polarized. Thus, for example, Laird Dalcastle, previously a friend to Covenanter and Royalist alike, reacts to his lady's religious bigotry by running successfully as a Cavalier Member of Parliament. At the same time, Hogg is careful not to attack religion as such: Lady Dalcastle's principles, we are told, "were not the tenets of the great reformers, but theirs mightily overstrained and deformed . . . until nature could not longer bear it."

Although ownership of the Altrive farm soon bankrupted him again, and sales of *The Justified Sinner* were disappointing, Hogg was by now a celebrity in correspondence with the likes not only of Scott but Robert Southey, Byron, and Wordsworth, whom Hogg visited several times at Rydal Mount and who commemorated his own, long-delayed visit to Altrive in his "Extempore Effusion Upon the Death of James Hogg." Through his friendship with the reviewer John Wilson, Hogg had become a main contributor to William Blackwood's new magazine, a monthly devoted to Tory politics and literary criticism. In October 1817 *Blackwood's* was the sensation of Edinburgh with its "Translation from an Ancient Chaldee Ms.," a satire in biblical chapter and verse of the city's leading Whigs. The immediate occasion of the "Chaldee Manuscript" was a booksellers' squabble between Blackwood and Archibald Constable, a publisher from whom Blackwood had previously finagled Scott's Waverley novels. The article launched the magazine and attracted to it several rising talents. The "Chaldee Manuscript" was the collective effort of Hogg, John Wilson, and John Gibson Lockhart. In March 1822 *Blackwood's* introduced the *Noctes Ambrosianae*, purportedly a series of after-hours dialogues on literature, politics, and local characters at Ambrose's in Edinburgh, in which Hogg, appearing in the low-comedy role of the Shepherd, stimulates the more genteel wits of Wilson (alias Christopher North), William Maginn, Lockhart, and company. The *Noctes* ended in February 1835. Whether the Shepherd represents Hogg's own views, how far Hogg was exploited by his *Blackwood's* friends, and how far he willingly let himself be exploited—the third possibility implying that the Shepherd is no persona but a deliberate self-parody by which Hogg mocks his audience's presumed superiority to him—are all open questions.

On New Year's Day 1832 Hogg arrived in London to negotiate publication of a collected edition of his works which he hoped would solve his perpetual pecuniary difficulties. Characteristically, his visit was a personal success—he was lionized—but a financial flop: the bookseller went bankrupt after publishing only one of the projected twelve volumes. It is this volume, *Altrive Tales* (1832), that includes the most complete version of Hogg's *Memoirs of the Author's Life*, a detailed account of his efforts to establish himself as a man of letters and of his miscellaneous dealings and double-dealings with Edinburgh booksellers and publishers. Sir Walter Scott's death in 1832 set Hogg to writing his long-intended reminiscences of their friendship. These were published in New York in 1834 as *Familiar Anecdotes of Sir Walter Scott*, and appeared in a pirated London edition later that year as *The Domestic Manners and Private Life of Sir Walter Scott*. Although Lockhart, Scott's son-in-law, found Hogg's anecdotes outrageous and later took revenge by caricaturing Hogg in his own "official" biography of Scott (1837-1838), Hogg's deep sense of indebtedness to Scott is unmistakable, despite the bluntness with which he recounts their disagreements. In 1835 a collection of Hogg's previously unpublished prose stories appeared as *Tales of the Wars of Montrose* and sold only three hundred copies; a cash gift from the prime minister, Sir Robert Peel, gave some relief that year.

All his life, Hogg had been a skilled and vigorous athlete. Each year he helped organize the St. Ronan's Border Games, where, as Lockhart reported in his *Life of Scott*, Hogg "exerted himself lustily" and rarely failed "to carry off some of the prizes, to the astonishment of his juniors." In 1835 Hogg had been ill for some time with what was thought to be jaundice. A hunting expedition in August seemed to help, but by the end of October he took to his bed. On 21 November 1835 he died and was buried in Ettrick Churchyard beside the legendary Will o' Phaup.

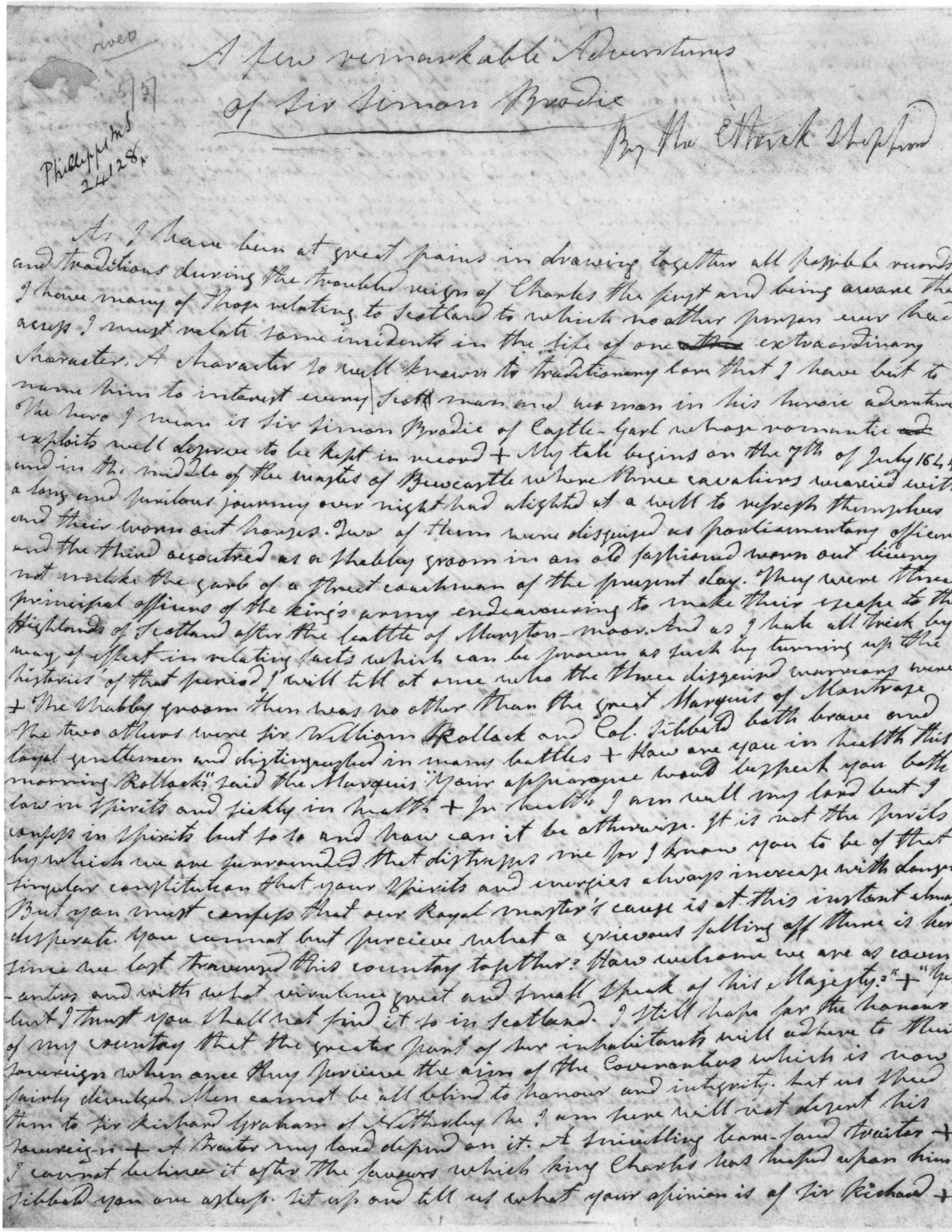

A few remarkable Adventures
of Sir Simon Brodie
By the Ettrick Shepherd

Phillipps MS 24128

As I have been at great pains in drawing together all possible records
and traditions during the troubled reign of Charles the first and being aware that
I have many of those relating to Scotland to which no other person ever had
access I must relate some incidents in the life of one ~~the~~ extraordinary
character. A character so well known to traditionary lore that I have but to
name him to interest every Scottish man and every man in his heroic adventures
The hero I mean is Sir Simon Brodie of Castle-Garl whose romantic
exploits well deserve to be kept in record + My tale begins on the 7th of July 1644
and in the middle of the wastes of Bewcastle where three cavaliers wearied with
a long and perilous journey over night had alighted at a well to refresh themselves
and their worn out horses. Two of them were disguised as parliamentary officers
and the third accoutred as a shabby groom in an old fashioned worn out livery
not unlike the garb of a street coachman of the present day. They were three
principal officers of the king's army endeavouring to make their escape to the
Highlands of Scotland after the battle of Marston-moor. And as I hate all trick by
way of effect in relating facts which can be proven as such by turning up the
histories of that period I will tell at once who the three disguised warriors were
+ The shabby groom then was no other than the great Marquis of Montrose
The two others were Sir William Rollock and Col. Sibbald both brave and
loyal gentlemen and distinguished in many battles + How are you in health this
morning Rollock?" said the Marquis "Your appearance would bespeak you both
low in spirits and sickly in health + "In health I am well my lord but I
confess in spirits but so so and how can it be otherwise. It is not the perils
by which we are surrounded that distresses me for I know you to be of that
singular constitution that your spirits and energies always increase with danger
But you must confess that our Royal master's cause is at this instant almost
desperate. You cannot but perceive what a grievous falling off there is here
since we last traversed this country together? How welcome we are as coun-
-ntries and with what virulence great and small speak of his Majesty?" + "Yes
but I trust you shall not find it so in Scotland. I still hope for the honour
of my country that the greater part of her inhabitants will adhere to their
sovereign when once they perceive the aims of the Covenanters which is now
fairly divulged. Men cannot be all blind to honour and integrity. Let us then
trust to Sir Richard Graham of Netherby he I am sure will not desert his
sovereign" + "A traitor my lord depend on it. A swindling base-hand traitor" +
I cannot believe it after the favours which King Charles has heaped upon him
Sibbald you are asleep. Sit up and tell us what your opinion is of Sir Richard +

Pages from the manuscript for a short story published in Tales of the Wars of Montrose *(HM 12410, Henry E. Huntington Library and Art Gallery)*

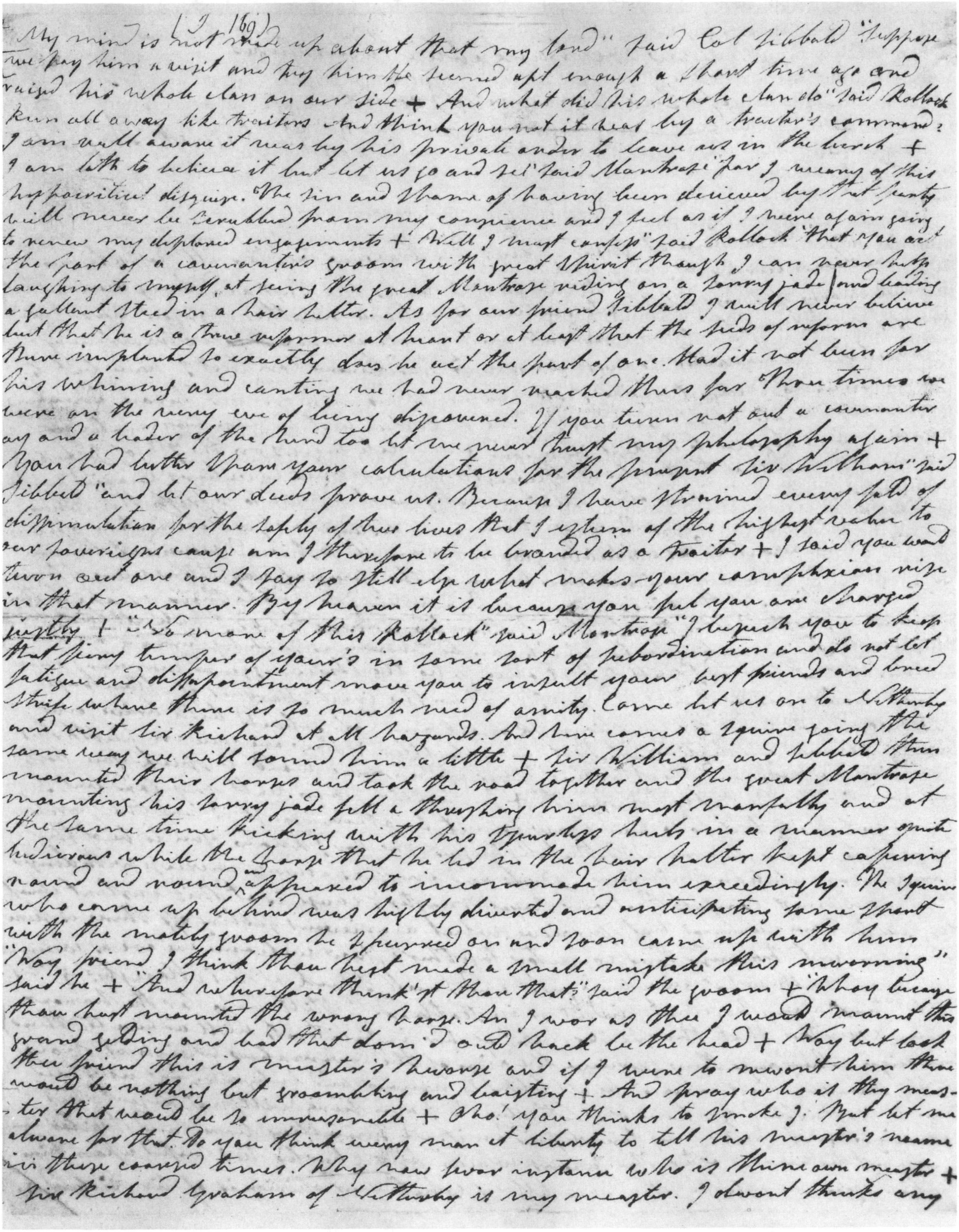
(J 169)
"My mind is not made up about that my lord" said Col Sibbald "Suppose
we pay him a visit and try him he seemed apt enough a short time ago and
raised his whole clan on our side + And what did his whole clan do" said Rollock
run all away like traitors And think you not it was by a traitor's command?
I am well aware it was by his private order to leave us in the lurch +
I am loth to believe it but let us go and see said Montrose for I weary of this
hypocritical disguise. The sin and shame of having been deceived by that party
will never be scrubbed from my conscience and I feel as if I were again going
to renew my deplored engagements + Well I must confess" said Rollock "that you act
the part of a covenanter's groom with great spirit though I can never help
laughing to myself at seeing the great Montrose riding on a sorry jade and leading
a gallant steed in a hair halter. As for our friend Sibbald I will never believe
but that he is a true reformer at heart or at least that the seeds of reform are
there implanted so exactly does he act the part of one. Had it not been for
his whining and canting we had never reached thus far. Three times we
were on the very eve of being discovered. If you turn not out a covenanter
ay and a leader of the herd too let me never trust my philosophy again +
You had better spare your calculations for the present Sir William" said
Sibbald "and let our deeds prove us. Because I have strained every fold of
dissimulation for the safety of these lives that I esteem of the highest value to
our sovereign's cause am I therefore to be branded as a traitor + I said you would
turn out one and I say so still else what makes your complexion rise
in that manner. By heaven it is because you feel you are charged
justly + "No more of this Rollock" said Montrose "I beseech you to keep
that fiery temper of your's in some sort of subordination and do not let
fatigue and disappointment move you to insult your best friends and breed
strife where there is so much need of amity. Come let us on to Netherby
and visit Sir Richard at all hazards. And here comes a squire going the
same way we will sound him a little + Sir William and Sibbald then
mounted their horses and took the road together and the great Montrose
mounting his sorry jade fell a thrashing him most manfully and at
the same time kicking with his spurless heels in a manner quite
ludicrous while the horse that he led in the hair halter kept capering
round and round and appeared to incommode him exceedingly. The squire
who came up behind was highly diverted and anticipating some sport
with the motly groom he spurred on and soon came up with him
"Nay friend I think thou hast made a small mistake this morning"
said he + "And wherefore think'st thou that" said the groom + "Why because
thou hast mounted the wrong horse. An I wor as thee I would mount this
grand gelding and lead that down ould hack be the head + Nay but look
thee friend this is master's horse and if I were to mount him there
would be nothing but grumbling and baisting + And pray who is thy master that would be so unreasonable + Oho! you thinks to smoke I. But let me
alone for that. Do you think every man at liberty to tell his master's name
in these cursed times. Why now for instance who is thine own master +
Sir Richard Graham of Netherby is my master. I dount thinks any

Since its rediscovery by André Gide in 1948, *The Private Memoirs and Confessions of a Justified Sinner* has been considered Hogg's greatest work. With its psychological sophistication, ironic framing, and rich sense of social history, the book has entered the canon of major nineteenth-century novels. Hogg's other writings are harder to assess. No doubt, he wrote too much too hastily—he was, after all, trying to earn a living by his pen. Victorian critics judged that his genius was impressive, but local rather than universal; and the bowdlerized, mediocre editions of his work, such as D. O. Hill's and Reverend Thomas Thomson's, tended to confirm this judgment. More recently, the influence of the Scottish nationalist movement has led to renewed appreciation of Hogg's writings precisely for their detailed awareness of local cultural conditions. Perhaps more than any other contemporary, Hogg not only understood but actually embodied in his own life the burgeoning conflict between the polite Edinburgh middle class, dependent for its values on the service industry of literary journalism, and the vanishing traditional values of the common folk. For he had a foot in both worlds.

Bibliography:

Edith C. Batho, "Bibliography," in her *The Ettrick Shepherd* (Cambridge: Cambridge University Press, 1927), pp. 183-222;

Batho, "Notes on the Bibliography of James Hogg, The Ettrick Shepherd," *Library*, fourth series 16 (December 1935): 309-326.

Biographies:

George Douglas, *James Hogg* (Edinburgh & London: Oliphant, Anderson & Ferrier, 1899);

Edith C. Batho, *The Ettrick Shepherd* (Cambridge: Cambridge University Press, 1927);

Alan Lang Strout, *The life and Letters of James Hogg, the Ettrick Shepherd*, volume 1 (1770-1825) (Lubbock: Texas Tech Press, 1946)—no more published.

References:

Douglas Gifford, *James Hogg* (Edinburgh: Ramsay Head Press, 1976);

R. P. Gillies, "Some Recollections of James Hogg," *Fraser's Magazine*, 20 (October 1839): 414-430;

David Groves, *James Hogg: The Growth of a Writer* (Edinburgh: Scottish Academic Press, 1988);

Gary Kelly, *English Fiction of the Romantic Period, 1789-1830* (London & New York: Longman, 1989), pp. 260-273;

Magdalene Redekop, "Beyond Closure: Buried Alive with Hogg's *Justified Sinner*," *ELH*, 52 (Spring 1985): 159-184;

Louis Simpson, *James Hogg: A Critical Study* (New York: St. Martin's Press, 1962);

Nelson C. Smith, *James Hogg* (Boston: Twayne, 1980);

Alan Lang Strout, "James Hogg's 'Chaldee Manuscript,' " *Publications of the Modern Language Association*, 65 (September 1950): 695-718.

Papers:

The National Library of Scotland in Edinburgh holds the largest collection of Hogg materials, including his letters. The Pierpont Morgan Library in New York possesses Hogg's manuscript for *Familiar Anecdotes of Sir Walter Scott*.

Theodore Hook

(22 September 1788 - 24 August 1841)

Louis J. Parascandola
Long Island University—Brooklyn Center

Theodore Hook

BOOKS: *The Soldier's Return; or What Can Beauty Do? A Comic Opera, in Two Acts* (London: Longman, Hurst, Rees & Orme, 1805; Philadelphia: Printed for Mathew Carey, 1807);

The Invisible Girl: A Piece in One Act, adapted from *Le Babillard*, by C. Maurice (London: Printed by and for C. & R. Baldwin, 1806; Baltimore: Printed by G. Dobbin & Murphy, 1807);

Catch Him Who Can! A Musical Farce, in Two Acts (London: Printed by and for C. & R. Baldwin, 1806);

Tekeli; or, The Siege of Montgatz: A Melo-drame, in Three Acts adapted from a play by René-Charles Guibert de Pixérécourt (London: Printed by and for C. & R. Baldwin, 1806; New York: D. Longworth, 1807);

The Fortress: A Melo-drama, in Three Acts, adapted from *La Forteresse du Danube*, by Pixérécourt (London: S. Tipper, 1807; Philadelphia: Published by Francis Shallus, 1808);

Music-Mad: A Dramatic Sketch (London: Printed by G. Sidney and sold by C. Chapple, 1808; New York: Published by the Longworths, 1812);

The Man of Sorrow, a Novel, as Alfred Allendale, 3 volumes (London: Printed for S. Tipper, 1808); republished as *Ned Musgrave: or, the Most Unfortunate Man in the World, a Comic Novel*, 1 volume (London: D. Bryce, 1854);

Safe and Sound: An Opera, in Three Acts (London: S. Tipper, 1809; New York: Published by D. Longworth, 1810);

Killing no Murder: A Farce, in Two Acts (London: Printed by W. Flint for S. Tipper, 1809; New York: Published by D. Longworth, 1809); revised as *A Day at an Inn: an Interlude, in One Act* (London: J. Pattie, 183?);

The Trial by Jury: A Comic Piece, in Two Acts (London: Sherwood, Neely & Jones, 1811; New York: Longworths, 1811);

Darkness Visible: A Farce, in Two Acts (London: C. Chapple, 1811; New York: Published by the Longworths, 1812);

Facts Illustrative of the Testament of Napoleon Bonaparte in Saint Helena (London: William Stockdale, 1819);

Tentamen; or, An Essay Towards the History of Whittington, Some Time Lord Mayor of London, as Vicesimus Blinkinsop (London: Printed for W. Wright, 1820);

Exchange no Robbery; or, the Diamond Ring: A Comedy in Three Acts (London: W. Wright, 1820);

Sayings and Doings: A Series of Sketches from Life (3 volumes, London: H. Colburn, 1824; 2 volumes, Philadelphia: H. C. Carey & I. Lea, 1824);

Sayings and Doings; or, Sketches from Life. Second Series (3 volumes, London: H. Colburn, 1825;

Hook circa 1800

2 volumes, Philadelphia: H. C. Carey & I. Lea, 1825);

Sayings and Doings; or, Sketches from Life. Third Series (3 volumes, London: H. Colburn, 1828; 2 volumes, Philadelphia: H. C. Carey & I. Lea, 1828);

Maxwell (3 volumes, London: H. Colburn & R. Bentley, 1830; 2 volumes, New York: Printed by J. & J. Harper, 1831; revised edition, 1 volume, London: R. Bentley, 1834);

The Life of General, the Right Honourable Sir David Baird, Bart, 2 volumes (London: R. Bentley, 1832);

The Parson's Daughter (3 volumes, London: R. Bentley, 1833; 2 volumes, Philadelphia: Carey, Lea & Blanchard, 1833; revised edition, 1 volume, London: R. Bentley, 1835);

Love and Pride (3 volumes, London: Whittaker, 1833; 2 volumes, Philadelphia: Carey, Lea & Blanchard, 1834); republished as *The Widow and the Marquess; or, Love and Pride,* 1 volume (London: R. Bentley, 1842);

Gilbert Gurney (3 volumes, London: Printed for Whittaker, 1836; 2 volumes, Philadelphia: Carey, Lea & Blanchard, 1836);

Jack Brag (3 volumes, London: R. Bentley, 1837; 1 volume, Philadelphia: Carey, Lea & Blanchard, 1837; revised edition, 1 volume London: R. Bentley, 1839);

Gurney Married: a Sequel to Gilbert Gurney (3 volumes, London: H. Colburn, 1838; 2 volumes, Philadelphia: Lea & Blanchard, 1839);

Births, Deaths, and Marriages (3 volumes, London: R. Bentley, 1839; 2 volumes, Philadelphia: Lea & Blanchard, 1839); republished as *All in the Wrong; or, Births, Deaths, and Marriages,* 1 volume (London: R. Bentley, 1842);

Precepts and Practice, 3 volumes (London: H. Colburn, 1840);

Fathers and Sons (3 volumes, London: H. Colburn, 1842; 2 volumes, Philadelphia: Lea & Blanchard, 1842);

Peregrine Bunce; or, Settled at Last, a Novel, completed by another author (3 volumes, London: R. Bentley, 1842; 1 volume, Philadelphia, Lea & Blanchard, 1844);

The Ramsbottom Letters (London: R. Bentley, 1872); republished as *The Ramsbottom Papers* (London: J. C. Hotten, 1874).

Collection: *The Choice Humorous Works, Ludicrous Adventures, Bon Mots, Puns and Hoaxes of Theodore Hook* (London: Hotten, 1873).

PLAY PRODUCTIONS: *The Soldier's Return, or, What Can Beauty Do?*, with overture and music by James Hook, London, Theatre Royal, Drury Lane, 23 April 1805;

The Invisible Girl, London, Theatre Royal, Drury Lane, 28 April 1806;

Catch Him Who Can!, with music by James Hook, London, Theatre Royal, Haymarket, 12 June 1806;

Tekeli; or, The Siege of Montgatz, with music by James Hook, London, Theatre Royal, Drury Lane, 24 November 1806;

The Fortress, with music by James Hook, London, Theatre Royal, Haymarket, 16 July 1807;

Music Mad, with music by James Hook, London, Theatre Royal, Haymarket, 27 August 1807;

The Siege of St. Quintin; or, Spanish Heroism, with music by James Hook, London, Theatre Royal, Drury Lane, 10 November 1808;

Killing no Murder, with music by James Hook, London, Theatre Royal, Haymarket, 21 August 1809; revised as *A Day at an Inn*, London, Lyceum, 25 August 1823;

Safe and Sound, with music by James Hook, London, Lyceum, 28 August 1809;

Ass-ass-ination, near Windsor, Orange House, 30 January 1810;

The Will, or the Widow; or, Puns in Plenty, near Windsor, Orange House, 30 January 1810;

The Trial by Jury, London, Theatre Royal, Haymarket, 25 May 1811;

Darkness Visible, London, Theatre Royal, Haymarket, 23 September 1811;

Exchange no Robbery; or, The Diamond Ring, London, Theatre Royal, Haymarket, 12 August 1820;

Over the Water, London, Theatre Royal, Haymarket, 23 September 1820.

OTHER: Michael Kelly, *The Reminiscences of Michael Kelly, of the King's Theatre Royal, Drury Lane, Including a Period of Nearly Half a Century with Original Anecdotes of Many Distinguished Persons, Political, Literary and Musical*, 2 volumes, ghostwritten by Hook (London: H. Colburn, 1826);

Alexandre Dumas, *Pascal Bruno: A Sicilian Story*, edited by Hook (London: H. Colburn, 1837; Philadelphia: Lea & Blanchard, 1839);

Harriet Maria Gordon Smythies, *Cousin Geoffrey, the Old Bachelor, a Novel*, 3 volumes, edited by Hook (London: R. Bentley, 1840);

Joseph Thomas James Hewlett, *The Parish Clerk*, 3 volumes, edited by Hook (London: H. Colburn, 1841);

Hewlett, *Peter Priggins, the College Scout*, 3 volumes, edited by Hook (London: H. Colburn, 1841);

Abraham Joseph Bénard (Fleury), *The French Stage and the French People, as Illustrated in the Memoirs of M. Fleury*, 2 volumes, edited by Hook (London: H. Colburn, 1841); republished as *Adventures of an Actor, Comprising a Picture of the French Stage during a Period of Fifty Years* (London: H. Colburn, 1842).

Theodore Hook once said of himself, "Give me a story to tell, and I can tell it, but I cannot create." This self-assessment aptly sums up the literary career of an author almost completely forgotten now, but one who was an important figure in the 1820s and 1830s and served as a link between eighteenth-century and Victorian novelists.

Theodore Edward Hook was born in London on 22 September 1788, to an artistic family. His father was James Hook, a noted musician who wrote more than two thousand songs; his mother, the former Miss Madden, wrote a farce titled *The Double Disguise* (1784); and his older brother, James, wrote librettos and novels.

Hook was a spirited youth, which resulted in his attending several schools, including Harrow, where two of his classmates were George Gordon, Lord Byron, and Robert Peel. There is a tale that, on Hook's first day at school, Byron dared Hook to heave a stone through the headmaster's window. Hook, characteristically, accepted the dare. The precocious youth soon started to write songs with his father and was regularly attending the theaters.

Hook's early literary work consisted of numerous melodramas and farces. In fact, he helped to introduce melodrama in England. His early plays *The Invisible Girl*, *Tekeli*, and *The Fortress*—produced in 1806 and 1807—were free translations from French melodramas. Byron, thinking about the elaborate escape in *Tekeli*, remarked in *English Bards, and Scotch Reviewers* (1809):

> Gods! o'er those boards shall Folly rear her head,
> Where Garrick trod, and Siddons loves to tread?
> On those shall Farce display Buffoon'ry's mask,
> And Hook conceal his heroes in a cask?

Hook next turned to farce. These works are undistinguished, relying on hackneyed plots usually involving cases of mistaken identities. As Myron F. Brightfield said in 1928, "the plays of Theodore Hook have no interest to-day for the student of literature. They are the work of a bright boy with an excellent memory and very little power of invention." Hook's playwriting served, however, as an apprenticeship during which he honed his natural talent for humor; in addition, he made important connections with such notables as Richard Brinsley Sheridan and actor Charles Mathews. His best-known play was *Killing no Murder*, a two-act farce which ran at the Haymarket for thirty-five performances in 1809. The play produced a stir because of its attacks on Methodists, and the licenser, a Methodist, would not permit the play to be performed until the offending lines were removed. Hook, a staunch defender of the Established Church, agreed but distributed printed copies of the suppressed scene. It would not be the last time Hook's strong conservative beliefs would cause a row.

Throughout his life Hook loved to mingle with the aristocracy. His passage into fashionable society was assured because of his musical skills and his reputation as a wit and a prankster. Perhaps his best-known prank was committed in 1810 when he vowed to make a woman who had angered him the talk of London. He proceeded to send more than four thousand letters to various merchants—one to an undertaker commissioning a made-to-order coffin—who descended en masse upon the unsuspecting woman's home.

Hook turned from playwriting in 1812 when he received an appointment as accountant-general and treasurer of the island of Mauritius. It was a position for which Hook was singularly unsuited, and he likely received the appointment because of his extemporaneous musical skills, which appealed to the Prince Regent (later George IV). It was a lucrative post, paying twenty-five hundred pounds a year, clearly an attraction to the high-living Hook who was heavily in debt. Hook seemed to be happy on the island, which had such amenities as a theater, a concert hall, and a racetrack. In 1818, however, Hook's idyllic stay suddenly ended when an unaccountable deficit was reported in the treasury.

Hook was forced to return to England, and while awaiting trial he turned his energies toward the Tory opposition to Queen Caroline, the estranged wife of George IV. He wrote a satire against her, *Tentamen; or, An Essay Towards the History of Whittington, Some Time Lord Mayor of London* (1820). Furthermore, he founded the short-lived periodical the *Arcadian* (1820) and the better-known magazine *John Bull* (1820-1841) almost entirely to attack the queen. *John Bull*, which Hook edited anonymously (though he was widely known to be responsible), created a tremendous stir with its vitriolic attacks on Caroline and her supporters. When she died in 1821, the magazine lost much of its impetus.

In 1821 Hook, though probably guilty only of negligence in the Mauritius affair, was declared to owe twelve thousand pounds. His political enemies may have contributed to his being declared guilty. At this point he moved to Somers Town, where he established a liaison with a woman who would later bear him five children, all left without any means of support on his death. In 1823 he was taken to a sponging house (a sort of debtors' prison) in Shire Lane and remained there until 1826. The experience at Shire Lane took a severe toll on his health.

While at Shire Lane Hook began writing fiction. Hook's novels generally reflect his conservative political bent, his interest in high society, and his keen sense of humor. Despite being carelessly written, the novels were quite popular when first published. The plots are loosely structured, and the major characters are vapid, although Hook was capable of creating vivid "humours" characters. Farcical touches are often combined with realistic descriptions of London life. Hook, who knew aristocratic London social circles well, was one of the first to exploit the growing interest in the "silver-fork novel" of the 1820s. William Hazlitt, in "The Dandy School" (*Examiner*, 18 November 1827), mocked Hook for his interest in fashionable life: "these privileged persons are not surely thinking all the time and every day of their lives of that which Mr. Theodore Hook has never forgotten since he first witnessed it, *viz.* that *they eat their fish with a silver fork*." The close attention to detail in these novels, particularly din-

Portrait in the Fraser's Magazine *"Gallery of Illustrious Literary Characters" (1830-1838)*

ing habits, however, often show Hook at his best, allowing him skillfully to ridicule vulgarians and would-be social climbers.

"Danvers," in the first series of Hook's popular *Sayings and Doings* (1824), reflects Hook's conservatism and his interest in fashionable living. The story, like the others in *Sayings and Doings*, is designed to illustrate a moral. This tale of a middle-class lawyer—who inherits a fortune, tries unsuccessfully to live above his station, and is happy only when he returns to his proper class—is meant to illustrate the saying: "Too much of a good thing is good for nothing." Hook published two further series of *Sayings and Doings* in 1825 and 1828. The ten stories in the three series are important for their emphasis on realism at a time when the Romantic novel was strongly in vogue. Other stories include "Merton" (a revision of *The Man of Sorrow*, published in 1808), "Gervase Skinner" (in which the title character is a reformed miser whose story illustrates the saying, "Penny wise and pound foolish"), and the curious Gothic tale "Martha the Gypsy" (set in 1820s London).

Hook followed this series of fiction with *Maxwell* (1830), *The Parson's Daughter* (1833), and *Love and Pride* (1833), all employing his knowledge of fashionable society. *Maxwell* bears some resemblance to "Newgate novels," popular criminal fiction of that period. The title character is a middle-class doctor who, while dissecting the "corpse" of a man hanged for a crime he did not commit, discovers the man is still alive. The book is in actuality an assault on the greed, hypocrisy, and pettiness of middle-class life. The main plot of *The Parson's Daughter* deals with the love affair of the highborn George Sheringham with Emma, daughter of a parson. They encounter many obstacles, including George's snobbish mother, but eventually they are united. The twist is that George has lost his fortune and Emma has gained her own. In *Love and Pride*, two stories, "Love" also deals with the reunion of two lovers who had been separated by chance, but the work is somewhat farcical in nature. "Pride" marks a return to the style of *Sayings and Doings*, exemplifying the saying that "Pride goes before a fall."

From 1830 through 1834 Hook also contributed stories to numerous periodicals, probably including *Blackwood's* and *Fraser's*. The editor of *Fraser's*, William Maginn, was a close friend of Hook's. In addition, Hook published a biography of a British officer, *The Life of General Sir David Baird* (1832).

Realizing that the vein of the fashionable novel had been exhausted, Hook relied more heavily on his old forte, farce, concentrating, usually unsympathetically, on middle-class characters. *Gilbert Gurney* (1836), generally regarded as Hook's best work, is somewhat autobiographical, chronicling the life of a hero who quits his study of law (Hook planned to study law at Oxford in 1810 and frequently satirized the legal profession) to attempt a career as a playwright. The plot is not nearly as interesting as the series of mishaps which befalls Gilbert and his erstwhile friend Daly before they miraculously, but predictably, arrive at a happy end. They are perpetrators and victims of a series of pranks. An example of the crude humor in the book involves a scene where the unsuspecting Daly spends the night lying with a corpse.

Hook was unable to duplicate the popularity of *Gilbert Gurney*. He tried to capitalize on its success with a poor sequel, *Gurney Married* (1838), which like its predecessor was first published in the *New Monthly Magazine*, a periodical edited by Hook from 1837 through 1841. *Jack Brag* (1837), like "Danvers," is a tale of a man who attempts to rise above his low birth but is only happy when he returns to his proper station, in Jack's case a humble life in the tallow business. *Peregrine Bunce* (1842), completed by another author after Hook's death in August 1841, tells of a mercenary man who attempts to arrange a loveless but "good" marriage in order to gain a legacy from a wealthy relative. In his final few years Hook, desperate for money, gave his name as editor to several books to which he actually contributed little.

Though his work is seldom read today, Hook was an important figure as a playwright, novelist, editor, and wit. Moreover, as Elliot Engel and Margaret F. King point out, Hook's novels, with their "exuberant profusion of realistic particulars, slapstick humour, and the delineation of contemporary middle-class life," influenced the early Charles Dickens, as well as William Makepeace Thackeray, and Anthony Trollope. Ironically, however, Hook may be best remembered in the portraits by other writers. Thackeray, though kind to Hook in his *Fraser's* reviews and a contributor himself to Hook's *New Monthly Magazine*, created a devastating caricature of him in the snobbish Mr. Wagg of *Vanity Fair* (1847-1848) and *Pendennis* (1848-1850). Benjamin Disraeli's Stanislaus Hoax in *Vivian Grey* (1826) and Lucian Gay in *Coningsby* (1844) provide more sympathetic portraits of Hook. Perhaps Gay, a man who wasted considerable abilities, is the most accurate fictional depiction of Hook. Unfortunately, one cannot read Hook without a sense of squandered talent.

Biographies:

John Gibson Lockhart, "Peregrine Bunce," *Quarterly Review* 72 (May 1843): 53-108;

R. H. Dalton Barham, *The Life and Remains of Theodore Edward Hook* (2 volumes, London: R. Bentley, 1849; revised edition, 1 volume, London: R. Bentley, 1855).

References:

Ernest A. Baker, *The History of the English Novel*, 10 volumes (London: Witherby, 1924-1939), VII: 206-221;

Myron F. Brightfield, *Theodore Hook and His Novels* (Cambridge: Harvard University Press, 1928);

Elliot Engel and Margaret F. King, *The Victorian Novel before Victoria: British Fiction during the Reign of William IV, 1830-37* (New York: St. Martin's Press, 1984).

George P. R. James

(9 August 1801 - 9 June 1860)

Raymond N. MacKenzie
University of St. Thomas

BOOKS: *The Ruined City, A Poem* (London: Printed for Henry Colburn, 1828);

Adia, or The Peruvians; The Ruined City; &c. (London: Henry Colburn, 1829);

Richelieu: A Tale of France (3 volumes, London: Henry Colburn, 1829; 2 volumes, New York: Printed by J. & J. Harper, sold by Collins & Hannay, 1829);

Darnley, or the Field of the Cloth of Gold (3 volumes, London: Henry Colburn & Richard Bentley, 1830; 2 volumes, New York: Printed by J. & J. Harper, sold by Collins & Hannay, 1830);

De L'Orme (3 volumes, London: Henry Colburn & Richard Bentley, 1830; 2 volumes, New York: Printed by J. & J. Harper, 1830);

The History of Chivalry (London: H. Colburn & R. Bentley, 1830; New York: Printed by J. & J. Harper, 1830);

Philip Augustus, or The Brothers in Arms (3 volumes, London: Henry Colburn & Richard Bentley, 1831; 2 volumes, New York: J. & J. Harper, 1831);

Henry Masterton, or the Adventures of a Young Cavalier (3 volumes, London: Henry Colburn & Richard Bentley, 1832; 2 volumes, New York: J. & J. Harper, 1832);

Memoirs of Great Commanders (3 volumes, London: Henry Colburn & Richard Bentley, 1832; 2 volumes, Philadelphia: E. L. Cary & A. Hart / Boston: W. D. Ticknor, 1835);

The String of Pearls (2 volumes, London: Richard Bentley, 1832; 1 volume, New York: Harper & Brothers, 1833);

The History of Charlemagne volume 1 of *France in the Lives of Her Great Men*, [no more published] (London: Longman, Rees, Orme, Brown, Green & Longman, 1832; New York: J. & J. Harper, 1832);

Delaware, or The Ruined Family (3 volumes, Edinburgh: Printed for Cadell, and Whittaker, London, 1833; 2 volumes, Philadelphia: Carey, Lea & Blanchard, 1833); republished as *Thirty Years Since, or The Ruined Family* 1 volume, (London: Simpkin, Marshall, 1848; New York: Harper, 1848);

Mary of Burgundy, or The Revolt of Ghent (3 volumes, London: Longman, Rees, Orme, Brown, Green & Longman, 1833; 2 volumes, New York: J. & J. Harper, 1833);

The Life and Adventures of John Marston Hall (3 volumes, London: Longman, Rees, Orme, Brown, Green & Longman, 1834; New York: Harper & Brothers, 1834); republished as *The Little Ball O'Fire, or The Life and Adventures of John Marston Hall* (London: Parry, 1848);

The Gipsey, A Tale (3 volumes, London: Printed for Longman, Rees, Orme, Brown, Green & Longman, 1835; 2 volumes, New York: Harper & Brothers, 1835);

My Aunt Pontypool (3 volumes, London: Saunders & Otley, 1835; 2 volumes, Philadelphia: Carey, 1836); republished as *Aims and Obstacles, A Romance* (New York: Harper & Brothers, 1868);

One in a Thousand; or, The Days of Henry Quatre (3 volumes, London: Longman, Rees, Orme, Brown, Green & Longman, 1835; 2 volumes, New York: Harper & Brothers, 1836);

On The Educational Institutions of Germany (London: Saunders & Otley, 1835);

The Desultory Man (3 volumes, London: Saunders & Otley, 1836; 2 volumes, New York: Harper & Brothers, 1836);

A History of the Life of Edward the Black Prince and of Various Events Connected Therewith Which Occurred During the Reign of Edward III, King of England, 2 volumes (London: Printed for Longman, Rees, Orme, Brown, Green & Longman, 1836; Philadelphia: Carey & Hart, 1842);

Eminent Foreign Statesmen, volumes 2-5, in *The Cabinet Cyclopaedia*, conducted by the Rev. Dionysius Lardner (London: Printed for Longman, Rees, Orme, Brown, Green & Longman, 1836-1838); volume 2 repub-

Engraving after an 1839 portrait by Houghton

lished as *Lives of the Cardinal de Richelieu, Count Oxenstiern—Count Olívarez and Cardinal Mazarin*, 2 volumes (Philadelphia: Carey, Lea & Blanchard, 1836); volume 3 republished in part in *Lives of Cardinal de Retz, Jean Baptiste Colbert, John de Witt, and the Marquis de Louvois*, 2 volumes (Philadelphia: Carey, Lea & Blanchard, 1837);

Attila, A Romance (3 volumes, London: Printed for Longmans, Rees, Orme, Brown, Green & Longman, 1837; 2 volumes, New York: Harper & Brothers, 1837);

The Robber, A Tale (3 volumes, London: Longman, Orme, Brown, Green & Longmans, 1838; 2 volumes, New York: Harper & Brothers, 1838);

The Life and Times of Louis the Fourteenth (4 volumes, London: Richard Bentley, 1838; 2 volumes, New York: Harper & Brothers, 1847);

A Book of The Passions (London: Longman, Orme, Brown, Green & Longmans / Paris: Delloy, 1839; Philadelphia: Lea & Blanchard, 1839; enlarged edition, Paris: Published by A. & W. Galignani, 1839); original contents republished as *Remorse and Other Tales* (New York: Bunce & Brothers, 1852);

The Huguenot: A Tale of the French Protestants (3 volumes, London: Printed for Longman, Orme, Brown, Green & Longmans, 1839; 2 volumes, New York: Harper & Brothers, 1839);

Charles Tyrrell; or, The Bitter Blood, 2 volumes (London: Richard Bentley, 1839; New York: Harper & Brothers, 1839);

Henry of Guise, or The States of Blois (3 volumes, London: Printed for Longman, Orme, Brown, Green & Longmans, 1839; 2 volumes, New York: Harper & Brothers, 1839);

The Gentleman of the Old School, A Tale (3 volumes, London: Printed for Longman, Orme, Brown, Green & Longmans, 1839; 2 volumes, New York: Harper & Brothers, 1839);

A Brief History of the United States Boundary Question (London: Saunders & Otley, 1839);

Blanche of Navarre, A Play (London: Longman, Orme, Brown, Green & Longmans, 1839; New York: Harper & Brothers, 1839);

The King's Highway, A Novel (3 volumes, London: Longman, Orme, Brown, Green & Longmans, 1840; 2 volumes, New York: Harper & Brothers, 1840);

The Man at Arms; or, Henri de Cerons: A Romance, 2 volumes (London: Richard Bentley, 1840; New York: Harper & Brothers, 1840);

Bertrand de La Croix, or The Siege of Rhodes (London: Published by J. Clements, 1841)—first published in *The Club Book*, 3 volumes (London: Printed for Cochrane & Pickersgell, 1831);

Corse de Leon, or The Brigand, A Romance (3 volumes, London: Longman, Orme, Brown, Green & Longmans, 1841; 2 volumes, New York: Harper & Brothers, 1841); republished as *The Brigand, or Corse de Leon, A Romance*, 1 volume (London: Smith, Elder, 1846);

The Ancient Regime: A Tale (3 volumes, London: Printed for Longman, Brown, Green & Longmans, 1841; 2 volumes, New York: Harper & Brothers, 1841); republished as *Castelneau; or, The Ancient Regime*, 1 volume (London: Simpkin, Marshall, 1849);

The Jacquerie; or, The Lady and the Page: An Historical Romance (3 volumes, London: Longman, Brown, Green & Longmans, 1841; 2 volumes, New York: Harper & Brothers, 1842);

Some Remarks on The Corn Laws with Suggestions for an Alteration in the Sliding Scale in a Letter to Col. Charles Wyndham, M.P. (London: John Olliver, 1841);

Morley Ernstein, or The Tenants of the Heart (3 volumes, London: Saunders & Otley, 1842; 1 volume, New York: Harper & Brothers, 1842);

A History of the Life of Richard Coeur-de-Lion King of England, 4 volumes (London: Saunders & Otley, 1842-1849; New York: J. & H. G. Langley, 1842-?);

The Commissioner; or, De Lunatico Inquirendo (Dublin: William Curry / London: Orr / Edinburgh: Fraser, 1843; New York: Harper & Brothers, 1851);

Forest Days, A Romance of Old Times (3 volumes, London: Saunders & Otley, 1843; 1 volume, New York: Harper & Brothers, 1843);

The False Heir (3 volumes, London: Richard Bentley, 1843; 1 volume, New York: Harper & Brothers, 1843);

Eva St. Clair and Other Collected Tales (2 volumes, London: Printed for Longman, Brown, Green & Longmans, 1843; 1 volume, Philadelphia: T. B. Peterson, 1853?);

Arabella Stuart, A Romance from English History (3 volumes, London: Richard Bentley, 1844; 1 volume, New York: Harper & Brothers, 1844);

Agincourt, A Romance (3 volumes, London: Richard Bentley, 1844; 1 volume, New York: Harper & Brothers, 1844);

Rose D'Albret; or, Troublous Times (3 volumes, London: Richard Bentley, 1844; 1 volume, New York: Harper & Brothers, 1844);

Arrah Neil; or, Times of Old (1 volume, New York: Harper & Brothers, 1844; 3 volumes, London: Smith, Elder, 1845);

The Smuggler, A Tale (3 volumes, London: Smith, Elder, 1845; 1 volume, New York: Harper & Brothers, 1845);

The Stepmother (London: Printed for private circulation, 1845; 3 volumes, London: Smith, Elder, 1846; 2 volumes, New York: Harper & Brothers, 1846);

Heidleberg, A Romance (3 volumes, London: Smith, Elder, 1846; 1 volume, New York: Harper & Brothers, 1846);

The Castle of Ehrenstein, Its Lords, Spiritual and Temporal, Its Inhabitants, Earthly and Unearthly (3 volumes, London: Smith, Elder, 1847; 1 volume, New York: Harper & Brothers, 1847);

A Whim and Its Consequences (3 volumes, London: Smith, Elder, 1847; 1 volume, New York: Harper, 1848);

The Convict, A Tale (3 volumes, London: Smith, Elder, 1847; 1 volume, New York: Harper & Brothers, 1847);

Russell, A Tale of the Reign of Charles II (3 volumes, London: Smith Elder, 1847; 1 volume, New York: Harper & Brothers, 1850);

The Life of Henry the Fourth, King of France and Navarre (3 volumes, London: T. & W. Boone, 1847; 2 volumes, New York: Harper & Brothers, 1847);

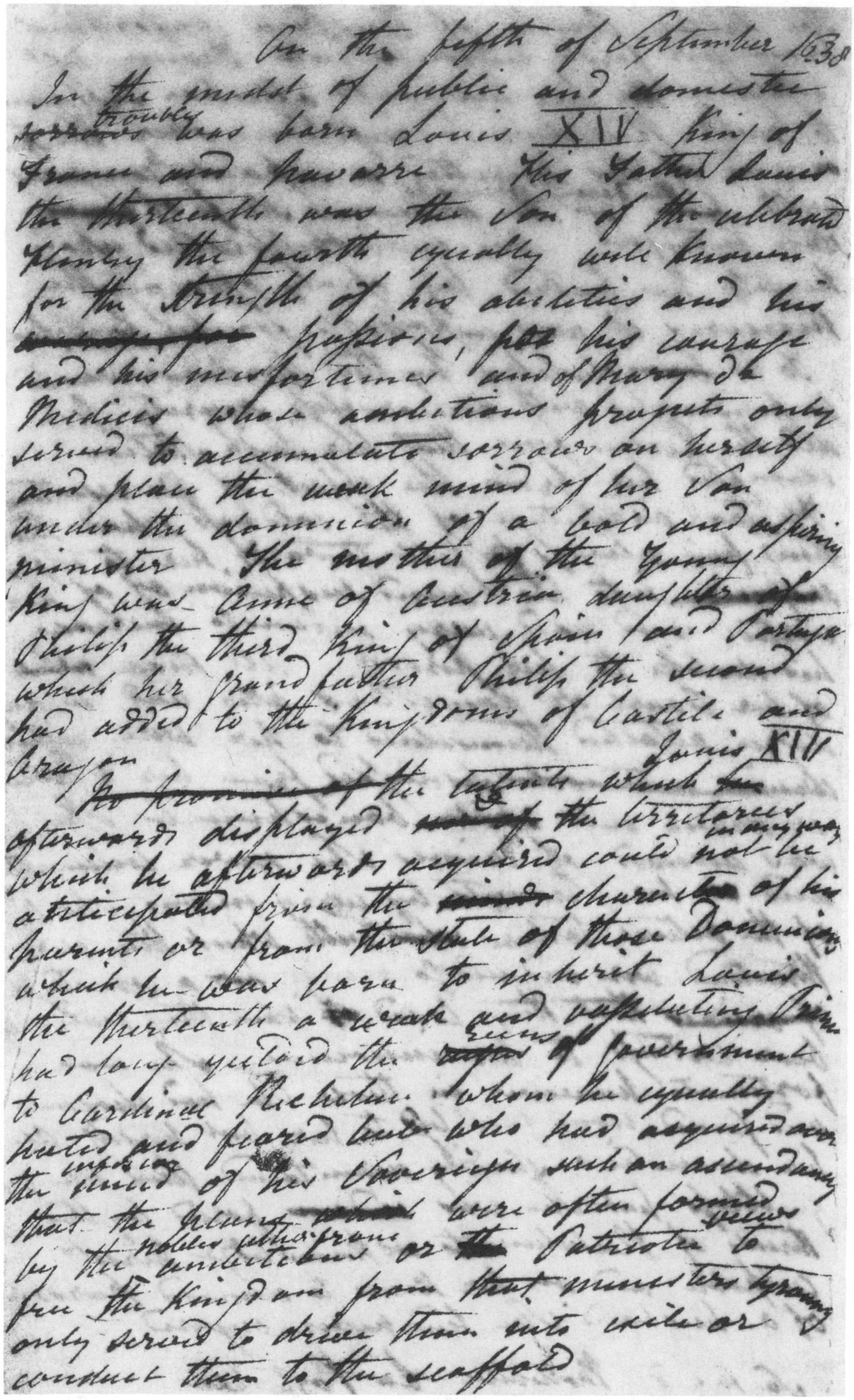

On the fifth of September 1638
In the midst of public and domestic
~~sorrows~~ troubles was born Louis XIV King of
France and Navarre. His Father Louis
the thirteenth was the Son of the celebrated
Henry the fourth equally well known
for the strength of his abilities and his
~~[illegible]~~ passions, for his courage
and his misfortunes and of Mary de
Medicis whose ambitious projects only
served to accumulate sorrows on herself
and place the weak mind of her Son
under the dominion of a bold and aspiring
minister. The mother of the young
King was Anne of Austria daughter ~~of~~
Philip the third King of Spain and Portugal
which her grandfather Philip the second
had added to the Kingdoms of Castile and
Aragon
~~No promise of~~ the talents which Louis XIV
afterwards displayed ~~[illegible]~~ & the territories
which he afterwards acquired could in any way not be
anticipated from the ~~[illegible]~~ character of his
parents or from the state of those Dominions
which he was born to inherit. Louis
the thirteenth a weak and vacillating Prince
had long yielded the ~~[illegible]~~ reins of government
to Cardinal Richelieu whom he equally
hated and feared but who had acquired over
the imposing mind of his Sovereign such an ascendancy
that the plans ~~which~~ were often formed
by the nobles either from ambition or ~~the~~ Patriotic views to
free the Kingdom from that minister's tyranny
only served to drive them into exile or
conduct them to the scaffold

Pages from the manuscript for The Life and Times of Louis the Fourteenth *(HM 11902, Henry E. Huntington Library and Art Gallery)*

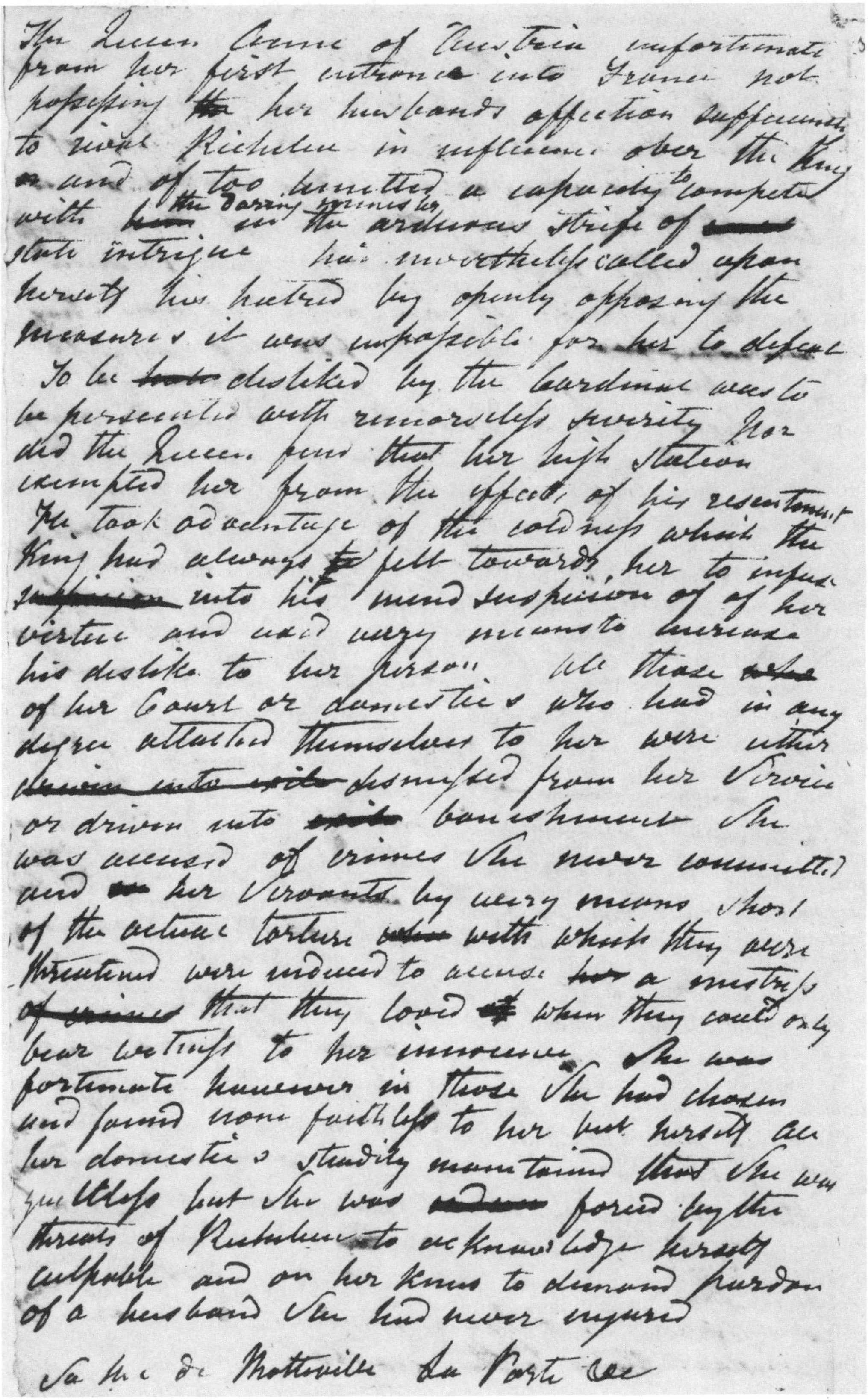
The Queen Anne of Austria unfortunate from her first entrance into France not possessing ~~the~~ her husbands affection sufficient to rival Richelieu in influence over the King ~~a~~ and of too limited a capacity to compete with ~~him~~ the daring minister in the arduous strife of ~~[illegible]~~ state intrigue had nevertheless called upon herself his hatred by openly opposing the measures it was impossible for her to defeat
To be ~~hated~~ disliked by the Cardinal was to be persecuted with remorseless severity nor did the Queen find that her high station exempted her from the effects of his resentment
He took advantage of the coldness which the King had always ~~to~~ felt towards her to infuse ~~suspicion~~ into his mind suspicion of of her virtue and used every means to increase his dislike to her person All those ~~who~~ of her Court or domestics who had in any degree attached themselves to her were either ~~driven into exile~~ dismissed from her Service or driven into ~~exile~~ banishment She was accused of crimes she never committed and ~~[illegible]~~ her Servants by every means short of the actual torture ~~[illegible]~~ with which they were threatened were induced to accuse ~~her~~ a mistress ~~of crimes~~ that they loved ~~of~~ when they could only bear witness to her innocence. She was fortunate however in those she had chosen and found none faithless to her but herself all her domestics steadily maintained that she was guiltless but she was ~~[illegible]~~ forced by the threats of Richelieu to acknowledge herself culpable and on her knees to demand pardon of a husband she had never injured
Vide Mde de Motteville La Porte &c

Beauchamp; or The Error (1 volume, New York: Harper & Brothers, 1847; 3 volumes, London: Smith, Elder, 1848);

Margaret Graham (1 volume, New York: Harper & Brothers, 1847; 2 volumes, London: Parry, 1848);

The Last of the Fairies (London: Parry and Company, 1848 [i.e., 1847]; New York: Harper & Brothers, 1848);

Sir Theodore Broughton; or, Laurel Water (3 volumes, London: Smith, Elder, 1846; 1 volume, New York: Harper & Brothers, 1848);

Camaralzaman: A Fairy Drama (London: Charles Ollier, 1848);

Gowrie, or, The King's Plot (London: Simpkin, Marshall, 1848; New York: Harper & Brothers, 1848);

An Investigation of the Circumstances attending the Murder of John Earl of Gowrie and Alexander Ruthven By Order of King James the Sixth of Scotland (London: Simpkin, Marshall, 1849);

The Woodman, A Romance of the Times of Richard III (3 volumes, London: T. C. Newby, 1849; 1 volume, New York: Harper, 1855);

The Forgery, or Best Intentions (3 volumes, London: T. C. Newby, 1849; 1 volume, New York: Harper & Brothers, 185-);

John Jones's Tales for Little John Joneses, 2 volumes (London: Cradock, 1849);

Dark Scenes of History (3 volumes, London: T. C. Newby, 1849; 1 volume, New York: Harper & Brothers, 1850);

The Old Oak Chest, A Tale of Domestic Life (3 volumes, London: T. C. Newby, 1850; 1 volume, New York: Harper, 1850);

Henry Smeaton, A Jacobite Story of the Reign of George the First (3 volumes, London: T. C. Newby, 1851 [i.e., 1850]; 1 volume, New York: Harper & Brothers, 1850);

The Connection between Literature, Science, and the Arts, An Address Delivered before the Literary Societies of Hamilton College, at Clinton, N.Y., July 22, 1851 (Utica: Seward & Thurber, 1851);

The Fate, A Tale of Stirring of Times (3 volumes, London: T. C. Newby, 1851; 1 volume, New York: Harper & Brothers, 1851);

Adrian, or the Clouds of the Mind, by James and Maunsell B. Field (2 volumes, London: T. & W. Boone, 1852; 1 volume, New York: D. Appleton, 1852);

Pequinillo, A Tale (3 volumes, London: T. C. Newby, 1852; 1 volume, New York: Harper & Brothers, 1852);

Revenge: A Novel, 3 volumes (London: T. C. Newby, 1852); republished as *A Story Without a Name*, 1 volume (New York: Stringer & Townsend, 1852); republished as *The Man in Black* (Philadelphia: T. B. Peterson, 1860);

A Life of Vicissitudes, 1 volume (New York: Harper & Brothers, 1852; republished as *The Vicissitudes of a Life*, 3 volumes (London: T. C. Newby, 1853);

An Oration on the Character and Services of the Late Duke of Wellington, Delivered Before The British Residents of Boston and Vicinity, and their American Friends at the Melocleon, November 10th, 1852 (Boston: Ticknor, Reed & Fields, 1853);

Agnes Sorrel, An Historical Romance (3 volumes, London: T. C. Newby, 1853; 1 volume, New York: Harper & Brothers, 1853);

Ticonderoga, or The Black Eagle, A Tale of Times Not Long Past (3 volumes, London: T. C. Newby, 1854; 1 volume, New York: Harper & Brothers, 1854); republished as *The Black Eagle, or Ticonderoga* (London: Routledge, 1859);

Prince Life: A Story for My Boy (London: T. C. Newby, 1852);

The Old Dominion, or The Southampton Massacre, A Novel (1 volume, New York: Harper & Brothers, 1856; 3 volumes, London: T. C. Newby, 1856);

Leonora D'Orco, A Historical Romance (3 volumes, London: T. C. Newby 1857; 1 volume, New York: Harper & Brothers, 1857);

Lord Montagu's Page, A Historical Romance (3 volumes, London: T. C. Newby, 1858; 1 volume, Philadelphia: Childs & Peterson, 1858);

The Cavalier, An Historical Novel, 1 volume (Philadelphia: T. B. Peterson and Brothers, 1859); republished as *Bernard Marsh, A Novel*, 2 volumes (London: Richard Bentley, 1864);

The Bride of Landeck (New York: Harper & Brothers, 1878).

Collection: *The Works of G. P. R. James*, 21 volumes (volumes 1-11: London: Smith, Elder, volumes 12-16: London: Parry, volumes 17-21: London: Simpkin, Marshall, 1844-1849).

OTHER: *Letters Illustrative of the Reign of William III from 1696 to 1708 Addressed to The Duke of Shrewsbury by James Vernon, Esq.*, 3 volumes, edited by James (London: Henry Colburn, 1841).

The Shrubbery in Upper Walmer, Kent, James's home in 1841-1843 and 1847

Though his books are seldom read today, G. P. R. James was one of the most prolific novelists of his time, popular both in Britain and in the United States. He produced more than ninety books, chiefly historical romances set in a wide variety of places and eras, and most of them were highly successful. One index of his popularity is to be found in the publishing figures of the Popular Library and Railway Library series, which produced cheap editions for travelers and casual readers. Between 1847 and 1860 the two series printed forty-seven titles by James; the nearest competitor in the series was Edward Bulwer-Lytton, with nineteen titles. There is also William Makepeace Thackeray's anecdote concerning a visit he made to his American publisher, James Harper, in 1852: Thackeray asked Harper who his most popular author was, and was abashed to hear that "James heads the list, far ahead of any author, as you can judge for yourself by glancing at the number of his books sold. He turns out a novel every six months, and the success is always the same, and tremendous."

The son of Pinkston and Jean Churnside James, George Payne Rainsford James was born in London, two doors down the street from the playwright Thomas Sheridan. James's grandfather, Robert James, was a good friend of Samuel Johnson and grew wealthy from his invention of a medication known as James's Powder for Fevers, which was enormously successful both in England and on the Continent. (There was a minor scandal when it was believed that the powder had caused Oliver Goldsmith's death, but modern scholars think this theory unlikely.) The novelist's father was also a doctor, and moved in affluent circles; he was physician to the Prince Regent (later George IV). When George James was thirteen, he was introduced to George Gordon, Lord Byron, who nicknamed him "Little Devil." Byron remained a favorite of James throughout his life, and something of the atmosphere of Byron's early verse romances permeates many of James's novels.

Byron's nickname indicated a part of a young James's personality—headstrong and adventurous. At the age of fourteen he joined the army to fight against Napoleon and just narrowly missed taking part in the Battle of Waterloo (June 1815). Later, he would write about this era in his life under the title of "Extracts from the Portfolio of an Adventure Seeker" (in *Harper's Monthly*, March 1853 - August 1855). He wandered about Europe for some time after being discharged from the army, and began to try his hand at writing. The earliest work that survives is

James in 1844 (engraving after a portrait by F. Cruickshank)

a series of six tales in imitation of the *Arabian Nights*, written by the time he was seventeen; the tales were published in 1832 as *The String of Pearls*. In 1816 he met Washington Irving at an inn in Bordeaux. Irving encouraged James in his literary efforts, but he did not begin work on his first novel until 1825. In some uncertainty as to the worth of it, he agonized over the first draft for some time (quite uncharacteristic of the mature James), but finally an aunt who had been a schoolmate of Sir Walter Scott paved the way for James to send the manuscript to Scott, asking his opinion of it. James waited three months for Scott's reply—which, when it finally arrived, was encouraging. This expert opinion was all James needed, and he sent the novel off to the publisher Henry Colburn. The novel was published in 1829 as *Richelieu: A Tale of France* and was an immediate success—so much so that Colburn offered him five hundred pounds for his next novel.

Set in 1685, during the Cinq-Mars rebellion, *Richelieu* is not James's best work, but it is in many ways typical. The main characters are fictional, while the historical characters and events are mostly backgrounded. The hero, the Comte de Bleneau, is wrongly thought by Richelieu to be mixed up in the Cinq-Mars plotting, and, after a series of duels, escapes, disguises, kidnappings, and intrigues, Bleneau is imprisoned and sentenced to death. There is a love interest in the character of Pauline de Beaumont, and the hero is accompanied in most of his adventures by two semicomic but courageous and faithful companions, Henry de la Mothe and Philip, a woodsman. At the climactic moment, Bleneau is saved from the executioner's block by a last-minute reprieve from the king, who has learned the truth. Bleneau is freed, and rides off to be reunited with Pauline. Taken strictly as an adventure story, *Richelieu* is fast-paced and readable, but the main characters are rather lifeless and uninteresting—criticisms that apply, to one degree or another, to many of James's works. And the novel suffers by comparison with Alfred de Vigny's *Cinq-Mars*, published in 1826.

His next novel, however, rises above these weaknesses and deserves a modern readership. *Darnley, or the Field of the Cloth of Gold* (1830) is set in England in 1520, about twenty years after the pretender Perkin Warbeck attempted to seize the throne of Henry VII. Its title character is a young nobleman whose father had been associated with Warbeck. Returning to his homeland to attempt to convince Henry VIII to reinstate his family to favor, Darnley chooses to prove himself to Henry first under an assumed name, planning to reveal his true identity only after the king has seen his true worth. Darnley is hindered in this by the machinations of Cardinal Thomas Wolsey, who is misled by Sir Payan Wileton into thinking Darnley is a traitor. Wolsey also figures in the love interest, deciding that Darnley's love, Lady Katrine, should marry someone else. Many of the plot elements come from the standard romance catalogue: disguises, mistaken identities, hairbreadth escapes, and the like are prominent. But the novel as a whole is better than a summary might sound. James's narrative persona in this novel is one of his best—a raconteur somewhat in the manner of Henry Fielding, willing to digress when the mood takes him, frequently addressing the reader directly in an easy and unstrained manner. His scenes of natural description are vivid and not overlong; there is a shipwreck scene late in the story that is one of James's most exciting moments. Many characters from all levels of society people the story, giving it a rich tapestrylike effect and giving the reader the sensation of seeing what English life in 1520 might really have been like. The main characters too are quite lifelike and interesting, much more than the mere counters of *Richelieu*. The villain, Wileton, is a fascinating creation. He is finally undone through the efforts of an old alchemist and astrologer, Sir Cesar, who adds a Spenserian flavor to the parts of the story wherein he figures. With the exception of Wileton, most of the characters are not one-dimensional. The historical figures, especially Henry and Wolsey, are interestingly drawn, and James does not let us calculate their next moves too soon; Wolsey in particular is effective, as the reader does not know until close to the end whether he is the standard Machiavellian or a real human capable of surprising the reader.

In *Darnley*, as in most of James's novels, he is at pains to convince the reader of the historical accuracy of the story. He frequently cites his sources, often quoting directly from them to prove some point about the customs or dress of the period and often insisting he is writing true history, not mere romance. By the standards of a modern historian, James would no doubt be found lacking, but it is important to remember that he saw the historical content of his work as serious, and his public did also. One of the reasons for the immense popularity of Walter Scott's Waverley novels was their historical content; a significant portion of the novel-reading public was getting its history from such novelists as James, Scott, Harrison Ainsworth, and Bulwer-Lytton, and these writers took their mission of educating their readers quite seriously. James reveals this attitude in a 10 July 1835 letter to Allan Cunningham, where he says he resents the lack of government support for his writing, and "though I would willingly devote my time and even my money to elucidate the dark points of our own history, yet encouragement from the public is small and from the Government does not exist, so that I lay down the pen in despair of ever seeing English History anything but what it is—a farrago of falsehoods and hypotheses covered over with the tinsel of specious reasoning from wrong data." Another instance of his attitude occurred in 1848: when the *Examiner* accused him of shoddy research in his novel *Gowrie* (1848), he published a lengthy pamphlet to prove his thesis that James VI had ordered the murder of John, Earl of Gowrie.

His complaint about recognition from the government was soon answered. His nonfiction *History of the Life of Edward the Black Prince* (1836) resulted in his appointment as historiographer royal to William IV. This appointment, in addition to the great gratification it gave James, is further proof of the early-nineteenth-century attitude toward work such as his and of the seriousness with which its historical content was viewed. Throughout the 1830s James produced a great many novels and several other substantial historical studies. His publisher gave him one thousand pounds in advance for his *Life and Times of Louis the Fourteenth* (1838), and the sales of his works continued to grow. Serious critics, however, did not give James the recognition he felt he deserved, and indeed some (including Thackeray) found him to be merely a purveyor of hackneyed plots and characters. He acquired

The house in Stockbridge, Massachusetts, where James lived in 1851 and 1852

the nickname of The Solitary Horseman, since so many of his novels opened with a lone horseman dramatically riding into the foreground. (He was rather fond of the nickname, though once he heard about it he made a point of never opening a novel that way again.)

One of James's traits that aroused a great deal of criticism was his sheer productivity: in 1839, for example, he published no fewer than seven books; ever since *Richelieu* his output had been staggering. He addressed this issue many times, both in the prefaces to his novels and in letters to friends and publishers, saying that he wrote better when he wrote quickly: his inspiration had no time to wane, and he was better able to keep the whole plan of the work in mind at one time. This productivity naturally resulted in charges of mechanical production of novels rather than true careful writing. Such charges exasperated James. As he wrote to Cunningham on 22 December 1833, "Why is it that I write too fast for that slow beast the Public? Is it because I rise earlier? or because I do it every day and cannot do without it? There are four and twenty hours in the day, are there not? Seven for sleep, four for dressing and feeding, four for reading, five for exercise and pleasure and four for writing. I cannot write less than five pages in an hour, which gives at the above calculation six thousand pages in a year of three hundred days.... There is no recourse but to write on and smother our executors under dust and manuscripts." James omits to mention here that he also found time for an active family and social life. He had married Frances Thomas on 3 December 1828, and they had four children. By all accounts James was an involved and conscientious husband and father, and he was also a convivial, social man, fond of conversation, who attracted a great many friends; though he never belonged to any literary circles, he counted as acquaintances many of the writers of his day.

The 1840s were as productive as the previous decade for James. During this time he also stood for Parliament and was very active in organizing reform of the copyright laws, championing the rights of writers whose works were being pirated. He was hardly disinterested in the issue himself, since many of his own novels were showing up in cheap, unauthorized editions in Britain and America. His work resulted in significant copyright reform. During this period, also, he began to experience financial difficulties. He was not independently wealthy (the profits from his grandfather's powders were long gone), and though he was paid well by the standards of the time for his work, he did not accumulate the kind of wealth that a modern writer of his stature and sales figures might. His problems began with the publication of a set of his *Collected Works*, which ap-

James in 1858

peared from 1844 to 1849. A complicated financial arrangement with the engraver went awry, and James was sued; he ended up having to pay out several thousand pounds, which virtually ruined his family. In desperation he decided to immigrate to America, where he hoped to start anew and make a living by writing and lecturing.

The family arrived in New York on 4 July 1850, and James soon set out to negotiate with the publisher James Harper, who offered James a disappointing arrangement that James nonetheless accepted. Shortly thereafter, he discovered Harper was paying less popular authors the same or more; after an angry confrontation, Harper relented and quadrupled James's payments. James then settled into life in Stockbridge, Massachusetts, and began a series of successful lectures. He also befriended Nathaniel Hawthorne and other American writers. And, of course, he continued to write. One of his most successful novels, *The Fate*, was printed in 1851. Dealing with the time of James II and the issue of limited monarchy and democracy, the novel was extremely popular in America; James was delighted to read in the *New York Evening Post* that the entire first chapter had been read aloud in the Supreme Court as an accurate description of the situation in England in James II's day. In *The Fate* James includes a defense of his repeating many of the same motifs in his novels on the grounds that it is human nature to repeat what we do best, and that the repetition is confined to a few of his many books, adding: "They are, perhaps, too many; but, though I must die, some of them will live—I know it, I feel it; and I must continue to write while this spirit is in this body." During this period he also befriended Maunsell B. Field, and the two collaborated on a novel (the first time James had tried collaboration) titled *Adrian* (1852).

James was also seeking out a government post to enhance his income, and in 1852 he was given the job of British consul in Norfolk, Virginia. There began the most trying and painful

Frances Thomas James after the death of her husband

period in James's life. Though he found Norfolk a dirty and unpleasant place to live, his real problems centered on the issue of slavery. He had never been forced to take a stand on slavery, but his general sentiment was the standard British one—that the institution should be abolished. Norfolk made him confront the issue more squarely than he would have wished. Soon after James's arrival, a slave ship came into port carrying some blacks who had been kidnapped from the West Indies. The slavers intended to sell them, but James defended them as British subjects and got them freed in court. He was soon the target of anonymous threats, and some of them became very real: no fewer than eight times, his house was attacked in the night by groups who tried to set it on fire. He feared for himself and for his family, and the disorganization of the British consul's office meant that his work offered little solace or escape. An outbreak of yellow fever in 1855 made his life, if possible, even more tense. In a sense James was responsible for the outbreak, for he had approved the docking of a ship carrying the disease (he had been assured by the captain, however, that the dead man on board had not had yellow-fever symptoms).

It would please the modern reader if James's antislavery sentiments had remained strong, but such was not the case. No doubt motivated by fear and a sense of isolation, he moderated his sentiments to placate the Virginians, and he gradually became a welcome member of Norfolk society. In 1856 the consul's office was moved to Richmond, which was an enormous improvement for James and his family. In that same year, he published one of his most remarkable novels, *The Old Dominion, or The Southampton Massacre*, which has as its subject the Nat Turner rebellion. The novel is a highly interesting document, but not for its main plot, which concerns the romance of a British soldier with a young Virginia woman, both of whom are insipid characters. The interest in the story for the modern reader is in its treatment of slavery. Nat Turner is, in the early sections of the novel, a lofty, mysterious, fascinating character, driven by his religious obsessions and highly articulate on the state of the slave—so articulate that the modern reader sympathizes with him entirely. James, however, does not, and he gradually reveals Turner to be no more than a misguided man driven into madness by the extreme positions he has taken. Turner starts his rebellion when he believes he sees a sign from God; when the hero later explains to him that the sign was merely an eclipse, Turner is dumbfounded, never having heard of such a thing before. The final attitude of the main characters is that, while they will free their own slaves, blacks as a race are not yet ready for freedom, and abolition must come slowly and gradually, only after the race is educated and improved to the point where they can handle freedom. Many of the worst and most offensive stereotypes of the era are employed in the novel, as the hero learns through observation that blacks are lazy, deceitful, and at best childlike. The main white abolitionist in the novel is a detestable, fanatic preacher named, tellingly, M'Grubber; he is murdered by the crazed and bloodthirsty blacks themselves, who afterward laugh about it, saying that they hope M'Grubber would be proud of them for doing what he taught them so well. While such a book no doubt improved James's relations with the Virginians, it makes sad reading today. As a document in the history of slavery in America, it is of some interest, for it details what the liberal antiabolitionist believed about the situation.

James's health was deteriorating during his years in Virginia; he began to suffer from gout, problems with his legs, heart palpitations, and diphtheria. He also began drinking heavily. In 1858, after numerous entreaties for a change of appointment, he was made consul of Venice, and he immediately moved with his family there. But in 1859 he began suffering attacks of paralysis, and his mental health deteriorated. His drinking increased, and he began to have fits of rage, gradually sinking into a state of depression and incoherence. He died in Venice on 9 June 1860, and is buried there. His wife and daughter moved back to America, settling with one of the sons in Eau Claire, Wisconsin. His wife died on 9 June 1891.

Despite his enormous output and his great popularity with his contemporaries, James remains a minor novelist. At his best—in *Darnley* and *The Fate*—he is a skillful teller of a good tale, and for audiences of his time he was a powerful and fascinating teacher of history. Like later minor novelists such as Charles Reade, his best work can still create for us the illusion of really being present at great historical moments. But for all his works might tell us about some of the details of history, they tell us relatively little about universal human concerns. It may be that this deficiency is almost inevitable with the genre of the historical novel itself, since apart from a few writers such as Scott, the great majority of historical novelists are forgotten in a generation or two. And, when the writer is unable to rise above the prejudices and blindnesses of his own era—as was James in *The Old Dominion*—we must regret that oblivion the less. In his defense, however, one cannot help but see James as a man worn down by a hostile environment, and turn back to his earlier works for their innocent, fast-paced action, and the sheer fun they still can provide.

Biographies:

Maunsell B. Field, *Memories of Many Men and of Some Women* (New York: Harper & Brothers, 1874);

S. M. Ellis, *The Solitary Horseman, or The Life & Adventures of G. P. R. James* (Kensington: Cayme Press, 1927);

James Meehan, "The Solitary Horseman in Virginia: Novelist G. P. R. James as British Consul, 1852-1858," *Virginia Cavalcade*, 27 (Autumn 1977): 58-67.

References:

Margaret Dalziel, *Popular Fiction 100 Years Ago: An Unexplored Tract of Literary History* (London: Cohen & West, 1957);

Avrom Fleishman, *The English Historical Novel: Walter Scott to Virginia Woolf* (Baltimore: Johns Hopkins Press, 1971);

James C. Simmons, *The Novelist as Historian: Essays on the Victorian Historical Novel* (The Hague: Mouton, 1973).

Lady Caroline Lamb

(13 November 1785 - 24 January 1828)

Cy Frost
University of Colorado at Denver

BOOKS: *Glenarvon* (3 volumes, London: Printed for Henry Colburn, 1816; 2 volumes, Philadelphia: Published by Moses Thomas, 1816);

Verses from Glenarvon To Which is prefixed the original introduction not published with the early editions of that work (London: Henry Colburn, 1816);

A New Canto (London, 1819);

Graham Hamilton (2 volumes, London: Printed for Henry Colburn, 1822; 1 volume, Philadelphia: H. C. Carey & I. Lee, 1822);

Ada Reis: A Tale, 3 volumes (London: John Murray, 1823);

Fugitive Pieces and Reminiscences of Lord Byron . . . also Some Original Poetry, Letters, and Recollections of Lady Caroline Lamb, edited by I. Nathan (London: Whittaker, Treacher, 1829).

Born on 13 November 1785 in London, Caroline Ponsonby was the third child and only daughter of Frederick Ponsonby, third Earl of Bessborough, and his wife, the former Lady Henrietta Frances Spencer. During her life Caroline inhabited the households of three aristocratic families. From age nine she lived with her maternal aunt, Georgiana, Duchess of Devonshire, at Devonshire House. Adjacent to Hyde Park, this mansion and its grounds dominated a huge area between Berkeley and Stratton Streets in Piccadilly. Described by Elizabeth Jenkins, Caroline Lamb's first biographer, as "the very temple of Society, frequented by a 'gorgeous train' headed by the Regent, Fox, and Sheridan," Devonshire House embodied the political and social power of eighteenth-century Whig aristocracy. Caroline's father, Frederick, was a Whig statesman and politician, her mother, Henrietta, a social virtuoso, adroit at the politics of Whig society. John Spencer, Caroline's maternal grandfather, held four peerages as a Whig member of the House of Commons; he was the grandson of Charles, third Earl of Sunderland, husband to Lady Anne Churchill, daughter of the redoubtable Sarah Jennings, Duchess of Marlborough, and John Churchill, Duke of Marlborough. Caroline herself would become an ardent Whig, known for her plangent and frequent toasts to Tory damnation.

A lack of information and subsequent biographical controversy obscure the events of her childhood. Caroline later told Sydney Owenson, Lady Morgan, that she spent the years from age four to nine in Italy under the care of a nurse, following a stroke suffered by her mother. Indeed, her mother was frequently ill, and while she did visit Naples, Florence, and Pisa during these years, it is unclear whether she did so to visit her daughter, who was already in residence there, or whether Caroline accompanied her mother on her travels. Caroline's education during this period appears to have been nonexistent, and, upon returning to England at age nine, she entered school as a virtual illiterate. For a time she attended a girl's seminary at Hans Place, Kensington, operated by Frances Rowden, formerly a governess to the Bessborough family. The Rowden school has been represented generally as a liberal and efficient institution, but Caroline, willful and headstrong, recklessly defied the school's requirements. One of Caroline's biographers, Henry Blyth, reports numerous occasions when her "tantrums," "dreadful lies," "outbursts," and other deployments of her "histrionic abilities" disrupted classroom decorum. Shortly after entering the Hans Place school, due to her defiance and to her mother's increasingly poor health, Caroline was sent to Devonshire House, where her maternal aunt, "the beautiful Duchess" of Devonshire, cared for Caroline along with her own children.

Alarmed by Caroline's recalcitrance, her maternal grandmother, Georgiana, Lady Spencer, sought the counsel of the family physician, a Dr. Warren, who diagnosed Caroline as being in a "highly nervous state," brought on, he supposed, by her too fertile and too agile brain. The doctor decided that Caroline should exercise her body more and her intellect less, thereby resting her

Lady Caroline Lamb (portrait by Thomas Phillips; Collection of the Duke of Devonshire, Chatsworth Settlement)

brain and, he presumed, her imagination. Dr. Warren prescribed that—because discipline and learning would endanger Caroline's fragile nervous system—she would not be placed under any restraint or be exposed to education of any type. As a result of Dr. Warren's "rest cure," Caroline ran unencumbered throughout Devonshire House and its gardens, receiving little more than custodial care. Thus unlimited temperamentally and foreclosed intellectually, Caroline languished at Devonshire House, receiving no further formal education until age fifteen. As she later wrote of this period, "I wrote not, spelt not. . . . I preferred washing a dog or polishing a piece of Derby-shire spar, or breaking in a horse, to any accomplishment in the world."

At age nineteen Caroline married William Lamb, later second Viscount Melbourne, Queen Victoria's adviser and first prime minister. Caroline was twelve years old when she met William during a visit she and her cousins made to his mother, Elizabeth, Lady Melbourne, at Brocket Park, the Melbourne estate in Hertfordshire. Lady Bessborough disapproved of her daughter's choice of a husband: although she liked William, she thought him possessed of weak character, and she disliked his mother; she nonetheless realized that Caroline's attachment was as inelastic as her will. The wedding took place on 3 June 1805 at the Bessborough residence in Cavendish

Square. Caroline Lamb later stated that she had been under a great strain during the ceremony, becoming hysterical, screaming, tearing her dress, and finally collapsing. Yet her biographers hasten to add that her account contradicts that of a presumably more equable chronicler, Lady Elizabeth Foster, a guest who, reporting on the wedding in a letter to her son, made no mention of Caroline's behavior beyond writing that she was nervous.

Caroline Lamb's hysteria prefigured a troubled marriage. Although she chose William Lamb and loved him, her restless mind, her enthusiastic defiance of convention, and her resistance to authority would not be bound by marriage. Not long after the wedding a "nervous disorder" overtook Caroline. Lady Spencer came to Brocket, where the newlyweds were spending their honeymoon, and conversed at length with her granddaughter, later writing to her daughter Georgiana, Duchess of Devonshire, that Caroline seemed to be physically well but that "her nervous agitations will grow to a very serious height if they are not checked." In the autumn, after she and William had settled into Melbourne House, his parents' home in London, Caroline found that she was pregnant, a discovery that bolstered her long-standing conviction that she should have been born male. Caroline frequently externalized this belief by dressing in boy's clothing: she especially preferred the uniforms worn by her pages. Caroline's diminutive body and close-cropped hair facilitated what she called "obscuring" herself within "the lovely garnish of a boy." During this period of the marriage, her mother wrote of Caroline that she was "so unlike a wife—[she] is more like a schoolgirl." On 31 January 1806 Caroline's pregnancy ended in miscarriage, causing physical suffering and an emotional trauma mitigated only somewhat by the subsequent birth on 29 August 1807 of Caroline's son and only surviving child, Augustus Lamb.

Caroline Lamb met George Gordon, Lord Byron, in 1812. The new wave of Romanticism held a strong appeal for her, although she found William Wordsworth and Samuel Taylor Coleridge insufficiently dramatic. Seeking a writer whose willful individualism and dramatic self-assertion matched her own, she found these traits in the work and the person of Byron. After reading a proof copy of Cantos I and II of *Childe Harold's Pilgrimage* (1812) lent to her by her friend Samuel Rogers, Lamb—intrigued with the poem's melodrama, its autobiographical apparatus, and particularly with its defiant and outcast pilgrim—resolved that she would meet its author. The opportunity presented itself on 25 March at a ball held at Melbourne House, where Caroline demanded that Rogers make the introduction. Rogers, annoyed by her eagerness, countered that Byron "has a club foot and bites his nails." "If he is as ugly as Aesop," she insisted, "I must meet him." But, according to her biographers, when she and Rogers approached Byron, they found him surrounded by a group of women, and Caroline turned away, spurning the introduction. That night she wrote in her journal a trenchant assessment of Byron, "Mad, bad and dangerous to know," a characterization that would become famous. Several days later Elizabeth Vassall Fox, Lady Holland, introduced Caroline to Byron at Holland House in Kensington. A passionate and stormy affair followed, one marked by Caroline's public proclamations of fealty and, when Byron began to withdraw from the liaison, by her overt and aggressive pursuit.

By the end of May 1812 Byron's interest in her had waned. Not to be dissuaded, she wrote him numerous letters and, upon receiving no satisfactory reply, took more direct action: on a day in late July, a disturbance in the street and hammering at the entrance of Byron's St. James Street rooms interrupted Byron's conversation with his friend John Cam Hobhouse. Byron opened the door to find a young man in heavy clothing; closer inspection revealed a disguised Caroline Lamb, who, underneath the man's outer attire, wore a page's uniform. After Byron persuaded her to change into clothing provided by a female servant, Caroline brandished a knife and threatened to stab herself, relenting only upon Byron's fevered intercession. Byron, further disenchanted by this and other public provocations, wrote to Caroline in November 1812 with the admonition, "I am no longer your lover." He subsequently married Caroline's cousin Annabella Milbanke—whose later sardonic portraits of Byron seem as subversive as Caroline's own—then separated from her and went into exile.

Desperate, Caroline retaliated by writing a novel based on the affair. *Glenarvon* (1816) attempts nothing less than the reimaging of Byron's *Childe Harold* self-portrait, the rewriting of Byron's Byron. Published anonymously on 9 May 1816 by Henry Colburn, *Glenarvon* has been regarded generally as a simple-minded roman à clef. Yet the novel aggressively contests Byron's

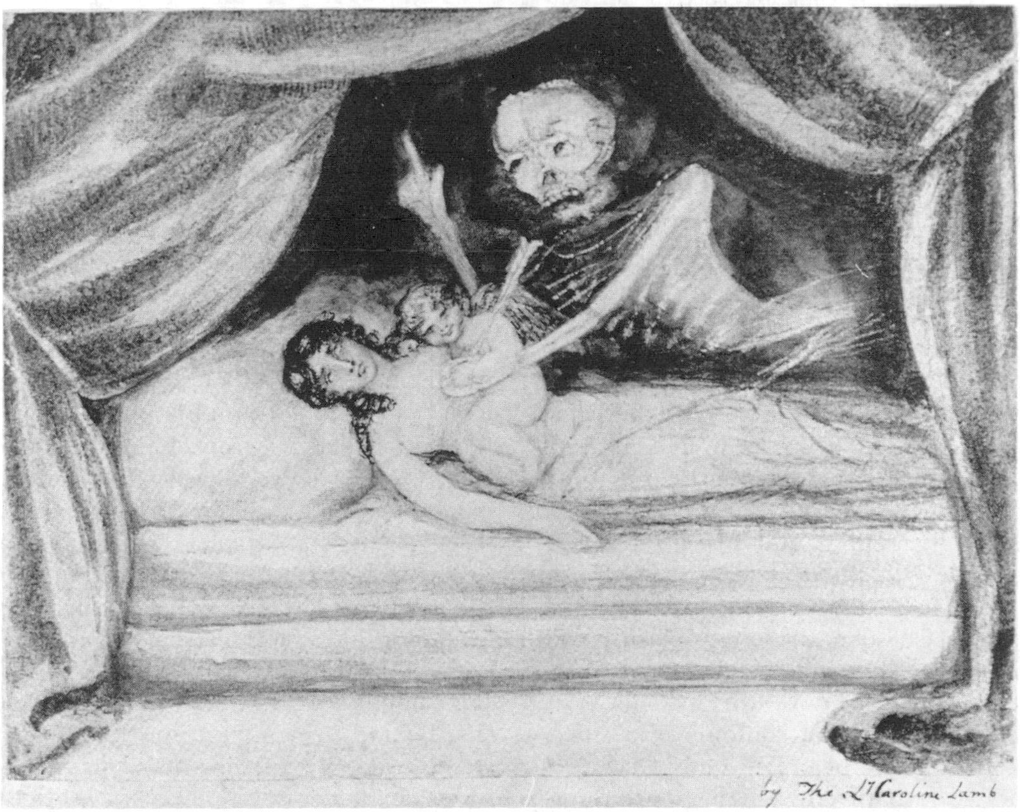

Lady Caroline Lamb's portrait of herself with her husband and son (top; Collection of the Honorable Lady Salmond) and her watercolor of a woman being stabbed by Cupid and Death (Sotheby's auction catalogue, sale number 3506, 15 December 1988)

fictive/public persona, that mythic figure perpetrated by *Childe Harold*. Calculating Byron's ego investment in his own mythmaking, Lamb refuses to corroborate his self-portrayal, insisting instead upon her own revisionary and retributive one. The identities of the three principal characters are never in doubt: Calantha, the heroine, is Caroline; Glenarvon is Byron; Lord Avondale is William. Set on the Irish estate of the duke of Altamonte, the Gothic and foreboding story marries an adolescent and naive Calantha to Lord Avondale, a worldly young officer amused at Calantha's innocence. For a time the couple thrives, but Lord Avondale's neglect and Calantha's unconventional and extravagant behavior lead to marital indifference. The couple spends time in London, where Calantha immerses herself in London society; they return to Ireland to find the country in upheaval. Calantha meets Glenarvon, leader of the Independent party, at the moment Avondale departs to put down rioting in another county. Calantha and Glenarvon fall in love and have an affair; Glenarvon departs for Wales, subsequently decides to marry Lady Mandeville, and writes Calantha a final letter that begins, "I am no longer your lover." Using in her text the very letter Byron wrote to end their affair, Lamb figures her alienation by using Byron's private correspondence to subvert the public production of his image. Throughout the novel Caroline depicts Glenarvon as unrelentingly guilt-ridden, morose, and self-serving. The end of the novel reveals the villain Viviani—kidnapper and child murderer—to be Glenarvon in disguise. Notwithstanding the severity of Lamb's indictment, there remains a eulogistic sense to the book that stems from a Romantic and transcendent nobility allowed to Glenarvon by the author. With the identity of its anonymous author clear and its portraits of Caroline's famous contemporaries only thinly veiled, the novel became an instantaneous succès de scandale, selling out three editions in the weeks following its publication.

Lamb completed her second novel in 1820 but insisted that Colburn not publish it for two years. *Graham Hamilton*, published anonymously in 1822, a less acute and more worldly book than *Glenarvon*, sketches only the contours of a story. The book concerns the beautiful Lady Orville, a profligate but good-natured woman, "the admiration of the whole world," whose "unbounded extravagance" causes her husband serious financial difficulty; Caroline based the character on her aunt, the duchess of Devonshire. Heeding the advice of Italian author and friend Ugo Foscolo to write a book "that will offend nobody," Lamb circumscribed her story within decorous limits. *Graham Hamilton*—absent the retributive fervor and sense of brandished power that characterize its predecessor—images only complacently and fails to assert itself. The book sold few copies.

By 1823 Lamb, excluded from society as a result of *Glenarvon*, completed *Ada Reis*, her third novel. Advancing an extraordinarily complicated and ultimately debilitating plot, the book features a handsome Byronish hero, Ada Reis, who, inspired by the adventures of the Corsairs, turns to pirating. Murdering his mistress Bianca Castamela for her infidelity, Ada Reis takes their daughter, whom he names Fiormonda, to his home in the Arabian desert. The two encounter Kabkarra, the personification of the Spirit of Darkness, who bestows upon Ada Reis a kingship in return for Ada Reis's vow of allegiance. Supervised by a wicked governess, Fiormonda reclines in the splendor provided by the spoils of her father's Faustian pact, but her infatuation with the dissolute villain Candulmar during a voyage with her father to Peru complicates that life. Candulmar abandons Fiormonda, who, despite other opportunities afforded by her beauty and Ada Reis's stature, continues to yearn for him. Ada Reis, following Kabkarra's leveling of Lima with an earthquake, finds himself in the midst of a primitive Indian tribe, separated from Fiormonda; Kabkarra guides Ada Reis through a mountain cave and into an underworld, where Kabkarra promises that Ada Reis will find his daughter, now the Empress of Hades. In a graphic and nightmarish scene, Ada Reis sees Fiormonda, bowed under the weight of a crown and seated at an extravagant banquet, and Bianca Castamela, his murdered mistress. Overjoyed at the vision of his former lover, Ada Reis approaches her, prepared to suggest that they reprise the affair; instead, he sees Bianca staring plaintively and preemptively at the man with whom she had committed the infidelity. In a rage Ada Reis stabs her, thereby condemning himself to eternal incarceration. Transported back to earth to the Oronooke Forests, Fiormonda lives as a recluse until her death, leaving behind in her tomb her history written on a scroll. *Ada Reis* takes as its main motif the innocent child corrupted by a wicked governess, a duplicitous lover, and the world's brutality. While a convoluted plot and mercilessly mechanical hero weaken its attraction, the novel, written with

Lady Caroline Lamb (watercolor by an unknown artist; Collection of Mary, Duchess of Roxburghe)

Lamb's typical narrative abandon, is imaginative and revealingly self-analytical. The book gratified Lamb more than any of her others and sold reasonably well.

Her marriage, though severely tested, had survived the affair with Byron and the succeeding years. In emotional flux and avoiding London, Caroline spent the time following the publication of *Ada Reis* at Hertfordshire, stationed romantically among the fields and forests of Brocket Park. Byron died in Greece on 19 April 1824, and the news of his death, delivered abruptly in a letter from William, caused Caroline to collapse and remain bedridden for two months. By the middle of July she had recuperated sufficiently to take a drive in her carriage up the hill from Brocket Park; as William rode before her, the two met a funeral procession in the road. William, inquiring, learned it was Byron's. He withheld the information from Caroline for a time, but she soon learned of it and collapsed once again. A month later, in August 1824, Caroline decided to travel to Paris, accompanied only by a maid. After a few months of aimlessly surveying France, she returned to England and—over the strenuous objections of William's relatives—to Brocket Park. In December 1827 Caroline was stricken with dropsy, a disease that caused her discomfort and some disfigurement. Taken to Melbourne House for specialized medical attention, she died there on 24 January 1828.

Known principally as Byron's most reckless lover and as the writer of a sensational novel based on their affair, Caroline Lamb has failed to achieve literary respectability. Her books have received only a brief and dismissive critical glance. Rarely distancing herself from the narrative voice, Caroline Lamb brashly and publicly medicated her wounds. She dispersed herself throughout her texts, unleashing her own transparent motives within her characters. Precisely because she sought to manage in fiction that which she could not manage in life, her work provokes compelling questions about the intimate bond between psyche and text, about the powers of authorial privilege, and about that peculiar nineteenth-century psychic dislocation known as "female nervousness." Beleaguered by tormenting questions of love and identity, Caroline Lamb remains a writer whose textual ambitions and anxieties invite critical attention as yet unreceived.

Biographies:

Elizabeth Jenkins, *Lady Caroline Lamb* (Boston: Little, Brown, 1932);

Henry Blyth, *Caro: The Fatal Passion* (New York: Coward, McCann & Geoghegan, 1973).

References:

David Cecil, *The Young Melbourne and the Story of His Marriage with Caroline Lamb* (Indianapolis & New York: Bobbs-Merrill, 1939);

Andrew Green, "Did Byron Write the Poem *To Lady Caroline Lamb?*" *Philological Quarterly*, 7 (October 1928): 338-344;

S. R. Townshend Mayer, "Lady Caroline Lamb," *Temple Bar*, 53 (June 1878): 174-192;

George Paston, "New Light on Byron's Loves. III. The Tragi-Comedy of Lady Caroline," *Cornhill Magazine*, 149 (June 1934): 641-655; 150 (July 1934): 1-16.

John Gibson Lockhart

(14 July 1794 - 25 November 1854)

Byron K. Brown
Valdosta State College

See also the Lockhart entry in *DLB 110: British Romantic Prose Writers, 1789-1839: Second Series.*

BOOKS: *Peter's Letters to His Kinsfolk,* as Peter Morris the odontist (3 volumes, Edinburgh: W. Blackwood / London: T. Cadell & W. Davies / Glasgow: Smith, 1819; 1 volume, New York: Printed by C. S. Van Winkle for A. T. Goodrich, Kirk & Mercein, C. Wiley, W. B. Gilley, and James Olmstead, 1820);

Letter to the Right Hon. Lord Byron. By John Bull, often attributed to Lockhart (London: Printed by & for William Wright, 1821);

Valerius: A Roman Story (3 volumes, Edinburgh: W. Blackwood / London: Cadell, 1821; 2 volumes, Boston: Wells & Lilly, 1821; revised edition, 1 volume, Edinburgh & London: W. Blackwood & Sons, 1842);

Some Passages in the Life of Mr. Adam Blair, Minister of the Gospel at Cross-Meikle: A Novel (Edinburgh: W. Blackwood / London: T. Cadell, 1822; Boston: Wells & Lilly, 1822);

Reginald Dalton (3 volumes, Edinburgh: W. Blackwood / London: T. Cadell, 1823; 2 volumes, New York: E. Duyckinck, 1823);

The History of Matthew Wald (Edinburgh: W. Blackwood / London: T. Cadell, 1824; New York: E. Duyckinck, Collins & Hannay, 1824);

Janus, or the Edinburgh Literary Almanack, by Lockhart and John Wilson (Edinburgh: Oliver & Boyd, 1826);

Life of Robert Burns (Edinburgh: Constable / London: Hurst, Chance, 1828; New York: W. Stodart, 1831);

The History of Napoleon Buonaparte, 2 volumes (London: John Murray, 1829; New York: J. & J. Harper, 1830);

Memoirs of the Life of Sir Walter Scott, Bart. (7 volumes, Edinburgh: R. Cadell / London: Murray and Whittaker, 1837-1838; 2 volumes, Philadelphia: Carey, Lea & Blanchard, 1837-1838; revised edition, 10 volumes, Edinburgh: Cadell / London: Murray & Whittaker, 1839); revised again and abridged as *Narrative of the Life of Sir Walter Scott, Bart.,* 2 volumes (Edinburgh: R. Cadell / London: Houlston & Stoneman, 1848);

The Ballantyne-Humbug Handled in a Letter to Sir Adam Ferguson (Edinburgh: R. Cadell / London: Murray & Whittaker, 1839);

Theodore Hook: A Sketch (London: Murray, 1852).

Editions: *Some Passages in the Life of Mr. Adam Blair. And The History of Matthew Wald* (Edinburgh & London: W. Blackwood & Sons, 1843);

Lockhart's Literary Criticism, edited by M. Clive Hildyard (Oxford: Blackwell, 1931);

John Bull's Letter to Lord Byron, edited by Alan Laing Strout (Norman: University of Oklahoma Press, 1947).

OTHER: *Lectures on the History of Literature, Ancient and Modern. From the German of Frederick Schlegel,* 2 volumes, translated by Lockhart (Edinburgh: W. Blackwood / London: Baldwin, 1818; Philadelphia: Thomas Dobson & Son, 1818);

The History of the Ingenious Gentleman Don Quixote of La Mancha. Translated from the Spanish of Cervantes by Motteux, 5 volumes, edited by Lockhart (Edinburgh: A. Constable / London: Hurst, Robinson, 1822);

Ancient Spanish Ballads, Historical and Romantic, translated by Lockhart (Edinburgh: Blackwood / London: Cadell, 1823; new edition, revised, London: John Murray, 1841; New York: Wiley & Putnam, 1842);

Poetical Works of Sir Walter Scott, 12 volumes, edited by Lockhart (Edinburgh: Robert Cadell, 1833-1834).

When Sir Walter Scott wrote that "Lockhart will *blaze,*" he noted the unusual promise that John Gibson Lockhart, his son-in-law, brought to the Scottish literary scene. Entering Edinburgh lit-

John Gibson Lockhart, 1830 (portrait by H. W. Pickersgill, R.A.; John Murray Collection)

erary society as one of the writers for *Blackwood's Edinburgh Magazine* who, with John Wilson and James Hogg, scandalized and titillated literary Scotland during the early years of William Blackwood's "Maga," Lockhart quickly established a reputation as a satirist, critic, translator, and magazine versifier. Although he never achieved the sustained literary brilliance that Scott predicted, Lockhart did lead a long and varied career as a man of letters, serving as editor of the *Quarterly Review* for twenty-eight years, helping to popularize German literary theory in England, and achieving a degree of immortality as Scott's biographer. Lockhart's four novels, written and published anonymously in as many years, are remarkably varied, including the first Oxford novel, the first classical novel written in English, and psychological studies of guilt and passion that anticipate the work of Emily Brontë and Nathaniel Hawthorne.

Born on 14 July 1794 in the manse of Cambusnethan, a small town in Lanarkshire, Lockhart was the oldest son of John Lockhart, a Presbyterian minister, by his second wife, Elizabeth Gibson Lockhart. During Lockhart's second year his family moved to nearby Glasgow, where his father had accepted a position as minister of the College Kirk. Young Lockhart's health was somewhat fragile, and as a result of childhood illness he became partially deaf, a condition which contributed to his natural reserve and his adult reputation for hauteur. Educated both at home and at Glasgow High School, he showed early promise as a scholar. At age eleven he enrolled in Glasgow University, where his extraordinary powers of memory and concentration compensated for his lack of industry. At the end of three years, he won the Blackstone prize in Greek and was awarded a Snell Exhibition to attend Balliol College, Oxford, where he enrolled in 1808.

While at Oxford, Lockhart laid the academic foundations for his later translations, criticism, and novels by reading widely in French, Italian, and Spanish as well as in Greek and Latin. At the same time he indulged his penchant for drawing caricatures of his professors, evincing a love of the satirical sketch that characterized his early writing. Lockhart left Oxford in 1813, at the age of nineteen, with a First in classics, then spent the next two years in Glasgow reading for the Scottish bar, corresponding with friends, and writing a first, lost novel tentatively titled "Romance of the Thistle." During this time he also learned German and so further prepared for his later work as a critic and novelist. In November 1815 he moved to Edinburgh to read more seriously for the bar, to which he was admitted in 1816.

Lockhart, the strikingly handsome and brilliant young Tory lawyer, was not well suited for a legal career, however; his proud reserve made him an indifferent speaker, and his literary ambitions soon brought him into association with the Blackwood group. In 1817 William Blackwood advanced him three hundred pounds for a translation of Friedrich von Schlegel's *Lectures on the History of Literature, Ancient and Modern* (1818). In preparation Lockhart spent part of 1817 in Germany, where he met Johann Wolfgang von Goethe, discovered the German psychological novel, and became enamored with German literary theory.

Soon after his return to Scotland in October 1817, he found John Wilson engaged in revitalizing Blackwood's new Tory magazine, begun in April of that year, by enlivening it with a more aggressive and controversial style. For the first issue of the revived periodical, published with a new title—*Blackwood's Edinburgh Magazine*—in October 1817, Lockhart helped Wilson and Hogg write "Translation from an Ancient Chaldee MS," a parody of scripture that outraged the literary and intellectual Edinburgh society it satirized. This work introduced Lockhart as "the Scorpion, who delighteth to sting the faces of men," and he quickly lived up to this description by writing a series of cleverly caustic "squibberies" under several aliases. Perhaps the best remembered of these are his contributions to the *Noctes Ambrosianae* (March 1822 - February 1835) and the series of articles titled "The Cockney School of Poetry" (October 1817 - August 1818), which Percy Bysshe Shelley blamed for hastening John Keats's death. These pieces won him instant notice—but also lasting notoriety, a reputation for reckless satire and critical severity which haunted him for the rest of his life.

When Lockhart met Sir Walter Scott in June 1818, he began a connection with the "Great Unknown" that shaped the rest of his life and literary career. Lockhart visited Scott's home at Abbotsford often during the succeeding months while he was writing the sketches of contemporary Scottish society he published as *Peter's Letters to His Kinsfolk* (1819). On 29 April 1820 he married Scott's elder daughter, Sophia. For the next five years, which Lockhart later recalled as happiest of his life, the young couple divided their time between Edinburgh and Chiefswood, their new home near Abbotsford on Sir Walter's estate. During this time Lockhart began work on several less ephemeral and less controversial projects, including the historical sections of the *Edinburgh Annual Register*, which Scott passed on to him, and translations of Spanish ballads, which appeared as a series titled "Horæ Hispanicæ" in *Blackwood's* (February 1820 - January 1821). In this same year, at age twenty-six, he began his brief career as a novelist.

Lockhart began *Valerius* in July, some three months after his wedding to Sophia. He always composed rapidly, and his first novel was no exception; in later years, John Wilson recalled that Lockhart finished the three volumes in as many weeks. Events, however, conspired to delay its publication. In the last three months of 1820 and the first month of 1821, John Scott, editor of the *London Magazine*, ran a virulent series of articles attacking Lockhart for his association with *Blackwood's Magazine*. In January 1821 Lockhart traveled to London and challenged Scott to a duel, but because of bungled arrangements and a series of misunderstandings, he returned to Scotland without receiving satisfaction. Soon afterward, Scott challenged Lockhart's representative, Jonathan Christie, who then met Scott and mortally wounded him on February sixteenth, two days after Lockhart's first child, John Hugh, was born in Edinburgh. The incident reinforced the danger and impropriety of Lockhart's early satire, and it emphasized the importance of establishing the less controversial literary reputation that Sir Walter was encouraging him to pursue. In Au-

Portrait of Sophia Scott, drawn by Lockhart sometime between June 1818 and their marriage in April 1820 (Collection of Mrs. Maxwell-Scott of Abbotsford), and a self-portrait that Lockhart painted in 1816 (from Andrew Lang, Life and Letters of John Gibson Lockhart, *1897)*

gust Sir Walter returned the proofsheets of *Valerius* to Lockhart, praising the novel as "most classical and interesting at the same time." Blackwood published the novel later that year.

Valerius recounts the adventures of Caius Valerius, the adolescent son of a Roman centurion and his British wife, who travels to Rome after his father's death to claim an inheritance. Through the eyes of this young outsider, Lockhart presents a panorama of Rome during the reign of Trajan, providing glimpses of the Roman world as it was challenged by the rising tide of Christian faith. As the novel ends, Valerius embraces the new faith, abandons Rome and his inheritance, and returns to Britain with a Christian bride.

Throughout, the novel offers diverse descriptions of Roman life. Valerius beholds the splendor of the Palatine, attends a luxurious Roman feast, hears the rhetoric of the Forum, enjoys a suburban dinner party, visits gloomy prisons holding Christian martyrs, fights the jostling crowds of the amphitheater, witnesses the horror of gladiatorial combat and the execution of a Christian martyr, falls by accident into an outlawed Christian assembly in the catacombs, and even finds himself in a barber's shop and a painter's studio. Through the major characters, Lockhart also explored the Roman mind at this important historical juncture. In the Sempronii, Valerius sees the nobility characteristic of the highest pagan ideals and practice. In the ambitious Stoic tutor Xerophrastes, he sees the emptiness of pagan philosophy. In Rubellia, the young widow who pursues his friend Sextus, he sees the darkness of pagan witchcraft and sorcery. In Thraso, the martyr, and Athanasia, the beautiful patrician girl he rescues and marries, he sees the courageous faith of the Christians.

Sir Walter Scott assured Lockhart that his maiden novel "cannot but produce a very deep sensation," and when *Valerius* appeared, its reviewers praised its original subject matter and the quality of its descriptions. These contemporary reviewers, however, also faulted its coldness and weakness of characterization. Furthermore, its style, as Francis Jeffrey noted in a review titled "Secondary Scottish Novels" (*Edinburgh Review*, October 1824), is "without idiom, without familiarity, and runs on even in the gay and satirical passages, in a rumbling roundabout, rhetorical measure, like a translation from solemn Latin, or some academical exercitations." In 1841 Lockhart extensively revised the novel, reducing its length by half and thereby improving it considerably. In its new edition, the novel went through at least four more printings.

In February 1822 Lockhart wrote to his brother Lawrence that he had converted one of their father's after-dinner stories into a second novel, *Some Passages in the Life of Mr. Adam Blair* (1822). As the novel opens, Adam, a young minister of powerful yet suppressed sexuality, suffers from physical and emotional privation following his wife's early death. Despite the kind attention of his parishioners and friends, he finds himself failing both physically and emotionally until he receives an unexpected visit from his dead wife's cousin, Charlotte Campbell. This sad and fallen woman takes up residence in Adam's house and becomes a mother to his daughter; as the young minister tries to restore her faith, their innocent association inevitably deepens into unrecognized passion. When a lawyer representing Charlotte's estranged husband arrives to remove her from Adam's household, Adam follows her to her lonely highland estate. Intending only to comfort Charlotte, he commits adultery with her, then, overcome by guilt, falls into a fever. Awakening to discover that Charlotte has died, Adam returns to Glasgow, confesses his guilt before an ecclesiastical court, and relinquishes his post. For ten years he lives a humble and blameless life as a yeoman farmer before he is reinstated by his generous patron and forgiving presbyters.

On one level, *Adam Blair* is a psychological study clearly influenced by Goethe and Henry Mackenzie, as well as by William Godwin and Charles Brockden Brown, whose novels Lockhart had reviewed for *Blackwood's* in December 1817 and February 1820, respectively. On another, it is a nostalgic re-creation of a Scottish faith, piety, and way of life that were rapidly vanishing at the beginning of the nineteenth century. At both levels, *Adam Blair* is strongly influenced by Lockhart's admiration for William Wordsworth. Throughout the novel Lockhart espouses a Wordsworthian confidence in the moral elevation of the yeomanry, and his portrayal of Adam's spiritual decline and recovery bears notable affinities to *The Excursion* (1814), a work Lockhart greatly admired. He closes the work with a passage from Wordsworth's "Lines left upon a Seat in a Yew-Tree."

Lockhart could not conceal his satisfaction with *Adam Blair*, and William Blackwood apparently shared his confidence in the novel, offering him three hundred pounds for the first edition and two hundred more for the second edition and the copyright. Some of Lockhart's Scottish readers, however, resented its description of a minister's moral failings. And while Lockhart defended the morality of his story in his private letters, he also tried to hide his anonymous authorship from his father. In 1824 *Adam Blair* was republished in a second and slightly revised edition. A measure of its continued popularity is evidenced by its occasional republication throughout the next three decades.

Soon after *Adam Blair* appeared, Lockhart completed and published an edition of Peter Anthony Motteux's translation of *Don Quixote*, a work which Sir Walter Scott had begun but asked him to finish. In the following year a collection of his translations from *Blackwood's* was published as *Ancient Spanish Ballads* (1823). This volume proved to be one of Lockhart's most popular, going through numerous editions throughout the nineteenth and early twentieth centuries. Also in 1823, Lockhart published his third novel, a triple-decker titled *Reginald Dalton*.

Reginald Dalton is a conventional romance in which the title character's adolescent dream of marrying a beautiful heiress and coming into possession of his ancient family seat, Grypherwast-hall, is fulfilled in dramatic and unexpected ways. During the course of the novel, his succession to the property is complicated by a swarm of schemers, including the hypocritical Sir Charles Catline and his daughter, Barbara; a conniving Scots lawyer, Mr. Ralph Macdonald; and a treacherous college friend, Frederick Chisney, all of whom hope to acquire the property for themselves.

At the same time *Reginald Dalton* is a novel of a young man's coming of age, his fall and restoration before his fortuitous accession to the property. Reginald, the only son of a widowed country vicar, goes to Oxford, where he slowly gives himself up to expensive and dissipating university amusements, even as he falls in love with Ellen Hesketh, the beautiful ward of an old Catholic priest. Reginald's extravagance during the first term exhausts his father's meager resources, and during his first visit home he confesses his folly to his forgiving father. When Reginald returns to Oxford, however, he discovers that his actual debt has exceeded his calculations and his fa-

Fenella dancing for Charles II, Lockhart's comic illustration of a scene in Sir Walter Scott's Peveril of the Peak *(Collection of Mrs. Maxwell-Scott of Abbotsford)*

ther's ability to pay, and he exonerates himself by avoiding his earlier companions, taking on editorial work, and finally becoming a sizar. Only after he proves his worthiness by taking responsibility for his extravagances and abandoning his dreams of Grypherwast-hall does he attain his inheritance.

Reginald Dalton is the first Oxford novel in English, and contemporary reviewers praised its lively and entertaining sketches of university life: the journey to Oxford, a town-and-gown row, a supper party, drinking bouts, a fox hunt, and a duel. The narrative voice is generally lively, and the tone rapidly shifts from the ironic to the melodramatic, from satiric to burlesque. Wordsworth's Benjamin the Waggoner and Peter Bell, for example, make a cameo appearance as drunken travelers who cause Reginald's Oxford-bound coach to wreck. While granting the novel power, most reviewers faulted its carelessness of production. Despite this weakness, *Reginald Dalton* was the most popular of Lockhart's novels. William Blackwood paid him one thousand pounds for it, twice the payment for *Adam Blair*. It went through several editions and printings between 1823 and 1880 and remained in print longer than any of his other novels.

Lockhart's final novel, *The History of Matthew Wald* (1824), appeared in the following year. This first-person narrative is represented as the posthumous memoirs of an old man who recalls how as a youth he was tormented by envy, resentment of real and imagined wrongs, and unrequited love. Despite fortune at least as great as misfortune, his passion, ambition, and dissimulation destroy his happiness, the objects of his affection, and finally his sanity. The memoirs end with a lurid description of the dreams and visions which tormented him in his madness. Appended to them is a letter from one of the old man's young acquaintances to another, recalling Wald in his old age as a hale, healthy old man, privately melancholy, perhaps, but a merry companion. The title page and closing letter are glossed with quotations from Wordsworth's "Matthew" poem, "The Fountain," suggesting, perhaps, that Wald's unexplained recovery was somehow Wordsworthian.

The History of Matthew Wald resembles Lockhart's earlier novels in several ways. In general outline it resembles *Reginald Dalton*: a young man comes of age, enters the world and acquires some polish, then gains an inheritance through the peculiarities of Scottish marriage law. It also shares several themes with Lockhart's earlier nov-

Lockhart's sketch of himself (center) riding with a man believed to be Sir Walter Scott (left; Collection of Mrs. Maxwell-Scott of Abbotsford)

els. Like *Reginald Dalton,* it satirizes religious hypocrisy and Methodism; like *Adam Blair,* it is a psychological study describing a character's fall and restoration while presenting some sympathetic portraits of rural clergy and Scottish yeomanry. Its tone, however, is uncharacteristically dark as the narrator's confessions of pride, vanity, shame, jealousy, resentment, ambition, and humiliation alternate with descriptions of his violent, obsessive, and destructive love. As Sir Walter Scott noted, it is "a painful tale very forcibly told—the worst is that there is no resting place—nothing from the title-page to the finis." The novel may owe something to James Hogg's *Private Memoirs and Confessions of a Justified Sinner,* which appeared in the same year. Both contain first-person confessions, discovered after the author's death, of unlovely emotions; both deal with themes of religious hypocrisy, fanaticism, and delusion. In his dark passions and obsessive love, Wald obviously anticipates Emily Brontë's Heathcliff.

Contemporary reviewers gave *Matthew Wald* mixed reviews. Most, like Scott, recognized its power and originality but were disturbed by its unremitting bleakness. Its description of madness was alternately praised and damned; its morality was defended and attacked. As in his other novels, the parts were superior to the whole, and its parts—the description of Mammy Baird, the story of Perling Joan, the account of John M'Ewan, the religious fanatic who commits murder—were most often singled out for praise. It was republished in 1840, before being collected with *Adam Blair* several times between 1843 and 1855.

In 1825 John Murray sent Benjamin Disraeli to Edinburgh to offer Lockhart the editorship of the *Quarterly Review.* Lockhart accepted, and at age thirty-one, he moved to London to assume the post he held for the next twenty-eight years. As the editor of England's preeminent Tory periodical, he was intimately involved in the literary currents and social issues of the day. During this time he continued to write for

John Gibson Lockhart (portrait by Sir Francis Grant; Scottish National Portrait Gallery)

Blackwood's even as he committed himself to his editorial duties, writing more than one hundred articles for the *Quarterly Review*, from book reviews (including a stinging review of Tennyson's *Poems* of 1833) to descriptions of dry rot.

After Lockhart left Chiefswood for London, he devoted his literary talents to biography rather than to fiction. His first biography was the *Life of Robert Burns* (1828), which he wrote for Murray's Family Library. It was quickly followed by *The History of Napoleon Buonaparte* (1829), chiefly an abridgment of Scott's *Life of Napoleon Buonaparte* (1827). His greatest work in this genre, though, was his *Memoirs of the Life of Sir Walter Scott, Bart.* (1837-1838). This life is infused with a depth of emotion often absent from Lockhart's work, and throughout the nineteenth century many readers compared it to James Boswell's *Life of Johnson* (1791). Lockhart devoted all proceeds from the sales of his Scott biography to help pay off the debts still attached to Abbotsford. Even its reception, though, was not without controversy, and in the year following its publication, Lockhart felt compelled to defend his portrayal of James and John Ballantyne's role in Sir Walter's financial collapse (*The Ballantyne-Humbug Handled in a Letter to Sir Adam Ferguson*). His last biography was a brief sketch of Theodore Hook's life, which appeared in the *Quarterly Review* in 1843 and was published as a separate volume in 1852.

Lockhart's later years were darkened by illness and family tragedy. His eldest son, immortalized as Hugh Littlejohn in Scott's *Tales of A Grandfather*, died in 1831. Sir Walter followed his grandson to the grave a year later. Sophia died in 1837, before she had seen all of her husband's biography of her illustrious father. With the death of Sir Walter Scott's last child in 1847, Lockhart's surviving son, Walter Scott Lockhart, became the laird of Abbotsford, but his profligacy soon estranged him from his father. In 1853 this son died, and Sir Walter's estate passed to Lockhart's only surviving child, his daughter Charlotte. In the same year Lockhart resigned from the *Quarterly Review* and wintered in Italy in a vain attempt to restore his failing health. There he renewed his early love of languages, spending hours a day acquainting himself with Hebrew and Arabic, renewing his knowledge of Italian, and reading Dante. In 1854 he abandoned all hopes of recovery and returned to England. After bidding farewell to friends and the scenes of happier days, he visited Abbotsford one last time. Refusing to spend his last days in the same room where his beloved father-in-law had died, Lockhart breathed his last in a small room overlooking the Tweed, adjacent to the dining room where Sir Walter had spent his final days. Lockhart was buried in Dryburgh Abbey, at Sir Walter Scott's feet.

John Gibson Lockhart's literary career was inseparable from Sir Walter Scott's, and he achieved his most enduring reputation as his father-in-law's biographer. As a novelist Lockhart was innovative, but not entirely successful. *Valerius* is original yet coldly executed. His later novels improved in emotional power and handling of dialogue, and they reflect, in interesting ways, the influence of German melodrama and of Wordsworth. They are, however, more successful in part than in whole, excelling in descriptive sketches and well-told episodes, but lacking in imaginative power. As editor and critic, Lockhart helped popularize German literary theory, but his work was largely ephemeral, hampered by his commitment to Tory ideology in the fiercely partisan atmosphere of the century in which he lived. In biography he found a literature most congenial to his talents and temperament.

Bibliographies:

Alan Lang Strout, *A Bibliography of Articles in Blackwood's Magazine, 1817-1825*, Texas Technological College Library Bulletin, no. 5 (Lubbock: Texas Tech Press, 1959);

Brian M. Murray, "The Authorship of Some Unidentified or Disputed Articles in *Blackwood's Magazine*," *Studies in Scottish Literature*, 4 (January-April 1967): 144-154.

Biographies:

George Robert Gleig, "John Gibson Lockhart," *Quarterly Review*, 116 (October 1864): 439-482;

Andrew Lang, *Life and Letters of John Gibson Lockhart*, 2 volumes (London: J. C. Nimmo, 1897);

Marion Lochhead, *John Gibson Lockhart* (London: John Murray, 1954).

References:

M. F. Brightfield, "Lockhart's *Quarterly* Contributors," *PMLA*, 59 (June 1944): 491-512;

Donald Carswell, *Scott and His Circle* (Garden City, N.Y.: Doubleday, Doran, 1930);

John Clive, "Peter and the Wallah: From Kinsfolk to Competition," in *History and Imagination: Essays in Honor of H. R. Trevor-Roper*, edited by Hugh Lloyd-Jones, Valerie Pearl, and Blair Wordon (New York: Holmes & Meir, 1982), pp. 311-325;

J. Cowley, "Lockhart and the Publication of *Marmion*," *Philological Quarterly*, 32 (April 1953): 172-183;

David Craig, Introduction to *Some Passages in the Life of Mr. Adam Blair, Minister of the Gospel at Cross-Meikle*, Scottish Reprints, no. 1 (Edinburgh: Edinburgh University Press, 1963), pp. v-xxv;

Frederic Ewen, "John Gibson Lockhart, Propagandist of German Literature," *Modern Language Notes*, 49 (April 1934): 260-265;

Francis Russell Hart, *Lockhart as Romantic Biographer* (Edinburgh: Edinburgh University Press, 1971);

M. Clive Hildyard, Introduction to *Lockhart's Literary Criticism*, edited by Hildyard (Oxford: Blackwell, 1931);

Henry James, *Hawthorne* (London: Macmillan, 1879; Ithaca: Cornell University Press, 1967), pp. 90-92;

J. D. Kern, E. Schneider, and I. Griggs, "Lockhart to Croker on the *Quarterly*," *PMLA*, 60 (March 1945): 175-198;

Joseph Kestner, "John Gibson Lockhart's *Matthew Wald* and Emily Bronte's *Wuthering Heights*," *Wordsworth Circle*, 13 (Spring 1982): 94-96;

Kestner, "Lockhart's *Peter's Letters to his Kinsfolk* and the Epistolary Genre," *Wordsworth Circle*, 11 (Autumn 1982): 228-232;

Marion Cleland Lochhead, "Coleridge and John Gibson Lockhart," in *New Approaches to Coleridge: Biographical and Critical Essays*, edited by Donald Sultana (London: Vision, 1981), pp. 61-79;

Gilbert Macbeth, *J. G. Lockhart, a Critical Study*, Illinois Studies in Language and Literature, 17, no. 3-4 (Urbana: University of Illinois Press, 1935);

Peter F. Morgan, "Lockhart's Literary Personality," *Scottish Literary Journal: A Review of Studies in Scottish Language and Literature*, 2 (July 1975): 27-35;

Coleman O. Parsons, "The Possible Origin of Lockhart's *Adam Blair*," *Notes and Queries*, 189 (17 November 1945): 203-206;

Thomas C. Richardson, "Character and Craft in Lockhart's *Adam Blair*," in *Nineteenth Century Scottish Fiction: Critical Essays*, edited by Ian Campbell (Totowa, N.J.: Barnes & Noble, 1979), pp. 51-67;

George Saintsbury, "Lockhart," in *The Collected Essays and Papers of George Saintsbury, 1875-1920* (London & Toronto: Dent / New York: Dutton, 1923), II: 1-30;

Virginia Woolf, "Lockhart's Criticism," in her *The Moment and Other Essays* (London: Hogarth Press, 1947), pp. 60-64.

Papers:

The largest collection of Lockhart materials is housed in the National Library of Scotland.

Mary Meeke

(? - October 1816?)

Ann W. Engar
University of Utah

SELECTED BOOKS: *Count St. Blancard, or the Prejudiced Judge*, 3 volumes (London: Printed for William Lane at the Minerva Press, 1795; facsimile, New York: Arno Press, 1977);

The Abbey of Clugny, 3 volumes (London: Printed for William Lane at the Minerva Press, 1795);

The Mysterious Wife, 4 volumes, as Gabrielli (London: Printed for W. Lane at the Minerva Press, 1797);

Palmira and Ermance, 3 volumes (London: Printed for William Lane at the Minerva Press, 1797);

The Sicilian, 4 volumes, as Gabrielli (London: Printed at the Minerva Press for William Lane, 1798);

Ellesmere, 4 volumes (London: Printed at the Minerva Press for William Lane, 1799);

Harcourt, 4 volumes, as Gabrielli (London: Printed at the Minerva Press for William Lane, 1799);

Anecdotes of the Altamont Family, 4 volumes, as Gabrielli (London: Printed at the Minerva Press for William Lane, 1800);

Which Is the Man?, 4 volumes (London: Printed at the Minerva Press for William Lane, 1801);

Mysterious Husband, 4 volumes, as Gabrielli (London: Printed at the Minerva Press for William Lane, 1801);

Midnight Weddings, 3 volumes (London: Printed at the Minerva Press for William Lane, 1802);

Independence, 4 volumes, as Gabrielli (London: Printed at the Minerva Press for Lane & Newman, 1802);

A Tale of Mystery, or Celina, 4 volumes (London: Printed at the Minerva Press for Lane & Newman, 1803);

Amazement!, 3 volumes (London: Printed at the Minerva Press for Lane, Newman, 1804);

The Nine Days' Wonder, 3 volumes (London: Printed at the Minerva Press for Lane, Newman, 1804);

Something Odd, 3 volumes, as Gabrielli (London: Printed at the Minerva Press for Lane, Newman, 1804);

The Old Wife and the Young Husband, 3 volumes (London: Printed at the Minerva Press for Lane, Newman, 1804);

The Wonder of the Village, 3 volumes (London: Printed at the Minerva Press for Lane, Newman, 1805);

Something Strange, 4 volumes, as Gabrielli (London: Printed at the Minerva Press for Lane, Newman, 1806);

There is a secret, find it out!, 4 volumes (London: Printed at the Minerva Press for Lane, Newman, 1808);

Laughton Priory, 4 volumes, as Gabrielli (London: Printed at the Minerva Press for Lane, Newman, 1809);

Stratagems Defeated, 4 volumes, as Gabrielli (London: Printed at the Minerva Press for A. K. Newman, 1811);

Matrimony, the height of bliss, or the extreme of misery, 4 volumes (London: Printed at the Minerva Press for A. K. Newman, 1812);

Conscience, 4 volumes (London: Printed at the Minerva Press for A. K. Newman, 1814);

The Spanish Campaign; or, The Jew, 3 volumes (London: Printed at the Minerva Press for A. K. Newman, 1815);

The Veiled Protectress; or, The Mysterious Mother, 5 volumes (London: Printed at the Minerva Press for A. K. Newman, 1819);

What Shall Be, Shall Be, 4 volumes (London: Printed at the Minerva Press for A. K. Newman, 1823);

The Parent's Offering to a Good Child: A collection of interesting tales (London: Deane & Munday / A. K. Newman, circa 1825);

The Birth-day present, or Pleasing tales of amusement and instruction (London: A. K. Newman, n.d., New York: King, 1830).

TRANSLATIONS: Augustus La Fontaine, *Lobenstein Village*, 4 volumes (London: Printed at

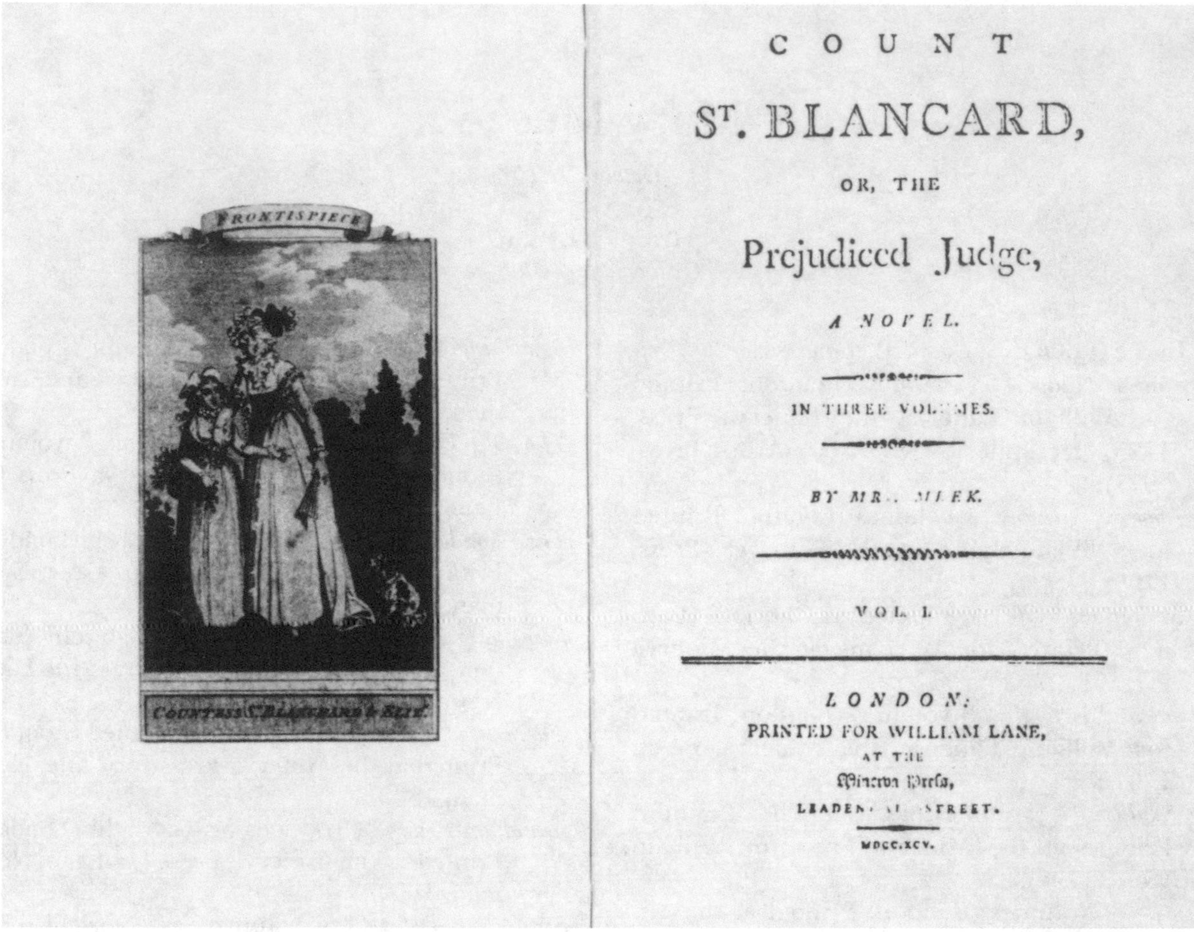

Frontispiece and title page for Meeke's first novel, in which she attempted to show "that friendship may prove sincere and permanent, even between men of very different rank in the world, provided they are both good characters"

the Minerva Press for Lane, Newman, 1804);

Ducrai Dumenil, *Julian, or My Father's House*, 4 volumes (London: Minerva Press, 1807);

The Unpublished Correspondence of Madame du Deffand with d'Alembert, Montesquieu, etc. (London: Printed for A. K. Newman, 1810);

Friedrich Gottlieb Klopstock, *The Messiah*, 2 volumes, parts 17-19 translated by Meeke, parts 1-16 translated by Mary Mitchell Collyer (London: J. Walker, 1811);

Sophie or Marie (Risteau) Cottin, *Elizabeth, or the exiles of Siberia*; Jacques Henri Bernardin de Saint-Pierre *Paul et Virginie*; and John Langhorne, *Solyman and Almena*. (London: Published by I. Tallis, 1814).

For more than twenty years Mary Meeke was one of the most popular and prolific writers of Gothic fiction for Minerva Press. Following the model of Ann Radcliffe, she wrote more than thirty novels with well-plotted, moral stories, in most of which a young person's hidden noble birth is gradually revealed. She also wrote nearly a dozen books under the pseudonym Gabrielli. Her books were favorites of such writers as Thomas Macaulay and Mary Mitford. Today they are seldom read: only one is available in a modern facsimile reprint.

Little is known about Mary Meeke's life. According to the *Dictionary of National Biography*, Mary "seems to have been the wife of Reverend Francis Meeke," who received his B.A. (1773) and M.A. (1776) from Christ's College, Cambridge, and "published a volume of poems in 1782." In October 1816 a Mary Meeke, widow of Reverend Francis Meeke, died at Johnson Hall, Staffordshire. This woman may have been Mary Meeke the novelist. Aside from these sketchy details, the only source of information about her is her work.

Her first novel, *Count St. Blancard, or the Prejudiced Judge* (1795), tells the story of a talented and handsome young doctor, Dubois, who falls in love with his best friend's sister, Adelaide de Ceare, but is prevented from paying court to her because of the difference in their ranks. Though he saves her from serious illness and later from rape, her father imprisons him in a dungeon while locking her away in a convent. Gradually the truth of Dubois's parentage is revealed: not the son of an apothecary, he is really the son of the man who is to judge his supposed crimes, President de Ransal. After the story of Dubois's parentage and birth gradually comes to light, his father grants him the title of Count St. Blancard, and he and Adelaide are happily united.

The strength of Meeke's work lies in her plots: she interweaves the stories of many lives and adds exciting complications such as illness, angry fathers, exile, imprisonment, robbery, trickery, secret marriages, masked men, and blackmail. There is little description: one scene follows quickly upon another. Aside from her plots, her novels are unremarkable. Her characters are flat with no change or growth over the course of the novel. The conversations are roughly handled: she has trouble distinguishing between direct and indirect discourse. Though she does use several points of view in *Count St. Blancard*—various lengthy sections of the story are presented from the perspective of the President, Jane the nursemaid, and the apothecary Rhubarbin, Dubois's foster father—the narrative voice seems the same.

Meeke's intent is primarily to entertain rather than to instruct her readers. Nevertheless, her own values come clearly through her stories. *Count St. Blancard* includes numerous attacks on Catholicism. Though they may stem from her position as a minister's wife, such attacks are common in Gothic fiction. She criticizes convent schools for paying too much attention to the birth and wealth of their students and writes of the power of money with "the holy fraternity of friars and Nuns." The nuns in the convent become much nicer to Adelaide when the President pays them, his wife gets a nun to break her vow of silence by paying her, and Adelaide bribes one of the lay sisters to post a letter for her. Meeke is satiric in her portrayal of the "good" superior of the convent, who is eager to ruin Adelaide's reputation until the President presents her with a handsome, weighty purse.

Meeke's feelings about Catholicism are clear-cut, but her views of the importance of rank and wealth are more complicated, especially in matters of marriage. In *Count St. Blancard* Meeke seems to take the middle-class position that merit is as important as money or social status and the romantic position that marriages should be love matches rather than business arrangements. Dubois has wealth and merit, which seem to qualify him as a lover to Adelaide in the author's eyes, if not in Adelaide's father's. Dubois's father, the President, married a woman of merit and family but no fortune. In one scene the President recreates an argument he had with his father in which he claimed marriage should be "for love rather than wealth or convenience." The President's love for his wife weathers seven years of enforced separation, and theirs is portrayed as a model marriage. Dubois's foster father, Rhubarbin, however, has a disastrous marriage. He married his master's wife for her money; she is a termagant who gives her husband no share of the business and leaves him as poor as when he began his employment. Rhubarbin is condemned for being mercenary and "thinking gold an infallible cure for almost every thing" but praised for his generosity and goodness in raising and educating Dubois. Monsieur de Ceare, Adelaide's father, though kind to his stepson, is pictured as the villain for his barbarous conduct in imprisoning the lovers because he has thought Dubois of inferior rank. In the final scenes of the novel, Adelaide is praised for being free from the pride and ambition which frequently accompany high birth, while Dubois is praised for adoring Adelaide "independent of her birth and riches."

Despite this emphasis on love and merit and condemnation of money and pride, the unpleasant realities of social class and the need for money persist. Dubois can marry Adelaide only when his true rank is revealed. Meeke emphasizes the superiority of people of rank and writes condescendingly of servants, merchants, and even Rhubarbin's cousin, who—though wealthy herself—promises to be "totally guided" by the President and his wife's wishes, even to the point of agreeing to marry whomever they dictate. Likewise, Meeke shows the misery of living without money in the stories of Rhubarbin, of the President's wife before her marriage, and of Jane the nursemaid, who dies in squalor. Thus, as much as love and virtue are valued, to live happily and independently one must have money and position.

One interesting aspect of *Count St. Blancard* is the diminished heroism of the hero. Meeke initially describes him as the perfect gentleman: he has a "most elegant figure," plays music and paints in his spare time, and is accomplished in his profession. In the first volume of the novel, he cures Adelaide and rescues her from the wicked Champagne. But in the second volume he is mostly absent, and in the third he is deathly ill. Rather than hearing him defy de Ceare and strongly claim his lady, the reader hears that "the movement of the carriage in these horrid roads was too much for the young man." The helplessness of the hero also has important consequences for the love story. The greatest outpourings of affection come not between the hero and heroine but from the parents, particularly the mother, to their newfound son. The mother's affection for her son borders on sensuality. In their first meetings "she listened to him in ecstasies, and when he looked another way, she gazed upon him in raptures." When Dubois hears the truth of her identity, he "would have flung himself upon his knees before her, but was prevented by her catching him in her arms, saying, 'My dear son, am I so blessed as to have you in my longing arms at last?' They remained silent for a few moments; the joy of both was too great to allow them to speak: it is impossible to form an idea of their mutual felicity." Dubois's scenes with Adelaide are tepid in comparison.

Meeke closes *Count St. Blancard* by claiming that she has merely translated the work and offers it as a "slight specimen of the late laws and customs" in France. The *Monthly Review* (1795) speculated that *Count St. Blancard* was "the labour of some industrious emigree; as the French idiom predominates." Yet the novel lacks description of the French city and countryside, and its serious moral tone seems as English as it does French. From her real translations it is apparent that Meeke was fluent in French.

Count St. Blancard was well received by the critics. The *Critical Review* (November 1795) called it "an entertaining and well-connected story," which "may agreeably beguile a leisure hour." The *Monthly Review*, picking up on Meeke's claims of offering her readers a view of French customs, said, "To those who seek amusement in tracing the former manners of France, we may recommend this little work. It may divert a solitary hour, without endangering youth or disgusting old age." In other words, the novel was viewed as light entertainment.

If Meeke was the wife of a clergyman who lived in a hall, she perhaps did not need to write for financial survival. Nevertheless, she wrote at a speedy rate which left little time for reflection or revision. *The Abbey of Clugny* (1795) soon followed *Count St. Blancard*. Like *Count St. Blancard*, *The Abbey of Clugny* includes satiric attacks on Catholicism. The tomb of the late Abbess is haunted because of her wickedness in life. Though prayers have been said for her soul, none has been very "efficacious." Father Onuphrious, the confessor, uses her tomb for midnight drunken feasts served on the coffin. In *The Abbey of Clugny* Meeke first made use of the supernatural: A ten-foot ghost with crossbones imprinted on its forehead interrupts the monks' revels. The "ghost" is later revealed to be the hero, Alexis, who had decided to punish the confessor for his hypocrisy and misdeeds.

These scenes have the most Gothic atmosphere of any in Meeke's novels. Meeke has little respect for the world of phantoms and little understanding of the psychology that creates such creatures. John Garrett, in comparing Meeke's Gothic trappings to Ann Radcliffe's portrayal of the irrational, introspective world, comments that in Meeke's novels "scenes of Gothic resonance are of rare occurrence, and, when they do appear, never succeed in conveying the stark, individual, and above all truthful impressions that Radcliffe's Gothic scenes never fail to evoke."

The Abbey of Clugny also received favorable critical notice. The *Monthly Review* (1796) commended the ease and vivacity with which the story was told and especially praised the ghost: "The effects . . . are well imagined, and spiritedly related." The reviewer again assumed that Meeke was either French or at least conversant with French manners and style. The *Critical Review* (April 1796) similarly praised the novel: "the incidents are well connected and interesting. . . . The story is not broken in upon by tiresome and impertinent episodes, so common with inferior novelists."

For her next novel Meeke assumed the pseudonym Gabrielli. The writer of the entry on Meeke in *British Authors of the Nineteenth Century* (1936) has supposed that this pen name may have been her maiden name and that she was of Italian descent. Meeke did not, however, translate any Italian works (though her novel *Something Odd* does have Italian quotations as chapter headings). Perhaps she used the pseudonym so as not to flood the market with too many Meeke novels at once or perhaps to have freedom to write in a little different style (though all her books seem much the same). Devendra P. Varma speculates that Meeke wrote under the pseudonym or even anonymously because of feminine conventions. To avoid savage criticism from reviewers, authors wrote anonymously or under the romantic guise of "by a lady." Gabrielli's *The Mysterious Wife*, at any rate, differs from Meeke's earlier novels in that the heroine—rather than the hero—is the one whose genealogy must be entangled. She is revealed to be the daughter of a duchess.

Gabrielli's second work, *The Sicilian* (1798), imitates Ann Radcliffe's *Sicilian Romance* (1790) and *The Italian* (1797). Like Meeke's earlier work, *The Sicilian* presents Catholic villains and female innocents who are preyed upon by male reprobates. Though the title leads the reader to believe that the novel is set in Sicily, much of the action occurs in the fashionable watering places of Bristol and verges on domestic comedy rather than high Gothic. The *Monthly Mirror* (March 1799) was not as enthusiastic as reviewers had been of Meeke's earlier novels: *The Sicilian* is "one of those works which possess just interest enough to prevent the reader's throwing the books aside in disgust."

In *Ellesmere* (1799), published under her own name, Meeke seems more disillusioned about romance and marriage than she was in *Count St. Blancard*. Lady Augusta Cameron sighs that "propriety . . . not romance" should guide young women in the choice of a spouse, and the hero, Clement, soberly considers his choice for a second marriage: "No longer the ardent lover ready to perform impossibilities to obtain the favour of the woman he had once so fervently adored, he could now calmly and dispassionately review his and her past conduct."

Meeke continued to write until her death. Though she introduced small variations in her novels, they continued to follow the formula of genealogical puzzles leading to revelation of the hero's or heroine's noble birth. Her novels moved more and more away from the Gothic genre, which was waning in popularity, to domestic fiction with some Gothic elements. Her narratives are always interesting and complicated, and she frankly admitted to aspiring no higher than commercial success. In the introductory chapter to *Midnight Weddings* (1802), she counseled authors to consult their publishers about material and style because publishers are "more competent judges" of trends in the taste of the literary public. Meeke's purpose is entertainment with an admixture of didacticism. In this she is successful. Francisca Julia wrote in the *Morning Post* in 1807 of the "well-told light fictions of Meeke," while it was said that Macaulay all but knew Meeke's books by heart, though in a 24 December 1832 letter to his sister Hannah he admitted they were "one just like another" and his tastes were, "I fear, incurably vulgar." Mary Mitford read Meeke's novels in her youth and reread at least six of them in her old age.

Meeke's works have not aged well, however. The *Dictionary of National Biography* condemned them for commonplace plots, poor literary style, and characters who "only faintly reflect contemporary manners." In this century her work was lambasted in *British Authors of the Nineteenth Century* (1936) as "pure trash of the commercial variety." More recently, John Garrett has pointed out Meeke's inferiority to Radcliffe and criticized her attempts to reconcile a middle-class outlook with the sublime horror of the Gothic. Along with the novels of Regina Maria Roche, Anna Maria Bennett, and Isabella Kelly, her work remains important as evidence of the popular tastes at the beginning of the nineteenth century.

References:

Dorothy Blakey, *The Minerva Press 1790-1820* (London: Printed for the Bibliographical Society at the University Press, Oxford, 1939);

Frederick S. Frank, *The First Gothics: A Critical Guide to the English Gothic Novel* (New York: Garland, 1987), pp. 235-241;

John Garrett, Introduction to *Count St. Blancard, or The Prejudiced Judge* (New York: Arno Press, 1977), pp. xv-xxix;

Montague Summers, *The Gothic Quest: A History of the Gothic Novel* (London: Fortune Press, 1938), pp. 30, 36, 100;

Devendra P. Varma, Foreword to *Count St. Blancard, or The Prejudiced Judge* (New York: Arno Press, 1977), pp. v-xiv.

Mary Russell Mitford

(16 December 1787 - 10 January 1855)

Mary Rose Sullivan
University of Colorado at Denver

See also the Mitford entry in *DLB 110: British Romantic Prose Writers, 1789-1832: Second Series.*

BOOKS: *Poems* (London: Printed for A. J. Valpy & sold by Longman, Hurst, Rees & Orme, 1810; enlarged edition, London: Printed by A. J. Valpy & sold by F. C. & J. Rivington, 1811);

Christina, the Maid of the South Seas, a Poem (London: Printed by A. J. Valpy for F. C. & J. Rivington, 1811);

Watlington Hill, a Poem (London: Printed by A. J. Valpy, 1812);

Narrative Poems on the Female Character in the Various Relations of Human Life, volume 1 [no more published] (London, 1813; New York: Eastburn, Kirk, 1813);

Julian, A Tragedy in Five Acts (London: G. & W. B. Whittaker, 1823; New York: W. B. Gilley, 1823);

Our Village, volume 1 (London: G. & W. B. Whittaker, 1824); volumes 2 and 3 (London: G. B. Whittaker, 1826, 1828); volumes 1-3 (New York: E. Bliss, 1828); volumes 4 and 5 (London: Whittaker, Treacher, 1830, 1832); volume 4 (New York: E. Bliss, 1830);

Foscari, a Tragedy in Five Acts and in Verse (London: Printed for G. B. Whittaker, 1826);

Dramatic Scenes, Sonnets, and Other Poems (London: G. B. Whittaker, 1827);

Rienzi, A Tragedy in Five Acts (London: J. Cumberland, 1828; Baltimore: Printed & published by J. Robinson, 1829; Boston: Press of the Boston Daily Advertiser, 1829; New York: Elton & Perkins, 1829);

Charles the First, an Historical Tragedy in Five Acts (London: J. Duncombe, 1834; Philadelphia: Carey & Hart, 1835);

Belford Regis, or Sketches of a Country Town (3 volumes, London: R. Bentley, 1835; 1 volume, Philadelphia: Carey, Lea & Blanchard, 1835);

Sadak and Kalasrade; or the Waters of Oblivion, a Romantic Opera in Two Acts (London: Fairbrother, 1836);

Country Stories (London: Saunders & Otley, 1837; Philadelphia: Carey, Lea & Blanchard, 1838);

Recollections of a Literary Life, or Books, Places, and People (London: R. Bentley, 1852; New York: Harper, 1852);

The Dramatic Works of Mary Russell Mitford, 2 volumes (London: Hurst & Blackett, 1854);

Atherton, and Other Tales (3 volumes, London: Hurst & Blackett, 1854; 2 volumes, Boston: Ticknor & Fields, 1854).

PLAY PRODUCTIONS: *Julian*, London, Theatre Royal, Covent Garden, 15 March 1823;

Foscari, London, Theatre Royal, Covent Garden, 4 November 1826;

Rienzi, London, Theatre Royal, Drury Lane, 9 October 1828;

Charles the First, London, Royal Victoria Theatre, 2 July 1834;

Sadak and Kalasrade, with music by Charles Parker, London, English Opera House, 20 April 1835.

OTHER: *Stories of American Life, by American Writers*, 3 volumes, edited by Mitford (London: H. Colburn & R. Bentley, 1830);

American Stories for Little Boys and Girls, Intended for Children Under Ten Years of Age, 3 volumes, edited by Mitford (London: Whittaker, Treacher, 1831);

Lights and Shadows of American Life, 3 volumes, edited by Mitford (London: H. Colburn & R. Bentley, 1832);

Findens' Tableaux, edited by Mitford (London: C. Tilt, 1838-1841);

Schloss's English Bijou Almanack for 1843. Poetically Illustrated by Miss Mitford (London: Schloss, 1843);

Fragments des oeuvres d'Alexandre Dumas choisis à l'usage de la jeunesse par Miss Mitford, selected

Mary Russell Mitford, circa 1825 (portrait by Benjamin Robert Haydon, Reading Museum and Art Gallery)

and translated by Mitford (Brussels: Pierre Rolandi, 1846).

Mary Russell Mitford, a minor poet and playwright, was most admired by her contemporaries for her writing in the genre known as the idyll. Her "little pictures," or informal sketches of rural English life, collected under the title *Our Village* (1824-1832), were among the most popular works of fiction in the first half of the nineteenth century and continue to be read, for their graceful style, genial tone, and precise observation of nature.

Born on 16 December 1787 in Alresford, Hampshire, Mary Russell Mitford was the only child of Mary Russell, a clergyman's daughter and lineal descendant of the ducal Bedfords, and George Mitford, son of a Northumberland surgeon. Although George Mitford studied for the medical profession and was always referred to as "Dr." Mitford, he seems not to have practiced medicine after his marriage in 1785, settling instead into his wife's Alresford estate and the life of a country gentleman. In the 1790s he moved the family to Berkshire, and in 1802, with the twenty-thousand-pound winnings from a sweepstakes ticket chosen by his ten-year-old daughter, Mary, he had built in the vicinity of Reading a comfortable estate known as Bertram House that served as home to the Mitfords for eighteen years. By 1820 Dr. Mitford's extravagant habits and gambling debts had depleted not only his daughter's winnings but his wife's considerable fortune, and, after a long court suit, the family was forced to move to a rented cottage in the small village of Three Mile Cross outside Reading. Mrs. Mitford died there in 1830; Dr. Mitford in 1842. Mary Russell Mitford lived on there until 1851, when she moved to the nearby village of Swallowfield.

A devoted daughter, unwilling to leave home, Mitford decided by 1820 on a professional writing career as a way to support the household. A precocious child, reading by the age of three, she had acquired a good background in English and French literature at the Chelsea boarding school, run by a M. de St. Quintin, that she attended from 1798 to 1802, and had published a volume of miscellaneous *Poems* in 1810 and some longer poems, including *Christina, the Maid of the South Seas* (1811). Samuel Taylor Coleridge was

Dr. George Mitford (portrait by John Lucas; from Constance Hill, Mary Russell Mitford and Her Surroundings, *1920)*

said to have helped her with at least one of these poems. Seeing the actor-manager William Macready perform at Covent Garden convinced her to try her hand at writing a historical drama, and although her first effort, "Fiesco," came to nothing—except for some poetic excerpts published in a journal, the *Museum*—she kept writing, with the encouragement of Thomas Noon Talfourd, an old Reading acquaintance who had become a London barrister with literary connections. Talfourd interceded with Macready, who brought out Mitford's second effort, *Julian*, at Covent Garden in March of 1823, where it ran for eight performances and earned her two hundred pounds. Her next historical drama, *Foscari*, set in the Venice of the doges, ran for fifteen performances at Covent Garden in 1826, and in 1828 her *Rienzi*, set in fourteenth-century Rome, received considerable acclaim, playing for thirty-four nights and establishing Mitford's name as a dramatist. Her next play, *Charles the First*, ran into difficulty with the censors, however, and did not appear until 1834 and then at the Victoria Theatre, beyond the lord chamberlain's reach. In 1835 she wrote the libretto for *Sadak and Kalasrade*, "a romantic opera," but failed to have two other plays, *Gaston de Blondeville* and *Inez de Castro*, produced at all. Another drama, *Otto of Wittelsbach*, written at the request of American actor Edwin Forrest in 1836 and worked on for the next four years, never reached the stage.

Even as she labored on her plays, Mitford was casting about for some more dependable source of income. Talfourd was impressed with some short, informal landscape descriptions she had written for a journal in 1819 and sent them to two journals with which he was connected; the *New Monthly*, edited by Thomas Campbell, refused them but the *Lady's Magazine* accepted them. Immediately on their appearance in December 1822, the sketches were hailed for their fresh and good-humored view of rural life. More were called for and supplied, and they proved so popular that Mitford arranged with publisher George

Whittaker to publish them in 1824 as *Our Village: Sketches of Rural Life, Character, and Scenery*. Within months the book was in its third edition, and Mitford continued to write similar sketches for other journals—leaving the *Lady's Magazine* after one editor absconded and another refused permission to reprint. Whittaker then brought the sketches out in separate volumes of *Our Village* at two-year intervals until 1832.

Clearly, despite her comparative success with drama, the idyll was Mitford's forte and the form with which her name henceforth would be associated. The sketches were particularly popular in America, being printed first in extracts in newspapers and then in pirated editions of *Our Village*. Her American reputation led to her being asked to edit volumes of American tales for young readers. Her tales and sketches were sought by decorative gift annuals such as the *Amulet* and *Friendship's Offering*, and in 1835 she brought out an extended story, which she called a "novel," set in Reading and called *Belford Regis*. *Country Stories* (1837) collects several tales first published in the annuals. Although her popularity as a fiction writer remained undiminished, these two volumes virtually brought to an end—except for a volume called *Atherton, and Other Tales* (1854)—her career in fiction.

Fame had taken its toll. The stories of the 1830s lacked the spontaneity and quaint humor of those written in the preceding decade. As literary pilgrims thronged to Three Mile Cross to see the originals of the people and places in *Our Village*, Mitford could no longer portray the life around her so candidly and had to draw more on imagination than on observation. Haste and fatigue also affected her, as she struggled to keep pace with her spendthrift father's debts. A letter to Elizabeth Barrett of 9 April 1842 describes a typical day:

> It will help you to understand how impossible it is for me to earn money as I ought to do, when I tell you that this very day I received your dear letter, and sixteen others; that then my dear father brought into my room the newspaper to hear the ten or twelve columns of news from India; then I dined and breakfasted in one, then I got up. By that time there were three parties of people in the garden; eight others arrived soon after—some friends, some acquaintances, and some strangers; the two first classes went away, and I was forced to leave two sets of the last, being engaged to call upon Lady Madalina Palmer. . . . She took me some six miles (on foot) in Mr. Palmer's beautiful plantations in search of that exquisite wild flower the buck-bean. . . .

Even after receiving a civil-list pension of one hundred pounds a year in 1837 she was forced to take on irksome editing tasks for the money. From 1838 to 1841 she edited the annual *Finden's Tableaux*, for which she solicited from friends contributions of poems and tales to accompany the engraved illustrations and wrote romances herself (such as "The Proud Ladye of Adlersberg," 1840). By the time of her father's last illness in the fall of 1842 she was unable to meet the deadline for another annual she had contracted to edit—a publishing curiosity called the *Bijou Almanack*, which was the size of a thumbnail and legible only through a magnifying glass—and had to call on her friend Elizabeth Barrett, an aspiring poet who had contributed to *Finden's*, to compose some of the handful of short poems that made up the text.

On Dr. Mitford's death in December 1842, old friends such as the literary critic Henry Chorley and the Reverend William Harness organized a public subscription that quickly reached some two thousand pounds and gave her the first leisure she had known in two decades. At age fifty-five she was ready for retirement and for a decade held out against all offers of writing assignments. She gave up a long-cherished idea of publishing her correspondence with Sir William Elford, an elderly dilettante she had met in 1810, but reclaimed letters to friends from a brief holiday in Bath in 1843 when she had visited Frances Trollope and Walter Savage Landor; those letters, along with notes from another rare excursion, to Taplow in 1848, were finally put to use in a late work, *Recollections of a Literary Life* (1852). Despite talk of moving—to Wales, to the Channel Islands, even to the Yucatán, which she had read about in an American travel book—she journeyed for the most part only around Reading, in country walks with her spaniel, Dash, and his successor, Flush. She read voraciously in memoirs, letters, and novels and maintained a prodigious correspondence. She knew personally most of the best-known writers of the day, from poets Joanna Baillie and Felicia Hemans to prose writers Jane Porter, Julia Pardoe, and Amelia Opie, and followed with particular interest the careers of prominent women such as Anna Jameson, Harriet Martineau, and George Sand. Marianne Skerrett, the queen's dresser,. supplied her with gossip about the new, young Queen Victoria, and

Mitford's cottage at Three Mile Cross, circa 1836 (lithograph by E. Havell)

painters Benjamin Robert Haydon and John Lucas sent her news from the art world.

Her most prized correspondent was Elizabeth Barrett Browning, whom she met in London in 1836 and with whom she forged a deep friendship that survived, despite disparity of age, temperament, and social class, until Mitford's death. After the first few years, when Mitford periodically journeyed the forty miles to London to visit the semi-invalid Elizabeth Barrett, their interchanges were confined mainly to paper, but it was on both sides a deeply satisfying sharing of views, confidences, and practical help. Both were intellectually independent but emotionally dominated by their fathers and plagued by physical weaknesses. They shared a taste for Elizabethan drama, Augustan essays, and Romantic memoirs, and particularly enjoyed the sensational French novels of Eugène Sue and Frédéric Soulié, supplied regularly to Three Mile Cross by way of Elizabeth Barrett's gift of a foreign library subscription. Mitford's special gift to Wimpole Street was Flush, offspring of her own spaniel Flush, sent to divert Elizabeth Barrett in her grief after the drowning of her brother. Mitford's later indiscreet revelation in *Recollections of a Literary Life* about her friend's trauma after that death strained but did not break the bonds of friendship, which had held through Barrett's surprise marriage in 1846 to Robert Browning and her move to Italy. Mitford thought of Barrett as her protégée, and a prediction that she made to her in late March 1842 conveys the warmth of affection for her young friend: "The position that I long to see you fill is higher, firmer, prouder than ever has been filled by woman. . . . My pride and my hopes seem altogether merged in you."

As a result of their discussions of French novelists, Mitford decided in 1846 to translate some excerpts from Balzac for young readers; she was challenged by the idea of putting his "vivid and coloured language" into "such English as should give some faint idea of his French." Her world had by now narrowed considerably: a series of accidents lamed her and the pain made her increasingly dependent on opium. She had to replace several servants—for theft, for drunkenness, and, in the case of her favorite maid, Kerrenhappuck, for deceiving her about an illegitimate child she had borne. Still, visitors to Three Mile Cross found the author of *Our Village* a lively conversationalist, as interested in discussing Napoleon III's politics as she was in showing her prize-winning geraniums. Short and stout, unstylish in costume and manner, she never played the bluestocking. Benjamin Haydon had captured her countrywoman sturdiness during the 1820s in

Mitford in 1829 (portrait by John Lucas; from W. J. Roberts, Mary Russell Mitford, *1913)*

what became known as the "Cook-maid" portrait, and John Lucas, thinking to give her more dignity, followed with a painting of her in an imposingly feathered hat. He corrected his mistake in 1852, however, by showing her—in what has become her best-known likeness (now in the National Portrait Gallery)—in old-fashioned bonnet and shawl, so as to preserve what he called her "characteristic of simplicity."

In the summer of 1851 Mitford managed a trip to the Crystal Palace exhibit in London and a reunion with Elizabeth Barrett Browning, who was visiting England with her husband and child. In September, her cottage literally uninhabitable from dampness and disrepair, Mitford packed up her "four tons of books" and moved to nearby Swallowfield, to a house large enough to accommodate her former maid, Kerrenhappuck, whom she had taken back into service, and "K's" child and husband, Sam Sweetman. Visitors included the young art critic John Ruskin and the American publisher James T. Fields. In this year also Henry Chorley lured her out of retirement to write a book of reminiscences and anecdotes about her favorite contemporary authors—including William Motherwell, Thomas Davis, and John Greenleaf Whittier—published in 1852 as *Recollections of a Literary Life, or Books, Places, and People.* It brought her renewed popularity and went quickly into American and French editions.

A fall from a pony chaise at the end of 1852 left Mitford almost totally confined to bed and chair, but she managed to write an autobiographical preface for a two-volume collection of her plays, published by Hurst and Blackett in 1854, and finally finished a last work of fiction, *Atherton, and Other Tales*, a book she had contracted for in 1836. She was still writing letters up to a few days before her death on 10 January 1855. Her executor, William Harness, immediately undertook to reclaim her letters from friends for publication but was prevented by the Mitford servants, "K" and Sam Sweetman, who claimed their mistress had given them rights to her papers. After Harness's death, his assistant, A. G. L'Estrange, succeeded in publishing an extensive collection of the letters which, together with supplementary volumes compiled by Henry Chorley, still constitute—despite errors of dating and transcription caused by difficulty in reading Mitford's handwriting—the best available record of her life and personality.

In assessing Mary Russell Mitford's career, later critics agree with her contemporaries that the *Our Village* idylls constitute her enduring achievement. Her poems, correct and conventional, she herself dismissed: "All sold well, and might have been reprinted; but I had (of this proof of tolerable taste I am rather proud) the sense to see that they were good for nothing" (letter to Elizabeth Barrett, 27 April 1842). Her dramas she regarded more highly, priding herself on clarity of exposition, but had no illusions about the low standards of dramaturgy in her day. She quoted approvingly the actor Charles Kemble's advice to her: "Think of the stupidest person of your acquaintance, and, when you have made your play so clear that you are sure that he would comprehend it, then you may venture to hope that it will be understood by your audience" (to Barrett, 16 August 1836). Mitford was constrained by the expectation that plays were primarily vehicles for the actor-manager and a means to make audiences feel instructed as well as entertained by exposure to "classical" themes. She followed the custom of borrowing subject matter—her *Foscari* covered the same ground as George Gordon, Lord Byron's poetic drama *The Two Foscari* (1821), just as Edward Bulwer-Lytton took her *Rienzi* material for his novel of the same title (1835)—but in the crowded field of writers using historical figures in their dramas she was considered to hold her own. A review in the *Athenaeum* (2 August 1845) of literary portrayals of Oliver Cromwell, including those by Sir Walter Scott, Victor Hugo, and Bulwer-Lytton as well as Mitford's in *Charles the First*, conceded that although none hit the mark squarely, "the lady probably came the nearest." A more positive endorsement came from America, where Charlotte Cushman played in *Rienzi* to admiring audiences in the 1830s, and from the composer Richard Wagner, who attributed the inspiration for his 1842 opera *Rienzi* to the influence of Mitford and Bulwer-Lytton. Her plays nevertheless remain, like others of that era, unread today, and her one lasting contribution to the drama may be her decision to do away with the conventional prologue and epilogue and let the action of the play stand on its own, a departure from tradition taken up by those who came after her.

Her idylls, on the other hand, are still very much read today, in countless popular editions such as the 1893 selection with an introduction by Anne Thackeray Ritchie, the 1982 World's Classics volume from Oxford University Press, and the 1987 centenary volume from Prentice-Hall with illustrations by John Constable, J. M. W. Turner, and George Stubbs. Despite their quintessentially English character and setting, the idylls have been translated into dozens of foreign languages; as early as 1842 Mitford heard to her delight that a homesick friend in Spain who asked for "an English-like book" was given a Spanish translation of *Our Village*.

The immediate appeal of these idylls is their wealth of lifelike detail, a quality that led reviewers to speak of Mitford's "Dutch painting." Much of what she described was drawn directly from life; the narrator's cottage in "Whitsun-Eve," for example, "very like a birdcage," and tiny garden, like a "framed canvas," are recognizably Mitford's own in Three Mile Cross. But even more appealing to readers than the convincingly real effect is the disarmingly candid, even intimate, voice of the narrator. In "The First Primrose" she ends a description of a local estate (actually the Mitfords' former manor) by saying: "This is an exact description of the home which, three years ago, it nearly broke my heart to leave. What a tearing up by the root it was! I have pitied cabbage-plants and celery, and all transplantable things, ever since. . . ." Like the personalized title, *Our Village*, the tone suggests an involvement in the life of the villagers and a sharing of their values and attitudes, so that even when the narrator laughingly records their quirks and follies her affection is evident. She is as fond of the coquettish Hetta Coxe as of the hardworking Hannah Bint, as interested in the misogynist mole catcher as in the courtly tavern owner. Her description of the latter's passionate pursuit of a visiting pastry cook is typically succinct: "During the week that the lady of the piecrust stayed, her lover almost lived in the oven." From the championship cricket match to the cow-

Portrait by Daniel Maclise in the Fraser's Magazine *"Gallery of Illustrious Literary Characters" (1830-1838)*

slip ball, no village event escapes her keen eyes and tart assessment. The combination of authorial sympathy and detachment was what Mitford most admired in the novels of Jane Austen, and, although she lacked Austen's ability to sustain plot and character, she often suggests the Austen manner of viewing village life as a microcosm of the larger social order.

In the Mitford village, gentry and laborers live in harmony with each other and with the seasons, as epitomized in the festival in "Our Maying," with its "honest English country dance" in which "the beflowered French hats, the silks and furbelows" are found "sailing and rustling amidst the straw bonnets and cotton gowns." Such idyllic scenes caused some critics to accuse Mitford of idealizing rural life rather than rendering it realistically, and certainly hers is a selective view of reality, as Elizabeth Barrett Browning suggested by labeling her friend "a prose Crabbe in the sun." Harsher aspects of country life—drunkenness, injustice, decay—exist in *Our Village* but, like the workhouse the narrator hurries by, they are kept in the background. Mitford, that passionate lover of the natural scene—never too busy to walk miles in search of "that exquisite wild flower the buck-bean"—had a deep sense of the essential oneness of humankind and nature and found it more evident in the country than in the city. "To live in the country is, in my mind, to bring the poetry of Nature home to the eyes and heart," she wrote to the city-bound Elizabeth Barrett (27 April 1842). In "The First Primrose" she recalls other such excursions to search out the first wildflowers of the season: "How profusely they covered the sunny open slope under the weeping birch, 'the lady of the woods'—and how often have I started to see the early innocent brown snake who loved the spot as well as I did, winding along the young blossoms, or rustling

Mitford in 1852 (portrait by John Lucas; from W. J. Roberts, Mary Russell Mitford, *1913)*

amongst the fallen leaves!" The serpent claims his place even in Mitford's Arcadia, but here it is innocent, loving, and equally entitled to share in nature's beauty.

This conviction of the essential unity of humans and external nature, together with her conviction of the dignity and worth of the humblest villager, mark her work as basically Romantic. Recent critics have found her writings more complex than usually has been recognized; P. D. Edwards, for one, sees her as a post-Romantic, her idylls "a modernized compound of traditional pastoral, Romantic social concern, Wordsworthian naturalism, novelistic human interest and lifelikeness, and at least glimpses of the evils and miseries so emphasized in traditional anti-pastoral, and in Crabbe and Cobbett." But, however much *Our Village* may anticipate the impulse toward realism in Victorian fiction, its enduring appeal lies in its sunny, affectionate view of the people and places of Mary Russell Mitford's rural world.

Letters:

The Letters of Mary Russell Mitford, Authoress of "Our Village," etc. Related in a Selection From Her Letters to Her Friends, 3 volumes, edited by A. G. L'Estrange (London: R. Bentley, 1870);

Letters of Mary Russell Mitford, second series, 2 volumes, edited by Henry Chorley (London: R. Bentley, 1872);

The Friendships of Mary Russell Mitford as Recorded in Letters From Her Literary Correspondents, 2 volumes, edited by L'Estrange (London: Hurst & Blackett, 1882);

Mary Russell Mitford: Correspondence with Charles Boner and John Ruskin, edited by Elizabeth Lee (London: Unwin, 1914);

Letters of Mary Russell Mitford, edited by R. Brimley Johnson (London: John Lane, 1925);

Miss Mitford and Mr. Harness: Records of a Friendship, edited by Caroline Duncan-Jones (London: Society for the Promotion of Christian Knowledge, 1955);

"The Correspondence of Mary Russell Mitford and Thomas Noon Talfourd (1821-1825)," edited by William A. Coles, M.A. thesis, Harvard University, 1956;

Women of Letters: Selected Letters of Elizabeth Barrett Browning and Mary Russell Mitford, edited by Meredith B. Raymond and Mary Rose Sullivan (Boston: G. K. Hall, 1987).

Biographies:

W. J. Roberts, *Mary Russell Mitford: The Tragedy of a Blue Stocking* (London: Andrew Melrose, 1913);

Vera Watson, *Mary Russell Mitford* (London: Evans, 1949).

References:

William A. Coles, "Mary Russell Mitford: The Inauguration of a Literary Career," *Bulletin of the John Rylands Library*, 40 (September 1957): 33-46;

P. D. Edwards, *Idyllic Realism from Mary Russell Mitford to Hardy* (New York: St. Martin's Press, 1988).

Papers:

Mitford materials are scattered throughout England and America. Collections of unpublished letters to Thomas Noon Talfourd are in the Harvard University Library, the John Rylands Library and the Bodleian Library; letters to other correspondents are in the Berkshire County Library, Reading, England, and the Henry E. Huntington Library, among other places. Mitford's diary covering the period 1 January 1819 to 11 March 1823 is in the British Library.

Hannah More

(2 February 1745 - 7 September 1833)

Ann Hobart
Trinity College

See also the More entry in *DLB 107: British Romantic Prose Writers, 1789-1832: First Series.*

SELECTED BOOKS: *The Search After Happiness: A Pastoral Drama* (Bristol: Printed & sold by S. Farley, 1773; republished with *Armine and Elvira,* by Edmund Cartwright (Philadelphia: Printed by James Humphreys, 1774);

The Inflexible Captive: A Tragedy (Bristol: Printed & sold by S. Farley, 1774; Philadelphia: Printed for John Sparhawk by James Humphreys, Jr., 1774);

Sir Eldred of the Bower, and The Bleeding Rock: Two Legendary Tales (London: Printed for T. Cadell, 1776);

Ode to Dragon, Mr. Garrick's house-dog, at Hampton (London: Printed for T. Cadell, 1777);

Essays on various subjects, principally designed for young ladies (London: Printed by J. Wilkie & T. Cadell, 1777; Philadelphia: Printed & sold by Young, Stewart & M'Culloch, 1786);

Percy: A Tragedy (London: Printed for T. Cadell, 1778);

The Works of Miss Hannah More in Prose and Verse (Cork: Printed by Thomas White, 1778);

The Fatal Falsehood: A Tragedy (London: Printed for T. Cadell, 1779);

Sacred Dramas, chiefly intended for young persons: the subjects taken from the Bible to which is added Sensibility, a poem (London: Printed for T. Cadell, 1782); augmented as *Sacred dramas, chiefly intended for young persons: the subjects taken from the Bible. To which are added: Reflections of King Hezekiah, Sensibility, a poem. And essays on various subjects, principally designed for young ladies* (Philadelphia: Printed for Thomas Dobson, 1787);

Florio: a tale, for fine gentlemen and fine ladies: and, The Bas Bleu; or, Conversation; two poems (London: Printed for T. Cadell, 1786);

Slavery, a poem (London: Printed for T. Cadell, 1788; New York: Printed by J. & A. M'Lean, 1788; Philadelphia: Printed by Joseph James, 1788);

Thoughts on the Importance of the Manners of the Great to General Society (London: Printed for T. Cadell, 1788; Philadelphia: Printed for T. Dobson, 1788);

Bishop Bonner's Ghost (Strawberry Hill: Printed by Thomas Kirgate, 1789);

An Estimate of the Religion of the Fashionable World (London: Printed for T. Cadell, 1791; Philadelphia: Printed for & sold by the Revd. M. L. Weems & H. Willis, 1793);

Village Politics, addressed to all the mechanics, journeymen, and day labourers in Great Britain, by Will Chip, a country carpenter (London: Printed for & sold by F. & C. Rivington, 1792);

Remarks on the speech of M. Dupont, made in the National Convention of France, on the subjects of religion and public education (London: Printed for T. Cadell, 1793); republished in *Considerations on Religion and Public Education, with Remarks on the Speech of M. Dupont, Delivered in the National Convention of France* (Boston: Printed by Weld & Greenough, 1794);

The Apprentice's Monitor; or Indentures in verse [single sheet] (Bath: Sold by S. Hazard and J. Marshall & R. White, London, 1795);

The Carpenter; or, the Danger of evil company [single sheet] (Bath: Sold by S. Hazard and J. Marshall & R. White, London: 1795);

The Gin-Shop; or, a Peep into a prison [single sheet] (Bath: Sold by S. Hazard and J. Marshall & R. White, London, 1795);

The History of Tom White the Postilion (Bath: Sold by S. Hazard and J. Marshall & R. White, London, 1795; Philadelphia: Published by B. Johnson, 1798);

The Market Woman, a true tale; or, Honesty is the best policy [single sheet] (Bath: Sold by S. Hazard and J. Marshall & R. White, London, 1795);

The Roguish Miller; or, Nothing got by cheating [single sheet] (Bath: Sold by S. Hazard and J. Marshall & R. White, London, 1795);

The Shepherd of Salisbury Plain (Bath: Sold by S. Hazard and J. Marshall & R. White, Lon-

Hannah More, 1787 (portrait by John Opie; from M. G. Jones, Hannah More, *1952)*

don, 1795; Philadelphia: Printed by B. & J. Johnson, 1800);

The Two Shoemakers (Bath: Sold by S. Hazard and J. Marshall & R. White, London, 1795); republished as *The History of the Two Shoemakers. Part I* (Philadelphia: Printed by B. & J. Johnson, 1800);

The Shepherd of Salisbury Plain. Part II (Bath: Sold by S. Hazard and J. Marshall & R. White, London, 1795; Philadelphia: Printed by B. & J. Johnson, 1800);

Patient Joe; or, the Newcastle Collier [single sheet] (Bath: Sold by S. Hazard and J. Marshall & R. White, London, 1795; Philadelphia: Printed & sold by J. Rakeshaw, 1808);

The Riot; or, Half a loaf is better than no bread [single sheet] (London: Sold by J. Marshall & R. White and S. Hazard, Bath, 1795);

The Way to Plenty: or, the second part of Tom White (London: Sold by J. Marshall & R. White and S. Hazard, Bath, 1795; Philadelphia: Printed by B. & J. Johnson, 1800);

The Honest Miller of Glocestershire [single sheet] (London: Sold by J. Marshall & R. White and S. Hazard, Bath, 1795);

The Two Wealthy Farmers; or, the History of Mr. Bragwell. Part I (London: Sold by J. Marshall & R. White and S. Hazard, Bath, 1795; Philadelphia: Printed by B. & J. Johnson, 1800);

The Two Wealthy Farmers; or, the History of Mr. Bragwell. Part II (Bath: Sold by S. Hazard and J. Marshall & R. White, London, 1795; Philadelphia: Printed by B. & J. Johnson, 1800);

Robert and Richard; or, the Ghost of poor Molly, who was drowned in Richard's mill pond (London: Sold by J. Marshall & R. White and S. Hazard, Bath, 1796);

The Apprentice Turned Master; or, the Second part of the Two Shoemakers (London: Sold by J. Marshall & R. White and S. Hazard, Bath,

1796); republished as *The History of the Two Shoemakers. Part II* (Philadelphia: Printed by B. & J. Johnson, 1800);

The History of Idle Jack Brown . . . Being the third part of the Two Shoemakers (London: Sold by J. Marshall & R. White and S. Hazard, Bath, 1796); republished as *The History of the Two Shoemakers. Part III* (Philadelphia: Printed by B. & J. Johnson, 1800);

The Shopkeeper Turned Sailor . . . Part I (London: Sold by J. Marshall & R. White and S. Hazard, Bath, 1796; Philadelphia: Printed by B. & J. Johnson, 1800);

Jack Brown in Prison . . . Being the fourth part of the History of the Two Shoemakers (London: Sold by J. Marshall & R. White and S. Hazard, Bath, 1796; republished as *The History of the Two Shoemakers. Part IV* (Philadelphia: Printed by B. & J. Johnson, 1800);

The Hackney Coachman; or, the Way to get a good fare (London: Sold by J. Marshall & R. White and S. Hazard, Bath, 1796);

Sunday Reading. On Carrying Religion into the Common Business of Life. A dialogue between James Stock and Will Simpson, the shoemakers (London: Sold by J. Marshall & R. White, 1796);

Turn the Carpet; or, the Two weavers: a new song, in a dialogue between Dick and John (London: Sold by J. Marshall & R. White and S. Hazard, Bath, 1796);

Betty Brown, the St. Giles's Orange girl (London: Sold by J. Marshall & R. White and S. Hazard, Bath, 1796; Philadelphia: Printed by B. & J. Johnson, 1800);

Sunday Reading. The Grand Assizes; or, General gaol delivery (London: Sold by J. Marshall & R. White and S. Hazard, Bath, 1796);

The History of Mr. Bragwell; or, the Two Wealthy Farmers. Part III (London: Sold by J. Marshall & R. White and S. Hazard, Bath; J. Elder, Edinburgh, 1796); republished as *The Two Wealthy Farmers; or, the History of Mr. Bragwell. Part III* (Philadelphia: Printed by B. & J. Johnson, 1800);

A Hymn of Praise for the Abundant Harvest of 1796 (London: Sold by J. Marshall & R. White and S. Hazard, Bath, 1796);

Sunday Reading. The History of the Two Wealthy Farmers . . . Part IV (London: Sold by J. Marshall & R. White and S. Hazard, Bath, 1796); republished as *The Two Wealthy Farmers; or, the History of Mr. Bragwell. Part IV* (Philadelphia: Printed by B. & J. Johnson, 1800);

The Two Wealthy Farmers, with the sad adventures of Miss Bragwell. Part V (London: Sold by J. Marshall & R. White and S. Hazard, Bath, 1796; republished as *The Two Wealthy Farmers; or, The History of Mr. Bragwell. Part V* (Philadelphia: Printed by B. & J. Johnson, 1800);

Black Giles the Poacher . . . Part I (London: Sold by J. Marshall & R. White and S. Hazard, Bath, 1796; Philadelphia: Printed by B. & J. Johnson, 1800);

The Cottage Cook; or Mrs. Jones's Cheap Dishes (London: Sold by J. Marshall & R. White; S. Hazard, Bath; and J. Elder, Edinburgh, 1796);

Sunday Reading. Bear ye one another's Burthens; or, the Valley of tears: a vision (London: Sold by J. Marshall & R. White; S. Hazard, Bath; and J. Elder, Edinburgh, 1796; Philadelphia: Benjamin Johnson, 1813);

Black Giles the Poacher. With the history of widow Brown's apple-tree. Part II (London: Sold by J. Marshall and S. Hazard, Bath, 1796; Philadelphia: Printed by B. & J. Johnson, 1800);

The Good Militiaman . . . being a new song by Honest Dan the ploughboy turned soldier (London: Sold by J. Marshall & R. White and S. Hazard, Bath, 1797);

Tawny Rachel, or, the Fortune teller (London: Sold by J. Marshall & R. White; S. Hazard, Bath; J. Elder, Edinburgh, 1797); republished as *The Fortune Teller* (Philadelphia: Published by B. Johnson, 1798);

The Two Gardeners (London: Sold by J. Marshall & R. White; S. Hazard, Bath; and J. Elder, Edinburgh, 1797);

The Sunday School (London: Sold by J. Marshall & R. White; S. Hazard, Bath; and J. Elder, Edinburgh, 1797);

The Day of Judgement; or, The Grand Reckoning (London: Sold by J. Marshall & R. White; S. Hazard, Bath; and J. Elder, Edinburgh, 1797);

The History of Hester Wilmot; or, the Second part of the Sunday School (London: Sold by J. Marshall & R. White; S. Hazard, Bath; and J. Elder, Edinburgh, 1797; Philadelphia: Sunday and Adult School Union, 1818);

Sunday Reading. The Servant Man turned Soldier; or, the Fair weather Christian (London: Sold by J. Marshall & R. White; S. Hazard, Bath; J. Elder, Edinburgh, 1797);

The History of Hester Wilmot; or, the New gown. Part II. Being a continuation of the Sunday School (London: Sold by J. Marshall; S. Hazard, Bath; and J. Elder, Edinburgh, 1797);

THE
SHEPHERD
OF
SALISBURY-PLAIN.

Sold by S. HAZARD,
(PRINTER to the CHEAP REPOSITORY for Religious and Moral Tracts,) at BATH;

By J. MARSHALL,
At the CHEAP REPOSITORIES, No. 17, Queen-Street, Cheap-Side, and No. 4, Aldermary Church Yard; and R. WHITE, Piccadilly, LONDON; and by all Booksellers, Newsmen, and Hawkers, in Town and Country.

Great Allowance to Shopkeepers and Hawkers.
Price 1d. or 4s. 6d. per 100. 2s. 6d. for 50. 1s. 6d. for 25.

[Entered at Stationers Hall.]

Title page for one of approximately fifty tracts in which More illustrated the rewards of virtue and piety for working-class readers

The Lady and the Pye; or, Know thyself (London: Sold by J. Marshall & R. White; S. Hazard, Bath; and J. Elder, Edinburgh, 1797);

Sunday Reading. The Strait Gate and the Broad Way, being the second part of the Valley of Tears (London: Sold by J. Marshall & R. White; S. Hazard, Bath; and J. Elder, Edinburgh, 1797);

The History of Mr. Fantom, the new fashioned philosopher and his man William (London: Sold by J. Marshall; S. Hazard, Bath; and J. Elder, Edinburgh, 1797; Philadelphia: Printed by B. & J. Johnson, 1800);

Sunday Reading. The Pilgrims. An allegory (London: Sold by J. Marshall; S. Hazard, Bath; and J. Elder, Edinburgh, 1797; Philadelphia: Printed & sold by Kimber, Conrad, 1808);

Dan and Jane; or, Faith and works. A tale (London: Sold by J. Marshall; S. Hazard, Bath; and J. Elder, Edinburgh, 1797);

The Two Wealthy Farmers; or, the Sixth part of the history of Mr. Bragwell and his two daughters (London: Sold by J. Marshall; S. Hazard, Bath; and J. Elder, Edinburgh, 1797);

The Two Wealthy Farmers; or, the Seventh and last part of the history of Mr. Bragwell and his two daughters (London: Sold by J. Marshall; S. Hazard, Bath; and J. Elder, Edinburgh, 1797);

The Plum-Cakes; or, the Farmer and his three sons (London: Sold by J. Marshall and S. Hazard, Bath, 1797);

'Tis All for the Best (London: Sold by J. Evans & J. Hatchard and S. Hazard, Bath, 1797?);

Strictures on the Modern System of Female Education. With a view of the principles and conduct prevalent among women of rank and fortune (2 volumes, London: Printed for T. Cadell, Jun. & W. Davies, 1799; facsimile, New York & London: Garland, 1974; Philadelphia: Printed by Budd & Bertram for Thomas Dobson, 1800; 1 volume, Charlestown:

Printed by Samuel Etheridge for E. Larkin, Boston, 1800);

The Works of Hannah More, including several pieces never before published (8 volumes, London: T. Cadell & W. Davies, 1801; enlarged, 19 volumes, 1818; enlarged, 11 volumes, London: T. Cadell, 1830); enlarged, with a memoir and notes, 6 volumes, London: H. Fisher, R. Fisher & P. Jackson, 1834; 2 volumes, New York: Harper & Brothers, 1837);

Hints Towards Forming the Character of a Young Princess, 2 volumes (London: Printed for T. Cadell & W. Davies, 1805);

Coelebs in Search of a Wife. Comprehending observations on domestic habits and manners, religion and morals (2 volumes, London: Printed for T. Cadell & W. Davies, 1808; 1 volume, New York: Published by David Carlisle, 1809; 2 volumes, New York: Published by T. & J. Swords, 1809);

Practical Piety; or, The Influence of the Religion of the Heart on the Conduct of the Life (London: Printed for T. Cadell, 1811; Boston: Munroe & Francis, 1811; Albany: Websters & Skinners, 1811; Burlington, N.J.: D. Allinson, 1811; Hartford, Conn.: Peter B. Gleason & Oliver D. Cooke, 1811);

Christian Morals (2 volumes, London: Printed for T. Cadell & W. Davies, 1813; New York: Eastburn, Kirk / Boston: Bradford & Read, 1813; New York: Published by D. Huntington, 1813);

An Essay on the Character and Practical Writings of St. Paul (2 volumes, London: T. Cadell & W. Davies, 1815; 1 volume, Boston: Wells, 1815; Philadelphia: Edward Earle / New York: Printed by T. & W. Mercein for Eastburn & Kirk, 1815);

Poems (London: Printed for T. Cadell & W. Davies, 1816; Boston: Wells & Lilly, 1817; enlarged edition, London: Cadell, 1829);

Moral Sketches of Prevailing Opinions and Manners, Foreign and Domestic; with Reflections on Prayer (London: Cadell & Davies, 1819; Boston: Wells & Lilly, 1819);

The Twelfth of August; or, the Feast of freedom (London: J. & T. Clarke, 1819; republished as *The Feast of Freedom; or, the abolition of domestic slavery in Ceylon; the vocal parts adapted to music by C. Wesley* (London: T. Cadell, 1827);

Bible Rhymes on the names of all the books of the Old and New Testament: with allusions to some of the principal incidents and characters (London: T. Cadell, 1821; Boston: Wells & Lilly, 1821);

The spirit of prayer. Selected and compiled by herself, from various portions exclusively on that subject, in her published volumes (London: T. Cadell, 1825; Boston: Cummings, Hilliard, 1826);

Miscellaneous Works, 2 volumes (London: Printed for T. Tegg, 1840).

Collections: *Cheap Repository*, 3 volumes (London: Sold by J. Marshall and S. Hazard, Bath, 1796-1797);

The Entertaining, Moral, and Religious Repository, 2 volumes (Elizabethtown, N.J.: Printed by Shepard Kollock for Cornelius Davis, New York, 1798-1799);

Cheap Repository, 3 volumes (Philadelphia: Printed by B. & J. Johnson, 1800).

PLAY PRODUCTIONS: *The Inflexible Captive: A Tragedy*, Bath, Theatre Royal, 18 April 1775;

Percy: A Tragedy, London, Theatre Royal, Covent Garden, 10 December 1777;

The Fatal Falsehood: A Tragedy, London, Theatre Royal, Covent Garden, 6 May 1779.

OTHER: Ann Yearsley, *Poems, on several occasions*, edited, with a preface, by More (London: Printed for T. Cadell, 1785).

Hannah More's claim to the title of novelist rests on a single work, *Coelebs in Search of a Wife* (1808). This book represented to many a remarkable divergence from More's literary practice and a potential contradiction of her frequently articulated objections to the reading and writing of novels. In *Strictures on the Modern System of Female Education* (1799), More had condemned contemporary novels derived from French models as a "pernicious source of moral corruption" and particularly regretted their growing popularity with young working-class women. But *Coelebs in Search of a Wife*, which depicted the courtship of a religiously principled young couple, was written to counter the questionable ethics of sentimental novels, and its didactic purport rescues More from any charge of inconsistency. From the beginning of her career she had aimed to improve literary culture and to raise moral standards through the medium of literature. A protégée of David Garrick and Samuel Johnson, who conceived of the stage as a vehicle for ethical instruction, she later collaborated with William Wilberforce, whose commitment to reforming the "manners and morals" of the English people became particularly urgent during the years of the French Revolution.

Though her works today hold only historical interest, Hannah More was one of the most widely read writers of her time. As a disciple of Evangelicalism, she contributed, moreover, to what would become a centrally defining strain of Victorian religious and cultural practice.

Hannah More was born at Stapleton, Gloucestershire, near Bristol, on 2 February 1745, fourth in a family of five sisters. Her father, Jacob More, a Tory and High Churchman, was master of a charity school at Stapleton under the patronage of Norborne Berkeley (later Baron Bottetourt). Hannah's mother, Mary Grace, was the daughter of a farmer. Jacob More educated his daughters—Mary, Elizabeth, Sarah, Hannah, and Martha—along with his schoolboys and prepared them sufficiently to open a school of their own. Established at Trinity Street, Bristol, in 1757 and moved to Park Street in 1767, the school profited from a growing interest in education for girls of the middle ranks, becoming one of the most reputable institutions of its kind in eighteenth-century England. The cooperation of the sisters in the superintendence of the school, which enabled them to retire from Park Street with a permanent income late in 1789, carried over into the philanthropic projects Hannah would initiate thereafter.

Of the five intelligent and resourceful young women, Hannah was clearly the most exceptional. At her request, Jacob More permitted Hannah to study Latin with James Newton at the Bristol Baptist Academy, but curtailed her lessons in mathematics when she began to surpass the achievements of her male classmates. She turned instead to the study of history and literature and, following instruction from the language masters at her sisters' school, read widely among English, French, Italian, and Spanish poets. From a very early age Hannah also wrote poetry and became known in Bristol for her *vers d'occasion*. One early effort, a "Morning Hymn," was forwarded by Dr. James Stonehouse, the sisters' Bristol mentor, to Samuel Johnson, who, on meeting Hannah in 1775, charmed her by reciting it. As an undergoverness at the Park Street school, More was also enabled to develop her talents as a dramatist. At age sixteen she wrote *The Search After Happiness: A Pastoral Drama* (1773), which she conceived as an alternative to the plays of questionable propriety that girls in boarding schools were permitted to perform. In *The Search After Happiness*, four young women seek the retreat of a wise widow to consult with her on their various moral failings. Envy, pedantry, novel reading, and laziness are each confessed in turn, and each is denounced as a violation of the true feminine character. The play was warmly received among educators—if not their students—and helped make the reputation of the Park Street establishment. By 1787, when it went into its ninth edition, *The Search After Happiness* had sold more than ten thousand copies. More's first effort was distinguished, as were all those that would follow, by its high morality and remarkable popularity.

More's early success as a playwright coincided with a failed romance, and the two circumstances combined to set the course of the first stage of her adult career. At age twenty-two she became engaged to William Turner, a wealthy middle-aged squire with a considerable estate at Wraxall. At first their courtship was decorously sentimental: Hannah wrote poetic inscriptions in praise of the estate, which Turner had painted on boards and mounted on trees "exactly," observed Charlotte Yonge in her biography of More, "like notices to trespassers." But a subsequently published poem dating from this period, "The Bleeding Rock," an imitation of Ovid which records the desertion of a nymph by her lover and her metamorphosis into a stone, resonates with the complications of the affair. Over a period of six years, Turner postponed the wedding date twice and failed to appear on the third. When More refused to set a fourth date, Turner, still insisting on his devotion, offered an annuity of two hundred pounds, which More at first declined. Through the intercession of Dr. Stonehouse, she eventually reconciled herself to Turner's endowment, which enabled her to make annual trips to London, where her talents enjoyed greater scope and encouragement.

Following her engagement to Turner, More began to pursue in earnest her interest in the drama. She frequented the recently founded Theatre Royal in Bristol, learning much about play production and making new friends among the actors and actresses she met there. During this period, she made use of a translation she had done of Pietro Metastasio's *Attilio Regolo* (1732) to write *The Inflexible Captive* (1774). More took her play to David Garrick, who in her view realized the moral potential of the stage to an unprecedented degree; Garrick, in some measure, returned her admiration. He personally arranged to produce More's *Inflexible Captive* at the Bath Theatre Royal, the most prestigious of the provincial the-

Barley Wood, near Bristol, the house the More sisters built in 1801 (watercolor by Capt. John Johnson, 1822; British Museum). Hannah More, who outlived the last of her sisters by two decades, left this home in 1828 to be near friends who could care for her.

aters. Garrick's involvement, which included the contribution of an epilogue, roused considerable interest among the fashionable world at Bath. Presented on 18 April 1775, the play was so well received that Garrick considered taking it to Drury Lane. More herself discouraged this plan, judging that *The Inflexible Captive*, which consists largely of declamations on honor by the elderly hero, Marcus Attilius Regulus, was not "sufficiently bustling for dramatic representation."

Garrick patronized More's next play, *Percy* (1778), from its inception: he criticized drafts that More sent to him from Bristol, wrote the prologue and epilogue, and orchestrated publicity and production at Covent Garden. A Border drama involving the houses of Douglas and Northumberland, *Percy* is based loosely on the twelfth-century romance of the Châtelain de Coucy and the Dame de Faiel. Percy's return from the crusades initiates a chain of events that results in the suicides of his former lover, Elwina, and her husband. Despite its static characters and lack of dramatic tension, contemporary theatergoers found the play a revelation. Opening on 10 December 1777 with Ann Barry as Elwina, *Percy* ran for a remarkable twenty-one nights. Four thousand copies of the play were sold by March 1778. It was revived several times during the eighteenth century, in 1787 with Sarah Siddons as Elwina. By then More was no longer attending the theater. Translated into French, *Percy* earned More admittance to the Rouen Academy of Arts, Sciences and Letters. More's third play, *The Fatal Falsehood* (1779), another tragedy of jealousy and betrayal, was not yet complete when Garrick died suddenly in January 1779. Though the reception for *Percy* secured its production at Covent Garden, *The Fatal Falsehood* suffered from the loss of Garrick's patronage and from a charge of plagiarism leveled by Hannah Cowley, another aspiring playwright who had submitted work to Garrick. The vituperative paper war which followed the opening of the play on 6 May 1779 contributed to More's determination to give up the theater, a decision which was perhaps inevitable after Garrick's death. More's Christian piety also played its part, as is indicated by the preface to the tragedies included in her collected *Works* (1801). There More maintained that the code of honor which tragedy exalts is not consistent with the Christian values of humility and resignation to the divine will.

During the years of her apprenticeship with Garrick, More was also welcomed to the assemblies of prominent bluestockings. Her social popularity grew with her literary reputation, which in turn came to rest on works that generously acknowledged her appreciation for the circles in which she was traveling. "Sensibility: An Epistle to the Hon. Mrs. Boscawen" (1782) was written to console More's friend Elizabeth Boscawen, widow of Adm. Edward Boscawen and a leading London hostess who was preoccupied with the welfare of her son, then serving as a soldier in America. More reminds Boscawen that great hearts are destined to suffer, but that it is to her fine sensibility that she owes the blessings of her life, not least of which is the host of illustrious friends to whom More alludes at the beginning of the poem. "Bas Bleu," which circulated for some time in manuscript before being published in 1786, celebrates the achievements of Mrs. Agmondesham Vesey in promoting the civilized art of conversation. Her Tuesday night assemblies were regularly attended by the Literary Club of Samuel Johnson, who in "Bas Bleu" is reverently called "the rigid Cato."

The quality of More's relationship with Johnson has been a matter of some debate. Much has been made of an incident cited in Hester [Thrale] Piozzi's *Anecdotes of the Late Samuel Johnson* (1786), in which Johnson responded to the adulation that More was always eager to bestow with the churlish recommendation "to consider what her flattery was worth before she choaked *him* with it." All other evidence indicates that Johnson appreciated More and promoted her work. Prior to the publication of More's ballads "The Bleeding Rock" and "Sir Eldred of the Bower" in 1776, Johnson arranged to read them with her. He approved the former and honored More by contributing one stanza to "Sir Eldred of the Bower," which tells the tale of a knight moved to murderous jealousy on discovering his beloved in the arms of her brother, whom he mistakes for a former lover. Johnson had dealt far less graciously with the poetry of Thomas Percy, whose edition of the *Reliques of Ancient English Poetry* (1765) inspired More's interest in the ballad form, and whose *Hermit of Warkworth* (1771) elicited from Johnson a celebrated parody. Johnson also praised "Bas Bleu" extravagantly, as More jubilantly confessed in an April 1784 letter to her sisters: "He said that there was no name in poetry that might not be glad to own it." In a 31 July 1784 letter to Sir William Forbes, James Beattie reported that "Johnson told [him], with great solemnity, that [Hannah More] was the most powerful versificatrix in the English language." The feminine form here is telling: Johnson does not praise More as a poet, but as a woman who wrote verses and who should be commended for doing so at all. But that Johnson valued More's companionship cannot be doubted, as is clear from their visit to Oxford in June of 1782, when Johnson solemnly escorted More through his university and his college, Pembroke. Johnson's association with More was commemorated on this occasion by what More recognized as "a very pretty piece of gallantry": as she reported to her sisters on 13 June, the master of Pembroke had hung a print of Johnson over the motto "And is not Johnson ours, himself an host?," a line from More's "Sensibility."

More's friendship with the Great Moralist is perhaps more easily explained than her relationship with the aristocratic skeptic Horace Walpole. Yet More and Walpole had friends in common and shared an intensely conservative political orientation: their letters written between 1784 and 1796 (a small but significant portion of Walpole's vast correspondence) testify to their mutual displeasure with events in France and with the activities of Republican sympathizers in England. They equally lamented contemporary feminist initiatives: it was in a 24 January 1795 letter to the receptive More that Walpole referred to Mary Wollstonecraft as "that hyena in petticoats." Walpole, moreover, who had a taste for light verse, appreciated More's poetry. He thought *Florio* (1786), which More dedicated to him, a "charming" poem and invited her to have her *Bishop Bonner's Ghost* (1789) printed on his press at Strawberry Hill. *Florio*, which tells the tale of a goodhearted young man of fashion drawn away from the dissipation of town life by the daughter of a country squire, anticipates the plot of *Coelebs in Search of a Wife* and hints at More's growing taste for contemplative retirement. *Bishop Bonner's Ghost*, a conceit celebrating the ecclesiastical character of More's friend and adviser Beilby Porteus, Bishop of London, dates from the early years of her affiliation with Evangelicalism.

A late project in More's career as bluestocking helps to account for her defection from the literary world. In the autumn of 1784, More was introduced to Ann Yearsley, a poor Bristol milk woman who had written poetry that had impressed More's Bristol connection. More adopted Yearsley as an object of patronage: she gave her lessons in composition, corrected her manuscripts, and raised a subscription among her

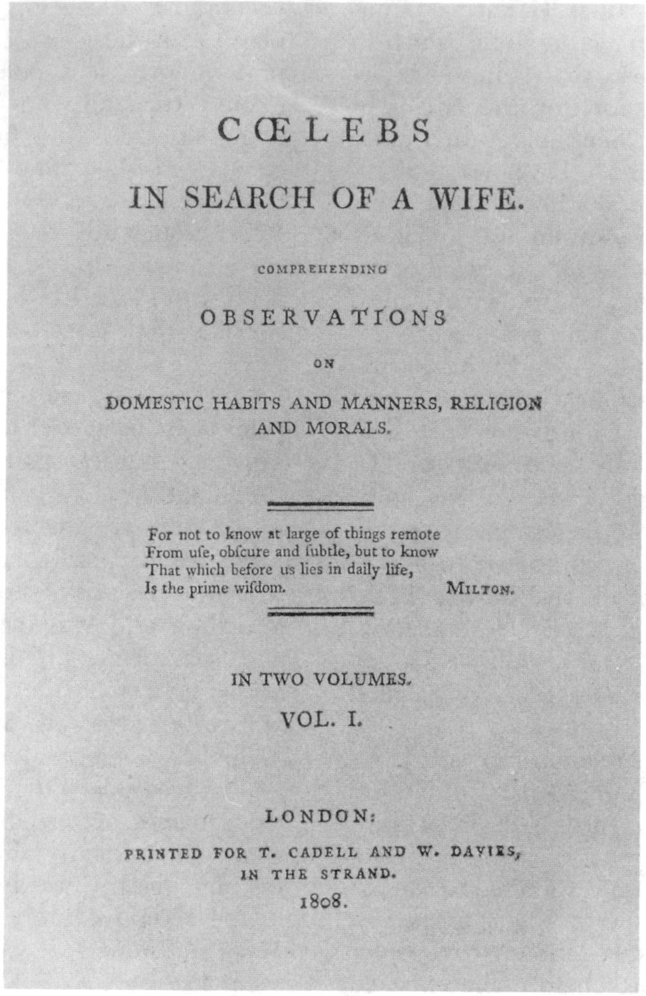

CŒLEBS

IN SEARCH OF A WIFE.

COMPREHENDING

OBSERVATIONS

ON

DOMESTIC HABITS AND MANNERS, RELIGION AND MORALS.

For not to know at large of things remote
From ufe, obfcure and fubtle, but to know
That which before us lies in daily life,
Is the prime wifdom. MILTON.

IN TWO VOLUMES.

VOL. I.

LONDON:

PRINTED FOR T. CADELL AND W. DAVIES, IN THE STRAND.

1808.

Title page for More's only novel (Special Collections, Thomas Cooper Library, University of South Carolina). Enormously popular with middle-class readers, the book was ridiculed by critics, including Sydney Smith, who interpreted its message as: "No Christian is safe who is not dull."

fashionable friends toward the publication of Yearsley's poems. The proceeds from the moderately successful first edition became a point of bitter controversy: Yearsley believed that she should receive royalties directly, while More insisted that they should be controlled by the subscribers. With the help of Yearsley, the press made much of the dispute. Though More demonstrated restraint in public, privately she expressed bitter resentment toward what she took to be Yearsley's ingratitude. Thereafter, More's philanthropy was guided by a conservative orientation that insisted on the submission of the lower orders and in no way encouraged the independence of an Ann Yearsley.

The shift in More's interests from literature and the stage to philanthropy and religion was secured by her affiliation in the late 1780s with Anglican Evangelicalism. When she was introduced to John Newton's *Cardiphonia* (1781) More embarked on an extensive reexamination of her own religious practice, affirming a commitment to a form of Christianity that stressed personal piety and charitable action in the world. At about the same time she became acquainted with the Charles Middletons, who won her sympathy for their great cause, the abolition of the slave trade. More's involvement with the abolitionist movement, recorded in her poem *Slavery* (1788), brought her into contact with prominent Evangelicals, most notably William Wilberforce, with whom she entered into lasting collaboration.

More and Wilberforce shared a passion for moral reform, which took as its first target the manners of the upper classes. The "great and the gay," of whose character and behavior More and Wilberforce both had firsthand knowledge, needed to be brought to a sense of their responsibilities as the leaders of society. In 1788 More published *Thoughts on the Importance of the Manners of the Great to General Society*, a "collection of loose and immethodical hints" directed against certain lapses peculiar to the upper classes, particularly sabbath-day entertainments and careless conversation in the presence of young people. The volume was an immediate best-seller, going through seven editions in several months. More's second essay, *An Estimate of the Religion of the Fashionable World* (1791), was considerably more trenchant than her first. Reflecting her strengthening identification with the Evangelical position, More's *Estimate of the Religion of the Fashionable World* is a frontal attack on the "practical irreligion" of the upper classes. She asserted that sin, hell, and the devil had become abstractions to these classes, who—regarding Christianity as a system of ethics alone—were unmindful of the need for personal salvation. The general neglect of religious instruction in the home and at school was for More both a cause and an effect of upper-class impiety. She censured the education in worldliness that boys received at public schools and deplored the display of nearly infant girls at "Baby Balls." Though *An Estimate of the Religion of the Fashionable World* did go into multiple editions, it did not meet with the uniformly warm reception generally reserved for her works: she was burned in effigy at the Westminster School, and a spirited doggerel encouraged children to "Foot it lively on the floor / Nor heed the carping Hannah More." But *Strictures on the Modern System of Female Education* (1799) was the most controversial—and influential—of More's essays for the great. Its thesis was that the reformation of society on a Christian foundation depended on the influence of pious and well-instructed women. The contemporary system of education for women of the upper ranks was designed to cultivate polite accomplishments alone and did not adequately prepare them for their duties as wives and mothers, which included the crucial task of indoctrinating their children in the Christian faith. A form of instruction that would render women more sober and dutiful was required. With this essay More defined the pattern gentlewoman of the Victorian period: charitable, unassuming, and obedient to strict standards of propriety. Her contemporaries, however, were offended by the antifeminism of *Strictures on the Modern System of Female Education* and by the insistence on human corruption that underlay More's argument for greater educational rigor. They detected in her parade of that "gloomy" doctrine a trace of Calvinism, which More as a good Anglican would have been horrified to avow. With *Strictures on the Modern System of Female Education* More truly began to suffer the consequences of her identification with Evangelicalism.

Meanwhile she was steadily demonstrating her commitment to its principles in her work among the lower orders. Collaborating with Wilberforce in the summer of 1789, More and her sisters laid out a plan to reform the countryside around Cheddar by establishing a series of charitable schools for the working classes. Grounded in her Tory politics and Evangelical religious beliefs, More's plan of instruction was "very simple and limited" and provided the poor no opportunity to raise themselves out of their prescribed social position: As More explained in a letter to Dr. Richard Beadon, named bishop of Bath and Wells in 1802, "They learn, on week days, such coarse works as may fit them for servants. I allow of no writing for the poor. My object is not to make fanatics, but to train up the lower classes in habits of industry and piety." This pedagogical program made More an obvious choice, when, in 1792, following the publication of Thomas Paine's *Rights of Man* (1791, 1792), people in high places looked for a popular writer to supply its antidote. Rumor had it that the prime minister, William Pitt the Younger, appealed to More to dispel the seditious doctrines circulating among the working classes; More herself claimed that Bishop Porteus persuaded her. The result was *Village Politics* (1792), a dialogue in a lively vernacular English between Jack Anvil, a village blacksmith who supports established order, and Thomas Hod, the village mason, who, having read *Rights of Man*, noisily demands a new constitution that will secure liberty and equality. In the course of the dialogue Anvil exposes the deception of revolutionary rhetoric and maintains that the English already enjoyed the rights for which the French were striving. Hod eventually abandons his imperfectly understood philosophy and swears his fidelity to "old England."

When part one of Paine's *Age of Reason* appeared in 1794, Porteus again turned to More, asking her to produce a tract that would counter Paine's indictment of the Church with a plain exposition of the evidence for Christianity. More regretfully refused since she was already deeply involved in a related project, the production and distribution of the Cheap Repository Tracts. Having contributed to the spread of literacy, she

More in November 1813 (drawing by Slater; from M. J. Jones, Hannah More, *1952)*

shared a growing concern that the lower orders be provided with safe reading materials. Working in collaboration with her sisters and receiving aid from members of the Clapham sect, More decided to bring out three tracts monthly—in the form of stories, ballads, and Sunday reading—which would stress the themes of morality, loyalty, and religion. To compete with the radical literature being circulated inexpensively among the poor, the tracts were initially produced in chapbook and broadsheet formats and sold at around a penny a copy, though bound editions eventually became available. By 1796 more than two million tracts had been sold, though how many of these had actually been paid for by working-class readers is unknown. From 1795 to 1798, 114 tracts were published, about 50 of which were written by More. Perhaps the most lastingly popular of these was *The Shepherd of Salisbury Plain* (1795). In this tract a West Country shepherd recounts his history to a passing gentleman, who—impressed with the poor man's piety and good management—arranges modest relief for him and his large family. This tale of quiet virtue rewarded is typical of the tracts, though readers are also reminded, as in the ballad *Turn the Carpet* (1796) and the story *'Tis All for the Best,* that Providence often works in less obvious ways. But while More labored tirelessly to produce good Christians and good citizens, there were those who perceived in her activities a latent threat to the establishment in Church and State. From 1800 to 1803, More was embroiled in a bitter controversy regarding the administration of her schools. The immediate pretext was her employment at Blagdon of a teacher accused of Methodism, but the dispute was fueled by a more general antipathy to Evangelicalism and to the principle of working-class education. During the Blagdon Controversy More was accused of usurping the prerogatives of the Anglican clergy and of spreading heterodox political and religious views—dangerous charges in that age of repression. Though she eventually cleared herself of these charges with Dr. Richard Beadon, Bishop of Bath and Wells, More's self-assurance was badly shaken by vicious attacks from the press.

More was roused from her self-doubt in 1805 by an appeal from Dr. Robert Gray, Prebendary of Durham, who persuaded her that her special talents were needed to write a guide for the education of Princess Charlotte Augusta, the heir presumptive to the throne. The year before, Dr. John Fisher, Bishop of Exeter, had assumed responsibility for the child's education, which, in the view of many, had formerly been sadly neglected by her dissolute parents, George, Prince of Wales, and Caroline of Brunswick. It was to Fisher that More dedicated her *Hints Towards Forming the Character of a Young Princess* (1805), rapidly produced to respond to a "national emergency." More's book proposed a curriculum suitable to form the moral character of the future sovereign. Natural science and the fine arts are rejected in favor of languages, literature, and history, the peculiar importance of which is elaborated throughout the greater part of the work. Sketchily documented and hastily written as it was, More's book pleased the court: the princess's grandmother Queen Charlotte invited More to Weymouth to consult with her and Martha, Lady Elgin, the princess's governess, about the child's education. What is more, the guide, which passed rapidly through six editions, seems to have rehabilitated More's public reputation, which had suffered somewhat during the Blagdon Controversy.

In 1808 More conceived the rather scandalous notion of writing a novel. Published anonymously in the same year, *Coelebs in Search of a Wife* was an enormous popular success. The first edition sold out in three days, and ten more editions appeared in the next nine months. The novel's popularity was not limited to England: before More's death in 1833, thirty thousand copies had been sold in America. The warm reception for *Coelebs in Search of a Wife,* which according to the critical standards of its time was a stilted and lifeless performance, can perhaps best be attributed to two sociological factors: the rise in popularity of Evangelicalism and the greater self-consciousness of a middle class eager for models of social comportment. Coelebs, the protagonist and narrator of the novel, is a serious young man of the upper middle class in search of his perfect bride. Passing first through fashionable London circles, where he finds no one to his taste, he arrives at the home of Mr. Stanley, the lifelong friend of his recently deceased father. Coelebs discovers in Stanley's daughter, Lucilla, all the qualities he had been looking for in a woman: without being "a Helen, a Saint Cecilia, or a Madame Dacier," she is elegant, sensible, and well bred. Above all, Coelebs deeply respects the Evangelical milieu in which she has been raised—a country estate where family and friends spend a large part of every day in rational conversation on religious topics. It was this feature of Evangelical life that Sydney Smith ridiculed in his strongly negative review of the novel for the *Edinburgh Review* (April 1809): "All the disciples of this school fall uniformly into the same mistake. They are perpetually calling upon their votaries for religious thoughts and religious conversation in everything, inviting them to ride, row, wrestle and dine out religiously. . . . No Christian is safe who is not dull." Remarkably, negative critical appraisals for *Coelebs in Search of a Wife* were not limited to secular journals. While some Evangelicals, including John Venn, saw in More's appropriation of the novel great potential for correcting the immoral and irreligious tendencies of the period, the reviewer for the *Christian Observer* (February 1809) discovered "some want of taste and strict delicacy" in the book. This review confused and angered More, who wrote no more novels.

In the 1810s More turned again to her preferred genre, the essay, producing four major didactic works that reiterated her themes of the war years, though in tones that reflected what she had suffered from criticism. In the prefaces to these volumes More acknowledged that she was in a sense "reproducing" herself and thanked her readers for their forbearance in accepting the repeated admonitions of a sincere woman who was conscious of her own shortcomings but wished nevertheless to be useful. Recognizing with a nostalgic reference to Johnson that the world into which she had been born had already passed away, she welcomed a new and increasingly middle-class audience, including "a great number of amiable young persons." *Practical Piety; or, The Influence of the Religion of the Heart on the Conduct of the Life* (1811) offered mild persuasion to accept the Christian way of life as the true path to happiness. It sold more copies than any of More's previous works, including *Coelebs in Search of a Wife. Christian Morals* (1813) provided direct instruction in Christian conduct to young people of social standing. More than ten

More at Barley Wood, 1820s (watercolor by an unknown artist; from M. G. Jones, Hannah More, *1952)*

thousand copies of this companion volume to *Practical Piety* were sold. Next came More's experiment in Christian biography, *An Essay on the Character and Practical Writings of St. Paul* (1815). More was no scholar and insisted that she intended only to represent Paul as a model of Christian conduct. Perhaps the most ambitious—and least successful—of More's efforts, the biography nevertheless sold seven thousand copies. *Moral Sketches*, a critique of postwar social customs and the difficulties they posed for Christian practice, followed in 1819. In it, More deplored the rapidity with which the English had forgotten their differences with France and made a case for religious instruction at home in lieu of the Grand Tour abroad. The first edition of *Moral Sketches* sold out on the day it appeared. These rather commonplace essays, with their emphasis on Christian morality rather than doctrine, helped to popularize Evangelicalism, which had been—and would continue to be—a stigmatized religious orientation.

In 1817 More's quiet years of essay writing were interrupted when, remembered for her *Village Politics* and her contributions to the Cheap Repository, she was asked to write tracts for the anti-Cobbett drive. Like many of More's later efforts, these texts simply restated, in less vital style, the views she had articulated during the 1790s. Indeed, some characters from that period, such as Mr. Fantom, were revived. In the face of working-class militancy and agitation for parliamentary reform, More insisted that the reasons for current distress could not be traced to any secular government but to the divine will. She continued to maintain that submission was the duty of the poor just as benevolence was the duty of the upper orders—a social program woefully inadequate to the needs of an increasingly urban and industrial England.

Hannah More died at Clifton Woods on 7 September 1833. Her works had already been collected three times: in 1801, 1818, and 1830. Other editions followed until 1853, after which demand for her writings dwindled away. Submitted to the rigorous standards of Victorian criticism, More's works did not stand up well: their original popularity had relied too heavily on her personality and connections, and on her capacity to respond with confidence to matters of contemporary concern. Historical interest now focuses on her *Cheap Repository Tracts* as a feature of counterrevolutionary activity in England and as precursors of the social fiction of the 1830s and 1840s. Feminist scholars find intriguing More's contradictory status as an advocate of feminine domesticity who nevertheless enjoyed great freedom and influence in the public sphere.

Bibliographies:

G. H. Spinney, "Cheap Repository Tracts: Hazard and Marshall Edition," *Library*, series 4, 20 (December 1939): 295-340;

Harry B. Weiss, "Hannah More's Cheap Repository Tracts in America," *Bulletin of the New York Public Library*, 50 (July 1946): 539-549; 50 (August 1946): 634-641.

Biographies:

William Roberts, *Memoirs of the Life and Correspondence of Hannah More* (4 volumes, London: R. B. Seeley & W. Burnside, 1834);

Charlotte Yonge, *Hannah More* (London: W. H. Allen, 1888; Boston: Roberts, 1888);

M. G. Jones, *Hannah More* (Cambridge: Cambridge University Press, 1952);

Jeremy Collingwood and Margaret Collingwood, *Hannah More* (Oxford & Batavia, Ill.: Lion, 1990).

References:

Catherine Gallagher, *The Industrial Reformation of British Fiction* (Chicago: University of Chicago Press, 1985);

Catherine Hall, "The Early Formation of Victorian Domestic Ideology," in *Fit Work for Women*, edited by Sandra Burman (New York: St. Martin's Press, 1979), pp. 15-32;

Elisabeth Jay, *The Religion of the Heart: Anglican Evangelicalism and the Nineteenth-Century Novel* (Oxford: Clarendon Press, 1979);

Elizabeth Kowaleski-Wallace, *Their Fathers' Daughters: Hannah More, Maria Edgeworth, and Patriarchal Complicity* (New York: Oxford University Press, 1991);

Mitzi Myers, "Hannah More's Tracts for the Times: Social Fiction and Female Ideology," in *Fetter'd or Free? British Women Novelists, 1630-1815*, edited by Mary Anne Schofield and Cecelia Macheski (Athens: Ohio University Press, 1986), pp. 264-284;

Susan Pedersen, "Hannah More Meets Simple Simon: Tracts, Chapbooks and Popular Culture in Late Eighteenth-Century England," *Journal of British Studies*, 25 (January 1986): 84-113;

Mary Poovey, *The Proper Lady and the Woman Writer* (Chicago: University of Chicago Press, 1984);

Harold V. Routh, "The Georgian Drama," in *The Cambridge History of English Literature*, 15 volumes, edited by A. W. Ward and A. R. Waller (New York: Macmillan / Cambridge: Cambridge University Press, 1933), XI: 284-314.

Papers:

A significant body of More's papers and letters was destroyed at the end of the nineteenth century by a descendant of William Roberts, More's first biographer. Part of her correspondence with the Garricks is at the Folger Shakespeare Library. Some of her correspondence with Wilberforce can be found at the Duke University Library, while correspondence with Wilberforce and other More materials are at the Huntington Library. Other documents, mostly letters, are located at the British Library; the Bodleian Library, Oxford; the John Rylands Library, Manchester; the Rush Rhees Library, University of Rochester; the Knox College Archives; the Historical Society of Pennsylvania; the New York Public Library; and the Pierpont Morgan Library.

Sydney Owenson, Lady Morgan

(25 December 1776? - 16 April 1859)

Kathleen Reuter Chamberlain
Emory and Henry College

BOOKS: *Poems, Dedicated by Permission to the Countess of Moira* (Dublin: Printed by Alex. Stewart and Phillips, London, 1801);

St. Clair, or, the Heiress of Desmond (Dublin: Printed by Brett Smith for Wogan, Brown, Halpin, Colbert, Jon Dornin, Jackson, and Metcalf, 1803; London: Harding & Highley / Dublin: Archer, 1803; Philadelphia: S. F. Bradford, 1807);

A Few Reflections, Occasioned by the Perusal of a Work entitled "Familiar Epistles," often attributed to Lady Morgan (Dublin: Printed by J. Parry, 1804);

The Novice of Saint Dominick (4 volumes, London: Printed for Richard Phillips, 1806; 2 volumes, Philadelphia: Printed for & published by T. S. Manning, 1807);

The Wild Irish Girl, 3 volumes (London: Printed for Richard Phillips, 1806; New York: Published by Alsop, Brannan & Alsop and twelve others, printed by D. & G. Bruce, 1807);

The Lay of an Irish Harp, or, Metrical Fragments (London: R. Phillips, 1807; Philadelphia: T. S. Manning, 1807);

Patriotic Sketches of Ireland, 2 volumes (London: Printed for R. Phillips by T. Gillet, 1807; Baltimore: Printed for G. Dobbin & Murphy, 1809);

Woman; or Ida of Athens (4 volumes, London: Longman, Hurst, Rees & Orme, 1809; 2 volumes, Philadelphia: Published by Bradford & Inskeep; Inskeep & Bradford, New York; Coale & Thomas, Baltimore, 1809);

The Missionary—An Indian Tale (3 volumes, London: Printed for J. J. Stockdale, 1811; 1 volume, New York: Published by Franklin and Butler & White, 1811); revised as *Luxima—A Tale of India* (London: C. Westerton, 1859);

O'Donnel—A National Tale (3 volumes, London: H. Colburn, 1814; 2 volumes, New York: Published by Van Winkle & Wiley, 1814);

France (2 volumes, London: Printed for H. Colburn, 1817; New York: Published by James Eastburn, printed by E. & E. Hosford, Albany, 1817; 1 volume, Philadelphia: Published by M. Thomas, James Maxwell, Printer, 1817);

Florence Macarthy, an Irish Tale (4 volumes, London: Printed for Henry Colburn, 1818; 2 volumes, Baltimore: N. G. Maxwell, 1819; New York: W. B. Gilley, 1819, Philadelphia: M. Carey & Sons, 1819);

Italy, 2 volumes (London: H. Colburn, 1821; New York: Printed by C. S. Van Winkle / Philadelphia: M. Carey & Sons, 1821);

Letter to the Reviewers of "Italy" (Paris, 1821);

The Life and Times of Salvator Rosa, 2 volumes (London: H. Colburn, 1824);

Absenteeism (London: H. Colburn, 1825);

The O'Briens and the O'Flahertys, a National Tale (4 volumes, London: H. Colburn, 1827; 2 volumes, Philadelphia: Carey, Lea & Carey, 1828);

The Book of the Boudoir, 2 volumes (London: Henry Colburn, 1829; New York: Printed by J. & J. Harper, sold by Collins & Hannay, 1829);

France in 1829-30 (2 volumes, London: Saunders & Otley, 1830; New York: J. & J. Harper, 1830);

Dramatic Scenes from Real Life (2 volumes, London: Saunders & Otley, 1833; 1 volume, New York: J. & J. Harper, 1833);

The Princess, or the Beguine (3 volumes, London: Bentley, 1835; 2 volumes, Philadelphia: Carey, Lea & Blanchard, 1835);

Woman and Her Master, 2 volumes (London: H. Colburn, 1840; Philadelphia: Carey & Hart, 1840);

The Book Without a Name, 2 volumes, by Lady Morgan and Sir T. Charles Morgan (London: Henry Colburn, 1841; New York: Wiley & Putnam, 1841);

Letter to Cardinal Wiseman (London: C. Westerton, 1851);

Sydney Owenson, Lady Morgan (engraving by William Holl after a drawing by Sir Thomas Lawrence)

Passages from My Autobiography (London: R. Bentley, 1859; New York: D. Appleton, 1859);

Lady Morgan's Memoirs: Autobiography, Diaries, Correspondence, 2 volumes, edited by W. Hepworth Dixon and Geraldine Jewsbury (London: W. H. Allen, 1862; revised, 1863).

PLAY PRODUCTION: *The First Attempt, or Whim of a Moment*, Dublin, Theatre Royal, 1807.

OTHER: *Twelve Original Hibernian Melodies, from the Works of the Ancient Irish Bards*, edited by Lady Morgan (London: Preston, 1805).

With her typical mixture of self-deprecation and self-dramatization, Sydney Owenson, Lady Morgan, referred to her most influential novel, *The Wild Irish Girl*, as a "little work" that had as its theme "circumstances of national import and national interest." In this case, the dramatization was justified. Published in 1806, *The Wild Irish Girl* brought both the wrongs and the glories of Ireland before the ordinary English reader in accessible form. Despite some literary deficiencies, the novel catapulted Owenson to a celebrity that lasted three decades, making her one of the major early spokespeople for the Irish cause. That she is so little known in the twentieth century is paradoxically a tribute to her success in her own time. Lady Morgan's combination of politics and literary popularity made her so potentially dangerous a figure that she was vilified in the establishment press, a medium whose verdicts usually dictate lasting reputations. These verdicts, coupled with Lady Morgan's no-longer-fashionable sentimental style, have relegated her to that most marginal of literary categories, "Lesser Writers." But her fiction, essays, and travel writings, which combine conventional literary trappings with shrewd political and social insights, show Lady Morgan to have had more ability and intelligence than history has accorded her.

The woman who would come to typify all that was picturesque and noble about Ireland in her persona of "the wild Irish girl' was probably born on Christmas Day 1776, though she so obscured her birth date that the precise year is unknown. Family legend held that she had been born at sea en route from England to Ireland, a story that, if true, would be symbolically appropriate given her lifelong desire to reconcile the English and the Irish. Her father, Robert Owenson (originally MacOwen), was an actor who specialized in that type later deplored as the "stage Irishman," but which in Robert Owenson's time helped build Irish pride though Gaelic songs and lore. From her father, Sydney learned the Irish history that formed the basis of her nationalistic views. Her connection with the theater may also have helped develop the talent for role-playing and self-marketing that stood her in good stead both before and during her years of celebrity.

After the death of her mother, Jane Hill Owenson, in 1789, Sydney and her sister, Olivia, attended boarding schools until their father's financial reversals forced them to accompany him on tour. These years of dreary poverty inspired Sydney to take over the family finances, first as a governess and then as a writer. As she told the story later, she decided upon writing after learning that Fanny Burney supported herself through literature.

Sydney Owenson did not approach her writing career with delusions of ease and glamour. Despite her lifelong penchant for casting herself as a "little Irish miss" who simply wrote from the heart, she clearly understood her market, combining political and romantic themes into popular entertainment that gained her fame and security. The title of her first work, *Poems, Dedicated by Permission to the Countess of Moira* (1801), suggests her willingness to combine art with patronage, though she always retained autonomy of content.

She followed the poems with her first novel, *St. Clair, or, the Heiress of Desmond* (1803). This epistolary work includes elements that became characteristic of her fiction: a compelling heroine and a liberal concern for the oppressed. The heroine of *St. Clair,* Olivia, is an idealized version of Owenson herself, as are most of her female protagonists. For this novel as well as all her writing, Owenson did copious research, as the many details of Irish history and customs attest. She usually underscored the accuracy of such material with footnotes, a device that often becomes intrusive. But Owenson's insistence on the literal truth of her picture of Ireland emphasizes the significance and innovation of her Irish themes. For many readers, Owenson's works provided the first serious corrective to English views of Irish "savagery" and "superstition."

After *St. Clair* came another novel, *The Novice of Saint Dominick* (1806), set in sixteenth-century France. Again, Owenson thoroughly researched the period. According to her biographer Lionel Stevenson, *The Novice of Saint Dominick* "anticipated the new type of historical fiction perfected a decade later by Scott." The heroine, Imogen, is another idealized Sydney, a character who demonstrates Owenson's interest in showing women as thinking and dynamic. Imogen travels freely while disguised as a troubadour and finally inherits enough money to educate herself and establish a successful salon. Though the novel is set in France, Owenson furthers her national interests by drawing parallels between the French suppression of Provençal language and culture and the English oppression of the Irish. Her next work, a collection of Irish songs translated from Gaelic, shows the scope of her efforts to rescue and popularize Irish culture. But it was her third novel, *The Wild Irish Girl,* that was to prove her greatest personal triumph.

From a twentieth-century point of view, *The Wild Irish Girl* is flawed. The pedantic footnotes, the romanticized characters, the self-consciously picturesque scenery, and the multisyllabic diction seem to offer little to modern taste. Nevertheless, a reader can still be caught up in the epistolary story of the Honorable Horatio M---, a young English ne'er-do-well whose father sends him to rural Ireland to mend his ways. M---'s letters initially show the usual English prejudices. Having been taught that the Irish are "turbulent, faithless, intemperate, and cruel," he protests that he would prefer exile to Siberia. But, as he travels under the name Henry Mortimer to obscure his English background, his contacts with noble natives and the beneficent Irish landscape lead him to support the Irish cause.

No small contributor to his conversion is "the wild Irish girl" herself, Glorvina, daughter of a destitute but proud descendant of early Irish royalty. Glorvina—elfin, intellectual, accomplished, and earnestly Irish—is not only a love interest, but also a touchstone for long discussions of Ireland's rich past and present woes. As Stevenson writes, "Mortimer's falling in love with Glorvina is taken as a matter of course, and his falling in love with Ireland is the real theme."

Portrait by Daniel Maclise from the Fraser's Magazine *"Gallery of Illustrious Literary Characters" (1830-1838)*

Both the book and the character of Glorvina captured the imaginations of Irish and English readers alike, so much so that Glorvina's red Celtic cloak and gold bodkin hair ornament became the rage in fashion. A character who was "wild" in the same way as Ireland—that is, artless, natural, and powerful—Glorvina was yet another version of Sydney Owenson. "The wild Irish girl" was a role that the author would play with great success in the drawing rooms of the English aristocracy and later in her own fashionable Dublin salon. Though she was often accused of exploiting Irish stereotypes to further her own social ambitions, one can also view Owenson's adoption of the "Glorvina" persona as an attempt to keep an appealing form of "Irishness" always in the minds of those with influence.

The Wild Irish Girl helped to create and to popularize a myth of Ireland that raised the consciousness of liberal English readers while educating Irish readers about their own heritage. Owenson's use of such ideas as Edmund Burke's belief in the power of the sublime and the Romantic concept of naturally benevolent rustics added an effective contemporary dimension to the otherwise hackneyed plot. This framework, well-adapted to the demands of popular fiction, allowed her to incorporate important elements of the "Irish problem" without overt political offense. Thomas Flanagan has called this combination of the popular and the nationalistic "sentimental patriotism," a term that need not be condescending.

In 1807 Sydney Owenson consolidated and extended her triumphs with a successful comic opera, another volume of poetry, and a collection of essays. By 1809 she had published her fourth novel, *Woman; or Ida of Athens*. Another professionally researched, market-oriented work, *Ida of Athens* is marred by hasty, careless composition. It tells the story of an intelligent Greek woman whose ideas about education and ethics are more important than the implausible plot. Combining her favorite topics—women and civil oppression—*Ida of Athens* also shows Owenson's political shrewdness. As the death of George Gordon, Lord Byron, would later poignantly demonstrate, the English were moved by the Greeks' struggle for freedom from the Turks. By capitalizing on this interest, Owenson scored another success while drawing pointed connections between the Greek plight and the Irish one.

Critical response to *Ida of Athens* and earlier works ranged from high praise to invective, a pattern that would continue throughout Owenson's career. Although her politics seem moderate to modern readers, many conservatives saw her as dangerously radical. Her most notoriously vindictive critic was John Wilson Croker, a contributor to the influential *Quarterly Review*. Croker attacked her works and her person from the publication of *St. Clair* onward, at one point even launching an investigation into her age and trying to strip her husband of his title. Writing for the *Freeman's Journal* in 1807, he accused her not merely of writing bad literature, but of "attempting to vitiate mankind—of attempting to undermine morality through sophistry. . . ." Such criticisms were echoed by others (though often more reasonably) for both political and literary reasons. The result was a reputation damaged for posterity.

In her own lifetime, however, the damage was mitigated by her popularity. She was so well-known that in 1809 she was invited to join the household of John James Hamilton, Marquis of Abercorn, one of the most pedigreed peers of the realm. Evidence suggests that Owenson was not eager to accept the offer, but in the end, the opportunity was too valuable to her career to be scorned. During her three years with the Abercorns she published only one novel, *The Missionary* (1811), set in India. Though it apparently impressed the youthful Percy Bysshe Shelley, the book was only moderately popular.

During 1811 and 1812, personal matters distracted her attention from literature. She had promised to marry the Abercorns' physician, an Englishman named Thomas Charles Morgan (who was knighted in 1811), though her letters show her reluctance to fulfill that promise. She and Morgan agreed to retain individual control over their money and were finally married on 20 January 1812. But whatever the new Lady Morgan's initial reservations, her marriage was apparently happy.

After the wedding, at her insistence, the couple left the Abercorn household. By 1813 they had established residence in fashionable Kildare Street, Dublin. Lady Morgan was also writing again. In 1814 she returned to her most popular form, the "national tale," with the publication of *O'Donnel*. This novel is less pedantic and more outspoken in its nationalistic sentiments than her previous fiction. Like many an able Irishman in Lady Morgan's time, O'Donnel has fled the enforced restrictions of his native country. The heroine is an equally able governess, who becomes a duchess, loses her husband, and marries O'Donnel after helping him to prominence. The significant innovation of *O'Donnel* is that the hero is Irish *and* a gentleman *and* a Catholic, attributes no fictional hero had hitherto combined. The book was tremendously successful, quickly selling out its first edition of two thousand copies.

The popularity of *O'Donnel* made Lady Morgan's publisher, Henry Colburn, anxious for more of her work. He sent her and her husband to France, newly opened to tourists after Napoléon's defeat at Waterloo (June 1815) and the subject of intense English interest. After two years of travel and research, Lady Morgan published her two-volume travel book *France* in 1817. The book was something of a sensation, sparking much controversy over its pro-Revolutionary sentiments—sentiments that could so easily be applied to Ireland. The public's eager response prompted Colburn to request a similar volume on Italy, which duly appeared in 1821. Then, refusing Colburn's offer to subsidize another travel book on Germany, the Morgans returned to Dublin.

Their travels had not dimmed Lady Morgan's Irish interests. In 1818 she had published another "national tale," *Florence Macarthy*, the story of a poor but aristocratic Irishwoman who makes her living as a novelist. The work incorporates social criticism with Lady Morgan's usual elaborate, romantic plot. *Florence Macarthy* also continues a satire of aristocratic life, based on her years with the Abercorns, that she had begun in *O'Donnel*. By the time *Italy* appeared, *Florence Macarthy* had gone through five editions.

Lady Morgan would write one more nationalistic tale, *The O'Briens and the O'Flahertys*, which appeared in 1827. Many critics consider this novel her best, despite its murky plot. Of all her "national tales," this one is the least optimistic, a work that, according to biographer Mary Campbell, "examines honestly the frustrations and final defeat of her own kind of romantic patrio-

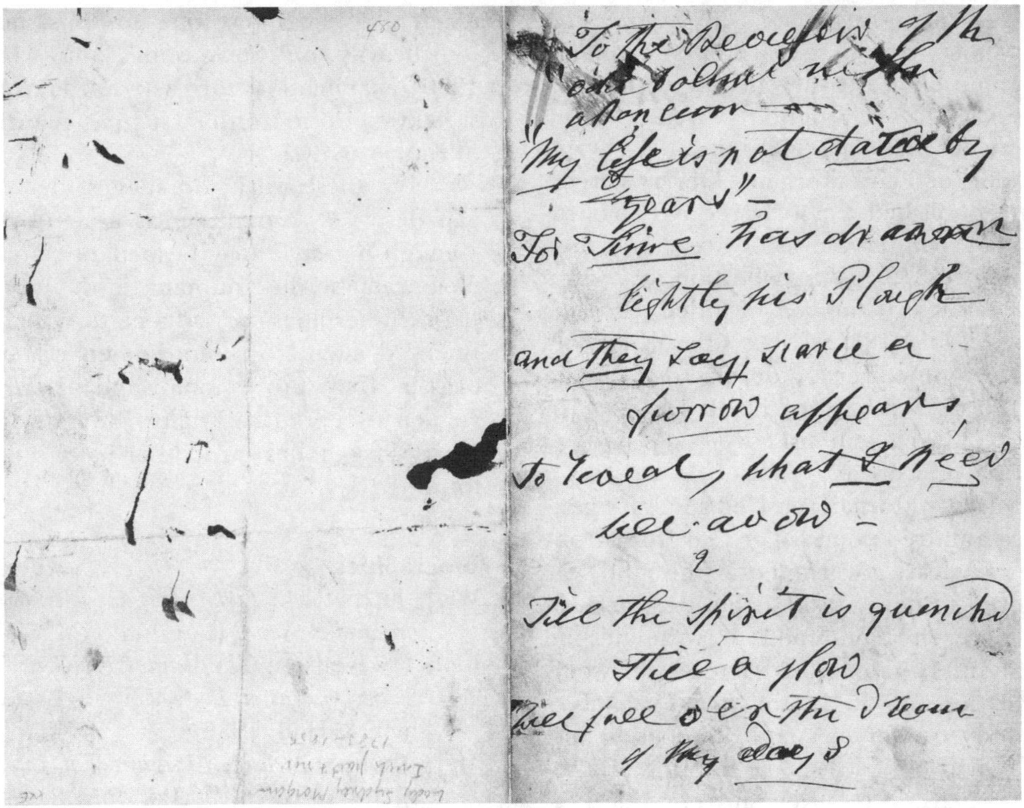

To the Reviewer of the
[illegible] Volume in the
Athenaeum —
"My Life is not dated by
years" —
For Time has drawn
lightly his Plough
and they say scarce a
furrow appears,
To reveal, what I need
not avow —
2
Till the spirit is quenched
like a flow
[illegible] o'er the dreams
of thy days

and brighten their
hours as they glow,
In the Sun-set of
memory's rays,
3
For as long as we feel
we enjoy —
and the heart sets
all dates at defiance
and forgetful of life
last alloy,
With Time makes a
Holy alliance

Then talk not to me
of "My age" —
I appeal from the Phrase
to the fact,
That I'm told in
your own brilliant page
I'm still young in [illegible]
Fancy, & Tact —
be loved —

Lady Morgan's response to an Athenaeum *review of* Passages from My Autobiography, *published when she was in her eighties (HM 36051, Henry E. Huntington Library and Art Gallery). Secretive about her age, she was offended by the reviewer's comment that she had "lived through the love, admiration, and malignity of three generations of men."*

tism." In literary terms, *The O'Briens and the O'Flahertys* shows a more mature, streamlined style than some of her earlier fiction, with fewer Gothic extravagances and tighter satire.

The end of her "national tales" was by no means the end of Lady Morgan's literary career. In 1824 she published a poorly received biography of Italian painter Salvator Rosa. *The Book of the Boudoir* (1829) is a collection of essays on a range of subjects, herself included. *Dramatic Scenes from Real Life* (1833) eschews her usual narrative for the immediacy of drama, though the content is mostly a rehash of her previous Irish writings. In 1835 she published *The Princess, or the Beguine*, her last novel.

In 1837 Lady Morgan received a literary pension of three hundred pounds per year from, ironically, the English government. She and Sir Charles moved to newly fashionable Belgravia, in London, where she continued to write despite failing eyesight. Her long-held interest in women found expression in *Woman and Her Master* (1840), a study of women's contributions to history that she had hoped to make the first of a series. In 1841 she collected the many periodical essays she had written with her husband in *The Book Without a Name*.

When Sir Charles Morgan died in 1843, his wife of thirty-one years was sincerely distraught; yet she did not retire. Instead, she dealt with her grief in her typical manner—by plunging energetically into hostessing, revising *The Missionary*, and working on her memoirs. A selection of these reminiscences, *Passages from My Autobiography*, appeared in January 1859. Lady Morgan died three months later, on April sixteenth.

She was not immediately forgotten. Many obituaries praised her, some predicting that her name and her work would live on. Her first biographer was W. J. Fitzpatrick, whose *Lady Morgan: Her Career, Literary and Personal* appeared in 1860. In 1862 W. Hepworth Dixon and Geraldine Jewsbury (Lady Morgan's secretary) edited her memoirs and correspondence. But beyond scattered references, she would not be examined seriously again until 1936, when Lionel Stevenson published his still-standard biography, *The Wild Irish Girl*. She received some brief (and sometimes hostile) attention in histories of Irish literature, but little in-depth scholarship appeared until a brief critical renaissance gave her some much-needed exposure in the late 1980s. These studies, however, added little to what was already known. Mary Campbell's 1988 biography, *Lady Morgan*, offers interesting insights, but it relies too heavily on Stevenson. James Newcomer's 1990 examination of selected novels is too sketchy to do more than suggest fruitful avenues of future analysis.

But these works do suggest that Lady Morgan deserves recognition as a significant writer. Though her style may be pedantic and her plots melodramatic, her humanistic themes and independent heroines created a pattern that clearly influenced later Irish and women writers. As one of the first professional and deeply political women writers in English, Sydney Owenson, Lady Morgan, has earned her place in literary history.

Biographies:

W. J. Fitzpatrick, *Lady Morgan: Her Career, Literary and Personal* (London: C. J. Skeet, 1860);

Lionel Stevenson, *The Wild Irish Girl: The Life of Sydney Owenson, Lady Morgan* (London: Chapman & Hall, 1936);

Mary Campbell, *Lady Morgan: The Life and Times of Sydney Owenson* (London, Sydney & Wellington: Pandora Press, 1988).

References:

Colin B. Atkinson and Jo Atkinson, "Sydney Owenson, Lady Morgan: Irish Patriot and First Professional Writer," *Eire-Ireland*, 15 (Summer 1980): 60-90;

James Cahalan, *The Irish Novel: A Critical History* (Boston: Twayne, 1988);

Thomas Flanagan, *The Irish Novelists 1800-1850* (New York: Columbia University Press, 1959), pp. 109-164;

James Newcomer, *Lady Morgan the Novelist* (Lewisburg, Pa.: Bucknell University Press, 1990);

Barry Sloan, *The Pioneers of Anglo-Irish Fiction 1800-1850* (Gerrards Cross, U.K.: C. Smythe / Totowa, N.J.: Barnes & Noble, 1987);

Elizabeth Suddaby and P. J. Yarrow, eds., *Lady Morgan in France* (Newcastle upon Tyne: Oriel Press, 1971).

Papers:

Lady Morgan's notebooks, correspondence, and commonplace books are in the Dublin National Library.

James Justinian Morier

(1782 or 1783? - 19 March 1849)

Laura Dabundo
Kennesaw State College

BOOKS: *A Journey Through Persia, Armenia, and Asia Minor to Constantinople in the Years 1808 and 1809* (London: Longman, Hurst, Rees, Orme & Brown, 1812; Philadelphia: M. Carey, 1816);

A Second Journey Through Persia, Armenia, and Asia Minor, to Constantinople, between the Years 1810 and 1816 (London: Longman, Hurst, Rees, Orme & Brown, 1818);

The Adventures of Hajji Baba of Ispahan (3 volumes, London: John Murray, 1824; 2 volumes, Philadelphia: A. Small, 1824);

The Adventures of Hajji Baba of Ispahan in England (2 volumes, London: John Murray, 1828; Philadelphia: Carey, Lea & Carey and J. Grigg, 1828);

Zohrab the Hostage (3 volumes, London: Richard Bentley, 1832; 2 volumes, New York: J. & J. Harper, 1833);

Ayesha: The Maid of Kars (3 volumes, London: Richard Bentley, 1834; 2 volumes, Philadelphia: Carey, Lea & Blanchard, 1834);

The Man of Honour and the Reclaimed, 2 volumes (London: Richard Bentley, 1834);

Abel Allnutt, a Novel (3 volumes, London: Richard Bentley, 1837; 1 volume, Philadelphia: E. L. Carey & A. Hart, 1837);

An Oriental Tale (Brighton: Printed by W. Leppard, 1839);

The Mirza, 3 volumes (London: Richard Bentley, 1841);

Misselmah, a Persian Tale (Brighton: Printed by W. Saunders, 1847);

Martin Toutrond: a Frenchman in London in 1831 (London: Richard Bentley, 1849).

OTHER: Wilhelm Hauff, *The Banished; a Swabian Historical Tale*, 3 volumes, edited by Morier (London: Henry Colburn, 1839);

Henriette Wach von Paalzow, *St. Roche, a Romance, from the German*, 3 volumes, edited by Morier (London: Richard Bentley, 1847).

James Justinian Morier, an English diplomat and writer, achieved renown during his lifetime chiefly for his imaginative *Adventures of Hajji Baba of Ispahan* (1824), based upon firsthand knowledge of Persian mores and culture. Although he is little known today, he was lauded by Charles Dickens, William Makepeace Thackeray, and Sir Walter Scott for his artistry and storytelling and his ability to transmute his personal observations into his "Oriental romances," works which now are recognized as competent specimens of Romantic fiction. The English novelistic tradition in which Morier participated has a respectable lineage originating in the first English translation of the *Arabian Nights* (1705-1708). Anglicized with Samuel Johnson's *Rasselas* (1759) and novels such as William Beckford's *Vathek* (1786), the vogue continued throughout the Romantic period with works such as Robert Southey's *Thalaba the Destroyer* (1801) and *The Curse of Kehama* (1810), George Gordon, Lord Byron's *The Giaour* (1813) and *The Corsair* (1814), and Thomas Moore's *Lalla Rookh* (1817). The "Oriental" tale continued to attract readers for the rest of the century.

Morier's ancestors were Huguenots displaced to Switzerland following the 1685 revocation of the Edict of Nantes (1598). The Moriers were eventually transplanted to England. Isaac Morier (1750-1817), the novelist's father, was the first of his family to become a British subject. Born in Smyrna, Turkey, he married Clara van Lennep, daughter of the Dutch consul general, who was also president of the Dutch Levant Company. In 1775 Isaac Morier was appointed first English consul general of the Levant Company at Constantinople, becoming British consul in 1806. All four of his sons served the British crown abroad and also on occasion worked on behalf of British commercial interests.

Isaac and Clara Morier's second son, James Justinian Morier, was born in Smyrna, probably in 1782 or 1783, although his exact birth date is uncertain. He spent much of his early life in

James Justinian Morier

Smyrna, where he came to know Moslem culture intimately. Where Morier was educated remains a mystery, although it is fairly certain that he went to school somewhere in England. According to some sources he attended Harrow, but his name does not appear in school records.

In 1807 Morier joined the diplomatic service as private secretary to Sir Harford Jones during his mission to the Persian court. Two years later Morier became secretary of legation in Tehran and in 1810 secretary of the embassy to Sir Gore Ouseley, ambassador extraordinaire to the Persian court. In Tehran Morier appears to have felt exhilarated by his work and surroundings but isolated and lonely. This tension may easily have contributed to the ironic perspective that later informed his fiction.

In 1812 Morier published his first book, *A Journey Through Persia, Armenia, and Asia Minor to Constantinople in the Years 1808 and 1809*. This travel book is considered one of the first serious books about the Middle East published in Europe. The book was well regarded by Morier's contemporaries. In fact Thomas Moore drew upon this volume for his popular *Lalla Rookh*.

In 1814 Morier was named chief British representative to the court of Persia, a post which enabled him to see much of the country. He remained in Persia until autumn 1815, and by December 1816 he had reached Constantinople. When he retired to England in 1817 on a government pension, he brought with him a wealth of incident, character, and setting on which to reflect and draw.

Morier's second travel book continued his account of his Eastern odyssey. *A Second Journey Through Persia, Armenia, and Asia Minor, to Constantinople* (1818) was as well received as his first effort, and some readers consider it better crafted because it is less a daily chronicle and a more "arranged" and "finished" accomplishment.

Morier had observed and reported the poverty of Middle Easterners subject to immensely rich despots, yet his social analysis rested upon a simplistic and common European prejudice. Both of Morier's travel books, like other Persian chronicles of the times, reflect a widespread notion of the Persian national character: warmth and cordiality mixed with hypocrisy and deceit. This condescending, ethnocentric notion became a major theme in all Morier's writings. Indeed, his travel writing whetted Morier's appetite for authorship. Morier realized that the scenes, personalities, and adventures he had described in his popular memoirs might be even more attractive to readers in fictionalized accounts of life in the Middle East. He had earlier been intrigued by Alain-René Lesage's *Gil Blas* (1715) as the sort of fiction he wished to write, and he borrowed the name of his best-known fictional character, Hajji Baba, from a young Persian medical student, whom he had served as an adviser in 1816-1819.

For the rest of Morier's life—with a hiatus in 1824-1826 when Britain sent him to Mexico as special commissioner for a treaty that now bears his signature—writing became his calling. He was married on 17 June 1820, to Harriet Greville, daughter of Sir William Fulke, a descendant of Fulke Greville, courtier to Elizabeth I and a biographer of Sir Philip Sidney. The Moriers settled in London and had one son, Greville, and one daughter, Mary Frances. Morier spent his final years in Brighton, where he died on 19 March 1849.

Morier's dedication to his craft was rewarded when his first novel was an immense success. *The Adventures of Hajji Baba of Ispahan* is a picaresque story married to the exotic tradition of the Oriental tale. Hajji Baba makes his way across the fascinating terrain of the Islamic Middle East. In large measure Morier's purpose in all his Middle Eastern writings seems to have been faithful depiction of the manners and mores that he had observed firsthand. His plots are realistic, his characters lifelike. No magic intrudes—as opposed to Southey's *Thalaba the Destroyer* or the familiar *Arabian Nights* tales of Sindbad and Ali Baba. Yet Morier's novel remained true to the spirit of the *Arabian Nights*, with the Eastern world and culture as its sphere and the vicissitudes of fame, fate, and fortune as its focus.

Satiric, suspenseful, and comic, as well as informative, provocative, and engrossing, *Hajji Baba* gave readers a sense of everyday life among all classes of people in the Middle East. The locale is principally Persia (now Iran), though the novel ranges into what is now Turkey, Afghanistan, Iraq, Georgia, and Turkestan as well.

Notwithstanding the exotic environs and meetings with dervishes, magicians, water carriers, executioners, medics, pipe and smoke vendors, and other colorful and seemingly alien folk, English readers could recognize that they and Hajji Baba's compatriots shared similar traits and foibles. Hajji Baba's own follies are not peculiar to him or his people; they derive from universal imprudence and impropriety. He is morally weak and physically energetic, gullible and cunning, generous and greedy, selfish and idealistic, affable and suspicious. His sins are recognizable to Christians as well as to Moslems.

Yet, for Morier and other Westerners of his time, the Moslem view seemed to absolve its adherents of responsibility for their fates. Not unlike Sindbad before him, Hajji Baba seems to suffer or prosper at the whim, evidently, of Allah. That is, his own behavior appears strangely irrelevant at times to the caprices of an omnipotent, omniscient, inescapable God. Hajji Baba's rises and falls, from one extreme to another, seem to Western minds nearly always unpredictable. Yet his vicissitudes are universal. Anyone, East or West, who has ever cursed his or her fate is kin to Hajji Baba.

As in Beckford's *Vathek*, Hajji Baba's amoral adventures are entrancing and beguiling, but, unlike Vathek, Hajji Baba does not control his own destiny, nor does he reach the evil extremes of Beckford's caliph, who chooses damnation in exchange for knowledge and power. Yet, unrestrained by moral scruples, Hajji Baba is open to experience—sometimes to his profit, often to his loss—certainly a more Romantic stance than the eighteenth-century one presented in *Vathek*. Hajji Baba maintains his faith, his spirits nearly always reviving, while the world remains unpredictable, unaccountable, and uncontrollable.

Hajji Baba was well received by Morier's contemporaries. Writing in the introduction to his *Talisman* (1825), Sir Walter Scott called Morier one of only two writers who "described the manners and vices of the Eastern nations not only with fidel-

Portrait in the Fraser's Magazine *"Gallery of Illustrious Literary Characters" (1830-1838)*

ity but with the humour of Le Sage and the ludicrous power of Fielding himself." The accuracy of Morier's portrait was confirmed by other Western visitors to the Middle East, as well as by natives of the region. Praised by John Gibson Lockhart, William Makepeace Thackeray, Charles Dickens, and Washington Irving, the book to others revivified *Gil Blas* and the anonymous *Lazarillo de Tormes* (1553), recreating French and Spanish picaros and surpassing the English efforts of Southey and Moore. The book went through several reprintings and new editions throughout the nineteenth century. In the twentieth century, at least a dozen editions have appeared.

Four years subsequent to the publication of *Hajji Baba* Morier attempted to repeat his performance with a sequel, *The Adventures of Hajji Baba of Ispahan in England* (1828). Here the satire of England that was implicit in the first book is more overt, as the ever-astounded protagonist makes his way through Britain as a representative of his government. The book might be compared to Canto XVI of Byron's *Don Juan* (1824), which describes Don Juan's escapades in England. While some reviewers compared it to Montesquieu's *Lettres persanes* (1721), fictional letters by two Persians visiting Paris, Morier's sequel was not as successful as its predecessor. Yet Morier's novels continued to be widely read and praised.

Morier's next novel, *Zohrab the Hostage* (1832), is once again set in Persia, but during an earlier period. *Zohrab* was followed by *Ayesha: The Maid of Kars* (1834). Although readers might have expected religious tolerance from a man so steeped in Middle Eastern culture, Morier's sense of the superiority of Christianity, one of his recurring themes, mars this book. Nonetheless, the titular figure, an enigmatic, beautiful, and fair young woman—indisputably Western—is intriguing. She foreshadows the equally misplaced and similarly described heroine of Rider Haggard's *She* (1887), who is also named Ayesha. Fascination with exoticism is often accompanied by a wish to locate the familiar at the heart of it. Consciously or not, Morier recognized that longing to make the world smaller, to find oneself or one's own in the distant and elusive. Perhaps he had come to this realization as a young English diplomat.

Morier's remaining novels also delineate collisions of Eastern and Western cultures, but they do not achieve the level of *Hajji Baba*, and critics, documenting increasing doses of melodrama, sentimentalism, and stock characterization, have consigned them to oblivion.

Morier's reputation rests with the fortunes of *Hajji Baba*—not a sorry legacy. If part of the strength and identity of Romantic literature comes from its range and breadth of imagination, then surely James Justinian Morier must not be denied his place in the ranks of the worthy.

References:

Terry H. Grabar, "Fact and Fiction: Morier's *Hajji Baba*," *Texas Studies in Literature and Language*, 11 (Fall 1969): 1223-1236;

George Krotkoff, "Hammer-Purgstall, Hajji Baba, and the Moriers," *International Journal of Middle East Studies*, 19 (February 1987): 103-108;

Ava Inez Weinberger, "The Middle Eastern Writings of James Morier: Traveller, Novelist, and Creator of Hajji Baba," Ph. D. dissertation, University of Toronto, 1984;

Arthur J. Weitzman, "Who Was Hajji Baba?" *Notes and Queries*, 217 (May 1970): 177-179.

Amelia Opie

(12 November 1769 - 2 December 1853)

Susan K. Howard
Duquesne University

BOOKS: *Dangers of Coquetry*, 2 volumes (London: Printed for W. Lane, 1790);

The Father and Daughter, A Tale, in Prose: With An Epistle from the Maid of Corinth to her Lover, and other poetical pieces (London: Printed by Davis, Wilks & Taylor and sold by Longman & Rees, 1801; New York: Printed & sold by John Harrison, 1802);

Poems (London: Printed for T. N. Longman & O. Rees by Taylor & Wilks, 1802);

Elegy to the Memory of the Late Duke of Bedford (London: T. N. Longman & O. Rees, 1802);

Adeline Mowbray; or, The Mother and Daughter (3 volumes, London: Longman, Hurst, Rees & Orme, 1805; Georgetown: Published by J. Milligan, Dinmore & Cooper, printers, 1808);

Simple Tales (4 volumes, London: Printed for Longman, Hurst, Rees & Orme, 1806; 2 volumes, Georgetown: Published at J. March's Bookstore, R. C. Weightman, printer, 1807);

The Warrior's Return and Other Poems (London: Longman, Hurst, Rees & Orme, 1808; Philadelphia: Published by Bradford & Inskeep, 1808);

Temper, or, Domestic Scenes (3 volumes, London: Longman, Hurst, Rees, Orme & Brown, 1812; 2 volumes, Boston: Bradford & Read, 1812; Boston: Printed by Watson & Bangs, 1812; New York: J. Eastburn, 1812);

Tales of Real Life (3 volumes, London: Longman, Hurst, Rees, Orme & Brown, 1813; 1 volume, Boston: S. G. Goodrich, 1827);

Valentine's Eve (3 volumes, London: Longman, Hurst, Rees, Orme & Brown, 1816; 2 volumes, Boston: Wells & Lilly, 1816);

New Tales (4 volumes, London: Longman, Hurst, Rees, Orme & Brown, 1818; 2 volumes, New York: Gilley, 1818; Philadelphia: M. Thomas, 1818);

Tales of the Heart (4 volumes, London: Longman, Hurst, Rees, Orme & Brown, 1820; 2 volumes, New York: William B. Gilley, Haly & Thomas, A. T. Goodrich, and Wiley & Halsted, 1820);

Madeline (2 volumes, London: Printed for Longman, Hurst, Rees, Orme & Brown, 1822; 1 volume, Boston: S. G. Goodrich, 1827);

The Negro Boy's Tale (London: Published by Harvey & Darton, 1824);

Illustrations of Lying, in All Its Branches (2 volumes, London: Longman, Hurst, Rees, Orme, Brown & Green, 1825; 1 volume, Boston: Published by Munroe & Francis and nine others, 1826);

Tales of the Pemberton Family, for the Use of Children (London: Harvey and Darton, 1825; Boston: Munroe & Francis, 1825);

The Black Man's Lament; or, How to Make Sugar (London: Printed for Harvey & Darton, 1826);

Detraction Displayed (London: Longman, Rees, Orme, Brown & Green, 1828; New York: Published by Orville A. Roorbach, W. E. Dean, printer, 1828; Philadelphia: Carey, Lea & Carey, sold in New York by G. & C. Carvill, in Boston by Munroe & Francis, 1828);

Lays for the Dead (London: Longman, Rees, Orme, Brown, Green & Longman, 1834).

OTHER: *Twelve Hindoo Airs with English words adapted to them*, music adapted by Edward Smith Biggs and words by Opie (London: Printed by Birchall, circa 1800);

A Second Set of Hindoo Airs with English words adapted to them, music by Biggs and words by Opie (London: Printed by Birchall, circa 1800);

John Opie, *Lectures on Painting, Delivered at the Royal Academy of Arts*, edited, with a memoir, by Amelia Opie (London: Longman, Hurst, Rees & Orme, 1809);

Mrs. Margaret Roberts, *Duty*, edited by Opie (3 volumes, London: Printed for Longman, Hurst, Rees, Orme & Brown, 1814; 2 vol-

Amelia Opie (portrait by John Opie; National Portrait Gallery, London)

umes, New York: Printed & published by I. Riley, 1815);

"The Last Voyage," in *The Amulet,* volume 3 (London: W. Baynes & Son and Wightman & Cramp, 1828), pp. 78-85;

"Poor Rosalie," in *The Amulet,* volume 8 (London: Frederick Westley & A. H. Davis, 1833), pp. 256-295.

SELECTED PERIODICAL PUBLICATIONS—UNCOLLECTED: "The Shipwreck," *European Magazine,* 83 (April 1823): 297-303;

"Recollection of Days in Belgium," *Tait's Edinburgh Magazine,* 7 (March 1840): 177-183; (June 1840): 293-301.

Amelia Opie's significance as a Romantic novelist lies in her timely, moving, and sometimes provocative domestic fiction. Like other Romantic novelists, Opie was concerned with the individual's changing relationship with society, and she chose to embody this relationship by depicting the individual's actions within the family unit. In this respect she must be considered alongside Maria Edgeworth and Elizabeth Inchbald, in the tradition of Frances Burney and Jane Austen, as a writer of the novel of manners.

Amelia Alderson Opie was born in Norwich in 1769, the only child of Dr. James Alderson and Amelia Briggs Alderson, who died when her daughter was fifteen. Though she received no formal education, young Amelia Alderson read the works of contemporary novelists, poets, and philosophers and took part in the political, religious, and literary discussions among her father and his guests, who included William Godwin and Thomas Holcroft, members of the Radical party. Her involvement with the Radicals became less intense after her marriage to the painter John Opie in London on 8 May 1798.

While some of Amelia Opie's early poetry and a novel, *Dangers of Coquetry* (1790), were pub-

The house in Colegate Street, Norwich, where Amelia Opie spent her childhood

lished before 1800, they received little critical consideration, and it was only with the publication of *The Father and Daughter* (1801) that her work met with popular success. The first printing of the novel, a surprisingly large one of 750 copies, was depleted within the year, and the novel continued to be popular well into the mid-nineteenth century. Critics responded favorably to the pathos of a father driven insane by his daughter's flight into the arms of a libertine and her subsequent repentance and filial redemption: Walter Scott later admitted to Opie that he had wept over the story. Assessments of its technical merits were less laudatory, however: a Dr. Brown, reviewing *The Father and Daughter* with Opie's *Poems* (1802) in the *Edinburgh Review* (October 1802), criticized Opie's static characterization and hackneyed plot, the "common history of every seduction in romance." These two reactions are typical of the responses which followed in the next twenty years to Opie's works.

Recent critics of *The Father and Daughter* have commented negatively on Opie's didacticism and noted the contradictions inherent in a story which decries Agnes Fitzhenry's victimization by an insensitive and unforgiving society, but also applauds the social stigma that precludes her fully rejoining society until she has suffered and worked to regain its respect.

Adeline Mowbray; or, The Mother and Daughter (1805) was loosely based on the life of Opie's friend Mary Wollstonecraft, who had married William Godwin in March 1797 and died the following September, a few days after having given birth to their daughter. Written in response to views against marriage espoused earlier by both Wollstonecraft and Godwin, *Adeline Mowbray* seems to offer two contradictory messages: it sentimentally presents the tragic consequences of Adeline's adherence to the doctrines of the Godwinian Frederic Glenmurray, while at the same time sanctioning that tragedy as socially necessary. After he falls in love with Adeline, Glenmurray proposes to her despite his previously stated opposition to the institution of marriage, but Adeline, who has embraced the principles stated in his books, refuses to marry him. Instead she lives with him "as his wife in the sight of God." This arrangement leads to social ostracism, estrangement from her mother, and her lover's death. Her attempt to reenter society, acceding to its demands, by marrying Glenmurray's cousin results in her misery and death. A reconciliation with her mother comes only as Adeline lies on her deathbed. Thus, while this novel may hint at a revolutionary view of personal freedom, one which might be expected, given Amelia Opie's own past actions—including her support of the Radicals during the Treason Trials of 1794—the message of *Adeline Mowbray* is ultimately conservative, coming down on the side of societal conformity and indicating the grave costs to the individual who explores new manners and mores alone.

In 1806 Opie published *Simple Tales*, which the reviewer for the *Edinburgh Review* (July 1806) criticized for its lack of originality in characterization and for stylistic deficiencies while praising the characters' closeness to nature. By this time Opie had gained recognition as a bluestocking; her home was open to artists and writers, and she included among her friends William Wordsworth, Walter Scott, Sarah Siddons, and Elizabeth Inchbald. With the death of her husband in 1807, Opie returned to live with her father in Norwich. There she edited her husband's lectures on painting, attaching a memoir of him, and published a book of poetry, *The Warrior's Return* (1808), which met with mixed reviews. In 1814, influenced by her friend Joseph John Gurney, she began to attend Quaker meetings. She was formally received into the Society of Friends in 1825.

The publication of her novel *Temper* in 1812 initiated her lifelong friendship with William Hayley, whose poem *The Triumphs of Temper* (1781) inspired her novel. Writing in 1901, William Dean Howells found Opie's heroine Emma Castlemain "offensively good" and the plot of the novel implausible. Certainly there are elements of the story that rely too heavily on coincidence, but Opie's female characterizations do achieve some psychological depth and validity. As Howells noted, Emma, like her mother, has "few moments of passive virtue": this characteristic is at once a source of their strength and of their weakness. When Agatha Torrington discovers her husband's infidelity, she takes Emma and leaves London; similarly, when Emma suspects that St. Aubyn loves another, she begins a series of flights away from him and all that reminds her of him. These women show admirable independence and self-respect, but Opie qualifies her approval by casting aspersions on their motives and by indicating that women can be only so active on their own behalf before they risk social censure.

Madeline (1822), which has attracted less critical attention than it deserves, makes a similar point. This novel is stylistically more polished than Opie's previous works and uses a complex narrative frame to relate the "history of a weak woman's heart." Madeline Munro is returned to her working-class Scottish family after years of living with an affluent English family. Through this rather unusual situation, Opie explores the conflicts between the English and the Scottish, between the landed aristocracy and the laboring poor, between parent and child, and between men and women—as well as the conflict within oneself. Unable to proclaim her marriage to the laird of Glencarron because their difference in social status would anger his family, Madeline realizes that she cannot live with the lie of a secret marriage or with Glencarron's idea of what she should be as a wife. She rebels against his reliance on her gentle, passive temper when it gives him freedom to neglect her. Like Agatha Torrington, Adeline Mowbray, and Agnes Fitzhenry, she leaves her unappreciative husband and earns her own living in London. Once again Opie reveals contradictory attitudes toward her heroine. While she questions society's approval of the passive woman, she ends this novel, as she does others, by blaming her heroine for the misfortunes caused in large part by male selfishness and greed. Madeline's journal concludes with self-recrimination for her "unreasonable desires" for reconciliation with her family.

Opie's later fiction attracted little critical comment. Her career as a fiction writer essentially ended with her formal admission into the Society of Friends in 1825: she left her novel "The Painter and His Wife," unfinished, thereby forfeiting a one-thousand-pound publisher's payment, since she felt its sensational subject matter might be viewed unfavorably by the Quakers. Opie's works after 1825 are blatantly didactic pieces, such as *Illustrations of Lying, in All Its Branches* (1825). While her Quaker friends approved of this work, and according to James Fenimore Cooper it enjoyed great popularity in America, literary critics in Britain found it too moralistic. Opie also joined the Abolitionist cause and wrote sentimental, ill-informed pieces on slavery. During the Revolution of 1830 she returned to France, where she had first traveled in 1802, to applaud Lafayette's ousting of Charles X and to indulge her own revolutionary sympathies. She toured

Illustration by John Opie in The Father and Daughter

Cornwall, her husband's birthplace, and there wrote *Lays for the Dead* (1834), a series of poetic remembrances. Though she began her memoirs, she died before finishing them.

Two of Opie's biographers, Jacobine Menzies-Wilson and Helen Lloyd, have suggested that Opie's works were popular with her contemporaries because of her "attractive personality" rather than because of their own merit. Yet they may have overstated the case. The popularity of *The Father and Daughter* and *Adeline Mowbray* outlived Opie, and these novels fairly represent their author's strengths—as well as her weaknesses—as a novelist. Though the technical aspects of her narratives were sometimes flawed, though her attitude toward her characters and their actions was not always consistent, and though she sometimes opted for the obvious moral ending rather than exploring the complexities of characterization hinted at in her best novels, she did offer an intelligent view of contemporary social issues and effectively showed how they impinged on people's lives. Yet these two works are among Opie's earliest and therefore indicate her lack of development as a novelist. While her later works, such as *Madeline*, are stylistically more polished, their didacticism is also more overt, their implausibility, sensationalism, and sentimentality more glaring. Mary Russell Mitford, though she had once compared Opie to Maria Edgeworth and Joanna Baillie, did not bother to read Opie's later fiction because "One knows the usual ingredients of her tales just as one knows the component parts of a plum-pudding. So much common sense (for the flour), so much vulgarity (for the suet), so much love (for the sugar), so many songs (for the plums), so much wit (for the spices), so much true morality (for the eggs), and so much mere mawkishness and insipidity (for the milk and water wherewith the said pudding is mixed)." Though this assessment gives some idea of the components of Opie's fiction, it ignores the important themes and the emotional power of her best work. As Elizabeth Barrett Browning noted in a 14 July 1838 letter to Mary Mitford: "With all her feeblenesses, yes, & silliness sometimes, she is very moving in her best stories."

Biographies:

Cecilia Lucy Brightwell, *Memorials of the Life of Amelia Opie* (Norwich: Fletcher & Alexander, 1854);

Brightwell, *Memoir of Amelia Opie* (London: Religious Tract Society, 1855);

Jacobine Menzies-Wilson and Helen Lloyd, *Amelia: The Tale of a Plain Friend* (London & New York: Oxford University Press, 1937).

References:

Jan Fergus and Janice Farrar Thaddeus, "Women, Publishers, and Money, 1790-1820," *Studies in Eighteenth-Century Culture*, 17 (1987): 191-207;

William Dean Howells, "Heroines of Miss Ferrier, Mrs. Opie, and Mrs. Radcliffe," in his *Heroines of Fiction*, 2 volumes (New York & London: Harper, 1901), I: 79-89;

Gary Kelly, "Amelia Opie, Lady Caroline Lamb, and Maria Edgeworth: Official and Unofficial Ideology," *Ariel*, 12 (October 1981): 3-24;

Kelly, "Discharging Debts: The Moral Economy of Amelia Opie's Fiction," *Wordsworth Circle*, 11 (Autumn 1980): 198-203;

Margaret Eliot MacGregor, *Amelia Alderson Opie: Worldling and Friend* (Northampton, Mass.: Smith College, 1933);

Anne Thackeray Ritchie, *A Book of Sibyls* (London: Smith, Elder, 1883).

Papers:

There are collections of Opie's papers in the British Library and the Huntington Library.

Thomas Love Peacock

(18 October 1785 - 23 January 1866)

William A. Davis, Jr.
College of Notre Dame of Maryland

See also the Peacock entry in *DLB 96: British Romantic Poets, 1789-1832; Second Series.*

BOOKS: *The Monks of St. Mark* (London: Privately printed, 1804);

Palmyra, and Other Poems (London: Printed by T. Bensley for W. J. & J. Richardson, 1806 [i.e., 1805]);

The Genius of the Thames: A Lyric Poem, in Two Parts (London: Published by T. Hookham, Jun. & E. T. Hookham and Manners & Miller, Edinburgh, 1810);

The Philosophy of Melancholy: A Poem in Four Parts with a Mythological Ode (London: Printed by William Bulmer for T. Hookham, Junior & E. T. Hookham; Gale & Curtis; and John Ballantyne, Edinburgh, 1812);

Sir Hornbook; or, Childe Launcelot's Expedition. A Grammatico-Allegorical Ballad (London: Printed for Sharpe & Hailes at the Juvenile Library, 1814 [i.e., 1813]);

Sir Proteus: A Satirical Ballad, as P. M. O'Donovan, Esq. (London: Printed for T. Hookham, Junr. & E. T. Hookham, 1814);

Headlong Hall (London: Printed for T. Hookham, Jun., 1816 [i.e., 1815]; Philadelphia: Published by M. Carey, sold by Wells & Lilly, Boston, 1816);

The Round Table; or, King Arthur's Feast (London: Printed & published by John Arliss and sold by Hoitts; Bowdery & Kerby, Jun.; Beilby & Knotts, Birmingham, 1817);

Melincourt, 3 volumes (London: Printed for T. Hookham, Jun. and Baldwin, Cradock & Joy, 1817; Published by Moses Thomas, printed by J. Maxwell, 1817);

Rhododaphne: or The Thessalian Spell. A Poem (London: Printed for T. Hookham, Jun., and Baldwin, Cradock & Joy, 1818; Philadelphia: M. Carey & Son, 1818);

Nightmare Abbey (London: Printed for T. Hookham, Jun.; and Baldwin, Cradock & Joy, 1818; Philadelphia: M. Carey & Son, 1819);

Maid Marian (London: Printed for T. Hookham, Jun., and Longman, Hurst, Rees, Orme & Brown, 1822);

The Misfortunes of Elphin (London: Published by Thomas Hookham, 1829);

Crotchet Castle (London: Published by T. Hookham, 1831);

Headlong Hall, Nightmare Abbey, Maid Marian, Crotchet Castle, revised editions, Bentley's Standard Novels, volume 57 (London: Richard Bentley, 1837);

Paper Money Lyrics, and Other Poems (London: Printed by C. & W. Reynell, 1837);

Gryll Grange (London: Parker, Son & Bourn, 1861);

The Works of Thomas Love Peacock, 3 volumes, edited by Henry Cole (London: Richard Bentley, 1875 [i.e., 1874]);

The Works of Thomas Love Peacock, The Halliford Edition, 10 volumes, edited by H. F. B. Brett-Smith & C. E. Jones (London & New York, 1924-1934).

OTHER: "Steam Navigation to India," *Edinburgh Review*, 60 (January 1835): 445-482;

Gl' Ingannati, or The Deceived, translated, with a preface, by Peacock (London: Chapman & Hall, 1862).

Thomas Love Peacock was an accomplished poet, essayist, opera critic, and satiric novelist. During his lifetime his works received the approbation of other writers (some of whom were Peacock's friends and the targets of his satire), literary critics (many of whom were simply his targets), and a notoriously vocal reading public. Today, Peacock's reputation rests almost exclusively on the merits of his seven novels, four of which—*Headlong Hall, Melincourt, Nightmare Abbey*, and *Maid Marian*—appeared in quick succession between 1815 and 1822. The remaining three—*The Misfortunes of Elphin, Crotchet Castle*, and *Gryll Grange*—were written and published at more leisurely intervals, *Gryll Grange* not appear-

Thomas Love Peacock and his mother, Sarah Love Peacock, circa 1805 (miniatures by Roger Kean; National Portrait Gallery, London)

ing until 1861, five years before Peacock's death. Peacock's novels record the intellectual, social, economic, and literary discussions (sometimes battles) of early-nineteenth-century England. They are, in one sense, "conversation novels," and many of the characters who take part in the various conversations were modeled after the leading personalities of Peacock's day. Peacock's novels have lost none of their appeal, however, for the subjects they address continue to inform the political and social dialogues. Their comedy still delights readers, and the conversations never go for long without a pause for comic action or comment.

Peacock was born in Weymouth, England, in 1785 to Samuel Peacock, a glass merchant, and Sarah Love, daughter of Thomas Love, then a retired master in the Royal Navy. When Peacock was three years old, he and his mother moved to the home of his maternal grandparents. (Several biographical accounts name the death of Peacock's father as the probable cause of this removal, but some uncertainty regarding the death of Samuel Peacock remains.) At age six Peacock entered a school at Englefield Green, then kept by John Harris Wicks. Several of the verse letters he wrote to family members during this time show an early interest and ability in social satire. Peacock seems to have been content at school and managed to impress his master, but the six years he spent at Englefield Green constituted Peacock's first and only formal education. By February 1800, Peacock was working as a clerk for the merchant house of Ludlow, Fraser, and Co. in London, but he remained in their employment only briefly. He began writing poems and incidental essays at this time, and in late 1805, *Palmyra*, his first collection of poems, was published and well received. The title poem, a study of apocalyptic ruin, represents Peacock's attempt at serious, learned poetry written in the style of his eighteenth-century forebears.

Shortly after the publication of *Palmyra*, Peacock became engaged to Fanny Falkner, a young woman from his neighborhood of Chertsey. The couple's engagement, which the interference of one of Miss Falkner's relatives soon brought to an end, was later recounted in the poem "Newark Abbey" (written in 1842). In 1808 Peacock served briefly as under secretary to Adm. Sir Home Popham aboard the HMS *Venerable*, which never left the harbor while Peacock was on board. The nature of his duties is not clear, but he was happy to go ashore after some six months to begin a walking tour of the Thames, soon afterward recounted in *The Genius of the Thames* (1810), an ode in two parts. The poem represents Peacock's attempt to describe the river and all that it means to him and to England. The tour of the Thames was followed by a journey to Wales, where Peacock finished his poem and met Jane Gryffydh, daughter of a Welsh parson. Peacock would propose marriage to her eight years later, but for the time being his mind seems to have been on poetry, which he continued to write and publish.

In October or November of 1812, Peacock met Percy Bysshe Shelley, who would soon come to depend on Peacock as a friend and as a literary critic/assistant. Shelley seems to have admired Peacock's poetry (especially *Palmyra*), despite the marked differences in the two poets' subjects and techniques. By this time Peacock had one more major poem, *The Philosophy of Melancholy* (1812), to his credit. As Peacock explains in his prefatory "General Analysis," the poem argues that contemplating mutability ennobles the mind, and that art and human relationships derive their "principal charms" and "endearing ties" from a philosophical consideration of mutability. Meanwhile the friendship of Peacock and Shelley continued to grow, and Peacock continued to write and to experiment with new subjects and literary forms. Two plays, *The Dilettanti* and *The Three Doctors*, neither of which was published or produced during Peacock's lifetime, were probably written during this time. A much more successful venture was *Sir Hornbook* (1813), subtitled *A Grammatico-Allegorical Ballad*, which provided instruction in grammar for children. Its hero, Childe Launcelot, conquers the parts of speech with the assistance of Sir Hornbook as they travel toward an understanding of language and prosody. The book went through five illustrated editions in five years, thanks to Peacock's talent for making grammar fun.

Peacock continued to travel, returning to Wales in 1813. At this time he was at work on two poems: the unfinished mythological epic *Ahrimanes*, written in Spenserian stanzas; and *Sir Proteus*, published in March 1814. The latter is a satiric attack on Robert Southey, the poet laureate, whose career Peacock had followed with some interest for several years. William Wordsworth, Samuel Taylor Coleridge, Walter Scott, and the periodical press also undergo satiric correction in *Sir Proteus*, but the focus of this pseudolearned poem is Southey, whose poems, Peacock's persona argues, are written without reference to taste, nature, or conscience. Shortly after the publication of *Sir Proteus*, Peacock learned of Shelley's elopement with Mary Godwin, daughter of William Godwin and Mary Wollstonecraft. Two weeks after the elopement, Shelley wrote a letter to his wife, Harriet, inviting her to join them on the Continent. In the same letter Shelley told Harriet that he had asked Peacock to look after her financial needs. Peacock evidently did as he was asked, motivated in part by his sympathy for Harriet and in part by his esteem for his friend.

In a quieter time, in 1795, Peacock had begun a letter to his mother with these lines: "DEAR MOTHER, I attempt to write you a letter/ In verse, tho' in prose, I could do it much better." It would take Peacock twenty years to try his skill at prose fiction, but inevitably he did so, and with important and far-reaching results. In 1815, with the Shelleys back in London and living near enough to make regular visits possible, Peacock began working on his first novel, *Headlong Hall*, published later that year. With its reliance upon characters who embody "opinions," its use of the country-house setting, its frequent departures into dramatic conversation, and its satiric intent, *Headlong Hall* proved to be much better than any of Peacock's still commendable poetic productions. This first novel was also to be the prototype for the majority of Peacock's later novels, for in subsequent works he modified, but never completely abandoned, the formula of *Headlong Hall*.

The novel is set at the country estate of Squire Harry Headlong, an individual who, "unlike other Welsh squires . . . had actually suffered certain phenomena, called books, to find their way into his house." Squire Headlong's thirst for knowledge takes him to Oxford in search of philosophers and men of taste, but he is told that none reside there. The disappointed squire decides to transform his well-stocked home into a meeting place for such individuals. His most important guests are Mr. Foster, a "perfectibilian"; Mr. Escot, a "deteriorationist"; Mr. Jenkison, a "statu-quo-ite"; and Reverend Dr. Gaster, an individual whose principal talent is eating well.

Peacock's characters agree on virtually nothing. They are not supposed to agree or for that matter to modify their own particular prejudices, to convince their listeners to change their views, or to take any real offense at the insults hurled at

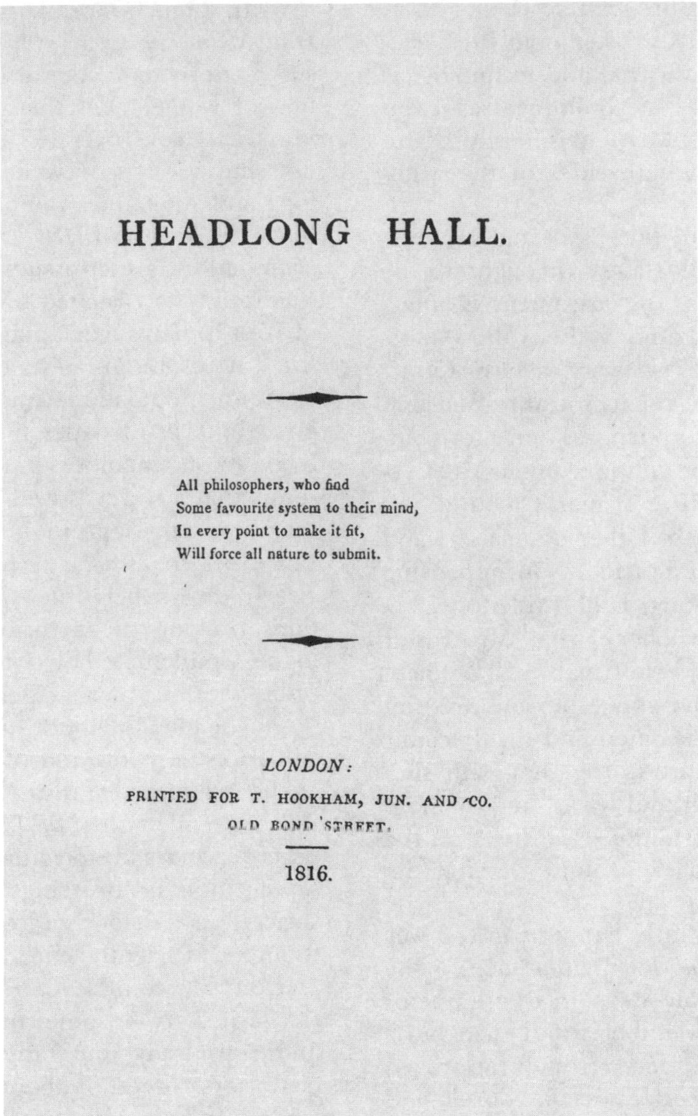

HEADLONG HALL.

All philosophers, who find
Some favourite system to their mind,
In every point to make it fit,
Will force all nature to submit.

LONDON:
PRINTED FOR T. HOOKHAM, JUN. AND CO.
OLD BOND STREET.

1816.

Title page for Peacock's first novel, his satiric treatment of what happens after Squire Harry Headlong departs from the custom of other Welsh squires and allows "certain phenomena, called books, to find their way into his house"

them from all sides. Their disagreements bring to life the purpose of the novel, which is announced on the title page:

All philosophers, who find
Some favourite system to their mind,
In every point to make it fit,
Will force all nature to submit.

The arguments commence on the first page of the novel and address topics that range from the ridiculous to the truly significant. A remark that "the day was none of the finest" occasions the response, "quite the contrary." Breakfast affords the characters an opportunity to argue about whether animal products should be included in an Englishman's diet. Next, the grounds of Headlong Hall provide the occasion for a dialogue on whether natural or artistically landscaped gardens are superior. The novel thus begins innocently with characters discussing subjects of questionable significance but bristling with satiric undertones. His audience won, Peacock turns to the more substantive issues.

The principal argument places Mr. Escot's contention that "original man" is superior to the modern specimen against Mr. Foster's belief that man is always improving both his inner self and the world around him. Escot brings to his argument an unlikely "proof" in the form of a giant skull, signifying, of course, that man was formerly larger and therefore better in every way than his shrunken relative. Foster points to factories as signs of man's industrial and technological advances; to Escot, the same buildings represent a mechanistic way of life. Mr. Jenkison, the "statu-quo-ite," finds merit in both sides of the argument.

The conversation of Mr. Escot and Mr. Foster develops in several stages throughout the novel. At various times, the argument is interrupted by other topics, among them the "transgressions" of periodical reviewers (a favorite target of Peacock), self-love versus social responsibility, the dinner menu, the purposes and shortcomings of novels written for young women, Mr. Cranium's theory of the nature of man ("a bundle or compound of faculties of other animals"), and Mr. Marmaduke Milestone's ideas on improving the grounds of Headlong Hall (Milestone believes in doing for shrubbery what Mr. Foster sees as the natural progress of man). All of these topics and their respective spokespersons are unified by a thin but well-executed and highly comic plot, which brings characters together with simple devices such as meals and walks, and by more dramatic means, such as minor explosions. At the end, a series of marriages promise varying degrees of happiness.

The fact that very little happens in the way of events in *Headlong Hall* hardly matters, for the point of the novel is to air ideas or, to use one of Peacock's terms, to blow bubbles and then burst them. Peacock's first readers strongly approved of the design and execution of the novel, and *Headlong Hall* appeared in a second edition after only six months in print. A third edition followed in 1822, and all of Peacock's subsequent novels bore the inscription "By the Author of Headlong Hall." Thomas Love Peacock had found his voice. It would not be long before he used it again.

During the winter of 1815-1816, Peacock and Shelley continued to visit and to read Greek together. Peacock also began working on *The Round Table; or, King Arthur's Feast* (1817), a children's poem that outlines the history of English royalty. Peacock's principal literary interests at this time, however, were two prose pieces: *Calidore*, an unfinished novel based upon Arthurian legends; and *Melincourt* (1817), an ambitious and highly topical novel written with the same spirit and with much the same intent as *Headlong Hall*.

In a much more leisurely way than *Headlong Hall*, *Melincourt* treats subjects such as original versus modern man, literary tastes, and the education of women, but the attention given to other ideas and controversies shows that Peacock was not simply out to rewrite his first novel. In this long and sometimes rambling novel (almost three times the length of *Headlong Hall*) Peacock's characters address such issues as West Indian slavery (the topic is occasioned by one character's boycott of West Indian sugar), political corruption (dramatized in an orangutan's victory in a Parliamentary election), population control, the causes of poverty, the evils of paper money, society's responsibility to its members, and the belief, held by some, that a society's well-being will increase if its members are kept in a state of general ignorance. As in *Headlong Hall*, the battle lines are clearly drawn between characters whose dispositions provide the occasion for a series of dialogues punctuated by loosely connected and often hilarious plot incidents.

The main plot in *Melincourt* concerns Mr. Sylvan Forester's slow and often interrupted pursuit of the rich and beautiful Anthelia Melincourt. Anthelia, "really romantic [and] unworldly," represents Peacock's ideal woman. Forester, the antithesis of "the kind of beings that constitute modern society," is Peacock's ideal man. The love plot, though sufficiently entertaining at its inception and the source of several comic incidents later in the novel, grows somewhat tedious as it rambles and runs away into tangents. Occasionally, the characters forget all about their love interests, as when Mr. Forester and friends suspend their search for the missing Anthelia, who has been kidnapped by another suitor, in order to engage new acquaintances in new discussions. Forester, of course, is on a higher sort of quest. His goals are to make others see that modern society needs reforming and to enlist their help in that cause. Thus there is a thematic parallel to Mr. Forester's winning of Anthelia: the slow, but eventually successful, conversion of Mr. Forester's friend, Sir Telegraph Paxarett, whose belief that "the practice of one individual, more or less, has little or no influence on general society" undergoes complete reversal. Sir Telegraph, however, does not change his ways without some resistance, as one especially revealing speech to Forester attests:

> When ecclesiastical dignitaries imitate the temperance and humility of the founder of that religion by which they feed and flourish: when the man

> in place acts on the principles which he professed while he was out: when borough-electors will not sell their suffrage, nor their representatives their votes: when poets are not to be hired for the maintenance of any opinion: when learned divines can afford to have a conscience: when universities are not a hundred years in knowledge behind all the rest of the world: when young ladies speak as they think, and when those who shudder at a tale of the horrors of slavery will deprive their own palates of a sweet taste, for the purpose of contributing all in their power to its extinction:—why then Forester, I will lay down my barouche.

This passage illustrates the range of Peacock's satire in *Melincourt* and the extent to which Peacock felt his society needed reform. Sir Telegraph does not, of course, wait for all of these required changes to take place before adopting his own reforming spirit, nor does Mr. Forester accomplish the change in his friend all by himself.

Melincourt, like *Headlong Hall,* includes a host of characters who contribute to both the serious and the not-so-serious moments in the novel. Peacock's characters—whether they represent serious thinkers who clearly have won their author's approval or strategically placed buffoons—all play parts in bringing to life the purpose of the novel, which is to expose social flaws and to show that individuals can and do change. In achieving this purpose, *Melincourt* offers fewer pauses for comedy than *Headlong Hall* and devotes most of its attention to arguments that are longer, more serious, and more complex than the arguments in the earlier novel. Nearly forty years after the publication of *Melincourt,* in the preface to the 1856 edition, Peacock reiterated the reasons for the novel's design: The "disputants," the main sources of the comedy, "have passed from the diurnal scene. Many of the questions, discussed in the dialogues, have more of general than of temporary application, and have still their advocates on both sides." Without going so far as to say that *Melincourt* is a serious book, one may say that its comedy is subservient to its social ideas and purposes in a degree that the comedy in *Headlong Hall* is not.

Melincourt was published in three volumes in 1817 at a price of 18 shillings. After this second novel, Peacock turned once more to verse and to his considerable knowledge of classical poetry. The result, published in February 1818, was *Rhododaphne*, a Greek love poem written in ode form and concerned with the traditional theme of supernatural interference in earthly love. Peacock enjoyed Mary Shelley's assistance with the transcription of the text and Percy Shelley's praise. George Gordon, Lord Byron, also found merit in Peacock's poem. Thus Peacock was beginning to win recognition in the literary world (John Keats, however, seemed not to like him). During the revision of his *Laon and Cynthia* (1817), Shelley actually solicited Peacock's help. Peacock was not, however, making much of a living by his writing and was by this time receiving some financial support from Shelley. This fact, along with others, may help to explain Mary Shelley's usual indifference to and occasional dislike for Peacock. On one occasion, for example, she referred to Peacock and Thomas Jefferson Hogg as members of Shelley's "menagerie." For his part, Peacock seems always to have kept the Shelleys' interests in mind and was instrumental in securing Mary Shelley's financial comfort following the death of her husband.

Not surprisingly, the Shelleys and their penchant for reform eventually proved to be irresistible subjects waiting for Peacock to translate into the medium of satiric fiction. With two satiric novels to his credit, Peacock was ready to try his skill once again. The result was *Nightmare Abbey*, which Peacock offered to the public in October 1818 for a price of 6s.6d. By far Peacock's least serious novel, *Nightmare Abbey* concerns the unhappy love interests of one Scythrop Glowry, as those interests take shape at various times in the persons of Miss Marionetta O'Carroll and Miss Celinda Toobad. One must approach with caution the idea that these characters represent deliberate portraits of Percy Shelley, his first wife, Harriet, and Mary Shelley. However, most readers of Peacock now agree with the editors of the Halliford Edition of Peacock's *Works*: "To regard Scythrop and his ladies as deliberate portraits, even of persons unknown to the public, would be as absurd as to ignore the resemblances."

The resemblances are, at the very least, thought provoking. Scythrop, whenever he is not moping in his tower over one woman or another (and he spends most of his time doing just that), gives vent to his "passion for reforming the world." He writes a pamphlet titled "Philosophical Gas; or, a Project for a General Illumination of the Human Mind." This "deep scheme for a thorough repair of the crazy fabric of human nature" sells a total of seven copies. Undaunted, Scythrop decides that the seven buyers, whoever they may be, shall be "the seven golden candle-

"A ghastly figure, shrouded in white drapery, with the semblance of a bloody turban on its head, entered and stalked slowly up the apartment"; frontispiece by J. Cawse for the revised, 1837 edition of Nightmare Abbey

sticks with which I will illuminate the world." One of these candlesticks turns out to be Celinda Toobad, whose sympathy for Scythrop's reform philosophy resembles Mary Shelley's sympathy for Shelley's ideas. Celinda, like Mary Shelley, also arrives in time to interrupt the progress of her philosopher's current love interest/commitment. When he is forced to be specific, Scythrop speaks (or hears others speak) on subjects by now familiar to Peacock's readers, including the education of women, modern versus ancient times, the importance of individual perception, and modern literature ("an intellectual blight . . . a delicious misanthropy and discontent, that demonstrates the nullity of virtue and energy"). This last subject is the special province of Mr. Flosky, a character who bears some resemblance to Coleridge and whose part in several lengthy conversations on life and literature is, by his own design (and Peacock's), quite unintelligible.

Perhaps because Scythrop does bear some resemblance to Shelley, the satire in *Nightmare Abbey* is never allowed to cut very deep. Although he might easily have done so, Peacock does not encourage his readers to take anyone in this novel very seriously. By a plan that seems to reverse the focus of *Melincourt*, Peacock turned his attention in *Nightmare Abbey* to the foibles of Scythrop, his ladies, and the rest of the guests at the Lincolnshire estate of Christopher Glowry. Mr. Flosky bears the brunt of Peacock's satire perhaps more than any other character, for he is exposed as a charlatan. He is forced to admit on more than one occasion that the darker, mysterious side of Romanticism is nothing more than a scheme concocted by Flosky so that he may gain advantage in the literary world. Yet the love story—not the reform theme—remains paramount through various plot incidents involving the primary and supporting characters. These incidents range from Mr. Asterias's search for a mermaid to the departure of Mr. Cypress (a character who resembles

Byron) for nowhere in particular in order "to seek." In short the seriousness of *Melincourt* is nowhere to be found in *Nightmare Abbey*. In its place one finds good-natured satire and comedy for the sake of laughter. Even Shelley, who read the novel in Italy, offered words of praise for its ability to amuse in a June 1819 letter to Peacock: "I am delighted with Nightmare Abbey. I think Scythrop a character admirably conceived & executed & I know not how to praise sufficiently the lightness chastity & strength of the language of the whole."

The periodical press responded with similar praise in the *Literary Gazette* (12 December 1818) and the *Monthly Review* (November 1819). Like Shelley, Byron found amusement in his caricature and asked Shelley to pass along his admiration to Peacock.

The literary world apparently liked the way Peacock wrote about its living practitioners in *Nightmare Abbey*, and Peacock continued to indulge his own sort of fascination with that world. In fact, during July 1818, Peacock began to look more closely at it and started to apply some shape to his thoughts with the "Essay on Fashionable Literature." This essay remained unfinished and was never published in Peacock's lifetime. The part that survives represents the beginning of what probably would have been a full-scale attack aimed at exposing the many forms of dishonesty upon which Peacock felt periodical writing was based. The final part of the surviving fragment is devoted to Peacock's rebuttal of an *Edinburgh Review* essay that had found fault, and very little else, in Coleridge's *Christabel* (1816). As the several caricatures of Coleridge elsewhere in Peacock's writings show, Peacock himself had found ideas and techniques not to his liking in Coleridge's writings. Nevertheless, the many reviews and quarterlies of Peacock's day represented, in his estimation, true enemies of truth and therefore irresistible targets.

While Peacock was preparing, and eventually laying aside, the "Essay on Fashionable Literature," he was also busy at work on his next novel, *Maid Marian* (1822). Even this project came to a halt, however, as Peacock's energies were diverted to two nonliterary pursuits. The first was his employment, commencing in January 1819, as assistant to the examiner at the India House, where he would continue to work his way up through positions of increasing responsibility until his retirement in 1856. Another assistant appointed in 1819 was the Utilitarian philosopher and historian of British India James Mill, then forty-six. Mill's son, John Stuart Mill, joined the India House in 1823.

Peacock's second nonliterary pursuit was his proposal of marriage to Jane Gryffydh, whom Peacock had met on his tour of Wales in 1811. Peacock had neither seen nor corresponded with his future wife since 1811, but the proposal, which he made by mail, was nevertheless accepted, and the couple was married on 20 March 1820. Peacock continued his employment at the India House, and in April 1821 he passed his probationary period and received an increase in salary from six hundred to eight hundred pounds per year. Literature was never far from his mind, and at various times Shelley called upon him to read and correct proofs of several poems.

Peacock, of course, felt that modern poetry needed more correction than a mere reading of proofs could provide, and in November 1820 his "The Four Ages of Poetry" appeared in the first (and last) number of *Ollier's Literary Miscellany*. Shelley escapes the ridicule leveled at "that egregious confraternity of rhymesters, known by the name of the Lake Poets," all of whom, maintains Peacock, are "studiously ignorant of history, society, and human nature." Peacock's thesis is that modern poetry abounds in everything poetically bad and sorely lacks everything poetically good. His argument that modern poetry is merely derivative, and badly so, is a clear challenge to the often-professed belief of the Romantic poets that their work represented something new. Shelley quickly answered Peacock's challenge with his "Defence of Poetry," but this essay, intended for the next number of *Ollier's Literary Miscellany*, did not appear in print until 1840.

In July 1821 Peacock's first child, Mary Ellen, was born. Peacock continued to pursue his work at the India House and soon returned to the writing project he had postponed in 1818. *Maid Marian*, Peacock's fourth novel, was published in April 1822 at a price of seven shillings. Based in part upon Joseph Ritson's anonymous *Robin Hood* (1795), *Maid Marian* was written, according to Peacock, in order to cast "oblique satire on all the oppressions that are done under the sun." The novel does not quite live up to its author's ambitious aims, but *Maid Marian* does provide readers with a brief look at an alternative society, however unattainable that society may be.

The story takes its direction from the main characters' involvement in two major pursuits. The first follows the Sheriff of Nottingham,

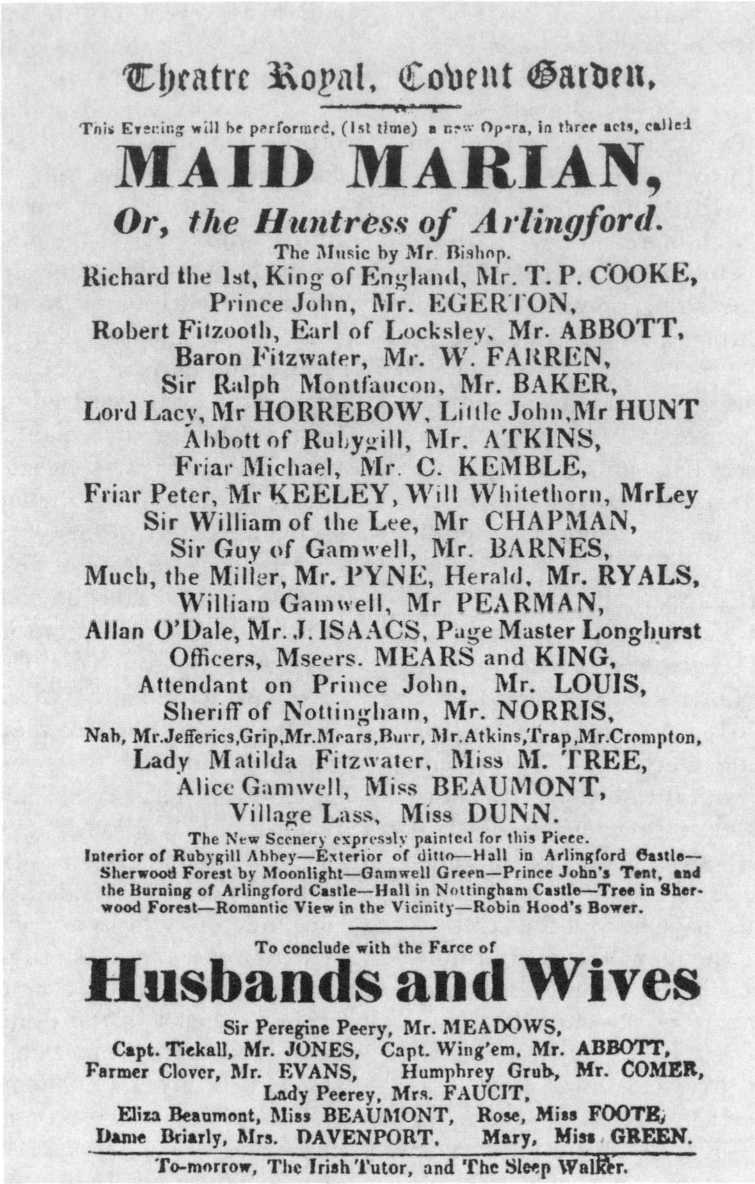

Theatre Royal, Covent Garden,

This Evening will be performed, (1st time) a new Opera, in three acts, called

MAID MARIAN,

Or, the Huntress of Arlingford.

The Music by Mr. Bishop.

Richard the 1st, King of England, Mr. T. P. COOKE,
Prince John, Mr. EGERTON,
Robert Fitzooth, Earl of Locksley, Mr. ABBOTT,
Baron Fitzwater, Mr. W. FARREN,
Sir Ralph Montfaucon, Mr. BAKER,
Lord Lacy, Mr HORREBOW, Little John, Mr HUNT
Abbott of Rubygill, Mr. ATKINS,
Friar Michael, Mr. C. KEMBLE,
Friar Peter, Mr KEELEY, Will Whitethorn, MrLey
Sir William of the Lee, Mr CHAPMAN,
Sir Guy of Gamwell, Mr. BARNES,
Much, the Miller, Mr. PYNE, Herald, Mr. RYALS,
William Gamwell, Mr PEARMAN,
Allan O'Dale, Mr. J. ISAACS, Page Master Longhurst
Officers, Mseers. MEARS and KING,
Attendant on Prince John, Mr. LOUIS,
Sheriff of Nottingham, Mr. NORRIS,
Nab, Mr.Jefferics,Grip,Mr.Mears,Burr, Mr.Atkins,Trap,Mr.Crompton,
Lady Matilda Fitzwater, Miss M. TREE,
Alice Gamwell, Miss BEAUMONT,
Village Lass, Miss DUNN.

The New Scenery expressly painted for this Piece.
Interior of Rubygill Abbey—Exterior of ditto—Hall in Arlingford Castle—Sherwood Forest by Moonlight—Gamwell Green—Prince John's Tent, and the Burning of Arlingford Castle—Hall in Nottingham Castle—Tree in Sherwood Forest—Romantic View in the Vicinity—Robin Hood's Bower.

To conclude with the Farce of

Husbands and Wives

Sir Peregine Peery, Mr. MEADOWS,
Capt. Tickall, Mr. JONES, Capt. Wing'em, Mr. ABBOTT,
Farmer Clover, Mr. EVANS, Humphrey Grub, Mr. COMER,
Lady Peerey, Mrs. FAUCIT,
Eliza Beaumont, Miss BEAUMONT, Rose, Miss FOOTE,
Dame Briarly, Mrs. DAVENPORT, Mary, Miss GREEN.

To-morrow, The Irish Tutor, and The Sleep Walker.

Playbill announcing the 3 December 1822 premiere of James Robinson Planché's operatic version of the novel in which Peacock attempted to cast "oblique satire on all the oppressions that are done under the sun"

Prince John, and Sir Ralph Montfaucon (an agent for King Henry) as they chase Robin Hood through Sherwood Forest in order to prosecute him for his various "crimes" against various authorities. The second pursuit follows Sir Ralph, Prince John, and Robin Hood as they vie for the hand of Matilda Fitzwater, daughter of the local baron, and known as Maid Marian in the society of Sherwood Forest. Only Robin Hood has a hope of obtaining this independent young lady, for Maid Marian, who is as skilled with words as she is with a bow and arrow, is not one to be intimidated by princes or barons, or by the power that they wrongly seek to exercise over others. She is, moreover, as Matilda Fitzwater, engaged to be married to her one true love, Robert, Earl of Huntingdon, also known as Robin Hood.

Peacock seems to be suggesting that individuals can and should try to emulate that which is noble in his two "outlaws," Robin and Marian, but he does so even while showing that their society is unrealistic and comically anarchistic. In other words, the foresters' laws provide a fitting retaliation to the various wrongdoings of the evil Prince John, but they are no answer to the complex problems facing any real society. The "principles" of their society have several obvious shortcomings. The foresters proclaim their government to be "legitimate" and follow this proclamation with another stating that all English laws, except for those that they deem convenient to obey, are null and void. Peacock's readers would have recognized that most tyrannous reigns begin with similar announcements. The foresters' system of "Equity" shows a similar susceptibility to abuse. They steal from the rich, but the poor receive only "a portion thereof as it may seem to us expedient to part with." In order to avoid all of the nastiness associated with stealing, the foresters "invite" their "guests" to pay for their dinners. The foresters' internal politics include unmistakable double meanings, for example: "In all cases a quorum of foresters shall constitute a court of equity, and as many as may be strong enough to manage the matter in hand shall constitute a quorum." Like other governments, the forest government has its share of pettiness: No one is allowed to call a forester by his or her given name, and anyone who does so must pay a fine or pay a fee for exemption from the rule to the friar, who has devised this plan for the purpose of enriching himself.

Although it is not "serious" satire in the sense that viable alternatives to social problems are offered, *Maid Marian* is an engaging and delightfully comic story, full of song and incident. The novel received favorable notices in the periodical press, and on 3 December 1822 an operatic version of the novel, augmented and scored by James Robinson Planché, was produced at Covent Garden theater. The opera ran for twenty-eight performances in fourteen months, received critical acclaim, and inspired an American production in 1824. The opera did not do well in America, however, and closed after one night at the Park Theatre in New York.

Peacock's enjoyment of the success of *Maid Marian* must have been tempered by a tragic event that occurred in the same year. On 8 July 1822 Percy Bysshe Shelley drowned off the coast of Italy. Peacock immediately began efforts to assist Mary Shelley in obtaining financial support from Shelley's father, Sir Timothy Shelley, who had always disapproved strongly of his son's manner of living. Peacock was successful in bringing the two parties to an agreement, despite their mutual dislike and many differences of opinion, receiving praise from both Mary and Sir Timothy for his efforts.

The 1820s were an especially active time for Peacock. In March 1823, a second daughter, Margaret Love Peacock, was born. In the same year Peacock purchased two cottages at Halliford and moved his young family and his mother there. The happy times at Halliford did not last long, however, for in January 1826, just two months short of her third birthday, Margaret Love Peacock died. Shortly afterward, the Peacocks adopted Mary Rosewell, a young girl from the neighborhood, but Jane Peacock's happiness proved to be only temporary. The death of Margaret triggered a mental breakdown in Jane Peacock that grew worse with time. She remained a nervous invalid until her death in 1851.

Despite these hardships, Peacock continued to prosper in his work at the India House. Through his colleague James Mill, he met the philosopher Jeremy Bentham, with whom he dined weekly for many years. Peacock also began writing literary review essays for publication in the *Westminster Review*. He would later write for several of the other leading journals on subjects ranging from steam navigation (one of his projects at the India House) to French literature. By the middle of the decade Peacock was at work on *Paper Money Lyrics*, his last collection of poetry, which was not published until 1837. During the years 1830-1834, Peacock busied himself with writing many operatic reviews for two periodicals, the *Globe* and the *Examiner*.

In February 1829 the *Literary Gazette* announced the impending publication of Peacock's next novel, *The Misfortunes of Elphin*, which soon afterward became available for purchase at the booksellers for a price of seven shillings. Very little is known about the composition history of the novel but the subject and tone suggest that it was written during the reform movement sweeping Britain in the late 1820s. The novel is concerned with political/social reform, but Peacock never forces the idea of nineteenth-century reform any further than the sixth-century Welsh setting will comfortably allow. In other words *The Misfortunes of Elphin* is a pleasant little story that is richly endowed with careful depictions of Welsh history and custom and that incidentally, though quite deliberately, uses the past in order to reveal some of the weaknesses of modern society.

Peacock's main target in this novel is negligent leadership. The primary offender is one Prince Seithenyn, high commissioner of royal embankment in the court of King Gwythno. One of Peacock's most memorable characters, Seithenyn is charged with maintaining the embankment, or sea wall, thereby ensuring the safety of King Gwythno's people so that they may continue to enjoy the privilege of keeping Gwythno happy and comfortable. Seithenyn, however, "executed [his post] as a personage so denominated might be expected to do: he drank the profits, and left the embankment to his deputies, who left it to their assistants, who left it to itself." The embankment, like the system of watch established to protect it, is quite rotten, and after years of neglect the wall collapses during a terrible storm. Hence the moral lesson of the novel: "The condition of the head, in a composite as in a simple body, affects the entire organization to the extremity of the tail." Peacock points to the modern application of his neatly imagined metaphor when he writes that he is "happy that our own public guardians are too virtuous to act or talk like Seithenyn. . . ."

When the governance of the flooded kingdom falls to Gwythno's more responsible son, Elphin, the society begins the process of reconstruction. Elphin is a king who provides for himself by fishing. His family consists of his queen, Angharad (who is Seithenyn's daughter), a foundling son named Taliesin, who becomes the best bard in Britain, and a daughter, Melanghel. They live a peaceful life until a pair of neighboring kings, who live by the principle that "might is right," begin to make trouble. Taliesin's virtuous actions—with the timely assistance of Seithenyn, still drunk after twenty years but now capable of doing good—and King Arthur himself rescue the kingdom. Good prevails, the virtuous are rewarded, and the evil are punished with a precision possible only in satiric romance.

The Misfortunes of Elphin received critical praise both for its satire and for its depiction of life in ancient Wales. The *Westminster Review* (April 1829), however, objected to Peacock's method of exalting the barbarous past over the enlightened present, a criticism that served to substantiate rather than to weaken Peacock's point in the novel. The *Cambrian Quarterly Magazine* (April 1829) had unreserved praise for the novel, calling it "the most entertaining book, if not the best, that has yet been published on the ancient customs and traditions of Wales." Despite the many favorable reviews, no subsequent edition of *The Misfortunes of Elphin* appeared in Peacock's lifetime.

While Peacock was engaged in writing opera reviews and other periodical essays, he was also composing his next novel, *Crotchet Castle*, published in 1831. Peacock's attention was, as always, divided among his several responsibilities, and while working on *Crotchet Castle* he was also studying the idea of regular steamship service between Great Britain and India (he submitted his findings to Parliament in 1834) and supervising the construction and fitting of steamships, several of which were designed to his specifications. Peacock evidently carried out his duties with great success, prompting one acquaintance to remark, "Mr. Peacock was meant for an Admiral."

As Carl Dawson has noted, *Crotchet Castle* marks Peacock's return "from the world of romance to the world of talk." The method of *Crotchet Castle* closely resembles the design of *Headlong Hall, Nightmare Abbey*, and *Melincourt*, with the arguments of characters (or caricatures) once more taking precedence over the love story, which once again ends with wedding bells. *Crotchet Castle*, like its predecessors, is the stage for a dozen or so "bubble-blowers," or characters who embody opinions, but Peacock's two main concerns in this novel are the unscrupulous business practices made possible by a paper-money economy and the problems associated with the "march of mind," one of the ideologies of the reform movement of the 1830s that promoted education for all.

The main combatants in the "march of mind" argument are the Reverend Dr. Folliott and the Scottish political economist Mr. MacQuedy, who holds the democratic position that "all minds are by nature alike. Education (which begins from their birth) makes them what they are." Hence the need for the diffusion of knowledge. The Reverend Dr. Folliott, another of Peacock's parsons who eats well and talks much, counters with his belief, borrowed from Pindar, that "All that is most excellent is so by nature." Mr. MacQuedy and the Reverend battle their way to rather equal shares of victory in this novel, in which the characters may be found "discussing every thing and settling nothing." The battles, not their outcomes, are of first importance in *Crotchet Castle*; yet Peacock does quite deliberately bring some of the controversies to predictable conclusions. Two medical men who promote unusual schemes involving inoculation become victims of their own love for experimentation, and in the conclusion to the paper-money theme young Crotchet experiences disappointment in love and the total collapse of his paper-money empire. Thus, on several occasions Peacock's charac-

Peacock at seventy-two (photograph by Maull & Co.)

ters end up in precisely the condition that their creator believed would best suit their counterparts in real life.

Crotchet Castle received a mixed critical response, the *Literary Gazette* (19 February 1831) calling Peacock "the wittiest writer in England" and the *Westminster Review* (July 1831) suggesting that Peacock redirect his attention to "the greater nuisances which prey upon the well-being of society." Peacock was doubtless pleased to see that his novel about controversies provided material for disagreement among the major periodicals of his day.

During the years following the publication of *Crotchet Castle* several changes took place in Peacock's life. In 1833 his mother died. Sarah Love Peacock had lived with her son and his family for many years, and Peacock had come to rely upon her as a literary collaborator. Her advice concerning his longer works was usually solicited and accepted. Peacock wrote little between 1834 and 1838, and published nothing from 1838 until 1851. Family cares and a promotion to the position of examiner at the India House allowed little time for literary pursuits. Happiness visited the family briefly in 1844 with Mary Ellen Peacock's marriage to Navy Lieutenant Edward Nicolls. Three months later, however, Nicolls was lost at sea and presumably drowned. Mary Ellen later gave birth to a daughter, Edith, who in later years assisted Peacock's first editors in assembling her grandfather's writings and reminiscences.

In 1851 Peacock, with the assistance of Mary Ellen, who in 1849 had married author George Meredith, wrote "Gastronomy and Civilization," which appeared in the December number of *Fraser's Magazine*. Shortly afterward Peacock published two sections of the three-part "Horae Dramticae," a series of reminiscences of the drama, in *Fraser's Magazine* (March and April 1852). Peacock approached the work with leisure, the final part appearing more than a year after his retirement from the India House in March 1856. Shortly after the publication of the last installment in October 1857, Mary Ellen, unhappy from the start with her marriage to Meredith, fled to Capri with painter Henry Wallis. Peacock never saw her again. In 1861, having returned to England alone, she died. Peacock did not attend her funeral.

In 1858, inspired by the publication of what he considered erroneous accounts of Shelley's life, Peacock began working on the periodical pieces known collectively as the "Memoirs of Percy Bysshe Shelley," the first of which appeared in the June 1858 issue of *Fraser's Magazine*. Peacock then decided to suspend work on his memoir until Thomas Jefferson Hogg completed his work on Shelley's life, but the furor raised over Hogg's work persuaded Peacock to continue his project. Peacock's account of Shelley's life—which continued in the January and March 1860 issues of *Fraser's*, with a "Supplementary Noticc" in March 1862—is drawn largely from personal knowledge and is considered by most scholars to be objective, yet guarded in its treatment of Shelley's more irrational acts and ideas.

Peacock's main literary interest at this time was *Gryll Grange*, which appeared serially from April through December 1860 in *Fraser's Magazine*. This novel, which was to be Peacock's last, was published as a book in February 1861. *Gryll Grange* closely resembles Peacock's other novels in both its spirit and its design, but the satire and the story are developed more gradually than in any of his earlier novels. *Gryll Grange* also shows an approach to character different (and some believe more realistic) from that in Peacock's previous fiction. The main characters, and many of the minor ones, are multidimensional in ways that their earlier counterparts are not: they enjoy full lives that have nothing to do with their opinions on social matters. In other words, the characters are free to live day to day *and* to engage in "discussion[s] on everything that presents itself."

In this novel most of Peacock's characters choose to devote the greater share of their energies to daily living, which as in many of the earlier novels, means the pursuit of love. *Gryll Grange* provides the stage for nine weddings, the majority of them arranged by Peacock's most favorably presented clergyman, the Reverend Dr. Theophilus Opimian. The closest that Peacock comes in his novels to self-portraiture, Reverend Opimian sincerely, and sensibly, speaks out against the pollution of the Thames, Parliamentary buffoonery, the craze for lectures on everything, "bank bubbles," "societies of all sorts, for teaching everybody everything," and many other matters, "however multiform, multifarious, and multitudinous." No lover of anything new, the Reverend prefers those ideas and things that have "an authority two thousand years old." He is not, however, consumed by his opinions, nor does he force his ideas upon his listeners the way a less carefully drawn spokesman might do. He is, for these reasons, a highly effective character—engaging his listeners without forcing them, and entertaining them without acting the fool.

The main action of *Gryll Grange* concerns the courtship of Miss Niphet, a shy but engaging young woman, and Lord Curryfin, a lecturer on fish (and therefore a target of Peacock's satire) who comes to his senses and shuts his mouth toward the end of the novel. The parallel courtship of Miss Gryll, the niece of Squire Gryll, and Algernon Falconer, a scholar who holds some strange ideas but who nevertheless enjoys his author's approval, rounds out the plot. Complications arise briefly when Lord Curryfin must decide between Miss Niphet and Miss Gryll (his affections originally leaned toward Miss Gryll), but everything works out in the end for both couples, and for the seven young virgins, former attendants of Mr. Falconer, and their affianced.

Before the nine weddings take place, Peacock has his characters stage an "Aristophanic comedy" during the Christmas holidays at Squire Gryll's estate. The play is a highly entertaining look at modern civilization seen largely through the eyes of Gryllus, a mythological character who prefers life as a pig to life as a human. Gryllus, taken on a tour of the modern world, finds that "improvements"—and here the reader is treated to a discussion of the social flaws traditionally invoked by Peacock—have made life worse. The play, a composition in verse, is a delightful piece of writing that treats many of Peacock's favorite topics in a new and imaginative way.

Gryll Grange received favorable notices in the *Spectator* (2 March 1861) and in the *Saturday Review* (16 March 1861), the latter commenting on the range of Peacock's learning as reflected in the characters' discussions and in the many explanatory footnotes. Peacock wrote *Gryll Grange* during an active period in which he also began, but eventually set aside, at least three prose tales. His last published work was the prose translation (1862) of an anonymous Italian play of the 1530s, *Gl' Ingannati*, which appeared in 1862. Peacock wrote nothing after this date, preferring to

Peacock in 1858 (portrait by Henry Wallis; National Portrait Gallery, London)

spend his days quietly, and preferably without visitors, in his library at Lower Halliford. He was troubled in his last years by an intestinal ailment. He died on 23 January 1866 and was buried in the New Cemetery at Shepperton.

An early discussion of Peacock's work—a review of *Nightmare Abbey* published in the *Literary Gazette* for December 1818—enunciates a concern that is still voiced by Peacock's readers and critics: "It would be difficult to say what his books are," wrote the anonymous reviewer, "for they are neither romances, novels, tales, nor treatises, but a mixture of all these combined." Yet Peacock remains important today not only because his novels are among the best of their type, but because the issues they address are universal. To read Peacock's best novels is to be reminded of the universality of human action and thought and of how susceptible to ridicule and/or revision the supposed triumphs of humanity really are.

Bibliographies:

Bill Read, "The Critical Reputation of Thomas Love Peacock," Ph.D. dissertation, Boston University, 1959;

Read, "Thomas Love Peacock: An Enumerative Bibliography," *Bulletin of Bibliography*, 24 (September-December 1963): 32-34; 24 (January-April 1964): 70-72; 24 (May-August 1964): 88-91;

William S. Ward, "Contemporary Reviews of Thomas Love Peacock: A Supplementary List for the Years 1805-1820," *Bulletin of Bibliography*, 25 (January-April 1967): 35.

Biographies:

Carl Van Doren, *The Life of Thomas Love Peacock* (London: J. M. Dent / New York: Dutton, 1911);

Felix Felton, *Thomas Love Peacock* (London: Allen & Unwin, 1973).

References:

Augustus H. Able, *George Meredith and Thomas Love Peacock: A Study in Literary Influence* (New York: Phaeton, 1970);

Bryan Burns, *The Novels of Thomas Love Peacock* (Beckenham, Kent: Croom Helm, 1985);

Marilyn Butler, *Peacock Displayed: A Satirist in His Context* (Boston: Routledge & Kegan Paul, 1979);

Olwen W. Campbell, *Thomas Love Peacock* (London: Arthur Barker, 1953; New York: Roy, 1953);

Benvenuto Cellini, *Thomas Love Peacock* (Rome: Edizioni Cremonese, 1937);

John K. Crabbe, "The Harmony of Her Mind: Peacock's Emancipated Women," *Tennessee Studies in Literature*, 23 (1978): 75-86;

Carl Dawson, *His Fine Wit: A Study of Thomas Love Peacock* (London: Routledge & Kegan Paul, 1970; Berkeley: University of California Press, 1970);

Dawson, *Thomas Love Peacock* (London: Routledge & Kegan Paul, 1968);

A. Martin Freeman, *Thomas Love Peacock: A Critical Study* (London: Martin Secker, 1911; New York: Mitchell Kennerley, 1911);

Keats-Shelley Memorial Bulletin, special Peacock issue, edited by Timothy Webb and Peter Garside, no. 36 (1985);

Lionel Madden, *Thomas Love Peacock* (London: Evans, 1967);

Jean-Jacques Mayoux, *Un Epicurien anglais: Thomas Love Peacock* (Paris: Nizet & Bastard, 1933);

Howard Mills, *Peacock: His Circle and His Age* (Cambridge: Cambridge University Press, 1969);

James Mulvihill, *Thomas Love Peacock* (Boston: Twayne, 1987);

Lorna Sage, ed., *Peacock: The Satirical Novels, A Casebook* (London: Macmillan, 1976);

J. I. M. Stewart, *Thomas Love Peacock*, Writers and Their Work, no. 156 (London: Published for the British Council and the National Book League by Longmans, Green, 1963).

Papers:

The major collections of Peacock's papers are in the British Library; the Bodleian Library, Oxford; and the Berg Collection and the Pforzheimer Library at the New York Public Library. Other papers are in the Archives of the Royal Literary Fund and at the Princeton University Library.

John William Polidori

(7 September 1795 - 27 August 1821)

Andrew M. Cooper
University of Texas at Austin

BOOKS: *Disputatio Medica Inauguralis, Quaedam de Morbo, Oneirodynia Dicto, Complectens* (Edinburgh: Excudebat Robertus Allan, 1815);

An Essay upon the Source of Positive Pleasure (London: Published by Longman, Hurst, Rees, Orme & Brown, 1818);

The Vampyre; a Tale (London: Printed for Sherwood, Neely & Jones, 1819; Albany, N.Y.: Printed by E. & E. Hosford, 1819; Boston: Munroe & Francis, 1819; Philadelphia: M. Thomas, 1819);

Ernestus Berchtold; or, the Modern Oedipus. a Tale (London: Printed for Longman, Hurst, Rees, Orme & Brown, 1819);

Ximenes, the Wreath, and Other Poems (London: Longman, Hurst, Rees, Orme & Brown, 1819);

The Fall of the Angels, a Sacred Poem (London: Printed by R. & A. Taylor for John Warren, 1821);

Sketches Illustrative of the Manners and Costumes of France, Switzerland, and Italy, plates by Richard Bridgens and text by Polidori (London: Baldwin, Cradock & Joy and Hatchard & Son, 1821);

The Diary of Dr. John William Polidori, 1816, Relating to Byron, Shelley, etc., edited by William Michael Rossetti (London: Elkin Mathews, 1911).

OTHER: "On Punishment of Death," *The Pamphleteer*, 8 (1816): 28-304.

When John William Polidori, then twenty years old and fresh from medical school, accepted George Gordon, Lord Byron's invitation to accompany him as personal physician on a tour of the Continent early in 1816, he had just the opportunity he needed to launch his literary career. According to Polidori's diary, John Murray, Byron's publisher and sometime friend, had secretly offered Polidori five hundred pounds to keep a journal recording everything about the trip—a project which, if adroitly managed, could enable Polidori to appear before the avid English public not as a Byron-monger but as a fit friend for his celebrated companion. Five months later, Polidori's hypersensitivity and resentfulness led Byron to dismiss him. Yet in the meantime he had participated in the famous ghost-story contest that resulted in Mary Shelley's *Frankenstein* (1818) and in an unfinished story by Byron that Polidori took over and rewrote as *The Vampyre* (1819). This novella, a typical *Schauerroman* ("shudder novel") that literalizes elements presented more obliquely in many other Romantic Gothic writings—including Samuel Taylor Coleridge's *Christabel*, which Byron recited the day after the ghost-story contest was begun—has gradually achieved much the same mythic status as *Frankenstein*.

As for the doctor's diary of his Continental tour, it remained unpublished until 1911, when his nephew William Michael Rossetti edited it with extensive commentary. Unfortunately, Rossetti had to work from the bowdlerized copy made by his maiden aunt Charlotte Polidori, who had destroyed the original manuscript after Rossetti had expressed interest in it some forty years earlier. Rossetti bravely affirms that the authority of her copy, which he says he supplemented with his own recollections of some of the deleted passages, "is only a shade less safe than that of the original." Polidori was no James Boswell (and Byron no Samuel Johnson), but the diary has served as an invaluable source of anecdotal information about Byron and the Shelleys during their period of first acquaintance.

In his own day Polidori remained obscure. His second novel, *Ernestus Berchtold; or, the Modern Oedipus* (1819; the subtitle deliberately echoes *Frankenstein; or The Modern Prometheus*), went largely unnoticed. His collection of verse *Ximenes, the Wreath, and Other Poems* (also published in 1819) was respectfully reviewed but soon forgotten. Polidori committed suicide by drinking poison at the age of twenty-five. The coroner's jury politely returned a verdict of "Died by the visitation of God," but Byron's diagnosis, reported by

John William Polidori, circa 1816 (portrait by F. G. Gainsford; National Portrait Gallery, London)

his biographer Thomas Moore, is probably more accurate: "It seems that disappointment was the cause of this rash act."

Polidori was born on 7 September 1795, the eldest son of Gaetano Polidori, a Tuscan scholar and translator who had settled in England, where he married an English lady, Anna Maria Pierce. Their daughter Frances became the mother of Dante Gabriel, William Michael, and Christina Rossetti. Polidori showed considerable precocity.

After attending a school in Somerstown and the Roman Catholic Ampleforth College in Yorkshire, Polidori studied medicine at the University of Edinburgh and received his doctorate at the exceptionally early age of nineteen. Apparently Polidori planned to become a man of letters like his father; in his diary (25 April 1816) he admitted that he was "ambitious for literary distinction." According to W. M. Rossetti, Polidori had completed the dramas *Ximenes, Boadicea*, and *Cajetan* ("Gaetano" in Italian) even before graduating from medical school. It seems he carried the manuscripts abroad and, with a characteristic mixture of naiveté, ambition, and conceit, showed one to Byron and the Shelleys for approval. "All agreed [it] was worth nothing," he candidly recorded in his diary (15 June 1816).

Unfortunately for Polidori, such was the unvarying response with which the Byron-Shelley circle greeted his literary efforts. In 1817 he completed a "medical tragedy"—possibly *Ximenes* with its similarity to Byron's *Manfred*—very likely the same drama he had shown Byron while working on it in Switzerland the previous summer. He submitted this work to the publisher John Murray, who forwarded it to Byron requesting "a *delicate*

Gaetano Polidori, father of the novelist and maternal grandfather of Dante Gabriel, Christina, and William Michael Rossetti (portrait by Dante Gabriel Rossetti, 1848; from William Michael Rossetti, ed., Dante Gabriel Rossetti: His Family Letters, *1895)*

declension." But Byron was merely provoked by Murray's italics, and perhaps also by his attempt to fob off an awkward situation. (Polidori may have believed that Murray's offer for the diary reflected an interest in his talent. Regardless, a rejection coming from Byron, who had already dismissed him, would hardly be easier to take.) The poet wrote back to Murray on 21 August 1817, enclosing the hilarious "Epistle to Murray," a rejection meant to be spoken by Murray himself:

Dear Doctor—I have read your play
Which is a good one in its way
Purges the eyes and moves the bowels
And drenches handkerchiefs like towels
With tears that in a flux of Grief,
Afford hysterical relief
To shatter'd nerves and quickened pulses
Which your catastrophe convulses.

Although we may agree with Byron that the melodramatic excesses of Polidori's dramas are thoroughly conventional, we need not accept the Byron-Shelley circle's blanket condescension toward him. Byron's letters, Mary Shelley's recollections in her 1831 introduction to *Frankenstein,* and the published anecdotes of Byron's friends Thomas Moore and Thomas Medwin all depict Polidori as a comical bungler. Clearly he played the role of odd man out among a tight little group of exiles. As Polidori was reminded over and over again that he was no match for the genius of his somewhat more experienced companions—he wrote in his diary (28 May 1816) that he felt "like a star in the halo of the moon, invisible"—the very impetuosity, candor, and ingenuousness that had made him congenial turned into petulance, querulousness, and jealousy.

The two men began their tour from Byron's London quarters on the morning of 23 April 1816, barely escaping the bailiffs who arrived to seize everything Byron left behind. Polidori's diary shows at the outset an aspect of self-parody that gradually wanes as the entries become more perfunctory and sporadic. On 26 April, the day they arrived in Ostend, he wrote a Wertherian description of how he had watched the "stern white cliffs" of Dover recede the day before, all the while "thinking on her who bade me join her remembrance with the last sight of my native soil." (The lady is unknown, if she ever existed; the writer's melodramatic pose resembles that of Byron's Juan at the beginning of Canto II of *Don Juan*, 1819.) Polidori went on to tell how, upon arriving at their hotel in Ostend, "Lord Byron fell like a thunderbolt upon the chambermaid," and Polidori reported "that I got a dreadful headache from the smell of paint in my bedroom, and that the tea was perfumed." The next day he noted: "Obliged to buy two books I did not want, because I let a quarto fall upon a fine girl's head while looking at her eyes." Any awe Polidori felt toward his patron soon wore off, and he wrote with ominous overconfidence to his sister Frances on 2 May, "I am very pleased with Lord Byron I am with him on the footing of an equal everything alike. . . ." One doubts if Byron ever reciprocated the attitude of his employee. As they continued their dilatory tour through the Low Countries along the Rhine to the borders of Switzerland, finally reaching Geneva, their destination, Polidori glutted his romantic appetite on the Gothic churches and cathedrals of Ghent, Antwerp, Brussels, and Cologne, and on the paintings of Nicolas Poussin, Claude Lorrain, Peter Paul Rubens, and Anthony Van Dyck. In a 1 May letter to Augusta Leigh, Byron confessed, "as for churches, and pictures, I have stared at them till my brains are like a guide-book," but Polidori made special arrangements to see private collections and continued his visits to picture galleries undeterred by a bout of feverish "Headache, vertigo, tendency to fainting, etc." (15 May). Indeed, Rossetti commented that Polidori "had some considerable native gift in sketching faces and figures with lifelike expression"—as one sees in the prose of his *Sketches Illustrative of the Manners and Costumes of France, Switzerland, and Italy* (1821). The views of the Rhine afforded at Koblentz, Moselle, and Mainz—"Scenes increasing in sublimity"—and, later, the Swiss and Italian Alps, would supply important backdrops to *The Vampyre* and *Ernestus Berchtold.*

The two travelers finally arrived at Lake Geneva on 25 May and settled at the Hôtel d'Angleterre in Sécheron. There they stayed until they moved into the elegant Villa Diodati on 10 June. Both men were excited at treading for the first time "classic ground" associated with the likes of Napoleon Bonaparte, Jean-Jacques Rousseau, Voltaire, and Anne-Louise-Germaine, Madame de Staël. Polidori enjoyed the added fillip of knowing that he alone shared the experience with his famous companion: "I *rode* first with L[ord] B[yron] upon the field of Waterloo; *walked* first to see Churchill's tomb; *bathed and rowed* first on the Leman Lake" (26 May)—but not for long. Claire Clairmont, Mary Shelley's stepsister and Byron's former lover, had been determinedly watching the hotel register. As soon as the travelers arrived she ambushed Byron with billets-doux, contrived a meeting, and overcame his lassitude. They resumed their affair. At the same time Byron struck up a friendship with Percy Shelley. Polidori's efforts to keep Byron for himself increasingly interfered with everybody's plans, making him a nuisance. After a few days reading and rowing on the lake amid the idyllic scenery, Polidori reported the first sign of trouble in his diary entry for 4 June: "Went on the lake with Shelley and Lord Byron, who quarrelled with me." This may have been either of two quarrels later related by Thomas Moore, who reported that Polidori, beaten by Shelley in a sailing match, challenged him to a duel. The pacifist Shelley merely laughed, but Byron, an excellent shot, offered to stand in for his new friend any time; Polidori could only sulk. In another of Moore's stories Polidori, while rowing, accidentally struck Byron on the kneecap with his oar. To Byron's carefully controlled response, "Be so kind, Polidori, another time, to take more care, for you have hurt me very much," the doctor alleg-

Villa Diodati, on Lake Geneva, the setting for the June 1815 ghost-story contest that was the genesis of Mary Shelley's Frankenstein *and Polidori's* The Vampyre

edly replied: "I am glad of it. I am glad to see you can suffer pain." Indeed, Polidori seems to have taken Byron's sangfroid as a personal reproach. Byron finally broke with him in September, fed up "with the eternal nonsense—& *tracasseries*—& emptiness—& ill-humour—& vanity of that young person" (letter to Murray, 17 June 1817). In justice, however, Byron added, "he has some talent—& is a man of honour,—and has dispositions of amendment. . . ." They parted amicably, and Polidori received seventy pounds for his services. As he explained in a 20 September 1816 letter to his father, "There was no immediate cause, but a continued series of slight quarrels. I believe the fault, if any, has been on my part; I am not accustomed to have a master, and therefore my conduct was not free and easy." According to Moore, Byron later commented that Polidori was "exactly the kind of person to whom, if he fell overboard, one would hold out a straw, to know if the adage be true that drowning men catch at straws."

Polidori continued his tour of Switzerland on foot, passing through Switzerland into Italy. Along the way he learned of the barbarism of the French invasion of 1793, the heroism of the Valaisians, and their betrayal by their Austrian allies. These scenes and events were used extensively in *Ernestus Berchtold*, which concerns the love affair and marriage of a young Swiss patriot to a lady ultimately discovered to be his sister. Early in October, Polidori reached Austrian-occupied Milan, where he frequented the opera and theater and became a regular visitor of the salons, meeting among others the poet Vincenzo Monti and the novelist Marie-Henri Beyle (Stendhal). But he was forced to quit the city when he provoked a ruckus while at the theater with Byron and his friend John Cam Hobhouse, who were passing through town. An Austrian grenadier's hat obstructed Polidori's view; with typical lack of circumspection, he complained vehemently, and was thrown into the guardhouse, where his nationality was insulted. He was released only through Byron's lordly intervention. Polidori never forgot this insult to his Italian blood. Ordered to leave town within twenty-four hours, he reported, "I got into the coach with only 5 louis in my pocket, . . . and left Milan with rage and grief so struggling in my breast that tears often started in my eyes, and all I could think of was revenge . . . , and a hope that before I left Italy there might be a rising to which I might join myself " (30 October).

Polidori's plan had been to visit relatives in Arezzo and possibly establish a medical practice in Florence or Rome. His diary ends in Pisa on 30 December 1816. Having become a superficial, often acerbic record of the dozens of new acquaintances he was making, it was no longer serving much purpose. In Pisa, Polidori served as physician to at least three members of the English colony there, all of whom—including Francis North, fourth Earl of Guilford—died under his care. Having made his way to Venice, he returned to England in April 1817 as traveling physician to Frederick North, the new earl of Guilford, and his sister-in-law, widow of the fourth earl (they survived the trip).

Polidori set up medical practice in Norwich, where he renewed his acquaintance with Elizabeth Martineau and her fifteen-year-old sister, Harriet. (In 1815, just after completing his medical degree, he had fallen in love with Elizabeth, but his affections had been unrequited.)

A serious concussion suffered in September 1817 hampered Polidori's attempts to establish his practice and his literary career. The *Norfolk Chronicle and Norwich Gazette* (20 September 1817) reported that Polidori was unconscious for four or five days. D. L. Macdonald asserts that he "almost certainly suffered some brain damage" and points out that his longer works, with one exception, were written or conceived before the injury. The one exception was *An Essay upon the Source of Positive Pleasure*, inspired by the accident and published in 1818. By August 1820 Polidori had abandoned both his literary and his medical careers and had decided to study law, enrolling at Lincoln's Inn in London on 7 November. His depression continued, and in less than a year he died by his own hand.

One senses his depression in *An Essay upon the Source of Positive Pleasure*, which, notwithstanding its title, dwells on the misfortunes of human life: "We come into the world weeping and we pass from the bed of sickness to our tomb." Doubtless thinking of his treatment by Byron, Polidori emphasizes how the aristocracy, instead of considering the talented but poor man as an equal, "are tempted by their pride, to insult him, and show the superiority of rank, by cutting slights and insolent sarcasms, which they may after repent, but cannot persuade themselves to correct." *Ximenes, the Wreath, and Other Poems*, one of three books he published in 1819, similarly reveals a note of personal desperation beneath its sentimental veneer. Its prefatory note, "To My Book," avers, "Thou art my only hope!" even as it goes on to say that "peace is found alone in death." The volume closes with a sonnet proclaiming its futility: "Farewell! Farewell! the hopes I've built on thee / Will fail too like the rest."

The Vampyre, however, was a major success. And yet its popularity may have only heightened Polidori's morbid feelings: when it first appeared, in the 1 April 1819 issue of the *New Monthly Magazine*, it was labeled "A Tale by Lord Byron." This attribution was omitted in the pamphlet edition of the story printed for Sherwood, Neely, and Jones at about the same time, but despite Byron's disclaimers and Polidori's protestations, Byron continued to be thought the author. French and German versions that appeared the same year were advertised as "a translation from the English of Lord Byron," and the story was included in editions of Byron's poetry published in Frankfurt in 1820 and in Zwickau in 1821, and also in the many Continental editions of Byron's work later in the century. A wildly popular stage adaptation was produced in Paris on 13 June 1820, and a "free translation" of this melodrama by James Robinson Planché was performed at the English Opera House on 9 August. Although his book went through six printings in two years, Polidori received only thirty pounds from Henry Colburn, publisher of the *New Monthly Magazine*.

This minor scandal over the story's true author probably put another nail in the coffin of Polidori's literary hopes. Evidently the confusion originated with a woman whom Polidori had met shortly after leaving Byron in 1816. This woman—who has sometimes been identified as Catherine, Countess Bruce, or a Madame Brélaz, whom he had met at the Bruces' Geneva salon—had told him she doubted if anybody could work up Byron's seemingly unpromising materials into a finished tale, thereby providing Polidori with his long-sought opportunity of competing successfully against his rival. Polidori left the manuscript in her keeping, and she or one of her friends sent it to Colburn, probably with an ambiguous letter implying the author was Byron. In repudiation, Byron then published his rather different, unfinished version of the story as "A Fragment" at the end of his *Mazeppa* in June 1819. Although John Murray made inquiries and reported to Byron on 27 April 1819 that Colburn seemed to be responsible for the confusion, some of Byron's friends believed Polidori had connivingly exploited Byron's name in order to further sales of the book. They thus secured his Victorian reputation as a liar and a leech. Yet much as Polidori needed money, he desired fame far more, and would not likely have traded the one for the other. In fact, Polidori appears to have acted in good faith. As he stated in a letter that Colburn agreed to publish in the May 1819 issue of the *New Monthly Magazine*: "though *the groundwork* is certainly Lord Byron's, its developement is mine. . . ."

In her retrospective account of the ghost-story contest, published as the introduction to the 1831 edition of *Frankenstein*, Mary Shelley claimed that "Poor Polidori had some terrible idea about a skull-headed lady, who was so punished for peeping through a keyhole—what to see I forgot—something very shocking and wrong of course; but . . . he did not know what to do with her. . . ." Evidently this story was abandoned, but Macdonald suggests that it may have been the germ for *Ernestus Berchtold*. Polidori himself gave an outline of Byron's projected plot for his story in the introduction to *Ernestus Berchtold*. Two friends travel from England to Greece, where the older one dies, but not before obtaining from his companion an oath to keep his death secret; returning home, the survivor is startled to find his companion "moving about in society," and is "horrified at finding that he made love to his former friend's sister." Byron's "Fragment" breaks off with the older man's death abroad. Beyond filling in the outline, Polidori contributes several elements that have become standard features of vampire fiction. His Lord Ruthven epitomizes the outcast villain-hero of Gothic fiction: gaunt, pallid, and basilisk-eyed, he is devoid of compassion yet strangely attractive. Ruthven is, literally, a lady killer, and he especially relishes virgins. Apparently he does not suck men's blood and never directly threatens his younger friend, Aubrey; yet there is a characteristically vampiric exchange of energy between the two men. As Aubrey sickens with the realization of what Ruthven is, the vampire grows increasingly healthy, but once Aubrey recovers, Ruthven reverts to his former emaciated state. Before dying, Ruthven arranges with local robbers to have his corpse dragged to a nearby mountain where it will be "exposed to the first cold ray of the moon." The plot's weak link is Aubrey's refusal to save his sister from marrying a vampire by revealing Ruthven's identity despite his oath of silence. On the other hand, considering that the story's main focus is the relationship between the two men, Aubrey's perverse adherence to his vow effectively masks the homoerotic side of their relationship by sustaining their rivalry for a female love object. There is much in this relationship that resembles the *ingénu* Polidori's relationship to his older, world-weary traveling companion of 1816.

It is unlikely that *The Vampyre* would have achieved such popularity, particularly on the Continent, had the true author's identity been recognized (Johann Wolfgang von Goethe, for one, claimed it was Byron's best work ever). Byron himself had already exploited vampire lore in his best-selling *Giaour* (1813). Nevertheless, *The Vampyre* remains the first tale in English explicitly about vampires. By emphasizing local color and folklore, Polidori's realism contributed to the general shift of Gothic fiction away from remote medieval locales toward plausible contemporary settings in which the supernatural is no longer explained away in the manner of Ann Radcliffe but is confronted in all its irrationality, hence the influence of *The Vampyre* on writers such as Sheridan Le Fanu and Bram Stoker. Polidori's greatest literary contribution, however, was once again to a work that would not bear his name. The day before the ghost-story contest, 15 June, Polidori made an intriguing entry in his diary: "[Percy] Shelley and I had a conversation about principles—whether man was to be thought merely an instrument." This was a subject on which Polidori was the resident expert: his medical thesis had been on somnambulism (a phenomenon closely connected with the new pseudoscience of mesmerism, thought transfer, and "animal magnetism"). Even if he somehow resisted his propensity to show off his knowledge, this conversation very likely makes the much-maligned doctor a crucial catalyst of Mary Shelley's *Frankenstein*.

Biography:

D. L. Macdonald, *Poor Polidori: A Critical Biography of the Author of* The Vampyre (Toronto, Buffalo & London: University of Toronto Press, 1991).

References:

Kenneth A. Bruffee, "Elegiac Romance," *College English*, 32 (January 1971): 465-476;

Robert R. Harson, "A Profile of John Polidori with a New Edition of *The Vampyre*," Ph.D. dissertation, Ohio University, 1966;

Mario Praz, "Chapter II: The Metamorphoses of Satan," in his *The Romantic Agony*, translated by Angus Davidson, second edition, corrected (London: Oxford University Press, 1970), pp. 55-94;

James Rieger, "Dr. Polidori and the Genesis of *Frankenstein*," in his *The Mutiny Within: The Heresies of Percy Bysshe Shelley* (New York: Braziller, 1967), pp. 237-247;

Montague Summers, *The Vampire, His Kith and Kin* (London: Kegan Paul, Trench, Trübner, 1928);

James B. Twitchell, *The Living Dead: A Study of the Vampire in Romantic Literature* (Durham, N.C.: Duke University Press, 1981), pp. 74-81, 104-115;

Henry R. Viets, "The London Editions of Polidori's *The Vampyre*," *Papers of the Bibliographical Society of America*, 63 (Second Quarter 1969): 83-103.

Papers:

Most of Polidori's papers, including Charlotte Polidori's transcription of his diary, are in the University of British Columbia Library. A few of his letters are at the British Library and the John Murray archives. Copies of his books with marginalia by Polidori are in the University of British Columbia Library and the Houghton Library, Harvard University.

Anna Maria Porter

(1780 - 21 September 1832)

Michael Adams
Albright College

BOOKS: *Artless Tales,* 2 volumes (London: Printed & sold for the author by L. Wayland, 1793, 1795);

Walsh Colville: or a Young Man's First Entrance into Life (London: Lee & Hurst / T. C. Jones, 1797);

Octavia: A Novel, 3 volumes (London: Longman & Rees, 1798);

The Lake of Killarney: A Novel (3 volumes, London: Printed for T. N. Longman & O. Rees, 1804; 2 volumes, Philadelphia: Printed for Thomas De Silver, 1810);

A Sailor's Friendship, and a Soldier's Love (2 volumes, London: Longman, Hurst, Rees & Orme, 1805; 1 volume, Baltimore: Printed & sold by Warner & Hanna, 1810);

The Hungarian Brothers (3 volumes, London: Printed by C. Stower for Longman, Hurst, Rees & Orme, 1807; 2 volumes, Philadelphia: Published by Bradford & Inskeep / New York: Inskeep & Bradford, printed by Robert Carr, 1809);

Don Sebastian, or the House of Braganza: An Historical Romance (4 volumes, London: Printed for Longman, Hurst, Rees & Orme, 1809; 2 volumes, Philadelphia: Printed by A. Small for M. Carey, 1810);

Ballad Romances, and Other Poems (London: Printed for Longman, Hurst, Rees, Orme & Brown, 1811; Philadelphia: M. Carey / Boston: Wells & Lilly, 1816);

Tales of Pity on Fishing, Shooting, and Hunting, Intended to Inculcate in the Mind of Youth, Sentiments of Humanity Toward the Brute Creation (London: Printed for J. Harris, 1814);

The Recluse of Norway (4 volumes, London: Longman, Hurst, Rees, Orme & Brown, 1814; 2 volumes, Philadelphia: A. Small, 1815; New York: Printed for I. Riley, 1815);

The Knight of St. John: A Romance (3 volumes, London: Printed for Longman, Hurst, Rees, Orme & Brown, 1817; 2 volumes, Philadelphia: Thomas, 1817; New York: J. Eastburn, 1817);

The Fast of St. Magdalen: A Romance (3 volumes, London: Printed for Longman, Hurst, Rees, Orme & Brown, 1818; 2 volumes, Boston: Wells & Lilly, 1819; New York: W. B. Gilley & C. Wiley, 1819);

The Village of Mariendorpt: A Tale (4 volumes, London: Longman, Hurst, Rees, Orme & Brown, 1821; New York, 1821);

Roche-Blanche, or the Hunters of the Pyrenees (3 volumes, London: Longman, Hurst, Rees, Orme & Brown, 1822; 2 volumes, Boston: Wells & Lilly, 1822);

Honor O'Hara: A Novel (3 volumes, London: Longman, Rees, Orme, Brown & Green, 1826; 2 volumes, New York: J. & J. Harper, 1827);

Tales Round a Winter Hearth, 2 volumes, by Anna Maria Porter and Jane Porter (London: Longman, Rees, Orme, Brown & Green, 1826);

Coming Out; and The Field of the Forty Footsteps, 3 volumes [volumes 1 and 2: *Coming Out,* by Anna Maria Porter; volume 3: *The Field of the Forty Footsteps,* by Jane Porter] (London: Printed for Longman, Rees, Orme, Brown & Green, 1828);

The Barony (3 volumes, London: Longman, Rees, Orme, Brown & Green, 1830; 2 volumes, New York: J. & J. Harper, 1830).

PLAY PRODUCTION: *The Fair Fugitives,* London, Theatre Covent Garden, 16 May 1803.

Though a popular novelist in her day, Anna Maria Porter, unlike her older sister Jane, neither deserved nor achieved lasting fame. Jane Porter's *The Scottish Chiefs* (1810), still in print today, has reached British and American readers in more than one hundred editions and printings. *The Hungarian Brothers* (1807), Anna Maria Porter's most-popular novel, saw the last of its roughly sixteen editions and printings in 1850. George Saintsbury attributes her diminished reputation, fairly, to her "amiable incompetence." Yet Porter was an influential author. Her novels articulate the spiritual progress of essentially good char-

acters in a corrupting world. This scheme—which justified the novel in a period when, for moral reasons, it was not universally approved—appealed particularly to members of the Anglican Evangelical movement, the core of Porter's audience, who helped to form public expectations for early nineteenth-century fiction. So Porter's novels warrant renewed attention.

The youngest of five children, Anna Maria Porter was born in Durham in 1780, after the death of her father, William Porter, a military surgeon. Soon after her birth, her mother, Jane Blenkinsop Porter, moved her family to Edinburgh. Maria and her sister, Jane, attended George Fulton's school, where both were prodigies. Five-year-old Maria performed so well, in fact, that when a panel of Edinburgh's leading educators examined the whole school, they placed her at the head of the class, before a girl of sixteen. By 1794 the family was living in London, and by the time Maria Porter turned sixteen she had published a two-volume collection of stories, appropriately titled *Artless Tales* (1793, 1795). Jane Porter, in contrast, did not publish her first novel until 1799, when she was twenty-three. According to A. M. Hall, family friends believed that "Jane's mind was of a more lofty order, she was intense, and felt more than she said, while Anna Maria often said more than she felt." Maria's writing often suffered from similar thoughtlessness, perhaps an effect of her premature entrance into literary life.

As Jane Porter later described it in a 13 October 1805 letter to Samuel Jackson Pratt, *Walsh Colville* (1797), Maria's first novel, is "a good warning, to young men, who are plunged into the same sea of Dissipations and Dangers" as the book's hero. In *Octavia* (1798) young women face the shifting morals of the fashionable world. While to the reviewer for the *British Critic* (March 1799) it seemed "a novel, without any particular merit, or any particular fault," another objected more strenuously: "Miss Porter may with care become respectable as a poetess; but we would advise her to relinquish the task of writing novels" (*Critical Review*, February 1798). She may have taken this advice seriously: in 1803 she wrote the text and lyrics for a musical drama called *The Fair Fugitives*. When it failed at Covent Garden on 16 May 1803, however, Porter returned to novels, with *The Lake of Killarney* (1804) and *A Sailor's Friendship, and a Soldier's Love* (1805).

Both novels are remarkably bad, ruined by tangled, improbable plots. In the first, Felix Charlemont, the earl of Roscommon's younger son, acknowledges his love for Rose de Blaquiere after, incredibly, he discovers fragments of her poetry adrift in a field. Rose breaks off their subsequent engagement because in the hallway outside his bedroom she finds a misplaced letter questioning Felix's sexual conduct. Of course they eventually marry, but Lady Roscommon secretly loves her stepson and, anxious to thwart his happiness, kidnaps Rose. This situation is even more absurd than it seems initially, since Rose, we discover, is Lady Roscommon's daughter. As they cross to Europe, Rose falls overboard, and when Felix finally reclaims her she is insane. Once she gives birth to their child, however, she recovers her sanity, miraculously "restored to more than her former charm."

Porter herself felt some need to apologize for *The Lake of Killarney*. In the preface she explains that she wrote it "merely as an amusement for the languid hours, which followed long and repeated fits of sickness," and her final words hardly invite one to read on: "I honestly confess my mediocrity, and prepare my readers for the unimportance of my work." The *Imperial Review* (October 1804) praised the novel because "it inculcates pure morality, it breathes elevated sentiment; it awakens no sympathies that are not . . . friendly to the cause of virtue." The *Monthly Review* (June 1805), however, with the preface in mind, delivered its verdict tongue-in-cheek: "the thread which connects the story together does not continually serve to conduct the reader along through the winding paths. We attribute this defect to the state of the author's health, which probably interrupted the chain of ideas, and weakened their mutual dependence on each other."

A Sailor's Friendship, and a Soldier's Love, no better and no worse than its immediate predecessor, was ignored by the press. Like all of Porter's novels it propagates evangelical values. In 1805, when Samuel Jackson Pratt solicited permission from Jane Porter to excerpt her work for a school anthology, she replied in a 13 October letter not only with information about her own books but with a special recommendation for *A Sailor's Friendship*: "Its style, and its sentiments, are so congenial with our own, that I should be glad to see specimens of 'Morality,' drawn from the pages. . . ." Readers who favor credible plots, characters drawn from life, and uncluttered prose would gladly substitute an extract for the whole.

Secluded in her family's new home in Thames Ditton, Surrey, Porter wrote *The Hungarian Brothers* (1807), a sprawling historical novel of the Napoleonic era, modeled after Jane Porter's *Thaddeus of Warsaw* (1803). Maria's two previous novels had not found much public approval, and those written after *Thaddeus of Warsaw* were novels of a different kind. Now she found her sister's style congenial; she could, according to the preface, "place her heroes in various situations, because the destinies of man are various," and "produce from the circumstances of the story some useful moral." And she could, like her sister, accomplish all of this to public acclaim.

Ann H. Jones explains the novel succinctly: "It is . . . about principle, duty, and self-control." Charles and Demetrius, the two brothers, are destitute sons of the late count of Leopolstat. At their mother's death, Charles, the elder, enters the Austrian army, educates his brother, and obtains a commission for him when he comes of age. Demetrius, unaware of their financial situation, lives a headstrong and imprudent life, though his basic impulses are good. Charles supports Demetrius with their meager legacy and himself lives, without debt or dishonor, on his military pay. He prospers as a soldier because he is brave, intelligent, and loyal; he falls in love with Adelaide—daughter of his greatest supporter, Field Marshal Ingersdorff—because he recognizes beauty, both physical and moral. Adelaide returns Charles's love because she recognizes both in him. Demetrius, in contrast, escapes one difficulty for another; yet Charles always supports him, and Demetrius finally improves himself according to Charles's example. As the *Monthly Review* (May 1808) noted, Porter had satisfied the expectations set forth in her preface: "In the consequences which arise to these persons from their different modes of conduct, a very valuable lesson is taught to young people."

The Hungarian Brothers, more carefully wrought than Porter's earlier novels, impressed

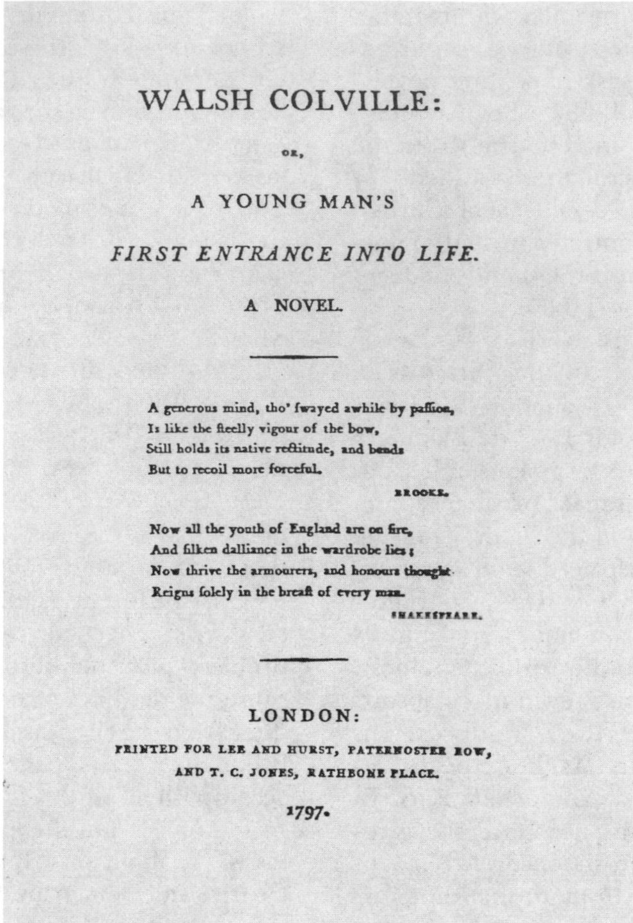

WALSH COLVILLE:

OR,

A YOUNG MAN'S

FIRST ENTRANCE INTO LIFE.

A NOVEL.

A generous mind, tho' ſwayed awhile by paſſion,
Is like the ſteelly vigour of the bow,
Still holds its native rectitude, and bends
But to recoil more forceful.

BROOKE.

Now all the youth of England are on fire,
And ſilken dalliance in the wardrobe lies;
Now thrive the armourers, and honour's thought
Reigns ſolely in the breaſt of every man.

SHAKESPEARE.

LONDON:

PRINTED FOR LEE AND HURST, PATERNOSTER ROW,
AND T. C. JONES, RATHBONE PLACE.

1797.

Title page for Anna Maria Porter's first novel, which Jane Porter called "a good warning, to young men, who are plunged into the same sea of Dissipations and Dangers" as the title character

her readers. The first half is exuberant and colorful. As the *Critical Review* (April 1808) remarked, "the incidents are striking . . . and many of the characters finely drawn," though, as with her earlier novels, the plot is "not always very probable." Halfway through the novel Marshal Ingersdorff reveals that Charles's father had once saved his life. In gratitude, he created the whole sequence of Charles's career, educated Adelaide to love someone just like Charles, recruited others to help in his elaborate scheme, and even disguised himself as a mysterious incognita to effect otherwise unlikely transitions in the plot. Ingersdorff explains that he did not arrive at this scheme on his own but had learned how to plot by reading novels. His confession reveals much about Porter's sense of herself as an author. In one chapter Goodness appears to be struggling against Fate; in the next, Ingersdorff undermines the moral integrity, not to mention verisimilitude, of the novel. *The Hungarian Brothers* ultimately suffers from its author's immaturity: she enjoys her role as contriver of plots and values her control over the story; indeed, she values our awareness of her control more than she values the novel itself.

The *Critical Review* (April 1808), which had once suggested that Porter give up writing novels altogether, received *The Hungarian Brothers* with cautious approval, but could not resist issuing another challenge: "On the whole, we think the work inferior to 'Thaddeus of Warsaw,' but not unworthy of its author." Having written one successful historical novel, Porter decided to write another, perhaps a better one. The result was *Don Sebastian* (1809). Don Sebastian was king of Portugal from 1557 to 1578, when he fought a disastrous battle against the Moors at Alcazar. Porter invents a life of trials for Sebastian, who survives the battle in her account, though by all historical accounts he died. The novel describes his enslavement by the Moors, and the ways in which it and other misfortunes temper his pride with humility. Finally, the *Critical Review* praised both "the arrangement of circumstances, and the discrimination of character." Modern readers will be less generous, but Porter had overcome many of her juvenile tendencies. Though less popular than its predecessor, *Don Sebastian* is the more subtle and accomplished novel.

Publication figures for *The Hungarian Brothers* and *Don Sebastian,* which together appeared in about eleven British and twelve American editions and printings, indicate a reliable audience. Porter, now fully established, could set aside novels temporarily, and attend to other literary interests. In this period she published her only volume of poetry, *Ballad Romances, and Other Poems* (1811). She followed it with a didactic work explained perfectly by its title: *Tales of Pity on Fishing, Shooting, and Hunting, Intended to Inculcate in the Mind of Youth, Sentiments of Humanity Toward the Brute Creation* (1814). In spite of more or less constant illness, Porter was a restlessly energetic writer; verse and stories were not enough to keep her mind occupied, and soon she returned to novels.

Porter's subsequent novels expose her imperialism. As Gary Kelly explains, "the Porter sisters gave medieval and renaissance history the character of idealized modern-day bourgeois life, thereby expropriating the 'national' past for the professional middle classes' vision of present and future." Porter's fiction, which traverses most of Europe and its history, willingly expropriates any national past to encourage English nationalism. Although her novels take place in foreign lands, her fictional world is always covertly English, Protestant Evangelical, and middle class. Don Sebastian, for instance, though originally Roman Catholic, converts to Protestantism, persuaded by his formerly Islamic wife, who has herself been converted to Protestantism by none other than an Englishwoman.

Porter shared cultural anxieties with her audience. In the preface to *The Recluse of Norway* (1814), she apologizes to her reader, whom she hopes "will not accuse me of apostatizing from my zealous attachment to the Reformed religion, by the necessity I was under, of making my hero of the Romish church." The *Critical Review* (April 1815) reacted with the sort of chauvinism that justified Porter's concern: "In these volumes, we felt much satisfaction, yet we could have wished that her selection of *names* to many well-drawn characters, had sounded more harmonious to an English reader." The book conforms to what had become her established pattern: its basically good hero suffers to improve and marries the woman whom finally he deserves.

With *The Recluse of Norway,* public admiration for Porter's fiction declined; her next novel, *The Knight of St. John* (1817), reclaimed some of it. One of the heroes, Cesario Adimari, who loses his patrimony in a centuries-old property dispute, hates his adversaries, the Cigali. Yet Giovanni Cigala, the knight of St. John, befriends Cesario, and attempts to compensate him for his losses. Initially, Cesario resists Giovanni's overtures; love affairs and the defense of Malta against the Turks in 1565 also interfere with the friendship. Yet, necessarily in Porter's universe of Christian possibility, Giovanni's Christ-like charity endures against Cesario's pride and stupidity.

The *European Magazine* (January 1818), "led by the title-page to anticipate a dry monkish chronicle," instead discovered "interesting events, a lively portraiture of man and of woman, calculated to engage human sympathies, and to captivate romantic imagination." The *Monthly Review* (March 1818) found the story far less satisfying, for though "Giovanni's fortitude and resignation, arising from Christian principles, are strikingly drawn . . . yet, as a whole, this romance is somewhat deficient in interest, and disfigured by puerilities." Some of the "puerilities" are all too familiar: when Cesario discovers Beatrice, the woman he loves, walking with Giovanni at a masked ball, he assumes that they have betrayed him (Beatrice, in fact, is attempting to do so); as he is about to reveal himself to them, he slips on the wet grass.

The *Monthly Magazine* (November 1817) accused Porter of falling behind the times, a far more significant fault than her "amiable incompetence": she seemed "insensible to the march of truth and philosophy, to the ceaseless development of the science of morals, and to the general and almost universal spread of those fraternal and *truly* Christian principles." The historical novel, though still fashionable, had lost its Evangelical audience which had developed new expectations: "Would it not then have been more pleasing, as well as a more useful, task, had Miss Porter employed her talents to represent the world as it is?"

Even with such hostility from the press, Porter wrote only historical fiction during the next decade. The pattern her novels took began to suffocate her art. She never developed away from ro-

Sir Robert Ker Porter, brother of Jane and Anna Maria Porter, served as historical painter to Alexander I of Russia and wrote books about his experiences in that country—as well as in Sweden, Spain, Portugal, and the Middle East—before his appointment as British consul in Venezuela.

mance into realism, certainly not in her next novel, *The Fast of St. Magdalen* (1818), which the *Monthly Magazine* (December 1818) described as "a work precisely after the same model which this author has adopted for all her productions, namely, a narrative founded on some historical anecdote, related in correct and not inelegant diction, inculcating moral principles, and breathing pious sentiments." The "anecdote" in this case is the fall and rise of the Medici from 1509 to 1512. The fortunes of the young warrior hero, Valombrosa, and the heroine, Ippolita, are bound inextricably with those of the Medici, ensuring a happy conclusion to their story. The novel suffers, as the *Edinburgh Monthly Review* (April 1819) suggested, from "hasty composition," a malady which had afflicted Porter's writing since *Walsh Colville*, and against which she apparently could not fortify herself. Ann H. Jones has remarked that in the novel "all her worst characteristics are seen almost in caricature." Nonetheless, the *Monthly Magazine* felt that the novel was, "at least, more interesting than her *Knight of St. John*."

Porter's next two novels accelerated her fall from public grace. *The Village of Mariendorpt* (1821), a novel about the Thirty Years' War, and *Roche-Blanche, or the Hunters of the Pyrenees* (1822), a story of France and England in the late sixteenth century, each appeared in single British and American editions. *The Knight of St. John* and *The Fast of St. Magdalen*, though by no means commercially as successful as *The Hungarian Brothers* or *Don Sebastian*, nonetheless each appeared in three British and two American editions. Neither *The Village of Mariendorpt* nor *Roche-Blanche* received a review, nor did any of Porter's subsequent books.

In 1822 the Porter sisters moved with their mother to a cottage in Esher, Surrey. The move was in some respects refreshing, for as Jane Porter explained, their new home "was cheerful and airy, on the summit of a hill . . . commanding all those various points which had rendered that perfectly rural spot an object of interest to all respectors of historical and poetical recollections." Though they began to write immediately upon their arrival, and continued to share their morning writings with each other and Mrs. Porter at tea, Maria's health was soon in decline; she even temporarily lost her sight. And though she had begun *Honor O'Hara* in 1822, she found herself unable to complete the project until her health had improved, three full years later.

In *Honor O'Hara* (1826), Porter returned to Ireland, from which she had long exiled herself in the interests of historical fiction. The story is a picture of domestic life, and a decided turn away from the often outlandish historical romances of the previous two decades. The novel appeared a few months after the two sisters published *Tales Round a Winter Hearth* (1826). The second volume is a short novel by Jane, *The Pilgrimage of Berenice*; the first is three stories by Maria: "Glenowan" and "Jeannie Halliday," both Scottish "folktales" of the sort she remembered hearing at her nurse's knee, and "Lord Howth," another contribution to the Matter of Ireland. These stories demonstrate that, when restrained, Porter had a pleasing imagination and a readable style: compared to her novels, "Jeannie Halliday" is positively elegant. *Coming Out* (1828), published with Jane's *The Field of the Forty Footsteps*, was another Irish and contemporary tale, neither commercially nor critically successful.

Porter concluded her career with *The Barony* (1830), a novel about love and anger between two neighboring families during the 1685 rebellion led by James Scott, Duke of Monmouth, illegitimate son of Charles II. Though tedious in places, the novel may be Porter's best, for the characters are psychologically convincing, the sequence of events plausible, the project of moral instruction sustained. Porter conceived the book with a generous spirit, remembering that "one should be earnest against the sin, compassionate of the sinner." Lord Villiers, the novel's rake, justifies that principle, as he ascends from depravity to a reformation both tentative and sincere, and therefore credible.

The Porter sisters, accustomed to unalloyed domestic happiness, wrote nothing after their mother died in 1831. Maria died in Bristol soon after, on 21 September 1832, of typhus contracted while visiting her brother William Ogilvie Porter. We do not estimate her legacy at much today, yet she led a successful life on her own terms. As A. K. Elwood reported, some of her contemporaries agreed with the terms and applauded the life: "You [Jane] and your sister were very young when you began to be authors; but you made a field of your own—you and she came forward, the first to teach in such works—the first to inculcate Christianity in stories of romance. You came forth with doctrines, that there was and is, the same moral law for man as for woman; that no other is sanctioned by Heaven; you declared it boldly, and have sustained it steadily." Though our own age may not listen, that is saying a lot, perhaps enough to justify fully Anna Maria Porter's short life and long art.

References:

A. K. Elwood, "Anna Maria Porter," in her *Memoirs of the Literary Ladies of England*, volume 2 (London: Henry Colburn, 1843);

A. M. Hall, "Memories of Miss Jane Porter," *The Art Journal*, new series 2 (1850): 221-223;

Ann H. Jones, *Ideas and Innovations: Best Sellers of Jane Austen's Age* (New York: AMS Press, 1986);

Nicholas A. Joukovsky, "Jane Porter's First Novel: The Evidence of an Unpublished Letter," *Notes and Queries* 235 (March 1990): 15-17;

Gary Kelly, *English Fiction of the Romantic Period* (London: Longman, 1989);

George Saintsbury, "The Growth of the Later Novel," in *The Period of the French Revolution*, volume 11 of *The Cambridge History of English Literature*, 14 volumes, edited by A. W. Ward and A. K. Waller (Cambridge: Cambridge University Press, 1907), pp. 285-310.

Jane Porter

(1776 - 24 May 1850)

Michael Adams
Albright College

BOOKS: *The Spirit of the Elbe: A Romance*, 3 volumes (London: Printed for T. Longman & O. Rees, 1799);

The Two Princes of Persia (London: Printed by J. Cundee for Crosby & Letterman, 1801);

Thaddeus of Warsaw (4 volumes, London: Printed by A. Strahan for T. N. Longman & O. Rees, 1803; 2 volumes, Boston: Published by Lemuel Blake, Lincoln & Edmands, printers, 1809);

Sketch of the Campaign of Count A. Suwarrow Ryminski (London: Longman, Hurst, Rees & Orme, 1804);

The Scottish Chiefs: A Romance (5 volumes, London: Printed for Longman, Hurst, Rees & Orme, 1810; 2 volumes, New York: D. Longworth, 1810; 3 volumes, Philadelphia: Bradford & Inskeep, 1810);

The Pastor's Fire-Side: A Novel (4 volumes, London: Longman, Hurst, Rees, Orme & Brown, 1815; 2 volumes, New York: W. B. Gilley, 1818);

Duke Christian of Luneburg, or Traditions of the Hartz, 3 volumes (London: Longman, Hurst, Rees, Orme, Brown & Green, 1824);

Tales Round a Winter Hearth, 2 volumes, by Jane Porter and Anna Maria Porter (London: Longman, Rees, Orme, Brown & Green, 1826);

Coming Out, and The Field of Forty Footsteps, 3 volumes [volumes 1 and 2: *Coming Out*, by Anna Maria Porter; volume 3: *The Field of Forty Footsteps*, by Jane Porter] (London: Longman, Rees, Orme, Brown & Green, 1828);

Sir Edward Seaward's Narrative of his Shipwreck and Consequent Discovery of Certain Islands in the Caribbean Sea: With a Detail of Many Extraordinary and Highly Interesting Events in His Life, from the year 1733 to 1749, as written in his own diary, edited by Jane Porter, 3 volumes (London: Longman, Rees, Orme, Brown & Green, 1831; New York: J. & J. Harper, 1831).

PLAY PRODUCTIONS: *Switzerland*, London, Theatre Royal, Drury Lane, 5 February 1819;

Owen, Prince of Powys, London, Theatre Royal, Drury Lane, 28 January 1822.

OTHER: *Aphorisms of Sir Philip Sidney*, 2 volumes, selected by Porter (London: Longman, Hurst, Rees & Orme, 1807).

Though virtually unread today, Jane Porter's *Thaddeus of Warsaw* (1803) was one of the first British historical novels. As Porter suggested in her preface to the Standard Edition (1831) of the novel, in *Waverley* (1814) Sir Walter Scott did her "the honour to adopt the style or class of novel of which 'Thaddeus of Warsaw' was the first:—a class which, uniting the personages of and facts of real history or biography, with a combining and illustrative machinery of the imagination, found a new species of writing in that day." Besides exerting this influence, Porter was immensely popular throughout the nineteenth century, both in Britain and in the United States. *Thaddeus* went through at least eighty-four nineteenth-century editions and printings, *The Scottish Chiefs* (1810) through roughly seventy-five. Harry E. Shaw writes that Scott superseded Porter because he "convince[d] his readers . . . that a novel about the past need not simply be a collection of historical bric-a-brac and antiquated speech . . . that it can have an interest for mature men and women." But nothing critics can say changes the fact that many, many mature men and women enjoyed Porter's best novels. They are not great novels, but if one can resist comparing them to books by Jane Austen and Scott, and can adopt an early-nineteenth-century sense of virtue and human possibility, one can still enjoy them today.

Born in Durham in 1776, Porter moved to Edinburgh with her mother, Jane Blenkinsop Porter, her three brothers, and her younger sister in 1780, the year after her father, William Porter, a military surgeon, died. She and her sister, Anna

After the king of Wurtemberg appointed her a canoness in the Chapter of Saint Joachim, Jane Porter frequently wore convent garb.

Maria, attended George Fulton's school, where both were prodigies. Her mother, though not a person of great means, kept an open house. Among her visitors was the young Walter Scott. By 1794 the Porters had migrated to London so that one of the brothers, Robert, might better pursue his vocation as a painter there. Mrs. Porter once again opened her house to literary persons, and to Robert's artist friends.

In 1797 Jane and Anna Maria assisted Robert and Thomas Frognall Didbin on an ill-fated periodical called *The Quiz* (1797-1798). Jane's first book, *The Spirit of the Elbe* (1799), proved an inauspicious beginning to her career as novelist. The *Monthly Review* (September 1799) was severely critical of this Gothic romance:

> That species of eloquence, which may be termed the false pathetic, pervades the whole work. The events are improbable, if not impossible; the spirits of the night are called to exercise their ghostly functions; and the characters are such as bear no similitude to any beings that we have ever known.

Undaunted, Jane Porter produced *The Two Princes of Persia* (1801), a very moralistic work in which two brothers, the princes Omra and Behauder, take instruction from their philosopher-teacher Sadi. The brothers have sharply contrasting personalities which resemble those of Jane and Anna Maria Porter, whom friends discriminated as "Il Penseroso" and "L'Allegro," respectively. Though the lessons were apparently drawn from life, and the *Anti-Jacobin Review* (April 1801) gave the book its "mite of approbation," *The Two Princes of Persia* seems to have been no more popular in 1801 than it would be today.

In her preface to the Standard Edition of *Thaddeus of Warsaw*, Porter remembers that during her first years in London, she saw many Polish refugees wandering in St. James's Park. One in particular caught her attention, "a gaunt figure, with melancholy and bravery stamped on his emaciated features." As she explains in her preface to the first edition, out of that figure she imagined Thaddeus Sobieski, a character "that prosperity could not inflate nor disappointments depress from pious trust and honorable action." A patriot in Poland's struggle for independence in 1794, Thaddeus loses his grandfather in battle and his mother to grief and strain, as Poland loses its last shred of liberty. He escapes to London, friendless and impoverished, perseveres amid his personal losses and shattered expectations, and exceeds what the reader can quite believe.

Other characters fall short of Thaddeus's standard. Lady Sara Roos and Euphemia Dundas, two ladies who compete for his attention, represent a world mostly petty and self-serving, immodest and frivolous. The novel has its surprises: when Thaddeus's closest friend, Pembroke Somerset, remarks optimistically that he has "an excellent father; who . . . will glory in loving you [Thaddeus] as a son," Porter opens into the ironic dimension of history. The old man is, of course, Thaddeus's natural father.

A critic for the *Monthly Review* (February 1804) commented that the first third of the novel, set in Poland, "is perhaps too deeply involved in bustle, and requires a larger portion of attention than the generality of novel readers are accustomed to bestow." Judging by the success of the book, however, most readers did not agree. Polish patriot Gen. Thaddeus Kosciuszko admired it and sent Porter a keepsake. Gen. William Gardiner, last British minister to the court of Stanislaus Augustus, when informed that Porter had never been in Poland, insisted that "no one could describe the scenes and occurrences there, in the manner it is done in that book, without having been an eye-witness." The novel is packed with vivid detail, and though one may not enjoy its insistent moralism, one cannot help but admire the novel's color and the writerly control Porter exercises over it. In the words of the *Imperial Review* (February 1804), the novel "is one of the few which, once opened, could not pass *unread*. The attention is arrested by the first page, and never suffered to diverge till the final denouement."

Yet in the twentieth century George Saintsbury could write that *Thaddeus* and *The Scottish Chiefs* are "almost utter, though virtuous and well intentioned, rubbish." A. D. Hook argues against the influence of *Thaddeus of Warsaw* on Scott, notes its deficiencies as a historical novel, and questions Porter's claim that in it she writes a "new species" of fiction, though Robert D. Hume has endorsed Porter's view. Recently, Ann H. Jones has discussed Evangelism as a potent element in Porter's imagination, shedding some light on Thaddeus Sobieski, who acts as a cipher for Christian idealism, and Porter's disdain for certain types of society. Jones also attributes interest in Porter's fiction to Evangelical influences in early-nineteenth-century taste, which Porter continued to satisfy in her other novels.

By 1804 the Porter sisters and their mother had moved to the village of Thames Ditton, Surrey; there she wrote *The Scottish Chiefs* (1810), which re-creates William Wallace's struggle (1297-1305) to liberate Scotland from Edward I. Porter had long nurtured a seed of Scottish romanticism, planted in her Edinburgh days by a poor neighbor named Luckie Forbes, who told the Porter children old tales and sang them ballads. In her "Retrospective Introduction" to the 1831 edition, Porter remembered having seen, peering out of the Edinburgh streets from their garret windows, widows of "The '45" (the 1745 rebellion of Scottish Jacobites, led by Charles Edward Stuart, the "Young Pretender" or "Bonnie Prince Charlie"). She also tells a remarkable story about meeting Jeannie Cameron, who supposedly rallied to the Pretender's standard and led two hundred of her kinsmen into battle at Prestonpans, Falkirk, and Culloden. Cameron would have been over ninety when this meeting is said to occur, and her exploits were wholly legendary. Porter's story suggests that she began to fictionalize Scottish history at an early age.

Porter's Wallace exceeds even Thaddeus Sobieski as an ideal of Christian behavior: he suffers worse trials with greater grace. He faces brutal opposition from the English, as well as con-

Portrait by Daniel Maclise in the Fraser's Magazine *"Gallery of Illustrious Literary Characters" (1830-1838)*

stant rebellion by the Scottish chiefs, who are jealous of his popularity and success and who suspect that he will usurp the Scottish throne. Lady Mar, wife of his most constant supporter, the earl of Mar, finally betrays Wallace because he spurns her love and ruins her ambition to become Scotland's queen. Her stepdaughter, Lady Helen, loves Wallace for his virtues rather than his power; she marries him immediately before his execution. The novel successfully conveys Porter's central theme, that virtue derives from character rather than from birth, but it succeeds somewhat clumsily because she contrives only the blackest evil and the most transcendent good.

The Scottish Chiefs met with a slightly less enthusiastic reception than *Thaddeus of Warsaw*, but it nonetheless marks the zenith of Porter's reputation. It also was translated into several languages, including German and Russian, and Napoleon feared its effects enough to proscribe its release in France. Typical of the reviews, the *British Critic* (March 1811) called the book "interesting" and proclaimed Wallace "one of the most perfect heroes that ever filled the pages of either history or romance." *Scots Magazine* (April 1810) suggested that Porter's "peculiar excellence consists . . . in her power of expressing ardent and enthusiastic passion . . . perhaps the highest excellence of composition which can be possessed by a work of fancy." But it also found significant faults: Porter "does not sufficiently know the art of letting herself down"; as a result, "bombast and meretricious ornament must be sought for, to fill up the pauses of real beauty." Her fundamental problem is an irresolvable conflict of history and entertainment, "as the events of real history are not arranged for the purpose of amusing the world." The reviewer questions, in effect, whether Porter's subject is really historical. In 1831 Porter responded: "What ballads were to the sixteenth-century, romances are to ours"; essentially, they are a type of history different than that which the reviewer expected.

The critics responded variously to Porter's next novel, *The Pastor's Fire-Side* (1815), good reviews mixed evenly with bad. The *Gentleman's Magazine* (February 1817) responded, insightfully, that the book "is a romance of the same class as 'Thaddeus' and 'The Scottish Chiefs' and in our judgment decidedly superior to those ingenious and highly popular productions." Porter's characters in *The Pastor's Fire-Side* are more fluid than those in her earlier novels, their moral successes tentative rather than given. In these newly dynamic characters, the reviewer recognizes Porter's peculiar strength: "In embodying the *Beau Ideal* of noble minds, Miss Porter is more eminently successful than any living writer." The *Critical Review* (February 1817), on the other hand, preferred static characters, an attitude with which, for moral reasons, the author herself agreed. Fortunately, as Ann H. Jones remarks, "Jane Porter the novelist at times got the better of Jane Porter the propagandist of Christian principles."

The novel focuses on the Duke de Ripperda, his son Louis, and that infamous Jacobite, Philip, Duke of Wharton, all of whom form a triangle of ascending and descending fortunes. Though Ripperda begins a fully honorable man, he later embraces Islam, and to avenge his political ruin he invades Spain under the emperor of Morocco. He arouses the reader's sympathy when he dies in his son's arms, divorced from his country, his better nature, and God. Louis begins the novel restless and superficial, but in reaction first to his father's integrity and later to his apostasy, he rises to selflessness that rivals Sobieski's or Wallace's. Wharton begins a scoundrel; yet his love for the pastor's grandniece, Cornelia, transforms him. He dies before they can marry, reformed but unrewarded.

When mingling good and evil in these more human characters, Porter risked failure she had previously avoided. For instance, she disturbed many readers who found the duke of Wharton more appealing than the less depraved Louis. The *British Critic* (June 1817) made a fair criticism when it wrote that *The Pastor's Fire-Side* "is certainly above the ordinary run of Romances; though the authoress, in aiming at a higher order of writing, has sometimes soared beyond the sphere both of her capacity and of her information." *The Pastor's Fire-Side* may well be Porter's most ambitious and sophisticated novel, but it is mostly overlooked today.

In 1822 the Porters moved from Thames Ditton to Esher, Surrey. During the last years at Thames Ditton, Porter temporarily set aside novels and wrote plays instead. *Bannockburn: A Novel, being a sequel to the Scottish Chiefs* (1821), though it bears Porter's name, is almost certainly by another writer. Her first play, "Egmont, or the Eve of St. Alyne," though Edmund Kean read and approved it, saw neither stage nor print. *Switzerland* (1819) and *Owen, Prince of Powys* (1822) were performed at Drury Lane, however, and both were dismal failures.

Through the Reverend Dr. James Stanier Clarke, his librarian, George IV suggested to Porter that she write a novel from the exploits of his ancestor, Duke Christian of Brunswick-Luneburg, which she did in *Duke Christian of Luneburg, or Traditions of the Hartz* (1824). Porter draws Duke Christian as a Protestant warrior-hero of monumental dimensions, but the novel fails in part because it does not develop sufficiently beyond mere illustration of Duke Christian's virtue, the liability, perhaps, of having been made to order. The book did satisfy the king, and it accurately describes Duke Christian's role in the Thirty Years' War; nonetheless, it marks a decline both in Porter's commercial and artistic success: it retreats from the psychological complexity and sophisticated structure of *The Pastor's Fire-Side*, and lacks the color and energy of *Thaddeus of Warsaw* and *The Scottish Chiefs*. Duke Christian is the least human, the least convincing, of Porter's central characters.

Next Porter collaborated with her sister on a two-volume collection of stories called *Tales Round a Winter Hearth* (1826). Jane contributed the last item to the first volume, "My Chamber in the Old House of Huntercombe," which explains how the narrator found the manuscript she records in the second volume, a short novel titled *The Pilgrimage of Berenice, A Record of Burnham Abbey*. Berenice is the daughter of Eustace de Bouillon, brother of Baldwin, the first king of Jerusalem. When Baldwin dies in 1118, Eustace returns to claim the throne, only to discover that his brother had bequeathed it to Baldwin du Bourg. In a fury of revenge, Eustace joins with the Caliph of Baghdad and offers him Berenice as an incentive to overthrow du Bourg. An English nobleman, the Count de Beaufort, intercepts a letter from de Bouillon to the Caliph and would have intervened if a lion had not attacked de Bouillon before de Beaufort could reach him. De Beaufort and Berenice fall in love and return to de Beaufort's estates in England, where Berenice founds the religious order that would preserve the manuscript account of her pilgrimage for so many years. The novel is plotted somewhat ineptly, and did not prove a success with Porter's well-established readership.

The sisters immediately collaborated again in *Coming Out, and The Field of Forty Footsteps* (1828), which met with the same tepid public reaction. In Jane's one-volume contribution, *The Field of Forty Footsteps,* a story of the English Civil War, the heroine, Betha Baldry, finds herself in a dilemma: on one hand she is daughter to Geoffrey Baldry, who has joined his interests with the Commonwealth; on the other, she is niece to Sir Eustace de Matchelowe, an exiled Royalist, to whom she is asked to send a letter that lists the regicides. During the novel Betha befriends the commander of the Parliamentary forces, Gen. Sir Thomas Fairfax, a good but underdeveloped character; Henry Stuart is captured in battle, and Betha's cousin, Arthur Matchelowe, liberates him; Geoffrey and his brother, Leonard, from sheer greed and ambition, kill each other in a duel. Betha is essentially ignored at the end of the novel, which is mostly a matter of skewed emphases, and of Porter's own pious Royalism. Betha, as a daughter of the Commonwealth, hardly has a chance against Porter's implicit criticism.

Betha Baldry and Berenice illustrate Porter's discomfort with heroines; her best novels depend for their success on an ideal of male heroism and a panoramic view of history. After *The Pastor's Fire-Side,* Porter's novels suffered from narrow scope. Both *The Pilgrimage of Berenice* and *The Field of Forty Footsteps* are large books crammed into single volumes, and they become absurd in miniature. In all respects, from the period in which she had briefly turned from fiction to drama, Porter's literary powers diminished. In order to rejuvenate them, she needed to do something wholly unlike anything she had done before, and in *Sir Edward Seaward's Narrative* (1831) she accomplished just that.

This novel is a shipwreck-and-survival narrative on the order of *Robinson Crusoe* (1719). Its protagonists are a Christian couple, Seaward and his wife, Elizabeth, who view their trial as one devised by God, their preservation as a gift from him, and conversion of the natives as their appointed mission. They take their stewardship of "Seaward's Islands" so seriously that, though they had regained civilization, they return to administer the islands for the Crown. Porter claimed that she had merely edited Seaward's journal for publication, and the Admiralty was taken by surprise for several days as they tried to verify the story. Finally, the *Quarterly Review* (December 1832) exposed several inaccuracies and fictions in the book, and recognized Porter's authorship. Edgar Allan Poe, who, according to Randel Helms, borrowed whole episodes from *Seaward* for *The Narrative of Arthur Gordon Pym* (1838), thought Porter's book more powerful than *Robinson Crusoe* in its verisimilitude. The *Quarterly Review* praised the book as "well worth a score of such productions as 'Thaddeus of Warsaw' . . . or 'The Scottish Chiefs.' "

Sir Edward Seaward's Narrative went through six nineteenth-century editions and printings, fewer even than *The Pastor's Fire-Side,* but enough to indicate a sure success. It might have marked the renewal of Porter's talent and influence, but domestic tragedy intervened, and she never wrote another book. Her mother died on 21 June 1831, after which the sisters moved to London. On 21 September 1832 Anna Maria died while the sisters were in Bristol visiting their brother William Ogilvie Porter. Porter lived on alone in London until 1842, when she visited her brother Sir Robert Ker Porter in Saint Petersburg. He died shortly after her arrival, and after Porter returned to London, it took nearly two years for her to settle his estate. In 1844 she removed to her brother William's house in Bristol and remained there until her own death on 24 May 1850.

Jane Porter began her career at her best, establishing in her early historical novels a subgenre of fiction fully realized by other authors, primarily Scott. Over the years she lost step with popular taste, but at one time she defined it. As S. C. Hall remembered more than a half century later, her books found "more than renown—popularity of the most extended order." *Thaddeus of Warsaw, The Scottish Chiefs, The*

Pastor's Fire-Side, and *Sir Edward Seaward's Narrative* are good books and still repay reading. Yet at the end of the nineteenth century, S. C. Hall asked of Porter what one still should ask today: "The 'Scottish Chiefs' was Jane Porter's most famous work. Who reads it now?"

References:

A. K. Elwood, "Anna Maria Porter," in her *Memoirs of the Literary Ladies of England*, volume 2 (London: Henry Colburn, 1843);

A. M. Hall, "Memories of Miss Jane Porter," *Art Journal*, new series 2 (1850): 221-223;

S. C. Hall, *Retrospect of a Long Life* (London: Bentley, 1883), pp. 386-388;

Randel Helms, "Another Source for Poe's *Arthur Gordon Pym*," *American Literature*, 41 (January 1970): 572-575;

A. D. Hook, "Jane Porter, Sir Walter Scott, and the Historical Novel," *Clio*, 5 (Winter 1976): 181-192;

Robert D. Hume, "Gothic Versus Romantic," *PMLA*, 84 (March 1969): 282-290;

Ann H. Jones, *Ideas and Innovations: Best Sellers of Jane Austen's Age* (New York: AMS Press, 1986);

Nicholas A. Joukovsky, "Jane Porter's First Novel: The Evidence of an Unpublished Letter," *Notes and Queries*, 235 (March 1990): 15-17;

Gary Kelly, *English Fiction of the Romantic Period* (London: Longman, 1989);

George Saintsbury, "The Growth of the Later Novel," in *The Period of the French Revolution*, volume 11 of *The Cambridge History of English Literature*, 14 volumes, edited by A. W. Ward and A. R. Waller (Cambridge: Cambridge University Press, 1907), pp. 285-310;

Harry E. Shaw, *The Forms of Historical Fiction: Sir Walter Scott and His Successors* (Ithaca: Cornell University Press, 1983);

Mona Wilson, "A Romantic Novelist," in her *These Were Muses* (London: Sidgwick & Jackson, 1924), pp. 119-142.

Walter Scott

(15 August 1771 - 21 September 1832)

Gary Kelly
University of Alberta

Sir Walter Scott (portrait by William Nicholson, R.S.A.; Scottish National Portrait Gallery)

See also the Scott entries in DLB 93: British Romantic Poets, 1789-1832: First Series *and* DLB 107: British Romantic Prose Writers, 1789-1832: First Series.

BOOKS: *The Eve of Saint John. A Border Ballad* (Kelso: Printed by James Ballantyne, 1800);

The Lay of the Last Minstrel (London: Printed for Longman, Hurst, Rees & Orme, and A. Constable, Edinburgh, by James Ballantyne, Edinburgh, 1805; Philadelphia: Printed for I. Riley, New York, 1806);

Ballads and Lyrical Pieces (Edinburgh: Printed by James Ballantyne for Longman, Hurst, Rees & Orme, London, and Archibald Constable, Edinburgh, 1806; Boston: Published & sold by Etheridge & Bliss and by B. & B. Hopkins, Philadelphia, 1807);

Marmion: A Tale of Flodden Field (Edinburgh: Printed by J. Ballantyne for Archibald Constable, Edinburgh, and William Miller & John Murray, London, 1808; Philadelphia: Hopkins & Earle, 1808);

The Lady of the Lake: A Poem (Edinburgh: Printed for John Ballantyne, Edinburgh, and Longman, Hurst, Rees & Orme and William Miller, London, by James Ballantyne, 1810; Boston: Published by W. Wells & T. B. Wait, printed by T. B. Wait, 1810; New York: E. Sargeant, 1810; Philadelphia: E. Earle, 1810);

The Vision of Don Roderick: A Poem (Edinburgh: Printed by James Ballantyne for John Ballantyne, Edinburgh, and Longman, Hurst, Rees, Orme & Brown, London, 1811; Boston: Published by T. B. Wait, 1811);

Rokeby: A Poem (Edinburgh: Printed for John Ballantyne, Edinburgh, and Longman, Hurst, Rees, Orme & Brown, London, by James Ballantyne, Edinburgh, 1813; Baltimore: J. Cushing, 1813);

The Bridal of Triermain, or The Vale of St. John. In Three Cantos (Edinburgh: Printed by James Ballantyne for John Ballantyne and for Longman, Hurst, Rees, Orme & Brown and Gale, Curtis & Fenner, London, 1813; Philadelphia: Published by M. Thomas, printed by W. Fry, 1813);

Waverley; or, 'Tis Sixty Years Since (3 volumes, Edinburgh: Printed by James Ballantyne for Archibald Constable, Edinburgh, and Longman, Hurst, Rees, Orme & Brown, London, 1814; 1 volume, Boston: Published by Wells & Lilly and Bradford & Read, 1815; 2 volumes, New York: Van Winkle & Wiley, 1815);

Guy Mannering; or, The Astrologer. By the Author of "Waverley" (3 volumes, Edinburgh: Printed by James Ballantyne for Longman, Hurst, Rees, Orme & Brown, London, and Archibald Constable, Edinburgh, 1815; 2 volumes, Boston: Published by West & Richardson and Eastburn, Kirk, New York, printed by T. W. White, 1815);

The Lord of the Isles: A Poem (Edinburgh: Printed for Archibald Constable, Edinburgh, and Longman, Hurst, Rees, Orme & Brown, London, by James Ballantyne, 1815; New York: R. Scott, 1815; Philadelphia: Published by Moses Thomas, 1815);

The Field of Waterloo: A Poem (Edinburgh: Printed by James Ballantyne for Archibald Constable, Edinburgh, and Longman, Hurst, Rees, Orme & Brown, and John Murray, London, 1815; Boston: T. B. Wait, 1815; New York: Van Winkle & Wiley, 1815; Philadelphia: Published by Moses Thomas, printed by Van Winkle & Wiley, 1815);

The Ettricke Garland; Being Two Excellent New Songs on The Lifting of the Banner of the House of Buccleuch, At the Great Foot-Ball Match on Carterhaugh, Dec. 4, 1815, by Scott and James Hogg (Edinburgh: Printed by James Ballantyne, 1815);

Paul's Letters To His Kinsfolk (Edinburgh: Printed by James Ballantyne for Archibald Constable, Edinburgh, and Longman, Hurst, Rees, Orme & Brown, and John Murray, London, 1816; Philadelphia: Republished by M. Thomas, 1816);

The Antiquary. By the Author of "Waverley" and "Guy Mannering" (3 volumes, Edinburgh: Printed by James Ballantyne for Archibald Constable, Edinburgh, and Longman, Hurst, Rees, Orme & Brown, London, 1816; 2 volumes, New York: Van Winkle & Wiley, 1816);

Tales of My Landlord, Collected and Arranged by Jedediah Cleishbotham, Schoolmaster and Parish-Clerk of Gandercleugh [*The Black Dwarf* and *Old Mortality*] (4 volumes, Edinburgh: Printed for William Blackwood and John Murray, London, 1816; 1 volume, Philadelphia: Published by M. Thomas, 1817);

Harold the Dauntless: A Poem (Edinburgh: Printed by James Ballantyne for Longman, Hurst, Rees, Orme & Brown, London, and Archibald Constable, Edinburgh, 1817; New York: Published by James Eastburn, printed by Van Winkle, Wiley, 1817);

Rob Roy; by the Author of "Waverley," "Guy Mannering," and "The Antiquary" (3 volumes, Edinburgh: Printed by James Ballantyne for Archibald Constable, Edinburgh, and Longman, Hurst, Rees, Orme & Brown, London, 1818 [i.e., 1817]; 2 volumes, New York: J. Eastburn, 1818; New York: Published by Kirk & Mercein, printed by E. & E. Hosford, Albany, 1818; Philadelphia: Published by M. Thomas, printed by J. Maxwell, 1818);

Tales of My Landlord, Second Series, Collected and Arranged by Jedediah Cleishbotham, Schoolmaster and Parish-Clerk of Gandercleugh [*The Heart of Mid-Lothian*], 4 volumes (Edinburgh: Printed for Archibald Constable, 1818; Philadelphia: M. Carey & Son, 1818);

Tales of My Landlord, Third Series, Collected and Arranged by Jedediah Cleishbotham, Schoolmaster and Parish-Clerk of Gandercleugh [*The Bride of Lammermoor* and *A Legend of Montrose*], 4 volumes (Edinburgh: Printed for Archibald Constable, Edinburgh, and Longman, Hurst, Rees, Orme & Brown and Hurst, Robinson, London, 1819; New York: Published by Charles Wiley, W. B. Gilley and A. T. Goodrich, printed by Clayton & Kingsland, 1819; Philadelphia: M. Thomas, 1819);

Provincial Antiquities and Picturesque Scenery of Scotland, text by Scott with plates by J. M. W. Turner and others (10 parts, Edinburgh: Printed by James Ballantyne, 1819-1826; 2 volumes, London: J. & A. Arch, 1826);

Miscellaneous Poems (Edinburgh: Printed for Archibald Constable, Edinburgh, and Hurst, Robinson, London, 1820);

Ivanhoe: A Romance; By "the Author of Waverley" &c. (3 volumes, Edinburgh: Printed for Archibald Constable, Edinburgh, and Hurst, Robinson, London, 1820 [i.e., 1819]; 2 volumes, Philadelphia: M. Carey & Son, 1820);

The Monastery: A Romance; By the Author of "Waverley" (3 volumes, Edinburgh: Printed for Longman, Hurst, Rees, Orme & Brown, London, and for Archibald Constable and John Ballantyne, Edinburgh, 1820; 1 volume, Philadelphia: Published by M. Carey & Son, 1820);

The Abbot; By the Author of "Waverley" (3 volumes, Edinburgh: Printed for Longman, Hurst, Rees, Orme & Brown, London, and for Archibald Constable and John Ballantyne, Edinburgh, 1820; 2 volumes, New York: J. & J. Harper, 1820; 1 volume, Philadelphia: M. Carey & Son, 1820);

Scott's parents, Walter and Anne Rutherford Scott, at the time of their marriage in 1758 (portraits attributed to Robert Harvie; Collection of Mrs. Maxwell-Scott of Abbotsford)

Kenilworth: A Romance; By the Author of "Waverley," "Ivanhoe," &c. (3 volumes, Edinburgh: Printed for Archibald Constable and John Ballantyne, Edinburgh, and Hurst, Robinson, London, 1821; Hartford: S. G. Goodrich, 1821; Philadelphia: M. Carey & Son, 1821);

The Pirate; By the Author of "Waverley," Kenilworth," &c. (3 volumes, Edinburgh: Printed for Archibald Constable, and Hurst, Robinson, London, 1822 [i.e., 1821]; 2 volumes, Boston: Wells & Lilly, 1822; 1 volume, Hartford: S. G. Goodrich and Huntington & Hopkins, 1822; 2 volumes, New York: E. Duyckinck, 1822; 1 volume, Philadelphia: H. C. Carey & I. Lea, 1822);

The Fortunes of Nigel; By the Author of "Waverley," "Kenilworth," &c. (3 volumes, Edinburgh: Printed for Archibald Constable, Edinburgh, and Hurst, Robinson, London, 1822; 2 volumes, New York: T. Longworth, 1822; Philadelphia: Carey & Lea, 1822);

Halidon Hill: A Dramatic Sketch (Edinburgh: Printed for Archibald Constable, and Hurst, Robinson, London, 1822; New York: S. Campbell, printed by E. B. Clayton, 1822; Philadelphia: H. C. Carey & I. Lea, 1822);

Peveril of the Peak; By the Author of "Waverley, Kenilworth," &c. (4 volumes, Edinburgh: Printed for Archibald Constable, Edinburgh, and Hurst, Robinson, London, 1822 [i.e., 1823]; 3 volumes, Philadelphia: H. C. Carey & I. Lea, 1823);

Quentin Durward; By the Author of "Waverley, Peveril of the Peak," &c. (3 volumes, Edinburgh: Printed for Archibald Constable, Edinburgh, and Hurst, Robinson, London, 1823; 1 volume, Philadelphia: H. C. Carey & I. Lea, 1823);

St. Ronan's Well; By the Author of "Waverley, Quentin Durward," &c. (3 volumes, Edinburgh: Printed for Archibald Constable, Edinburgh, and Hurst, Robinson, London, 1824 [i.e., 1823]; Philadelphia: H. C. Carey & I. Lea, 1824);

Redgauntlet: A Tale of the Eighteenth Century; By the Author of "Waverley" (3 volumes, Edinburgh: Printed for Archibald Constable, Edinburgh, and Hurst, Robinson, London, 1824; 2 volumes, Philadelphia: H. C. Carey & I. Lea, 1824);

Tales of the Crusaders; By the Author of Waverley [*The Betrothed* and *The Talisman*] (4 volumes, Edinburgh: Printed for Archibald Constable, Edinburgh, and Hurst, Robinson, London, 1825; New York: Published by E. Duyckinck, Collins & Hannay, Collins, E. Bliss & E. White, and W. B. Gilley, printed by J. & J. Harper, 1825; 2 volumes, Philadelphia: H. C. Carey & I. Lea, 1825);

Letter to the Editor of the Edinburgh Weekly Journal from Malachi Malagrowther, Esq. on the Proposed Change of Currency and Other Late Alterations, As They Affect, or Are Intended to Affect, the Kingdom of Scotland (Edinburgh: Printed by James Ballantyne for William Blackwood, 1826);

A Second Letter to the Editor of the Edinburgh Weekly Journal, from Malachi Malagrowther, Esq.: On the Proposed Change of Currency, and Other Late Alterations, As They Affect, or Are Intended to Affect, the Kingdom of Scotland (Edinburgh: Printed by James Ballantyne for William Blackwood, 1826);

A Third Letter to the Editor of the Edinburgh Weekly Journal, from Malachi Malagrowther, Esq.: On the Proposed Change of Currency, and Other Late Alterations, As They Affect, or Are Intended to Affect, the Kingdom of Scotland (Edinburgh: Printed by James Ballantyne for William Blackwood, Edinburgh, and T. Cadell, London, 1826);

Woodstock; or, the Cavalier: A Tale of the Year Sixteen Hundred and Fifty-One; By the Author of "Waverley, Tales of the Crusaders," &c. (3 volumes, Edinburgh: Printed for Archibald Constable, Edinburgh, and Longman, Rees, Orme, Brown & Green, London, 1826; 2 volumes, Philadelphia: H. C. Carey & I. Lea, 1826);

The Life of Napoleon Buonaparte, 9 volumes (Edinburgh: Printed by Ballantyne, for Longman, Rees, Orme, Brown & Green, London, 1827; Philadelphia: Carey, Lea & Carey, 1827);

The Miscellaneous Prose Works of Sir Walter Scott, Bart., 6 volumes (Edinburgh: Cadell, 1827; Boston: Wells & Lilly, 1829);

Chronicles of the Canongate. By the Author of "Waverley," &c. ["The Highland Widow"; "The Two Drovers"; "The Surgeon's Daughter"] (2 volumes, Edinburgh: Printed for Cadell, Edinburgh, and Simpkin & Marshall, London, 1827; 1 volume, Philadelphia: Carey, Lea & Carey, 1827);

Religious Discourses. By a Layman (London: Henry Colburn, 1828; New York: Printed by J. & J. Harper, sold by Collins & Hannay, 1828);

Chronicles of the Canongate: Second Series; By the Author of "Waverley" &c. [*The Fair Maid of Perth*] (3 volumes, Edinburgh: Printed for Cadell, Edinburgh, and Simpkin & Marshall, London, 1828; 1 volume, Philadelphia: Carey, Lea & Carey, 1828);

Tales of a Grandfather: Being Stories Taken from Scottish History, first-third series (9 volumes, Edinburgh: Printed for Cadell, 1828-1830 [i.e., 1827-1830]; 8 volumes, Philadelphia: Carey, Lea & Carey, 1828-1830);

Anne of Geierstein; or, The Maiden in the Mist; By the Author of "Waverley," &c. (3 volumes, Edinburgh: Printed for Cadell, Edinburgh, and Simpkin & Marshall, London, 1829; 2 volumes, Philadelphia: Carey, Lea & Carey, 1829);

The History of Scotland, 2 volumes, in *The Cabinet Cyclopædia, Conducted by Rev. Dionysus Lardner* (London: Printed for Longman, Rees, Orme, Brown & Green and John Taylor, 1830);

The Doom of Devorgoil: A Melo-drama. Auchindrane; or, the Ayrshire Tragedy (Edinburgh: Printed for Cadell, Edinburgh, and Simpkin & Marshall, London, 1830; New York: Printed by J. & J. Harper, 1830);

Letters on Demonology and Witchcraft (London: J. Murray, 1830; New York: J. & J. Harper, 1830);

Tales of a Grandfather: Being Stories Taken from the History of France (3 volumes, Edinburgh: Cadell, 1831; 2 volumes, Philadelphia: Carey & Lea, 1831);

Tales of My Landlord: Fourth and Last Series Collected and Arranged by Jedediah Cleishbotham, Schoolmaster and Parish-Clerk of Gandercleugh [*Count Robert of Paris* and *Castle Dangerous*] (4 volumes, Edinburgh: Printed for Robert Cadell, Edinburgh, and Whitaker, London, 1832; 3 volumes, Philadelphia: Carey & Lea, 1832);

The Journal of Sir Walter Scott, 3 volumes, edited by John Guthrie Tait and W. M. Parker (Edinburgh: Oliver & Boyd, 1939-1949).

Editions: *Waverley Novels*, 48 volumes, with Scott's prefaces and final revisions (Edinburgh: Cadell, 1829-1833);

Miscellaneous Prose Works, 30 volumes, edited by John Gibson Lockhart (Edinburgh: R. Cadell, 1834-1846);

The Miscellaneous Works of Sir Walter Scott, 30 volumes (Edinburgh: A. & C. Black, 1870-1871);

The Waverley Novels, Centenary Edition, 25 volumes (Edinburgh: A. & C. Black, 1870-1871);

The Waverley Novels, Dryburgh Edition, 25 volumes (London & Edinburgh: A. & C. Black, 1892-1894);

The Waverley Novels, Border Edition, 48 volumes, edited by Andrew Lang (London: J. C. Nimmo, 1892-1894; Boston: Estes & Lauriat, 1893-1894);

The Poetical Works of Sir Walter Scott, With the Author's Introductions and Notes, edited by J. Logie Robertson (London: H. Frowde, 1894);

Lives of the Novelists (London, New York & Toronto: Oxford University Press, 1906);

Minstrelsy of the Scottish Border, edited by Thomas Henderson (London: Harrap, 1931);

Private Letters of the Seventeenth Century, edited by Douglas Grant (Oxford: Clarendon Press, 1947);

The Life of John Dryden, edited by Bernard Kreissman (Lincoln: University of Nebraska Press, 1963);

The Journal of Sir Walter Scott, edited by W. E. K. Anderson (Oxford: Clarendon Press, 1972);

The Prefaces to the Waverley Novels, edited by Mark A. Weinstein (Lincoln: University of Nebraska Press, 1978);

The Letters of Malachi Malagrowther, edited by P. H. Scott (Edinburgh: Blackwood, 1981);

Scott on Himself: A Collection of the Autobiographical Writings of Sir Walter Scott, edited by David Hewitt (Edinburgh: Scottish Academic Press, 1981).

OTHER: *The Chase, and William and Helen: Two Ballads from the German of Gottfried Augustus Bürger*, translated by Scott (Edinburgh: Printed by Mundell & Son for Manners & Miller and sold by T. Cadell, Jun. & W. Davies, 1796);

Goetz of Berlichingen, With the Iron Hand: A Tragedy. Translated from the German of Goethe, translated by Scott (London: Printed for J. Bell, 1799);

"The Fire King," "Glenfinlas," "The Eve of Saint John," "Frederick and Alice," and "The Wild Huntsmen," in *Tales of Wonder; Written and Collected by M. G. Lewis, Esq., M.P.*, 2 volumes (London: Printed by W. Bulmer for the author & sold by J. Bell, 1801), I: 62-69, 122-136, 137-147, 148-152, 153-163;

Minstrelsy of the Scottish Border, 2 volumes, edited by Scott (Kelso: Printed by James Ballantyne for T. Cadell, Jun. & W. Davies, London, and sold by Manners & Miller and A. Constable, Edinburgh, 1802); enlarged edition, 3 volumes (Edinburgh: Printed by James Ballantyne for Longman & Rees, London, and sold by Manners & Miller and A. Constable, Edinburgh, 1803; revised, 1810; Philadelphia: Carey, 1813);

Sir Tristrem: A Metrical Romance of the Thirteenth Century; by Thomas of Erclidoune, edited and completed by Scott (Edinburgh: Printed by James Ballantyne for Archibald Constable, Edinburgh, and Longman & Rees, London, 1804);

Original Memoirs, Written during the Great Civil War: Being the Life of Sir Henry Slingsby, and Memoirs of Capt. Hodgson, edited by Scott (Edinburgh: printed by J. Ballantyne for A. Constable, 1806);

The Works of John Dryden, 18 volumes, edited, with a biography, by Scott (London: Miller, 1808);

Joseph Strutt, *Queenhoo-Hall: A Romance; and Ancient Times: A Drama*, 4 volumes, edited by Scott (Edinburgh: Printed by J. Ballantyne for J. Murray, London, and A. Constable, Edinburgh, 1808);

Memoirs of Capt. George Carleton, An English Officer. . . . Written by Himself, edited by Scott (Edinburgh: Printed by J. Ballantyne for A. Constable and J. Murray, London, 1808);

Memoirs of Robert Carey, Earl of Monmouth, edited by Scott (Edinburgh: A. Constable, 1808);

The State Papers and Letters of Sir Ralph Sadler, Knight-Banneret, edited, with an introductory essay, by Scott (Edinburgh: Printed for Archibald Constable and for T. Cadell & W. Davies, William Miller, and John Murray, London, 1809);

A Collection of Scarce and Valuable Tracts [The Somers Tracts], second edition, 13 volumes, edited by Scott (London: Printed for T. Cadell & W. Davies, 1809-1815);

English Minstrelsy: Being a Selection of Fugitive Poetry from the Best English Authors, 2 volumes, edited by Scott (Edinburgh: J. Ballantyne, 1810);

The Poetical Works of Anna Seward; with Extracts from Her Literary Correspondence, 3 volumes, edited by Scott (Edinburgh: J. Ballantyne, 1810);

Scott's birthplace, the College Wynd (top), one of the steep, narrow lanes in the Old Town section of Edinburgh (New York Public Library); and George Square, Edinburgh (bottom; Scottish National Portrait Gallery). Scott lived with his family at number 95 George Square from 1775 until his marriage in 1797.

Secret History of the Court of James the First, 2 volumes, edited by Scott (Edinburgh: Printed for J. Ballantyne, 1811);

The Works of Jonathan Swift, 19 volumes, edited, with a biography and notes, by Scott (Edinburgh: Constable, 1814);

The Border Antiquities of England and Scotland, 2 volumes, includes an introduction by Scott (London: Printed for Longman, Hurst, Rees, Orme & Brown, 1814, 1817);

James, eleventh Baron Somerville, *Memorie of the Somervilles*, 2 volumes, edited by Scott (Edinburgh: Constable, 1815);

Ballantyne's Novelist's Library, 10 volumes, edited, with biographical prefaces, by Scott (London: Hurst, Robinson, 1821-1824);

Memorials of the Haliburtons, edited by Scott (Edinburgh: Printed by J. Ballantyne, 1824).

Walter Scott was the most influential novelist in world literature. The sources of his fiction were diverse and included extensive reading in medieval and Renaissance verse romance and detailed memory of English literary classics, especially Shakespeare. His novels may be read as critical responses to his eighteenth-century forerunners in the novel and to contemporary women writers of "national tales" and "historical romances." His work is informed by a specialist's knowledge of seventeenth-century history and literature, a sound education in Scottish Enlightenment history and sociology, a strong and highly personal reaction to the revolutionary crises of his day, and his experience as a best-selling narrative poet. Scott fashioned the historical novel as a major vehicle for inventing a supposedly "national" culture, history, identity, and destiny that would unite all regions and classes during an age of rapid and often violent change. Accordingly his novels, like his narrative poems, were not only best-sellers in their time but widely imitated then and thereafter, inspiring generations of nation builders in Europe and around the world through the nineteenth and into the twentieth century.

Yet Scott came from relatively obscure social and intellectual background on the margins of Europe. He was born in Edinburgh, the son of Anne Rutherford Scott, the well-educated daughter of a professor of medicine at Edinburgh University, and Walter Scott, a staunchly Presbyterian, Scottish lawyer descended from a Border farming family. His father's grandfather, an earlier Walter Scott, had joined the Jacobite uprising of 1715 and was later nicknamed "Beardie" because he swore not to shave until the Stuarts were restored to the throne. His son Robert Scott, the novelist's grandfather, is said to have quarreled with the old man and expressed his rebellion by declaring himself a Whig, or supporter of the Hanoverian line of George I. These conflicts were revived in the young Walter Scott's literary imagination as a continuing theme of his novels. Scott's family had become urbanized when his father left the family's roots in the land to become a professional man. This choice was again opting for the "new" Scotland over the "old," the future over the past. The Union of Scotland and England in 1707 had directed the attention of the Scottish landed magnates to politics, Parliament, and patronage at London, while the Scottish professional men educated at the great Scottish universities, with their progressive, modern curriculum, became leaders in Scottish society and culture, which were soon as advanced as anywhere in Europe, at least in Edinburgh, Glasgow, and Aberdeen and their hinterlands of the Scottish Lowlands. The Scottish Highlands remained another country, notoriously as backward as anywhere in Europe, looked down upon yet romanticized by their "enlightened" compatriots.

The Scottish university towns in particular were centers of a Scottish Enlightenment driven by professional men and their interests, especially by the lawyers, including Scott's father and Scott himself, who followed his father into that profession. This Enlightenment was a broad intellectual and cultural movement critical of both the mystifications of feudal and court government and the "superstition" and unreason of the common people. On the positive side, the Scottish Enlightenment promoted what would now be called "modernization"—science and technology for an efficient and productive agrarian and manufacturing economy, a higher level of "national" self-awareness to ensure social coherence and stability without recourse to autocratic government, the reform of laws and civil administration to ensure social and economic opportunity and equity, and the modification of social conventions and conduct to achieve a higher level of civil society. In time the promoters of these aims became dominant in countries other than Scotland. The Scottish Enlightenment could be seen as prophetic of modern Western society; one of the prophets and popularizers of the Scottish Enlightenment was Walter Scott. It is therefore not surprising that he has become a popular author in "modern-

Scott at age six (miniature by an unknown artist; Scottish National Portrait Gallery)

izing" societies throughout Europe and around the world, from the Far East to Latin America.

One reason for his popularity was that he retained a strong sense of the tension between "tradition" and "progress." He was born into the forward-looking "town gentry," but he self-consciously retained imaginative as well as personal links with his ancestral lands in the Borders and with the culture and community those lands had shaped over time. At eighteen months, Scott contracted polio, which left his right leg lame, and spent much time convalescing at his grandfather's farm. Here he learned to love sports and outdoor activity despite his handicap, heard tales of the old Jacobite days and of religious persecutions of the previous century, acquired a devotion to the beauty of the Border country, and developed a lifelong interest in the popular lore of the region as well as the traditional chapbook literature of the common people. This lore and literature left a deep impression on his imagination and later made him unusually sensitive to the otherness of plebeian culture to his own professional mentality. At the same time he became unusually well situated to be a leader in appropriating this lore and literature to the new professional middle-class idea of "national" identity, history, culture, and destiny, both in his activities as a folklorist during the 1790s and even more in his best-selling poems and novels.

Scott had a much more ambivalent attitude toward the Scottish national church, to which his father was strongly attached, than to other aspects of his cultural inheritance. The strong element of Calvinism in Presbyterianism repelled Scott and later inclined him to prefer the episcopalian church. This choice did involve complex crossing of loyalties, for episcopalianism was the established religion in the Church of England. Furthermore, the conflict between these two forms of Protestantism was deeply embedded in the history of Britain and especially the English Civil War and ensuing conflicts of the seventeenth-century. These conflicts were perpetuated to some extent in the eighteenth century in struggles between Tories and Jacobites on one hand and between Whigs and Hanoverians on the other. In other words, Scott's preferred form of religion was the dominant one in England, but a form of dissent in Scotland, whereas Presbyterianism was the dominant religious and cultural force in Scotland but a sect of religious Dissent in England. On the theological level, some Presbyterians' Calvinist belief in predestination, emphasis on purity of faith, and insistence on unmediated contact between the individual and the deity contrasted with the episcopalian belief in free will, emphasis on good works as well as true faith, and acceptance of the mediating, earthly role of the church. This contrast had important intellectual, cultural, and political consequences on the secular level, reinforcing regional, social, and cultural differences within Britain as potential sources of conflict and disharmony. This potential became manifest in the 1790s, when Presbyterians and other religious Dissenters in England were associated with support for the French Revolution as a harbinger of the religious toleration they had long been demanding. In Scotland some forms of Presbyterianism were associated with opposition to state interference in religion and other matters. This opposition could easily be seen as hostility to the present order of government. Thus Scott's preference for episcopalianism over his father's religion had complex significance and considerable personal and artistic consequence for him.

Scott began his formal education in 1775-1776 at Bath in England, where he was sent to seek treatment for his lameness. He was fond of literature and especially narrative verse and struck some observers as quite precocious. In October 1779 he was sent to the old High School in Edinburgh, where he was only a mediocre student; but he had an inquiring mind and strong memory and great physical and intellectual energy. He assimilated anything in narrative form, from historiography to Renaissance verse romance, and even as a schoolboy he could entertain his mates with his skill as a storyteller. During this time he became particularly fond of chivalric romance and history of bygone heroism. After leaving the High School in 1783, Scott spent some time with an aunt at Kelso in the Border country, where he attended the local grammar school and met James Ballantyne. Later in 1783 Scott entered Edinburgh University at the age of twelve (not unusually early at that time). The philosophical and cultural ideas he picked up there shaped his outlook for the rest of his life.

In March 1786 he was apprenticed to his father to train for five years as a Writer to the Signet, or practitioner of Scottish law. An illness interrupted his university education in 1788, but he returned in 1789, attending among others Dugald Stewart's lectures in moral philosophy and the lectures in Scots law and civil law given by David Hume, nephew and namesake of the philosopher. Through the law lectures in particular Scott gained an insight into the development of Scottish civil society from feudalism to the modern age; this insight would have a strong influence on his novels. Like other students and young professionals, Scott joined literary and philosophical societies that met regularly to discuss learned topics of current interest. Although called to the bar in 1792 Scott was little interested in getting into professional practice and later said that he would have gone into the military had it not been for his lame right leg. Instead he read widely from the large circulating library founded by the Scottish poet Allan Ramsay and run by James Sibbald. He also spent a good deal of time traveling around Scotland, especially in the Borders but also in the Highlands, collecting folk ballads. One of his sources was Margaret Hogg, the mother of James Hogg, a shepherd whom Scott later helped in a career as journalist, poet, and novelist.

Like many young men of the time, Scott was interested in both popular and avant-garde culture. With some friends he took up the literature of the contemporary German Sturm und Drang group, a nationalistic cultural movement reacting against the French Enlightenment and its German imitators. The Sturm und Drang writers were more interested in local folk sources of national identity than in Enlightenment cosmopolitanism. Just as these writers felt German culture was overshadowed by the French Enlightenment, the official culture at the courts of many German states, so many young Scots professionals resented the dominant influence of English culture in Scotland. Furthermore, Sturm und Drang writers acknowledged a debt to Scottish writing such as James Macpherson's literary forgeries, the poems of Ossian. The philosopher of the Sturm und Drang, Johann Gottfried Herder, fashioned an influential cultural anthropology inspired by the example of "Ossian" and calling for a return to the culture of the "folk" as the basis of national revival. Scott was probably less interested in Sturm und Drang cultural politics than in the energy and novelty of their work and their aura of being avant-garde. Nevertheless, the parallels between the literature of the Sturm und Drang and Scott's later poems and novels would prepare the way for their influence on the Continent. Meanwhile, Scott contented himself with "translating"—his command of German was in fact very shaky—Gottfried August Bürger's art ballad "Lenore," which he retitled "William and Helen," other poems by Bürger and by Johann Wolfgang von Goethe, and several German plays. He published two poems from Bürger, anonymously, in 1796 and his version of Goethe's historical drama *Goetz von Berlichingen* (1733), under his own name, in 1799.

In the early 1790s Scott experienced a painful collision between the ideals of this progressive Sentimental culture and more traditional and conventional social practices and values. He fell deeply in love with Williamina Belsches, but it seems her family did not consider Scott a good enough match, and she married someone else. The disappointment left a deep impression, and even years later Scott found recollection of her could stir emotions he would rather not face. On 24 December 1797 he married a Frenchwoman, Charlotte Carpenter (Anglicized from Charpentier), probably the illegitimate daughter of Ar-

Scott and Charlotte Carpenter circa 1797, the year of their marriage (miniatures by unknown artists; Collection of Mrs. Maxwell-Scott of Abbotsford). Scott is wearing the uniform of the Royal Edinburgh Volunteer Light Dragoons.

thur Hill, second Marquis of Downshire. They had a successful if dispassionate marriage, and four children—Charlotte Sophia (born 1799), Walter (born 1801), Anne (born 1803), and Charles (born 1805).

Apart from the broad cultural movements of the Scottish Enlightenment and the pre-Revolutionary culture of Sensibility, the most important influences on the young Scott were the unprecedented events of the French Revolution and its aftershocks in Britain and in Scotland. Scott responded strongly to the political and social crises of the 1790s and became an ardent opponent of what was called "Jacobinism," or plebeian and middle-class revolutionary ideology, whether in France or Britain. Artisan political protest and professional middle-class "Jacobinism" were particularly prominent in Scotland in the early 1790s, and the repression of them was particularly harsh there. In 1797 Scott himself helped organize a unit of volunteer cavalry, the Edinburgh Light Dragoons. This troop, like others of a similar kind throughout Britain, was made up mostly of middle-class citizens, ostensibly to resist a threatened French invasion but also to intimidate rebellious, pro-French workers. During one skirmish with men rioting over the high price of food in the spring of 1800, Scott narrowly escaped injury but found he could not bring himself to cut down the man who tried to strike him. Scott the writer did revel in representing martial spirit, but he also represented strongly the horrors and misery of war. He certainly entered into military training with enthusiasm in the 1790s. But his professional future had to be attended to as well, and in 1798, thanks to personal influence, he was appointed to the office of sheriff-depute of Selkirkshire in the Border country, an office which he performed faithfully over many years.

Meanwhile, Scott was reading widely in the popular literature, history, and mythology of Britain and Europe and writing imitations of traditional oral ballads. In 1802 and 1803 he published his first work of importance, *Minstrelsy of the Scottish Border*, an edition of ballads he had collected himself. This collection was a major contribution to the subject then known as "popular antiquities," later known as "folklore." Like others of his time, Scott viewed the oral narratives and songs of the common people in light of the humanist tradition of textual criticism that assumed an "original" text from which all others were descended. Yet he also showed awareness of the quite different, communal and unhistorical textuality of oral culture. The difference between written and oral cultures would later surface in his novels. *Minstrelsy of the Scottish Border* also led to friendship with its printer and publisher, his acquaintance from Kelso grammar school days, James Ballantyne, and his brother John. Their personal, literary, and business relationship was entangled with Scott's successes and failures until the end of his life. Scott was also proud of the fact that he made six hundred pounds, then a very considerable sum, from *Minstrelsy of the Scottish Border*. The following year, 1804, he published an edition of the medieval romance *Sir Tristrem*.

Scott achieved his first major literary success in 1805 with a long narrative poem, *The Lay of the Last Minstrel*. In the same year he became the silent partner in the publishing firm of John Ballantyne, thus keeping one eye on business and the other on poetry. *The Lay of the Last Minstrel* was obviously a development of his folkloristic and antiquarian interests. Similar to folkloristic narrative poems of the late eighteenth century, it appropriates folk- and art-ballad forms to the verse romance and an Enlightenment glamorization of medieval chivalry, with touches from the Gothic novel. The larger aim was to dramatize a "national" culture supposedly rooted in the country's distinctive landscape and the resulting life and character of its "people," but in fact the poem represents an "imagined community" beyond the dangerous social and regional divisions of the 1790s. This aim was based on the Scottish Enlightenment vision of a progressive, unified society, and it was the common ground between Scott's poems and novels.

Although Scott later claimed to have begun a novel in 1805—which he resumed writing in 1813 and published in 1814 as *Waverley*—he would have been aware that poetry had a much higher cultural standing than prose fiction at that time and that poetry was considered a proper endeavor even for a professional man and a lawyer. The novel, by contrast, was considered a "woman's" form. It is true that the narrative poem combining romantic adventure with antiquarian scholarship had been developed in the late eighteenth century partly by women writers such as Hannah Cowley, but the form was still well within the masculine side of the gendered order of literary discourse. Alongside the sublime and manly art of poetry, Scott also continued his conventionally masculine work as a scholar, with an edition of the works of seventeenth-century poet, critic, and dramatist John Dryden, published in 1808. This eighteen-volume collection was one of many such editorial tasks he would undertake with the aim of establishing a professionally treated body of English "classics," a "national" literature as the basis for a modern educational curriculum that would unite Britons in a common print culture. Even so, Scott suspected that many prospective professional clients might distrust a lawyer who was also a poet, and to provide more financial security he obtained in 1806 the reversion of another public legal post, that of principal clerk of the Court of Session. This position too was no sinecure, and Scott had to do the work without pay for several years while he waited for the actual holder to retire or die.

A literary labor that was partly a rehearsal for his historical novels was his editing and completing *Queenhoo-Hall* (1808), an unfinished prose romance by the antiquarian Joseph Strutt. At about the same time Scott broached with James Ballantyne the possibility of republishing a series of "romances of wonder," with notes and introductions by Scott, and to include well-known English novels, translations from German and other contemporary literatures, and selections of Persian, Arabic, and other oriental tales. This project fell through, but in 1808 Scott was paid the extraordinary sum of one thousand pounds by the enterprising publisher Archibald Constable for the poem *Marmion*. Scott's partnership with James Ballantyne, as the printer of his works, was also proving profitable. Scott continued to pull the strings of literary patronage for others, including the shoemaker-poet John Struthers, whom he helped to find a publisher, and the German scholar Henry Weber, whom Scott helped promote new editions of metrical romances. These were only two of the writers Scott helped in his lifetime. As he later told John Gibson Lockhart, "there was hardly one of all my schemes that did not afford me the means of serving some poor devil of a brother author"—and sisters, too, as Scott later helped the careers of women writers such as the novelist Susan Ferrier. When offered the post of poet laureate in 1813, he turned it down but used his influence to get it conferred on his friend Robert Southey, whom he thought needed the money.

Scott was able to arrange things other writers could not, largely because he was both commercially successful and socially astute. By 1810 he was a literary lion, on familiar terms with important noblemen, politicians, writers, and public figures. These relationships were also due in part to his ability to combine conservative social and political views with active promotion of various progressive projects and causes. One of his major literary achievements was to show the apparent inevitability and desirability, yet the social and cultural cost, of "progress" in a post-Revolutionary age. Scott's poems and novels are often set near similar crises in the past, showing how they were or could have been prevented from deteriorating into the kind of revolution he and his compatriots saw in France and feared in Britain. Scott was a modern but unwavering Tory throughout his life and, whenever he could, worked to further conservative social and political views against what he saw as the destabilizing forces of political "innovation." Though himself a "new man," risen from the professions by his own merit, he never doubted that the landed gentry were the natural leaders of society and the nation. In 1809 he helped found the Tory *Quarterly Review* to counterbalance the Whig *Edinburgh Review*, the first of a new breed of professional critical and literary magazines replacing those of the eighteenth century. Yet Scott also had close ties to the *Edinburgh Review*—a sign of his ability to get along with men of differing political and cultural values. At about the same time he helped reorganize the Royal Edinburgh Theatre on a more professional footing. Though not a successful playwright himself, Scott saw his novels adapted by others into popular and durable dramas. Throughout Europe there were more nineteenth-century grand operas based on his works than on those of any other writer except William Shakespeare.

As yet, however, Scott was known as a best-selling poet, and in 1810 he published another success, *The Lady of the Lake*. The poem was an immediate sensation, sold twenty thousand copies in just months, and was said to have created an entirely new tourist industry for the Highland sites described in the poem. Scott made twenty-two hundred pounds from the first edition alone, apart from his profits as partner in Ballantyne's firm, which again printed his work. He had need of the money. He and his family, like other genteel urban professional people, spent summers and holidays in the country at Ashestiel, a rented house on the River Tweed. In 1811, however, Scott bought the modest farm of Clarty Hole lower down the Tweed and began transforming it into a gentleman's estate, building a fake baronial castle named Abbotsford. He had joined the landed gentry, the social ambition of most successful professional men in Britain. Additions to the house and estate strained even Scott's prodigious literary earnings and business profits; yet Abbotsford remained an ever-varying pleasure to him. Here he enjoyed the interests and pursuits of a gentleman, including outings with his much-beloved dogs (some of whom appear in his novels), carried out the local duties and benefactions expected of a landlord, received a constant stream of visitors, and worked on his novels and other literary projects. Scott also became concerned to pass down his newly acquired estate and status to his children, and especially his son Walter, whom he encouraged to enter the genteel military profession.

As a "new man" Scott had a strong interest in "feudalizing" his own social status, identity, and estate. He self-consciously assumed the role of semifeudal retainer to important noblemen with whom he was distantly related. He took a feudal fancy to regarding the house of Buccleuch as the "chief" of his "clan" and was a genuine friend to three successive dukes of that family. Yet in April 1824, when his son Walter complained that his prospective bride's family had a vulgar surname (Jobson) and had made their money in "trade," Scott replied that in the present-day aristocracy of wealth or talent was equal to any; moreover, his own family was only distantly noble "and therefore, though gentlemen, are much like what the French call Gentillatres and the highlanders Duniewassels." Meanwhile, at Abbotsford Scott combined fake antiquity with modern convenience, ornamenting the house with antiques suitable to its architectural appearance yet installing such innovations as gas lighting (Scott was a shareholder in the gas company). He aimed to be a progressive landlord yet laid out his lands with fake historic sites and promoted schemes such as the transplanting of mature trees that could enable a new estate to appear long-established within its builder's lifetime.

Scott's next poem, *The Vision of Don Roderick* (1811), was not as successful as he hoped, and though he was paid three thousand pounds for its successor, *Rokeby* (1813), his popularity as a poet seemed to be waning. He published another

Scott in the ruins of Hermitage Castle, 1808 (portrait by Henry Raeburn; Collection of the Duke of Buccleuch and Queensberry, K.T.)

poem, *The Bridal of Triermain* (1813), anonymously to test the perceptiveness and loyalty of the reading public, but the work was widely recognized as his. Keeping up his contributions to building an institution of national literature, he published an edition of Jonathan Swift's works in 1814. As an editor Scott had high standards for accuracy and scholarship, and though Swift, like Dryden, was coming to be regarded as an "indecent" writer, Scott refused to bowdlerize or "castrate" the texts of either Swift or Dryden. In the same year he published a literary experiment, *Waverley; or, 'Tis Sixty Years Since*, the historical novel he supposedly began in 1805 and actually advertised as a forthcoming book for 1809-1810. Scott published the work anonymously and did not expect much from it. He also knew that, while being a best-selling poet might not seriously compromise either his standing in the legal profession or his newly acquired gentility, appearing as a novelist was another thing altogether. Not only was the novel generally (if erroneously) thought to be mainly written and read by women (and therefore widely regarded as subliterary), it was also highly commercialized and associated with the decadent court culture that had left Britain in difficulties during the Napoleonic wars. Publishing a novel might even undermine Scott's reputation (and profits) as a successful poet.

Nevertheless, if anyone in the Romantic period appreciated the ideological and artistic potential of the novel, past and present, it was Scott, and his own novels were formed from the elements he admired in his predecessors and contemporaries. In a variety of prefaces and essays later collected as *Lives of the Novelists* (1906), Scott reflected on their work, revealing the sources of his own. He saw Henry Fielding as "the father of the English novel" and, significantly, "a painter of national manners." Like Fielding, Scott uses an omniscient third-person narrator to give tonal unity to his novels, relies on picaresque adventures to display his themes, presents characters as representative social types, and relies on the romance plot of testing a young man's character by experience of the contradictions and relativities in the

Abbotsford as it appeared during Scott's lifetime

wider world. Scott even throws the hero of *Waverley* into the same historical event in which Fielding's Tom Jones is caught up—the Jacobite rebellion of 1745. Fielding's major achievement, according to Scott, was his high degree of integration of plot and episode, "the felicitous contrivance, and happy extrication of the story, where every incident tells upon and advances the catastrophe, while, at the same time, it illustrates the characters of those interested in its approach."

Scott rated his compatriot Tobias Smollett as high as Fielding but deplored Smollett's desultory arrangement of episodes. Scott saw Smollett's achievement as "vivacity" of representation in details, characters, and episodes, contrasted to the circumstantial minuteness of realism in the novels of Alain-René Lesage, Daniel Defoe, and Samuel Richardson. They often carried realism to a tedious extent, Scott felt, obstructing the progress of what he called "narration," or the connection of parts into a sequence always moving forward to the "catastrophe," or climax of the story. Many critics have accused Scott himself of loose narrative structure, but his formal interest was in "vivacity" of characters and episodes at once realistic and figural, thereby fusing the historical and literary, or poetic. This fusion was the basis of his appeal to readers for the next century and his legacy to successors such as Stendhal, Allessandro Manzoni, Honoré de Balzac, Thomas Carlyle, Charles Dickens, Anthony Trollope, George Eliot, and Leo Tolstoy.

The other major aspect of novel form for Scott was "style," by which he meant both narrative mode, or the construction of the "author" as a model consciousness in the text, and style in the usual sense of language, sentence structure, rhythm, tone, figures of speech, and diction. "Style" in this large sense was for Scott a moral and even political issue more than an aesthetic one. For example, of the "Sentimental" novelists Scott disliked Laurence Sterne and preferred his own countryman Henry Mackenzie. Scott felt that both depicted the passions successfully, but Mackenzie rightly rejected Sterne's "licence of wit, and flights of imagination, retrenched, in great measure, his episodical digressions, and altogether banished the indecency and buffoonery to which [Sterne] had too frequent recourse." Where Sterne had "a beautiful trope," Mackenzie had "a moral truth" and wrote "pure musical Addisonian prose." In other words, Sterne used "style" to create an idiosyncratic and individualistic textual voice, but Mackenzie followed the essayist Joseph Addison in aiming for a voice of educated, cultivated consensus.

This distinction was not merely formal. During a revolutionary age when all literary forms were used in political debate, formal and stylistic options were inextricably tied to political positions. In the 1790s the pre-Revolutionary cultural movement known as Sensibility came to be seen as a forerunner of Revolutionary politics. The idiosyncratic and individualistic authorial "voice" characteristic of Sentimental literature was used by Revolutionary sympathizers in Britain, "English Jacobins," as a device for authenticating their political views without recourse to traditional cultural institutions and discourses. In opposition, a Fieldingesque or Addisonian rhetorical posture was often adopted by "Anti-Jacobin" British writers. Later, in the aftermath of the Revolution debate, such a style became associated with literature of national reconciliation. This was the literary movement which Scott joined, and it is not surprising that his first novel is dedicated to Mackenzie as "our Scottish Addison."

Among his other contemporaries, Scott most admired women novelists such as Maria Edgeworth and Jane Austen. He claimed that Edgeworth was a major inspiration, especially her Irish tales such as *Castle Rackrent* (1800), "The Absentee" (1812), and *Ormond* (1817). These tales incorporate Irish life and lore in stories advocating a coalition of professional middle class and landed gentry able to unite Britain and lead it from feudal to capitalist paternalism. Edgeworth assigns social and regional characters dialect speech, making them more realistic and socially representative, but she also locates such non-standard language within a textual structure dominated by the standard written English used by the narrator and the wise characters in the tale. Thus Edgeworth constructs a linguistic universe implicitly favoring those with "standard" English, the form used by professionals and just then emerging as the basis of a "national" dialect because it belonged to no particular place or region of Britain. Edgeworth's tales also adapt the romance journey and novel of education to depict a young man encountering a society divided by class, religion, and merely local and regional interest, yet learning his proper social role and responsibilities in a national context. Scott took Edgeworth's fictional form and instilled it with the wide range of learning, allusion, and reference that readers would expect from a writer with a man's education, professional experience, and access to public and political life. Edgeworth's achievement was recognized in her time, but Scott's development of it finally established the place of the novel in the emergent institution of national literature.

Scott was also one of the first to recognize Jane Austen's achievement, which he saw as different from his own. He praised *Emma* (1816) in the October 1815 issue of the *Quarterly Review* (published in March 1816) and—after reading *Pride and Prejudice* (1813) "for the third time at least"—in March 1826 he commented in his journal, "The Big Bow-wow strain I can do myself like any now going, but the exquisite touch which renders ordinary commonplace things and characters interesting from the truth of the description and sentiment is denied to me." This remark reflects a common view of women novelists as specialists, by their very nature, in subjectivity, domesticity, and the details of local, daily "reality." Scott was also being unjust to himself. His novels of description incorporate topography, architecture, costume, customs, laws, lore, and historical narrative, developing the work of other women predecessors or contemporaries such as Clara Reeve, Sophia Lee, and Ann Radcliffe. Furthermore, many critics praised Scott for showing the relation between large historical movements and everyday life and private relationships. Scott's comment on Austen registers his preference for constructing characters in terms more social than subjective and his reluctance to represent powerful feelings and intimate relationships. This reluctance may have an autobiographical basis in his early disappointment in love and the pessimistic, depressive side of his character, but it is also a reaction to Romantic fascination with extreme individualism ranging from Byronism to the cult of Napoleon Bonaparte. Scott sided with many conservative men and women writers in emphasizing duties rather than "rights" and the inescapably social nature of the individual.

Scott's aversion to Romantic subjectivity, as antisocial or even revolutionary, may have combined with his reluctance to confront his own deepest feelings and his ambivalence about the social and cultural status of the novel. Nevertheless, these attitudes had important artistic consequences in his experiments with narrative framework and persona. The early successors to *Waverley* were published as "by the author of *Waverley*." But *The Black Dwarf* and *Old Mortality* were published together as *Tales of My Landlord* (1816), ostensibly assembled by the provincial antiquarian and poet Peter Pattieson and edited after his untimely death by the pedantic Jedediah

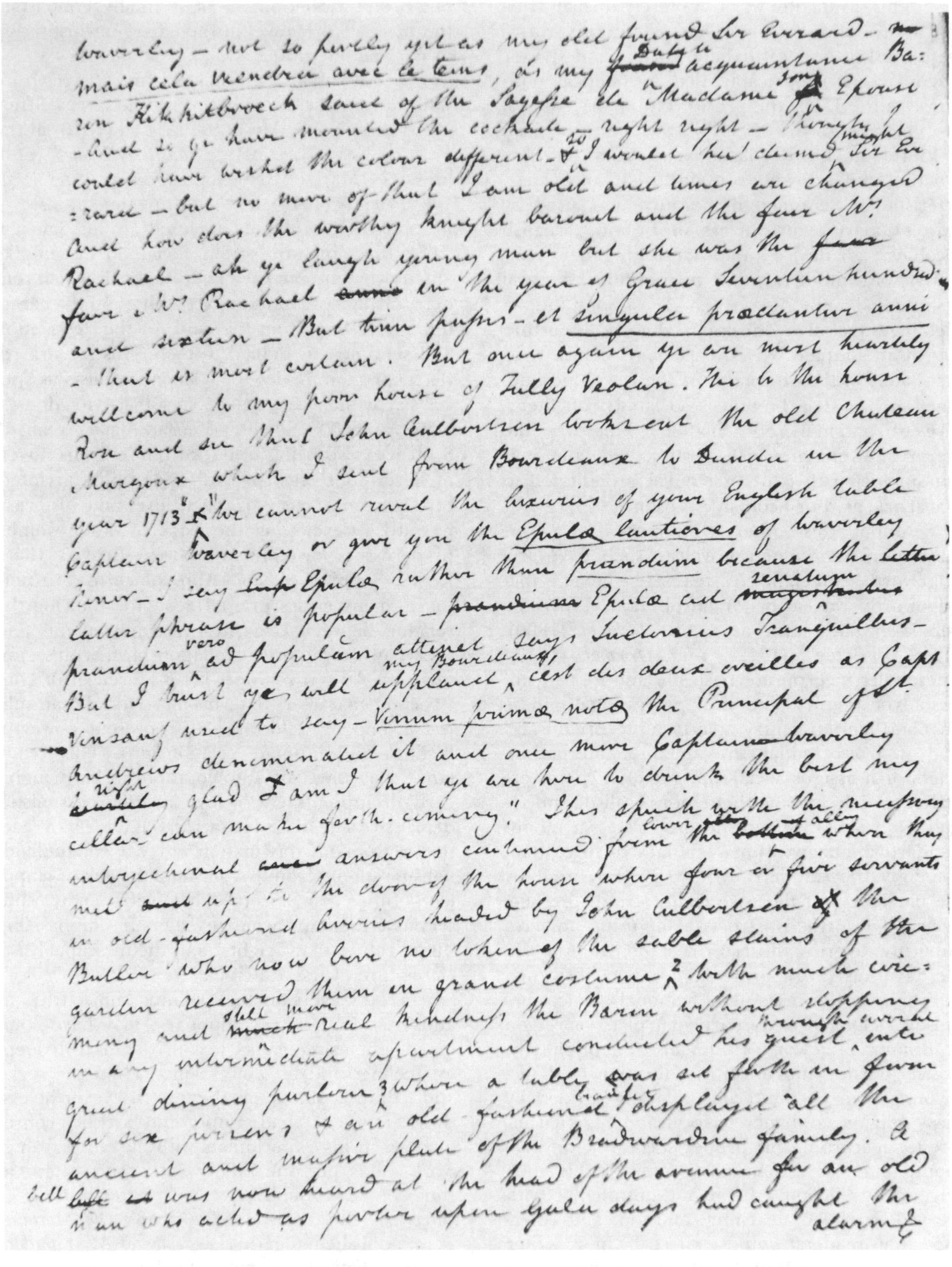
Waverley – not so portly yet as my old friend Sir Everard –
mais cela viendra avec le tems, as my Dutch acquaintance Ba:
ron Kikkitbroeck said of the Sagesse de Madame son Epouse
– And so ye have mounted the cockade – right right – Though I
could have wished the colour different – & so I would ha' deemed might Sir Eve
:rard – but no more of that I am old and times are changed
And how does the worthy knight baronet and the fair Mrs
Rachael – ah ye laugh young man but she was the fair
fair Mrs Rachael in the year of Grace Seventeen hundred
and sixteen – But time passes – et singula praedantur anni
– that is most certain. But once again ye are most heartily
welcome to my poor house of Tully Veolan. Hie to the house
Rose and see that John Cultbertson looks out the old Chateau
Margoux which I sent from Bourdeaux to Dundee in the
year 1713 – we cannot rival the luxuries of your English table
Captain Waverley or give you the Epulae lautiores of Waverley
Honor – I say Epulae rather than prandium because the latter
latter phrase is popular – Epulae ad senatum
prandium vero ad populum attinet says Suetonius Tranquillus –
But I trust ye will applaud my Bourdeaux, c'est des deux oreilles as Capt
Vinsauf used to say – Vinum primae notae the Principal of St.
Andrews denominated it and once more Captain Waverley
right glad I am that ye are here to drink the best my
cellar can make forth-coming." This speech with the necessary
interjectional answers continued from the lower alley where they
met up to the door of the house where four or five servants
in old-fashioned liveries headed by John Cultbertson the
Butler who now bore no token of the sable stains of the
garden received them in grand costume with much cere:
mony and still more real kindness the Baron without stopping
in any intermediate apartment conducted his guest through a
great dining parlour where a table was set forth in form
for six persons & an old-fashioned beaufet displayed all the
ancient and massive plate of the Bradwardine family. A
bell was now heard at the head of the avenue for an old
man who acted as porter upon Gala days had caught the
alarm &

Page from the manuscript for Waverley *(Adv. MS. I.I.O, f. 31v; National Library of Scotland)*

Cleishbotham, whose surname could be translated as "flog-bottom" or perhaps "rubbish dump." Cleishbotham is schoolmaster in the village of Gandercleugh, symbolically "the central part—the navel . . . of this our realm of Scotland." It may have been the grimness of *Old Mortality* as a tale of seventeenth-century religious and political fanaticism that induced Scott to introduce these figures to mediate between past and present; yet he carried this narrative persona through four series of *Tales of My Landlord*. In *Ivanhoe* (1819) Scott introduced another narrative persona, Laurence Templeton, who addresses his work to the Reverend Doctor Dryasdust, Fellow of the Antiquarian Society. *The Monastery* (1820) purports to be a manuscript received by Captain Cuthbert Clutterbuck ("cluttered bench or desk") from a French Benedictine monk of Scottish descent who has been driven into exile by the French Revolution. In the "Introductory Epistle" of *Kenilworth* (1821) Captain Clutterbuck recounts a meeting with "the Author of Waverley" in which the latter replies to his critics and defends the artistry of his novels. This preface is perhaps Scott's most interesting reflection on his own work. Even after Scott revealed publicly his authorship of the Waverley Novels he published two series of *Chronicles of the Canongate* (1827 and 1828) supposed to be the work of Chrystal Croftangry, "a Scottish gentleman of the old school," trained as a lawyer but now with "a fortune, temper, and person, rather the worse for wear"—rather like Scott himself. Through these various masks Scott not only comments on his own work but also plays with literary theoretical issues. These include the fictional or rhetorical character of any narration, the instability of narratorial identity, the contingent nature of any narrative act, and the commercial nature of literature.

The relationship of fiction and history, much debated by Scott's critics in his own time and throughout the nineteenth century, is discussed in the introduction to *The Betrothed*, which was published with *The Talisman* as *Tales of the Crusaders* (1825). This introduction purports to be minutes of a meeting of prospective "shareholders designing to form a joint-stock company, united for the purpose of writing and publishing the class of works called the Waverley Novels." Various of Scott's personae show up to give their opinions on the prospects of the project, but the "chairman," who is "the Eidolon, or image of the author," becomes irritated with their reluctance and threatens to go ahead on his own:

> I will leave you and your whole hacked stock in trade—your caverns and your castles—your modern antiques, and your antiquated moderns—your confusion of times, manners, and circumstances—your properties, as player-folk say of scenery and dresses—the whole of your exhausted expedients, to the fools who choose to deal with them. I will vindicate my fame with my own right hand . . . in a word, I will write HISTORY!

One persona comments, "The old gentleman forgets he is the greatest liar since Sir John Mandeville"—supposed author of a fourteenth-century book of fictitious travels. Another persona replies, "Not the worse historian for that, . . . since history, you know, is half fiction." Scott is playing with the relativity of historical discourse, drawing the reader's attention to the fact that the past is transmitted through documents and evidence that never speak for themselves but must always be interpreted by fallible and prejudiced humans, and therefore historiography is as constructed as fiction. These prefaces and personae broach important issues around Scott's innovations as a novelist; yet the stories of the novels bear little trace of such critical self-reflection and are narrated confidently and authoritatively, much in the manner of the Enlightenment "philosophical history" that informs the social and historical vision of the Waverley Novels.

Certainly Scott was ambivalent about the Waverley Novels and their success. He repeatedly both disparaged and boasted of them in his journal and private conversations. He thought a truly "great" man such as Arthur Wellesley, first Duke of Wellington, would hardly give such works a thought, and he compared them to "lines" of cheap manufactured goods. Yet he was bemused and even amazed by his own fertility of imagination and saw the work as both craft and heroic adventure. He spoke of writing as a form of artisanship, using the term *wrought* instead of *wrote*, and he determined to discharge his huge financial debt in almost knightly fashion, declaring, "My own right hand shall do it." Even his manner of composition was a mixture of casualness and confidence, improvisation and method, brashness and bravery. He would start with the germ of story, characters, and setting in a particular situation and move forward through the plot, improvising as he went along. When he reached an impasse he would take vigorous exercise, a dose of socializing, or an extra glass of wine at dinner to ensure good sleep, and he would rise to find the way ahead clear. He wrote quickly, relying on James Ballantyne to fill in punctuation, catch blunders, and so on. He used one side of a sheet of paper and when he had finished a stint of composition he would go back, making changes and additions on the blank facing page. His handling of proofs and revisions was sometimes careless, more often scrupulous.

The Waverley Novels are appropriately named after the first of them, for *Waverley* has the formal and thematic characteristics that Scott reworked in various ways through almost two decades and over two dozen novels. The leisurely opening chapters describe the youth of Edward Waverley, whose surname suggests his character. Significantly, this character resembles that of the inexperienced and impressionable protagonist of anti-Jacobin novels of the 1790s, who is all too easy ideological prey for courtly intriguers out to disturb the social order for their own ends. Scott displaces the counterrevolutionary theme to the Scottish past, but many elements of the Revolution debate haunt *Waverley*. Waverley is caught between a dual political ancestry, with his Whig and Hanoverian father, now deceased, on one side and his Tory and Jacobite uncle, appropriately named Sir Everard (ever-hard, or diehard), on the other. Raised by his uncle, Waverley has developed a romantic Jacobitism that is reinforced by his extensive reading in courtly chivalric romances of an earlier era, giving him the character of a quixote. Scott here is true to a particular line of Scottish Enlightenment thought that was highly critical of feudal chivalry as false ideals not maintained in practice. The Enlightenment writers, and Scott in *Waverley*, preferred to reconstruct chivalry as a new, bourgeois, and domestic ideal of the gentleman, and this ideal is in fact what Waverley achieves after all his misadventures with the false chivalry of the Jacobite rebellion.

True to character, Sir Everard chooses a military career for his nephew. On joining his regiment in Scotland, Waverley stops to visit his uncle's old Jacobite friend, the Baron of Bradwardine, who lives on a dilapidated estate on the borders of the Lowlands and the Highlands, where time has stood still since an earlier age of semifeudal gentry culture. Though Bradwardine and his retinue are comic, the comedy indicates the remoteness of the place, in more ways than one, from mainstream society. Bradwardine's alienation from his times is dangerous because it opens the way for his estate to become a pathway between the Highlands and the Lowlands for social outsiders, including criminals. The estate also leads Waverley deeper into the feudal Scottish past when he visits Glennaquoich, the Highland domain of clan MacIvor.

Here the past is not a relic but an illusion, carefully created as a show by the Frenchified clan chief, Fergus, in order to exploit the feudal loyalties of his people for the new cause of Charles Edward Stuart, known as "Bonnie Prince Charlie," the "Young Pretender." Fergus, like the other Jacobites, has spent so much time in exile in France with his "king" that he has become more French than Scottish; that is, he has become skilled in the arts of courtly intrigue. Such intrigue, as Scott's readers would know, was supposed to depend on the use of women as seducers, and Fergus in fact uses his sister Flora, who is genuinely attached to and expert in her people's traditions, to inveigle the romantic Waverley into sympathy for the Stuart cause. In this respect Flora is Scott's version of woman as repository of the "national" culture, depicted in such earlier novels as Sydney Owenson's *Wild Irish Girl* (1806) and Germaine, Madame de Staël's *Corinne* (1807). Scott's version of the character is less positive, however. Flora is the star of the theatrical shows of "traditional" Scottish culture stage-managed by her brother at Glennaquoich to dazzle the ignorant (the clan followers) and the gullible (Waverley). That Flora should be used as a tool by her own brother shows the moral bankruptcy of what Fergus represents. As readers of Scottish Enlightenment social criticism would know, theatrical displays similar to those put on by Fergus were supposed to be a major way that autocratic court government and "priestcraft" (the MacIvors are of course Catholics) maintained their illusion of power and their ideological and cultural sway over the nation at large. Though the reader is allowed to see behind the scenes and thus detect the illusion in a way Waverley is not, both the courtly and the "primitive" characters at Glennaquoich are sharply realized by Scott, with peculiar traits and characteristic speech, thereby impressing the reader with their power to impress the callow hero. Scott's justly celebrated "realism" of characterization was not a mere artistic achievement—he would have considered that to be effete aestheticism—but part of a politically motivated rhetorical strategy, something he would have considered the proper business of any serious writer and artist.

Three of Scott's four children: Walter (top), who was an officer in the Eighteenth Hussars (portrait by Sir William Allan); Sophia (bottom left), who married John Gibson Lockhart (portrait by William Nicholson); and Anne (bottom right), who never married and cared for her father during his last years (portrait by William Nicholson; all portraits from the Collection of Mrs. Maxwell-Scott of Abbotsford)

Complex circumstances, including the plotting of Fergus, the complicity of Flora, and the undeniably regal charisma of Prince Charles, lead Waverley to join the Jacobite rebellion almost despite himself. Waverley's relative malleability represents Scott's pessimistic view, in the aftermath of cataclysmic Revolutionary events, that history comes to bear on the ordinary individual without much clear understanding of it or choice on his or her part. In fact, in the Waverley Novels one who tries to make history often comes to a bad end. Such pessimism is somewhat at odds with the optimistic rationalism of the pre-Revolutionary Scottish Enlightenment and could be considered Scott's version of Romantic irony. Significantly, Waverley plays the role of mere bystander at the Jacobite victory of Preston-pans, though he manages to save an English officer, Colonel Talbot, from being put to death. Swept along by others, Waverley then follows the prince's army into England, where the people are expected to flock to the Stuart banner. They do not, and in the withdrawal back to Scotland, Waverley is separated from the army and forced into hiding. Though he is now a traitor, his growing awareness of the cruelties of rebellion and war, the duplicities of politics, the self-interested intriguing of the Jacobites, and his own place as a political pawn have already alienated him from the Pretender's cause.

Fortunately Colonel Talbot's influence gains Waverley a pardon, and after the final defeat of the Jacobites he witnesses the trial of the still-defiant Fergus and his still-loyal Highland followers. Waverley now sees the Highlanders as survivors of a primitive and outmoded social culture and thereby the dupes of decadent court politics. They stand for the common people misled by selfish leaders, be those leaders courtly autocrats or revolutionary democrats. Even in defeat and death, however, the valor and virtues of the Highlanders are recognized, as Scott characteristically insists that much can be said for those who must pass away in the name of progress and the national destiny. Flora appropriately retires to a French convent, a symbol in Enlightenment social criticism of sterile and unproductive "superstition." Waverley does manage to have the Bradwardine estate restored to the baron and to have the manor itself restored from the ravages of war—an apt symbol of the constitution retaining its old, traditional form but with new materials. As Flora predicted, Waverley settles down with the wisely feminine and domestic Rose Bradwardine to the life of a benevolent landed gentleman, doing what he can for the clan MacIvor, and perhaps becoming someone rather like the narrator, and still an instrument, though in a different sphere, of history as the production over time of "modern" Britain.

Waverley embodies in novel form a concern for social harmony, national unity, and enlightened, tolerant leadership. This concern was certainly prominent in public debate at the time Scott probably conceived and perhaps partly wrote the novel, in 1808; he may even have had this concern as early as he claimed to have begun the novel, in 1805. Yet the social and national outlook in 1808 and 1809 was bleak, and the novel also embodies more optimistic beliefs—in the possibility of social reconciliation, triumph over an alien political ideology, and renewed progress—characteristic of the years 1813 and 1814, when Scott finished the novel. At the same time these concerns are articulated through a well-established, widely diffused Scottish Enlightenment sociology of a supposedly "national" identity that was shaped over time by particular landscapes, modified by inherited institutions and culture, expressed in social practices (including speech, dress, "manners," domestic architecture, and so on), and lived out daily at the local level. Of necessity, then, *Waverley* and its successors are novels of description because the actual or assumed factuality of this descriptive material validates Scott's representation of the past as an analogue to and influence on the present. *Waverley* addresses some of the most pressing concerns of the later stages of the international struggle against Napoleon and the spirit of the Revolution that he claimed to represent. Scott's realism of representation and energy of figurative historical allusion aestheticized these concerns, making them available for the imaginative grasp of his readers. It is hardly surprising that readers responded enthusiastically.

Waverley sold quickly and was widely attributed to Scott, but he did not publicly acknowledge his authorship of it and its many successors until 1827. This secrecy required an elaborate system of copyists and the collaboration of Scott's close friend and business partner, James Ballantyne, who also acted as a self-appointed spokesman for the reading public, sometimes to Scott's irritation. By the time Scott published *Waverley* his career as a poet was virtually over. He later said, perhaps half jokingly, that he turned to the novel and away from poetry in face of the emergent

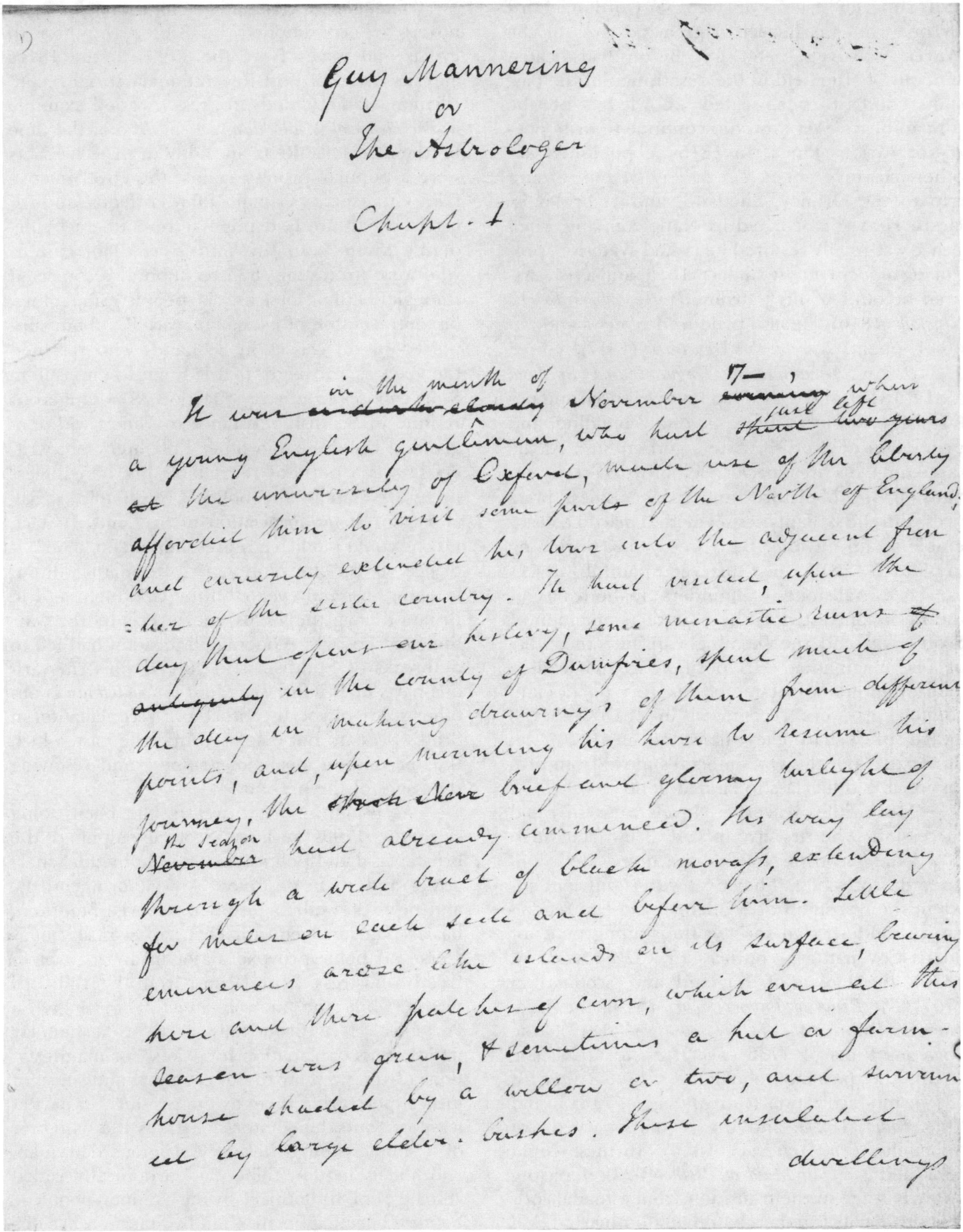
Guy Mannering
or
The Astrologer

Chapt. 1.

It was in the month of November 17— when a young English gentleman, who had just left the university of Oxford, made use of the liberty afforded him to visit some parts of the North of England, and curiosity extended his tour into the adjacent frontier of the sister country. He had visited, upon the day that opens our history, some monastic ruins in the county of Dumfries, spent much of the day in making drawings of them from different points, and, upon mounting his horse to resume his journey, the brief and gloomy twilight of the season had already commenced. His way lay through a wide tract of black morass, extending for miles on each side and before him. Little eminences arose like islands on its surface, bearing here and there patches of corn, which even at this season was green, & sometimes a hut or farm-house shaded by a willow or two, and surrounded by large elder-bushes. These insulated dwellings

First page of the manuscript for Guy Mannering *(MA 436, Pierpont Morgan Library)*

and superior talent of George Gordon, Lord Byron, who was himself a great admirer of the Waverley Novels. Scott felt Byron had beaten him out of "the field in the description of the passions, and in deep-seated knowledge of the human heart." Yet Scott did continue to write poetry of various kinds. In 1815 he published another narrative poem, *The Lord of the Isles*, after a trip to the Orkney, Shetland, and Hebrides islands. He was fascinated by Napoleon, and when peace was finally restored he visited Waterloo, producing a poem on the subject (1815) and a fictionalized account of his journey, *Paul's Letters To His Kinsfolk* (1816). He also produced reviews and another poem, *Harold the Dauntless* (1817), edited *The Border Antiquities of England and Scotland* (1814, 1817), and continued his busy social and political life, business interests, estate building, and promotion of Scottish writers and culture. At the same time, his breakneck speed of work, costly expansion of Abbotsford, and risky business practices with the Ballantynes seemed to place a considerable strain on him. For three years, beginning in March 1817, he suffered painful attacks caused by gallstones—reminders of the frailty of the flesh contrasted to the boundless ambition of Scott's will and the seemingly infinite fecundity of his imagination. His position as the leading man of letters in Britain and his Tory politics and connections were recognized in 1818 with the award of a baronetcy (gazetted in 1820), an honor that put the seal on Scott's move from professional middle class to landed gentry.

Meanwhile, Waverley Novels came in rapid succession. The first group and a few later ones, called the "Scottish Novels," are now widely considered Scott's best. They deal with significant crises in the transition of Scotland from late feudalism to modern civil society: the "killing time" of Stuart-Covenanter conflict (in *Old Mortality*, 1816), the Union of England and Scotland in 1707 (*The Bride of Lammermoor*, 1819), the Jacobite rebellion of 1715 (*Rob Roy*, 1817), the Porteous Riots of 1736 (*The Heart of Midlothian*, 1818), the Jacobite rebellion of 1745 (*Waverley*, 1814), modernization (*Guy Mannering*, 1815, and *Redgauntlet*, 1824), and the revolutionary threat to stability (*The Antiquary*, 1816). To these could be added *The Fair Maid of Perth* (1828), depicting an early stage in the transition from a feudal society with a court monarchy relying on martial skill and the exercise of main force to a mercantile and bourgeois society relying on market forces and laws.

Though representations of the past, these novels are conditioned by Scott's response to events and issues from the 1790s to the 1810s and his vision of post-Revolutionary social reconciliation, stability, and progress. A good example is *The Heart of Midlothian*, set in 1736 at the time of the Porteous Riots in Edinburgh. The riots were a popular protest against the government's failure to execute Captain John Porteous, an officer who had aroused popular resentment by ordering his men to fire into a crowd of citizens who were protesting the execution of a convicted smuggler, killing at least six people. Smuggling, or contravention of excise tax, was illegal but supported by all classes in Scotland, who resented the taxes as a foreign, that is English, imposition. Scott chooses to portray the riots as a dangerous residue of Scottish resistance to Union with England, a Union he and other Enlightenment writers saw as a perhaps regrettable but nonetheless necessary step in the political, economic, social, and cultural modernization of Scotland. In fact, no one could publish a representation of "mob" violence in the Revolutionary aftermath without bringing to mind events on the Continent and in Britain during the 1790s; more recently the wartime and postwar economic dislocation had led to outbreaks of Luddism and "bread riots" in various parts of Britain. *The Heart of Midlothian* is another study of social conflict and reconciliation in Scott's present, but displaced into the past, which thus becomes a means of grasping and resolving the issues of the present.

As usual, and as novelists had been doing since the 1790s at least, Scott exemplified the broad social and political issues in individual characters and their destinies. A wellborn, courtly, and ne'er-do-well Englishman, George Staunton, has become involved with a band of Scottish smugglers and helps provoke a riot in an attempt to free his mistress, Effie Deans, from the Tolbooth prison while the mob is exacting revenge on Porteous. Here Scott falls back on a familiar middle-class explanation for "riots," or manifestations of the popular moral economy and sense of justice, portraying them as the product, in part at least, of "outside agitators." Effie is the daughter of a simple though devoutly religious dairyman, and she is in the Tolbooth—sardonically called "the heart of Midlothian" by the common people—because her illegitimate child by Staunton has disappeared. In fact the child has been abducted by Meg Murdockson, the mother of Madge Wildfire, who was also seduced by Staunton and who has become half-crazed after her own child died and she was abandoned by Staunton. Meg wants revenge on Effie and so has taken Effie's child to replace Madge's. Under a harsh, religiously inspired law against infanticide, Effie must pay with her life for being unable to account for her bastard child's whereabouts. Staunton fails to persuade Effie to escape, however, and after the riot Effie is tried and condemned to death.

Effie might have been saved if her sister Jeanie had been prepared to lie in court, and even the sisters' father, Davie Deans, comes close to asking Jeanie to do so, though it goes directly against his strict religious principles. Jeanie has absorbed these principles from her father, however, and cannot lie, even to save a sister. Instead, Jeanie, hitherto a quiet and unassuming model of femininity, resolves to try a more womanly way to free her sister than the ways of masculine criminal violence, the male-dominated law, or worldly transgression. She will travel to England to seek a royal pardon for Effie in an interview with Queen Caroline, who is certain, Jeanie believes, to respond to a plea from another woman. Others—including the man she loves, the minister Reuben Butler—try to dissuade her from this apparently quixotic quest, or at least persuade her to send her appeal in a letter. But Jeanie does not share the learned Reuben's faith in the power of writing; she has the common people's confidence in the greater efficacy of the spoken word. Female quixotes were common enough in counterrevolutionary novels of the 1790s and the early decades of the nineteenth century, and Scott's heroine is in part a variation on these. She is not a satiric "female philosopher" or comic feminist, inspired by revolutionary ideas, but rather a completely domestic woman inspired by conventionally feminine virtues of family loyalty, forgiveness, and peaceful mediation.

On her journey to London Jeanie is beset by hazards arranged through the machinations of Meg Murdockson and her criminal confederates. Another danger is her first encounter with a form of Christianity that seems very different from her own, though equally inspiring. This Christianity is Church of England Anglicanism, the English equivalent of the Scottish episcopalianism preferred by Scott. Jeanie encounters this temptation, coincidentally, in the church presided over by the father of that Staunton who had seduced her sister Effie. Jeanie goes on to London, however, where she discovers the good side of the Scots' reputation for sticking together when outside their own country. She is assisted by Scots in London and in particular by John, Duke of Argyle and Greenwich, an actual historical character. A powerful man at court yet a patriotic Scot, an honest statesman, and a progressive landlord, Argyle is, as his dual title indicates, the new model of a *British* peer, though his rivals at court try to undermine him by portraying him as more Scottish and thus anti-English. Argyle is struck by Jeanie's naturalness and by the opportunity her cause offers of helping reconcile the queen, who is deeply resentful of the lynching of her officer Porteous, to her Scottish subjects. Argyle takes up his countrywoman's cause and brings about the interview that enables Jeanie, as she imagined, to move the queen as more than a queen—as a woman—and obtain Effie's pardon. Jeanie's womanly feelings succeed in mending the breach in her family and local community caused by antisocial individualism, sexual and legal transgression, and religious and social intolerance. A feminine version of the voice of the people, guided by a true statesman, succeeds in mending a dangerous breach in the nation caused by the same individualism, court intrigue, and national prejudice. For over two decades moral writers and social critics had called on women to exercise such heroism in domestic life in order to save the nation; Scott novelizes and historicizes this call in *The Heart of Midlothian*.

This reconciliation is not the end of the novel, however. Scott goes on in a fourth volume to describe Argyle's recruitment of Jeanie and Reuben Butler for his Scottish estate, a model of the economic and social future being developed on lands symbolically straddling the Scottish Lowlands and the Highlands. Here Jeanie and her family flourish and spread their domestic virtues through the society around them. Years later, however, Jeanie and her family are visited by Effie and Staunton, now married, living in luxury, and successful at playing the game of court society. But the price of their "success" is high. They are forced to maintain false identities and guard carefully against exposure, and they have been providentially punished for their earlier errors by remaining childless. Finally, in a melodramatic coincidence Staunton is killed, unwittingly, by his own son, Effie's bastard child, who had grown up to become a half-savage outlaw in the Highlands. A common view among critics is that Scott added this last volume to his novel mainly to pad the work out for greater profit. But these chapters make an important point in relation to the

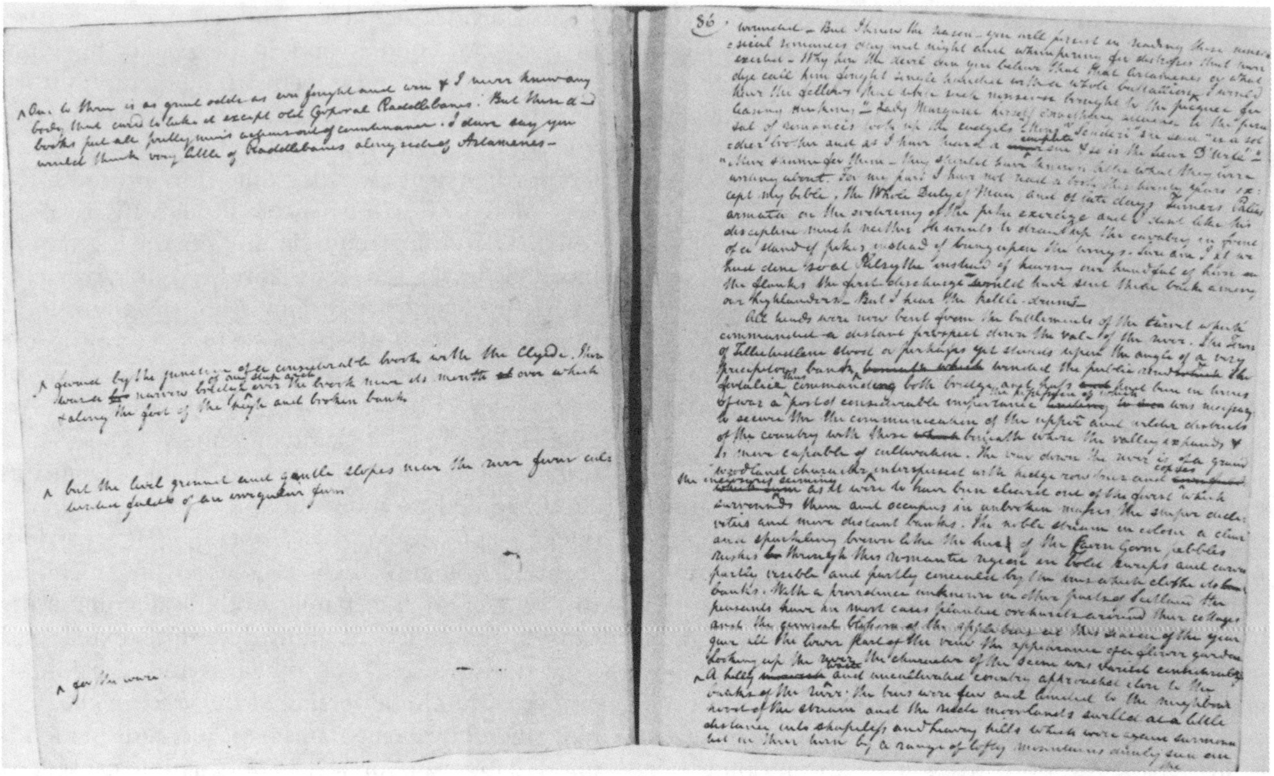

Pages from the manuscript for Old Mortality *(MA 445, Pierpont Morgan Library)*

growing social alienation within Britain in the late 1810s. The events of the last volume illustrate central themes of Scottish Enlightenment political economy: the emptiness of court culture, the destructiveness of plebeian savagery, and the productive union of commons and nobles in a hierarchical yet progressive harmony. At the same time, Jeanie's effective feminization of social and political issues, while remaining thoroughly feminine and domestic, may be read as an answer to feminist attempts to feminize politics during the 1790s.

In *Ivanhoe: A Romance* (1819) Scott treats the same themes in a new and different way. The subtitle is an important generic marker, since the "novel" and the "romance" were carefully distinguished at that time. The novel was supposed to deal mainly with manners in "real" life in a more or less contemporary setting; the romance was supposed to license extravagant characterization and actions that were thought characteristic of a bygone world and its literature of verse romance. This extravagance is certainly found in *Ivanhoe*, though in other respects it is a "modern novel" in medieval costumes and furnishings. More important, in *Ivanhoe* Scott begins to explore the origins of modern Britain and Europe, especially their social differences and conflicts, in the Middle Ages and the Renaissance. Once again Scott projects the conflicts of his present into the past, and more obviously than before he rewrites the struggles of the 1790s as a warning to Britain and Europe in the Revolutionary aftermath. By apparently historicizing the present, Scott gains for his views on the present the authority of history. Opening present conflicts to the remedies of history was envisaged by the Scottish Enlightenment as a necessary evolution from savagery to civilization. *Ivanhoe* represents the conflict and reconciliation of Anglo-Saxons and Normans in England. Under King John—who is acting as regent for his brother King Richard, away on the mad project of the Crusades—England lacks strong government and degenerates into contending upper-class interests, represented by selfish Norman barons and sullen Saxon chiefs, and popular rebellion, represented by Locksley (or Robin Hood) and his men. Readers could draw their own conclusions about the parallel between this situation and that of Britain in 1819, with good King George III long absent from the throne due to insanity, and the nation presided over rather than ruled by the decadent Prince Regent (later George IV). *Ivanhoe* introduces two foreign elements, one positive and one negative, into this internal social conflict. On one hand there are the rich Jew Isaac of York and his daughter Rebecca. Isaac helps finance the heroic deeds of the novel's hero, and Rebecca heals the hero's wounds. Capitalism and healing power represent progressive forces of modernization not yet domesticated in England. On the other hand there are the Knights Templar, a secret society in which Western chivalric heroism has been contaminated by too much contact with the decadent Orient during the Crusades. In this way decadent court culture is represented as alien—a familiar theme in social criticism of the time—and imperialism is represented as opening the door to contamination by the alien.

The novel develops these themes in three movements. In the first, the young Saxon knight Wilfred of Ivanhoe returns from the Crusades to reclaim his birthright. He has been disinherited by his father, who hopes to reestablish the Saxon monarchy through a marriage between his ward, Rowena, and the Saxon lord Athelstane, who are descendants of lines that ruled England before the Norman conquest. Ivanhoe fights as the anonymous knight "El Desdichado," or "The Disinherited," in a great tournament at Ashby-de-la-Zouche and overcomes all opponents, including Brian de Bois-Guilbert, an arrogant Norman. Ivanhoe is wounded in the fray and tended by Rebecca, who is skilled in physic. The next movement opens with the capture of Ivanhoe, Rebecca, Isaac, Rowena, Cedric, and Athelstane by the Norman robber-baron Front-de-Boeuf, who takes his prisoners to his castle of Torquilstone. He plans to extort a ransom from Isaac while Bois-Guilbert intends to force Rebecca to become his mistress. Another Norman, Maurice de Bracy, plans to force Rowena into marriage with him in order to get her inheritance. Much of this skulduggery could be found in modern dress in Gothic romances or novels of high society, and there is not much that is necessarily medieval about it. Nevertheless, Scott does give a convincingly evil character to this selfish and shortsighted exercise of local tyranny. Torquilstone is soon besieged by a united force of Locksley's band and oppressed peasants, led by King Richard. He has returned from the Crusades and is traveling incognito, somewhat like the good king of popular chapbook tales, who disguises himself and travels about, free from the deceptions of courtly flatterers, to see at first hand how his subjects live. After the Saxon woman Ulrica, who was forced to become Front-de-Boeuf 's mistress years earlier, sets fire to Torquilstone, it is captured and the villains are killed, taken prisoner, or forced to flee.

The final movement of the novel takes place at Coningsburgh castle, where the Templar Bois-Guilbert has fled with his captive, Rebecca. His actions have violated Templar vows, but the visiting head of the order decides to blame Rebecca and try her for having "enchanted" the knight. Though Ivanhoe is still weak from the wounds he received at Ashby, he undertakes to defend Rebecca in trial by combat against Bois-Guilbert. During the fight Ivanhoe is near defeat when his opponent suddenly collapses and dies from an excess of his own strong passions—appropriately self-defeated from within. At this moment Richard reveals his identity and reclaims royal authority. Cedric accepts his son back into the family, and Rowena and Ivanhoe are to be wed in a prefiguratively modern English line uniting formerly distinct and hostile peoples. At the same time, the alien elements in England, good and bad, Jewish and Templar, are forced to leave. *Ivanhoe* shows some sympathy for the Jews, influenced by Maria Edgeworth's critique of anti-Semitism in her recent novel *Harrington* (1817), but Scott remained convinced that what were seen as negative characteristics of the Jewish people were too ingrained to be reformed or integrated into the new Britain, just as, for all the mixed qualities of Isaac and good qualities of Rebecca, they could not be assimilated into medieval England.

Significantly, the female representatives of the novel's various cultures—Rowena, Rebecca, and Ulrica—are clearly meant to be more sympathetic and appealing than the masculine or manly ones, just as the feminine or feminized versions of these cultures are more sympathetic and appealing than the masculine versions. In fact, the female cultural representatives are seen to be victims of male representatives of their own and other cultures. Even the ideal male representatives—Ivanhoe, Locksley, and Richard—seem largely ineffective: Ivanhoe is incapacitated by wounds for much of the novel, Locksley is an outlaw, and the situation unfolded in the novel has arisen because of Richard's idealistic but irresponsible absence in the Holy Land, to which he is to return at the end of the novel. Scott here follows a strong antifeudal, antichivalric line in Scottish Enlightenment history and theory of the rise of civil society. Philosophers such as David Hume

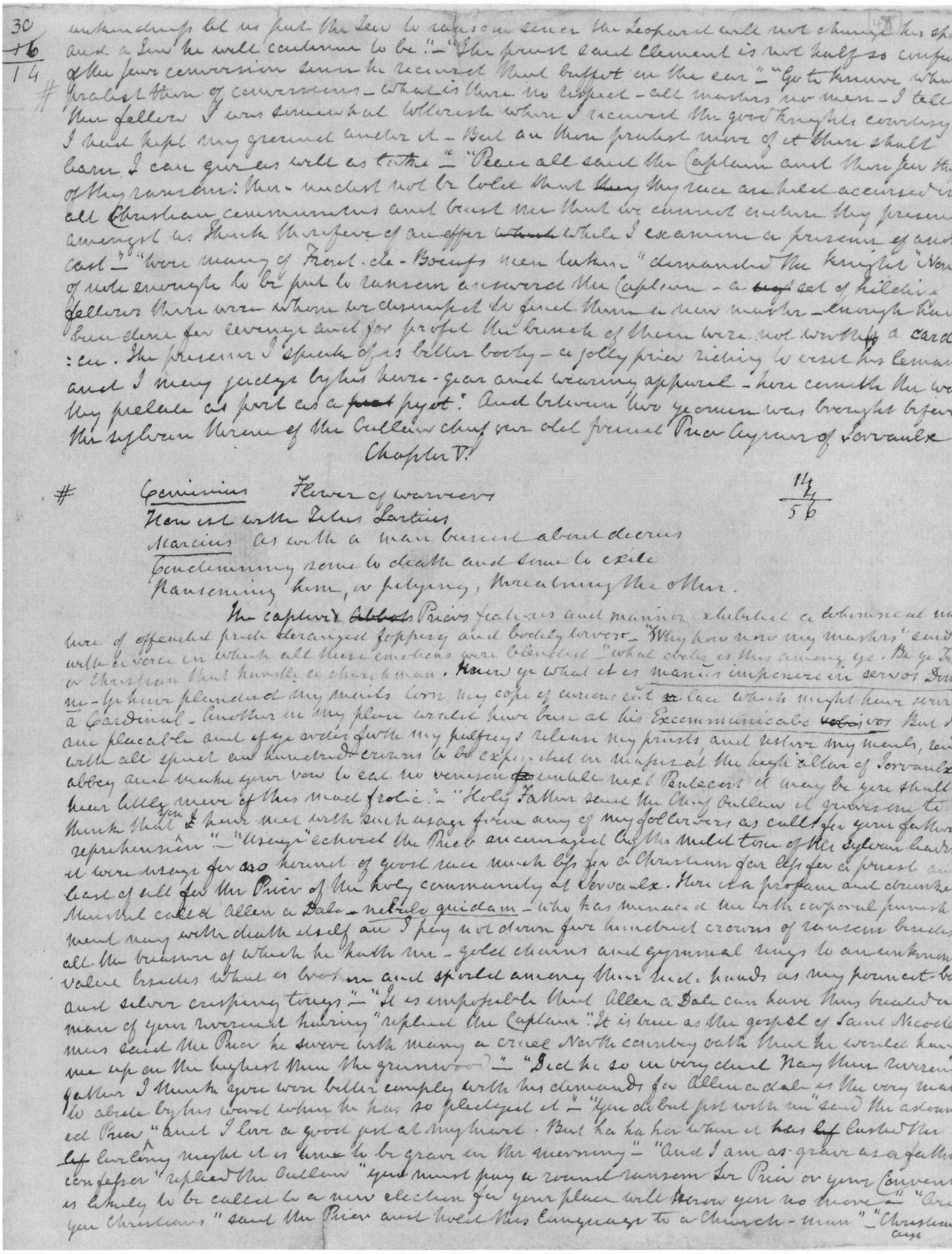

30
16
14

unkindness let us put the Jew to ransom since the Leopard will not change his spots and a Jew he will continue to be." — "The priest said Clement is not half so comfortable of the Jews conversion since he received that buffet on the ear" — "Go to knave what prattlest thou of conversions — what is there no respect — all masters no men — I tell thee fellow I was somewhat bolterish when I received the good knights courtesy or I had kept my ground under it — But an thou pratest more of it thou shalt learn I can give as well as take" — "Peace all said the Captain and thou Jew think of thy ransom: thou needest not be told that thy race are held accursed in all Christian communities and trust me that we cannot endure thy presence amongst us. Think therefore of an offer while I examine a prisoner of another cast" — "Were many of Front-de-Boeufs men taken" demanded the knight "None of note enough to be put to ransom answered the Captain — a set of hilding fellows there were whom we dismissed to find them a new master — enough had been done for revenge and for profit the bunch of them were not worth a cardecu. The prisoner I speak of is better booty — a jolly friar riding to visit his leman and I may judge by his horse-gear and wearing apparel — here cometh the worthy prelate as pert as a pyot." And between two yeomen was brought before the sylvan throne of the Outlaw chief our old friend Prior Aymer of Jorvaulx.

Chapter V.

14
56

Cominius Flower of warriors
How is't with Titus Lartius
Marcius As with a man busied about decrees
Condemning some to death and some to exile
Ransoming him, or pitying, threatening the other.

The captive Priors features and manner exhibited a whimsical mixture of offended pride deranged foppery and bodily terror — "Why how now my masters" said he with a voice in which all these emotions were blended "what order is this among ye. Be ye Turks or Christians that handle a churchman. Know ye what it is manus imponere in servos Domini — Ye have plundered my mails torn my cope of curious cut lace which might have served a Cardinal — Another in my place would have been at his Excommunicabo vos But I am placable and if ye order forth my palfreys release my priests and restore my mails, and with all speed count out an hundred crowns to be expended in masses at the high altar of Jorvaulx abbey and make your vow to eat no venison until next Pentecost it may be you shall hear little more of this mad frolic." — "Holy Father said the Chief Outlaw it grieves me to think that you have met with such usage from any of my followers as calls for your fatherly reprehension" — "Usage" echoed the Priest encouraged by the mild tone of the sylvan leader "it were usage for no hound of good race much less for a Christian far less for a priest and least of all for the Prior of the holy community at Jorvaulx. Here is a profane and drunken minstrel called Allen a Dale — nebulo quidam — who has menaced me with corporal punishment nay with death itself an I pay not down four hundred crowns of ransom besides all the treasure of which he hath me — gold chains and gymmal rings to an unknown value besides what is broken and spoiled among their rude hands as my pouncet-box and silver crisping tongs" — "It is impossible that Allen a Dale can have thus treated a man of your reverend bearing" replied the Captain "It is true as the gospel of Saint Nicodemus said the Prior he swore with many a cruel North country oath that he would hang me up on the highest tree in the greenwood" — "Did he so in very deed Nay then reverend father I think you were better comply with his demands for Allen a dale is the very man to abide by his word when he has so pledged it" — "You do but jest with me" said the astounded Prior "and I love a good jest at my heart. But ha ha ha when it has lasted the lee-long night it is time to be grave in the morning" — "And I am as grave as a father confessor" replied the Outlaw "you must pay a round ransom Sir Prior or your Convent is likely to be called to a new election for your place will know you no more" — "Are you Christians" said the Prior and hold this language to a Church-man" — "Christians

Beginning of chapter 5 in the manuscript for Ivanhoe *(MA 440, Pierpont Morgan Library)*

and Adam Smith represented feminine influence as a major force in the evolution of feudalism and chivalry from a martial to a civic culture. In the aftermath of the Revolution debate of the 1790s, this view of women's role in forging civil society merged with an ideal of domestic woman as repository of the national culture and conscience and inspiration for moral and social reform. *Ivanhoe*, with *The Heart of Midlothian* and other Waverley Novels, represents that ideal.

Ivanhoe is now regarded in the English-speaking world as one of Scott's lesser novels, yet it was probably the most influential of his novels in other countries. One reason for this fact may be the language of *Ivanhoe*. Unlike the Scottish novels, it has no Scots dialect to challenge the translator, and the represented speech of all characters is a bookish, pastiche Shakespearean—what the later Scottish novelist Robert Louis Stevenson referred to as "tushery," after the expletive *tush* supposedly marking the speech of many characters in Scott's medieval novels. The main reason for the popularity of *Ivanhoe* outside of Britain, however, was that its representation of nation-making addressed the interests of middle-class nationalists not only in Europe but in parts of the world that were or soon would be shaking off colonial rule. *Ivanhoe* circulated not only as a novel in translation and in various imitations, but was turned into several dramatic versions and operas. Its cultural influence was thought to be so pervasive that Mark Twain later blamed it for causing the American Civil War by inspiring Southern "gentlemen" with false ideals of chivalry.

To Scott, however, *Ivanhoe* was only one success of many that had to follow if he were to continue his own meteoric rise to the status of gentleman. For a while he worked this new "line" of medieval novels. At the same time, he continued to develop in these novels his concern for the present state of Britain, which Scott saw as lurching from one crisis to another and always on the edge of the abyss of revolution. *The Monastery: A Romance* (1820) and its sequel *The Abbot* (1820) turn to the period of the Protestant Reformation, a revolution in religion more than in politics, according to Enlightenment historians. *Kenilworth: A Romance* (1821) turns to Elizabethan court intrigues and shows their tragic effects on the lives of otherwise virtuous individuals. Scott comes closer to modern times, but in a remote society, in *The Pirate* (1821), dealing with the conflict of tradition and change and set in the Orkney Islands, where he had visited seven years earlier. *The Fortunes of Nigel* (1822) represents court society again, this time during the reign of James I and the emergence of a new political consensus after centuries of conflict and war between Scotland and England. These novels are largely disregarded now, and some are among those that later gave Scott a reputation as a mere writer of swashbuckling adventure stories for adolescent boys rather than for mature adults. Certainly some of these novels have proved more suitable for conversion into swashbuckling films and comic books than the Scottish novels favored by literary critics.

Meanwhile Scott's personal and family fortunes continued in prosperous course. His daughter Sophia married the young writer and critic John Gibson Lockhart in 1820, providing Scott with an able lieutenant. Lockhart was not only a convinced Tory (like Scott), but he was also a leading young intellectual. He contributed to the new and lively Edinburgh *Blackwood's Magazine* and in 1819 published a satiric, fictionalized account of Edinburgh society, *Peter's Letters to His Kinsfolk*. After his marriage, he published a historical novel, *Valerius* (1821), set in Roman times. But Lockhart was more in tune than Scott with the Romantic interest in divided subjectivity, as seen in his later novels, *Adam Blair* (1822), *Reginald Dalton* (1823), and *Matthew Wald* (1824). In 1825 Lockhart was appointed editor of the influential *Quarterly Review* and wrote no more novels.

Scott's preeminence as an inventor of tradition was recognized in 1822 when he was made manager for the state visit to Edinburgh of the recently crowned George IV, the first visit of a Hanoverian monarch to Scotland. Scott disliked the king and used to refer to him as "our fat friend," echoing Beau Brummell, but he drew on all his extensive social and political connections and antiquarian lore to make the event into a symbol of national and historical reconciliation. Scott was also partly responsible for recovering the long-disused Scottish regalia in 1818.

Despite such exertions Scott published three novels in 1823. Two of these, *Peveril of the Peak*, set in the English Civil War period, and *Quentin Durward*, set at the time of monarchic struggle between France and Burgundy, deal with Scott's continuing concern over the unity of Britain and the progress of European civil society in the face of antisocial passions such as revenge or excessive personal ambition and the narrowly selfish interests of factions and social groups at the expense of the national interest. *St. Ronan's Well*, set in Scot-

Scott in 1822 (portrait by Sir Henry Raeburn; Scottish National Portrait Gallery)

land and in modern times, recognizes the skill in depicting passion and psychological struggle by women novelists from Frances Burney through Mary Brunton and Jane Austen to Lady Caroline Lamb and Susan Ferrier. Scott is true to his own strength, however, in emphasizing that disharmony in the individual is the internalization of social conflict. Balzac and Stendhal criticized Scott for lack of "passion," but like many in his time he associated passion with decadent, erotic court culture and the sublime yet destructive personal ambition of historical figures such as Cromwell and Napoleon. *St. Ronan's Well* confronts these subjective and social forces, especially as erotic passion, though Scott was finally dissuaded by Ballantyne from treating the subject with the frankness he first intended.

Scott's next novel, *Redgauntlet: A Tale of the Eighteenth Century* (1824), is considered by many to be one of his best, perhaps because it returns to the Scottish matter of the first group of Waverley Novels. It depicts the continuing political intrigues of Jacobites—led by the proud baron after whom the novel is titled—after the failure of the 1745 uprising. His uncompromising and fatal loyalty to the Stuart past motivates the plot, based on Redgauntlet's scheme to ensnare the Waverley-type hero, Darsie Latimer, in the Jacobite cause. The novel includes both an autobiographical sketch in the character of Alan Fairford, close friend of the hero, and an experiment in first-person narration unusual for Scott. In view of Scott's notorious reticence in dealing with the deeply subjective, in himself or in his fictional characters, it is significant that he here shows indulgence of personal passions having a disastrous effect on personal as well as national destiny. The inset story, "Wandering Willie's Tale," is a masterpiece of the genre and demonstrates from the viewpoint of the folk's wisdom the hellish cruelty of the old Scottish lairds and the necessity of standing up to them. The novel ends optimistically, with the errant hero and his friend properly integrated into society on the side of rational progress. Yet the dark passions and cruelties of the past are deflected, suppressed, and marginalized rather than resolved. If *Redgauntlet* is a coda to the first batch of Scottish Waverley Novels then it is one that looks back more to *The Bride of Lammermoor* than to the confident progressivism of *Waverley* or *The Heart of Midlothian*, and it introduces disturbing disharmonies into the major keys of the earlier works.

Scott was perhaps becoming cloyed with his own success. He was anxious over his continued flirting with financial disaster, and he became yet more pessimistic about Britain's ability to preserve its hard-won civil society and empire in the face of new social forces, worsening social alienation, and increasing social conflict. The world no longer seemed to make sense in terms of the Scottish Enlightenment political economy that had informed the thinking of Scott and his generation and enabled them to grasp unprecedented and cataclysmic historical events. Scott continued, however, to transpose and displace such personal and public concerns into his fusion of history and fiction. In *The Betrothed* and *The Talisman*, published together as *Tales of the Crusaders* (1825), he gives a disturbingly "realistic" version of the world idealized by Romantic medievalists (including at times Scott himself) to ennoble middle-class culture. In these novels Scott again articulates an Enlightenment view of chivalry and the Crusades as grand historical examples of passion and self interest masquerading as civility and civili zation; but in fact the Crusaders are no better than the decadent or barbaric societies they attacked.

Woodstock; or, the Cavalier (1826) is set during the seventeenth-century English Civil War, but the events depicted parallel the struggle in the 1820s among court monarchy, various factions of the landed gentry and middle class, and the politicized lower class. This struggle is represented in the novel through the complex relationships among the historical characters of young Charles II and Oliver Cromwell; an aptly named Cavalier, Roger Wildrake; a loyalist squire and keeper of the lodge, Sir Henry Lee; Sir Henry's nephew, the moderate parliamentarian officer Colonel Markham Everard; the Presbyterian minister Nehemiah Holdenough and his Anglican opponent, the royalist plotter Rochecliffe; and the plebeian soldier Joseph Tomkins and other various lower-class characters. The principal mediating agent is the virtuous, feminine, and domestic Alice Lee, Sir Henry's daughter. The setting is a royal lodge at Woodstock, outside Oxford, which has been confiscated by Parliament. The lodge is similar to the one that once was the hideaway of Rosamund Clifford, unfortunate mistress of Henry II and heroine of a popular chapbook story. Scott often uses such chapbook classics to inform his novels; and here he uses the story as a backdrop to the novel's political and amorous intrigues. The lodge is the secret refuge of young Charles II, fleeing from the royalist defeat at Worcester, and the novel depicts the various religious, social, and political factions of the "Interregnum" and the inability of even a great military leader such as Cromwell to create the national consensus necessary to civil society. Scott suggests that the fate of the nation rather depends on individual heroes and heroines at the local level uniting in families, as Alice Lee and Markham Everard finally do, to reproduce their values into succeeding generations.

Scott was now at the height of his personal success and influence. He led in founding a new Edinburgh Academy, where sons of the gentry and middle class would be educated together, with a modern curriculum including the new subject of English composition and literature. In February 1825 the marriage of Scott's older son, Walter, to an heiress, Jane Jobson, seemed to ensure the continuation of Scott's personal social success into the future. Accordingly, he made over his estate of Abbotsford to his son, reserving the right to raise a mortgage on the property if needed. In July Scott toured Ireland with his daughter Sophia and her husband, Lockhart, partly to visit Maria Edgeworth, with whom he had corresponded for some years and whose "Irish tales" he had long admired and proclaimed as the model for his novels of Scottish life. In Ireland Scott found that he was a public figure, greeted by crowds in the street. On 14 May 1826, however, his wife died; though theirs had not been a particularly close marriage, Scott missed her a great deal. Public loss followed personal. In the same year a crisis in business credit caused the bankruptcy of several publishers, including Archibald Constable, whose failure also dragged down Ballantyne's firm and thus Scott himself. Early in 1827 he publicly revealed his authorship of the Waverley Novels to avoid conflict of interest in dealing with his creditors. He was able to save Abbotsford and thus preserve his family's gentry status, but ironically it was partly Scott's desire to expand Abbotsford at any cost that helped bring on his and his partners' ruin. Aware of Scott's importance as a literary and public figure, the creditors treated him respectfully and even generously. But he still would have to discharge an enormous debt of £130,000 by his own efforts. The stress damaged his health and probably hastened his death.

Scott (fourth from left) with family and friends, 1825; Archibald Constable, James Hogg, John Gibson Lockhart, Anne Scott, Lady Scott, Sophia Scott Lockhart, Maria Edgeworth, Walter Scott (son), Anne Scott (niece), Harriet Edgeworth, Charles Scott, and Robert Shortreed (painting by William Stewart Watson; from a 1901 edition of Lockhart's Memoirs of the Life of Sir Walter Scott, Bart.)

Yet he continued producing not only Waverley Novels but also other works reflecting on the issues of the day. In the nonfiction *Letters of Malachi Malagrowther* (1826) Scott follows the example of Jonathan Swift's *Drapier's Letters* (1724) and adopts a fictitious public persona to defend Scottish financial and monetary independence from England. Perhaps in recognition, reference to Scott appeared on Scottish bank notes, even in the twentieth century. In 1827 Scott published his massive, nine-volume *Life of Napoleon Buonaparte*, which he had been working on since 1825. He gives some attention to the Revolution that Napoleon claimed to embody and portrays the ancien régime falling from its own corruption and the influence of French philosophes such as Jean-Jacques Rousseau and Voltaire. Scott acknowledges Napoleon's major role in restoring stability and progress after the divisions and bloodshed of the Revolution. He praises Napoleon's genius for government and his extensive professionalization of the French state, rebuilding it on merit. But he also deplores Napoleon's inevitable vanity and ambition, resulting in the devastation of Europe, the deaths of millions, and his own downfall. Though the book was too massive to become a popular classic such as Thomas Carlyle's *History of the French Revolution* (1837), Scott's *Life of Napoleon Buonoparte* was well received by political thinkers and historians in Britain as well as France. In a different historiographical key, Scott published between 1827 and 1831 a nine-volume history of Scotland for children, in three series of *Tales of a Grandfather* (1827-1830); a fourth series (1831) deals with the history of France. Even this work was touched with personal sorrow, however: it was written for Scott's adored grandson, John Hugh Lockhart, who died at age ten on 15 December 1831.

Scott returned to fiction for adults with three short stories, the first series of *Chronicles of the Canongate* (1827). These tales present in short compass and sharper outline the conflicts of past and present, self and society that were represented in the novels. "The Surgeon's Daughter" shows the Orientalization of the British in India through a villain resembling those of Anti-Jacobin novels in the 1790s. In "The Highland Widow" remorseless Jacobitism again collides with the political and social realities of modern Scotland, leading to the unnecessary death of the widow's son rather than his return to traditional Highland life. In "The Two Drovers" differences of culture and a combination of circumstances lead to the Highland drover's murdering his English friend and being executed for the crime.

Scott's next novel, *The Fair Maid of Perth* (1828), the second series of *Chronicles of the Canongate*, continues and sharpens some of the themes in the first series. Set in a fourteenth-century Scottish commercial town, it presents a variety of dangerous and at times bloody conflicts between savage feudal clans, a weak and corrupt court and aristocracy, and a self-interested town middle class. Each of these groups lacks internal harmony and leadership, leading them into unnecessary conflict with each other. Their differences focus on courtship of "the fair maid of Perth," the romantic and idealistic daughter of a leading merchant. It is the smith Harry Wynd who survives intrigues against him, prevails in physical combat, and claims the "fair maid" as his bride. In the process he learns that brute force alone cannot unite a society, and she learns that such force is sometimes necessary to ensure the civil society that is the way of the future, just as Scott thought it was for Britain in the late 1820s.

Anne of Geierstein; or, The Maiden in the Mist (1829) mounts a similar argument. It involves the fifteenth-century conflicts between the emergent yeoman democracy of Switzerland and the powerful but unstable Charles the Bold, Duke of Burgundy, the rising monarchy of France and the feeble kingdom of Provence, and Lancastrian and Yorkist barons in England. Amid this turmoil two English nobles calling themselves Philipson—but in fact the exiled earl of Oxford and his son Arthur—attempt to raise money for Margaret of Anjou, widow of Henry VI, so that she can attempt to revive the recently defeated Lancastrian cause. But their efforts are impeded by Margaret's own relentless ambition, the enmity and greed of German robber barons, the machinations of the Vehme-gericht secret society, and the turmoil caused by the arrogance of the powerful Charles the Bold, Duke of Burgundy. Young Philipson is also distracted from his political mission by his love for Anne of Geierstein, a woman at once intellectual, noble in blood, democratically Swiss by upbringing, determinedly feminine and domestic, yet active in supporting heroic virtues of others. She is an obvious contrast to the scheming but ineffective Margaret. As ineffective in a different way is Margaret's father, King René of Provence, who is more interested in courtly-love rituals and the latest troubadour love poem than in defending his culturally sophisticated but financially bankrupt kingdom against the predatory designs of France and Burgundy.

The analogy, between this set of mainly historical characters and the situation of Britain and Europe in the late 1820s, is subtle and complex. Readers would know that the Lancastrian cause eventually rose again to triumph at Bosworth Field in 1485, ending centuries of baronial conflict and civil war and founding the Tudor dynasty in a union of Yorkists and Lancastrians that was to prove the basis of modern England and Britain. The course of the novel suggests that this settlement was due less to Margaret's unfeminine intervention in politics than to the fortitude, loyalty, and perseverance of obscurer individuals such as the Philipsons. Implicitly, the solution to internal conflicts in the past may work again in the present. This solution, achieved by civic heroism on the individual and domestic level, sets up another contrast, between the future Tudor monarchy and its successors and the differing powers of France, Burgundy, Switzerland, and Provence.

France here, as in Scott's own day, is cast as a duplicitous, despotic, and expansionist state. Burgundy is a commercially developed, prosperous, and even luxurious state suitably represented by its arrogant, impulsive, and extravagant ruler, Charles the Bold. But it is a state lacking national coherence and unity, selling and sold to the highest bidder, emblematically dependent on treacherous Italian mercenaries for its military power. Switzerland, by contrast, is a democratic federation of independent communities, not quite a nation-state, but already having a common character derived from the rugged landscape and the agrarian economy appropriate to it and united by religion and culture. Not surprisingly, the Swiss can mount a formidable military force when necessary. Whereas Switzerland is rough and unsophisticated but strong, Provence is civilized to the point of decadence, living on its past as a source of medieval court culture but morally as well as financially bankrupt. In the course of the novel two of these states, the wealthy Burgundy and the impoverished Provence, disappear into the abyss of history, while the emergent states of France and Switzerland have their

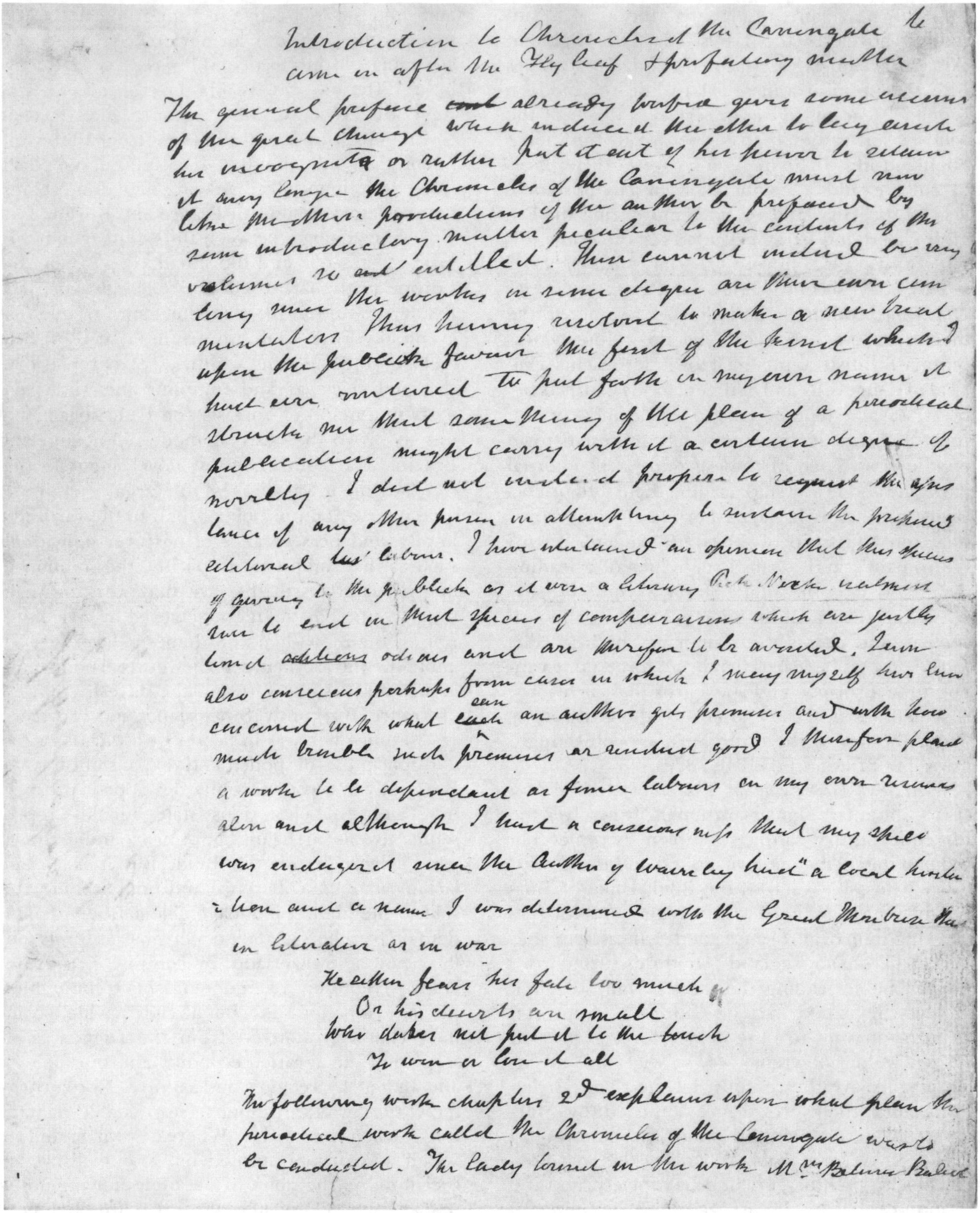
Introduction to Chronicles of the Canongate to come in after the Fly leaf & prefatory matter

The general preface ~~cont~~ already before gives some account of the great change which induced the author to lay aside his incognito or rather put it out of his power to retain it any longer. The Chronicles of the Canongate must now like the other productions of the author be prefaced by some introductory matter peculiar to the contents of the volumes so entitled. There cannot indeed be any long … the works in some degree are their own commentators. Thus having resolved to make a new trial upon the publick favour the first of the kind which I had ever ventured to put forth in my own name it struck me that something of the plan of a periodical publication might carry with it a certain degree of novelty. I did not indeed propose to request the assistance of any other person in attempting to sustain the proposed editorial labours. I have entertained an opinion that this species of giving to the publick as it were a literary Pick Nick is almost sure to end in that species of comparisons which are justly termed odious and are therefore to be avoided. I am also conscious perhaps from cases in which I may myself have been concerned with what ease an author gets promises and with how much trouble such promises are rendered good. I therefore placed a work to be dependant as former labours on my own resources alone and although I had a consciousness that my shield was endangered since the Author of Waverley had "a local habitation and a name" I was determined with the Great Montrose that in literature as in war

He either fears his fate too much
Or his deserts are small
Who dares not put it to the touch
To win or lose it all

The following work chapters 2d explains upon what plan the periodical work called the Chronicles of the Canongate was to be conducted. The lady turned in the work Mrs Baliol Baliol

Draft of an addendum Scott wrote in 1831 for the introduction to Chronicles of Canongate, *First Series, in the 1829-1833 edition of his novels (HM 1982, Henry E. Huntington Library and Art Gallery)*

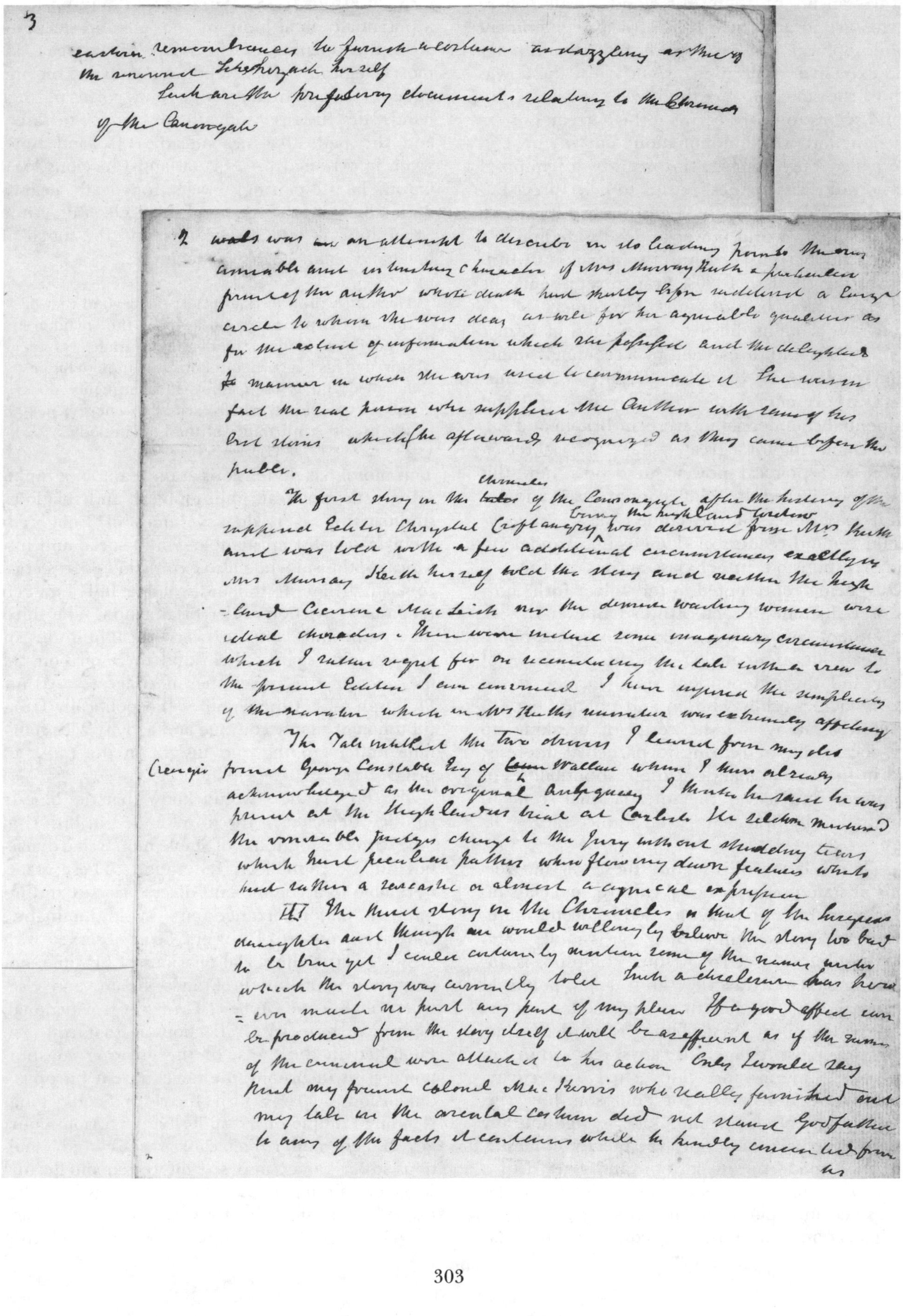

3

certain remembrances to furnish a costume as dazzling as that of the renowned Scheherazade herself

Such are the prefatory documents relating to the Chronicles of the Canongate

2 works was an attempt to describe in its leading points the very amiable and interesting character of Mrs Murray Keith a particular friend of the author whose death had shortly before saddened a large circle to whom she was dear as well for her agreeable qualities as for the extent of information which she possessed and the delightful manner in which she was used to communicate it. She was in fact the real person who supplied the Author with some of his best stories which she afterwards recognized as they came before the public.

The first story in the Chronicles of the Canongate after the history of the supposed Editor Chrystal Croftangry being the Highland Widow was derived from Mrs Keith and was told with a few additional circumstances exactly as Mrs Murray Keith herself told the story and neither the Highland Cicerone MacLeish nor the demure waiting women were ideal characters. There were indeed some imaginary circumstances which I rather regret for on reconsidering the tale with a view to the present Edition I am convinced I have injured the simplicity of the narrative which in Mrs Keiths narrative was extremely affecting

The Tale entitled the Two Drovers I learned from my old friend George Constable Esq of Wallace Craigie whom I have already acknowledged as the original Antiquary. I think he said he was present at the Highlanders trial at Carlisle He seldom mentioned the venerable judges charge to the Jury without shedding tears which had peculiar pathos when flowing down features which had rather a sarcastic or almost a cynical expression

The third story in the Chronicles is that of the Surgeons daughter and though we would willingly believe the story too bad to be true yet I could certainly mention some of the names under which the story was currently told. Such a circumstance has however not made me push any part of my plan. If a good effect can be produced from the story itself it will be as efficient as if the name of the criminal were attached to his action. Only I would say that my friend Colonel MacKerris who really furnished out my tale in the oriental costume did not stand Godfather to any of the facts it contains while he kindly consented from his future ahead of them for good or ill. These events are in accord with Scottish Enlightenment "philosophical history," which held that luxury and excessive "civilization" would cause the downfall of the state. During the novel the fate of England seems to hover between the extremes of extinction and world domination, but in the end the exiled Englishmen, reinforced by a feminized version of Swiss virtues, return to help direct England away from the abyss and toward its future as a dominant world power in Scott's lifetime.

Crudely translated into the situation in Britain during the late 1820s, France represents the old style of duplicitous court government, which Scott saw brought down by revolution in France in the 1790s and threatened by a seemingly imminent revolution in Britain in the late 1820s. Burgundy represents the increasingly powerful and influential commercial interests in Britain and Europe, clamoring for a greater share of social recognition and political power; in Scott's view this new group lacked the solid economic base and political experience of the landed class. Provence would remind readers of flamboyant, scandalous, and irresponsible upper-class society of the late 1820s, being represented in the "silver-fork" novels of Benjamin Disraeli, Edward Bulwer-Lytton, and others. Switzerland is closer to Scott's political ideal, but, as an analogy for the aristocracy of labor and the independent small farmer, it too clearly lacks worldly wisdom and political experience. It is always on the verge of breaking up into local units or retiring to parochial interests, and in the end it abandons the responsibilities of its power and leaves the international scene to domination by France, or what France represents here.

The relationships among these varying versions of state power, national culture, and class hierarchy are of course exemplified by Scott in individual characters and their vicissitudes and relationships. The hero, Arthur Philipson, is another version of Waverley, and at key points in the novel he, like the contending states, wavers on the edge of an abyss. Though the abyss is actual, the most dangerous abyss is within, in Philipson's moral and intellectual subjectivity. The novel is not named for Philipson, however, but for Anne of Geierstein. Once again a morally and intellectually superior, yet ideally domestic, woman is made the inspiration and reward of a young man of good heart and sound principles but as yet uncertain character, courage, and public dedication. Three times (Scott liked the folklore pattern of triads) Anne saves Philipson from a potentially fatal lapse of courage and decision. Near the opening of the novel she appears almost magically when Philipson wavers on the edge of a mountain ledge and, offering her hand, stirs his resolution to step across to safety and the path that lies ahead. A second time, when imprisoned by a brutal and rapacious local baron, he despairingly waits for death near a dark abyss in the floor of his cell. But Anne again appears out of darkness, and the touch of her hand again steels his resolution:

> Her touch produced an effect far beyond that of the slight personal aid which the maiden's strength could have rendered. Courage was restored to his heart, vigour and animation to his benumbed and bruised limbs; such influence does the human mind, when excited to energy, possess over the infirmities of the human body.

This moral has dimensions at once autobiographical, artistic, political, philosophical, and religious, summarizing as it does volumes of Enlightenment materialist epistemology and social and historical optimism while also expressing Scott's episcopalian belief in the indissoluble link between religious conviction and ethical action. The third time Anne intervenes to warn the Philipsons of a secret plot against them and their mission. At the end of the novel the marriage of Arthur Philipson and Anne signifies the politically fruitful union of manly courage and activity with feminine understanding and insight in the cause of progress.

Scott's readers would know that the bloody conflicts depicted in the novel ended in historical time with the founding of stable monarchic dynasties and a republican federation. These states were able to accommodate diverse classes and interests in nations arranged in a world-dominating European concert of powers. Scott observed with growing alarm the social divisions of his time, not only in Britain, but in France, Spain, and elsewhere in Europe. *Anne of Geierstein* is a fictional, figurative, historicist reflection of that concern. Published in the midst of the growing constitutional crisis in Britain, the novel gave a European dimension but a British focus to Scott's long-standing critique of irresponsible, luxurious court government and ruling class, restless and ambitious lower ranks, and self-interested intellectual schemers aiming to fish in troubled waters. Yet his vision of the way forward seems overshadowed by doubt. This doubt soon seemed con-

Scott reading the proclamation issued by Mary, Queen of Scots, before her marriage to Henry Stuart, Lord Darnley (portrait by Sir William Allan; National Portrait Gallery, London)

firmed. When Scott revised the novel in 1831 for his "Magnum Opus" edition of the Waverley Novels, France had just had another revolution and Britain again seemed on the verge of one. Significantly, Scott now decided to close his text with a note including this remark by the medieval historian Philippe de Commines: "Such changes and revolutions in states and kingdoms, God in his providence has wrought before we were born, and will do again when we are in our graves; for this is a certain maxim, that the prosperity or adversity of Princes are wholly at his disposal."

The success of *Anne of Geierstein* with the reading public indicates that many of them shared his doubts. Though this success showed that Scott retained his popularity as a novelist, he and his publisher Robert Cadell were anxious, though for different reasons, to extract every bit of profit from the Waverley Novels. After several novels had come out, Scott would market them again in various formats and prices, aimed at different levels of the book-buying public. Triple-decker, or three-volume, novels were not only expensive but considered ephemeral reading, priced to be bought by circulating libraries and rented out to subscribers. Enterprising publishers tried to enlarge this market with cheaper reprints of works that had proved popular on their first appearance. Scott and Ballantyne put out such a series in 1820 as the Novelist's Library. The Waverley Novels were obvious candidates for similar treatment, and Cadell brought out an edition with "revisions," notes, and prefaces by Scott to give the novels a fresh appeal. This edition, which Scott called his "Magnum Opus," was published in the form of a five-shilling volume each month from 1829 until 1833. It was to be not only a money-spinner but a monument to Scott as a living "classic."

In February 1830 his years of strenuous literary labor, active public life, and good living caught up with Scott, and he suffered a severe stroke, one of several that would relentlessly incapacitate him. For the time being, however, he recovered and plunged into new work. He produced a study of "superstition," *Letters on Demonology and Witchcraft* (1830), a subject that infused his poems and novels and that had interested him since his days of collecting folk ballads and translating German Sturm and Drang literature in the 1790s. Sensing that his body was failing him, he became more determined than ever to cast off his debt of "honor," as he called it, by producing more Waverley Novels, egged on by Cadell, who was eager to get as much as he could from "the Wizard of the North" before the end. Scott's last two novels, *Count Robert of Paris* and *Castle Dangerous*, were published in 1832 as the fourth and last series of *Tales of My Landlord*. Both return to the theme of medieval chivalry as an ideology and culture inspiring a ruling class and uniting an entire society—indeed an entire civilization—despite its divisions and differences. Set in Byzantium during the eleventh century, *Count Robert of Paris* dramatizes the confrontation of the youthful, energetic, but uncouth feudal culture of Western Europe, represented by Count Robert and his warrior-wife, Brenhilda, with the decadent and Orientalized classical culture of antiquity, as the Crusaders pass through the capital of the eastern Roman Empire on their way to liberate the Holy Land from the equally energetic, youthful, and expansionist Islamic world. *Castle Dangerous* is set in the fourteenth century on the border of England and Scotland. Like *The Three Perils of Man* (1822), by Scott's friend James Hogg, *Castle Dangerous* shows the follies and disasters that can arise from chivalric codes of arms and love, especially when intertwined and taken to excess.

As Scott's health declined, a navy ship, the *Barham*, was made available by the Whig government to transport him to the Mediterranean in hopes the climate there would at least prolong his life. Since he was well known as a Tory, Scott was gratified by this compliment to him. As he prepared to leave England, a reform bill was defeated by the House of Lords and political disturbances broke out in the capital and throughout Britain. Scott's worst fears, of a revolution, seemed about to be realized after four decades. Nevertheless, he enjoyed the trip south. He was received in Malta, Naples, and Rome as an international celebrity. He learned that his last two novels had sold well, and Cadell offered two thousand pounds, sight unseen, for a projected new Waverley Novel on the siege of Malta by the Turks in 1565. From Naples Scott thought of visiting the Aegean, so celebrated in poetry and life by Byron. Scott even contemplated returning to poetry with a verse romance set on the island of Rhodes. But the plan to travel further east had to be given up, and while returning home through Germany, Scott suffered further strokes, leaving him physically paralyzed. Anxious to die at home, he was hurried back to Abbotsford. Almost to the last he tried to take pen in hand to spin out more Waverley Novels. He lingered for a few weeks in semiconsciousness. At last he lost his long-sustained emotional and mental self-control, breaking into uncontrollable rages and screaming for hours at a time. He died quietly, however, surrounded by his family, on 21 September 1832, during a beautiful autumn afternoon. Shortly afterward the enormous debt he had undertaken to discharge was finally cleared. The proceeds from further editions of his works made Robert Cadell rich. A monumental biography (1837, later revised) by Lockhart set Scott up as a pattern for the successful man of letters over the next century.

Scott produced his novels in the aftermath of a European struggle of political ideologies, systems, and empires, and in a Britain racked with crises caused by deep economic and social changes and dislocation. Scott does register regret for loss of some old values, particularly individual and collective strength of conviction, and what George Eliot, Scott's greatest admirer among the Victorians, called "the pathos, the heroism often accompanying the decay and final struggle of old systems." Scott also recommended a conservative progressivism under a predominantly rural social hierarchy; he shows little interest in urbanization or industrialization, two of the major changes of his time. Like Edmund Burke, Scott disliked middle-class self-interest, feared lower-class political revolution, and envisaged a professionalized gentry exercising cultural and political leadership, mediating between other classes, protecting the weak against predatory interests, preserving the best of the past against cultural or political "innovation," improving the present without rending the social fabric, and advancing Britain's international and imperial interests against less "civilized" nations. Like Burke, Scott found inspiration for reconstructing Britain in a chivalry imbued with professional middle-class values. Scott's poems and novels focus on what he saw as the historical vicissitudes of this chivalry, moving from the matter of Scotland to that of England, Christendom, and Europe.

The political and social implications of the Waverley Novels were certainly recognized in their time. As William Hazlitt remarked in *The Spirit of the Age* (1825), "The political bearing of

Portrait by Daniel Maclise in the Fraser's Magazine *"Gallery of Illustrious Literary Characters" (1830-1838)*

the *Scotch Novels* has been a considerable recommendation to them." Hazlitt also thought that, as a result, "young ladies" would not like them, though there is not much evidence to support this opinion. In 1833 the working-class radical Richard Carlile declared that Scott's alluring fictions had obstructed "the circulation of knowledge in the body politic," helping "kings, and priests, and lords" to keep the common people down. Yet in the same year Harriet Martineau, the greatest woman popularizer of political economy in the century, praised Scott for teaching his age the great lesson of social reconciliation, including (though unwittingly) "the rights of woman." On the other hand Mark Twain claimed, in *Life on the Mississippi* (1883), that the Waverley Novels were the major obstacle to progress after the French Revolution because they made readers in love "with decayed and swinish forms of religion; with decayed and degraded systems of government; with sillinesses and emptinesses, sham grandeurs, sham gauds, and sham chivalries of a brainless and worthless long-vanished society." Twain thought that whereas Miguel de Cervantes' *Don Quixote* (1605) "swept the world's admiration for the mediæval chivalry-silliness out of existence," Scott's *Ivanhoe* "restored it." In consequence, said Twain, Scott did "more real and lasting harm, perhaps, than any other individual who ever wrote."

Certainly there was in Scott's own time a determination to appropriate him and his work to new kinds of Romantic nationalism and commercialized chauvinism. These trends took on an imperial dimension as Scottish emigrants carried a sentimental patriotism around the world during the nineteenth century, renaming strange foreign places after scenes and sites from Scott. Places from Scott's Edinburgh to faraway New Zealand were "Scottified." When the prison in Edinburgh was rebuilt in the 1820s according to the latest utilitarian principles, it was given a false medieval facade to make it look like something from Scott, and the central railway station in Edinburgh was named Waverley. In Canada the boat taking tourists out into the thundering waters below Niagara Falls was named the *Maid of the Mist* after the heroine of Scott's *Anne of Geierstein.* Scott's poetic and novelistic world has entered into popular and commercialized culture beyond Scotland and Britain, and the real world will bear the marks of Scott's fictitious worlds for generations to come, whether or not his works ever become popular classics again.

Such popularity made Scott's works suspect to serious intellectuals and critics even in his own time. Yet early critical comments on the Waverley Novels generally recognized them as an unprecedented, if uneven and controversial, intellectual and artistic achievement. Critical debate focused on the intellectual, aesthetic, and social effects of the novels through their combination of history and fiction. As a young man Thomas Babington Macaulay thought Scott had shown the historian how to relate individual and domestic experience to the public, political, and national scene, but Stendhal thought Scott's emphasis on the social and public domains inhibited his ability to represent complex subjectivity. Italian novelist Allesandro Manzoni, who had been profoundly influenced by Scott, later wrote, "A great poet and a great historian may be found in the same man without creating confusion, but not in the same work." More representative of opinion in Britain was the view of the lawyer and historian Sir Archibald Alison that Scott had invented a new species of writing which "unites the learning of the historian with the fancy of the poet; . . . which teaches morality by example, and conveys information by giving pleasure; and which, combining the charms of imagination with the treasures of research, founds the ideal upon its only solid and durable base—the real." Thomas Carlyle, whose polemical *Past and Present* (1843) is a Victorian nonfiction version of *Ivanhoe,* praised the Waverley Novels for showing "that the bygone ages of the world were actually filled by living men, not by protocols, state-papers, controversies and abstractions of men." Popularized history was a major instrument of national culture and education in the nineteenth century, and not surprisingly Scott's novels were often adapted and illustrated as children's books and textbooks.

With the rise of literary modernism and professional academic criticism in the twentieth century, however, Scott's poems and novels fell out of favor and out of the literary canon, though retaining some following with the reading public. Response divided into extremes of "Scottolatry" on one hand and dismissal by professional and academic criticism on the other. There was an outburst of both kinds of response at the bicentenary in 1932. Since then Scott has been gradually regaining critical esteem, though he has not yet become again a popular classic. Herbert J. C. Grierson's edition of Scott's letters (1932-1937), Edgar Johnson's monumental biography (1970), and W. E. K. Anderson's edition of his journal (1972) provided new insight into Scott's life, thought, and writing, enabling readers and critics to go beyond the version of Scott that Lockhart created for the Romantics and Victorians. A critical edition of the Waverley Novels from Edinburgh University Press will further this impulse. Scholars and critics have pointed out Scott's incorporation of medieval romance, Shakespeare, the Bible, chapbook literature, and folklore into the Waverley Novels, his debt to the Scottish Enlightenment, his pervasively political interests, the extent of his influence on many national literatures around the world, the complexity of his personality and writings, and finally his formal artistry in service of that complexity. The work of David Daiches in the 1950s and Duncan Forbes in 1971 prepared the way for a revival of serious critical attention to Scott as an intellectual and political thinker. Perhaps the most important stimulus to renewed interest in these aspects of Scott was the English translation (1962) of the Marxist critic Georg Lukács's book on the historical novel and nineteenth-century bourgeois liberalism (1937). A new generation of scholars and critics is now reconsidering Scott in relation to Marxist, feminist, and other theoretical approaches developed since the 1960s. In an irony Scott would have enjoyed, a new "Scott industry" labors both to re-create and to justify Scott's enormous popularity and influence in the past.

Letters:

The Letters of Sir Walter Scott, 12 volumes, edited by Sir Herbert J. C. Grierson, assisted by Davidson Cook, W. M. Parker, and others (London: Constable, 1932-1937).

Bibliographies:

Greville Worthington, *A Bibliography of the Waverley Novels* (London: Constable, 1931);

William Ruff, *A Bibliography of the Poetical Works of Sir Walter Scott, 1796-1832* (Edinburgh: Edinburgh Bibliographical Society, 1938);

James Clarkson Corson, *A Bibliography of Sir Walter Scott: A Classified and Annotated List of Books and Articles Relating to His Life and Works, 1797-1940* (Edinburgh & London: Oliver & Boyd, 1943);

Jill Rubenstein, *Sir Walter Scott: A Reference Guide* (Boston: G. K. Hall, 1978).

Biographies:

John Gibson Lockhart, *Memoirs of the Life of Sir Walter Scott, Bart.* (7 volumes, Edinburgh: Cadell, 1837-1838; revised, 10 volumes, 1839);

Sir Herbert Grierson, *Sir Walter Scott, Bart.: A New Life Supplementary to and Corrective of Lockhart's Biography* (London: Constable, 1938);

Hesketh Pearson, *Sir Walter Scott: His Life and Personality* (New York: Harper, 1955);

Edgar Johnson, *Sir Walter Scott: The Great Unknown*, 2 volumes (New York: Macmillan, 1970).

References:

James Anderson, *Sir Walter Scott and History; With Other Papers* (Edinburgh: Edina Press, 1981);

Alan Bell, ed., *Scott Bicentenary Essays: Selected Papers Read at the Sir Walter Scott Bicentenary Conference* (Edinburgh & London: Scottish Academic Press, 1973);

Alan Bold, ed., *Sir Walter Scott: The Long-forgotten Melody* (London: Vision Press, 1983);

David Brown, *Walter Scott and the Historical Imagination* (London & Boston: Routledge & Kegan Paul, 1979);

Alice Chandler, *A Dream of Order: The Medieval Ideal in Nineteenth-Century Literature* (Lincoln: University of Nebraska Press, 1970);

A. O. J. Cockshut, *The Achievement of Sir Walter Scott* (London: Collins, 1969);

Daniel Cottom, *The Civilized Imagination: A Study of Ann Radcliffe, Jane Austen, and Sir Walter Scott* (Cambridge & New York: Cambridge University Press, 1985);

Thomas Crawford, *Scott*, revised and enlarged edition, Scottish Writers Series (Edinburgh: Scottish Academic Press, 1982);

David Daiches, *Sir Walter Scott and His World* (New York: Viking, 1971);

Donald Davie, *The Heyday of Sir Walter Scott* (London: Routledge & Kegan Paul, 1961);

D. D. Devlin, *The Author of Waverley: A Critical Study of Walter Scott* (London: Macmillan, 1971);

Nicholas Dickson, *The Bible in Waverley: or, Sir Walter Scott's Use of the Sacred Scriptures* (Edinburgh: A. & C. Black, 1884);

Avrom Fleishman, *The English Historical Novel: Walter Scott to Virginia Woolf* (Baltimore: Johns Hopkins Press, 1971);

Duncan Forbes, "The Rationalism of Sir Walter Scott," *Cambridge Journal*, 7 (October 1953): 20-35;

Kurt Gammerschlag, "The Making and Un-Making of Sir Walter Scott's *Count Robert of Paris*," *Studies in Scottish Literature*, 15 (1980): 95-123;

Mark Girouard, *The Return to Camelot: Chivalry and the English Gentleman* (New Haven & London: Yale University Press, 1981);

Robert C. Gordon, *Under Which King? A Study of the Scottish Waverley Novels* (Edinburgh: Oliver & Boyd, 1969);

Francis R. Hart, *Scott's Novels: The Plotting of Historic Survival* (Charlottesville: University Press of Virginia, 1966);

John O. Hayden, ed., *Scott: The Critical Heritage* (London: Routledge & Kegan Paul, 1970);

James T. Hillhouse, *The Waverley Novels and Their Critics* (Minneapolis: University of Minnesota Press, 1936);

Andrew D. Hook, "Jane Porter, Sir Walter Scott and the Historical Novel," *Clio*, 2 (Winter 1976): 181-192;

Gary Kelly, *English Fiction of the Romantic Period 1789-1830* (London & New York: Longman, 1989);

James Kerr, *Fiction Against History: Scott as Storyteller* (Cambridge: Cambridge University Press, 1989);

Mary Lascelles, *The Story-Teller Retrieves the Past: Historical Fiction and Fictitious History in the Art of Scott, Stevenson, Kipling, and Some Others* (Oxford: Clarendon Press, 1980);

Georg Lukàcs, *The Historical Novel*, translated by Hannah Mitchell and Stanley Mitchell (London: Merlin Press, 1962);

David Marshall, *Sir Walter Scott and Scots Law* (Edinburgh: W. Hodge, 1932);

Graham McMaster, *Scott and Society* (Cambridge: Cambridge University Press, 1981);

Jane Millgate, *Scott's Last Edition: A Study in Publishing History* (Edinburgh: Edinburgh University Press, 1987);

Millgate, *Walter Scott: The Making of the Novelist* (Toronto: University of Toronto Press, 1984);

Jerome Mitchell, *Scott, Chaucer, and Medieval Romance: A Study in Sir Walter Scott's Indebtedness to the Literature of the Middle Ages* (Lexington: University Press of Kentucky, 1987);

Coleman O. Parsons, *Witchcraft and Demonology in Scott's Fiction: With Chapters on the Supernatural in Scottish Literature* (Edinburgh & London: Oliver & Boyd / New York: Clarke Irwin, 1964);

James Reed, *Sir Walter Scott: Landscape and Locality* (London: Athlone Press, 1980);

Harry E. Shaw, *The Forms of Historical Fiction: Sir Walter Scott and His Successors* (Ithaca, N.Y.: Cornell University Press, 1983);

Graham Tulloch, *The Language of Walter Scott* (London: André Deutsch, 1980);

Alexander Welsh, *The Hero of the Waverley Novels* (New Haven & London: Yale University Press, 1963);

Judith Wilt, *Secret Leaves: The Novels of Sir Walter Scott* (Chicago & London: University of Chicago Press, 1985).

Papers:

Collections of manuscripts, letters, documents, and memorabilia are held by the Henry W. and Albert A. Berg Collection and the manuscript division of the New York Public Library, the Boston Public Library, the British Museum, the Folger Shakespeare Library in Washington, D.C., the Forster Collection in the Victoria and Albert Museum, the Houghton Library and the Widener Library of Harvard University, the Henry E. Huntington Library, the Pierpont Morgan Library, the National Library of Scotland, the Carl Pforzheimer Library in the New York Public Library, the library of Princeton University, and the library of the University of Rochester.

Mary Wollstonecraft Shelley
(30 August 1797 - 1 February 1851)

Eleanor Ty
Wilfrid Laurier University

BOOKS: *Mounseer Nongtongpaw; or, The Discoveries of John Bull in a Trip to Paris* (London: Printed for the Proprietors of the Juvenile Library, 1808);

History of a Six Weeks' Tour through a part of France, Switzerland, Germany, and Holland, with Letters descriptive of a Sail round the Lake of Geneva, and of the Glaciers of Chamouni (London: Published by T. Hookham, jun., and C. & J. Ollier, 1817);

Frankenstein; or, The Modern Prometheus (3 volumes, London: Lackington, Hughes, Harding, Mavor & Jones, 1818; revised edition, 1 volume, London: Henry Colburn & Richard Bentley, 1831; 2 volumes, Philadelphia: Carey, Lea & Blanchard, 1833);

Valperga: or, The Life and Adventures of Castruccio, Prince of Lucca, 3 volumes (London: G. & W. B. Whittaker, 1823);

The Last Man (3 volumes, London: Henry Colburn, 1826; 2 volumes, Philadelphia: Carey, Lea & Blanchard, 1833);

The Fortunes of Perkin Warbeck (3 volumes, London: Henry Colburn & Richard Bentley, 1830; 2 volumes, Philadelphia: Carey, Lea & Blanchard, 1834);

Lodore (3 volumes, London: Richard Bentley, 1835; 1 volume, New York: Wallis & Newell, 1835);

Lives of the Most Eminent Literary and Scientific Men of Italy, Spain, and Portugal, volumes 86-88 of *The Cabinet of Biography*, in *Lardner's Cabinet Cyclopedia*, conducted by Reverend Dionysius Lardner (London: Printed for Longman, Orme, Brown, Green & Longman and John Taylor, 1835-1837; republished in part as *Lives of the Most Eminent Literary and Scientific Men of Italy*, 2 volumes (Philadelphia: Lea & Blanchard, 1841);

Falkner (3 volumes, London: Saunders & Otley, 1837; 1 volume, New York: Harper & Brothers, 1837);

Lives of the Most Eminent Literary and Scientific Men of France, volumes 102 and 103 of *The Cabinet of Biography* (London: Printed for Longman, Orme, Brown, Green & Longman, 1838, 1839); republished in part as *Lives of the Most Eminent French Writers*, 2 volumes (Philadelphia: Lea & Blanchard, 1840);

Miniature of Mary Shelley, painted after her death by Reginald Easton, who based this portrait on a sketch made by Edward Ellerker Williams in 1821 or 1822, on Mary Shelley's death mask, and on the advice of her son and daughter-in-law (Bodleian Library, Oxford)

Rambles in Germany and Italy in 1840, 1842, and 1843, 2 volumes (London: Edward Moxon, 1844);

The Choice—A Poem on Shelley's Death, edited by H. Buxton Forman (London: Printed for the editor for private distribution, 1876);

Tales and Stories, edited by Richard Garnett (London: William Paterson, 1891);

Proserpine & Midas: Two Unpublished Mythological Dramas, edited by A. Koszul (London: Humphrey Milford, 1922);

Mary Shelley's Journal, edited by Frederick L. Jones (Norman: University of Oklahoma Press, 1947);

Mathilda, edited by Elizabeth Nitchie (Chapel Hill: University of North Carolina Press, 1959);

Collected Tales and Stories, edited by Charles E. Robinson (Baltimore & London: Johns Hopkins University Press, 1976);

The Journals of Mary Shelley, 2 volumes, edited by Paula Feldman and Diana Scott-Kilvert (Oxford: Clarendon Press, 1987).

Editions: *The Last Man*, edited by Hugh J. Luke, Jr. (Lincoln: University of Nebraska Press, 1965);

Frankenstein, or The Modern Prometheus, edited by M. K. Joseph (Oxford & New York: Oxford University Press, 1969);

Frankenstein, or The Modern Prometheus [1818 text], edited by James Rieger (New York: Bobbs-Merrill, 1974).

OTHER: *Posthumous Poems of Percy Bysshe Shelley*, edited, with a preface and notes, by Mary Shelley (London: Printed for John & Henry L. Hunt, 1824);

The Poetical Works of Percy Bysshe Shelley, 4 volumes, edited, with a preface and notes, by Mary Shelley (London: Edward Moxon, 1839);

Essays, Letters from Abroad, Translations and Fragments. By Percy Bysshe Shelley, 2 volumes, edited, with a preface and notes, by Mary Shelley (London: Edward Moxon, 1840).

By the time she was nineteen, Mary Wollstonecraft Shelley had written one of the most famous novels ever published. Embodying one of the central myths of Western culture, *Frankenstein; or, The Modern Prometheus*, first published in 1818, tells the story of an overreacher who brings to life the monster who inhabits one's dreams, a tale which still stands as a powerful and enduring example of the creative imagination. Nearly two hundred years later, the story of his creation still inspires stage, film, video, and television productions. In addition to *Frankenstein*, Mary Shelley wrote six other novels, a novella, mythological dramas, stories and articles, various travel books, and biographical studies. By 1851, the year of her death, she had established a reputation as a prominent author independent of her famous husband, Percy Bysshe Shelley.

The daughter of the two great intellectual rebels of the 1790s, William Godwin and Mary Wollstonecraft, Mary Shelley (née Godwin) was born on 30 August 1797 in London. Eleven days after her birth, her mother, the celebrated author of *A Vindication of the Rights of Woman* (1792), died of puerperal fever, leaving Godwin, the author of *An Enquiry Concerning Political Justice* (1793), to care for Mary and her three-year-old half sister, Fanny Imlay (to whom he gave the name Godwin). Godwin could find no words to articulate his grief at the loss of the woman with whom he had fallen passionately in love thirteen months before, at the age of forty. In spite of their ethical opposition to the institution of marriage, he and Wollstonecraft had married only five months earlier in order to give their child social respectability.

Bereft of his companion, Godwin dealt with his affliction in the only way he knew, by intellectual reasoning and reflection. The day after her funeral, he began to sort through Mary Wollstonecraft's papers, and by 24 September he had started working on the story of her life. His loving tribute to her, published in January 1798 as the *Memoirs of the Author of a Vindication of the Rights of Woman*, is a sensitive but full and factual account of the life and writings of his wife, including Wollstonecraft's infatuation with the painter Henry Fuseli; her affair with American speculator and former officer in the American Revolutionary Army, Gilbert Imlay, the father of her illegitimate daughter, Fanny; and her two unsuccessful attempts at taking her own life. Godwin's noble intention was to immortalize his wife, whom he considered to be a "person of eminent merit." Instead of expressing admiration, however, the public condemned Wollstonecraft as licentious, and read her attempted suicides in terms of her lack of religious convictions. When Godwin had declared in the *Memoirs* that "There are not many individuals with whose character the public welfare and improvement are more intimately connected" than his subject, he could not have predicted how accurately and with what irony this statement would become true. For at least the next hundred years the feminist cause was to suffer setback after setback because of society's association of sexual promiscuity with those who advocated the rights of women. In the index to the *Anti-Jacobin Review* of 1798, for example, "See Mary Wollstonecraft" is the only entry listed under "Prostitution," and the Wollstonecraft listing ends with a cross-reference to "Prostitution." Such was the complex and ambiguous heritage Mary Shelley received from her mother. She was to grow up with what Anne K. Mellor had described as a "powerful and ever-to-be frustrated need to be mothered," as well as with the realization that the parent she had never known was both celebrated as a pioneer reformer of woman's rights and education, and castigated as an "unsex'd female."

Godwin immediately became the chief object of her affections, as he was her primary caretaker for the first three years of her life. Having studied progressive educational authorities, from Jean-Jacques Rousseau to his contemporaries, Godwin also attempted to adopt many of Wollstonecraft's child-care practices. Precocious, sensitive, and spirited, Mary became his favorite child. He called her "pretty little Mary" and relished evidence of her superiority over Fanny. He supervised their early schooling and took them on various excursions—to Pope's Grotto at Twickenham, to theatrical pantomimes, and to dinners with his friends James Marshall and Charles and Mary Lamb. Mary Shelley's attachment to her father was to become intense and long lasting.

The idyll ended when the Godwin's housekeeper and governess, Louisa Jones, left their residence, The Polygon, with one of Godwin's more tempestuous and irresponsible protégés, George Dyson. Godwin had been looking for a wife since 1798 and met Mary Jane Clairmont on 5 May 1801. Susceptible to her flattery, Godwin immediately saw in "Mrs." Clairmont—a self-proclaimed "widow," with a six-year-old son, Charles, and a four-year-old daughter, Jane—the ideal helpmate and mother. Young Mary Shelley's stepmother was in reality Mary Jane Vial, spinster, who had lived with expatriate mercantile families in France and in Spain. Marshall summed her up as a "clever, bustling, second-rate woman, glib of tongue and pen, with a temper undisciplined and uncontrolled; not bad-hearted, but with a complete absence of all the finer sensibilities."

Mary Shelley's relationship with her stepmother was strained. The new Mrs. Godwin resented Mary's intense affection for her father and was jealous of the special interest visitors showed in the product of the union between the two most radical thinkers of the day. Not only did she demand that Mary do household chores,

Mary Shelley circa 1814 (sketch by an unknown artist; St. Pancras Public Libraries)

she constantly encroached on Mary's privacy, opening her letters and limiting her access to Godwin. Nor did she encourage Mary's intellectual development or love of reading. While her daughter, Jane (who later called herself Claire), was sent to boarding school to learn French, Mary never received any formal education. She learned to read from Louisa Jones, Godwin, and his wife, and followed Godwin's advice that the proper way to study was to read two or three books simultaneously. Fortunately, she had access to her father's excellent library, as well as to the political, philosophical, scientific, or literary conversations that Godwin conducted with such visitors as William Wordsworth, Charles Lamb, Samuel Taylor Coleridge, Thomas Holcroft, John Johnson, Humphry Davy, Horne Tooke, and William Hazlitt. For example, on 24 August 1806 Mary and Jane hid under the parlor sofa to hear Coleridge recite "The Rime of the Ancient Mariner," a poem which later haunted both *Frankenstein* (1818) and *Falkner* (1837).

Despite a wildly fluctuating income—based largely on the Juvenile Library of M. J. Godwin and Company, a publishing enterprise devised by Mrs. Godwin—the physical needs of the children were provided. Mary's favorite pastime as a child was to "write stories," and in 1808 her thirty-nine-quatrain reworking of Charles Dibdin's five-stanza song *Mounseer Nongtongpaw* was published by the Godwin Juvenile Library. This version became so popular that it was republished in 1830 in an edition illustrated by Robert Cruikshank. Meanwhile, as Mary became a young woman, the tension with Mrs. Godwin increased. Mellor argues that Mary "construed Mrs. Godwin as the opposite of everything that she had learned to worship in her own dead mother"—as conservative, philistine, devious, and manipulative, where Wollstonecraft was freethinking, intellectual, open, and generous. In the summer of 1812 Godwin sent his precious only daughter to visit William Baxter, an acquaintance who lived in Dundee, Scotland. With the Baxter family, Mary experienced a happiness she had rarely known. She grew fond of Baxter, and a friendship soon developed between Mary and his two daughters, Christina and Isabel. This close-knit family was to provide Mary with a model of domestic affection and harmony that would surface later in her fiction. The dunes, the beach, and the barren hills near Dundee inspired Mary, and she would later describe this scenery in her novella *Mathilda* (written in 1819-1820).

On her return to London in November 1812, Mary met for the first time Godwin's new, young, and wealthy disciple, Percy Bysshe Shelley, and his wife, Harriet Westbrook Shelley. The son of a man of fortune, Percy had received a superior education at Eton and briefly at Oxford. Before the age of seventeen, he had published two Gothic romances, *Zastrozzi* (1810) and *St. Irvyne* (1811), and now, influenced by Godwinian precepts, he desired to benefit humanity more directly. Percy Shelley shared Godwin's belief that the greatest justice is done when he who possesses money gives it to whomever has greatest need of it. Therefore it was not long before Shelley was supporting Godwin financially. When Mary next met the tall, frail-looking, elegant Percy, on 5 May 1814, she viewed him as a generous young idealist and as a budding genius. He, in turn, had become dissatisfied with his wife and was affected by Mary's beauty, her intellectual interests, and, above all, by her identity as the "daughter of William and Mary."

By June 1814 Shelley was dining with the Godwins almost every day. Chaperoned by Jane, Mary and Percy went for daily walks, sometimes to St. Pancras Church to visit Wollstonecraft's grave, where Mary had earlier gone to read her mother's works. Inevitably, on 26 June, they declared their love for each other. Percy saw Mary as a "child of love and light," and in his dedicatory stanza for *The Revolt of Islam* (1817) wrote of her: "They saw that thou wert lovely from thy birth, / Of glorious parents, thou aspiring Child." Upon discovering the relationship, Godwin, while still accepting Percy Shelley's money, forbade him from visiting the house. Mary tried to obey her father's injunction, but Percy's attempted suicide soon convinced Mary of the strength of his love, and on 28 July 1814 she fled with him to France, accompanied by Jane Clairmont.

Recollecting her years with Percy, Mary wrote in her journal on 19 December 1822: "France—Poverty—a few days of solitude & some uneasiness—A tranquil residence in a beautiful spot—Switzerland—Bath—Marlow—Milan—The Baths of Lucca—Este—Venice—Rome—Naples—Rome & misery—Leghorn—Florence Pisa—Solitude The Williams—The Baths—Pisa—These are the heads of chapters—each containing a tale, romantic beyond romance." The eight years Mary and Percy Shelley spent together were indeed characterized by romance and melodrama. During this period Mary and Percy, both extremely idealistic, lived on love—because of extended negotiations over the disposition of the estate of Percy's grandfather—without money, constantly moving from one placed to another. Mary gave birth to four children, only one of whom survived to adulthood. The first, a girl, was born prematurely and died eleven days later in 1815; William, born in 1816, died of malaria in 1819; Clara Everina, born in 1817, perished from dysentery the next year; Percy Florence, born in 1819, died in 1889. In 1822 Mary miscarried during her fifth pregnancy and nearly lost her life. With the suicides of Fanny Godwin and Harriet Shelley in 1816, death was much on her mind. Numerous critics—among them Ellen Moers, Sandra Gilbert, and Susan Gubar—have pointed out the link between the themes of creation, birth, and death in *Frankenstein* and Mary Shelley's real-life preoccupation with pregnancy, labor, maternity, and death.

Before Mary Shelley wrote her most popular novel, she published *History of a Six Weeks' Tour through a part of France, Switzerland, Germany, and Holland, with Letters descriptive of a Sail round the Lake of Geneva, and of the Glaciers of Chamouni* (1817), which was based on journal entries and long letters home to Fanny. For this work Mary had as a literary model her mother's *Letters Written during a Short Residence in Sweden, Norway, and Denmark* (1796), a book that, according to Godwin, "calculated to make a man in love with its author." While describing the countryside with enthusiasm and accuracy, Shelley writes from a foreigner's perspective. She complains, for instance, of the squalor and the dirt in French villages, and of the disgusting behavior of Germans.

In 1815, shortly after the death of her first baby, Shelley recorded a dream that may or may not have had a direct influence on the plot of *Frankenstein*. On 19 March 1815 she recorded in her journal: "Dream that my little baby came to life again—that it had only been cold & that we rubbed it before the fire & it lived." Her anxieties about motherhood and the inability to give life may have led her to write the tale of the aspiring scientist who succeeds in creating a being by unnatural methods. For example, Frankenstein's act has been read, by Robert Kiely and Margaret Homans among others, as an attempt to usurp the power of the woman and to circumvent normal heterosexual procreation.

In *Frankenstein*, Shelley dramatizes some of her ambivalent feelings about the proto-Victorian ideology of motherhood. As Mary Poovey has argued, Shelley desired to conform to the ideals of what a proper wife and mother should be, but her attachment to Percy, who was still legally married to Harriet, and the ménage à trois with Jane Clairmont (who over the next five years changed her name three times, from Jane to Clara to Clare and finally to Claire) involved her in an unconventional, if not romantically original, domestic arrangement. Condemned by her beloved father, who believed that she "had been guilty of a crime," the seventeen-year-old Mary, not yet a wife and no longer a mother, was insecure and increasingly dependent on Percy for emotional support and familial commitment. He, on the other hand, caught up in his excited passions, was eager to live out his theory of "free love," encouraging Claire's affections. In the early part of 1815 Percy's friend Thomas Jefferson Hogg came to stay with Mary, Percy, and Claire for six weeks, during which time Percy urged Mary, despite her reluctance, to reciprocate Hogg's sexual overtures.

Though Claire continued in Mary and Percy's household until 1820, she was temporarily diverted by an affair with George Gordon, Lord Byron, during the spring of 1816. Persuading Percy and Mary to accompany her to Switzerland to meet Byron, Claire set off with the Shelleys in early May 1816 and eventually moved into a chalet on the banks of Lake Geneva, within walking distance from Villa Diodati, where Byron and his physician, Dr. John William Polidori, were staying. Byron and Percy became close friends, sailing together on the lake and having literary and philosophical discussions in the evenings. Both Mary and Percy found Byron fascinating and intriguing. He was handsome, capricious, cynical, and radiated an intellectual energy. Mellor surmises that "The intellectual and erotic stimulation of [Percy] Shelley's and Byron's combined presence, together with her deep-seated anxieties and insecurities, once again erupted into Mary's consciousness as a waking dream or nightmare," becoming "the most famous dream in literary history."

In the 1831 edition of *Frankenstein* Mary Shelley's introduction explains how she, "then a young girl, came to think of and to dilate upon so very hideous an idea." On a rainy evening in June 1816, they all gathered at the fireside to read aloud *Fantasmagoriana, ou Recueil d'histoires d'apparitions de spectres, revenants, fantômes, etc.* (1812), a French translation of a German book of ghost stories. At Byron's suggestion, they each agreed to write a horror story. The next day Byron read the beginning of his tale, Shelley "commenced one founded on the experiences of his early life," and Polidori had "some terrible idea about a skull-headed lady who was so punished for peeping through a key-hole." Mary wanted to think of a story "which would speak to the mysterious fears of our nature and awake thrilling horror—one to make the reader dread to look round, to curdle the blood, and quicken the beatings of the heart." The others dropped their stories, but kept asking Mary: "Have you thought of a story?" to which she had to reply with "a mortifying negative." Finally, one night, after a discussion among Byron, Polidori, and Percy Shelley concerning galvanism and Erasmus Darwin's success in causing a piece of a *vermicello* to move voluntarily, she fell into a reverie of waking dream where she saw "the pale student of unhallowed arts kneeling beside the thing he had put together." She felt the terror for the artist who endeavored "to mock the stupendous mechanism of the Creator

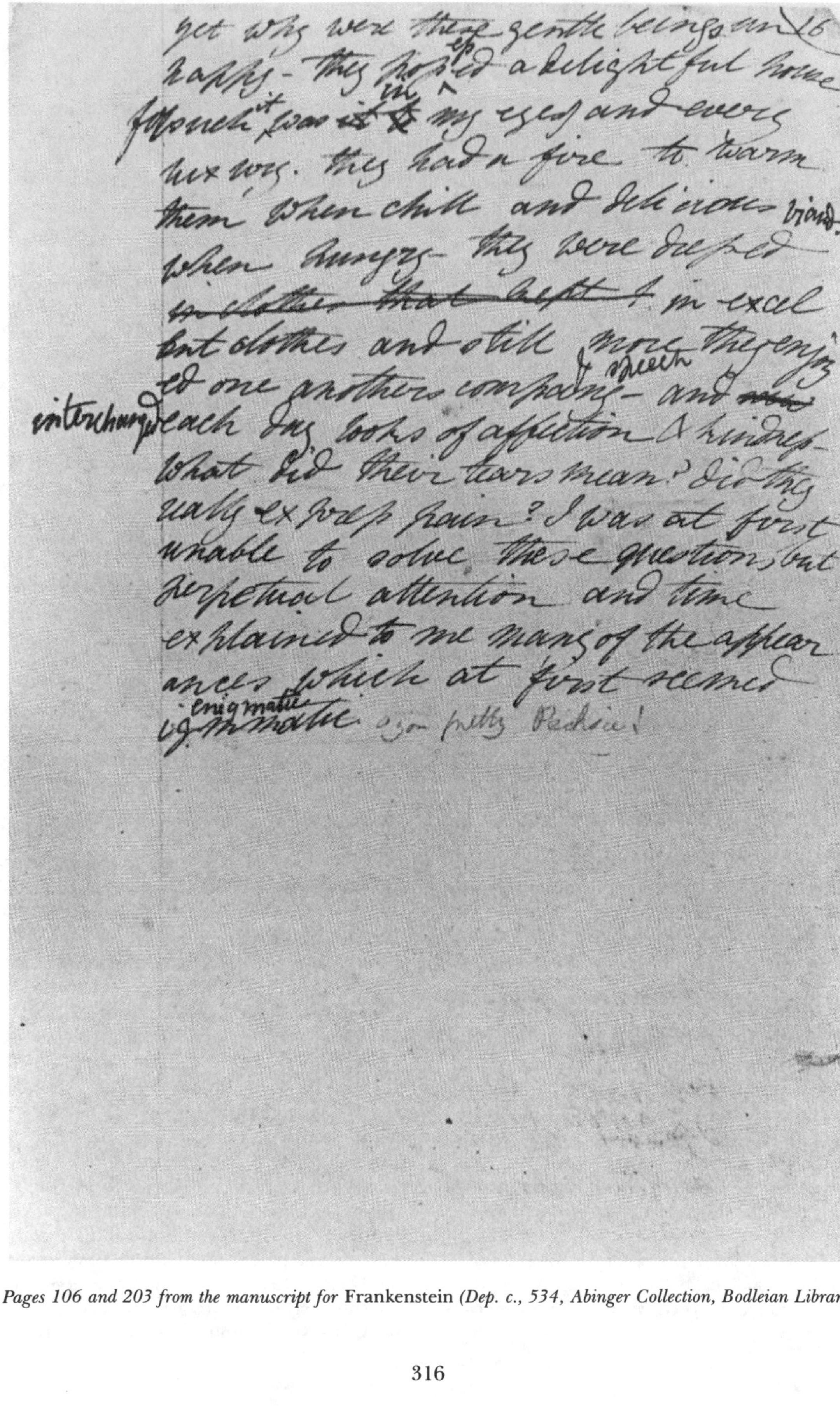
yet why were ~~these~~ gentle beings un- 16
happy - they possessed a delightful house
(for such it was in my eyes and every
luxury. they had a fire to warm
them when chill and delicious viands
when hungry - they were dressed
~~in clothes that kept~~ in excellent clothes and still more they enjoyed one anothers company & speech - and ~~saw~~
interchanged each day looks of affection & kindness.
What did their tears mean? did they
really express pain? I was at first
unable to solve these questions but
perpetual attention and time
explained to me many of the appearances which at first seemed
enigmatic ~~inigmatic~~ o you pretty Pecksie!

Pages 106 and 203 from the manuscript for Frankenstein *(Dep. c., 534, Abinger Collection, Bodleian Library, Oxford)*

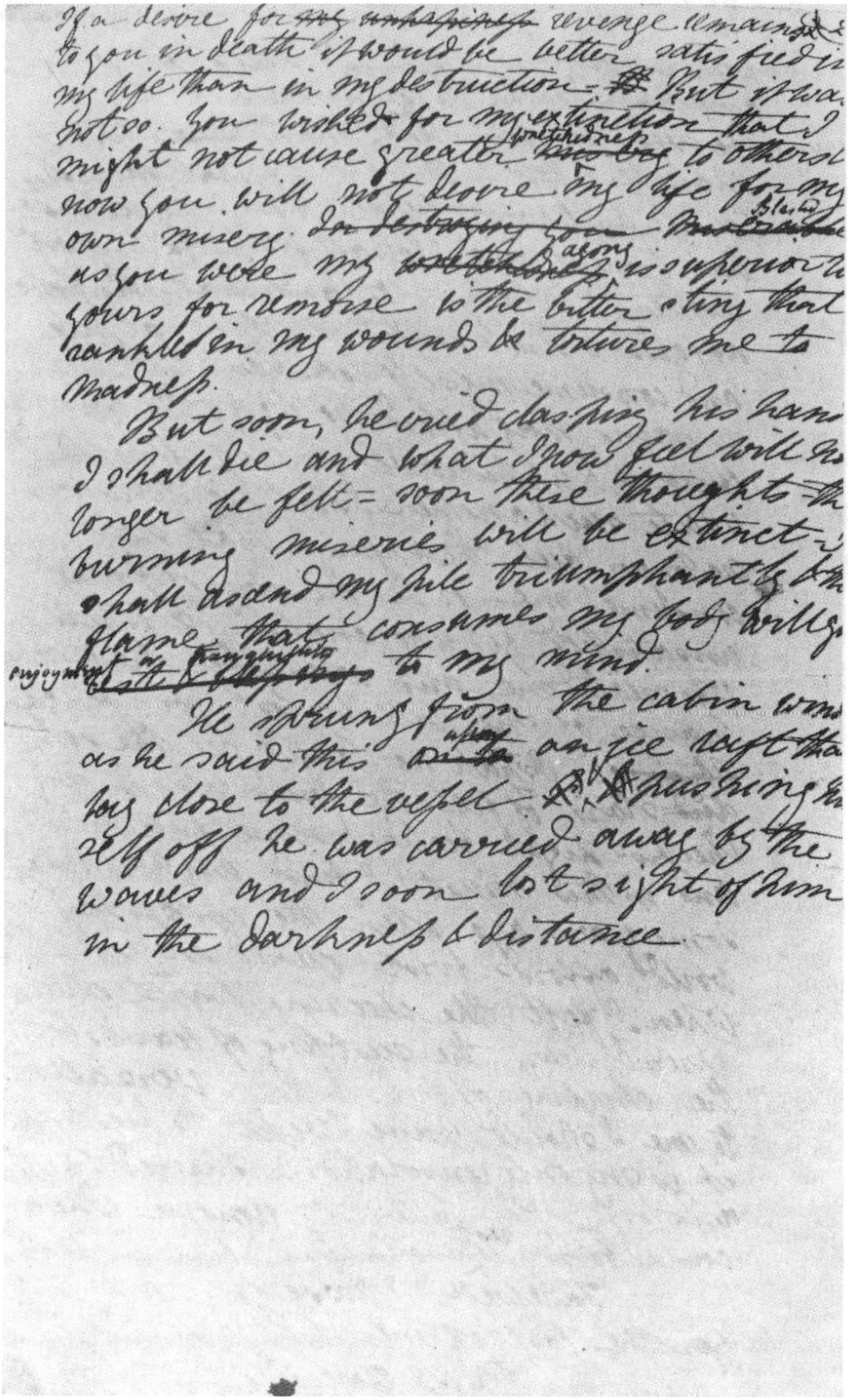
If a desire for revenge remained to you in death it would be better satisfied in my life than in my destruction. But it was not so. You wished for my extinction that I might not cause greater wretchedness to others & now you will not desire my life for my own misery. Blasted as you were my agony is superior to yours for remorse is the bitter sting that rankles in my wounds & tortures me to madness.

But soon, he cried clasping his hands I shall die and what I now feel will no longer be felt — soon these thoughts & burning miseries will be extinct. I shall ascend my pile triumphantly & the flame that consumes my body will give enjoyment to my mind.

He sprung from the cabin window as he said this upon an ice raft that lay close to the vessel & pushing himself off he was carried away by the waves and I soon lost sight of him in the darkness & distance.

of the world" by giving the "spark of life" to a "hideous corpse." Next morning, after the poets went off sailing, she started work on what was to become chapter 4 of *Frankenstein,* which begins, "It was on a dreary night of November. . . ."

Encouraged by Percy, Mary developed the little ghost story into a novel, which she finished in May of 1817 at Marlow and published in March 1818. To those who have not read the book, the name Frankenstein is often associated with the monster rather than its creator. The mistake is perhaps not altogether erroneous, for as many critics point out the creature and his maker are doubles of one another, or doppelgängers. Their relationship is similar to that between the head and the heart, or the intellect and the emotion. The conception of the divided self—the idea that the civilized man or woman contains within a monstrous, destructive force—emerges as the creature echoes both Frankenstein's and narrator Robert Walton's loneliness: all three wish for a friend or companion. Frankenstein and his monster alternately pursue and flee from one another. Like fragments of a mind in conflict with itself, they represent polar opposites which are not reconciled, and which destroy each other at the end. For example, the creature enacts the repressed desires of its maker, alleviating Victor Frankenstein's fear of sexuality by murdering his bride, Elizabeth Lavenza, on their wedding night. Identities merge, as Frankenstein frequently takes responsibility for the creature's action: for instance, after the deaths of the children William and Justine, both of which were caused by the creature, Frankenstein admits they were "the first hapless victims to [his] unhallowed arts."

In a recent reading of *Frankenstein,* Mellor demonstrates a link between events, dates, and names in the novel and those in Mary Shelley's life. Mellor argues that the novel is born out of a "doubled fear, the fear of a woman that she may not be able to bear a healthy normal child and the fear of a putative author that she may not be able to write. . . . the book is her created self as well as her child." Dated 11 December 17— to 12 September 17—, the letters that form the narration of the novel—from Walton to his sister Margaret Walton Saville (whose initials are those of Mary Wollstonecraft Shelley)—are written during a period similar in duration to Mary Shelley's third pregnancy, during which she wrote *Frankenstein.* Mellor discovered that the day and date on which Walton first sees the creature, Monday, 31 July, had coincided in 1797, the year in which Mary Shelley was born. This fact and other internal evidence led Mellor to conclude that the novel ends on 12 September 1797, two days after Mary Wollstonecraft's death: "Mary Shelley thus symbolically fused her book's beginning and ending with her own—Victor Frankenstein's death, the Monster's promised suicide, and her mother's death from puerperal fever can all be seen as the consequence of the same creation, the birth of Mary Godwin the author."

The theme of creation is highlighted by the many references to *Paradise Lost* (1667), John Milton's epic rendition of the biblical story of Genesis, which becomes an important intertext of the novel. "Did I request thee, Maker, from my clay / To mould me man? Did I solicit thee / From darkness to promote me?—," from book 10, is quoted as the epigraph, and Milton's poem is one of the books the creature reads. The monster is caught between the states of innocence and evil: like Adam he is "apparently united by no link to any other being in existence," but as an outcast and wretch he often considers "Satan as the fitter emblem" of his condition. Victor Frankenstein, too, is at once God, as he is the monster's creator, but also like Adam, an innocent child, and like Satan, the rebellious overreacher and vengeful fiend. Throughout the novel there is a strong sense of an Edenic world lost through Frankenstein's single-minded thirst for knowledge.

Frankenstein is also cast as a Promethean figure, striving against human limitations to bring light and benefit to mankind. While he advises Walton to "Seek happiness in tranquillity and avoid ambition," he nevertheless invites his listeners to share in the grandeur of his dreams, to glory in his ability to create a sublime facsimile of the human self. Frankenstein's fall, after all, results not from his creative enterprise, but from his failure and inability to give love to his creature. Indeed, another central concern of the novel is the conflict of individual desire against that of familial and social responsibility. George Levine writes: "*Frankenstein* spells out both the horror of going ahead and the emptiness of return. In particular, it spells out the price of heroism." Unlike her mother, Mary Wollstonecraft, and unlike the Romantic poets generally, Shelley advocates self-denial and social harmony over self-assertion, confrontation, and the individualistic, imaginative act. In her novel she shows that Frankenstein's quest is an act of selfish obsession, one that destroys his domestic relationships. He is contrasted with the mariner Robert Walton, whose

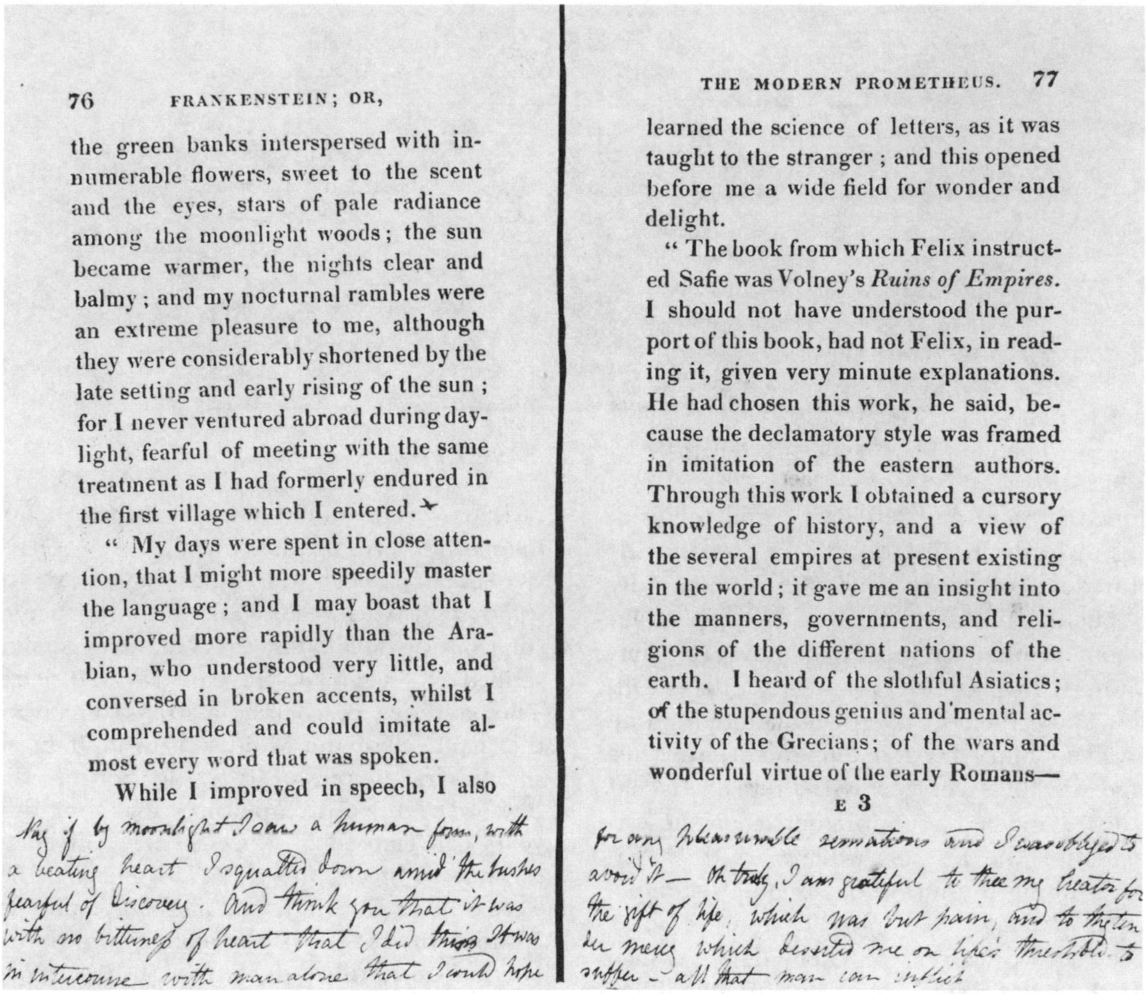

76 FRANKENSTEIN; OR,

the green banks interspersed with innumerable flowers, sweet to the scent and the eyes, stars of pale radiance among the moonlight woods; the sun became warmer, the nights clear and balmy; and my nocturnal rambles were an extreme pleasure to me, although they were considerably shortened by the late setting and early rising of the sun; for I never ventured abroad during daylight, fearful of meeting with the same treatment as I had formerly endured in the first village which I entered.

"My days were spent in close attention, that I might more speedily master the language; and I may boast that I improved more rapidly than the Arabian, who understood very little, and conversed in broken accents, whilst I comprehended and could imitate almost every word that was spoken.

While I improved in speech, I also

Nay if by moonlight I saw a human form, with a beating heart I squatted down amid the bushes fearful of discovery. And think you that it was with no bitterness of heart that I did this? It was in intercourse with man alone that I could hope

THE MODERN PROMETHEUS. 77

learned the science of letters, as it was taught to the stranger; and this opened before me a wide field for wonder and delight.

"The book from which Felix instructed Safie was Volney's *Ruins of Empires.* I should not have understood the purport of this book, had not Felix, in reading it, given very minute explanations. He had chosen this work, he said, because the declamatory style was framed in imitation of the eastern authors. Through this work I obtained a cursory knowledge of history, and a view of the several empires at present existing in the world; it gave me an insight into the manners, governments, and religions of the different nations of the earth. I heard of the slothful Asiatics; of the stupendous genius and mental activity of the Grecians; of the wars and wonderful virtue of the early Romans—

E 3

for any pleasurable sensations and I was obliged to avoid it — Oh truly, I am grateful to thee my creator for the gift of life, which was but pain, and to thy tender mercy which deserted me on life's threshold to suffer — all that man can inflict

Pages from a copy of the 1818 edition of Frankenstein *that Mary Shelley gave to a Mrs. Thomas in 1823, annotated by Shelley (PML 16799, Pierpont Morgan Library)*

concern for others ultimately wins over his ambition to reach the "region of beauty and light."

Finally, the use of the nightmarish murders, the demonlike monster, the terror of the unknown, and the destruction of the idyllic life in nature by a dark, ambiguous force places *Frankenstein* in the tradition of the Gothic novel. Like other Gothic authors, Shelley situates good and evil as a psychological battle within human nature. Both Frankenstein and the creature initially have "benevolent" feelings and intentions, but eventually both become obsessed with ideas of destruction and revenge. Shelley's novel successfully manipulates the conventions of the genre, replacing the stock Gothic villain with morally ambiguous characters who reflect the depth and complexities of the human psyche.

After *Frankenstein,* Shelley wrote the novella *Mathilda,* which was never published in her lifetime. A rough draft was originally titled "The Fields of Fancy" (after Wollstonecraft's unfinished tale "Cave of Fancy," written in 1787). *Mathilda,* though not exclusively autobiographical, includes many self-revealing elements. For example, the three characters—Mathilda, her father, and Woodville the poet—are obviously Mary Shelley, Godwin, and Percy Shelley. The tale is in the form of memoirs addressed to Woodville, composed by a woman who expects to die at age twenty-two. Written during the late summer and autumn of 1819, when Mary was struggling with the depression from the deaths of two children in nine months, *Mathilda* is at once angry, elegiac, full of self-recriminations, and charged with self-pity. Like Mary Shelley's own nativity, Mathilda's birth causes the death of her mother, who has only shortly before been blissfully wedded to Mathilda's father. Mathilda is

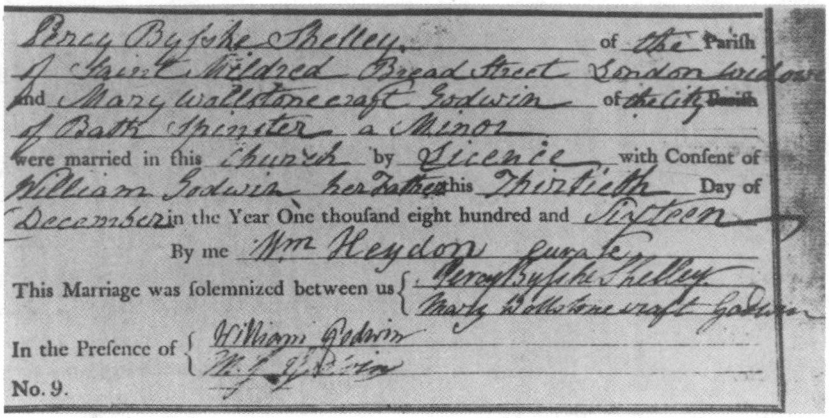
Percy Bysshe Shelley of the Parish of Saint Mildred Bread Street London widower and Mary Wollstonecraft Godwin of the City of Bath Spinster a Minor were married in this Church by Licence with Consent of William Godwin her Father this Thirtieth Day of December in the Year One thousand eight hundred and Sixteen

By me Wm Heydon Curate

This Marriage was solemnized between us { Percy Bysshe Shelley / Mary Wollstonecraft Godwin

In the Presence of { William Godwin / M. J. Godwin

No. 9.

The Shelleys' marriage certificate (Bodleian Library, Oxford)

abandoned by him and left lonely and unloved, growing up with an austere aunt in Scotland. At his return sixteen years later, she is ecstatically happy, but the felicity is brief, as he, full of agony, soon admits his incestuous love for her. This father's love could be read as wish fulfillment on Mary Shelley's part; Godwin, though he had forgiven Mary for her elopement after her marriage on 30 December 1816, remained cold and callous, unable to comfort her when she was grieving after the loss of William in 1819. Instead of exalting the incestuous bond, Mellor believes that *Mathilda* "calls into question the bourgeois sexual practices of her day, . . .which defined the young, submissive, dutiful, daughter-like woman as the appropriate love-object for an older, wiser, economically secure and 'fatherly' man." When Mathilda flees from her father, he kills himself, and Mathilda, after staging her own suicide, goes off to mourn him in a remote area of Scotland.

Mathilda's relationship with the poet of "exceeding beauty"—whom she meets in Scotland—reveals Mary Shelley's awareness of her contribution to the gulf that had developed between her and Percy at this time. As Percy's poem "To Mary" suggests, Mary had become cold and withdrawn by late 1819, but she was not insensitive to the pain she was inflicting on him. In *Mathilda* the heroine criticizes herself: "I became unfit for any intercourse . . . I became captious and unreasonable: my temper was utterly spoilt. . . . I had become arrogant, peevish, and above all suspicious." Her self-examination leads her to remorse and wretchedness, and—dying of consumption—she concludes: "having passed little more than twenty years upon the earth I am more fit for my narrow grave than many are when they reach the natural term of their lives."

Shelley began writing her next novel, *Valperga*, in April 1820 while in Florence and was still working on it in Pisa that fall. Percy Shelley described it in an 8 November 1820 letter to Thomas Love Peacock as a work "illustrative of the manners of the Middle Ages in Italy, which she has raked out of fifty old books." Bonnie Rayford Neumann emphasizes that four difficult years had elapsed in Mary Shelley's life between the novel's inception in 1817, while the Shelleys were still in England, and its completion in the autumn of 1821. As the change in title from "Castruccio, Prince of Lucca" to *Valperga* suggests, the book Shelley finally produced was quite different from the one she had originally intended. The focus of the novel published in 1823 is not on Castruccio, an exiled, ambitious adventurer who returns to his native city and becomes its demoniac tyrant, but on the inhabitants of Valperga, the ancestral palace and home of the heroine, Euthanasia. As Neumann points out, *Valperga* shares with *Frankenstein* and *Mathilda* the theme of "initiation—or fall—from the innocent, happy illusions of childhood into the reality of adulthood with its knowledge of loneliness, pain, and death." In the novel Euthanasia awakens to the realization that her lover, of whom she had "made a god . . . believing every virtue and every talent to live in his soul," was in reality deceitful, cruel, and self-serving. Castruccio is responsible not only for Euthanasia's unhappiness and death but for the misery and eventual demise of Beatrice, another fanatically religious girl. The tragedy of both women stems largely from their self-delusion, their illusory belief in Castruccio's goodness and love despite all external evidence.

In 1822 Shelley was to suffer her greatest loss, the death by drowning of Percy Shelley on 8 July. Ironically, just about a month before his decease he had saved her from bleeding to death when she miscarried during her fifth pregnancy. Their relationship had had its difficulties. Mary secretly blamed Percy for the death of their daughter Clara, and she became severely depressed and withdrawn after William's death. Unable to find emotional support and affection from Mary, Percy had sought consolation elsewhere. Emily W. Sunstein surmises that Percy and Claire "may have become lovers in 1820." Moreover, in 1821 Percy became fond of and flirted with Jane Williams, wife of Edward Williams (who was to drown with Shelley), and composed verses to her. He also became enraptured of Emilia Viviani, the nineteen-year-old daughter of the governor of Pisa and the woman for whom he wrote *Epipsychidion* (1821). Mary, aware of his dissatisfactions and his interest in other women, had trusted that time would heal the breach between them. Percy's sudden death left Mary in a psychological turmoil, with feelings of "fierce remorse" and guilt. To atone for her guilt, she committed herself to the immortalization of her husband. She decided to write his biography and publish a definitive collection of his poems. Later she created an idealized portrait of him in her next novel, *The Last Man* (1826). Her desire to glorify Percy was blocked, however, by his father, who was embarrassed by any public mention of his revolutionary and atheistic son. Mary contented herself with appending long biographical notes to her 1824 and 1839 editions of his poetry, notes which, as Mellor points out, "deified the poet and rewrote their past history together."

In February 1824, about a year and a half after Percy's drowning, Mary began to write her darkest and gloomiest novel, *The Last Man*. In his introduction to the novel Hugh J. Luke, Jr., points out that Shelley was "boldly experimenting with the novel form, attempting to expand its boundaries." *The Last Man* is a work of science fiction, an apocalyptic prophecy, a roman à clef, a Bildungsroman, a dystopia, a Gothic horror, and a domestic romance. Envisioning a horrifying and disastrous future world in a nightmarish state, it chronicles the disappearance of the inhabitants of earth as people are killed by war, emotional conflict, or a mysterious plague comparable to or worse than that described by Daniel Defoe's *Journal of the Plague Year* (1722). Conceived partly out of a desire to immortalize Percy, the figure of Adrian, Earl of Windsor, is a Romantic idealist, lofty, full of courage and self-sacrificing beliefs. He is a republican who dreams of the day when countries will "throw off the iron yoke of servitude, poverty will quit us, and with that, sickness." In the midst of epidemic and disease he expresses hope for liberty and peace, the union and cooperation of all mankind. But, though he is a paragon, he remains single, unable to find his soul mate. Mellor points out the ambivalence toward Percy Shelley manifested in the portrait of Adrian. Adrian resembles Percy in appearance. He is a "tall, slim, fair boy, with a physiognomy expressive of the excess of sensibility and refinement"; he seems angelic, with his gold "silken hair," and "beaming countenance." Benevolent, sincere, and devoted to love and poetry, he nevertheless is impractical and excessively emotional. Implicit in the portrait, argues Mellor, is a criticism of Percy as a narcissistic egoist insensitive to the needs of his wife and children. Unthinkingly, Adrian causes his own death and that of Clara's by drowning, leaving Lionel Verney alone, as the "last man" on earth. Verney's situation mirrors Mary's, especially after Byron's death in Greece on 19 April 1824. She wrote in her journal on 14 May 1824: "The last man! Yes I may well describe that solitary being's feelings, feeling myself as the last relic of a beloved race, my companions extinct before me—" The next day she lamented: "At the age of twenty six I am in the condition of an aged person—all my old friends are gone . . . & my heart fails when I think by how few ties I hold to the world. . . ."

After Percy's death Mary developed a strong friendship with Jane Williams, believing that the two of them would live together forever. Jane, however, admitted her preference for Thomas Jefferson Hogg in 1827, and also betrayed Mary by spreading malicious tales to their friends about how Mary's "coldness" and "temper" had made Percy unhappy in their last year together. Though she received offers of matrimony from men such as John Howard Payne, an American actor-dramatist, and Prosper Mérimée, a cynical French novelist and dandy, Shelley never remarried. As she wrote to Edward John Trelawny on 14 June 1831, in answer to his half-serious proposal: "Mary Shelley shall be written on my tomb." The men who did interest her—including poet Bryan Waller Procter, American author Washington Irving, and Aubrey Beauclerk, whom Emily W. Sunstein speculates may

Mary Shelley in 1840 (portrait by Richard Rothwell; National Portrait Gallery, London)

have been Shelley's lover briefly in 1833—were not willing to commit themselves to her. She was to spend the rest of her life as a devoted mother to Percy Florence Shelley and a devoted daughter to Godwin, whom she continued to support emotionally and financially until his death in 1836.

The Fortunes of Perkin Warbeck, published in 1830, was perhaps Shelley's least successful novel. Impressed by the popularity of Sir Walter Scott's historical romances, Shelley attempted one based on the historical figure Perkin Warbeck, who claimed to be the younger son of Edward IV, Richard, Duke of York, escaped from the Tower of London—after Richard III's henchmen killed his elder brother—and raised in Flanders. When Warbeck attempted to take the throne of Henry VII for the Yorkists, his pretension was supported by James IV of Scotland who wed him to his cousin Princess Katherine Gordon. Shelley was under some constraints in the composition of the novel. Believing in his royal identity, she created Perkin Warbeck as a stereotypically perfect, benevolent, and honest character, and then had to manipulate that character to adhere to the facts of history. William Walling describes the book as "essentially a lifeless novel, although it deserves our respect for the quality of the intelligence which is intermittently displayed in it," while Bonnie Rayford Neumann says that the novel "has none of the power and passion of her earlier ones; by the time she removes Richard from the Procrustean bed, not only does she have no hero, but she is almost devoid of a story as well."

During the years 1828 to 1838 Shelley also kept busy by writing more than a dozen stories for a popular annual gift book, *The Keepsake*. In

Sir Percy Florence Shelley and Jane, Lady Shelley (Alexander Hay Collection, Mitchell Library, State Library of New South Wales, Sydney)

1831 the revised edition of *Frankenstein* was published by Colburn and Bentley in their Standard Novels series. This version places more emphasis on the power of fate and the lack of personal choice in human lives. Nature is no longer seen as organic; it becomes a mechanistic force capable of creating, preserving, and destroying. Even Shelley's belief in the ideology of the loving, egalitarian family is undercut, as most instances of domestic affection prove ineffectual. By 1831 Shelley viewed herself as she presented her hero, as a victim of destiny.

Shelley's last two novels, *Lodore* (1835) and *Falkner* (1837), are semi-autobiographical, and both repeat the triangle of characters found in *Mathilda*: father-daughter-lover. The most popular and successful of her novels since *Frankenstein*, *Lodore* was the first of Shelley's novels to have a sentimental, happy ending. Ignored by her mother, the heroine, Ethel, is taken to America by her father, Lord Lodore, and is left alone when he is killed in a duel. In London she falls in love with the financially desperate Edward Villiers and marries him. Their experiences of insecurity are reminiscent of the early years that Mary and Percy shared together. Villiers is haunted by creditors and forced to flee, but unlike Shelley, Ethel is reconciled with her mother, who, it turns out, has been their secret benefactress. Unable to fully portray the mother-daughter relationship she never had, Shelley resorted to a sentimentalized and unrealistic ending.

In *Falkner* Shelley once again emphasizes a father-daughter relationship, this time between an orphaned girl, Elizabeth Raby, and her rakish, Byronic guardian, Falkner. Haunted by a dark and mysterious past, Falkner is horrified to find that Elizabeth loves Gerard Neville, the son of the woman he once destroyed. The descriptions of Falkner's guilt and the psychological tortures he inflicts upon himself and his daughter make the novel one of Shelley's best works. Elizabeth, caught between her lover's desire for revenge and her adoptive father's secret obsession, becomes the link which ultimately enables all to live in domestic peace. *Falkner* is an appropriate finale to Mary Shelley's novel writing as it encapsulates many of her concerns and uses her greatest novelistic strengths—the portrayal of an agonized hero struggling with himself, the conflicts created by love and domestic duty, the problem of the absent mother, the concept of fate and victimization, the Gothic terror of the unknown—elements she had dexterously manipulated and precociously displayed in the writing of *Frankenstein* nineteen years earlier.

Before working on *Falkner*, Shelley had written three volumes in *The Cabinet of Biography*, part of the Reverend Dionysius Lardner's *Cabinet Cyclopedia*, and after completing her last novel she devoted her energies to nonfiction and editing her husband's works. Her last book, an account of summer tours on the Continent with her son and his college friends, was published in 1844. By then she was in ill health, and in 1848 she began to suffer what were apparently the first symptoms of the brain tumor that eventually killed her. The disease was not diagnosed until December 1850 when she began to experience numbness in her right leg and impaired speech. Within a little more than a month she was almost completely paralyzed, and she died in London on 1 February 1851, having asked to be buried with her mother and father. Her son and daughter-in-law, Jane, Lady Shelley, had the bodies of her parents exhumed and buried them with her in the churchyard of St. Peter's, Bournemouth. A memorial sculpture to Mary and Percy Shelley was commissioned by Percy Florence and Jane Shelley and installed at nearby Christchurch Priory.

Letters:

Letters of Mary Shelley, edited by Henry H. Harper (Norwood, Mass.: Plimpton, 1918);

The Letters of Mary W. Shelley, edited by Frederick L. Jones (Norman: University of Oklahoma Press, 1944);

My Best Mary: The Selected Letters of Mary Wollstonecraft Shelley, edited by Muriel Spark and Derek Standford (London: Wingate, 1953);

The Letters of Mary Wollstonecraft Shelley, 3 volumes, edited by Betty T. Bennett (Baltimore: Johns Hopkins University Press, 1980, 1983, 1988).

Bibliographies:

W. H. Lyles, *Mary Shelley: An Annotated Bibliography* (New York: Garland, 1975);

Frederick S. Frank, "Mary Shelley's *Frankenstein*: A Register of Research," *Bulletin of Bibliography*, 40 (September 1983): 163-188.

Biographies:

Shelley Memorials, edited by Jane, Lady Shelley (London: Smith, Elder, 1859);

Helen Moore, *Mary Wollstonecraft Shelley* (Philadelphia: Lippincott, 1886);

Florence A. Marshall, *The Life and Letters of Mary Wollstonecraft Shelley*, 2 volumes (London: Bentley, 1889);

Lucy Madox Rossetti, *Mrs. Shelley* (London: W. H. Allen, 1890);

Richard Church, *Mary Shelley* (London: G. Howe, 1928; New York: Viking, 1928);

Rosalie Glynn Grylls, *Mary Shelley* (London & New York: Oxford University Press, 1938);

Muriel Spark, *Child of Light—A Reassessment of Mary Wollstonecraft Shelley* (Hadleigh, Essex: Tower Bridge Publications, 1951); revised as *Mary Shelley—A Biography* (New York: Dutton, 1987);

Eileen Bigland, *Mary Shelley* (London: Cassell, 1959; New York: Appleton-Century Crofts, 1959);

Noel B. Gerson, *Daughter of Earth and Water: A Biography of Mary Wollstonecraft Shelley* (New York: Morrow, 1973);

Jane Dunn, *Moon in Eclipse—A Life of Mary Shelley* (London: Weidenfeld & Nicolson, 1978);

Emily W. Sunstein, *Mary Shelley: Romance and Reality* (Boston, Toronto & London: Little, Brown, 1989).

References:

Harold Bloom, ed., *Mary Shelley: Modern Critical Views* (New York: Chelsea House, 1985);

Sylvia Bowerbank, "The Social Order vs. The Wretch: Mary Shelley's Contradictory-Mindedness in *Frankenstein*," *ELH*, 46 (Fall 1979): 418-431;

Richard J. Dunn, "Narrative Distance in *Frankenstein*," *Studies in the Novel*, 6 (Winter 1974): 408-417;

Sandra Gilbert and Susan Gubar, *The Madwoman in the Attic* (New Haven: Yale University Press, 1979);

Devon Hodges, "*Frankenstein* and the Feminine Subversion of the Novel," *Tulsa Studies in Women's Literature*, 2 (Autumn 1983): 155-164;

Margaret Homans, *Bearing the Word: Language and Female Experience in Nineteenth Century Women's Writing* (Chicago: University of Chicago Press, 1986);

Mary Jacobus, "Is There a Woman in This Text?," *New Literary History*, 14 (Autumn 1982): 117-141; republished in her *Reading Woman* (New York: Columbia University Press, 1986);

Barbara Johnson, "My Monster/My Self," *Diacritics*, 12 (Summer 1982): 2-10;

Robert Kiely, *The Romantic Novel in England* (Cambridge: Harvard University Press, 1972);

George Levine and U. C. Knopeflmacher, eds., *The Endurance of Frankenstein* (Berkeley & Los Angeles: University of California Press, 1979);

Peter McInerney, "*Frankenstein* and the Godlike Science of Letters," *Genre*, 13 (Winter 1980): 455-475;

Anne K. Mellor, *Mary Shelley: Her Life, Her Fiction, Her Monsters* (New York & London: Methuen, 1988);

Bonnie Rayford Neumann, *The Lonely Muse—A Critical Biography of Mary Wollstonecraft Shelley* (Salzburg, Austria: Institut für Anglistik und Amerikanistik, Universtät Salzburg, 1979);

Elizabeth Nitchie, *Mary Shelley—Author of Frankenstein* (New Brunswick, N.J.: Rutgers University Press, 1953);

Jean de Palacio, *Mary Shelley dans son oeuvre* (Paris: Klincksieck, 1969);

Mary Poovey, *The Proper Lady and the Woman Writer: Ideology as Style in the Works of Mary Wollstonecraft, Mary Shelley, and Jane Austen* (Chicago & London: University of Chicago Press, 1984);

Fred V. Randel, "*Frankenstein*, Feminism and the Intertextuality of Mountains," *Studies in Romanticism*, 23 (Winter 1984): 515-533;

Marc A. Rubenstein, "My Accursed Origin: The Search for the Mother in *Frankenstein*," *Studies in Romanticism*, 15 (Spring 1976): 165-194;

Lee Sterrenburg, "*The Last Man*: Anatomy of Failed Revolutions," *Nineteenth-Century Fiction*, 33 (December 1978): 324-347;

Martin Tropp, *Mary Shelley's Monster* (Boston: Houghton Mifflin, 1976);

William Veeder, *Mary Shelley & Frankenstein: The Fate of Androgyny* (Chicago: University of Chicago Press, 1986);

William Walling, *Mary Shelley* (New York: Twayne, 1972).

Papers:

The largest collection of Mary Shelley's papers is in Lord Abinger's Shelley Collection on deposit at the Bodleian Library, Oxford. Most of these papers have been microfilmed. Other significant collections of letters are in the Carl H. Pforzheimer Library, New York Public Library; the Huntingdon Library; the John Murray Collection; and the British Library.

Horatio (Horace) Smith

(31 December 1779 - 12 July 1849)

John H. Rogers
Vincennes University

See also the entry on Horatio (Horace) Smith and James Smith in *DLB 96: British Romantic Poets, 1789-1832: Second Series.*

BOOKS: *A Family Story* (London, 1799);

The Runaway, or the Seat of Benevolence, 4 volumes (London: Printed for Crosby & Letterman, 1800);

Trevanion, or Matrimonial Matters, 4 volumes (London: Earle, 1801);

Horatio, or Memoirs of the Davenport Family (London, 1807);

Highgate Tunnel: or, The Secret Arch. A Burlesque Operatic Tragedy, in Two Acts, as Momus Medlar, Esq. (London: Printed for John Miller, 1812);

Rejected Addresses, by Horace and James Smith (London: Printed for John Miller, 1812; New York: Published by James Eastburn, 1813);

Horace in London, by Horace and James Smith (London: John Miller, 1813; Boston: Cummings & Hilliard / New York: Eastburn, Kirk / Cambridge: Hilliard, Metcalf, 1813);

First Impressions: or Trade in the West. A Comedy. In Five Acts (London: T. Underwood, 1813);

Amarynthus the Nympholept (London: Longman, Hurst, Rees, Orme & Brown, 1821);

Gaities and Gravities (3 volumes, London: H. Colburn, 1825; 2 volumes, Philadelphia: H. C. Carey & I. Lea / New York: Collins, 1826);

The Tor Hill (3 volumes, London: H. Colburn, 1825; 2 volumes, Philadelphia: H. C. Carey & I. Lea, 1825);

Brambletye House, or, Cavaliers and Roundheads (London: Colburn, 1826; Boston: Wells & Lilly, 1826);

Reuben Apsley (3 volumes, London: H. Colburn, 1827; 2 volumes, Philadelphia: Carey, Lea & Carey, 1827);

Zillah: A Tale of the Holy City (4 volumes, London: H. Colburn, 1828; 2 volumes, New York: J. & J. Harper, 1829);

The New Forest (3 volumes, London: H. Colburn, 1829; 2 volumes, New York: J. & J. Harper, 1829);

Walter Colyton: A Tale of 1688 (3 volumes, London: H. Colburn, 1830; 2 volumes, New York: J. & J. Harper, 1830);

The Midsummer Medley for 1830: A Series of Comic Tales (London: H. Colburn & R. Bentley, 1830);

Festivals, Games and Amusements, Ancient and Modern (London: H. Colburn & R. Bentley, 1831; New York: J. & J. Harper, 1831);

Tales of the Early Ages (3 volumes, London: H. Colburn, 1832; 2 volumes, New York: J. & J. Harper, 1832);

Gale Middleton: A Story of the Present Day (3 volumes, London: R. Bentley, 1833; 1 volume, Philadelphia: Carey, Lea & Blanchard, 1834);

The Involuntary Prophet: A Tale of the Early Ages (London: R. Bentley, 1835);

The Tin Trumpet; or, Heads and Tales, for the Wise and Waggish; To Which are added, Poetical Selections, by the late Paul Chatfield, M.D. [pseud.]. *Edited by Jefferson Saunders* [pseud.] (London: Whittaker, 1836; Philadelphia: E. L. Carey & A. Hart, 1836);

Jane Lomax, or A Mother's Crime (3 volumes, London: H. Colburn, 1838; 2 volumes, Philadelphia, 1838);

The Moneyed Man, or The Lessons of a Life (3 volumes, London: H. Colburn, 1841; 2 volumes, Philadelphia: Lea & Blanchard, 1841);

Adam Brown, the Merchant (3 volumes, London: H. Colburn, 1843; 1 volume, New York: Harper, 1843);

Arthur Arundel: A Tale of the English Revolution (3 volumes, London: Colburn, 1844; 1 volume, New York: Harper, 1844);

Love and Mesmerism (3 volumes, London: Colburn, 1845; 1 volume, New York: Harper, 1846).

Horace Smith, circa 1825 (engraving after a portrait by John James Masquerier)

Collection: *The Poetical Works of Horace Smith*, 2 volumes (London: H. Colburn, 1846).

PLAY PRODUCTIONS: *Highgate Tunnel*, as Momus Medlar, Esq., London, Theatre Royal, Lyceum, 2 July 1812;
The Absent Apothecary, London, Theatre Royal, Drury Lane, 10 February 1813;
First Impressions; or, Trade in the West, London, Theatre Royal, Drury Lane, 30 October 1813.

OTHER: *Memoirs, Letters and Comic Miscellanies in Prose and Verse of the late James Smith*, 2 volumes, edited by Horace Smith (London: H. Colburn, 1840; Philadelphia: Carey & Hart, 1841).

The period of the late eighteenth and early nineteenth centuries is known as the time in which there was a "shift of sensibility," the time when the Augustan Age gave way to the new voices of the Romantic period. This era is marked not only by the arrival of strong new poetic voices but also by a considerably larger reading public. This period also saw the rise of the literary amateurs, authors for whom literature was less a central concern than a by-product of their social and professional lives. The lives and works of most of these writers are largely forgotten today, but the study of a representative writer, such as Horatio (Horace) Smith, can provide both a broader perspective on the major literature of his time and an index to the tastes of the new reading public.

Baptized Horatio, Horace Smith was the son of Mary Bogle Smith, daughter of a dissenting minister, and Robert Smith, a London solicitor who became assistant to the solicitor of the ordnance. Possessed of knowledge and interests that were by no means limited to his profession, Robert established a charity hospital and a smallpox-inoculation clinic for the poor and was active in raising funds for them. He wrote comic verses for his own amusement and was always interested in history. In 1787 Robert Smith became a fellow for life of the Society of Antiquaries, and he be-

Horace Smith and his brother James (portrait by G. H. Harlow; private collection; from Anthony Burton and John Murdoch, Byron: An exhibition to commemorate the 150th anniversary of his death in the Greek War of Liberation, 19 April 1824, *Victoria and Albert Museum, 1974)*

came a fellow for life of the Royal Society in 1796.

Horace Smith's parents taught him the classics, French, Italian, and the composition of English poetry at home before sending him to the Chigwell School in Essex in 1787. In 1791 he moved from the Chigwell School to the Alfred House Academy in Middlesex, where he spent the next four years. Smith became a clerk in the countinghouse of merchant Robert Kingston in 1796. In 1806, with financial help from his father, Smith became a partner in Smith and Chesmer, Merchants and Insurance Brokers. Using inside information from his father's official dispatches, he amassed a fortune before leaving the firm in 1812 to join the London Stock Exchange.

While he worked diligently at his profession, Smith's main interests were the literary and theatrical life of his time. He produced his first novel, *A Family Story*, in 1799. This highly moral tale of the happiness of domestic life, published under the name Mr. Smith because Horace was unsure how his father would react to the book, was sufficiently successful that Smith followed it with *The Runaway, or the Seat of Benevolence* (1800), concerning the rich recluse Mr. Somers, who is so moved by the pitiful story of a ragged beggar, Theodore, that he takes the beggar in; *Trevanion* (1801), a story of secret marriage and its baleful effects; and *Horatio, or Memoirs of the Davenport Family* (1807). These early novels are indications of Smith's remarkable ability to gauge the taste of the contemporary reading public, but they are obviously juvenile works, sentimental family chronicles that have attracted little notice since their publication. Horace Smith's successful career as a novelist came much later, after he had spent more than two decades as a writer of poetry and essays.

In 1799-1800 Smith began contributing to the *Gentleman's Magazine*, and over the next ten years he produced occasional poems and essays for such publications as Thomas Hill's *Monthly Mirror*. This decade of journalistic work served to sharpen Smith's literary skills and to introduce him into the literary and theatrical society of London.

In 1805 Smith published a poem in the *Gentleman's Magazine* deploring the public preference for theatrical exhibitions and dumb shows over superior dramas such as Richard Cumberland's *West Indian* (1771) and *The Jew* (1794). Cumberland agreed with the poem's sentiments, and was so pleased with the poetic tribute that he arranged to meet Smith. Cumberland introduced Smith to such important figures of the time as the dramatic publisher John Miller and Charles William Ward ("Portsoken Ward" as Horace termed him), the secretary of the Drury Lane theater.

In 1810 Smith married a woman who bore him two children, Eliza and Horatio Shakespeare Smith. After the death of his first wife, who did not have the approval of his father, Smith married a Miss Ford on 17 March 1818. They had two daughters, Rosalind and Laura Smith.

Smith's best and most successful literary work, *Rejected Addresses* (1812), resulted from an unusual episode in English literary history. In 1809 the Drury Lane theater had been destroyed by fire. When the new theater building was completed in 1812, a committee had the idea of holding a competition for a poetic address to be spoken on opening night. The committee received 112 submissions, including one by Horace Smith, but the addresses were of such generally abysmal quality that the committee rejected all of them and asked George Gordon, Lord Byron, to supply a poem suitable for the occasion. The committee's decision, unsurprisingly, caused a terrific outcry from the would-be candidates for poetic fame, as Ward had feared. According to Arthur H. Beavan, while dining with James Smith, Horace's elder brother, Ward accurately prophesied, "Won't there be a d——d row when the award is given! They'll be wanting the rejected Addresses published, just to show the public what they were like." Taken with this idea, James Smith improvised some suitable verses; Ward was amused at the concept and urged James to make fun of all the other poets in verses of his own. James repeated this idea to Horace, and in less than six weeks, in time for the Drury Lane opening, the two brothers wrote the twenty-one parodies that make up *Rejected Addresses*. These insightful and delightful parodies of William Wordsworth, Byron, Samuel Taylor Coleridge, George Crabbe, and other, lesser Romantic poets and poetasters were immediately successful. The volume ran through five editions in 1812, thirteen by 1813, twenty-two by 1851, and appeared in new editions in 1888, 1899, 1904, and 1929. For the rest of their lives Horace and James Smith were known as the authors of *Rejected Addresses* or as the "Rejected Addressees."

Attempting to capitalize on the great success of *Rejected Addresses*, Horace and James Smith published *Horace in London* (1813), imitations of Horace's odes that they had written for the *Monthly Mirror*. The poems are of little merit, but the popularity of *Rejected Addresses* carried *Horace in London* through four editions by 1815.

After the publication of *Horace in London*, Horace Smith's life and literary pursuits underwent a significant change. In 1816 Smith met Percy Bysshe Shelley, who made such a profound and lasting impression on Smith that the two became great friends. According to Beavan, Shelley found it "odd that the only truly generous person I ever knew who had money to be generous with, should be a stockbroker," and he paid poetic tribute to Smith in his "Letter to Maria Gisborne." When Shelley left England, Smith took charge of his business affairs and saw to the publication of Shelley's *Oedipus Tyrannus; or, Swellfoot the Tyrant* in 1820. Late in his life Smith remembered Shelley as "this singular being, infinitely the most extraordinary character my long life has known." So strong was Shelley's impact that Smith decided to follow Shelley to Italy, leaving London in 1821, the year in which he published, anonymously, his last volume of poetry, *Amarynthus the Nympholept*.

Although Smith planned to join Shelley in Italy, his wife, who had just given birth to their daughter Rosalind, became too ill to continue the journey, so the family settled in Versailles, where Smith became associated with a large number of English expatriates. While residing in France he contributed to Thomas Campbell's *New Monthly Magazine* and John Scott's *London Magazine*, tried unsuccessfully to establish an English newspaper, and through his correspondence became a link between the literary societies of France and England.

Robert Smith, father of Horace and James Smith, circa 1830 (engraving after a miniature by an unknown artist)

In 1825 Smith returned to England, settled at Tunbridge Wells, and began the series of novels that would occupy him throughout the remaining twenty years of his literary career. Though in their time these novels were extremely popular in both England and America, they have now sunk into oblivion. They were written not to impress posterity but to please Smith's contemporary readers, who embraced them avidly. *Brambletye House, or, Cavaliers and Roundheads* (1826), the first of Smith's successful historical romances, is representative of the strengths and weaknesses of his work in this form.

This story of the dashing Cavalier Sir John Compson, his stalwart son Jocelyn, and their adventures while trying to escape the wrath of Oliver Cromwell and his Puritan followers was written solely to entertain, and so it does. The Cromwellian and early Restoration periods afford Smith great opportunities to describe battles, sieges, desperate flights from the enemy, brave soldiers and romantic heroines, picturesque scenery, and all the other staples of historical romance from the time of Ann Radcliffe to that of Barbara Cartland. Aside from such surface excitements, however, neither *Brambletye House* nor any of its successors has much to offer a serious reader. The plots are improbable; the characters are stereotypes; the dialogue tends toward humorous rustic or pseudoarchaic dialect; the writing is frequently stilted (*Brambletye House* begins "It was on a dark and gusty night of Autumn"); and the books abound in "gadzookery."

Of the more than a dozen historical romances that followed *Brambletye House*, *Reuben Apsley* (1827), set in the time of James II; *Zillah: A Tale of the Holy City* (1828), set in Jerusalem during the period just before Herod's capture of the city in 37 B.C.; and *Arthur Arundel: A Tale of the English Revolution* (1844), in which Smith returns to the period of the English revolution, are perhaps the best. But all of Smith's novels are derivative, imitative of the original work of Walter Scott. Horace Smith, always an accurate and honest critic of his own work, freely acknowledged his source in his 4 July 1826 letter to Scott, sent with a copy of *Brambletye House*: "As I never proposed any other object to myself, in my novel of *Brambletye House*, than to produce a humble imitation of that style which you have so successfully introduced into the department of literature, I was so far gratified by the sale of the first two editions, as it proved that I had made some little approach toward my model." Smith could effectively imitate the author of *Peveril of the Peak* (1822) or *Woodstock* (1826); he did not, however, continue to develop into the kind of writer who could produce *The Heart of Midlothian* (1818) or the Waverley novels. Horace Smith's work as a novelist thus occupies a minor place in the history of prose fiction, though it deserves some attention from students of the history of popular taste.

In the preface to his 1845 novel, *Love and Mesmerism*, Smith announced to his readers that it would be his last work of fiction. During the last few years of his life he wrote a series of essays for the *New Monthly Magazine*, including several entertaining reminiscences of the Romantic poets he had known in his youth. Horace Smith died at Tunbridge Wells on 12 July 1849.

Biographies:

P. G. Patmore, *My Friends and Acquaintances* (London: Saunders & Otley, 1854);

Epes Sargeant, "Biographical Memoir," in *Rejected Addresses*, edited by Sargeant (New York: Hurd & Houghton, 1866), pp. ix-xxiii;

Arthur H. Beavan, *James and Horace Smith* (London: Hurst & Blackett, 1899).

References:

Edmund Blunden, "The Rejected Addresses," in his *Votive Tablets* (London: Cobden-Sanderson, 1931), pp. 199-204;

Stuart Curran, "The View From Versailles: Horace Smith on the Literary Scene of 1822," *Huntington Library Quarterly*, 40 (August 1977): 357-371;

Abraham Hayward, "James Smith," in his *Biographical and Critical Essays*, 2 volumes (London: Longman, Brown, Green, Longman & Roberts, 1858), I: 131-148;

Ian Jack, *English Literature 1815-1832* (Oxford: Clarendon Press, 1963);

Francis Jeffrey, "Rejected Addresses," *Edinburgh Review*, 20 (July-November 1812): 434-451;

Walter Jerrold, "The Centenary of Parody," *Fortnightly Review*, 98 (new series 92) (July-December 1912): 223-234;

George Kitchen, *A Survey of Burlesque and Parody in English* (London: Oliver & Boyd, 1931);

Robert W. Lowe, "The Real Rejected Addresses: A Chapter in the History of Theatrical Literature," *Blackwood's Magazine*, 153 (May 1893): 742-750;

Donald H. Reiman, Introduction to *Rejected Addresses* (New York & London: Garland, 1977); also published in *Amarynthus* (New York & London: Garland, 1977).

Caroline Anne Bowles Southey

(6 December 1786 - 20 July 1854)

Lauren Pringle De La Vars
Saint Bonaventure University

BOOKS: *Ellen Fitzarthur: A Metrical Tale* (London: Printed for Longman, Hurst, Rees, Orme & Brown, 1820);

The Widow's Tale and Other Poems (London: Longman, Hurst, Rees, Orme & Brown, 1822);

Solitary Hours (Edinburgh: William Blackwood / London: T. Cadell, 1826; New York: Wiley & Putnam, 1846);

Chapters on Churchyards (2 volumes, Edinburgh: William Blackwood, 1829; 1 volume, New York: Wiley & Putnam, 1842);

The Cat's Tail, being the History of Childe Merlin. A Tale, as Baroness de Katzleben (Edinburgh: William Blackwood / London: T. Cadell, 1831);

Tales of the Factories (Edinburgh: William Blackwood, 1833);

The Birth-Day; A Poem, in Three Parts, to Which Are Added, Occasional Verses (Edinburgh; William Blackwood & Sons, 1836; New York: Wiley & Putnam, 1845);

Robin Hood: A Fragment, By the Late Robert Southey and Caroline Southey, with Other Fragments and Poems by R. S. and C. S. (Edinburgh: William Blackwood & Sons, 1847);

The Poetical Works of Caroline Bowles Southey, Collected Edition (Edinburgh & London: William Blackwood & Sons, 1867).

OTHER: "The Little Brook and the Star," in *The Literary Souvenir, or Cabinet of Poetry and Romance*, edited by Alaric A. Watts (London: Longman, Rees, Orme, Brown & Green, 1828), pp. 289-304;

"Inflexibility" and "Bridget Plantagenet," in *The Literary Souvenir*, edited by Watts (London: Longman, Rees, Orme, Brown & Green, 1829), pp. 176-189 and 270-288;

Robert Southey, *The Life of the Rev. Andrew Bell*, volume 1, edited by Caroline Bowles Southey (London: John Murray, 1844).

SELECTED PERIODICAL PUBLICATIONS—UNCOLLECTED: "To the Author of 'The Shepherd's Calendar,' " *Blackwood's Edinburgh Magazine*, 15 (June 1824): 655-658;

"La Petite Madelaine," *Blackwood's Edinburgh Magazine*, 30 (August 1831): 205-227;

"Devereux Hall," *Blackwood's Edinburgh Magazine*, 32 (October 1832): 486-504;

"The Early Called," *Blackwood's Edinburgh Magazine*, 37 (January 1835): 82-94; 37 (February 1835): 196-209;

Review of *The Seven Temptations*, by Mary Howitt, *Blackwood's Edinburgh Magazine*, 37 (April 1835): 643-649;

"Fanny Fairfield," *Blackwood's Edinburgh Magazine*, 39 (February 1836): 198-208; 39 (March 1836): 391-403; 39 (April 1836): 497-513;

"This Time Two Years," *Blackwood's Edinburgh Magazine*, 41 (June 1837): 752-761;

"Mr. Howitt's 'Homes and Haunts of the Poets' " [letter], *Athenaeum*, 23 January 1847, p. 96.

In its neglect of both her personal and artistic virtues, literary history has not been kind to Caroline Anne Bowles. Literary historians may recognize her only through the disapproving eyes of the Wordsworth circle, as Robert Southey's calculating wife during his senility and as "wicked stepmother" to his children. Caroline Southey's entire life and career cannot be judged, however, by the gossip of one group about her four-year marriage with the poet laureate. At the time of her wedding to Southey, her friend of twenty years, she was at the height of her popularity as a poet and storyteller. Although she was never as celebrated as Felicia Hemans or Mary Russell Mitford, her poems and tales have much in common with theirs in tone and subject, and British readers of the 1820s and 1830s relished the pathos and piquancy of Caroline Bowles's writings.

Caroline Anne Bowles was born at Buckland Cottage, near Lymington, Hampshire, England, the only child of Capt. Charles Bowles

Caroline Anne Bowles and her dog Mufti in 1833, six years before her marriage to poet laureate Robert Southey (portrait by an unknown artist; from Edward Dowden, ed., The Correspondence of Robert Southey with Caroline Bowles, *1881)*

and Anne Burrard Bowles, on 6 December 1786. Her idyllic childhood among the Hampshire forests and streams is described thoughtfully in her long autobiographical poem, *The Birth-Day* (1836). From her own account in *The Birth-Day*, her letters to Anna Eliza Bray, and a friend's reminiscences, it seems that she must have been an engaging young woman. She was slight and pretty (though her face was somewhat marked by smallpox), fond of "rhyming and scribbling," sketching, fishing, dancing, listening to family legends, and tending her pets. The deaths of first her father and then her mother left her alone in 1817, despondent and impoverished; a generous relative's settling a small annuity on her allowed her to retain her home. Anxious to use her time wisely and not unwilling to augment her small income, she concentrated on developing her talent for writing.

Her first long work was a weepy metrical verse narrative, published in 1820 as *Ellen Fitzarthur*, two years after she had taken the bold step of sending it to Robert Southey. With no connections in the literary world, she had learned of Southey's kindness to another aspiring poet, Henry Kirke White, and determined to seek the same indulgence from the poet laureate. She was not disappointed. Something in her modest and self-deprecating letter stirred Southey (as a letter from young Charlotte Brontë twenty years later did not) to exert himself in suggesting revisions and using his influence to find a publisher for *Ellen Fitzarthur*. Her temerity in introducing herself to Southey began a devoted literary and personal friendship, carried on through regular correspondence and infrequent visits, and culminating in their marriage in 1839. The progress of this friendship is documented in Edward Dowden's edition of their correspondence, though it is regrettable that the majority of the letters in that volume are Southey's: many of Bowles's letters had been lost and Dowden omitted many others that, to him, "lack[ed] the kind of interest which extends to strangers."

In spite of her frequent references in letters to her loneliness, ill health, and melancholy prospects, she did enjoy her quiet life. Alone at Buckland Cottage after the death of her old nurse in 1824, she traveled rarely, busying herself with writing poetry and stories—as well as letters to numerous friends, sketching and painting, spoiling her menagerie of pets (Southey's pets and hers often exchanged greetings through their owners' correspondence), and visiting her rural neighbors, whose stories and peculiarities she detailed in her writings. She was a proper English country lady, slightly eccentric in her habits and dress, conservative in her politics, self-effacing but intrepid. In 1869 John Forster reported one story, possibly apocryphal, which has her volunteering as magistrate of her district during the stack-burning riots of November 1830.

The self Caroline Bowles reveals in her letters to Southey "possessed more liveliness and satiric talent than might have been expected from the authoress of 'Chapters on Churchyards,' " remarked Richard Garnett in the *Dictionary of National Biography*. She teased Southey, noted for his upright character, with her trenchant assessments of personages known to both. Both enjoyed a good piece of fun: Bowles's whimsical poem *The Cat's Tail* (1831), illustrated by George Cruikshank, is easily a match for Southey's typographically droll "The Story of the Three Bears." As her friend "E. O." wrote in the *Cornhill Magazine* (August 1874), Bowles was a natural storyteller, a trait inherited from her mother and her French grandmother, Madelaine Burrand: "She had a quaint caustic style of telling an anecdote that was entirely her own; and in ghost stories she was inimitable. . . . her strong sense of the ridiculous, and her utter absence of sentimentality, disappointed comparative strangers, who expected something pathetic from the writer of so many touching poems." Cheerful and amusing, she was a welcome guest at house parties, which in those days lasted for days or weeks. At one Christmas party she concocted an elaborate trick which involved "a bundle of torn letters which the hostess had picked up in the corridor, . . . the signatures . . . missing. They contained strictures, more or less true, on everyone's manners, aspirations, and general character; and so well was the deception kept up that it was not traced to its proper source for some time." "My autobiography would not be unentertaining," she mused to Southey (26 February 1828).

These happy qualities in Caroline Bowles seem incompatible with those of the stereotypically genteel, languid, melancholy poetess. But it was as just such a poetess that she began to enjoy a measure of success, though all her books, until after her marriage to Southey, were published anonymously. *Ellen Fitzarthur*, the tragic tale of a deserted sweetheart, attracted little notice, but that notice was not discouraging. In 1822 she published *The Widow's Tale and Other Poems*, a collection of poems on lost loves and untimely deaths, somewhat improved artistically, critics agreed, from the uneven verse of her first publication. In the mid 1820s she began a twelve-year connection with *Blackwood's Edinburgh Magazine* as a contributing poet, reviewer, essayist, and fiction writer. Most of her early contributions were published by William Blackwood in 1826 as *Solitary Hours*, which proved quite successful. With this book, an interesting mix of poems, familiar essays, and a long tale, "The Smuggler," her reputation as a noteworthy writer, though still an anonymous one, rose. Her essay on "Beauty" impressed Sara Coleridge, who responded with an essay "On the Disadvantages Resulting from the Possession of Beauty," and a second edition of *Solitary Hours*, appearing under her married name in 1839, proved the lasting appeal of the collection. The poems included in *Solitary Hours*, with titles such as "Autumn Flowers," "A Mother's Lament," "To a Dying Infant," "Farewell to My Friends," are characteristic of all her short poems, for the most part set firmly in the sentimental, even bathetic, tradition, with some typical variations: playing with dialect in Robert Burns's apostrophic style, using neomedieval diction and settings. Representative Victorian views of Bowles's poems in general stress their sweet femininity, grace, and pathos. As D. M. Moir commented in 1851:

> We therein find all the varied impulses of a gentle nature, all the finer feelings of a woman's heart. No man could have written such poetry—at least no man has ever yet done so: it breathes of "a purer ether, a diviner air" than that respired by the *soi-disant* lords of the creation; and in its freedom from all moral blemish and blot—from all harshness and austerity of sentiment—

from all the polluting taints that are apt to cleave to human thought, and its expansive sympathy with all that is holy, just, and of good report—it elevates the heart even more than it delights the fancy. . . . The heart of no Englishwoman was ever more certainly in its right place than that of Caroline Bowles.

Later in the century Alfred H. Miles agreed, adding that she "had a far better idea of the difference between true and false sentiment than most of the women poets of her time." Caroline Bowles's poems testify to her belief that tender and elevated sentiment was the stuff of good women's poetry; her comment on Felicia Hemans's poetry in a 9 July 1827 letter to Blackwood substantiates this point: "Many write with as much feeling, some with taste as refined and as melodious diction, but no other woman that I know of with such loftiness and holiness of thought as Mrs Hemans, except . . . the gifted Joanna [Baillie]."

In his "Monologue, or Soliloquy on the Annuals" (*Blackwood's*, December 1829), Blackwood's chief reviewer, John Wilson, calling hers a "delightful genius," named Bowles "by far the most profoundly pathetic female writer of the age." With such success in poetry, her diverting her talents into writing prose, and specifically into prose fiction, demonstrates her feeling that poetry as written by women could not hold all that she wanted to express. (Weary of the "very pretty poetry" of the annuals and gift books, she complained to Southey on 21 October 1833, "I am sick to death of the sweet Swans my sisters . . . , and think to myself 'I would rather be a kitten, and cry mew than one of those same ballad metremongers.' ") One critic accused her of egotism, a quality deemed unattractive in Romantic women writers. That a certain egotism is necessarily involved in publishing a several-thousand-line poem about one's childhood development of self is unquestioned, though Wordsworth's *Prelude* (1850) likely elicited no such detraction. But the first-person narrator of *The Birth-Day*, the poet's "I," is unusual in Bowles's poetry. It may have been this same egotism, this strong interest in herself, that pushed Caroline Bowles into prose. As Hervey suggests, her small annuity freed her to please herself and not the public in her writing, and she wrote what "best harmonized with her tastes." In her own essays (such as "Thoughts on Letter-Writing" in *Solitary Hours*) she adopted the confident subjective stance of the male narrator in the Romantic familiar essay and transposed that same stance into her fictional tales as well.

Bowles tried to accommodate her publishers' ideas of what women writers ought to write, though not always with the best grace. Responding to Southey's praise of her amusing dramatic sketch "Inflexibility," which appeared in *The Literary Souvenir* for 1829, she observed on 22 December 1828:

Such things are rather entertaining and easy to compose, but somehow all the worthies I have ever written for think fit to discourage my comic vein. Whenever I treat the Monster [William Blackwood] in that way he thanks me for "the admirable production," but hints that "in the pathetic I am super-admirable." I sent "Inflexibility" to the Goth [Alaric A. Watts, editor of *The Literary Souvenir*], and he thanked me too—"It was very clever, but unfortunately he was overpowered with contributions of that description: would I write him something serious?" So you see they *will* have me "like Niobe, all tears."

Caroline Bowles, and her writing, suffered from the Romantic double standard. When she wrote as a poetess should—sadly, sweetly, selflessly—her work was highly praised. There can be no doubt that she was gifted in writing just that kind of poem and tale, and Bowles deserved that praise, though tastes have changed and a modern reader may snicker just at the point where she hoped to draw forth a tear. But she was also gifted in writing in her own voice, subjectively and satirically.

The "I" of Caroline Bowles is apparent in her prose masterpiece, the essays and tales published in *Blackwood's Edinburgh Magazine* from 1824 to 1829 and republished in two volumes as *Chapters on Churchyards* (1829). These tales retained public favor, slight as it was, longer than any of her poems: according to Mrs. Margaret Oliphant some fifty years later, they were "almost the only relics of her that have a faint survival." Some critics, such as Richard Garnett, have extrapolated the tone of the collection from its lugubrious title; but these are not simply "pathetic novelettes," though all center on death and the graveyard. Much as other fiction writers of the period, including Washington Irving and Mary Russell Mitford, treated English country life, Bowles uses the English country graveyard as a microcosm of all that is simple, religious, constant, and good in rural England, shaken as it was by agricultural revolution in the 1820s. In "Common

Robert Southey in 1828, ten years after the beginning of his correspondence with Caroline Bowles (engraving after a portrait by Sir Thomas Lawrence)

ground"—even more than in Thomas Gray's *Elegy Written in a Country Church Yard* (1751)—the churchyard is the repository for the past of each village, each family's story, each individual's life. Each of the three long tales—"Broad Summerford," "Andrew Cleaves," and "The Grave of the Broken Heart"—begins or ends in a churchyard, as does each tale embedded in Bowles's monologue, which comprises the first nine chapters.

Chapters on Churchyards is Bowles's most successful work because its organic form allowed her the latitude to exercise all her talents, in pathos and comedy, in descriptions of nature and of personalities, in poetic turns of phrase without the restraints of rhyme and meter. The first half of the book is a charming monologue, nine chapters in which Bowles, as herself, muses about churchyards she has visited and the tales pertaining to them. The first three chapters show her range. A tender description of the quaint country custom of planting perennials on a spouse's grave moves smoothly into a satiric anecdote about the inevitable loss of interest in gardening after a hasty remarriage: "sow annuals" is Bowles's advice. Chapter 2 joins practical comments on proper landscaping and placement of churchyards with an exquisite meditation on the beauty of the church, meadow, and stream at sunset, and ends with a treacly tableau at the rectory window, of the curate and his wife readying their dimply baby for bed. Chapter 3 presents a witty, Chaucerian analysis of the village churchgoers filing through the churchyard on their way to Sunday service.

Bowles's genius for extreme sentimentalism is evident in the two-part story of Andrew

Cleaves, the most popular tale of *Chapters on Churchyards*; it is also arguably her fictional masterpiece because of its careful portrayal of character. Heir of William Wordsworth's Michael and forebear of George Eliot's Silas Marner, Andrew Cleaves is a hard, grasping loner whose brief marriage for money leaves him with a child to raise. His overwhelming love for little Josiah restores him to full humanity and Christian concord. But, tragically, Josiah falls in with bad company, squanders Andrew's considerable life savings, and is executed, repentant. Andrew, a grieving, destitute old man, is soon buried with his son. The village is horrified at reports of a ghostly presence seen nightly above Andrew's grave. Investigation reveals that Andrew's aged white horse, faithful to the end, has broken down the churchyard wall and, after visiting nightly, has finally died across the new-mounded grave. Though the overall death toll of characters in *Chapters on Churchyards* is only slightly higher than that in Mitford's *Our Village* (1832), Bowles's deaths are much more richly melodramatic. Each tragic end is garnished with every conceivable heartrending circumstance: penury, faithless love, innocent beauty cut off in its prime, forlorn pets expiring on their masters' graves.

Contemporary reaction to the "bright and tender" and "too painful" tales in *Chapters on Churchyards* provoked Bowles's fullest explanations of her method in writing fiction. Southey, whose opinions she often sought and considered, wrote to her on 17 August 1829, "You are a *cruel* writer, for you imagine tales which I, with all my love for the writer, and with all my admiration for the passages that catch my eye, cannot bear to read. . . . In my future fiction I will make everybody happy as far as I can, for the sake of making myself so while I write, and will tell no sad stories, unless they are true ones." Bowles replied on 8 September:

> You are as deliberately cruel as I am. Do you break one's heart less with melancholy truths than if you tried it with mournful fiction? And be it known to you, that (except in the story of Andrew Cleaves) I have only been guilty of working upon prepared canvas. Circumstances within my own knowledge, or recollection of my mother's inexhaustible traditionary store, supplied me with abundant materials. I wish you joy of your determination to make all your creatures happy. I find it much easier to kill them out of the way, and then I take special care, when my work is done, never to read a page of it.

Mary Howitt and Maria Jane Jewsbury wrote to tell her of their enthusiasm for the newly published *Chapters on Churchyards*, Jewsbury singling out "The Grave of the Broken Heart" as particularly excellent. Some years later Caroline Southey responded to Anna Maria Bray's praise of "Andrew Cleaves": "It seems to me that that style of writing—the deep tragic—is by far the easiest, and, as most addressed to the passions, by no means the best. My husband used quite to disapprove of it, and scolded me for writing 'Andrew Cleave,' at the same time that he said, that after writing that I must not talk of incapacity. But he called it 'wicked writing' " (3 November 1841).

As she pointed out to Southey in her letter of 8 September 1829, Bowles rarely drew on her own creativity for the plots of her stories; instead, her custom was to recast stories of her own family and their friends told to her by her mother and grandmother. "Broad Summerford," of *Chapters on Churchyards*, tells the story of the declining years and happy deaths of two of her mother's relatives, the pastor of Broad Summerford and his twin sister. Bowles begins by confessing her source for the tale she continues in the first person: her mother was "rich in old tales, and family legends, and all sorts of traditionary lore—. . . and many a fire-light hour have I sat on the low footstool at her feet, listening . . . ; and often, in after life, I have caught myself speaking to others of those places, persons, and circumstances, as if I had been contemporaneous with the former, and familiar with the latter, from personal observation and experience." In the same way "La Petite Madelaine," published in *Blackwood's* in August 1831, was Bowles's conscious fictionalization of her French grandmother's childhood and marriage to an Englishman, inspired, as she confides to the reader at the outset, by her recent encounter with a distant relative.

Besides "Andrew Cleaves," however, Bowles wrote at least one other tale from her own imagination. From the modern viewpoint "The Little Brook and the Star," which appeared in Watts's *Literary Souvenir* for 1828, is a rather subversive piece. It is a moral tale, directed to a juvenile audience as are many of her poems (on 28 April 1829 she quipped to Southey, the laureate: "I expect, if . . . there is a royal nursery in my time, to be made laureate to that same"), but with an unorthodox message. The tale begins conventionally, introducing the main character, "a certain little Brook that might have been the happiest creature in the world, if it had . . . been content with the station assigned to it by an unerring Providence." The authorial "I" consistently assures the reader of the authenticity of the tale and adds wry comments on the action. At first the little brook is happy in her forest seclusion, under the loving regard of the single star whose light pierces the foliage. When her woodland friends bring rumors of a wide and exciting world, however, the little brook becomes dissatisfied with her quiet life. Vain and light-minded, she gains her heart's desire when woodcutters expose her to the flirtatious twinkles of the expanse of stars overhead and the burning admiration of the sun. But her pleasure wanes as herds slurp and wallow in her now-muddy pools, and the sun's fierce thirst dooms her to complete evaporation. At this point the reader expects the traditional didactic ending: the brook should repent and die, shamed, a lesson to all young women not to aspire to carnal or worldly adventure. The message of the semireclusive Bowles, writing from her cottage in the New Forest, is, ironically, that knowledge is preferable to innocence: that the little brook, "refined by rough discipline—purified by adversity," is more fit to unite with her beloved star than she ever would have been had she stayed quietly in the forest.

Modern assessment of Caroline Bowles's writing ought to consider the influence of her constant correspondent and literary adviser Robert Southey, but some critics have overstated her debt to him; in *British Authors of the Nineteenth Century* (1936) one says, "Her literary reputation is based primarily upon her intimate association with Southey, under whose influence she wrote," an unrealistic evaluation considering her success as an anonymous writer and a lack of documentary evidence. Even with the recognition that Dowden may have omitted relevant material from his collection of their correspondence, it is still noteworthy that after her first poem *Ellen Fitzarthur* their letters show no evidence of Southey's previewing her work before publication, only his praise of published work. She rarely discussed her work in progress; their literary discussions focus instead on his writing and publishing. What there is in the letters of Southey's response to her work indicates that he was partial to her pathetic lyrics, but urged her to write poems closer to prose, feeling that her genius lay in that form. In his 27 January 1831 letter he suggested that she recast the incidents of some of her lyrics into less ornamented "simple narrative," to provide "the most close and faithful picture." One of his earliest letters to her (17 June 1818) asserts women's superiority in writing prose and their deficiencies in writing poetry; in this vein he sympathized with her inability to master the intricate metrical pattern of his *Thalaba the Destroyer* (1801), the pattern in which they began in November 1823 to compose their collaborative poem, *Robin Hood* (never finished, though she published a fragment in 1847, after Southey's death).

Bowles continued to write poetry and prose fiction throughout the 1830s, though only two volumes of her poetry were published: *Tales of the Factories* (1833), a condemnation of industrial atrocities preceding Caroline Norton's and Elizabeth Barrett Browning's similar poems, and *The Birth-Day* (1836). Her *Blackwood's* fiction of the 1830s represents no departure from the successful themes and tone of *Chapters on Churchyards*; it was never collected. Upon her marriage to Southey on 5 June 1839, she ceased writing for publication, occupied as she soon was with the task of caring for Southey in his mental infirmity.

Caroline Bowles and Robert Southey were married eighteen months after the death of Southey's beloved wife of forty-two years, Edith Fricker Southey. That summer Southey's mental capacity deteriorated rapidly; by the autumn his recollections of a lifetime of reading and writing were gone, and he was unable to exert himself intellectually. Some chroniclers claim that he recognized Caroline and was grateful for her company until nearly the last year of his life, when he sank into complete insensibility; others state that he was oblivious to the persons around him as early as the autumn of 1839. He died on 21 March 1843.

The controversy over Caroline Bowles's conduct in marrying Southey and during their blighted marriage dominates Victorian biographical reference to her. Some commentators felt that Bowles married Southey in order to benefit financially and that as his guardian she behaved unreasonably and cruelly; others felt that she had acted out of love and in Southey's best interests, that she had jeopardized her financial security by the marriage, and, indeed, that she had foreseen the catastrophe of his mental failure and sacrificed her happiness to ease his final years. Unfortunately, no full account of the situation exists: decorum often prevented disclosure of pertinent information. For instance, William Henry Smith, the author of a piece on Southey in the March and April 1851 issues of *Blackwood's*, demurs,

Greta Hall, Robert Southey's Keswick home. Caroline Bowles visited this house for the first time in 1823 and lived here after her marriage to Southey in 1839.

"Strangers as we are, it would ill become us to dwel upon, or amplify this part of the narrative" dealing with Southey's second marriage, and the editor of the autobiography of Anna Eliza Bray, Caroline Southey's correspondent throughout Robert Southey's illness, comments that the bulk of Mrs. Southey's letters, which "pour out the very secrets of her heart," are "of far too painful and too confidential a character for publication." As late as 1927, Edith Morley stated in her edition of the correspondence of Henry Crabb Robinson that "it did not seem necessary to publish" a good amount of information about the Southey family quarrel.

The quarrel involved as principals Katharine Southey and Caroline Bowles Southey. Kate, Southey's youngest surviving daughter and the only one living at home, was nearly thirty at the time of her father's marriage. Her father had expected that she and her sister Bertha would be shocked by his decision to remarry, but hoped that they would become reconciled. Announcing his engagement, he wrote to them on 15 October 1838: "Some natural tears it will call forth. But that I have done well and wisely . . . I am sure you will perceive, and that the change in my condition . . . will be to Kates comfort and yours. I am perfectly satisfied Caroline will be to you as an elder sister. . . ." The Southey daughters were at the Wordsworths' when they received the news, and Wordsworth hinted to Crabb Robinson that their violent reactions did not bode well for Caroline Southey's acceptance in the family. In a March 1839 letter Robert Southey told Walter Savage Landor that Kate's welfare was a key reason for his remarriage. Landor, believing Caroline was in her thirties, reported to Rose Paynter in May that Southey "has known the lady for twenty years—that there is a just proportion between their ages, and that, having but one daughter single, and being obliged to leave her frequently, she wants a friend and guide at home. Nothing is more reasonable, nothing more considerate and kind. Love has often made other wise men less wise, and sometimes other good men less good; but never Southey." Relations between the women at Greta Hall seemed harmonious during the first few months of Robert Southey's deterioration. A thirdhand report, from Catherine Clarkson to Crabb Robinson, noted that "Mrs. Southey declined interfering with domestic affairs that she might devote herself entirely to him & that all the family are delighted with her" (4 December 1839).

By the summer of 1840 Kate and Caroline Southey were at odds. Southey's biographer Jack Simmons reasons that Kate's jealousy of her stepmother and Caroline's iron rule in the sickroom, combined with the strain on both women of Southey's sad condition, caused the rift. One dramatic result was Kate's leaving Greta Hall and moving in with the Wordsworths at Rydal Mount. Wordsworth volunteered as a mediator between Kate and Caroline Southey, but his own account (to Crabb Robinson, early in 1841) shows that he withheld information from each side and had already made up his mind that Caroline Southey was in the wrong. Landor, Southey's irascible friend, was convinced that Wordsworth "fermented the misunderstanding and mischief between those of Southey's children who opposed the second wife and those who befriended her" (3 November 1839). All the Southeys and their friends took sides. Southey's children Bertha and Cuthbert, the Wordsworth clan, Sara Coleridge, and Crabb Robinson sided with Kate; Southey's daughter Edith May and her husband, John Wood Warter, and Southey's younger brother, Dr. Henry Herbert Southey, as well as Landor and Anna Maria Bray, sided with Caroline Southey.

Depending on the allegiance of their sources, biographical retrospectives either praise or blame Caroline Southey. One of her strongest supporters was William Jerdan, whose chapter on Robert Southey in *Men I Have Known* (1866) spends a disproportionate amount of text championing Caroline Southey: "It seems to me that a resentful spirit against the lady who became his second wife led to imputations upon her conduct by no means deserved; and was, in short, an ebullition of anger, founded on partial views, and seriously unjust. . . . his suffering wife had for three years to endure the hostile censures of his [children], and be calumniated for making an 'idiot' of the man she had for years almost adored, and whose process towards that sad condition neither began with nor was accelerated by her." Jerdan records that Southey's mental debility was marked near the end of their year-long engagement (on which Bowles had insisted, to regain her own health so as not to be an encumbrance to Southey), but that Bowles married the failing Southey in spite of her tragic prevision. Landor concurred in his 4 April 1843 letter pleading (futilely) for Richard Monckton Milnes's assistance in procuring a government pension for her: "Before she married him she was well aware into what a state she was hastening, and she married him because she felt certain that no other would take the same care of him as she would. What saint or martyr ever reached this sublimity of self-devotion?" Landor rejoiced in writing a short poem in her honor nine years later, "On Mrs. Southey's Pension," when she was granted a crown pension.

It is difficult to see Caroline Bowles Southey as the villain in the Southey family quarrel, especially since the rancor seems to come from her opponents, and little from her. Even Wordsworth conceded that she genuinely desired to resolve the quarrel with Kate Southey. In spite of the unhappiness of her situation, uprooted from her lifelong home and finding no solace in her new one, she was devoted to Southey and unflagging in her attempts to alleviate his sufferings. In a poignant letter to Anna Maria Bray, dated 24 May 1841, Caroline Southey wrote:

> There is no living creature near me now to whom I can think aloud. Every day my heart seems, not contracting, but closing in more and more upon feelings which I dare not dwell on within myself; for that which softens and unnerves I cannot risk. I am grown much harder than I was. I shall, I hope, become more so every day, for I have need of it.

Some bits of poetry she wrote in these years are particularly affecting. A sonnet she wrote to Southey on his sixty-seventh birthday prays that "the mysterious veil" shrouding him "from this world and all its woes" will lift him from darkness into light; the beginning of this poem tells of their hopeful engagement and its bitter denouement:

> Come, friend! true friend! join hands with me, he
>   said.
> Join hand and heart for this life's latest stage,
> And that to come unending. I engage,
> God being gracious to me, as we tread
> The dim descent, to be to thee instead
> Of all thou leav'st for my sake! On our way,

If not with flowers and summer sunshine gay,
Soft light yet lingers, and the fadeless hue
Of the Green Holly. Be of courage! Come!
Thou shalt find friends, fear not: warm, loving,
true,
All who love me.—He said, and to his home
Brought me. Then sank, a stricken man. . . .

Caroline Southey did not attend her husband's funeral on the wet, cold morning of 23 March 1843, according to a 25 March letter of Edward Quillinan, Wordsworth's son-in-law. Nor did she invite Wordsworth, but he and Quillinan came anyway, Wordsworth having confirmed that Kate and Cuthbert Southey wanted him to attend. Hartley Coleridge recorded that the feuding factions stood apart and did not speak to each other as Southey was laid to rest in the parish churchyard; Quillinan noted, "Poor Kate says that she has now got her father back again." Within a few weeks Wordsworth, the new poet laureate, and Quillinan were ungenerously anxious to make it known that Caroline Southey had done very well for herself financially by her marriage to Southey, contrary to what the newspapers were saying about her impoverished state.

After her husband's death Caroline Southey moved back to her beloved Buckland Cottage and spent her remaining eleven years tending Southey's reputation. She planned to edit Southey's correspondence and began collecting letters from his friends, but she was forestalled by his literary executors, Henry Taylor and Cuthbert Southey. (Cuthbert Southey edited his father's *Life and Correspondence* [1849, 1850], including only the briefest mention of Caroline Bowles.) She did edit the first volume of Robert Southey's biography of educator Dr. Andrew Bell, a project he had left unfinished at the onset of his decline (the biography was published in 1844, with Cuthbert Southey listed as author of the second and third volumes). In 1847 she published, with a lengthy introductory essay, a volume of later poems by herself and Southey, including the fragment of "Robin Hood" they had worked on in the 1820s. One last appearance in print was controversial; in a letter published in the 23 January 1847 issue of the *Athenaeum* she rebuked William Howitt for "cast[ing] dirt on the name of Robert Southey" in his *Homes and Haunts of the Most Eminent British Poets* (1847), which she had not seen, but had read of in an *Athenaeum* review. The next issue of the *Athenaeum* censured Mrs. Southey's haste in condemning Howitt, quoting his book's high praise for her.

Her last years were quiet ones, devoted to writing letters and reading, brightened by occasional visits to her stepdaughter Edith May and the satisfaction of being awarded a Civil List pension in 1852. She died ("The event had long been expected," said one obituary) at Buckland Cottage on 20 July 1854.

Caroline Bowles Southey, if she is remembered as a writer at all, is likely remembered as one among the bouquet of "Modern English Poetesses" celebrated in Henry Nelson Coleridge's 1840 article. But Landor cited her prose, not her poetry, as exceptional, claiming that she had "written admirable things. There is one chapter on 'Churchyards,' which the united faculties of Sterne and Addison would scarcely have produced." Richard Garnett, too, asserted that her literary reputation should rest on her prose *Chapters on Churchyards*: "Though very unpretending, these are frequently both powerful and pathetic. Miss Bowles's gifts were rather those of a storyteller than of a poet, and her poetry is generally the better the nearer it approaches to prose." Her stories were certainly to the taste of her late-Romantic audience, the readers of *Blackwood's* and the annuals, and her prose writings—satiric, sentimental, and subjective—are central to any study of Romanticism in popular literature.

Letters:

The Correspondence of Robert Southey with Caroline Bowles, edited by Edward Dowden (Dublin: Hodges, Figgis, 1881);

"The Correspondence of Caroline Anne Bowles Southey to Mary Anne Watts Hughes," edited by Vernon Louis Schonert, Ph.D. dissertation, Harvard University, 1957.

References:

Anna Eliza Bray, *Autobiography*, edited by John A. Kempe (London: Chapman & Hall, 1884);

J. F. Burnet, "Caroline Bowles," *Fortnightly Review*, new series 173 (May 1953): 338-342;

Henry Nelson Coleridge, "Modern English Poetesses," *Quarterly Review*, 66 (September 1840): 374-418;

Janet E. Courtney, *The Adventurous Thirties: A Chapter in the Women's Movement* (London: Oxford University Press, 1933); pp. 33-43;

Kenneth Curry, ed., *New Letters of Robert Southey*, 2 volumes (New York & London: Columbia University Press, 1965);

John Dennis, ed., *Robert Southey: The Story of His Life Written in His Letters* (London & New York: Bell, 1894);

E. O., "Robert Southey's Second Wife," *Cornhill Magazine*, 30 (August 1874): 217-229;

John Forster, *Walter Savage Landor: A Biography* (Boston: Fields, Osgood, 1869), pp. 556-563;

T. K. Hervey(?), "Caroline Southey," *Athenaeum*, 5 August 1854, pp. 969-970;

William Jerdan, "Robert Southey," in his *Men I Have Known* (London & New York: George Routledge & Sons, 1866), pp. 406-420;

Justice [pseud.], "Mrs. Southey's Grievance," *Athenaeum*, 30 January 1847, pp. 125-126;

Alfred H. Miles, "Caroline (Bowles) Southey," in *The Poets and the Poetry of the Nineteenth Century*, 10 volumes, edited by Miles (London: Hutchinson, 1892-1897);

D. M. Moir, *Sketches of the Poetical Literature of the Past Half-Century* (Edinburgh: William Blackwood & Sons, 1851);

Margaret Oliphant, *Annals of a Publishing House: William Blackwood and His Sons, Their Magazine and Friends*, 3 volumes (Edinburgh: William Blackwood & Sons, 1897-1898);

Oliphant, *The Literary History of England in the End of the Eighteenth and Beginning of the Nineteenth Century*, 3 volumes (London: Macmillan, 1882), I: 327;

William Henry Smith, "Southey," *Blackwood's Edinburgh Magazine*, 69 (March 1851): 349-367; 69 (April 1851): 385-405;

Edmund Tew, "Dr. Southey and Thomas Carlyle," *Notes and Queries*, sixth series 3 (9 April 1881): 284-285;

Oliver Warner, "Miss Bowles Visits Southey," *Country Life*, 101 (2 May 1947): 808-809;

John Wilson, Review of *The Birth-Day*, *Blackwood's Edinburgh Magazine*, 41 (March 1837): 404-427.

John Sterling

(20 July 1806 - 18 September 1844)

Eric W. Nye
University of Wyoming

BOOKS: *Arthur Coningsby*, 3 volumes (London: Published by Effingham Wilson, 1833);

Poems (London: Edward Moxon, 1839);

The Election: A Poem, in Seven Books (London: John Murray, 1841);

The Poetical Works of John Sterling [unauthorized edition], edited by Rufus W. Griswold (Philadelphia: Herman Hooker, 1842);

Strafford. A Tragedy (London: Edward Moxon, 1843);

Essays and Tales, by John Sterling, Collected and Edited, with a Memoir of His Life, 2 volumes, edited by Julius Charles Hare (London: John W. Parker, 1848);

The Onyx Ring, edited, with a biographical preface, by Charles Hale (Boston: Whittemore, Niles & Hall, 1856).

A man of letters whose career began toward the end of the Romantic period, John Sterling is relatively unknown today. How this obscurity came to be is one of the puzzles of literary history. Born into the best society, eminent among the brightest of his generation at Cambridge University, befriended early by John Stuart Mill and Thomas Carlyle, Sterling demonstrated his talent successfully in virtually every literary mode. His poetry was trumpeted with extravagance by John Wilson in *Blackwood's Magazine* and solicited for publication in America by Ralph Waldo Emerson. His verse tragedy, *Strafford* (1843), was well reviewed by Margaret Fuller and G. H. Lewes. His aphorisms—really prose poems—and essays filled the pages of the most prominent journals of his day. His contemporaries cherished their communications with him and carefully preserved his letters. Selections from his correspondence, richly laced through with literary observations, were published after his death from tuberculosis at age thirty-eight. His travel writings, the result of futile attempts to find a better climate for his feeble frame, have never been collected, though the available specimens are brilliant narratives, rivaling the best of that genre. In some ways the least of his achievements were in prose fiction. Even here two novels are attributed to him (though one of these is very doubtfully assigned), as well as a novella published on both sides of the Atlantic, and a series of prose tales and romances that *Blackwood's* purchased eagerly in the late 1830s. Nearly all his work was published anonymously or pseudonymously and attracted a select though small circle of admirers. During his short life, Sterling never consolidated his literary reputation with the general public, and subsequent critics, rather than appraise his work directly, have found it much easier to echo the opinions of Thomas Carlyle's tendentious *Life of John Sterling* (1851). Begun as a tribute, that work evolved into a case study in the dangers of Coleridgean speculation, as exemplified to Carlyle by Sterling. Carlyle's friendship mattered much to Sterling, but the posthumous biography effectively canceled with its rhetorical force Sterling's own modest, hard-earned, diverse reputation.

The son of Edward and Hester Coningham Sterling, John Sterling was born at Kames Castle, a rundown estate on the Isle of Bute, where his father, a retired captain of militia, had taken up farming. Three years later, in autumn 1809, Edward Sterling gave up his attempt to establish himself as a gentleman farmer and took his family to live in the village of Llanblethian, near Cowbridge in Glamorganshire, where he was appointed adjutant of the Glamorganshire Militia. In 1812 he began a career as a political writer when the *Times* published some of his letters under the pseudonym *Vetus*, and in spring 1815, after they had spent seven months living in France, he and the family settled in London, where he eventually established a permanent connection with the *Times*.

In October 1824 John Sterling entered Trinity College, Cambridge, where his energetic reading in the libraries later influenced his experiments in prose fiction. He became acquainted with European models of romantic fiction, au-

Portrait by B. de la Cour, 1830 (location of original unknown; from Anne Kimball Tuell, John Sterling: A Representative Victorian, *1941)*

thors such as Victor Hugo, Ludwig Tieck, Johann August Musæus, Friedrich de la Motte Fouqué, E. T. A. Hoffmann, Jean Paul Richter, Novalis, and above all Johann Wolfgang von Goethe. The seeds from such reading were nourished by Sterling's attachment to the intellectual salon surrounding Samuel Taylor Coleridge, whom Sterling probably met through his tutor, Julius Charles Hare, who was later one of the executors of Coleridge's will. Sterling became devoted to Coleridge, serving as disciple and amanuensis at a time when Coleridge's interest in German fiction was strong. Hare owned perhaps the finest library in England of German literature of his time. Coleridge, Hare, and the Germans made up a formidable constellation of influence over young Sterling, a constellation that would have been envied by Carlyle, then at work on his own translations of Goethe's *Wilhelm Meister's Apprenticeship* (1824), *German Romance* (1827), and a *Life of Friedrich Schiller* (1825). A leading member of the Apostles Club and the Union Society, Sterling left Cambridge for a period in the late 1820s and soon became well established in London literary circles, at first through writing for the *Athenaeum*. Then in July 1828 he and friends bought the jour-

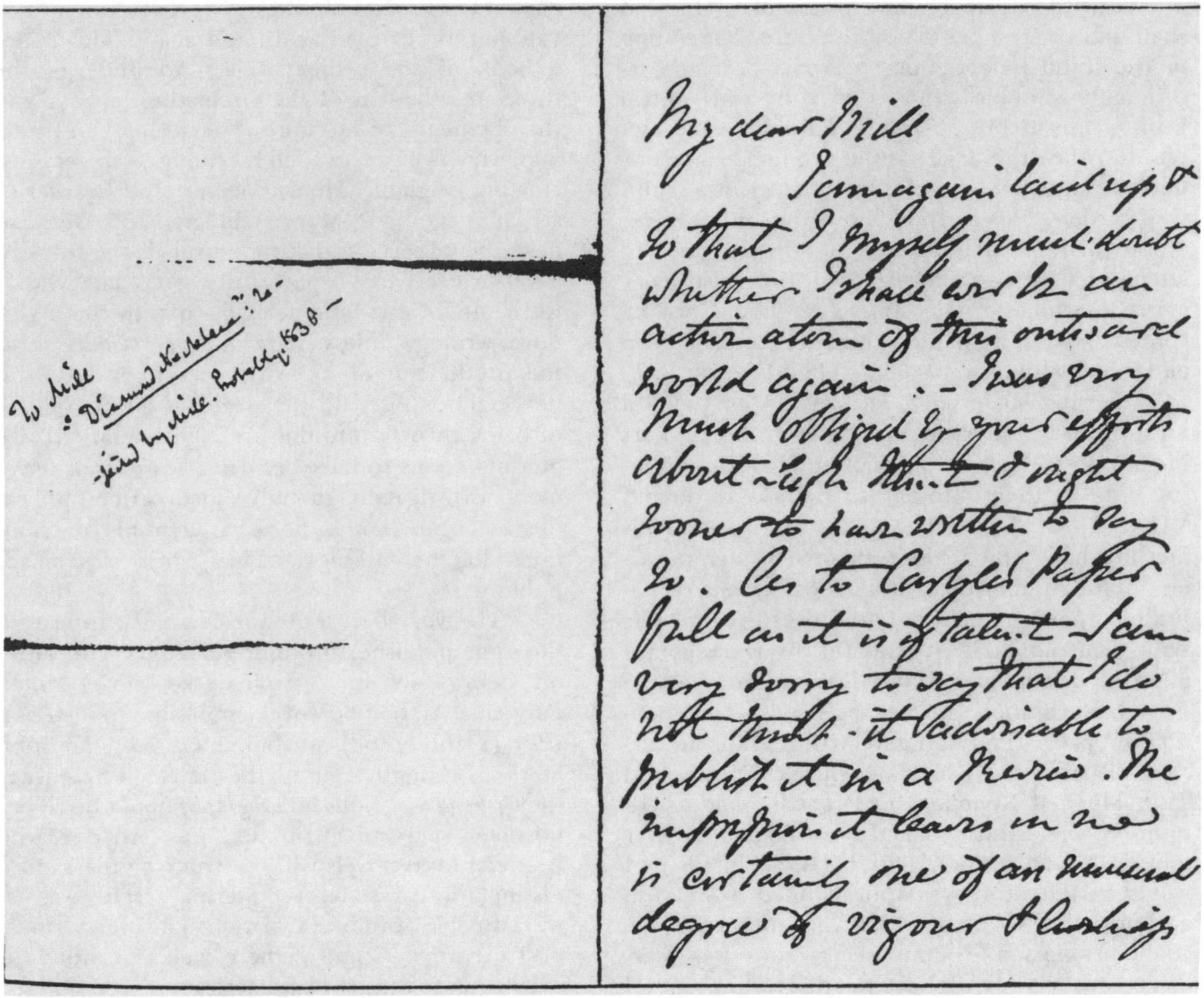

To Mill
: Diamond Necklace": 2e-
-fixed by Mill. Probably 1838 -

My dear Mill
I am again laid up &
so that I myself must doubt
whether I shall ever be an
active atom of this outward
world again. — I was very
much obliged by your efforts
about Leigh Hunt & ought
sooner to have written to say
so. As to Carlyle's Paper
full as it is of talent I am
very sorry to say that I do
not think it advisable to
publish it in a Review. The
impression it leaves on me
is certainly one of an unusual
degree of vigour & flashing

Part of a letter, probably written in 1836, in which Sterling advised John Stuart Mill not to publish an article by Thomas Carlyl in the London and Westminster Review *(from Anne Kimball Tuell,* John Sterling: A Representative Victorian, *1941) The note at left is in Carlyle's hand.*

nal and merged it with the *Literary Chronicle* to form the *Athenaeum and Literary Chronicle*, which he helped to edit during its early years.

Sterling's earliest efforts in the short prose tale, which appeared in the *Athenaeum* during 1828 and 1829, bear comparison with Nathaniel Hawthorne's or Edgar Allan Poe's, which they predate. They might also be compared with contemporary poetic evocations of imaginary worlds by Sterling's fellow Cambridge Apostle, Alfred Tennyson. Either highly symbolic or self-consciously allegorical, the tales are often set in worlds of fairy or myth or antiquity. Very often their thrust is didactic or at least parabolic.

During the same period, Sterling was also at work on a novel, *Arthur Coningsby*. Published in January 1833 by Effingham Wilson, it was advertised as written "several years ago" and is se early in the fervid decade of the 1790s. Lik Carlyle's *Sartor Resartus* (1833-1834), *Arthur Coningsby* is a Bildungsroman, more particularly a species of crisis biography. Despite advice to the contrary in the front matter, the reader familiar wit Sterling's life will have difficulty avoiding the association of the characters with real persons. It i the story of a young man in his early twentie who abandons his expectations in England, wanders into the conflict of powerful factions and ideals in revolutionary France, and emerges chastened and alone, intent on immigrating to the American frontier. Sterling's character articulates the Everlasting No! for which Carlyle's protagonist is well known, rejects the political impulses of both France and England, and concludes with a cryptic postscript from Aeschylus: "He that shall deliver thee exists not in nature." Operating on the grand scale, the plot of *Arthur Coningsby* occasionally stumbles and is fraught with outrageous coincidences, Gothic episodes, and set pieces. A favorite device is the extended conversation of characters strolling in a gallery or a sculpture garden. This method allows the author to exercise his speculations on aesthetics and to attempt balancing political, social, and artistic concerns. Sterling's *Arthur Coningsby* should not be confused with Benjamin Disraeli's better-known and more optimistic *Coningsby* (1844).

Sterling suffered a serious loss of political idealism in the debacle ensuing from his support of Gen. José Maria de Torrijos and his band of insurgents in their attempt to depose Ferdinand VII of Spain. In the late 1820s and early 1830s Sterling had rallied his influential contemporaries in the Cambridge Union Society and Cambridge Apostles to support the overthrow of this tyrannical monarch. Just as the previous generation in Britain had drawn inspiration from the French Revolution, so Sterling's sought a repetition in Spain. Tennyson and Arthur Hallman carried dispatches. Richard Chenevix Trench and John Mitchell Kemble sailed to Gibraltar to administer the funds collected in England. After months of frustration and delay a shipload of would-be liberators was apprehended by Spanish authorities in November 1831 and summarily executed at Málaga. Among the victims was Sterling's cousin Capt. Robert Boyd. Sterling's novel is partly an attempt to exorcise the despair that ensued from this episode.

Despite its anonymous publication by Effingham Wilson, better known for radical political tracts than novels, *Arthur Coningsby* achieved modest success. Mill and Coleridge applauded it privately. Carlyle was impressed. Among about two dozen contemporary reviews, the *Satirist* (3 February 1833) remarked, "the three volumes abound in vivid paintings and high intellectual imaginings—political, metaphysical, philosophical, moral, and, above all, religious. As a novel—highly interesting and attractive, solid, instructive, and entertaining throughout—we pronounce it a performance of high talent." The *Times*, for which Sterling's father worked, devoted more than a column to comments and extracts (5 February 1833). The *Courier* review (23 March 1833) exclaimed, "All Hail! Arthur Coningsby!—Here is another book at last, which, though a novel, and in three volumes, may be purchased to place on the shelves of a permanent private library, to read again and again. This is not a book of the ordinary class, to undergo the three months run of the circulating library, and then be heard of no more. The author can think, and, what is more, can tell his thoughts in very fascinating language. He will need no puff-power to set him going." More tellingly, the *Spectator* began by observing that the novel "is the work of a very clever, nay a powerful writer, but who at the same time is little acquainted with the art of novel-writing; unless, indeed, *Arthur Coningsby* is the production of an early season of life, and now only exposed to the world as an alternative of being thrown into the fire" (26 January 1833). Sterling seems to have regarded his own achievement with disdain, though shortly after publication he began another book based on his contributions to the *Athenæm*. This work was never published.

The year before *Arthur Coningsby* appeared, the same publisher brought out a powerful satire on George IV in a triple-decker novel called *Fitzgeorge*. An obituary of the publisher in the *Bookseller* (1 July 1868) attributed *Fitzgeorge* to John Sterling, though later in the nineteenth century the *Dictionary of National Biography* noted how "impossible" such an attribution was. Anyone who has read both novels will be struck by the radical dissimilarity of style. Yet Sterling's style was always capable of radical variation. The high seriousness of *Arthur Coningsby* here yields to ludicrous events and comic characterization. Could the same young author who narrates the claustrophobic bloodbaths of the Reign of Terror also sketch the Augustan fancies of the Prince of Wales's toilet? The mode of allusion in *Fitzgeorge* is akin to the grand tradition of English satire. The writer seems mature and sententious, with a Whig attitude to reform. The same cannot be said of Sterling in *Arthur Coningsby*. The authorship of *Fitzgeorge* remains a mystery; it was probably not John Sterling who wrote this novel.

On 2 November 1830, while awaiting the outcome of Torrijos's expedition to Spain, Sterling had married Susanna Barton, of the Anglo-Irish family of Bordeaux wine merchants still in trade as Barton-Guestier. Not long after their wedding, he suffered a pulmonary attack that contributed to his decision to sail to Saint Vincent, in the West Indies, and assume management of a sugar plantation in which he had an interest. A son, the first of their seven children, was born to the Sterlings in Saint Vincent in October 1831.

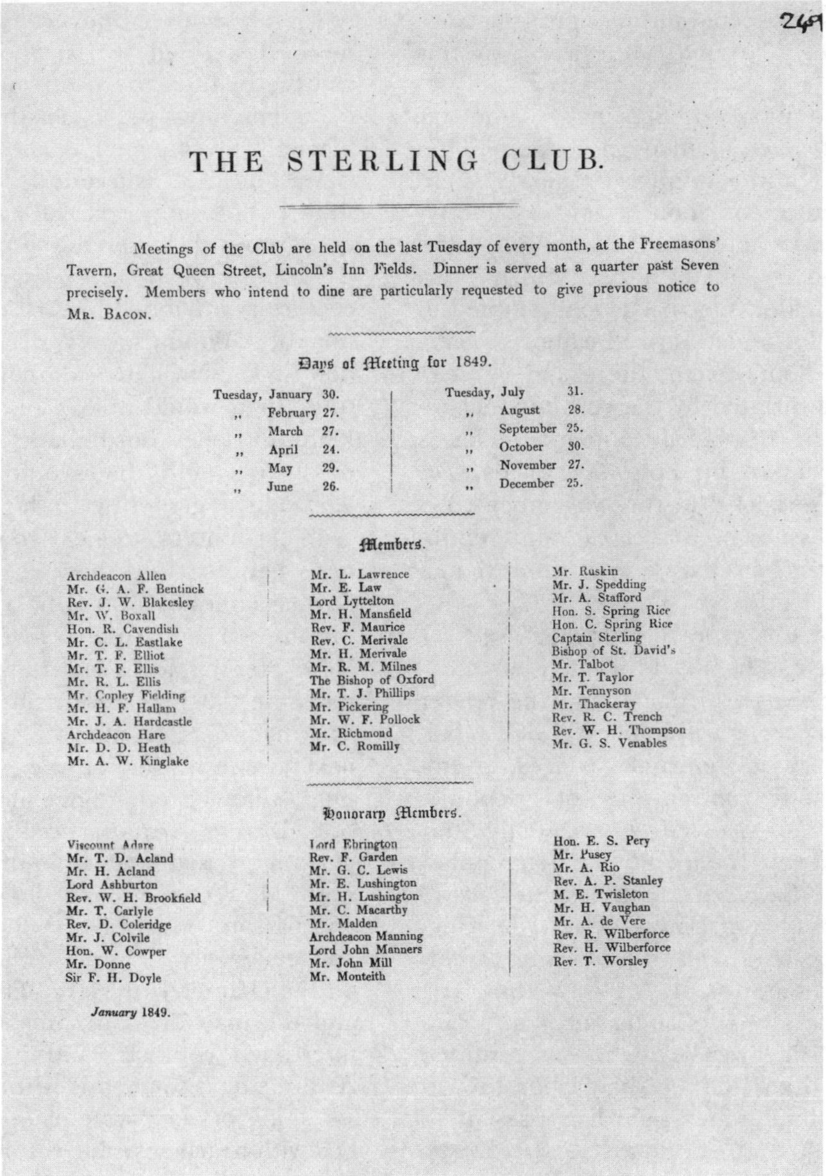

249

THE STERLING CLUB.

Meetings of the Club are held on the last Tuesday of every month, at the Freemasons' Tavern, Great Queen Street, Lincoln's Inn Fields. Dinner is served at a quarter past Seven precisely. Members who intend to dine are particularly requested to give previous notice to Mr. Bacon.

Days of Meeting for 1849.

Tuesday, January	30.	Tuesday, July	31.
,, February	27.	,, August	28.
,, March	27.	,, September	25.
,, April	24.	,, October	30.
,, May	29.	,, November	27.
,, June	26.	,, December	25.

Members.

Archdeacon Allen
Mr. G. A. F. Bentinck
Rev. J. W. Blakesley
Mr. W. Boxall
Hon. R. Cavendish
Mr. C. L. Eastlake
Mr. T. F. Elliot
Mr. T. F. Ellis
Mr. R. L. Ellis
Mr. Copley Fielding
Mr. H. F. Hallam
Mr. J. A. Hardcastle
Archdeacon Hare
Mr. D. D. Heath
Mr. A. W. Kinglake
Mr. L. Lawrence
Mr. E. Law
Lord Lyttelton
Mr. H. Mansfield
Rev. F. Maurice
Rev. C. Merivale
Mr. H. Merivale
Mr. R. M. Milnes
The Bishop of Oxford
Mr. T. J. Phillips
Mr. Pickering
Mr. W. F. Pollock
Mr. Richmond
Mr. C. Romilly
Mr. Ruskin
Mr. J. Spedding
Mr. A. Stafford
Hon. S. Spring Rice
Hon. C. Spring Rice
Captain Sterling
Bishop of St. David's
Mr. Talbot
Mr. T. Taylor
Mr. Tennyson
Mr. Thackeray
Rev. R. C. Trench
Rev. W. H. Thompson
Mr. G. S. Venables

Honorary Members.

Viscount Adare
Mr. T. D. Acland
Mr. H. Acland
Lord Ashburton
Rev. W. H. Brookfield
Mr. T. Carlyle
Rev. D. Coleridge
Mr. J. Colvile
Hon. W. Cowper
Mr. Donne
Sir F. H. Doyle
Lord Ebrington
Rev. F. Garden
Mr. G. C. Lewis
Mr. E. Lushington
Mr. H. Lushington
Mr. C. Macarthy
Mr. Malden
Archdeacon Manning
Lord John Manners
Mr. John Mill
Mr. Monteith
Hon. E. S. Pery
Mr. Pusey
Mr. A. Rio
Rev. A. P. Stanley
M. E. Twisleton
Mr. H. Vaughan
Mr. A. de Vere
Rev. R. Wilberforce
Rev. H. Wilberforce
Rev. T. Worsley

January 1849.

Announcement of the 1849 meetings of the club founded in 1838 to honor John Sterling (MS 19432, f. 249, National Library of Scotland)

After his home and library were destroyed by a hurricane and after persecution by other planters for his liberal attitudes toward slavery, Sterling took his family back to England in August 1832. By the following summer the Sterlings were visiting Germany. In Bonn he met his Cambridge tutor, Julius Hare, who had become rector of Herstmonceux in Sussex. Having already given serious consideration to becoming a clergyman, Sterling accepted an offer to serve as Hare's curate, taking orders and being ordained a deacon on Trinity Sunday 1834. He served for less than a year before ill health forced him to retire.

The mid 1830s marked an acceleration in Sterling's intellectual maturity, even as his physical health declined. Through his reading of Continental literature and philosophy he became one of the most advanced thinkers in England, specifically in matters of German biblical hermeneutics. He advised John Stuart Mill in composing his classic *Logic* (1843) and easily exceeded Carlyle in theological studies. Carlyle regarded these as Sterling's years of confusion, from which Carlyle himself emancipated the younger man, but Carlyle never fully appreciated the theological basis of Sterling's mature creative thought and analysis.

Neither did Carlyle accept Sterling's growing commitment to poetry, drama, and fiction at this time.

The second phase of Sterling's fiction appeared in *Blackwood's Edinburgh Magazine* beginning in 1837 and running for nearly three years. Published anonymously or pseudonymously, these works, interspersed with aphorisms and pages of poetry, made a powerful impression on Ralph Waldo Emerson, who attempted to find a publisher for an authorized edition of Sterling's works. To some extent the shape of Sterling's fiction was dictated by the conventional requirements of the *Blackwood's* audience. This is especially apparent in his episodic novella, *The Onyx Ring*, first serialized in the November 1838 and succeeding issues of *Blackwood's* and republished in America as a separate work more than a decade after his death.

As in *Arthur Coningsby* the form of *The Onyx Ring* is problematic. The novel form tended to encourage Sterling's digressiveness, and the reader finds a profusion of tales within tales, as well as ballads within tales, lyrics, journal passages, epistolary episodes, and paraphrases of recondite mythology. If *Arthur Coningsby* is essentially Sterling's "Resolution and Independence" from political life, *The Onyx Ring* represents his attempts to reconcile the conflicting claims of Carlyle, Goethe, Hare, and others over his evolving career. The nominal protagonist of *The Onyx Ring*, Arthur Edmonstone, despairs at his inequality with the beautiful Maria Lascelles, who has confided her devotion to him. Rather than labor toward the means of winning her guardian's assent to their marriage, Arthur succumbs to the arcane offer of an onyx ring from a mysterious old man, whom he meets at midnight in Temple Church. By wearing the onyx ring, Arthur receives the power to merge his being with that of any other person for precisely one week at a time. This series of out-of-body experiences enables him to reflect on human existence from various perspectives. His final incarnation is that of a blithe, old, crippled basketmaker. The crisis of the plot occurs when the basketmaker discloses to the elevated Maria that she is in fact his granddaughter, changed in infancy for the moribund child of the Lascelles family. Reconciled with poise to her new station, Maria finds herself deprived of her last relation by the basketmaker's sudden death. The reader wonders about Arthur, who has chosen that particularly unfortunate week to occupy the old man's being. But Arthur arrives as himself again and happily claims the hand of the newly descended Maria. Such is the frame tale. But the real quality of this novella is in the series of intervening personae that Arthur inhabits. Though his character is necessarily inchoate, the characters who surround him are powerfully drawn. The female characters in *The Onyx Ring*, too, are much better developed than the romantic heroines of *Arthur Coningsby*.The first circle of characters inhabited by Arthur is drawn from his normal station in society, the familiars of his London circle. Sir Charles Harcourt possesses the fortune that would make him eligible to marry Maria Lascelles, but he lacks the depth of soul or power of mind that would win her affection. Through a gathering at his country house Arthur encounters his next four temporary identities. The first of these is that of the simple farmer James Wilson, who chooses this week to propose to his rural beloved and is accepted. Here Sterling idealizes cottage virtues and narrates the touching death of one family member, who had been swept off to London. Arthur's next avatar is that of the world explorer Hastings, whose exotic tales enlivened Wilson's fireside. During Arthur's occupation, Hastings falls in with gypsies and is injured in one of their raids. He recuperates in the cottage of the country parson, Musgrave, whose otherworldliness and generosity suggest strongly that he is based on the character of Hare. The man of the world and the man of God come into some especially interesting conflicts, and it is no wonder that Arthur's next sojourn is with Musgrave. The parson ministers in the poorhouse and at the deathbed with nearly invisible results. When he encounters a profound poem, he is at a loss for a response. Arthur's next week is spent in the person of the poet himself, apparently modeled on Goethe. This man comes as near as anyone to winning Maria's heart from its pledge to Arthur. He possesses a comprehensive sensibility to nature, matters of the spirit, science, and history. Clearly to John Sterling the career of poet was at this time most appealing. Yet, as chance would have it, during the poet's foray with Maria to a ruined church, the two are driven by a storm to seek refuge with an articulate recluse named Collins. Collins is probably the best developed of the characters in this procession, and he is, by all accounts, patterned as a literary portrait of Carlyle. Collins disapproves of the poet's idleness and lack of earnest striving. His creed sounds much like the Carlylian doctrines of work and salvation. The

Hillside, Sterling's house near Ventnor on the Isle of Wight, where he spent the last two years of his life

conflict of these two representative figures, Collins and the poet, is elaborated with great skill by Sterling, himself caught between them. Collins, like Sterling himself, takes a transcendental view of politics and tries forever to exorcise his self-reproach for having persuaded a young idealist to expose himself to death in a political cause, just as Sterling had exposed his cousin in the Spanish affair. In Collins's dialogue Sterling has captured precisely the Carlylian idiom of the 1830s. Elsewhere in the tale, too, Sterling shows the maturity of his narrative powers and the versatility of his own style. His cottage scenes invite comparison with Charles Dickens, and his metaphysical apparatus with Hawthorne or Poe.

Sterling's final years before his death from tuberculosis in 1844 were spent composing in modes other than fiction and in sporadic trips abroad in the hope of improving his health. His poems were collected by Moxon in 1839, and despite Emerson's intercession appeared in an unauthorized edition in America three years later. His verse satire *The Election* was published by Murray in 1841 and reviewed by Mill as the best poetic satire since Byron's. His reviews of Carlyle (*London and Westminster Review*, October 1839) and Tennyson (*Quarterly Review*, September 1842) are among the very finest on their subjects and are often reprinted. Though his circle of admirers was small, it included many significant figures in Victorian church, state, literature, and academy. The membership list of the Sterling Club, formed in 1838 to honor him with periodic dinner meetings, reads like an index of eminent Victorians. Sterling struggled to remain a complete man of letters in an age when the various requisites of that calling were being parceled off into fragments. Like Coleridge, Sterling wanted to combine faith and the imagination, historical Christianity and the modern experiment. Like Goethe he hoped to unify the worlds of science and nature, of phenomena and metaphenomena. Like Carlyle he wanted to heal the troubled spirits of his contemporaries. That these profound ambitions fell short of complete fulfillment in his short life is hardly surprising.

Letters:

Letters to A Friend, edited by William Coningham (Brighton: Arthur Wallis, 1848?); revised and enlarged as *Twelve Letters Originally Printed for Private Circulation* (London: John Ollivier / Brighton: A. Wallis, 1851);

A Correspondence Between John Sterling and Ralph Waldo Emerson with a Sketch of Sterling's Life by the Editor, edited by Edward Waldo Emerson (Boston & New York: Houghton, Mifflin, 1897);

Letters from John Sterling to George Webbe Dasent, 1838-1844, edited by John R. Dasent (Edinburgh: David Douglas, 1914).

Biographies:

Julius Charles Hare, "Sketch of the Author's Life," in *Essays and Tales, by John Sterling, Collected and Edited, with a Memoir of His Life,* 2 volumes, edited by Hare (London: John W. Parker, 1848), I: i-ccxxxii;

Thomas Carlyle, *The Life of John Sterling* (London: Chapman & Hall, 1851);

Anne Kimball Tuell, *John Sterling: A Representative Victorian* (New York: Macmillan, 1941).

References:

Peter Allen, *The Cambridge Apostles: The Early Years* (Cambridge & New York: Cambridge University Press, 1978);

John Bromley, *The Man of Ten Talents: A Portrait of Richard Chenevix Trench, 1807-86, Philologist, Poet, Theologian, Archbishop* (London: S.P.C.K., 1959);

Thomas and Jane Welsh Carlyle, *The Collected Letters of Thomas and Jane Welsh Carlyle,* Duke-Edinburgh edition, 15 volumes to date, edited by Charles Richard Sanders, Kenneth J. Fielding, Clyde de L. Ryals, Ian M. Campbell, and others (Durham, N.C.: Duke University Press, 1970-);

Samuel Taylor Coleridge, *Collected Letters of Samuel Taylor Coleridge,* 6 volumes, edited by Earl Leslie Griggs (Oxford: Clarendon Press, 1956-1971);

N. Merrill Distad, *Guessing at Truth: The Life of Julius Charles Hare (1795-1855)* (Shepherdstown, W. Va.: Patmos Press, 1979);

Ralph Waldo Emerson, *The Letters of Ralph Waldo Emerson,* 6 volumes, edited by Ralph L. Rusk (New York: Columbia University Press, 1939);

Caroline Fox, *Memories of Old Friends: Being Extracts from the Journals and Letters of Caroline Fox of Penjerrick, Cornwall, from 1835 to 1871,* edited by Horace N. Pym (London: Smith, Elder, 1882);

Robert Barclay Fox, *Barclay Fox's Journal,* edited by R. L. Brett (London: Bell & Hyman, 1979);

Catharine B. Johnson, ed., *William Bodham Donne and his Friends* (London: Methuen, 1905);

Frederick Maurice, ed., *The Life of Frederick Denison Maurice Chiefly told in his own Letters,* 2 volumes (London: Macmillan, 1884);

John Stuart Mill, *Autobiography* (London: Longmans, Green, Reader & Dyer, 1873); edited by Jack Stillinger (Boston: Houghton Mifflin, 1969);

Mill, *The Earlier Letters of John Stuart Mill, 1812-1848,* 2 volumes, edited by Francis E. Mineka (Toronto: University of Toronto Press / London: Routledge & Kegan Paul, 1963);

Margaret Oliphant, *Annals of a Publishing House: William Blackwood and His Sons, Their Magazine and Friends,* 3 volumes (New York: Scribners, 1897-1898);

Ralph L. Rusk, *The Life of Ralph Waldo Emerson* (New York & London: Columbia University Press, 1949);

Joseph Slater, ed., *The Correspondence of Emerson and Carlyle* (New York: Columbia University Press, 1964);

Samuel Smiles, *A Publisher and His Friends: Memoir and Correspondence of the Late John Murray,* 2 volumes (London: John Murray, 1891);

Maria Trench, ed., *Richard Chenevix Trench, Archbishop: Letters and Memorials,* 2 volumes (London: Kegan Paul, Trench, 1888).

Papers:

The largest collections of John Sterling's manuscripts are at the Beinecke Library, Yale University; the Houghton Library, Harvard University; the National Library of Scotland; and the King's College Library, Cambridge.

Edward John Trelawny

(13 November 1792 - 13 August 1881)

William D. Brewer
Appalachian State University

See also the Trelawny entry in *DLB 110: British Romantic Prose Writers, 1789-1832: Second Series.*

BOOKS: *Adventures of a Younger Son,* 3 volumes (London: Henry Colburn & Richard Bentley, 1831; New York: J. & J. Harper, 1832);

Recollections of the Last Days of Shelley and Byron (London: Edward Moxon, 1858; Boston: Ticknor & Fields, 1858); revised and enlarged as *Records of Shelley, Byron, and the Author,* 2 volumes (London: Basil Montagu Pickering, 1878; New York: Scribner, 1887).

OTHER: "Sahib Tulwar (Master of the Sword)," in *Heath's Book of Beauty,* edited by Marguerite, Countess of Blessingham (London: Longman, Orme, Brown, Green & Longmans, 1839), pp. 196-206.

George Gordon, Lord Byron, is reputed to have said of his friend Edward John Trelawny that "Trelawny would be a good fellow if he could spell and speak the truth." As Byron explained to his mistress Teresa Guiccioli, "since [Trelawny's] adolescence he has tried to realize the type of my Corsair. He keeps the poem under his pillow and they say that in the seas of India he aimed at creating such a personality by his deeds and behaviour." But while Byron seemed skeptical about the authenticity of Trelawny's autobiography, Trelawny's other contemporaries accepted him essentially at face value, and this acceptance enabled Trelawny to pull off the most daring literary hoax of the Romantic era. Although he had compiled a relatively mediocre career as a midshipman in the British Navy until leaving (still as a midshipman) in 1812, Trelawny managed to convince the world that he had deserted the navy, joined up with a privateer named de Ruyter, and lived the life of a corsair in the Indian Ocean, killing both men and animals with ruthless ferocity. In essence Trelawny created an entire past for himself based on his Byronic fantasies. *Adventures of a Younger Son* (1831) and *Recollections of the Last Days of Shelley and Byron* (1858) established Trelawny as an important figure of the Romantic period. In fact many reviewers of *Adventures of a Younger Son* assumed that Trelawny was the model for the heroes of Byron's *Giaour* (1813), *Corsair* (1814), and *Lara* (1814), despite the fact that Trelawny did not actually meet Byron until 1822. Although much of *Adventures of a Younger Son* is fabricated and although he often revised and distorted the truth in *Recollections of the Last Days of Shelley and Byron,* Trelawny was a gifted storyteller, and one senses that his readers believed him because they wanted to. Whatever its inaccuracies, *Recollections of the Last Days of Shelley and Byron* is the most fascinating and vividly realized memoir of the Pisan circle, far surpassing Thomas Medwin's and Leigh Hunt's efforts, and the fanciful *Adventures of a Younger Son* is a gripping and powerfully imagined tale of adventure in exotic climes. To the bluestockings of Victorian England, Trelawny became the embodiment of the Romantic hero, and he lived long enough to excite Algernon Charles Swinburne's admiration and to provide a partial model for the Squire Trelawny of Robert Louis Stevenson's *Treasure Island* (1883). Yet to the modern reader Trelawny is most significant as the friend of Shelley and Byron, for Trelawny was the man who befriended and cremated Shelley and who accompanied Byron on his fatal journey to Greece.

Trelawny was born on 13 November 1792, possibly in Cornwall, to Charles and Maria Trelawny. (In 1798 his father received a large inheritance from a cousin named Owen Salusbury Brereton and took that cousin's surname.) As Trelawny claims in the relatively factual part of *Adventures of a Younger Son,* his father was a domestic tyrant who vented most of his wrath on Trelawny, the younger son of the family. At an early age Trelawny developed a hatred of authority: he often told the story, set down in *Adventures of a Younger Son,* of how he murdered his father's pet raven, a sinister and tyrannical bird

Edward John Trelawny, 1822-1823 (portrait by W. E. West; private collection; from William St Clair, Trelawny: The Incurable Romancer, *1977)*

who guarded the family fruit garden. The five-year-old Trelawny expressed his resentment against his abusive and stingy father by gibbeting the raven twice, stoning him, clubbing him, and then drowning the bird in a duck pond. While home life was hardly pleasant for the young Edward John, school was worse. He and his slightly older brother, Harry (born in early 1792), were sent at age eight to a school in Bristol run by the Reverend Samuel Seyer, a man notorious for his severity. One of Seyer's former pupils later spoke of being caned an average of three times a day for a period of seven years. If one can believe the *Adventures of a Younger Son*, Trelawny learned little at this school but an increased loathing of discipline: he led a group of boys who flogged their tutor; then, after being struck, he boldly attacked the Reverend Seyer and was expelled from the school when he set fire to the room in which he was imprisoned.

After this disaster at the boarding school, Trelawny's father, in an effort to rid himself of his rebellious younger son, sent Trelawny into the Royal Navy at the age of twelve. Although Trelawny later glorified his career as a sailor and privateer, in reality he was miserable, in constant conflict with his superiors and never experiencing the adventures his romantic soul craved. He was shunted from ship to ship as a difficult and unpopular midshipman and was often punished by being sent up to the masthead to sit, hanging onto the rigging, for hours. Trelawny's biographer William St Clair surmises that on the masthead Trelawny first began imagining the stories which were later written down in *Adventures of a Younger Son*. The victim of the petty tyrants of a British naval vessel, Trelawny pictured himself leading a mutiny against them, like his hero Fletcher Christian of the *Bounty*, or deserting the navy he hated to join up with privateers like Robert Surcouf, a French corsair who was the scourge of British shipping in the Indian Ocean. The facts of Trelawny's life were, however, far different from his fantasies, and, after being wounded during the assault of Java in 1811, Trelawny quit the navy in the following year, still a midshipman.

In May 1813 Trelawny provoked his father's wrath again by marrying a woman named Caroline Addison: he was twenty and she was even younger. A daughter was born in 1814. Two years later, while Caroline was pregnant with a second daughter, Trelawny discovered that his wife was having an affair with a Captain Coleman. In the wake of a messy divorce, which became final in 1819, Trelawny reached a kind of nadir. He responded to failure as a naval man and as a husband by completely repudiating his past. Although his family and Caroline had known him as John Trelawny, he decided that he was henceforth to be called Edward; although he had left the navy a midshipman, he "promoted" himself to the rank of captain. And he began a program of self-education, enthusiastically reading Byron's Eastern tales as well as the works of the lesser known Percy Bysshe Shelley. In particular, Byron's *Corsair* gave shape to Trelawny's fantasies about his naval career, and it was only a matter of time before Trelawny made the acquaintance of his two literary heroes. As luck would have it, a hunting companion of Trelawny's, Edward Ellerker Williams, had become Shelley and Byron's intimate friend, and Trelawny was invited to join the poets at Pisa to help them design sailboats. Trelawny met both poets in January 1822.

To the circle at Pisa, Trelawny, whom Mary Shelley called that "kind of half Arab Englishman," became the embodiment of a Byronic hero, more Byronic, if possible, than Byron himself. Certainly Trelawny, who had dark, weather-beaten features and an imposing physique, looked the part, and his tales of adventure entranced his admiring audience. The stories of Trelawny's desertion from the navy and his adventures with the great privateer de Ruyter were probably first told in Pisa. In the company of Byron, the greatest literary name of the day, and Shelley, whose atheism and revolutionary principles he both admired and sought to emulate, Trelawny felt compelled to invent a past which would gain him attention and respect. And, having invented a fantastic life history, Trelawny continued to insist upon its validity until the end of his days, until he himself seems to have come to believe in it. Inspired by Trelawny's tales, Shelley began to write a drama about a pirate separated from his true love. This work was never finished, but Trelawny's stories may well have influenced a work that Byron did complete: *The Island* (1823), a narrative poem based on the adventures of the mutineers of the *Bounty*. But while Trelawny worshiped Shelley, he felt slightly antagonistic toward Byron, perhaps because Byron was an impediment to Trelawny's quest to become *the* Byronic hero. In the *Recollections of the Last Days of Shelley and Byron*, Byron is described as stingy and vain, whereas Shelley is presented as a man of lofty spirit and ideals.

Shelley's death by drowning in July 1822 brought Trelawny's friendship with him to a tragic close. Trelawny was the designer of Shelley's boat, the *Don Juan*, which turned out to be overmasted and generally unseaworthy. In later accounts of Shelley's drowning, Trelawny went to great lengths to argue that Shelley, Williams, and the boy who accompanied them were rammed by a large fishing vessel, possibly because they were suspected of carrying booty. Yet the documents Trelawny had in hand when he began writing *Recollections of the Last Days of Shelley and Byron* in 1858 supported the view that the *Don Juan* simply was too unseaworthy to survive a storm. Trelawny seems to have edited these documents to clear himself of negligence in his friend's death. After Shelley's disfigured corpse was washed ashore, Trelawny arranged and performed an elaborate cremation on the beach and burned his hand badly when he pulled Shelley's smoldering heart from the ashes. Without Shelley the Pisan circle soon broke up, and on 21 July 1823 Byron and Trelawny left Italy to join the Greeks in their struggle for independence from the Ottoman Empire.

Byron was more cautious than Trelawny, and while he remained on the Ionian Islands sizing up the situation, Trelawny donned Albanian garb and went in search of action. Unfortunately, the warlord with whom Trelawny ultimately cast his lot was Odysseus Androutsos, a brigand and turncoat who would fight for either the Greeks or the Turks, depending on which side had the upper hand. After Byron's sudden death at Missolonghi on 19 April 1824, Trelawny drifted more and more into Odysseus's orbit, and in 1825 the wily bandit cemented his relationship with the eccentric Englishman by arranging for Trelawny's marriage to his thirteen-year-old half sister, Tersitsa. But Odysseus's fortunes began to de-

Trelawny in 1837 (portrait by E. Duppa; National Portrait Gallery, London)

cline as the other revolutionary factions in Greece began to receive money from England, and in a desperate attempt to maintain his power he allied himself with the Turks. Then, leaving Trelawny in command of his fortified cave, he left to seek the protection of the Greek warlord of Athens. Trelawny's defense of the cave was brief. Two Englishmen who had joined him in the cave tried to assassinate Trelawny by shooting him in the back at point-blank range, but one of the guns failed to go off, and, although two balls from the other gun entered Trelawny's body, he lived. His jaw smashed, he survived by ingesting liquids and egg yolks. He was rescued, three teeth missing, his right arm paralyzed, and his jaw scarcely able to open, by a Maj. d'Arcy Bacon, and taken aboard a British navy vessel. His Greek adventures were at an end, but during the time he spent in Greece he was finally able to become the corsair of his imagination, to prove himself more Byronic than Byron himself.

In the years that followed the Greek expedition, Trelawny's marriage to Tersitsa broke up, leaving him with a daughter named Zella (he later was to name the child bride of *Adventures of a Younger Son* Zela). He subsequently proposed to Mary Shelley and to her stepsister, Claire Clairmont, but both women wisely turned him down. Finally he settled in Florence, near Walter Savage Landor and Charles Armitage Brown (John Keats's friend), and began to write down the tales with which he had entertained the Pisan circle years before. With Mary Shelley's help, *Adventures of a Younger Son* was published anonymously in 1831. The first part of the book is a fairly accurate portrait of Trelawny's early life and naval career, but the remainder is largely fantasy. The book's unnamed protagonist leaves his frigate in Bombay and, after beating his former lieutenant half to death in a tavern, turns against

England and the hated East India Company and joins up with the French privateer de Ruyter. The two sail across the Indian Ocean, leaving death and destruction in their wake: although Trelawny's protagonist recognizes that he is excessively violent, he often seems to relish his brutal acts of vengeance. In the course of his adventures he murders a half-dozen men, not to mention a violent old woman and a club-wielding "orang-outang," and he seldom feels even a pang of remorse. During one of the book's many slaughters, a dying Arab entrusts his daughter to the protagonist's care, and the young girl, Zela, becomes his bride. She accompanies him on the remainder of his adventures, often saving his life, until she is wounded by sharks and finished off by poisoned nutmegs supplied by a jealous Javanese widow. After her death the grieving hero cremates her on the beach in a scene obviously drawn from Trelawny's cremation of Shelley. *Adventures of a Younger Son* has no real plot, and de Ruyter and Zela often seem more like Byronic abstractions than real people. But as a vividly rendered tale of sanguinary exploits in exotic seas *Adventures of a Younger Son* is superb—Trelawny was a gifted storyteller, and he fascinated his readers in 1831 just as he had earlier charmed the Pisan circle. The fact that the protagonist claims to be a traitor to England, joining Napoleon's side to attack British shipping, seems to have bothered no one. Although the book was published anonymously, the British public immediately identified the protagonist with Trelawny, the friend of Byron and adventurer in Greece, and he soon found himself lionized.

Few of Trelawny's contemporaries questioned the accuracy of *Adventures of a Younger Son*, and it was considered an autobiography rather than a novel. In an article published in 1956, however, Lady Anne Hill finally separated the truth from the fiction. By laboriously going through naval records, she found that Trelawny never did desert, and that he had remained a midshipman in the British Navy rather than becoming a captain on a French privateer: 125 years after the publication of *Adventures of a Younger Son*, Trelawny's hoax was exposed. Subsequent criticism has considered the book as a novel with autobiographical elements rather than as a work of nonfiction.

After the success of *Adventures of a Younger Son*, which was translated into several languages, including French and German, Trelawny left England to explore America. His stay in the United States during 1832-1834 was not a pleasant one: he hoped to fight in a seemingly imminent war between South Carolina and the Union, but the conflict did not materialize, and Trelawny nearly drowned while trying to swim across the Niagara River. On his return his adoring public begged him to write further about his adventures with de Ruyter, and he obliged, writing "Sahib Tulwar (Master of the Sword)" for the 1839 volume of *Heath's Book of Beauty*, a bluestocking annual edited by Lady Blessington. In this short story the hero of *Adventures of a Younger Son* and de Ruyter climb the Himalayas to meet a renowned swordsman, who turns out to be of American extraction. Sahib Tulwar proves to be as ferocious and bloodthirsty as the younger son and de Ruyter put together, fighting the British and his own comrades as the whim strikes him. He is, in fact, not unlike Odysseus Androutsos. One can be sure that the bluestockings loved the story, but it was the last younger-son tale that Trelawny ever wrote. In 1841 he married Augusta Goring and settled into domestic life with her on a farm at Usk. They had three children.

Trelawny's second and perhaps most important book, published in 1858, was *Recollections of the Last Days of Shelley and Byron*, an account of the months he spent with the poets in Pisa, his trip to Greece with Byron, and his subsequent adventures with Odysseus. Although this work was much more accurate and truthful than *Adventures of a Younger Son*, it was written thirty-five years after the events it describes, and Trelawny was never one to prefer the truth to the inspiration of his own romantic imagination. Thus it does not surprise us to read that Trelawny withdrew Byron's shroud to discover that *both* the poet's feet were clubbed, although all of the medical evidence indicates that only the right foot was deformed. This passage certainly bothered Trelawny's Victorian audience, who objected strenuously to his unseemly curiosity at Byron's deathbed—such an invasion of the dead poet's privacy, many felt, could have been perpetrated only by a cad. On the other hand, the fact that Trelawny had aligned himself with Odysseus, a traitor to the Greek Revolution, seems to have bothered no one. Although this memoir was not without controversy, it soon became a great success. *Adventures of a Younger Son* was republished, and a new generation of readers enjoyed the exploits of Trelawny and de Ruyter.

Trelawny's powers of description make *Recollections of the Last Days of Shelley and Byron* captivating reading, even when it may be inaccurate. He

The North West Passage, *by John Everett Millais (Tate Gallery, London). Trelawny at eighty-two was the model for the man.*

describes, for example, Shelley's lying at the bottom of a pool, "stretched out on the bottom like a conger eel," quietly waiting to drown. Whether this incident occurred or not, the passage vividly depicts Shelley's death wish and prefigures, in an almost poetic way, Shelley's later death by drowning. In 1878 Trelawny published the book in expanded form as *Records of Shelley, Byron, and the Author*. The new title reflected Trelawny's own rise in stature: as one of the last survivors of the Romantic era, he had become by 1878 a legendary figure who had simply outlived those who could contradict him. Although Trelawny added new materials to the 1878 edition it is not, overall, substantially different from the first edition.

Trelawny's long life ended on 13 August 1881 after a fall. True to his Shelleyan ideals, he proclaimed his atheism on his deathbed, and his remains were buried next to Shelley's in Rome. Although *Adventures of a Younger Son* was a great success during Trelawny's life, and is still entertaining reading today, it is as the friend of Byron and Shelley that Trelawny will longest be remembered. He was, in a sense, a self-invented man. He rewrote his past in a successful effort to gain celebrity, and his credulous admirers ultimately gave him credit for inspiring (rather than being inspired by) the Byronic hero. Unlike many tellers of tall tales, he was never made to admit the falsity of his stories. To many Victorians, including the Pre-Raphaelites, he was the epitome of Romantic heroism, and when he was eighty-two John Everett Millais used him as a model for a painting titled *The North West Passage*. Trelawny is shown as an old man listening to an account of the search for the Northwest Passage. The caption reads: "It can be done and England should do it." While recent criticism has exposed Trelawny's misrepresentations and reduced his legendary stature, he remains significant as a gifted storyteller who helped shape his contemporaries' notions of the Byronic hero and who left us with vivid portraits of two of the greatest poets of the Romantic age.

Letters:

Letters of Edward John Trelawny, edited by H. Buxton Forman (London & New York: Oxford University Press, 1910).

Biographies:

Margaret Armstrong, *Trelawny: A Man's Life* (New York: Macmillan, 1940);

Rosalie Glynn Grylls, *Trelawny* (London: Constable, 1950);

William St Clair, *Trelawny: The Incurable Romancer* (New York: Vanguard Press, 1977).

References:

Betty T. Bennett, ed., *The Letters of Mary Wollstonecraft Shelley*, 3 volumes (Baltimore: Johns Hopkins University Press, 1980-1987);

Lady Anne Hill, "Trelawny's Family Background and Naval Career," *Keats-Shelley Journal*, 5 (Winter 1956): 11-32;

Leslie Marchand, "Trelawny on the Death of Shelley," *Keats-Shelley Memorial Bulletin*, no. 4 (1952): 9-34;

Donald H. Reiman, ed., *Shelley and his Circle: 1773-1822*, volumes 5, 6, and 8 (Cambridge, Mass.: Harvard University Press, 1973-1986);

Cecil Roberts, "And Did Trelawny Lie?," *Books and Bookmen*, 19 (October 1973): 62-66.

Papers:

The Houghton Library at Harvard University has the manuscripts for *Adventures of a Younger Son* and *Records of Shelley, Byron, and the Author*. Trelawny's letters and other documents can be found in several locations, including the Carl H. Pforzheimer Library at the New York Public Library, the Keats-Shelley Memorial Library in Rome, and the Bodleian Library at Oxford University.

Checklist of Further Readings

Abrams, M. H. *The Mirror and the Lamp: Romantic Theory and the Critical Tradition.* New York: Oxford University Press, 1953.

Abrams. *Natural Supernaturalism: Tradition and Revolution in Romantic Literature.* New York: Norton, 1973.

Altick, Richard. *The English Common Reader: A Social History of the Mass Reading Public, 1800-1900.* Chicago: University of Chicago Press, 1957.

Armstrong, Nancy. *Desire and Domestic Fiction: A Political History of the Novel.* New York: Oxford University Press, 1987.

Baker, Ernest A. *The History of the English Novel,* 10 volumes. London: Witherby, 1924-1939.

Barnett, George L., ed. *Eighteenth-Century British Novelists on the Novel.* New York: Appleton-Century-Crofts, 1968.

Briggs, Asa. *A Social History of England.* London: Weidenfeld & Nicolson, 1983.

Brown, Julia Prewitt. *A Reader's Guide to the Nineteenth-Century English Novel.* New York: Macmillan / London: Collier Macmillan, 1985.

Butler, Marilyn. *Jane Austen and the War of Ideas.* Oxford: Clarendon Press, 1975.

Davis, Lennard J. *Factual Fictions: The Origins of the English Novel.* New York: Columbia University Press, 1983.

Day, Geoffrey. *From Fiction to the Novel.* London & New York: Routledge & Kegan Paul, 1987.

Eagleton, Terry. *The Function of Criticism: From 'The Spectator' to Post-Structuralism.* London: Verso, 1984.

Ellis, Kate. *The Contested Castle: Gothic Novels and the Subversion of Domestic Ideology.* Urbana: University of Illinois Press, 1989.

Ferris, Ina. "Repositioning the Novel: *Waverly* and the Gender of Fiction." *Studies in Romanticism,* 28 (Summer 1989): 291-301.

Gallagher, Catherine. *The Industrial Reformation of British Fiction: Social Discourse and Narrative Form, 1832-1867.* Chicago: University of Chicago Press, 1985.

Gaull, Marilyn. *English Romanticism: The Human Context.* New York: Norton, 1988.

George, M. Dorothy. *London Life in the XVIIIth Century.* London: Kegan Paul, Trench, Trübner / New York: Knopf, 1925.

Gilbert, Sandra M., and Susan Gubar. *The Madwoman in the Attic: The Woman Writer and the Nineteenth-Century Literary Imagination.* New Haven: Yale University Press, 1979.

Kelly, Gary. *English Fiction of the Romantic Period, 1789-1830.* London & New York: Longman, 1989.

Kelly. *The English Jacobin Novel, 1780-1805.* Oxford & New York: Clarendon Press, 1976.

Kiely, Robert. *The Romantic Novel in England.* Cambridge, Mass.: Harvard University Press, 1972.

Leavis, Q. D. *Fiction and the Reading Public.* London: Chatto & Windus, 1965.

Lovell, Terry. *Consuming Fiction.* London & New York: Verso, 1987.

Lowenthal, Leo. *Literature, Popular Culture, and Society.* Englewood Cliffs, N.J.: Prentice-Hall, 1961.

McGann, Jerome. *The Romantic Ideology: A Critical Investigation.* Chicago: University of Chicago Press, 1983.

McKeon, Michael. *The Origins of the English Novel, 1600-1740.* Baltimore: Johns Hopkins University Press, 1987.

Mudge, Bradford K. "The Man with Two Brains: Gothic Novels, Popular Culture, Literary History." *PMLA*, 107 (January 1992): 92-104.

Neuburg, Victor. *Popular Literature, From the Beginning of Printing to the Year 1897: A History and Guide.* Harmondsworth, U.K. & New York: Penguin, 1977.

The New Cambridge Modern History, volume 8: *The American and French Revolutions, 1763-1793*, edited by A. Goodwin, and volume 9: *War and Peace in an Age of Upheaval, 1793-1830*, edited by C. W. Crawley. Cambridge: Cambridge University Press, 1965.

Newton, Judith Lowder. *Women, Power, and Subversion: Social Strategies in British Fiction, 1778-1860.* Athens: University of Georgia Press, 1981.

Poovey, Mary. *The Proper Lady and the Woman Writer: Ideology as Style in the Works of Mary Wollstonecraft, Mary Shelley, and Jane Austen.* Chicago: University of Chicago Press, 1984.

Saintsbury, George. *The English Novel.* London: Dent, 1913.

Sales, Roger. *English Literature in History, 1780-1830: Pastoral and Politics.* New York: St. Martin's Press, 1983.

Spencer, Jane. *The Rise of the Woman Novelist: From Aphra Behn to Jane Austen.* Oxford: Blackwell, 1986.

Spender, Dale. *Mothers of the Novel: 100 Good Women Writers before Jane Austen.* London & New York: Pandora, 1986.

Taylor, John Tinnon. *Early Opposition to the English Novel: The Popular Reaction from 1760 to 1830.* New York: King's Crown Press, 1949.

Thompson, E. P. *The Making of the English Working Class.* London: Gollancz, 1963; revised, 1980.

Tompkins, J. M. S. *The Popular Novel in England, 1770-1800.* Lincoln: University of Nebraska Press, 1961.

Tymn, Marshall B., ed. *Horror Literature: A Core Collection and Reference Guide.* New York: Bowker, 1981.

Watson, George, ed. *The New Cambridge Bibliography of English Literature*, volume 3: 1800-1900. Cambridge: Cambridge University Press, 1969.

Watt, Ian. *The Rise of the Novel: Studies in Defoe, Richardson, and Fielding*. London: Chatto & Windus, 1957.

Williams, Ioan. *The Realist Novel in England: A Study in Development*. London: Macmillan, 1974.

Williams, ed. *Novel and Romance, 1700-1800: A Documentary Record*. London: Routledge & Kegan Paul, 1970.

Wolff, Robert Lee. *Nineteenth-Century Fiction: A Bibliographical Catalogue Based on the Collection Formed by Robert Lee Wolff*, 5 volumes. New York & London: Garland, 1981.

Yeazell, Ruth Bernard. *Fictions of Modesty: Women and Courtship in the English Novel*. Chicago: University of Chicago Press, 1991.

Contributors

Michael Adams .... *Albright College*
Samuel I. Bellman .... *California State Polytechnic University, Pomona*
William D. Brewer .... *Appalachian State University*
Byron K. Brown .... *Valdosta State College*
Kathleen Reuter Chamberlain .... *Emory and Henry College*
Andrew M. Cooper .... *University of Texas at Austin*
Laura Dabundo .... *Kennesaw State College*
William A. Davis, Jr. .... *College of Notre Dame of Maryland*
Lauren Pringle De La Vars .... *Saint Bonaventure University*
Ann W. Engar .... *University of Utah*
Cy Frost .... *University of Colorado at Denver*
Jacqueline Gray .... *University of Colorado at Boulder*
Ann Hobart .... *Trinity College*
Susan K. Howard .... *Duquesne University*
Gary Kelly .... *University of Alberta*
David E. Latané, Jr. .... *Virginia Commonwealth University*
Raymond N. Mackenzie .... *University of St. Thomas*
Eric W. Nye .... *University of Wyoming*
Louis J. Parascandola .... *Long Island University—Brooklyn Center*
Myra L. Rich .... *University of Colorado at Denver*
John H. Rogers .... *Vincennes University*
Beverly Schneller .... *Millersuille University*
Mary Rose Sullivan .... *University of Colorado at Denver*
Eleanor Ty .... *Wilfrid Laurier University*

Cumulative Index

Dictionary of Literary Biography, Volumes 1-117
Dictionary of Literary Biography Yearbook, 1980-1990
Dictionary of Literary Biography Documentary Series, Volumes 1-9

Cumulative Index

DLB before number: *Dictionary of Literary Biography,* Volumes 1-117
Y before number: *Dictionary of Literary Biography Yearbook,* 1980-1991
DS before number: *Dictionary of Literary Biography Documentary Series,* Volumes 1-9

A

B

C

D

E

F

G

H

Cumulative Index

K

L

M

O

P

Q

R

S

T

U

V

W

ISBN 0-8103-7593-1
90000
9 780810 375932

(Continued from front endsheets)

80: *Restoration and Eighteenth-Century Dramatists,* First Series, edited by Paula R. Backscheider (1989)

81: *Austrian Fiction Writers, 1875-1913,* edited by James Hardin and Donald G. Daviau (1989)

82: *Chicano Writers,* First Series, edited by Francisco A. Lomelí and Carl R. Shirley (1989)

83: *French Novelists Since 1960,* edited by Catharine Savage Brosman (1989)

84: *Restoration and Eighteenth-Century Dramatists,* Second Series, edited by Paula R. Backscheider (1989)

85: *Austrian Fiction Writers After 1914,* edited by James Hardin and Donald G. Daviau (1989)

86: *American Short-Story Writers, 1910-1945,* First Series, edited by Bobby Ellen Kimbel (1989)

87: *British Mystery and Thriller Writers Since 1940,* First Series, edited by Bernard Benstock and Thomas F. Staley (1989)

88: *Canadian Writers, 1920-1959,* Second Series, edited by W. H. New (1989)

89: *Restoration and Eighteenth-Century Dramatists,* Third Series, edited by Paula R. Backscheider (1989)

90: *German Writers in the Age of Goethe, 1789-1832,* edited by James Hardin and Christoph E. Schweitzer (1989)

91: *American Magazine Journalists, 1900-1960,* First Series, edited by Sam G. Riley (1990)

92: *Canadian Writers, 1890-1920,* edited by W. H. New (1990)

93: *British Romantic Poets, 1789-1832,* First Series, edited by John R. Greenfield (1990)

94: *German Writers in the Age of Goethe: Sturm und Drang to Classicism,* edited by James Hardin and Christoph E. Schweitzer (1990)

95: *Eighteenth-Century British Poets,* First Series, edited by John Sitter (1990)

96: *British Romantic Poets, 1789-1832,* Second Series, edited by John R. Greenfield (1990)

97: *German Writers from the Enlightenment to Sturm und Drang, 1720-1764,* edited by James Hardin and Christoph E. Schweitzer (1990)

98: *Modern British Essayists,* First Series, edited by Robert Beum (1990)

99: *Canadian Writers Before 1890,* edited by W. H. New (1990)

100: *Modern British Essayists,* Second Series, edited by Robert Beum (1990)

101: *British Prose Writers, 1660-1800,* First Series, edited by Donald T. Siebert (1991)

102: *American Short-Story Writers, 1910-1945,* Second Series, edited by Bobby Ellen Kimbel (1991)

103: *American Literary Biographers,* First Series, edited by Steven Serafin (1991)

104: *British Prose Writers, 1660-1800,* Second Series, edited by Donald T. Siebert (1991)

105: *American Poets Since World War II,* Second Series, edited by R. S. Gwynn (1991)

106: *British Literary Publishing Houses, 1820-1880,* edited by Patricia J. Anderson and Jonathan Rose (1991)

107: *British Romantic Prose Writers, 1789-1832,* First Series, edited by John R. Greenfield (1991)

108: *Twentieth-Century Spanish Poets,* First Series, edited by Michael L. Perna (1991)

109: *Eighteenth-Century British Poets,* Second Series, edited by John Sitter (1991)

110: *British Romantic Prose Writers, 1789-1832,* Second Series, edited by John R. Greenfield (1991)

111: *American Literary Biographers,* Second Series, edited by Steven Serafin (1991)

112: *British Literary Publishing Houses, 1881-1965,* edited by Jonathan Rose and Patricia J. Anderson (1991)

113: *Modern Latin-American Fiction Writers,* First Series, edited by William Luis (1992)

114: *Twentieth-Century Italian Poets,* First Series, edited by Giovanna Wedel De Stasio, Glauco Cambon, and Antonio Illiano (1992)

115: *Medieval Philosophers,* edited by Jeremiah Hackett (1992)

116: *British Romantic Novelists, 1789-1832,* edited by Bradford K. Mudge (1992)

117: *Twentieth-Century Caribbean and Black African Writers,* First Series, edited by Bernth Lindfors and Reinhard Sander (1992)